Doing Justice to History

OXFORD MONOGRAPHS IN INTERNATIONAL HUMANITARIAN AND CRIMINAL LAW

This series emerged through the vision of the late Antonio Cassese. Since then the series has published original and innovative works on challenging issues in international humanitarian law and international criminal justice, primarily by emerging authors. Given the ever-growing intersection of these areas with other fields of international law such as the jus ad bellum, and disciplines such as criminology, sociology, and history, the scope of the series also incorporates these perspectives. Fresh approaches and new ideas for improving conceptual and practical challenges are welcomed. The series editors encourage submissions from around the world, and will consider edited collections, although the primary focus is on authored works.

ALSO PUBLISHED IN THIS SERIES

The Humanitarian Civilian
How the Idea of Distinction Circulates Within and Beyond International Humanitarian Law
Rebecca Sutton

Rules of Engagement and the International Law of Military Operations
J.F.R. Boddens Hosang

To Serve the Enemy
Informers, Collaborators, and the Laws of Armed Conflict
Shane Darcy

Internationalized Armed Conflicts in International Law
Kubo Mačák

Doing Justice to History

Confronting the Past in International Criminal Courts

BARRIE SANDER

OXFORD
UNIVERSITY PRESS

OXFORD
UNIVERSITY PRESS

Great Clarendon Street, Oxford, OX2 6DP,
United Kingdom

Oxford University Press is a department of the University of Oxford.
It furthers the University's objective of excellence in research, scholarship,
and education by publishing worldwide. Oxford is a registered trade mark of
Oxford University Press in the UK and in certain other countries

First Edition published in 2021
Impression: 1

Published in the United States of America by Oxford University Press
198 Madison Avenue, New York, NY 10016, United States of America

British Library Cataloguing in Publication Data
Data available

Library of Congress Control Number: 2020947987

ISBN 978–0–19–884687–1

DOI: 10.1093/oso/9780198846871.001.0001

Printed and bound by
CPI Group (UK) Ltd, Croydon, CR0 4YY

Series Editors' Preface

Dr Barrie Sander's monograph is an original and important contribution to scholarship on the historiography and methodology of international trials. This profound study comes at a time of growing fatigue with international criminal justice and its institutions in certain previously supportive quarters, alongside dampened enthusiasm, even cynicism, about their efficacy as responses to situations of mass atrocity.

Dr Sander meticulously examines not just what he calls 'the struggle for historical justice' (discursive contests between different actors vying for judicial acknowledgement of their preferred interpretations of the past) but proves how historical narratives are construed and communicated at international criminal courts and tribunals through individuals at particular times and their actions/inactions at certain stages of legal proceedings and afterwards.

He has been able to do this through application of a tri-partite conceptual framework: focusing on the *actors* involved in *struggles for historical justice*, the *questions* around which such struggles tend to be structured, and the *practices* through which such struggles are conducted. He takes us through the historical function of international courts and processes of international justice, exploring in particular *how* such courts construct historical narratives about both the culpability of the accused and the broader mass atrocity contexts in which they are alleged to have participated.

Through Dr Sander's expert dissection of the charging of crimes, the interpretation of normative categories, as well as legal doctrine on modes of participation and defences, readers are provided with a window into the way that judicial narratives are formed. His skilled analysis then shows readers something else that is new and important. We see how certain objectives can be pursued to the detriment of others; how supposedly objective principles of legality and culpability can deflect attention from the structural causes of mass violence, and favour the interests of dominant States, most notably those with vested interests in the outcome and the reasons therefor. Critically, Dr Sander also shows what is avoided or excluded in judicial representations of history, what is exaggerated or over-stated, what is left out by accident and deliberately. And, he also provides his readers with a sociological analysis of the impact that these judicial narratives have had in the outside world.

Many have sensed with increasing discomfort that something is awry, but Dr Sander has become the one to identify and analyse what has really been happening. This is no flat legal analysis, but one in which a talented scholar has been able to bring law and the legal process both to light and life. One of the reasons why Dr Sander has been able to achieve this is because he has successfully drawn from other disciplines, and these complement his dominantly legal approach. His innovative and structured methodology brings forth rich and illuminating insights that will surely influence academic discourse in this area for some time to come.

Three decades into the modern revival of the international justice project, Dr Sander does not believe its proponents can continue to hide behind the excuse that matters of fairness, propriety, legality, and legitimacy will come in time. Delivery on the promises that international criminal justice has made (or have been made on its behalf) cannot be forever delayed without a loss of faith or a feeling of betrayal. His point is well-made. Dr Sander, though is not merely a passive diagnostician of international criminal justice's maladies, but also seeks to palliate, if not cure them.

His prescription is to 'critically contextualise' the histories constructed in the decisions and judgments of international criminal courts in a holistic, trifocal way. The components of this are through looking 'backwards' to evaluate the processes by which they came to be, 'forwards' to the ongoing debates and contestations that they provoke, and 'sideways' to other mechanisms that construct post-atrocity stories. The last of these activities relies on a level of good faith dialogue which is often sorely lacking in traumatised societies.

Dr Sander is well aware of this, so rather than asserting that the various storytellings ought to be treated as ends in themselves, or capable of creating (or imposing) closure, he considers them to be better viewed with greater humility, as providing at most a discursive beginning for individuals and for communities to engage with, view, and debate the past. As such, to build upon his metaphor he usefully employs, they ought to be looked at as monuments, not in the sense of monumental iconic pieces with lapidary lessons, but as sites where memory and the past can be debated. This careful conclusion is the outcome of his close, nuanced, and clear-eyed appraisal of the merits, limits, and failings of international criminal tribunals.

Furthermore, and consistently with the above, although much of the book is focused on courts and tribunals, it is no example of judicial fetishism. Instead, it rightly looks more broadly to other institutions and actors involved with international criminal justice, none of which are in themselves authoritative and have their own constraints and limits. Despite these, they are a vital part of the creation of the collective, if not shared, memories of deeply troubled times and need to be apprised 'within the wider horizons of possibility'. Hence, Dr Sander's conclusion is critical, but cautiously optimistic.

Dr Sander is to be commended for this study, the first of its kind in our series. It confronts issues that go to the very foundation of the system of international criminal justice, and the reasons why it was created. We are proud to publish Dr Sander's monograph.

The Editors

Acknowledgements

Writing this book has been a long and stimulating journey, one that has challenged me to reflect not only on my object of study—international criminal justice—but also my own positionality in the world. Along the way, I have had the good fortune of being supported by many inspiring and thought-provoking individuals and communities. I am grateful to them all.

This book is based on my doctoral thesis, undertaken at the Graduate Institute of International and Development Studies (Graduate Institute), under the supervision of Professor Andrea Bianchi. I am particularly grateful to have been supervised by Andrea, whom I initially met when I took his class on international legal theory—a course which I view as pivotal to the way I think about international law. I would like to thank Andrea for his encouragement, responsiveness, constructive feedback, and, most of all, for providing me with the intellectual space for my creativity to develop. I would also like to thank the other members of my thesis committee—Professor Paola Gaeta (Graduate Institute) and Professor Gerry Simpson (London School of Economics)—for taking the time to carefully review my manuscript and provide valuable feedback on my research.

I would also like to thank a number of other scholars, colleagues, friends, and family for their support during this process. In Geneva: Jason Rudall, Leslie-Anne Duvic Paoli, Antonio Coco, and Patryk Labuda. At Harvard: Samuel Moyn, Pekka Phjankoski, and Luisa Lourenço. In Copenhagen: Mikael Madsen, Mikkel Christensen, Shai Dothan, Jakob Holtermann, Marina Aksenova, Kerstin Carlson, Juan Mayoral, Günes Ünüvar, and Tom Daly. In Brazil: Michael Mohallem, Luca Belli, Nico Zingales, and Matias Spektor. Around the world: Jean d'Aspremont, Duncan Hollis, Mark Drumbl, Kjersti Lohne, Christine Schwöbel-Patel, Karen Engle, Sofia Stolk, Marieke de Hoon, Larissa van den Herik, Meg deGuzman, Morten Bergsmo, and Russell Buchan. For their invaluable friendship: Aaron, Andy, Mike, Adam, Tom, Sabs, Dom, Agnes, Anne-Laure, Chris, Josefien, Olga, Kate, Elle, Lily, Laura, Suria, Marina, and Kerry. And my close family: Julie, Suzie, Mike, Natasha, and Craig.

I am also grateful for the support provided by Harvard Law School, iCourts, and Fundação Getúlio Vargas for hosting me at various stages of my research, and to the Graduate Institute and Geneva Academy for providing invaluable support during my time in Geneva. In addition, I would like to thank the University of Virginia and the Graduate Institute for awarding me an Albert Gallatin Fellowship to fund my year at Harvard Law School.

I would also like to extend a special thank you to the team at Oxford University Press, in particular Jack McNichol and Merel Alstein for their support throughout the publishing process, as well as the team at Newgen Knowledge Works for their incredible work on the production of the book.

Last, but by no means least, I would like to thank my wife, Zhaneta, my daughter, Valentina, and my parents, who have been constantly at my side during this process, offering their continued support, guidance, and empathy. This book is above all for them.

Contents

Table of Abbreviations

AFRC	Armed Forces Revolutionary Council
CDF	Civil Defence Forces
CUP	Cambridge University Press
DRC	Democratic Republic of the Congo
GLAN	Global Legal Action Network
ICC	International Criminal Court
ICTR	International Criminal Tribunal for Rwanda
ICTY	International Criminal Tribunal for the former Yugoslavia
ILC	International Law Commission
IMF	International Monetary Fund
IMT	International Military Tribunal
IMTFE	International Military Tribunal for the Far East
JCE	Joint Criminal Enterprise
KLA	Kosovo Liberation Army
LRA	Lord's Resistance Army
NATO	North Atlantic Treaty Organization
OUP	Oxford University Press
PrepCom	Preparatory Committee
RAF	Rwandan Armed Forces
RPF	Rwandan Patriotic Front
RUF	Revolutionary United Front
SCSL	Special Court for Sierra Leone
SGBV	Sexual and Gender-Based Violence
TRC	Truth and Reconciliation Commission
UN	United Nations
UNAMIR	United Nations Assistance Mission in Rwanda
VJ	Yugoslav Army
VRS	Bosnian Serb Army

1
Introduction

I. Doing Justice to History

'We are living in a fake news era' was the response of Syrian President Bashar al-Assad to a report released by Amnesty International concerning prison deaths in Syria.[1] 'There is no such thing as Rohingya. It is fake news' was the reaction of an officer in Rakhine's state security ministry amid international accusations that the military in Myanmar were conducting a campaign of ethnic cleansing against the Rohingya Muslims.[2] 'Misinformation, fake news and politicization of human rights' was the message put forward by Philippine Foreign Affairs Secretary, Alan Cayetano, at the United Nations (UN) General Assembly in an attempt to justify his government's 'war on drugs'.[3] Around the world, political leaders have seized upon the phrase 'fake news' as a tool for defending their policies and attacking their critics. Indeed, such is the frequency with which the term has been used that Collins Dictionary even decided to make 'fake news' its official 'Word of the Year' for 2017.[4]

Yet, while the term 'fake news' may be experiencing a spike in popularity, the phenomenon of political leaders and groups dismissing allegations of mass atrocities as false or fictitious is nothing new. Indeed, a major concern for survivors of mass atrocities has been the fear that their experiences will be dismissed by the public as mere fabrication. Consider, for example, the opening passages of Holocaust survivor Primo Levi's *The Drowned and The Saved*, in which he recalls the public inclination to reject early reports of Nazi annihilation camps on account of their 'vast proportions', 'extreme cruelty', and 'intricate motivation'.[5] Levi notes that public dismissal was even foreseen by the SS militiamen themselves, who would cynically admonish the prisoners that even if they were fortunate to survive the death camps, the acts of the Nazis would be dismissed by the public as 'too monstrous to be believed'.[6]

Denial, it seems, is part and parcel of the commission of mass atrocities.[7] Little wonder, therefore, that episodes of mass violence have typically been accompanied by a yearning to find out 'what happened' and uncover 'the truth', a desire that sometimes emerges collectively as a social movement to confront the past.[8]

[1] '"Fake News," Trump's Obsession, Is Now a Cudgel for Strongmen' *The New York Times* (12 December 2017).
[2] '"No Such Thing as Rohingya", Myanmar Erases a History' *The New York Times* (2 December 2017).
[3] Human Rights Watch, 'Philippines's "Denier-in-Chief" Defends Murderous Drug War: Foreign Secretary Touts "Sovereignty" to Deflect Foreign Criticism' (28 September 2017).
[4] 'Fake News Is "Very Real" Word of the Year for 2017' *The Guardian* (2 November 2017).
[5] P Levi, *The Drowned and the Saved* (R Rosenthal trans, Abacus 1988) 1.
[6] Ibid.
[7] S Cohen, *States of Denial: Knowing About Atrocities and Suffering* (Polity Press 2001).
[8] M Osiel, *Mass Atrocity, Collective Memory, and the Law* (Transaction Publishers 1997) 266.

Doing Justice to History. Barrie Sander, Oxford University Press (2021). © Barrie Sander.
DOI: 10.1093/oso/9780198846871.003.0001

Over the course of the past century, the field of international criminal justice in general, and international criminal courts in particular, has emerged as one of society's most prominent responses to this desire.[9] During this period, not only have international criminal courts become normalised, but also the vocabulary of international criminal law has become an entrenched part of international discourse, permeating discussions in both legal and political commentary.[10]

The establishment of international criminal courts has contributed to the judicialisation of history.[11] As communities—both local and international—have struggled to make sense of mass atrocities, not only has it become more common for historians to rely on the idiom of international criminal law, but also expectations have increasingly been placed on international criminal courts to render authoritative historical accounts of the mass atrocity situations that fall within their purview. History, in other words, has been put on trial.

The relevance of history to international criminal justice has been acknowledged in the rhetoric that has tended to accompany the work of international criminal courts. In particular, the aspirational claims that have surrounded such courts have often reflected a faith in their capacity to produce clear and authoritative historical accounts concerning not only the behaviour of the accused on trial, but also the broader contexts within which they previously operated. For example, the British Chief Prosecutor at Nuremberg, Sir Hartley Shawcross, famously declared that the tribunal would provide 'a contemporary touchstone and an authoritative and impartial record to which future historians may turn for the truth, and future politicians for warning'.[12] Former President of the International Criminal Tribunal for the former Yugoslavia (ICTY), Judge McDonald, once stated that an important aim of the tribunal was 'to establish as judicial fact the full details of the madness that transpired in the former Yugoslavia'.[13] This perspective was eventually endorsed on the ICTY's official website, which lists as one of the tribunal's principal achievements 'creating a historical record, combatting denial and preventing attempts at revisionism'.[14] Similarly, former President of the International Tribunal for Rwanda (ICTR), Judge Pillay, once claimed that the tribunal was establishing 'a record which will help keep alive the world's collective memory' of what happened in Rwanda in 1994.[15]

[9] On the construction of the field of international criminal justice, see generally, F Mégret, 'International Criminal Justice as a Juridical Field' (2016) XIII *Champ Pénal*.

[10] SMH Nouwen and WG Werner, 'Monopolizing Global Justice: International Criminal Law as Challenge to Human Diversity' (2015) 13 *Journal of International Criminal Justice* 157.

[11] RJ Evans, 'History, Memory, and the Law: The Historian as Expert Witness' (2002) 41 *History and Theory* 326, 326.

[12] 'Twelfth Day, Tuesday, 4 December 1945: Morning Session', *Trial of the Major War Criminals before the International Military Tribunal, Nuremberg, 14 November 1945–1 October 1946: Volume III: Proceedings 1 December 1945–14 December 1945* (Nuremberg IMT 1947) 91, 92.

[13] 'Annual Report of the International Tribunal for the Prosecution of Persons Responsible for Serious Violations of International Humanitarian Law Committed in the Territory of the Former Yugoslavia since 1991' UN Docs A/53/219 S/1998/737 (1998) [296].

[14] 'Achievements', ICTY Website, accessible at: http://www.icty.org/en/about/tribunal/achievements (last accessed 2 June 2020).

[15] 'The Rule of Law and the Role of the Individual in the Pursuit of Human Rights by Judge Navanethem Pillay, President of the ICTR', *Friedrich-Ebert Stiftung 2003 Human Rights Award* (20 May 2003).

More recently, international criminal courts have been characterised as 'important tools for ensuring the right to the truth'.[16] References to the right to the truth have even begun to appear in international criminal proceedings. For instance, Judge Steiner in a single-judge decision of the International Criminal Court (ICC) Pre-Trial Chamber in the case of *Katanga and Ngudjolo* expressly recognised that 'the victims' core interest in the determination of the facts, the identification of those responsible and the declaration of their responsibility is at the root of the well-established right to the truth for the victims of serious violations of human rights'.[17]

These sentiments—which are far from isolated—have heightened expectations that international criminal courts are capable of acting as mechanisms of historical closure.[18] In particular, according to what has been termed the 'authoritative narrative theory',[19] judges are expected to cut through the adversarial narrative contestation of the prosecution, defence, and, in some contexts, victim participants at trial, to render authoritative historical narratives in their judgments. According to this perspective, judges act as positivist historians, imposing consensus on contrasting and conflicting evidence, by selecting one narrative in preference to others, and ultimately by conferring the mantle of fact on the narratives they construct and validate in their judgments.[20]

Although useful as a point of departure for thinking about the relationship between history and international criminal justice, the authoritative narrative theory begs a number of questions. What determines the scope and content of the historical narratives constructed within the judgments of international criminal courts? Which actors exert most influence over the process of historical narrative construction in different institutional contexts? What tends to be included and foregrounded within, as well as marginalised and excluded from, the narratives constructed within international criminal judgments? And to what extent are the histories constructed within international criminal courts consistent and authoritative both within and beyond the courtroom?

This book aims to address these questions by examining how the past has been confronted within three sets of international criminal courts: first, the International Military Tribunal (IMT) at Nuremberg and the International Military Tribunal for the Far East (IMTFE) at Tokyo; second, the UN ad hoc tribunals, namely the ICTY, the ICTR, and the Special Court for Sierra Leone (SCSL); and finally, the ICC. By critically examining the scope and content of the histories constructed within the judgments of these courts and by surfacing the influence of different actors and

[16] 'Study on the Right to the Truth: Report of the Office of the United Nations High Commissioner for Human Rights' UN Doc E/CN4/2006/91 (8 February 2006) [61].

[17] *Prosecutor v Germain Katanga and Mathieu Ngudjolo Chui* (Decision on the Set of Procedural Rights Attached to Procedural Status of Victim at the Pre-Trial Stage of the Case, Pre-Trial Chamber) ICC-01/04-01/07-474 (13 May 2008) [32].

[18] See, in this regard, JE Alvarez, 'Rush to Closure: Lessons of the Tadić Judgment' (1997–1998) 96 *Michigan Law Review* 2031, 2036 (referring to the 'model of closure' as 'a kind of Weberian "ideal type"' that has 'provided the single, coherent rubric to justify *ad hoc* international tribunals').

[19] TW Waters, 'A Kind of Judgment: Searching for Judicial Narratives After Death' (2010) 42 *George Washington International Law Review* 279, 285.

[20] EH Reiter, 'Fact, Narrative, and the Judicial Uses of History: *Delgamuukw* and Beyond' (2010) 8 *Indigenous Law Journal* 55, 78.

contexts over the precise orientation of judicial narratives, this study seeks to develop a deeper understanding of the emancipatory potential and limits of international criminal courts.

To date, relatively little scholarship has been undertaken in this area. In fact, whereas sophisticated work has extensively explored the construction of historical narratives within *domestic* atrocity trials,[21] scholarship on the relationship between history and *international* criminal courts has been far more limited.[22] Existing analyses have tended to focus on examining the relationship between history and particular categories of crime or modes of participation,[23] or unveiling how history has been constructed within isolated institutional contexts.[24] Likewise, leading treatises on international criminal law have devoted limited space to the relationship between history and international criminal justice.[25] This book begins to address this lacuna in the literature. The purpose of this opening chapter is to introduce the book's principal themes and arguments.

[21] See, for example, H Arendt, *Eichmann in Jerusalem: A Report on the Banality of Evil* (revised and enlarged edition, Penguin Books 1994); Osiel (n 8); L Douglas, *The Memory of Judgment: Making Law and History in the Trials of the Holocaust* (Yale University Press 2001); LY Bilsky, *Transformative Justice: Israeli Identity on Trial (Law, Meaning, and Violence)* (University of Michigan Press 2004); D Pendas, *The Frankfurt Auschwitz Trial, 1963–1965: Genocide, History, and the Limits of the Law* (CUP 2006); S Löytömäki, *The Law and Politics of Memory: Confronting the Past* (Routledge 2014); and KJ Heller and G Simpson (eds), *The Hidden Histories of War Crimes Trials* (OUP 2013). For important contributions that begin to look beyond domestic atrocity trials, see, in particular, M Koskenniemi, 'From Impunity to Show Trials' (2002) 6 *Max Planck Yearbook of United Nations Law* 1; G Simpson, *Law, War & Crime—War Crimes Trials and the Reinvention of International Law* (Polity Press 2007) Chapter 4; and G Baars, *The Corporation, Law and Capitalism: A Radical Perspective on the Role of Law in the Global Political Economy* (Brill 2019).

[22] The two studies that bear most similarity to the present book are NA Combs, *Fact-Finding Without Facts—The Uncertain Evidentiary Foundations of International Criminal Convictions* (CUP 2010); and RA Wilson, *Writing History in International Criminal Tribunals* (CUP 2011). Neither, however, is a substitute for the present work. In terms of scope, both studies focus primarily on the trials and judgments of ad hoc international criminal tribunals. Substantively, Combs' study explores the *fact-finding competencies* of the ICTR, the SCSL, and the Special Panels in the Dili District in East Timor. As such, Combs' book is concerned less with the historical narratives that are constructed within international criminal courts and more on identifying the evidentiary fact-finding impediments that have confronted such courts in particular contexts. Wilson's study seeks to understand why *historical evidence* concerning the contexts in which crimes occur has been relied upon by international prosecutors and defence counsel within different international criminal courts. As such, Wilson's book is concerned less with examining the scope and content of the historical narratives ultimately constructed within the judgments of international criminal courts and more with understanding what motivates different actors to rely on historical-contextual evidence in particular institutional settings.

[23] See, for example, C Fournet, *The Crime of Destruction and the Law of Genocide: Their Impact on Collective Memory* (Ashgate 2007); M Osiel, *Making Sense of Mass Atrocity* (CUP 2009); and N Henry, *War and Rape: Law, Memory and Justice* (Routledge 2011).

[24] See, for example, JN Shklar, *Legalism—Law Morals, and Political Trials* (Harvard University Press 1964); D Bloxham, *Genocide on Trial: War Crimes Trials and the Formation of Holocaust History and Memory* (OUP 2001); T Kelsall, *Culture under Cross-Examination: International Justice and the Special Court for Sierra Leone* (CUP 2009); B Elberling, *The Defendant in International Criminal Proceedings: Between Law and Historiography* (Hart Publishing 2012); K Bachmann and A Fatić, *The UN International Criminal Tribunals: Transition without Justice?* (Routledge 2015); D Zarkov and M Glasius (eds), *Narratives of Justice in and out of the Courtroom* (Springer 2014); T Waters (ed), *The Milošević Trial: An Autopsy* (OUP 2014); and KC Priemel, *The Betrayal: The Nuremberg Trials and German Divergence* (OUP 2016).

[25] See, for example, R Cryer et al, *An Introduction to International Criminal Law and Procedure* (3rd edn, CUP 2014) 38–40.

II. The Struggle for Historical Justice

While it is well established that international criminal courts author narratives about mass atrocity situations,[26] contestation remains over the extent to which international criminal courts should be expected to write history in practice.[27]

For some, international criminal trials should be designed to focus strictly on their adjudicative function of determining the culpability of the accused for alleged transgressions of criminal prohibitions and never shaped to satisfy wider sociopolitical objectives.[28] According to this *adjudicative* conception of justice, a court's consideration of history should be strictly limited to what is required to determine the criminal responsibility of the accused, and subordinated to the demands of adhering to liberal principles of criminal law aimed at safeguarding the rights of the accused to a fair and impartial trial.[29] Historical truth, on this account, is only important to the extent that it is considered a prerequisite for doing justice to the accused,[30] a point vividly illustrated by Jeremy Bentham's famous metaphor of 'Injustice, and her handmaid Falsehood'.[31] To the extent that international criminal courts render historical narratives in the process of determining the culpability of the accused, these histories should be considered unavoidable by-products or incidental consequences of carrying out their primary adjudicative function.[32] The sole questions with which international criminal courts should concern themselves are whether a particular crime has occurred and whether the accused may be held criminally responsible for it.

For others, focusing international criminal trials narrowly on their adjudicative function constitutes an overly restrictive view of justice.[33] Relying instead on *sociopolitical* conceptions of justice, adherents to this view believe that international criminal courts should be seen not simply as procedural devices for determining individual culpability, but as didactic and therapeutic mechanisms for achieving a range of broader sociopolitical objectives. For instance, a wide range of stakeholders have asserted the value of establishing a historical record for contributing to the reconciliation of divided local communities.[34] In a similar vein, it has often been claimed that historical

[26] B Sander and JvH Holtermann, 'Symposium: Doing Justice to Truth in International Criminal Courts and Tribunals' *Humanity* (3 July 2017).

[27] See similarly, L Arbour, *War Crimes and the Culture of Peace* (University of Toronto Press 2002) 33–34.

[28] The most prominent defence of this position remains Arendt (n 21).

[29] M Damaška, 'What Is the Point of International Criminal Justice?' (2008) 83 *Chicago-Kent Law Review* 329, 341 and 360.

[30] J Doak, 'The Therapeutic Dimension of Transitional Justice: Emotional Repair and Victim Satisfaction in International Trials and Truth Commissions' (2011) 11 *International Criminal Law Review* 263, 276.

[31] J Bentham, *Rationale of Judicial Evidence: Volume I* (Hunt and Clarke 1827, reprinted, Garland 1978) 22. See also, S Haack, 'Epistemology Legalized: Or, Truth, Justice, and the American Way' (2004) 49 *The American Journal of Jurisprudence* 43, 43 (arguing that Bentham's metaphor serves as a powerful reminder that 'justice requires not only just laws, and just administration of those laws, but also factual truth—objective factual truth').

[32] See, for example, R Zacklin, 'The Failings of Ad Hoc International Tribunals' (2004) 2 *Journal of International Criminal Justice* 541, 544; and R May and M Wierda, 'Evidence before the ICTY', in R May et al (eds), *Essays on the ICTY Procedure and Evidence: In Honour of Gabrielle Kirk McDonald* (Kluwer 2001) 249, 253.

[33] See, for example, Douglas (n 21) 2.

[34] See, for example, *Prosecutor v. Miroslav Deronjić* (Sentencing Judgment, Trial Chamber) IT-02-61-S (30 March 2004) [133]; MC Bassiouni, 'The Need for International Accountability', in MC Bassiouni (ed),

records may serve as warning signs to future generations, enabling them to learn from past mistakes and avoid the recurrence of prior episodes of mass violence.[35] In order to enhance the sociopolitical value of judicially constructed historical narratives, adherents to sociopolitical perspectives have sometimes advocated for international criminal courts to permit prosecution and defence counsel to paint with a broader historical brush, widening 'the spatial and temporal frame of courtroom storytelling in ways that allow litigants to flesh out their competing interpretations of recent history, and to argue these before an attentive public'.[36]

Taking this debate as its point of departure, *Chapter 2* shifts analytical focus away from the normative questions of *whether* and *to what extent* international criminal courts *should* conduct historical inquiries, towards a concern for examining *which* historical narratives *are* constructed in practice, *whose* histories *are* made to matter, and *which* actors *exert* particular influence over the scope and content of such narratives in different institutional contexts. As Gerry Simpson has put it, 'the larger question is not *whether* to make history but rather ... what sort of histories *are* made by international criminal tribunals'.[37]

In this study, I contend that international criminal courts constitute confrontational terrains in which a range of different actors struggle for public and official judicial acknowledgement of their preferred interpretations of the past.[38] Importantly, any attempt to narrate history, regardless of the context, will always be dependent on assumptions and choices (including which facts to select, how to order them, and what relationships those facts can be made to figure) that are far from neutral or mechanical.[39] As Martha Minow observes, 'history is never one story, and ... no telling can fully escape the preoccupations of the moment or the political concerns of the authors'.[40] As such, the narratives constructed within the judgments of international criminal courts are always the product of the situated choices of the different actors who interact within international criminal proceedings. These actors are engaged in a struggle to ensure that their preferred version of history receives a judicial seal of approval.[41] I characterise this contest as *a struggle for historical justice*—an intense competition for judicial recognition of each actor's preferred interpretation of the past.[42]

International Criminal Law: Volume III, International Enforcement (Martinus Nijhoff Publishers 2008) 3, 25; and S Brammertz, 'Address on the Occasion of the ICTY's 20th Anniversary' (27 May 2013).

35 DF Orentlicher, *Shrinking the Space for Denial: The Impact of the ICTY in Serbia* (Open Society Justice Initiative 2008) 15.

36 Osiel (n 8) 296.

37 G Simpson, 'International Criminal Justice and the Past', in G Boas et al, *International Criminal Justice: Legitimacy and Coherence* (Edward Elgar 2012) 123, 128 (emphasis added).

38 See, in this regard, Cohen (n 7) 225 (discussing the significance of the distinction between 'knowledge' and 'acknowledgement').

39 T Skouteris, 'Engaging History in International Law', in JM Beneyto and D Kennedy (eds), *New Approaches to International Law* (TMC Asser Press 2012) 99, 104.

40 M Minow, *Between Vengeance and Forgiveness: Facing History after Genocide and Mass Violence* (Beacon Press 1998) 143.

41 See similarly, Priemel (n 24) 14 ('trials provide an arena in which history ... is the very subject of a contest over which version of events will be read into the judgment with both sides hoping the judicially prevailing view ... will ultimately evolve into historiographical consensus').

42 The term 'historical justice' has rarely appeared in existing scholarship. Where it has been used, the phrase has generally been relied upon to refer to historical accountability processes rather than the judicial

The struggle for historical justice generally—though not always—culminates in the production of an international criminal judgment, which, despite being presented in conclusive and universalist terms, always entails the construction of a particular narrative about the past.[43] By recognising and foregrounding particular aspects and perspectives of mass atrocity situations whilst at the same time marginalising and excluding others from view, international criminal judgments constitute forms of legitimation.[44] The legitimating qualities of judgments also characterise the judicial decisions that precede them, but it is the judgment that represents the authoritative climax of international criminal proceedings. As Timothy Waters explains, 'it is judgment—grounded in the procedural integrity of the trial and sitting at the apex of the process—that produces the dispositive, displacing authority claimed for international criminal law's interpretation of violent conflict'.[45]

In order to facilitate this study's examination of the struggle for historical justice and the legitimating qualities of international criminal judgments in different institutional contexts, *Chapter 2* elaborates a framework for illuminating how different actors have influenced the scope and content of judicially constructed historical narratives in practice. This framework identifies the *actors* involved in struggles for historical justice, the *questions* around which such struggles tend to be structured, and the *practices* through which such struggles are conducted.

The framework first distinguishes the different *actors* who participate in struggles for historical justice within international criminal courts. Such struggles often have more interested parties than the original conflict, ranging from prosecutors, defendants, victims, and judges, to States and civil society groups.[46] Importantly, the agency of these actors is exercised against a background of contextual constraints, encompassing not only the set of circumstances external to such actors, but also their internal context, including their past experience and presuppositions.[47] It is through

acknowledgement of particular historical narratives. See, for example, R Teitel, *Transitional Justice* (OUP 2000) 69*ff.* (exploring 'the historical response to evil legacies and the question of what role historical accountability plays in liberal transition' under the banner of 'historical justice'); and K Neumann, 'Historians and the Yearning for Historical Justice' (2014) 18 *Rethinking History* 145, 147 (noting that in the aftermath of situations of mass atrocity, there is often 'an intense yearning for historical justice, that is, for redress of past wrongs'). For critical discussions of the different conceptions of justice that are related to international criminal courts, see generally, F Mégret, 'What Sort of Global Justice Is 'International Criminal Justice'?' (2015) 13 *Journal of International Criminal Justice* 77; and Nouwen and Werner (n 10).

[43] S Löytömäki, 'Law and Memory: The Politics of Victimhood' (2012) 21 *Griffith Law Review* 1, 18. See also, L van den Herik, 'International Criminal Law as a Spotlight and Black Holes as Constituents of Legacy' (2016) 110 *AJIL Unbound* 209, 209 ('Since the reach of international criminal tribunals is legally, politically, and practically limited, omissions, or black holes, are unavoidable').

[44] Simpson (n 21) 88–91 and 101–104; B Leebaw, *Judging State-Sponsored Violence, Imagining Political Change* (CUP 2011) 17–18 and 175; and Henry (n 23) 125–130. See also, V Nesiah, 'The Trials of History: Losing Justice in the Monstrous and the Banal', in R Buchanan and P Zumbansen (eds), *Law in Transition: Human Rights, Development and Transitional Justice* (Hart Publishing 2014) 289, 304 (highlighting how transitional justice institutions operate as 'official gatekeepers—privileging some histories while obscuring others').

[45] Waters (n 19) 281.

[46] R Steinke, *The Politics of International Criminal Justice: German Perspectives from Nuremberg to The Hague* (Hart Publishing 2012) 12.

[47] A Bianchi, 'Textual Interpretation and (International) Law Reading: The Myth of (In)determinacy and the Genealogy of Meaning', in PHF Bekker et al (eds), *Making Transnational Law Work in the Global Economy: Essays in Honour of Detlev Vagsts* (CUP 2010) 34, 41.

the practices and interactions of different actors that historical narratives are constructed and contested within international criminal proceedings.

The framework next identifies the particular *questions* around which struggles for historical justice have typically been structured. In general, such struggles have entailed contestation over the questions of whether particular categories of *crimes* have been committed and whether criminal responsibility for their commission may be attributed according to particular categories of *culpability*—encompassing modes of participation doctrines and grounds for excluding responsibility and mitigating punishment—to particular categories of *persons*. Crucially, these questions are contested at different junctures throughout the international criminal justice process, spanning the drafting of statutory frameworks, the selection and charging of accused persons for prosecution, and the evaluation of evidentiary materials and legal arguments at trial and within the decisions and judgments of international criminal courts.

Identifying these questions illuminates the specificity of international criminal law. As Tor Krever explains, international criminal law 'takes as its focus the particular, never the general: the specific international legal norm breach, the specific war crime, the specific act of violence, or at a slightly wider remove, the specific conflict with its several or many crimes and violations of human rights or international norms'.[48] At the same time, although these questions are oriented towards the specific and the particular, they also require an examination of selective aspects of the social contexts within which accused persons previously operated—both as a means of identifying whether particular crimes have been committed, as well as for ascertaining whether such crimes can be attributed to the accused.[49] It is through this process of selectively contextualising the behaviour of the accused on trial that international criminal courts not only seek to make the acts and omissions of the accused intelligible so that their culpability can be determined, but also become embroiled in constructing broader narratives that recount more generally 'what happened' during the mass atrocity situations under examination.

The final aspect of the framework concerns the different types of *practices* by which actors engage in struggles for historical justice within international criminal courts. Specifically, two types of practices are distinguishable:[50] first, *evidentiary* practices, which include the collection, admissibility, presentation, scrutiny, and evaluation of evidentiary materials, as well as the adoption, revision, and interpretation of concomitant rules of procedure and evidence; and second, *legal* practices, which include drafting, interpretative, charging, and defensive practices concerning legal categories, as well as the attendant sources, principles of justice, and rules of interpretation that guide their recognition and application in different institutional contexts. It is through these legal and evidentiary practices that mass atrocity situations are transformed into

[48] T Krever, 'International Criminal Law: An Ideology Critique' (2013) 26 *Leiden Journal of International Law* 701, 722.

[49] See similarly, Damaška (n 29) 336; and Wilson (n 22) 21–22.

[50] See similarly, K Campbell, 'Reassembling International Justice: The Making of "the Social" in International Criminal Law and Transitional Justice' (2014) 8 *International Journal of Transitional Justice* 53, 63 (distinguishing between 'practices of determining legal findings, which serve as the axiological foundation of the legal determination of responsibility and punishment' and 'fact-finding practices, which serve as the epistemic foundation of the legal determination of "fact" ').

a legal form, with the result that certain aspects of such events are acknowledged and foregrounded, whilst other aspects are marginalised and excluded.[51]

Although both evidentiary and legal practices exert influence over the scope and content of the historical narratives constructed within international criminal courts, the present study focuses primarily on the relationship between legal categories and historical narration. Legal categories—encompassing jurisdictional requirements, admissibility criteria, and sentencing factors—may be likened to narrative grids within which fact patterns must be specifically framed to fit to ensure their legal relevance in any particular case.[52] As Lawrence Douglas argues, 'history and memory do not simply enter a trial, as if offered an open ticket of admission', but rather '*filter* into the trial through certain legal or juridical categories that shape its form and substance'.[53] At the same time, however, this study illuminates how legal categories have also proven to be adaptable in the face of novel factual circumstances through the process of legal interpretation.[54]

By revealing the influence of different actors over the questions of whether particular categories of crimes have been committed (the *crime* question) and whether criminal responsibility for their commission may be attributed according to particular categories of culpability (the *culpability* question) to particular categories of persons (the *prosecutorial targets* question), this book reveals the dynamics of struggles for historical justice within international criminal courts and the different forms of legitimation that characterise their judgments as a result. In forging this path, this study situates itself within a body of critical scholarship whose prime interest lies in 'understanding' international criminal justice as part of an effort to 'upset international criminal justice's balance, expose some of its contradictions, increase its anxiety, and situate it within a larger horizon of possibilities'.[55]

III. The Prosecutorial Targets Question

All criminal justice systems are subject to an inevitable degree of selectivity. What distinguishes the field of international criminal justice is the sheer *scale* of its selectivity. As former ICTY Prosecutor Louise Arbour explains, whereas a domestic prosecutor is rarely called upon to be selective in relation to the commission of serious crimes, an international prosecutor 'has to be highly selective before committing resources to investigate or prosecute, and must work in a manner that can complement domestic

[51] See, in this regard, P Bourdieu, 'The Force of Law: Toward a Sociology of the Juridical Field' (1987) 38 *Hastings Law Journal* 805, 831–832.

[52] See, for example, Wilson (n 22) 9 ('Because courts *follow* law's own exceptional principles rather than those of historical inquiry, they can reduce complex histories to a defective legal template, and thereby distort history') (emphasis added).

[53] L Douglas, 'The Didactic Trial: Filtering History and Memory into the Courtroom' (2006) 14 *European Review* 513, 515–516 (emphasis in original).

[54] L Douglas, 'Perpetrator Proceedings and Didactic Trials', in A Duff et al (eds), *The Trial on Trial: Volume 2: Judgment and Calling to Account* (Hart Publishing 2006) 191, 196–199.

[55] F Mégret, 'International Criminal Justice: A Critical Research Agenda', in C Schwöbel (ed), *Critical Approaches to International Criminal Law: An Introduction* (Routledge 2014) 17, 21 and 46.

legal systems'.[56] In *Chapter 3*, I examine the practices that have influenced the selection of prosecutorial targets in different institutional settings and the implications that have followed for the scope and content of the historical narratives constructed by international criminal courts in their judgments.

An important starting point for this discussion is the recognition that the statutory frameworks of international criminal courts have generally been restricted to determining the criminal responsibility of *individuals*. This restriction has proven significant, not only precluding international criminal courts from formally determining the responsibility of collective entities, but also necessitating a high degree of selectivity regarding which individuals to target for prosecution. In turn, this high degree of selectivity has tended to transform the individuals on trial into symbols of the systems of criminality to which they once belonged and, in some cases, still support.[57] As Frédéric Mégret observes, individual defendants 'are almost never reduced to their "bare individuality" but always stand, in at least some symbolic manner, for broader systemic problems to which they are associated'.[58] This symbolism is reinforced by the fact that the contextual elements of the crimes adjudicated by international criminal courts and the collective elements of modes of participation often require judges to examine the broader social contexts within which individual defendants previously operated. Viewed from this perspective, the narrative significance of selecting who to target for international prosecution becomes clear, such determinations serving to define not only which individuals are called to answer for their alleged crimes, but also which aspects of the broader systems of criminality with which they are affiliated are examined in the process.

In order to illuminate which individuals have been targeted for prosecution within different international criminal courts, *Chapter 3* examines selectivity at two levels: first, *situational* selectivity, which concerns the mass atrocity situations that have been selected for investigation; and second, *case* selectivity, which concerns the individuals that have been targeted for prosecution within the situations selected for investigation.

In terms of *situational* selectivity, international criminal courts have predominantly been established as ad hoc responses to specific crisis situations in accordance with the interests of powerful States—whether as a means of punishing the vanquished and legitimating new structures of global governance (the Nuremberg IMT and the Tokyo IMTFE), assuaging public opinion by giving an impression of 'doing something' in response to a particular crisis situation (the ICTY and ICTR), or responding to a request for assistance with respect to a conflict situation that is of minimal concern or threat to their own political interests (the SCSL). The focus on situations that tend not to clash with the interests of powerful States has continued at the ICC where, in contrast to other international criminal courts, the Prosecutor has been empowered—subject to a number of legal and practical constraints—to determine which situations

[56] L Arbour, 'Progress and Challenges in International Criminal Justice' (1997) 21 *Fordham International Law Journal* 531, 534.

[57] See similarly, GP Fletcher, 'The Storrs Lectures: Liberals and Romantics at War: The Problem of Collective Guilt' (2002) 111 *Yale Law Journal* 1499, 1514.

[58] Mégret (n 42) 88 and 90.

to investigate. In particular, whether as a result of jurisdictional and admissibility limitations built into the ICC's statutory framework, or through the strategic facilitation or withholding of State cooperation and resources, the political context has generally proven to be a significant determinant of the situational focus of the ICC Prosecutor in practice. For instance, the ICC Prosecutor has generally moved relatively swiftly to initiate investigations into situations referred to it by States Parties or the Security Council, whilst proceeding with varying levels of enthusiasm towards initiating investigations into particular situations *proprio motu* depending on the level of support garnered from the international community at particular moments of time. In general, therefore, international prosecutors have either declined to investigate or been obstructed from pursuing investigations into situations which have the potential to threaten the interests of powerful States.

With respect to *case* selectivity, international prosecutors have generally targeted only a small number of individuals from a far larger pool of potential indictees within the situations they have investigated. In particular, three categories of case selectivity are distinguishable: first, *factional* selectivity, which concerns the prosecutorial practice of targeting individuals belonging to particular groups within mass atrocity situations to the marginalisation or complete exclusion of others; second, *functional* selectivity, which concerns the prosecutorial practice of targeting individuals who performed particular roles during the conflict—for example, high-ranking or low-ranking, political, military, or economic—to the marginalisation or complete exclusion of others; and finally, *procedural* selectivity, which concerns the inability to prosecute particular individuals on technical or procedural grounds, in particular their lack of fitness to stand trial or death prior to arrest, trial, or judgment. In *Chapter 3*, I identify a number of trends that have emerged with respect to each of these categories of case selectivity across different international criminal courts.

In terms of *factional* selectivity, for example, international prosecutors have either avoided or been prevented from targeting individuals protected by States on whose cooperation they are reliant and/or which are particularly powerful within the international community in general. In this vein, Allied personnel were not subject to prosecution at the IMT and IMTFE, North Atlantic Treaty Organization (NATO) personnel were subject to only a half-hearted investigation at the ICTY, members of the Rwandan Patriotic Front were not prosecuted at the ICTR, peacekeepers were not investigated at the SCSL, while the ICC Prosecutor has tended to de-prioritise prosecutions against members of factions aligned with the interests of the entities responsible for referring situations to it for investigation.

In terms of *functional* selectivity, international prosecutors have predominantly targeted political and military leaders perceived to bear the highest levels of responsibility for their participation in the commission of crimes. The preference for prosecuting *leaders* reflects the collective character of the crimes adjudicated by international criminal courts, which often—though not always—are set in motion by remote 'intellectual' architects and physically perpetrated by an executive machinery on the ground. Importantly, however, international prosecutors have also evinced a willingness to opportunistically prosecute mid-to-lower ranking individuals based on factors that include ease of apprehension, access to evidence, the extent of their participation, the character of their crimes, and strategic incentives to prepare the ground for more complex higher profile cases in the future.

The preference for prosecuting *political and military* figures reflects the fact that such actors are typically perceived to bear the greatest degree of responsibility for the commission of crimes, particularly in light of their participation in the orchestration of mass atrocities. The result of this preference, however, has been to marginalise or neglect the prosecution of other actors, including, most notably, individuals who use their positions within *private business entities* to participate in the commission of crimes. The relative neglect of prosecutions against private businesspersons stems from a range of factors including evidentiary obstacles, attribution challenges, and the interests of States in working with rather than against private businesses in the aftermath of mass atrocity situations.

Finally, as regards *procedural* selectivity, international criminal courts have been confronted with a not insignificant number of potential indictees and defendants who have been deemed unfit to stand trial or passed away prior to prosecution or verdict. Since no mechanisms exist for rendering judgments posthumously, in such circumstances judges are denied the opportunity to narrate history. As Mark Drumbl argues, the death of defendants prior to their verdicts being rendered demonstrates 'the expressive vulnerabilities' of international criminal proceedings.[59]

With respect to both situational and case selectivity, therefore, the targets of international prosecutions have primarily been selected in accordance with the political contexts within which international criminal courts have been forced to operate. While accident has played a role, particularly where individuals have died prior to prosecution or verdict, a clear thread running through the selection of targets for international prosecution has been the dominant influence of imbalances of power both between and within States beyond the courtroom. As Gerry Simpson observes, 'to a visitor from Mars perusing the historical record as set out in international tribunals for the past 60 years, the impression given would be that, with the exception of Bosnian Muslims and Croats tried at the ICTY, war crimes, crimes against humanity and genocide are carried out only by those states (or rebel groups) opposed to the interests of the North Atlantic elite'.[60]

Given the dominant influence of the political context on the selection of prosecutorial targets, the final part of *Chapter 3* identifies a number of strategies that have sometimes been deployed by defendants and their counsel in an effort to counter the hegemonic orientation of international criminal prosecutions.[61] Specifically, two strategies are examined: first, a strategy of *rupture* whereby defendants have sought to delegitimise the trial by illuminating crimes allegedly committed by individuals from States on whose behalf the prosecution has been brought; and second, a strategy of *rebuttal* whereby defence counsel have sought to construct a counter-narrative to the prosecution's theory of the case, which specifically relies on crimes committed by other parties to the conflict as a means of demonstrating that either the acts allegedly

[59] MA Drumbl, *Atrocity, Punishment, and International Law* (CUP 2007) 177.

[60] Simpson (n 37) 144.

[61] See, in this regard, L May, *Genocide: A Normative Account* (CUP 2010) 249 ('a vigorous defense often means enlarging the scope of people who can be held responsible for a crime').

perpetrated by the accused were not criminal at the time of commission or the prosecution had failed to meet its burden of proof. In terms of their impact, however, although such strategies have sometimes resonated with audiences beyond the courtroom, they have generally had limited success in influencing the narrative orientation of the judgments of international criminal courts. As a result, the focus of international criminal courts has tended to remain oriented towards the production of apologetic historical narratives that accord with the interests of States on whose cooperation prosecutors have been reliant and/or which are particularly powerful within the international community more generally.[62]

IV. The Crime Question

Categories of crime perform an important narrative function within international criminal courts, not only defining the harms for which accused persons may potentially be held criminally responsible, but also influencing which aspects of their social context will be rendered visible in the process. In *Chapter 4*, I examine the practices that have influenced the range and definition of crimes adjudicated within international criminal courts and the implications for the scope and content of the historical narratives constructed within their judgments. In particular, I reveal how the range and definition of crimes have been shaped by different actors at particular junctures within international criminal justice processes, including the drafting of statutory frameworks, the selection of charges to include in indictments, and the interpretation of crime categories in judicial decisions and judgments. Crucially, the relative importance of these junctures and the relative influence of different actors has tended to vary depending on the institutional context in which the struggle for control over the selection and meaning of categories of crime has been conducted.

At Nuremberg and Tokyo, for example, the range and definition of crimes adjudicated by the IMT and IMTFE were shaped primarily in accordance with the interests of the Allied States. For instance, during the drafting of the Nuremberg and Tokyo Charters, the interests of the Allies were unambiguously prioritised over concerns raised about the retroactive character of the categories of crime under discussion. The inclusion of crimes against peace in the Nuremberg and Tokyo Charters, for example, reflected the prioritisation of the interests of the United States both in proving that the German war had been illegal in its inception as well as ensuring the punishment of Japanese aggression.

The charging practices of prosecutors at the IMT and IMTFE were similarly dominated by Allied interests, both in terms of the extensive scope of the indictments, as well as their focus on particular crimes and incidents. For instance, the Nuremberg indictment included controversial charges related to the execution of 11,000 Polish officers in the Katyn Forest despite the widespread belief that the Soviets had been responsible

62 See similarly, Damaška (n 29) 361 ('international prosecutions are instituted mainly against citizens of states that are weak actors in the international arena or fail to enjoy the support of powerful nations'); and I Brownlie, *Principles of Public International Law* (7th edn, OUP 2008) 604 ('Political considerations, power, and patronage will continue to determine who is to be tried for international crimes and who [is] not').

for the massacre, while the Tokyo indictment included provocative charges of murder for killings committed as part of an illegal war despite their contradiction with the well-established distinction between the legality of going to war (*jus ad bellum*) and the legality of the conduct of war (*jus in bello*).

In their judgments, the judges of the IMT and IMTFE managed to side-step validating some of these more controversial charges, but were nonetheless powerless to examine crimes and incidents that had been purposefully omitted from the Nuremberg and Tokyo indictments as a result of Allied interests including, for example, various forms of sexual and gender-based violence and the bombing of civilian population centres. At the same time, the judges proved willing to give a judicial seal of approval to the legal validity of the crime categories that the Allies had included in the Nuremberg and Tokyo Charters despite retroactivity concerns that had been raised by the defence. The judges also adhered to the more restrictive aspects of the drafting of these crime categories, including the requirement that crimes against humanity had to be committed 'in execution of or in connection with any crime within the jurisdiction of the Tribunal'.[63] This war-nexus requirement—a deliberate attempt by the Allied drafters to preclude setting a precedent that might apply to Allied behaviour beyond the context of the Second World War—had significant implications for the Nuremberg IMT's historical record, resulting in the narrative exclusion of atrocities committed prior to the outbreak of war in 1939 from the tribunal's judgment.

While the pervasive theme that characterised the Nuremberg and Tokyo tribunals was one of Allied domination, the range and definition of crimes adjudicated by the UN ad hoc tribunals were shaped by a more diverse set of factors. In terms of drafting, for example, although States remained primarily responsible for delimiting the general categories of crime that fell within the subject-matter jurisdiction of the ad hoc tribunals, their statutory frameworks benefited from a wider range of inputs, including the involvement of the UN Secretary-General and the views of civil society groups. From a narrative perspective, the final texts of the Statutes that emerged from these drafting processes were notable in several respects.

Most importantly, the Statutes restricted the subject-matter jurisdiction of the ad hoc tribunals to war crimes, crimes against humanity and—in the case of the ICTY and ICTR—the crime of genocide,[64] thereby marking a shift away from the 'aggressive war paradigm' that had characterised the Nuremberg and Tokyo tribunals, towards an 'atrocity paradigm'.[65] As a result, questions concerning the allocation of responsibility for the initiation of the conflicts in the former Yugoslavia, Rwanda, and Sierra Leone generally fell beyond the purview of the judgments of the ad hoc tribunals.

The Statutes also recognised certain forms of criminality whose precise status under conventional or customary international law was uncertain at that time, a prominent example being the recognition of individual criminal responsibility for serious

[63] Article 6(c), Nuremberg Charter; Article 5(c), Tokyo Charter.

[64] Article 5 of the Statute of the SCSL empowered the Special Court to prosecute persons who had committed certain crimes under Sierra Leonean law, though these were not prosecuted in practice.

[65] L Douglas, 'From IMT to NMT: The Emergence of a Jurisprudence of Atrocity', in KC Priemel and A Stiller (eds), *Reassessing the Nuremberg Military Tribunals: Transitional Justice, Trial Narratives, and Historiography* (Berghahn Books 2012) 276, 285–288 (locating the beginnings of the shift in the Nuremberg Military Tribunals).

violations of Article 3 common to the Geneva Conventions 1949 and Additional Protocol II in the Statutes of the ICTR and SCSL. By progressively developing the law within the Statutes of the ad hoc tribunals, the drafters sought to empower judges to ensure the continued relevance of international criminal law to contemporary conditions of armed conflict and mass atrocity.

Beyond progressively developing the law, the Statutes were also notable for the laconic terms in which they were drafted, each elaborating little more than a list of crime categories with minimal guidance concerning the applicable law, rules of interpretation, or elements of crimes. By drafting the Statutes in such terse terms, the drafters unambiguously delegated significant discretion to the judges to identify the precise scope and content of the categories of crime through their case law.

The challenge of illuminating the meanings of the rudimentary crime categories that had been included in their statutory frameworks was duly accepted by the judges of the ad hoc tribunals. Particularly in their early decisions and judgments, judges found themselves confronted with a set of crime categories whose scope and content had remained both vague and relatively static for decades and a set of novel factual circumstances that reflected the evolving nature of atrocities and conflicts that had emerged in the second half of the twentieth century. In this context, the judges predominantly opted to progressively develop the meaning of the categories of crime within their Statutes so as to ensure their continued relevance to modern-day conditions. As Beth van Schaak explains, by relying upon 'a series of interpretive devices, analytical claims, and methodological choices', the ad hoc tribunals 'allowed defendants to be prosecuted for offenses … that were not part of positive law at the time the defendants acted', engaging in what became a 'dramatic, if unacknowledged, form of judicial lawmaking'.[66] In *Chapter 4*, I examine how the categories of war crimes and crimes against humanity were adapted to the privatisation of contemporary violence, while the crime of genocide was expanded to encompass more localised geographies of violence. In addition, I reveal how the prohibited acts recognised within each of these general crime categories were modernised to reflect not only more diverse forms of criminality, but also the ways in which different forms of violence intersect.

Beyond the central importance of judicial interpretation, the charging practices of prosecutors at the ad hoc tribunals also played a significant role in determining which crime categories were adjudicated in particular cases. Notably, in contrast to the State-dominated charging practices at the IMT and IMTFE, both the scope and focus of the charges at the ad hoc tribunals were influenced by a wider range of factors.

With respect to the *scope* of indictments, over time prosecutors at the ad hoc tribunals shifted their strategy away from bringing near-comprehensive charges that attempted to reflect the full alleged criminality of defendants towards a preference for charges that were more modestly representative of their alleged criminality. This shift was triggered both by lessons learned from prior prosecutorial practices, as well as pressure from States to speed up the completion of their mandates. The latter pressure also led judges to become more interventionist in managing the scope of indictments,

[66] B van Schaak, '*Crimen Sine Lege*: Judicial Lawmaking at the Intersection of Law and Morals' (2008) 97 *Georgetown Law Journal* 119, 172.

whilst spurring prosecutors at the ICTY and ICTR to rely on negotiated forms of justice in an effort to further reduce the size of their caseloads.

In terms of the *focus* of indictments, beyond the jurisdictional limitations of their mandates and the availability of evidence, prosecutors were influenced by a range of factors in determining the precise charges to bring in particular cases. In *Chapter 4*, I illustrate the different factors at play by examining the fluctuating record of the ICTR concerning the prosecution of sexual violence crimes. Relevant factors that shaped the charging record in practice included the investigative strategies and prosecutorial priorities of different prosecutors, sporadic witness testimony, civil society activism, the exercise of judicial discretion, and State pressure.

In contrast to the UN ad hoc tribunals, the ICC is a permanent international court with primarily prospective and potentially worldwide jurisdiction. These characteristics have proven influential in determining the range and definition of crimes categories adjudicated by the Court in practice.

Since the ICC was designed to be a judicial institution which could, in theory at least, have jurisdiction over the nationals of the States involved in its establishment, the crime categories included in the ICC Statute and further elaborated in the Elements of Crimes were drafted with a heightened degree of definitional precision. Reflecting the delicate consensus-building negotiation process that preceded its finalisation, the ICC Statute contains both progressive and restrictive elements.

Some of the more progressive elements of the ICC Statute—for example, the inclusion of war crimes in non-international armed conflicts—reflect the receptivity of the drafters to the then-emerging jurisprudence of the ad hoc tribunals. Other elements—such as the inclusion of a broad range of sexual and gender-based crimes and the crime of recruiting and using child soldiers—owe more to the influence of civil society groups. Ultimately, however, many of the more progressive dimensions of the ICC Statute were only accepted subject to certain restrictions, which reflected the difficult compromises forged during the drafting process. For example, although gender-based persecution was recognised in the ICC Statute, 'gender' was defined ambiguously to refer to 'the two sexes, male and female, within the context of society'—the notion of 'two sexes' responding to concerns raised by a number of conservative and religious States and civil society groups that the inclusion of gender as a ground of persecution might compel them to recognise rights based on sexual orientation, while the reference to 'within the context of society' responding to the interests of other States and civil society groups that advocated for a broader socially constructed notion of gender.[67] In a similar vein, although the crime of aggression was recognised and—by amendment—defined in the ICC Statute, the interests of more powerful States are reflected in the restrictive conditions that must be satisfied before the ICC can exercise jurisdiction over the crime. As a result, the narrative orientation of the Court is likely to remain focused on war crimes, crimes against humanity, and the crime of genocide for the foreseeable future.

The detailed elaboration of crime categories in the ICC Statute and the Elements of Crimes, together with the ICC's primarily prospective jurisdiction, have afforded

[67] Article 7(3), ICC Statute.

judges less leeway or need to progressively develop the meaning of such categories within their case law. As such, whereas judicial creativity proved to be one of the dominant influences over the scope and content of the historical narratives constructed in the judgments of the ad hoc tribunals, in practice it has been the charging practices of the ICC Prosecutor that have proven to be a more significant influence over the scope and orientation of the historical narratives constructed in ICC judgments.

In terms of the *scope* of the charges, the ICC Prosecutor has predominantly brought narrow charges concerning a limited number of crimes and a small number of incidents. In *Lubanga*, for example, the Prosecutor limited the charges to the war crimes of conscripting, enlisting, and using child soldiers,[68] while in *Katanga and Ngudjolo*, the Prosecutor brought thirteen counts of war crimes and crimes against humanity, all of which focused on a single attack that took place on 24 February 2003.[69] As a result, the narratives constructed in the judgments of the ICC to date have tended to focus more narrowly on a limited number of incidents and themes of criminality.

This narrow charging strategy is primarily a reflection of the institutional design of the ICC, which was established by States with the potential to investigate multiple mass atrocity situations. In addition, the ICC Prosecutor has also been confronted by a number of external political constraints, including fluctuating security concerns, a limited budget, and dependency on State cooperation to conduct effective investigations. While the Prosecutor has on occasion brought more extensive charges—the Pre-Trial Chamber confirmed seventy counts of crimes against humanity and war crimes in the case of *Ongwen*, for example—the Office of the Prosecution's most recent strategy plan suggests that, looking to the future, the Prosecutor intends to give heightened consideration to the possibility of bringing 'narrower but stronger cases' that focus on 'key aspects of victimisation, particular incidents, areas, time periods, or a single accused'.[70]

In terms of the *focus* of the charges, beyond the jurisdictional limitations of the ICC and the availability of evidence, the precise charges brought in any particular case at the ICC have hinged on a diversity of factors. In *Chapter 4*, I illustrate the different influences at play by examining the fluctuating record of the ICC Prosecutor concerning the prosecution of sexual and gender-based crimes. Particularly significant has been the shift in investigative strategy away from a focused and phased approach to investigations under former ICC Prosecutor Luis Moreno-Ocampo towards in-depth, open-ended investigations under Fatou Bensouda. This shift, together with a number of other institutional reforms, appears to have been at least partially responsible for the more consistent inclusion of sexual and gender-based crimes within charging documents, as well as improvements in the number of cases and charges confirmed at the confirmation of charges stage of proceedings. Beyond the investigative strategy and priorities of the ICC Prosecutor, other relevant factors that have shaped the charging

[68] *Prosecutor v Thomas Lubanga Dyilo* (Decision on the Confirmation of Charges, Pre-Trial Chamber) ICC-01/04-01/06-803-tEN (29 January 2007) [9]–[12].

[69] *Prosecutor v Germain Katanga and Mathieu Ngudjolo Chui* (Decision on Confirmation of Charges, Pre-Trial Chamber) ICC-01/04-01/07-717 (30 September 2008) [573]–[581] (confirming 10 of the 13 counts).

[70] ICC Office of the Prosecutor, 'Strategic Plan 2019–2021' (17 July 2019) [24].

record at the ICC include the exercise of judicial oversight and the influence of civil society groups and victims' legal representatives.

Ultimately, this comparative analysis reveals how the range and definition of categories of crimes adjudicated within international criminal courts have been contingent on the situated choices of different actors operating in particular institutional contexts. Similar to the selection of prosecutorial targets, States have played an important role, influencing both the jurisdictional limits of international criminal courts, as well as the scope and focus of the crimes charged in particular cases. However, particularly at the UN ad hoc tribunals and the ICC, a wider range of practices have also proven influential, including most prominently the judicial creativity of judges in progressively developing the meaning of crime categories as well as the evolving investigative and prosecutorial priorities of international prosecutors in defining the scope and focus of the charges.

Although the substantive focus of international criminal courts has fluctuated over time, *Chapter 4* concludes by identifying a number of forms of criminality that have consistently been marginalised despite falling within the scope of their subject-matter jurisdiction—specifically, sexual violence against men and boys, environmental harms, and war crimes concerning the conduct of hostilities. In practice, the marginalisation of these forms of violence has been the product of a range of factors, including inadequate sensitivity of investigators, lawyers, and judges; evidentiary challenges; and uncertainties and ambiguities in the law. By surfacing these factors, I reveal how the structure and architecture of international criminal law, together with the practices of different actors operating within international criminal courts, have shaped the (in)visibility of different forms of violence within the histories constructed in international criminal judgments.

V. The Culpability Question

The vast majority of crimes adjudicated by international criminal courts are manifestations of 'system criminality', a term that typically refers to two features of such offences:[71] first, the *collective* participation of large numbers of individuals in their perpetration; and second, the *systemic* authorisation or enablement of their commission. The collective and systemic dimensions of system crimes have raised a number of thorny questions for international criminal courts tasked with determining when and how criminal responsibility for such offences may be attributed to individuals.

In confronting questions of attribution, international criminal courts have generally been mindful of the principle of personal culpability, the animating concern of which is to ensure that criminal responsibility is attributed to individuals and their punishment calibrated in ways that respect individual agency.[72] In the context of

[71] E van Sliedregt, *Individual Criminal Responsibility in International Law* (OUP 2012) 20–22; and A Smeulers, 'Punishing the Enemies of All Mankind' (2008) 21 *Leiden Journal of International Law* 971, 976–981.

[72] D Robinson, 'A Cosmopolitan Liberal Account of International Criminal Law' (2013) 26 *Leiden Journal of International Law* 127, 131 and 140.

determining individual criminal responsibility for system crimes, adhering to the principle of personal culpability has confronted international criminal courts with the vexing question of whether and how the collective and systemic dimensions of mass atrocity situations may alter the normative expectations that may reasonably be placed on individuals operating in such environments.[73] According to a range of studies in the field of social science, mass atrocity contexts may both *expand* the agency of individuals by enabling them to achieve a greater amount of violence and harm than could otherwise be achieved alone, as well as *diminish* individual agency through their subjection to different forms of situational pressures.[74] As such, when confronting questions of attribution in their case law, international criminal courts have had to determine the extent to which the social contexts in which accused individuals operated should be deemed *legally relevant* to the determination of their criminal responsibility.

In tackling this question, international criminal courts have had to steer a course between 'an absurd and ahistorical individualism', which ignores the social contexts in which individual actions occur, and 'a reductive structural determinism', which characterises individuals as mere puppets of the social structures within which they operate.[75] In *Chapter 5*, I examine some of the categories of culpability that have been recognised by international criminal courts for the purpose of attributing criminal responsibility for system crimes to individuals in different institutional contexts. In particular, two types of culpability categories are distinguished: first, *modes of participation doctrines*, by which international criminal courts connect individuals to the commission of crimes; and second, *grounds for excluding responsibility and desert-based mitigating factors in sentencing*, by which international criminal courts exclude the responsibility or mitigate the punishment of individuals in light of the situational pressures of their social contexts.[76] These categories perform a significant narrative function within international criminal judgments, defining not only the types of acts and omissions that can link and disconnect individuals to and from the commission of system crimes, but also the extent to which their social contexts are relevant for rendering their behaviour intelligible for this purpose.

Modes of participation doctrines are typically free-standing categories, although sometimes are incorporated into the definition of an offence, as is the case for certain inchoate crimes which criminalise conduct when the prohibited harm has not yet occurred.[77] In practice, modes of participation doctrines serve a dual narrative function in the judgments of international criminal courts. First, such doctrines perform the function of *linking individuals with particular crimes*,[78] defining not only whether individuals can be connected to particular crimes, but also how individuals are connected

[73] Ibid 140–142.

[74] KJ Fisher, *Moral Accountability and International Criminal Law: Holding Agents of Atrocity Accountable to the World* (Routledge 2012) 77–78.

[75] Simpson (n 21) 71.

[76] On 'desert-based mitigating factors', see D Husak, 'Partial Defenses', in D Husak, *The Philosophy of Criminal Law: Selected Essays* (OUP 2010) 311, 313; and K Ambos, *Treatise on International Criminal Law: Volume I: Foundations and General Part* (OUP 2013) 303.

[77] A Zahar and G Sluiter, *International Criminal Law: A Critical Introduction* (OUP 2008) 220; A Ashworth and J Horder, *Principles of Criminal Law* (7th edn, OUP 2013) 6.

[78] JD Ohlin, 'Second-Order Linking Principles: Combining Vertical and Horizontal Modes of Liability' (2012) 25 *Leiden Journal of International Law* 771, 772.

to their commission.[79] As Kai Ambos explains, each mode of participation doctrine constructs a particular narrative about 'the role, function, position, or status of the participants/accused in the given criminal organization and the quality and weight of their contribution to the criminal context or collective group/crime'.[80] Second, modes of participation doctrines *represent the dynamics of collective action and the complex organisational structures* by which system crimes are carried out.[81] By identifying the role of individuals within particular contexts, modes of participation doctrines represent the social phenomena of system crimes in different ways, emphasising particular characteristics of their perpetration and affecting the ways in which historical events are portrayed.[82] As Mikaela Heikkilä explains, modes of participation doctrines not only seek to represent the criminal behaviour of an individual offender, but also strive to 'mirror the context of action in which the individual offender behaves criminally'.[83]

In practice, a range of modes of participation doctrines have been formulated by international criminal courts in an effort to represent the myriad forms that participation may take in situations of mass atrocity. Different doctrines enable distinct narratives to be constructed about the roles and contributions of the individuals on trial as well as the dynamics of the collective contexts within which they operated. In *Chapter 5*, I examine a selection of modes of participation doctrines through which international criminal courts have determined the criminal responsibility of the alleged masterminds of system crimes, namely: the inchoate crime of *conspiracy* at the Nuremberg IMT and Tokyo IMTFE; *joint criminal enterprise* at the UN ad hoc tribunals; and different forms of *perpetration* at the ICC. My analysis reveals a propensity on the part of judges to redevelop modes of participation doctrines rooted in domestic legal systems to fit the particular characteristics of mass atrocity environments—moulding different doctrines to fit the factual circumstances of particular cases—with the attendant risk of jeopardising the stability and fairness of the criminal law.[84] I also reveal how the narratives constructed through recourse to these doctrines have varied in at least two key respects: first, in terms of the strength of the connection or link required between defendants and the crimes with which they are charged; and second, in terms of the range of different degrees of participation for which such categories impose the same culpability label. In general, the weaker the required connection between an individual and the crimes, and the broader the range of degrees

[79] N Jain, *Perpetrators and Accessories in International Criminal Law: Individual Modes of Responsibility for Collective Crimes* (Hart Publishing 2014) 7–8; and H van der Wilt, 'Srebrenica: On Joint Criminal Enterprise, Aiding and Abetting and Command Responsibility' (2015) 62 *Netherlands International Law Review* 229, 239.

[80] Ambos (n 76) 86–87.

[81] M Osiel, 'Choosing among Alternative Responses to Mass Atrocity: Between the Individual and the Collectivity' *Ethics & International Affairs* (18 September 2015).

[82] M Heikkilä, *Coping with International Atrocities through Criminal Law: A Study into the Typical Features of International Criminality and the Reflection of these Traits in International Criminal Law* (Åbo Akademi University Press 2013) 230 and 259–260.

[83] Ibid 236.

[84] E van Sliedregt, 'The Curious Case of International Criminal Liability' (2012) 10 *Journal of International Criminal Justice* 1171, 1185; D Guilfoyle, 'Responsibility for Collective Atrocities: Fair Labelling and Approaches to Commission in International Criminal Law' (2011) 64 *Current Legal Problems* 255, 266; H van der Wilt, 'Joint Criminal Enterprise and Functional Perpetration', in A Nollkaemper and HG van der Wilt (eds), *System Criminality* (CUP 2009) 158, 166.

of participation encompassed within particular modes of participation doctrines, the easier international criminal courts have found it to attribute criminal responsibility to alleged masterminds of system crimes, but at the risk of over-inflating their agency and passing over the complexity of the institutional dynamics of the environments within which they operated.

Even if an international criminal court is able to establish that a particular crime has been committed and to identify the participation of an individual in the crime's commission, there exist a range of grounds for excluding responsibility and desert-based mitigating factors on the basis of which an individual's culpability may either be excluded or reduced. In practice, these categories also perform an important narrative function, not only defining the circumstances when the link between defendants and the commission of crimes may be broken or mitigated, but also the aspects of a defendant's social context that are legally relevant and irrelevant—and thereby rendered visible or invisible—for the purpose of determining their culpability.

In general, international criminal courts have adopted a restrictive approach to grounds for excluding responsibility and desert-based mitigating factors, identifying only a narrow and tightly defined range of situational pressures on the basis of which the criminal responsibility of individuals may be excluded or their punishment in some way mitigated. In *Chapter 5*, I illustrate this trend by examining the extent to which an individual's criminal responsibility has been excluded or their punishment mitigated as a result of two types of situational pressures: first, situations that involve the physical or psychological *coercion* of an individual to act in a wrongful manner—encompassing a review of the scope and content of the defence of duress and a range of coercion-related factors in sentencing; and second, situations that result in diminishing an individual's *cognition* of wrongdoing—encompassing a review of the scope and content of the defence of mistake of law. By only recognising a restrictively defined range of grounds for excluding responsibility and desert-based mitigating factors, international criminal courts have conveyed the message that most situational pressures encountered in mass atrocity situations could reasonably have been resisted by defendants. In narrative terms, the result of this restrictive approach has been to decontextualise the behaviour of defendants, excluding or at the very least marginalising those aspects of a defendant's social context which have implicitly been deemed merely *explanatory* of their behaviour as opposed to *exculpatory or mitigating*.

Ultimately, through this comparative analysis of categories of culpability I reveal a tendency on the part of international criminal courts to *selectively contextualise* the behaviour of the defendants on trial for the purpose of determining their culpability. On the one hand, international criminal courts have formulated a range of inchoate crimes and modes of participation doctrines through which they have sought to reflect how the collective and systemic character of mass atrocity situations may expand individual agency. On the other, international criminal courts have recognised only a narrow and restrictively defined set of grounds for excluding responsibility and desert-based mitigating factors on the implicit assumption that most of the situational pressures that characterise mass atrocity situations could reasonably have been resisted by defendants. As a result, the narratives constructed in the judgments of international criminal courts have tended to demonstrate greater concern for identifying links between individuals and system crimes than attempting to understand how individuals may be acculturated into violence by situational pressures stemming from the collective and systemic dimensions of the mass atrocity contexts in which they operated.

VI. Beyond the Purview of International Criminal Judgments

Although international criminal courts have not been blind to the collective and systemic contexts in which system crimes are typically carried out, in practice the scope and focus of judicial contextualisation has been restricted by the selection of individuals targeted for prosecution, the range and definition of crimes adjudicated, and the categories of culpability relied upon in particular cases. As Mirjan Damaška argues, the historical narratives constructed in international criminal judgments are inevitably restricted by the fact that 'judges cannot sufficiently disentangle themselves from the webs of legal relevancy'.[85]

Against this background, *Chapter 6* conducts a more detailed examination of those aspects of mass atrocity situations that have tended to be marginalised or excluded from the narratives of international criminal courts. In particular, three aspects of mass atrocity situations that have received little or no attention within international criminal judgments are examined: first, the structural and slow violence that tends to exist prior to, during, and after the outbreak of situations of mass atrocity; second, the interventions of international actors, including the policies and practices of colonial powers, international financial institutions, and international peacekeeping forces; and finally, the roles performed by bystander communities and resisters during episodes of mass violence.

By illuminating these narrative blind spots, international criminal courts are revealed to be somewhat 'carnivalesque' in their depiction of mass atrocity situations:[86] just like the mirrors of a carnival funhouse, international criminal courts have tended to greatly exaggerate one aspect of mass atrocities, namely the actions of local political and military figures and the immediate collective contexts within which they operated, whilst at the same time distorting and minimising others, including the myriad structural and international interventions that establish some of the conditions of possibility for mass violence. As Vasuki Nesiah has put it, 'moments of *anti-impunity* against perpetrators of international crimes are also moments of *impunity* for injustices committed by systemic inequality'.[87]

Importantly, to shine a spotlight on the narrative exclusions of international criminal courts is neither to belittle the acts of violence committed by the individuals convicted by international criminal courts nor to suggest that such courts should necessarily broaden their narrative frames. Rather, highlighting these blind spots more modestly serves to call attention to the narrative limits of international criminal courts

[85] Damaška (n 29) 336.

[86] The 'carnivalesque' image is taken from DO Pendas, *The Frankfurt Auschwitz Trial, 1963–1965: Genocide, History, and the Limits of the Law* (CUP 2006) 294.

[87] V Nesiah, 'Doing History with Impunity', in K Engle et al (eds), *Anti-Impunity and the Human Rights Agenda* (CUP 2016) 95, 96 (emphasis added).

and to highlight the risk that their judgments may undermine more nuanced understandings of human agency in mass atrocity contexts, whilst legitimating some of the structural and slower forms of violence that they marginalise or exclude.[88]

VII. Narrative Pluralism Within and Beyond International Criminal Courts

Having illuminated the scope and content of the historical narratives constructed in the judgments of international criminal courts, *Chapter 7* critically reflects on the expectations of historical finality and closure that have typically accompanied the rendering of international criminal judgments.[89] Specifically, I argue that the historical narratives constructed within the judgments of international criminal courts tend to be neither static nor final, but subject to a process of ongoing contestation and evolution over time both within and beyond the courtroom.[90]

Within the courtroom, despite the asserted finality of international criminal judgments and the deployment of doctrines such as judicial notice, through which international criminal courts may nurture consensus and prevent challenges to particular facts in future cases, judicially constructed narratives are often less final and uniform than is generally assumed. In particular, two types of narrative pluralism may arise within the international criminal courtroom: first, *inter-court* narrative pluralism, which arises where the judgments of different courts examine the same mass atrocity situation from different perspectives; and second, *intra-court* narrative pluralism, which arises where narratives constructed within an international criminal judgment are revisited in later cases adjudicated by the same court. The roots of narrative pluralism within the courtroom are varied, including differences that arise between cases relating to the availability and evaluation of evidence, the charging practices of international prosecutors, and the judicial interpretation of legal categories such as crimes and modes of participation.

Even where international criminal courts manage to achieve *inter-court* and *intra-court* narrative consistency, a range of social psychological and practical factors have often generated a gap between the intended meaning of such narratives and their public or social meaning amongst different audiences *beyond* the courtroom. *Social psychological* factors include motivational and cognitive biases that influence how individuals perceive the world and themselves.[91] As a result of these biases, members of

[88] See similarly, E Dauphinee, 'War Crimes and the Ruin of Law' (2008) 37 *Millennium: Journal of International Studies* 49; Krever (n 48); G Baars, 'Making ICL History: On the Need to Move beyond Pre-Fab Critiques of ICL', in C Schwöbel (ed), *Critical Approaches to International Criminal Law: An Introduction* (Routledge 2014) 196; and SMH Nouwen, '"As You Set out for Ithaka": Practical, Epistemological, Ethical, and Existential Questions about Socio-Legal Empirical Research in Conflict' (2014) 27 *Leiden Journal of International Law* 227, 254–255.

[89] The chapter is an adapted version of B Sander, 'History on Trial: Historical Narrative Pluralism within and beyond International Criminal Courts' (2018) 67 *International and Comparative Law Quarterly* 547.

[90] See similarly, D Buss, 'Expert Witnesses and International War Crimes Trial: Making Sense of Large-Scale Violence in Rwanda', in D Zarkov and M Glasius (eds), *Narrative of Justice In and Out of the Courtroom: Former Yugoslavia and Beyond* (Springer 2014) 23, 43; and Douglas (n 54) 198.

[91] See generally, S Ford, 'A Social Psychology Model of the Perceived Legitimacy of International Criminal Courts: Implications for the Success of Transitional Justice Mechanisms' (2012) 45 *Vanderbilt Journal of*

local communities torn apart by conflict often interpret judicially constructed narratives against the background of their communal attachments to particular factions to the underlying conflict, as well as attendant self-serving narratives of collective victimhood. *Practical* factors that influence narrative reception include the geographical, cultural, and linguistic remoteness of international criminal courts, which sometimes result in judicially constructed narratives failing to reach members of local communities at all.[92] In other instances, judicial narratives only reach local audiences after first being filtered through international and/or local carrier groups.[93] In particular, national politicians and local media outlets have often proven particularly influential in shaping how judicially constructed narratives are received and understood by local audiences in post-conflict societies.[94] Taken together, these social psychological and practical factors reveal that rather than serving as bulwarks against denialism, it is more common for both the authority and interpretation of the judicially constructed historical narratives to remain contested long after their initial construction.

VIII. Conclusion

Michael Marrus once observed that for professional historians, 'the narrative that emerges from his or her pen depends directly upon the kinds of questions asked at the beginning'.[95] This book reveals how the scope and content of the historical narratives to emerge from the pens of international criminal courts in their judgments are the product of struggles for historical justice that culminate in the judicial legitimation of particular understandings of the past to the marginalisation and exclusion of others.

In *Chapter 8*, I reflect on three strands of legitimation that pervade the judgments of the international criminal courts examined in this study. In particular, I suggest that the historical narratives constructed in international criminal judgments have generally been: *apologetic*, shaped and restricted in significant respects in accordance with the balance of power between and within States beyond the courtroom; *spectacular*, foregrounding a narrow set of egregious physical, direct, and immediate forms of violence to the neglect of other types of harm; and *narrowly contextualised*, in ways that

Transnational Law 405; M Milanović, 'Establishing the Facts about Mass Atrocities: Accounting for the Failure of the ICTY to Persuade Target Audiences' (2016) 47 *Georgetown Journal of International Law* 1321; and M Milanović, 'Courting Failure: When Are International Criminal Courts Likely to Be Believed by Local Audiences?', in KJ Heller et al (eds), *The Oxford Handbook of International Criminal Law* (OUP 2020) 261.

[92] JN Clark, 'The Impact Question: The ICTY and the Restoration and Maintenance of Peace', in B Swart et al (eds), *The Legacy of the International Criminal Tribunal for the Former Yugoslavia* (OUP 2011) 55, 76.

[93] Henry (n 23) 119–122.

[94] See, for example, E Ramulić, 'Victims' Perspectives', in RH Steinberg (ed), *Assessing the Legacy of the ICTY* (Martinus Nijhoff Publishers 2011) 103, 105; R Hodžić, 'A Long Road Yet to Reconciliation: The Impact of the ICTY on Reconciliation and Victims' Perceptions of Criminal Justice', in RH Steinberg (ed), *Assessing the Legacy of the ICTY* (Martinus Nijhoff Publishers 2011) 115, 117; and M Klarin, 'The Impact of the ICTY Trials on Public Opinion in the Former Yugoslavia' (2009) 7 *Journal of International Criminal Justice* 89, 90.

[95] MR Marrus, 'History and the Holocaust in the Courtroom', in R Smelser (ed), *Lessons and Legacies V: The Holocaust and Justice* (Northwestern University Press 2002) 215, 232.

focus on localised systems of criminality rather than broader international networks, emphasise military and political figures at the expense of economic actors, and direct attention towards the ways in which the collective and systemic qualities of system crimes may expand individual agency to the neglect of the dilemmas and ambiguities of agency experienced within the spectrum of human relationships that exist in mass atrocity situations.

Reflecting in particular on how international criminal courts tend to be structurally constrained in their ability to address demands for historical justice that challenge the existing international political order, the study concludes by offering two perspectives that may open up avenues for orienting the practices of international criminal courts towards a more emancipatory politics: first, a strategic expressivist perspective concerned with whether and how different actors may mobilise the expressive power of the vocabulary and practices of international criminal justice processes to advance their strategic agendas; and second, a critical perspective concerned with contextualising the historical narratives constructed within the judgments of international criminal courts, viewing them in more humble terms as moments of discursive beginning rather than instances of historical closure.

Saul Friedlander famously described the Holocaust as 'an event which tests our traditional conceptual and representational categories, an "event at the limits"'.[96] Whenever societies respond to mass atrocity situations, there is always an inevitable incompleteness and inadequacy to such efforts, a gap between the justice individuals and communities strive for and the institutional means at their disposal by which they attempt to deliver it.[97] This book modestly aims to contribute to the process of illuminating this gap, as well as a sobering of some of the ambitious hopes and aspirations that have traditionally been invested in international criminal courts.

[96] S Friedlander, 'Introduction', in S Friedlander (ed), *Probing the Limits of Representation: Nazism and the 'Final Solution'* (Harvard University Press 1992) 1, 3.

[97] See similarly, Nouwen and Werner (n 10) 176 ('human law, culture and conventions will *always* be short of the justice we strive for because justice is mediated by men'); and Minow (n 40) 5 (recognising 'the incompleteness and inescapable inadequacy of each possible response to collective atrocities').

2
The Struggle for Historical Justice

In the field of international criminal justice, appeals to history have been advanced from multiple perspectives. There are, in fact, at least three ways in which the relationship between history and international criminal justice has been conceived.[1]

First, there are *histories of international criminal justice*—narrative accounts of the origins and trajectory of the field. A frequently invoked narrative, for example, presents the judicialisation of the field through the metaphor of a physical journey, beginning at Nuremberg, continuing in The Hague, and culminating in Rome.[2] By depicting the institutional development of the field as a linear series of events, scholars and practitioners have been able to generate a sense of disciplinary movement and orient the field towards progress.[3] As David Koller explains, individual episodic developments in the field become 'no longer isolated phenomena to take on their own accord, but rather milestones falling on an invisible line of progress from injustice to a more rudimentary, and finally, to a more advanced international law'.[4] These types of narratives have also been invoked by international prosecutors in their opening statements—a tactic aimed at shoring up the legitimacy of international prosecutions.[5]

In contrast to evolutionary histories of international criminal justice, more critically oriented accounts have sought to disrupt conventional narratives and assumptions about the origins and development of the field.[6] Emily Haslam, for example, has discussed the nineteenth-century slave trade trial of Joseph Peters, specifically comparing the centrality of African testimony in the trial with how it was reported at the time, so as to expose contemporary scholarship's marginalisation of the contribution of Africans to the development of international criminal law and to disrupt conventional assumptions of African victims as passive recipients of, rather than agents in,

[1] I draw here on a typology elaborated by Matthew Craven in the context of examining the relationship between history and international law. M Craven, 'Introduction: International Law and Its Histories', in M Craven et al (eds), *Time History and International Law* (Martinus Nijhoff Publishers 2007) 1, 7.

[2] D Koller, '... and New York and The Hague and Tokyo and Geneva and Nuremberg and ... : The Geographies of International Law' (2012) 23 *European Journal of International Law* 97, 99–105.

[3] F Johns et al, 'Introduction', in F Johns et al (eds), *Events: The Force of International Law* (Routledge 2011) 1, 2.

[4] Koller (n 2) 100.

[5] See generally, S Stolk, '"The Record on Which History Will Judges Us Tomorrow": Auto-History in the Opening Statements of International Criminal Trials' (2015) 28 *Leiden Journal of International Law* 993 (referring to such invocations of history by international prosecutors as 'auto-history').

[6] See generally, I Tallgren and T Skouteris (eds), *The New Histories of International Criminal Law: Retrials* (OUP 2019). Critical histories are not unique to the field of international criminal justice. See, for example, S Marks, 'Human Rights in Disastrous Times', in J Crawford and M Koskenniemi (eds), *The Cambridge Companion to International Law* (CUP 2012) 309, 316 (re-telling and re-imagining the story of the international protection of human rights as a tragedy so as to illuminate 'presuppositions, tendencies and effects that are unremarkable, or at any rate generally unremarked, within the romantic story of human rights').

Doing Justice to History. Barrie Sander, Oxford University Press (2021). © Barrie Sander.
DOI: 10.1093/oso/9780198846871.003.0002

international criminal justice.[7] As Haslam explains, 'To the extent that the construction of international criminal law's subjects is linked to a particular version of international criminal legal history, a retelling, or broadening, of that history can contribute to re-positioning the ways in which international criminal law's subjects are framed.'[8] Underpinning these more critically oriented historical accounts are both an awareness of the contingencies of the field, and a concern for 'exposing the hidden margins of possibility within the present, unearthing the fractures and lines of flight disclosed by the seemingly impenetrable political forces of the day'.[9]

Beyond histories of international criminal justice, there are also studies of *international criminal justice in history*—examinations of the influence of particular practices within the field of international criminal justice on 'the wider world of politics, economics, or sociology against which it is deployed, or within which it is inserted'.[10] For instance, several studies have explored the impact of the International Criminal Court (ICC) Prosecutor's one-sided strategy of prosecuting members of the Lord's Resistance Army (LRA) for crimes allegedly committed during the conflict in Northern Uganda. According to Nouwen and Werner, for example, the ICC Prosecutor's strategy has enabled the Ugandan government to portray itself as a 'friend of mankind', fighting to uphold the universal norms of the international community, whilst instrumentalising the stigmatising power of the ICC's indictments to transform the LRA from an enemy of the government into an 'enemy of humanity'.[11] Indeed, the more the ICC has portrayed itself as a neutral and apolitical institution, the more attractive it has become as a tool to delegitimise the opponents of the Ugandan government.[12] In this way, rather than serving as a peacemaker, the ICC has become a weapon that can be deployed against non-state actors, a political tool for stigmatising LRA violence and validating the Ugandan government's monopoly on the legitimate use of force.[13] In this regard, Adam Branch has observed how—buoyed by its heightened legitimacy in the international community as a result of the ICC arrest warrants against the LRA commanders—the Ugandan government was able to launch military incursions into the eastern regions of the Democratic Republic of the Congo, as well as obtain assistance from the US military to carry out Operation Lightning Thunder in 2008 in an attempt to capture the LRA commanders.[14] According to Branch, it is even conceivable that the Ugandan government invited the ICC to intervene against the LRA 'not to help bring the war to an end but to entrench it and to obtain support for its military

[7] E Haslam, 'Silences in International Criminal Legal Histories and the Construction of the Victim Subject of International Criminal Law: The Nineteenth-Century Slave Trading Trial of Joseph Peters', in C Schwöbel (ed), *Critical Approaches to International Criminal Law: An Introduction* (Routledge 2014) 180, 181, 183, and 188–191.

[8] Ibid 190.

[9] B Golder, 'Beyond Redemption? Problematising the Critique of Human Rights in Contemporary International Legal Thought' (2014) 2 *London Review of International Law* 77, 107.

[10] Craven (n 1) 7.

[11] SMH Nouwen and WG Werner, 'Doing Justice to the Political: The International Criminal Court in Uganda and Sudan' (2010) 21 *European Journal of International Law* 941, 962.

[12] Ibid 963.

[13] F Mégret, 'Practices of Stigmatization' (2013) 76 *Law and Contemporary Problems* 287, 297. See also, M Kersten, *Justice in Conflict: The Effects of the International Criminal Court's Interventions on Ending Wars and Building Peace* (OUP 2016) 66–79.

[14] A Branch, *Displacing Human Rights: War and Intervention in Northern Uganda* (OUP 2011) 191.

campaign'.[15] In this way, the ICC's intervention in Uganda serves to illustrate the potential for the ICC to provide a convenient pretext to legitimise military interventions in other States, as well as law enforcement activity against political opponents.[16] In such instances, the ICC becomes embedded within justificatory narratives that seek to legitimise the use of force, the vocabulary of international criminal law serving to facilitate 'a neutral and universalist mode of emancipatory intervention'.[17]

The present study is situated within a third dimension of the relationship between history and international criminal justice—*history in international criminal justice*—which encompasses the different ways in which international criminal courts are domains of historical production. Within international criminal courts, history is constructed and contested in various forms by a range of actors throughout the entire international criminal justice process. For instance, historical narratives are constructed by international prosecutors in their charging documents.[18] In addition, history is also contested as part of the daily struggle between the antagonists in international criminal trials. As Paul Gewirtz explains, within criminal trials 'one side's narrative is constantly being met by the other side's counter-narrative (or side-stepping narrative), so that "reality" is always disassembled into multiple, conflicting and partly overlapping versions, each version presented as true, each fighting to be declared "what really happened"'.[19] Beyond narrative contestation at trial, through their archives, international criminal courts also serve as 'bookkeepers of history',[20] preserving a broad range of materials that may otherwise have been lost or destroyed.[21] Importantly, the production of history within international criminal courts is not static, but subject to ongoing contestation within audiences beyond the courtroom—often via carrier groups such as local politicians, the media, civil society groups, and court outreach departments, which selectively filter the historical narratives constructed within the courtroom to those beyond it.[22]

Viewed in this light, there are multiple sites of historical production within international criminal courts, ranging from the pre-trial and trial stages of proceedings to the judgment and storage of materials in judicial archives (see Figure 2.1 below).

In this context, the present study examines international criminal proceedings as struggles for historical justice—adversarial confrontations in which different actors compete for judicial validation of their preferred narratives of the past. Adopting this perspective, this study is interested in the scope and content of the historical narratives constructed within the judgments of international criminal courts. Through

[15] Ibid 192.
[16] Ibid 186.
[17] D Kennedy, *The Dark Sides of Virtue: Reassessing International Humanitarianism* (Princeton University Press 2004) 23.
[18] T Meron, 'Answering for War Crimes: Lessons from the Balkans', in T Meron, *War Crimes Law Comes of Age: Essays* (OUP 1998) 278, 283.
[19] P Gewirtz, 'Narrative and Rhetoric in the Law', in P Brooks and P Gewirtz (eds), *Law's Stories—Narrative and Rhetoric in the Law* (Yale University Press 1996) 2, 8.
[20] JJ Savelsberg and RD King, 'Law and Collective Memory' (2007) 3 *Annual Review of Law and Social Science* 189, 193.
[21] D Luban, 'Demystifying Political Violence: Some Bequests of ICTY and ICTR' (2016) 110 *AJIL Unbound* 251, 252.
[22] N Henry, *War and Rape: Law, Memory and Justice* (Routledge 2011) 119–122.

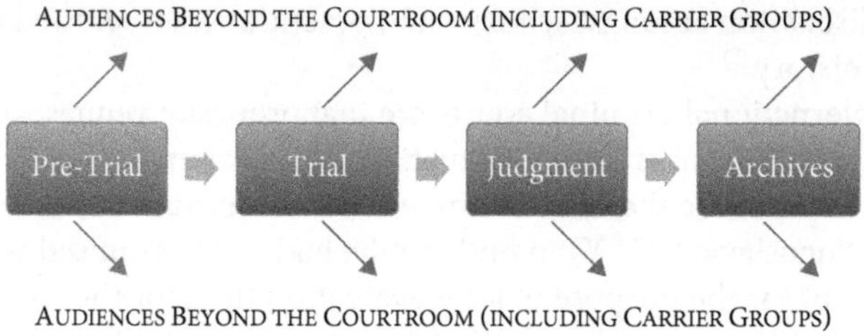

Figure 2.1: The Flow of Historical Narratives Through the International Criminal Process

their judgments, international criminal courts act as epistemic engines, constructing historical narratives concerning not only the culpability of the individuals targeted for prosecution but also the broader mass atrocity situations within which they previously operated.[23] Significantly, since international criminal prosecutions are inherently structured to examine particular episodes of the past, this historical function of international criminal courts is inescapable. As Mark Osiel observes, 'judges are *inevitably* understood to be engaging in "writing history" and influencing collective memory, whether or not they so intend'.[24]

The purpose of the present chapter is to establish the study's theoretical foundations. To this end, I begin by situating the present study within the context of existing scholarly debates concerning the historical function of international criminal courts, in particular the contestation that has arisen over the precise scope that the historical inquiries facilitated by such courts should be expected to take (Section I). The chapter then turns to introduce this study's analytical perspective, which is premised on the characterisation of international criminal courts as confrontational terrains that are host to struggles for historical justice (Section II). In order to facilitate a critical examination of these struggles, the chapter elaborates a framework for exploring how the practices of different actors have influenced the scope and content of the historical narratives constructed in the judgments of international criminal courts in different institutional contexts (Section III). The chapter concludes by explaining the significance of this framework for the remainder of the study (Section IV).

I. The Contested Historical Function of International Criminal Courts

The extent to which international criminal courts *should* construct historical narratives about the episodes of mass violence examined in their trials has become part of

[23] B Sander and JvH Holtermann, 'Symposium: Doing Justice to Truth in International Criminal Courts and Tribunals' *Humanity* (3 July 2017).

[24] M Osiel, *Mass Atrocity, Collective Memory, and the Law* (Transaction Publishers 1997) 241 (emphasis added).

an absorbing discussion amongst scholars and practitioners interested in the link between law and history.[25]

For some, international criminal courts are inappropriate venues for detailed historical expositions into mass atrocity situations. For example, when the accused in *Karadžić* tried to persuade the Trial Chamber of the International Criminal Tribunal for the former Yugoslavia (ICTY) to find that he had been promised immunity from prosecution, if not for the purpose of legal evaluation then for the records of history, the judges rejected the accused's submission noting that 'the Chamber's purpose is not to serve the academic study of history'.[26] In a similar vein, Holocaust historian Michael Marrus has argued that 'trials cannot and should not be expected to do the job of historians to teach history'.[27]

Others have written with greater enthusiasm about the didactic potential of international criminal courts, arguing that the construction of a historical record should be considered one of their central functions. For example, Robert Kempner, an assistant German American Prosecutor at the International Military Tribunal (IMT), famously referred to the Nuremberg trials as 'the greatest history seminar ever held in the history of the world'.[28] More recently, former ICTY Judge Patricia Wald argued that 'insofar as history is itself composed of a compilation and distillation of many views of the same events, there can be little question that the exquisitely detailed accounts of wartime atrocities, elicited in month- and year-long trials, contribute mightily to the process'.[29]

In this section, I contend that these contrasting perspectives on the historical function of international criminal courts reflect distinct conceptions of justice, the underlying assumptions of which serve to inform normative preferences concerning the appropriate scope of the historical inquiries facilitated within international criminal courts in practice:[30] on the one hand, an *adjudicative* conception, which favours a narrower optic forensically focused on determining the culpability of the accused; and on the other, *sociopolitical* conceptions that favour a more expansive degree of historical contextualisation in pursuit of fulfilling a broader range of sociopolitical objectives.

[25] In particular, a number of studies have discussed the relative merits of conducting relatively narrower or broader historical inquiries within international criminal courts. See, for example, L Arbour, *War Crimes and the Culture of Peace* (University of Toronto Press 2002) 33–34; E Stover, *The Witnesses: War Crimes and the Promise of Justice in The Hague* (University of Pennsylvania Press 2005) 21–23; Henry (n 22) 21–27; and A Hol, 'The Theatre of Justice: On the Educational Meaning of Criminal Trials', in C Brants et al, *Transitional Justice: Images and Memories* (Ashgate 2013) 71, 75–76.

[26] *Prosecutor v Radovan Karadžić* (Decision on the Accused's Holbrooke Agreement Motion, Trial Chamber) IT-95-5/18-PT (8 July 2009) [46]. See similarly, *Prosecutor v Stanišić and Simatović* (Decision Pursuant to Rule 73*bis*(D), Trial Chamber) Case No IT-03-69-PT (4 February 2008) [21] ('the Tribunal was established to administer justice, and not to create a historical record').

[27] MR Marrus, 'History and the Holocaust in the Courtroom', in R Smelser (ed), *Lessons and Legacies V: The Holocaust and Justice* (Northwestern University Press 2002) 215, 216.

[28] Quoted in L Douglas, *The Memory of Judgment: Making Law and History in the Trials of the Holocaust* (Yale University Press 2001) 2 (noting that Kempner was referring to both the Nuremberg IMT and the Nuremberg subsequent proceedings).

[29] PM Wald, 'Foreword: War Tales and War Trials' (2008) 106 *Michigan Law Review* 901, 911.

[30] This section draws on B Sander, 'Unveiling the Historical Function of International Criminal Courts: Between Adjudicative and Sociopolitical Justice' (2018) 12 *International Journal of Transitional Justice* 334, 337–340.

A. An Adjudicative Conception of the Historical Function

According to the *adjudicative* conception of justice, international criminal courts should only facilitate historical inquiries into episodes of mass violence to the extent required to determine the criminal responsibility of the accused on trial. As Hannah Arendt famously argued in her prominent elaboration of this position, 'the purpose of a trial is to render justice, and nothing else; even the noblest of ulterior purposes . . . can only detract from the law's main business: to weigh the charges against the accused, to render judgment, and to mete out punishment'.[31] Accordingly, for Arendt, '[a]ll the things that the defendant did not come into contact with, or that did not influence him, must be omitted from the proceedings of the trial and consequently from the report on it'.[32]

Adherents to the adjudicative conception of justice generally argue that rendering a wide-ranging historical account is an illegitimate judicial concern, the introduction of which may distort the underlying liberal legalist values put in place for the protection of the accused. Ian Buruma, for example, has argued that '[w]hen the court of law is used for history lessons, the risk of show trials cannot be far off'.[33] To become entangled with such issues can only lead to 'poor justice or poor history, probably both'.[34] To the extent that international criminal courts are required to delve into the broader context as part of their determination of the culpability of the accused, the historical narratives constructed as a result should be considered unavoidable by-products or incidental consequences of carrying out their primary adjudicative function.[35] As former President of the International Criminal Tribunal for Rwanda (ICTR) Judge Byron once argued, since 'the purpose of a criminal trial is to establish individual guilt, not to establish the historical truth about the conflicts', the ICTR only 'establishes a factual record of the genocide and the atrocities to the extent that they are the framework of findings on individual criminal responsibility'.[36]

The adjudicative conception of justice advocates a strict subordination of the pursuit of historical truth to the demands of the desert-based constraints designed to safeguard the accused from arbitrary prosecution or punishment.[37] In the international criminal context, these constraints are given expression in the form of the

31 H Arendt, *Eichmann in Jerusalem: A Report on the Banality of Evil* (revised and enlarged edition, Penguin Books 1994) 253.

32 Ibid 286.

33 I Buruma, *The Wages of Guilt: Memories of War in Germany and Japan* (Atlantic Books 2009) 142.

34 Osiel (n 24) 80 (describing this as the 'prevailing opinion' concerning attempts to combine justice and history).

35 See, for example, N Eltringham, '"We Are not a Truth Commission": Fragmented Narratives and the Historical Record at the International Criminal Tribunal for Rwanda' (2009) 11 *Journal of Genocide Research* 55, 57 (observing, on the basis of a series of interviews conducted at the ICTR, that while judges tend to concede that international criminal trials lead to the production of historical records, they also insist that such records are 'unintentional').

36 B Elberling, *The Defendant in International Criminal Proceedings: Between Law and Historiography* (Hart Publishing 2012) 201 (citing ICTR Judge Byron).

37 See generally, D Robinson, 'International Criminal Law as Justice' (2013) 11 *Journal of International Criminal Justice* 699; and D Robinson, 'A Cosmopolitan Liberal Account of International Criminal Law' (2013) 26 *Leiden Journal of International Law* 127.

liberal criminal law principles of legality, culpability, and fairness,[38] rooted in domestic criminal justice systems and international human rights law.[39] To construct history within international criminal courts without sufficient regard for these principled constraints would risk international criminal trials becoming nothing more than instrumentalised tools to obtain certain or near-certain convictions of accused individuals.[40]

According to the adjudicative perspective, therefore, international criminal courts should resist the temptation to broaden the scope of their historical narratives beyond what is deemed legally relevant to determine the culpability of the accused. As Mirjan Damaška has argued, 'it is best for judges to limit their inquiries into the larger context to the very minimum required' and to 'fasten their attention upon what they do best: establish whether particular individuals—especially those in positions of power—committed specific wrongs'.[41]

B. Sociopolitical Conceptions of the Historical Function

While the adjudicative conception of justice has found favour with many scholars and practitioners,[42] others argue that the adjudicative perspective underappreciates the didactic potential of international criminal trials.[43] Relying instead on *sociopolitical* conceptions of justice, these scholars and practitioners believe that international criminal courts may legitimately broaden their historical perspective in order to improve their contribution towards sociopolitical objectives beyond their adjudicative mandate. In this regard, whereas the adjudicative perspective views the accused as the primary audience of international criminal courts, sociopolitical perspectives are also concerned, to a far greater degree, with audiences beyond the courtroom.

Importantly, it should not be thought that sociopolitical conceptions of justice encompass only one position. In fact, there exists significant dissensus between adherents to sociopolitical perspectives concerning which non-adjudicative goals should legitimately fall within the mandate of international criminal courts, how such goals should be prioritised, and how international criminal proceedings should be designed to ensure their fulfilment.[44] Nonetheless, adherents to sociopolitical perspectives

[38] See generally, K Ambos, *Treatise on International Criminal Law: Volume I: Foundations and General Part* (OUP 2013) 87–97.

[39] JD Ohlin, 'LJIL Symposium: Where to Find the Liberal Principles of Criminal Law' *Opinio Juris* (10 April 2013).

[40] D Robinson, 'The Identity Crisis of International Criminal Law' (2008) 21 *Leiden Journal of International Law* 925, 931.

[41] M Damaška, 'What Is the Point of International Criminal Justice?' (2008) 83 *Chicago-Kent Law Review* 329, 341 and 360.

[42] See, for example, RA Wilson, *Writing History in International Criminal Tribunals* (CUP 2011) 5 (observing, based on empirical interviews with ICTY personnel, that many staff members 'adhere to some version of the doctrine of liberal legalism' and 'generally endorse a fairly restricted crime-based evidentiary approach to determining individual criminal responsibility').

[43] See, for example, Douglas (n 28).

[44] See similarly, C Stahn, 'Between 'Faith' and "Facts": By What Standards Should We Assess International Criminal Justice?' (2012) 25 *Leiden Journal of International Law* 251, 258.

share the view that at least some sociopolitical objectives may legitimately fall within the mandates of international criminal courts.

Equally, it should not be thought that those favouring sociopolitical conceptions of justice are unconcerned with the demands of desert-based constraints. As Lawrence Douglas explains:[45]

> [T]he notion that a trial can succeed as pedagogy yet fail to do [adjudicative] justice is crucially flawed. To succeed as a didactic spectacle in a democracy, a trial must be justly conducted insofar as one of the principal pedagogic aims of such a proceeding must be to make visible and public the sober authority of the rule of law.

In other words, one would struggle to find supporters of sociopolitical conceptions of justice who seriously dispute the importance of international criminal courts safeguarding the rights of the accused through adherence to liberal legalist constraints. At the same time, it is in the context of articulating *what is required* by these liberal criminal law principles that the distinction between adjudicative and sociopolitical perspectives proves influential since it is generally considered that the further an international criminal trial strays from its adjudicative task in pursuit of broader sociopolitical objectives, the greater *the risk* that the liberal legalist constraints designed to safeguard the rights of the accused may be diluted in practice.[46]

Adherents to sociopolitical conceptions of justice tend to favour broadening the historical parameters of international criminal trials beyond what is strictly required to determine the culpability of the accused on trial based on the perceived instrumental value of historical narratives for achieving a diversity of sociopolitical objectives including deterring future atrocities, reconciling divided communities, and healing the psychological wounds of victims.

For example, a range of stakeholders have advocated for international criminal courts to enlarge their historical frames on the basis of the perceived therapeutic value of historical narratives for victims of mass atrocities. The relationship between victims and historical narration within international criminal courts is complex, with victims generally taking on the dual role of beneficiaries and contributors to such narratives. As Sofia Stolk explains, international criminal courts have a 'double commitment to deliver authoritative truth *to* the victims while simultaneously including and authorising truth-telling *by* the victims'.[47] Underlying this double commitment is a belief that victims stand to benefit from both the construction and production of historical narratives within international criminal courts.

[45] Douglas (n 28) 3.

[46] See, for example, S Ford, 'Fairness and Politics at the ICTY: Evidence from the Indictments' (2013) XXXIX *North Carolina Journal of International Law and Commercial Regulation* 45, 57 ('as trials become more and more political, they inevitably become less fair, because the focus shifts from a determination of guilt through fair procedures to concerns about the consequences of the trial.'); and JI Turner, 'Defense Perspectives on Law and Politics in International Criminal Trials' (2008) 48 *Virginia Journal of International Law* 529, 537 ('The further a trial strays from its focus on the adjudicative function, the more likely it is to disregard the defendant's rights in pursuit of non-legal purposes').

[47] S Stolk, 'The Victim, the International Criminal Court and the Search for Truth: On the Interdependence and Incompatibility of Truths about Mass Atrocity' (2016) 13 *Journal of International Criminal Justice* 973, 977 (emphasis in original).

In terms of *production*, by rendering authoritative historical narratives in their judgments, it is claimed that international criminal courts can provide victims with a form of social acknowledgement of both their victim and survivor status that signals society's renewed solidarity with them, as well as a form of social condemnation of the perpetrator's acts.[48] On this account, historical records are 'products' delivered by international criminal courts to victims, directly responding to their desire to have a declaration of 'what happened' by an authoritative body.[49]

In terms of *construction*, it is claimed that victims may be empowered by contributing to the development of the historical narratives within international criminal judgments whether through formally participating in trials or acting as witnesses.[50] Specifically, the act of testifying or participating in international criminal trials has been said to provide an effective coping mechanism for victims, engaging them in a cathartic process in which they are able to purge the past and find closure.[51] By empowering victims to write their own history, the trial is said to dramatise what Shoshana Felman has termed 'a conceptual revolution' in the victims whereby they acquire 'historical authority, that is to say, *semantic authority* over themselves and over others'.[52] Through the trial process, victims, previously objects of mass atrocities, are said to re-acquire their status as subjects, to shift their social status from victim to survivor, and even to provide a voice to other victims who were not able to survive the conflict.[53]

Leaving aside the critiques to which these claims have been subjected,[54] the perceived benefits and importance of responding to the needs of victims have often led to calls for the expansion of the historical frames of international criminal courts, whether in the form of calls to expand the charges against the accused,[55] or to amend rules of procedure to allow greater space for victims to present not only their knowledge about what happened during particular episodes of mass violence but also their experiences of suffering.[56]

Beyond supporting the interests of victims, the impulse to broaden the historical scope of international criminal trials is also reflected in the sentiments of those seeking

[48] J Doak, 'The Therapeutic Dimension of Transitional Justice: Emotional Repair and Victim Satisfaction in International Trials and Truth Commissions' (2011) 11 *International Criminal Law Review* 263.

[49] Stolk (n 47) 981.

[50] This paragraph draws on B Sander, 'The Expressive Limits of International Criminal Justice: Victim Trauma and Local Culture in the Iron Cage of the Law' (2019) 19 *International Criminal Law Review* 1019–1020.

[51] C Fournet, 'Mass Atrocity: Theories and Concepts of Accountability – On the Schizophrenia of Accountability', in R Henham and M Findlay (eds), *Exploring the Boundaries of International Criminal Justice* (Ashgate 2011) 27, 44.

[52] S Felman, 'Theaters of Justice: Arendt in Jerusalem, the Eichmann Trial, and the Redefinition of Legal Meaning in the Wake of the Holocaust' (2000) 1 *Theoretical Inquiries in Law* 465, 498 and 502 (emphasis in original).

[53] For Primo Levi, the desire of survivors to tell their stories could even be characterised as 'an immediate and violent impulse, to the point of competing with our most elementary needs'. P Levi, *The Drowned and The Saved* (R Rosenthal trans, Abacus 1988), 64.

[54] See generally, Sander (n 50).

[55] See critically, A Branch, 'Truth Beyond the ICC' *Humanity* (10 July 2017).

[56] See, in this regard, Stolk (n 47) 984–987 (distinguishing between victims contributing knowledge to the ICC concerning 'the facts' and 'their experiences', the former contributing to 'a discourse of truth', the latter to 'a discourse of suffering').

to enhance the capacity of international criminal courts to deter future atrocities and reconcile divided local communities. Former ICTY Judge Schomburg, for example, once claimed that 'there is no peace without justice; there is no justice without truth, meaning the *entire* truth and nothing but the truth'.[57] Similarly, Mark Osiel has argued that 'if courts are to influence collective memory of ... historical episodes in persuasive ways, they must admit a wider range of evidence and argument than are often cognizable within strictly legal terms'.[58] For Osiel, international criminal trials should be 'unabashedly designed as monumental spectacles' in order to maximise their capacity to generate a discursive form of solidarity amongst conflicting groups within societies torn apart by episodes of mass violence.[59]

As these examples illustrate, sociopolitical conceptions of justice tend to favour broadening the historical narrative frames of international criminal courts in light of their perceived instrumental value. As Louise Arbour explains, to adhere to a sociopolitical perspective is generally 'to commit to the exposition of the larger picture, to paint the broad and complex historical fresco, not only to expose and record individual guilt but to exploit the dramatic stage of the trial to construct the collective memories upon which both victims and perpetrators, indeed whole nations, will be cleansed of their brutal past'.[60]

C. Shifting Analytical Perspective

Reflecting on the debate between adjudicative and sociopolitical conceptions of the historical function of international criminal courts, it is possible to view these perspectives less as static positions and more as opposing lines of argumentation that can be deployed to support or critique the practices of international criminal courts.[61] To adopt an *adjudicative* mode of argumentation is to advocate a more forensic understanding of a court's historical function—whether by promoting a narrower narrative frame or applying principled constraints in a more restrictive manner. To adopt a *sociopolitical* mode of argumentation is to advocate a less constrained understanding of a court's historical function—whether by promoting a broader narrative frame or applying principled constraints in a more diluted manner. The tension between these modes of argumentation flows from the contradictory assignments of international criminal courts,[62] which are at once expected to act as criminal courts rendering formal justice to the accused *and* transitional justice mechanisms rendering

[57] *Prosecutor v Miroslav Deronjić* (Sentencing Judgment, Trial Chamber) IT-02-61-S (30 March 2004) (diss op Schomburg) [6] (emphasis added).

[58] Osiel (n 24) 97.

[59] Ibid 3.

[60] Arbour (n 25) 34.

[61] See generally, D Robinson, 'Inescapable Dyads: Why the International Criminal Court Cannot Win' (2015) 28 *Leiden Journal of International Law* 323 (introducing the notion of 'inescapable dyads' in the discourse of international criminal justice—opposing poles of critique that may be deployed against the practices of international criminal courts)

[62] See similarly, ibid 330 ('[E]ach side of the dyad is based in *values that can be credibly regarded as values underlying international criminal justice.*') (emphasis in original).

representational justice to the mass atrocity situation in the interests of victims and society.[63]

Against this background, the present study seeks to shift analytical focus away from the normative questions of *whether* and *to what extent* international criminal courts *should* write history, towards a concern for examining *which* histories *are* constructed within the judgments of such courts in practice. As Nicola Henry argues, the pertinent question is not whether it is right to intentionally use legal processes to construct history, but rather 'how law shapes or produces history ... and how law reproduces hegemonic relations of power that in turn shape how historical events are to be remembered'.[64] Since international criminal courts are inescapably embroiled in the construction of history, the present study seeks to understand *whose* histories are recorded in practice.[65]

II. Unveiling the Struggle for Historical Justice

In recent years, the historical function of international criminal courts has increasingly been examined by reference to their expressive qualities.[66] Mark Drumbl, for example, has compared international criminal courts to theatrical spectacles that 'narrate history and thereby express shared understandings of the provenance, particulars, and effects of mass violence'.[67] In a similar vein, Leora Bilsky has characterised the criminal courtroom as 'a field of human drama', endowed with the capacity to 'transform dry and distant history or abstract ideological worldviews into a living story with a name, a face, and a body'.[68] Some scholars have even referred to international criminal trials as 'show trials', not in the pejorative sense that their results are preordained, but because they constitute pedagogical performances targeted at a range of audiences both within and beyond the courtroom.[69] Lawrence Douglas, for example, has argued that 'to call Holocaust trials show trials ... is to state the obvious' since they evidently constitute 'dramas of didactic legality' specifically orchestrated 'to show the world the facts of astonishing crimes and to demonstrate the power of law to reintroduce order into a space evacuated of legal and moral sense'.[70]

[63] F Mégret, 'Joinder, Fairness, and the Goals of International Criminal Justice', in T Waters (ed), *The Milošević Trial: An Autopsy* (OUP 2014) 120, 128 ('[T]he constant tension between a strict forensic understanding of their mandate and one more geared toward transitional justice has yielded one of the most productive dynamics in the international tribunals' history').

[64] Henry (n 22) 27.

[65] J Klabbers, 'Book Review' (2004) 15 *European Journal of International Law* 1055, 1058.

[66] See generally, B Sander, 'The Expressive Turn of International Criminal Justice: A Field in Search of Meaning' (2019) 32 *Leiden Journal of International Law* 851.

[67] MA Drumbl, *Atrocity, Punishment, and International Law* (CUP 2007) 174.

[68] LY Bilsky, *Transformative Justice: Israeli Identity on Trial (Law, Meaning, and Violence)* (University of Michigan Press 2004) 3.

[69] See, for example, D Luban, 'State Criminality and the Ambition of International Criminal Law', in T Isaacs and R Vernon (eds), *Accountability for Collective Wrongdoing* (CUP 2011) 61, 75; and Osiel (n 24) 65. See also, Arendt (n 31) 266 (recognising that a criminal trial can be designed as 'a show' provided the script is focused narrowly on the acts of the accused and not programmed in advance to achieve a certain outcome); and D Garland, *Punishment and Modern Society: A Study in Social Theory* (OUP 1990) 67 (referring to 'show-case' trials in the domestic criminal context).

[70] Douglas (n 28) 3.

Building on this body of scholarship, this study contends that a significant expressive dimension of international criminal courts resides in their judgments. In particular, by constructing historical narratives, authenticating them as truths, and disseminating them to the public, the judgments of international criminal courts constitute important societal mechanisms for publicly and officially acknowledging particular interpretations of the past. In this context, 'acknowledgement' refers to the process whereby knowledge about the past that is retained in private consciousness becomes officially sanctioned and enters the public sphere.[71] According to this perspective, the judgments of international criminal courts constitute expressive devices that serve to transform private versions of the past into public historical narratives.[72]

The question remains, however: *whose* histories are acknowledged in practice? In tackling this question, this study contends that the historical narratives constructed within the judgments of international criminal courts are the product of the situated choices of the different actors who interact within international criminal justice processes.[73] In other words, international criminal courts are confrontational arenas in which history is the subject of a struggle over which interpretation of events will be validated in their judgments—an intense contest for judicial recognition of each actor's preferred version of the past.[74]

To characterise international criminal courts as host to struggles for historical justice is to recognise both the *constructed* nature and *legitimating* qualities of the historical narratives rendered in their judgments.

A. The Constructed Nature of Judicial Narratives

According to what has been termed the foundationalist perspective,[75] international criminal courts merely reflect the truth rather than construct it.[76] The popularity of this view is traceable to our human desire for an authoritative and objective account of the past in the aftermath of mass atrocities. As Mark Osiel explains, episodes of mass violence are not the types of situations in respect to which 'we feel comfortable about letting a hundred interpretive flowers bloom', such events generally triggering 'the residual positivist … in virtually everyone'.[77]

Yet, historiography has long questioned the notion that the past is an object 'out there' that can be readily unearthed, in favour of emphasising interpretation,

[71] S Cohen, *States of Denial: Knowing About Atrocities and Suffering* (Polity Press 2001) 225 (relying on the distinction between 'knowledge' and 'acknowledgement' first made by philosopher Thomas Nagel).

[72] S Löytömäki, 'Law and Memory: The Politics of Victimhood' (2012) 21 *Griffith Law Review* 1, 18.

[73] See similarly, but with a focus on the expressive qualities of international criminal trials rather than judgments, T Meijers and M Glasius, 'Trials as Messages of Justice: What Should Be Expected of International Criminal Courts?' (2016) 30 *Ethics & International Affairs* 429.

[74] KC Priemel, *The Betrayal: The Nuremberg Trials and German Divergence* (OUP 2016) 14.

[75] T Skouteris, *The Notion of Progress in International Law Discourse* (TMC Asser Press 2010) 24 (referring to 'the so-called foundationalist view that knowledge can be grounded on a meta-theoretical, decisive, or transcendental base').

[76] See, for example, JE Alvarez, 'Crimes of States/Crimes of Hate: Lessons from Rwanda' (1999) 24 *Yale Journal of International Law* 366, 448 (referring to 'the assumptions of many international lawyers that international trials only reflect truth but do not construct it').

[77] Osiel (n 24) 265 and fn76.

perspective, and limitations caused by language and other forms of subjectivity.[78] As John Berger famously put it, 'The past is never there waiting to be discovered, to be recognized for exactly what it is. History always constitutes the relation between a present and its past.'[79] According to these more critical accounts of history, the past exists in a 'pre-jigsawed state', a condition that requires the historian 'to cut and shape it into a narrative explanation'.[80] As such, history is not simply about identifying particular facts, but also more importantly about the possible sets of relationships that those facts can be made to figure.[81] According to Thomas Skouteris, for example, 'the same historical fact can be read differently by different discourses (e.g. law, history, sociology, economics, art, history), while within each discourse there are different readings over space and time'.[82] From this perspective, any attempt to narrate the past is always premised on assumptions and choices (such as which facts to refer to and what relationships can be drawn between them) that are far from neutral or mechanical.[83] As Alun Munslow argues, 'precision in the generation of facts is literally meaningless unless and until those facts (as propositions or events under a description) are turned into stories, explained further with arguments, and offered as sustained and coherent ideological positions'.[84] Viewed in this light, the historical narratives rendered within the judgments of international criminal courts may be characterised as contingent on the choices of the different actors who interact within international

[78] S Löytömäki, 'Legalisation of the Memory of the Algerian War in France' (2005) 7 *Journal of the History of International Law* 157, 176–177. See also, H White, 'Narrativity in the Representation of Reality', in H White, *The Content of the Form: Narrative Discourse and Historical Representation* (John Hopkins University Press 1990) 1, 24 (noting that any search for objectivity will always represent 'a desire to have real events display the coherence, integrity, fullness, and closure of an image of life that is and can only be imaginary'); Osiel (n 24) 241 ('Writing history is now understood as necessarily involving a choice between alternative interpretive framings, a fact that endows historiography with a similarity to fiction and mythmaking'); and R Teitel, *Transitional Justice* (OUP 2000) 70 ('When history takes its "interpretive turn," there is no single, clear, and determinate understanding or "lesson" to draw from the past, but, instead, recognition of the degree to which historical understanding depends on political and social contingency').

[79] J Berger, *Ways of Seeing* (BBC and Penguin Books 1972) 11. See also, EH Carr, *What is History?* (2nd edn, Palgrave 1986) 24 (arguing that history is 'a continuous process of interaction between the historian and his facts, an unending dialogue between the present and the past').

[80] A Munslow, *Deconstructing History* (2nd edn, Routledge 2006) 160. See also, H White, 'The Historical Text as Literary Artifact', in H White, *Tropics of Discourse: Essays in Cultural Criticism* (John Hopkins University Press 1978) 81, 96 (defining a narrative as 'the syntagmatic dispersion of events across a temporal series presented as a prose discourse, in such a way as to display their progressive elaboration as a comprehensible form').

[81] White (n 80) 94.

[82] T Skouteris, 'Engaging History in International Law', in JM Beneyto and D Kennedy (eds), *New Approaches to International Law* (TMC Asser Press 2012) 99, 112. See also, Osiel (n 24) 258 ('there are necessarily many stories—consistent with known facts—that can be told about the history of a given community and the relations among its subgroups').

[83] Skouteris (n 82) 104. See also, White (n 80) 84 (noting that facts are transformed into narratives 'by the suppression or subordination of certain of them and the highlighting of others, by characterization, motific repetition, variation of tone and point of view, alternative descriptive strategies, and the like').

[84] Munslow (n 80) 172. See also, A Funkenstein, 'History, Counterhistory, and Narrative', in S Friedlander (ed), *Probing the Limits of Representation: Nazism and the 'Final Solution'* (Harvard University Press 1992) 66, 68 (noting how facts 'gain their meaning and even their very factuality from the context in which they are embedded, a context reconstructed solely by the historian, whose narrative makes and shapes the fact'); and H White, 'The Fictions of Factual Representation', in H White, *Tropics of Discourse: Essays in Cultural Criticism* (John Hopkins University Press 1978) 121, 134 ('What is at issue here is not, What are the facts? but rather, How are the facts to be described in order to sanction one mode of explaining them rather than another?').

criminal proceedings—together with the institutional contexts within which such choices are made.

Importantly, to recognise the constructed nature of judicial narratives is not to be equated with the idea that there are no criteria available for judging their plausibility.[85] Critical historians have readily acknowledged that it is possible to distinguish between good and bad historiography on the basis of criteria such as responsibility to the rules of evidence, fidelity to the factual record, logical consistency, coherence of argumentation, and depth of narrative detail.[86] Equally, however, critical historians have also sought to emphasise that what counts as an adequate representation of a historical event must be adjudged to be relative to the time, place, and context of its formulation.[87] As such, a central concern for critical historians has been to illuminate the constructed nature of historical narratives and to deconstruct the biases and presuppositions on which such constructions are based. As Hayden White explains:[88]

> The important distinction from a post-modernist point of view is not between ideology and objectivity but between ideological constructions of history that are more or less open about the 'constructed' nature of their versions of history and more or less willing to make of their own modes of production elements of their contents.... If postmodern notions of history are informed by a critique of the ideology of objectivism, this does not necessarily mean that they are opposed to the truth and committed to lie, delusion, fantasy, or fiction. It means rather that ... post-modernism recognizes that 'reality' is always as much constructed in discourse as it is discovered in the historical record. Which means that post-modernist 'objectivity' is aware of *its* own constructed nature and makes this work of construction the subject of its discourse.

As this passage indicates, critical historians do not deny the necessity of referencing the past through the available evidence, but merely question more foundationalist claims to an 'ultimate referentially and knowing history'.[89]

Viewed in this light, the present study may be understood as an attempt to recognise and illuminate the constructed nature of the historical narratives rendered within the judgments of international criminal courts. In other words, rather than examining

[85] See, in this regard, K Jenkins, *Refiguring History: New Thoughts on an Old Discipline* (Routledge 2003) 13 (noting that the critical perspective of history does not lead to the conclusion that 'we must therefore accept that everyone else's discursive "reality" and historical constructs are all *equally* correct or all *equally* wrong'. For, 'although there is no *ultimate*, objective foundation for our historical positions (or our moral decisions), we do still make decisions on the basis of preferences according to the tools at hand in any given social formation, we do still put worlds under descriptions, and we are still able to give (relative to such descriptions) argumentative support for them to those who might decide to listen to it and engage in conversation').

[86] White (n 80) 97; H White, *The Content of the Form: Narrative Discourse and Historical Representation* (John Hopkins University Press 1990) 4–5 and 78; H White, 'Historical Emplotment and the Problem of Truth', in S Friedlander (ed), *Probing the Limits of Representation: Nazism and the 'Final Solution'* (Harvard University Press 1992) 37, 38.

[87] H White, 'Response to Arthur Marwick' (1995) 30 *Journal of Contemporary History* 233, 244.

[88] H White, 'Postmodernism and Textual Anxieties', in B Strath and N Witoszek (eds), *The Postmodern Challenge: Perspectives East and West* (Rodopi BV 1999) 27, 38.

[89] Munslow (n 80) 153.

the historical narratives rendered within international criminal courts against an objective standard of truth, this study is concerned with revealing the actors and practices that have shaped *how* history is constructed in particular institutional contexts.[90]

B. The Legitimating Qualities of Judicial Narratives

To recognise the constructed nature of judicial narratives is to appreciate their particularity. Through their judgments, international criminal courts act as 'official gatekeepers', privileging some histories at the expense of others.[91] In performing this task, judges are engaged in a process that is at once destructive and reconstructive. Having afforded the antagonists the opportunity to put forward their preferred versions of the past and subjected them to scrutiny at trial,[92] judges seek on the one hand to effectively kill off and delegitimise judicially unpersuasive interpretations of the past and on the other to declare their own as authoritative.[93] This dual role is reminiscent of Robert Cover's depiction of judges as both 'people of violence' and 'people of peace'.[94] As 'people of violence', judges seek to invalidate historical accounts that conflict with their own judicially constructed narratives, while as 'people of peace', they seek to promote renewed solidarity around the narratives they declare as authoritative.[95]

By authorising particular versions of the past in their decisions and judgments, international criminal courts inescapably perform a legitimation function—recognising and foregrounding particular perspectives of mass atrocity situations whilst at the same time marginalising and excluding others from view.[96] As Bronwyn Leebaw has argued, the result is 'deeply paradoxical': institutions that have been promoted as a basis for challenging denial end up legitimating selective forgetting.[97]

[90] See similarly, EH Reiter, 'Fact, Narrative, and the Judicial Uses of History: *Delgamuukw* and Beyond' (2010) 8 *Indigenous Law Journal* 55, 66.

[91] V Nesiah, 'The Trials of History: Losing Justice in the Monstrous and the Banal', in R Buchanan and P Zumbansen (eds), *Law in Transition: Human Rights, Development and Transitional Justice* (Hart Publishing 2014) 289, 304.

[92] TW Waters, 'A Kind of Judgment: Searching for Judicial Narratives After Death' (2010) 42 *George Washington International Law Review* 279, 290.

[93] See, in this regard, P Bourdieu, 'The Force of Law: Toward a Sociology of the Juridical Field' (1987) 38 *Hastings Law Journal* 805, 837–838.

[94] R Cover, 'Nomos and Narrative', in M Minow et al (eds), *Narrative, Violence, and the Law: The Essays of Robert Cover* (University of Michigan Press 1993) 95, 155 ('Judges are people of violence. Because of the violence they command, judges characteristically do not create law, but kill it. Theirs is the jurispathic office. Confronting the luxuriant growth of a hundred legal traditions, they assert that *this one* is law and destroy or try to destroy the rest. But judges are also people of peace. Among warring sects, each of which wraps itself in the mantle of a law of its own, they assert a regulative function that permits a life of law rather than violence. The range of the violence they could command (but generally do not) measures the range of the peace and law they constitute.') (emphasis in original).

[95] See, in this regard, M Minow, 'The Work of Re-Membering: After Genocide and Mass Atrocity' (1999) 23 *Fordham International Law Journal* 429, 430 (referring to this process as one of 're-membering', a process of 'reconstituting a community of humanity against which there can be crimes ... and within which victims and survivors can be reclaimed as worthy members').

[96] See generally, G Simpson, *Law, War & Crime—War Crimes Trials and the Reinvention of International Law* (Polity Press 2007) 88–91 and 101–104; Henry (n 22) 125–130; and V Nesiah, 'Doing History with Impunity', in K Engle et al (eds), *Anti-Impunity and the Human Rights Agenda* (CUP 2016) 95.

[97] B Leebaw, *Judging State-Sponsored Violence, Imagining Political Change* (CUP 2011) 175.

To recognise the legitimating qualities of international criminal courts is to highlight their definitional qualities.[98] Through their judgments, international criminal courts construct identities, define past wrongdoings as crimes, and delineate boundaries between guilt and innocence, right and wrong, blamers and blamed, victims and perpetrators.[99] Importantly, as Lucinda Finley explains, 'through its definitions and the way it talks about events, law has the power to *silence* alternative meanings—to suppress other stories'.[100] Silences are often as, if not more, significant than what is spoken within the judgments of international criminal courts.[101] In particular, silences are more than simply the absence of voice, but are themselves charged with meaning, representing 'the residue' of the exercise of voice, 'stories not available, not accepted, not listened to at all'.[102] By framing the past in particular ways, international criminal courts focus attention on particular aspects of mass atrocity situations to the displacement of others.[103] Viewed from this perspective, the judgments of international criminal courts may be characterised as not only moments of historical acknowledgement and remembrance, but also acts of institutionalised amnesia and oblivion.

The legitimating qualities of judgments have already been discussed in scholarly accounts of *domestic* atrocity trials. In particular, a number of studies have demonstrated how the narratives constructed within domestic criminal judgments have legitimated particular understandings of the past, typically in line with the interests of the State in which and on whose behalf such prosecutions have been conducted.[104] With respect to the Holocaust trials of Barbie, Papon, and Touvier, for example, Richard Wilson has observed how the French courts 'blew with the political wind'.[105] Particularly contentious was the finding of the French Court of Cassation that for an act to constitute a crime against humanity it must have been committed 'in the name of a State practising a policy of ideological supremacy',[106] a requirement that not only shielded French

[98] Z Miller, 'Effects of Invisibility: In Search of the "Economic" in Transitional Justice' (2008) 2 *International Journal of Transitional Justice* 266, 267.

[99] See similarly, D Buss, 'Performing Legal Order: Some Feminist Thoughts on International Criminal Law' (2011) 11 *International Criminal Law Review* 409, 411; and S Löytömäki, *The Law and the Politics of Memory: Confronting the Past* (Routledge 2014) 10.

[100] LM Finley, 'Breaking Women's Silence in Law: The Dilemma of the Gendered Nature of Legal Reasoning' (1989) 64 *Notre Dame Law Review* 886, 888 (emphasis added). See similarly, Miller (n 98) 267 ('Despite its claims to exposure, revelation and memorialization, the project of transitional justice may simultaneously perpetuate invisibility and silence'); and E Dauphinee, 'War Crimes and the Ruin of Law' (2008) 37 *Millennium: Journal of International Studies* 49, 65 (pointing to 'the inherent risk that law already contains—a certain blindness to its conflation of justice and judgment—a certain inattention to what it erases and ignores in its efforts to illuminate what it privileges').

[101] See similarly, DS Koller, 'The Faith of the International Criminal Lawyer' (2008) 40 *New York University Journal of International Law and Politics* 1019, 1066; S Kendall, 'Critical Orientations: A Critique of International Criminal Court Practice', in C Schwöbel (ed), *Critical Approaches to International Criminal Law: An Introduction* (Routledge 2014) 54, 66; and K Engle et al, 'Introduction', in K Engle et al (eds), *Anti-Impunity and the Human Rights Agenda* (CUP 2016) 1, 7.

[102] Reiter (n 90) 66.

[103] On 'framing', see generally, AB Houge and K Lohne, 'End Impunity! Reducing Conflict-Related Sexual Violence to a Problem of Law' (2017) 51 *Law & Society Review* 755.

[104] See generally, B Sander, 'Justice as Identity: Unveiling the Mechanics of Legitimation in Domestic Atrocity Trials' (2018) 16 *Journal of International Criminal Justice* 203.

[105] Wilson (n 42) 34–35.

[106] *Fédération Nationale des Déportés et Internés Resistants et Patriotes et Autres v Klaus Barbie*, Cass Crim, 20 December 1985 [1986] ILR 78, translated by C Fournet, *Genocide and Crimes Against Humanity: Misconceptions and Confusion in French Law and Practice* (Hart Publishing 2013) 13.

conduct in Algeria from scrutiny, but also impeded critical examinations of the relationship between the French Vichy regime and Nazi Germany during the Second World War.[107] As Martti Koskenniemi has argued, in these types of cases, domestic criminal courts find themselves entering 'the terrain where national identities are constructed out of interpretations of the nation's past'.[108]

In contrast to existing accounts of *domestic* atrocity trials, the courts examined in the present study—the Nuremberg IMT, the Tokyo International Military Tribunal for the Far East (IMTFE), the ICTY, the ICTR, the Special Court for Sierra Leone (SCSL), and the ICC—are distinguished by the fact that their establishment derives from *international* legal acts or instruments.[109] By critically examining the scope and content of the narratives constructed within the judgments of these courts, the present study seeks to illuminate the forms of legitimation that characterise *international* criminal courts in different institutional contexts.

III. A Framework for Examining Struggles for Historical Justice

Once it is acknowledged that international criminal courts are inevitably engaged in the construction of history, the tasks of the judge and the historian begin to appear strikingly similar. As Charles Maier has observed, 'the trial, like the writing of history, and the judge along with the historian, both pre-eminently aspire to produce a coherent narrative: one that explains and interprets as well as records'.[110] Yet, if it is the construction of historical narratives that unites judges and historians, it is the distinct contexts within which they conduct this task that divides them.[111]

[107] See similarly, Fournet (n 106) 44; Douglas (n 28) 195; and L Sadat Wexler, 'The Interpretation of the Nuremberg Principles by the French Court of Cassation: From Touvier to Barbie and Back Again' (1994) 32 *Columbia Journal of Transnational Law* 289, 346 and 355.

[108] M Koskenniemi, 'From Impunity to Show Trials' (2002) 6 *Max Planck Yearbook of United Nations Law* 1, 25. See also, Teitel (n 78) 115 ('Transitional truth-tellings are not atomized narratives, not radical new beginnings, but, rather, always stand in contingent relation to the state's existing historical legacies').

[109] R O'Keefe, *International Criminal Law* (OUP 2015) 88. On the contestation that has arisen amongst scholars concerning what makes a court 'international' in nature, see generally, W Schabas, *Unimaginable Atrocities: Justice, Politics, and Rights at the War Crimes Tribunals* (OUP 2012) 17–21.

[110] CS Maier, 'Doing History, Doing Justice: The Narrative of the Historian and of the Truth Commission', in RI Rotberg and D Thompson, *Truth v. Justice: The Morality of Truth Commissions* (Princeton University Press 2000) 261, 271. See similarly, KC Priemel and A Stiller, 'Introduction: Nuremberg's Narratives: Revising the Legacy of the "Subsequent Trials"', in KC Priemel and A Stiller (eds), *Reassessing the Nuremberg Military Tribunals: Transitional Justice, Trial Narratives, and Historiography* (Berghahn Books 2012) 1, 4 (identifying 'the narrative as a crucial junction' between lawyers and historians); and Wilson (n 42) 8 (noting that both lawyers and historians rely on 'overarching narratives to organize individual facts, visual images, and other forms of evidence into a coherent whole').

[111] See similarly, Wilson (n 42) 6–8, 144–145, and 216–218 (noting 'the distinctively legal ways of knowing that arise from specialized legal precepts' and revealing how 'modern law still constitutes a distinctive system of knowledge that is guided by its own principles for comprehending human behaviour'); Savelsberg and King (n 20) 190 ('law is subject to a particular set of institutional rules . . . that color the collective memory produced in legal institutions and through legal processes in ways that differ distinctly from memories produced by historians or in the worlds of politics, art, and religion'); and Teitel (n 78) 89 ('the choices between criminal and historical inquiries turn out hardly to present a choice between truth and justice. The question, instead, is what sort of "truth"?').

International criminal courts operate in the midst of struggles for historical justice—contests between different actors for their preferred versions of history to receive a judicial seal of approval. In order to illuminate the constructed nature and legitimating qualities of the historical narratives rendered within their judgments, this study relies upon a framework that distinguishes the *actors* involved in struggles for historical justice, the *questions* around which such struggles are structured, and the *practices* through which such struggles are conducted.

A. The Actors

Struggles for historical justice generally have more interested actors than the underlying conflicts that form their focus—ranging from prosecutors, defendants, victims, and judges, to States and civil society groups. Although these actors have not always expressly identified themselves as narrative entrepreneurs,[112] it is often apparent from their public statements that they consider themselves strongly invested in securing judicial validation of their favoured versions of events.

Prosecutors and *defendants*, for example, have generally not shied away from stressing the importance they place on securing judicial approval for their preferred interpretations of the past. In his opening statement in the case of *Norman et al*, for instance, the SCSL Prosecutor emphasised that 'it is vitally important that the brutality and savagery of this war are exposed and chronicled so that we have an official record of the horrors that befell this nation'.[113] In a similar vein, in the case against *Radovan Karadžić* at the ICTY, the defendant stressed that he was motivated 'first of all, to determine the truth, the truth about our conflict, to determine the truth as I say, and then to defend myself in the second place'.[114]

Beyond prosecutors and defendants, *victims* of mass atrocities also tend to be heavily invested in the scope and content of the historical narratives constructed within the judgments of international criminal courts. In fact, it is not uncommon for local communities to experience competitive victimhood in the aftermath of episodes of mass violence, with different groups struggling for recognition of their specific narratives of victimhood.[115] In many situations, members of rival groups within local communities torn apart by conflict experience 'a strong wish—and thus also strive—to establish that their ingroup was subjected to *more* injustice and suffering at the hands of the outgroup than the other way around'.[116] With this in mind, demands for historical

[112] See similarly, Mégret (n 13) 294–295 (arguing that an examination of practices of stigmatisation within international criminal courts 'might be revealing precisely in the sense that it allows us to conceptualize what international criminal lawyers *really* do, what their social function is beyond law's own rhetoric about itself, and, as it were, its ideological self-presentation') (emphasis in original).

[113] *Prosecutor v Norman, Fofana, and Kondewa* (Transcript, Trial Chamber) SCSL-04-14-T (3 June 2004) 15. On the historical dimensions of the opening statements of international criminal trials, see generally Stolk (n 5).

[114] *Prosecutor v Radovan Karadžić* (Transcript, Status Conference) IT-95-5/18-PT (17 September 2008) 43.

[115] Löytömäki (n 72) 18.

[116] M Noor et al, 'When Suffering Begets Suffering: The Psychology of Competitive Victimhood Between Adversarial Groups in Violent Conflicts' (2012) 16 *Personality & Social Psychology Review* 351, 352.

justice within local communities often translate into demands for the validation of their already entrenched internal narratives about the conflict, encompassing not only an evasion of responsibility for any crimes committed by the faction with which they identify, but also a cloak of collective victimhood whereby each group views itself as the principal victim of wrongs committed by other groups during the conflict.[117]

States, for their part, also have strong interests in the narratives authored within international criminal judgments. As Mirjan Damaška explains, since the crimes adjudicated by international criminal courts are typically the product of organised collective activity, 'entities including state governments may in some cases feel as if they were themselves on trial along with the indicted individuals'.[118] For instance, if an individual acted pursuant to a State policy, their prosecution will often raise questions concerning the responsibility of the State in question.[119] State interests may also be implicated by judicial examinations of the broader context of such crimes, encompassing, for example, questions concerning who initiated a conflict, what goals the warring factions pursued, and what relationships existed between different groups.[120] Beyond concerns about being negatively implicated in judicial narratives, States may also be interested in trying to steer the focus of judicial narratives towards the stigmatisation of their enemies—whether through limiting the jurisdictional scope of international criminal courts or selectively cooperating with their investigations.

Civil society groups have also long expressed an interest in shaping the scope and content of the historical narratives constructed within international criminal courts. Importantly, different constituencies within civil society often compete for attention, each advocating a particular view concerning which crimes and individuals should be prioritised for prosecution. As Frédéric Mégret explains, 'For pacifists, aggression is the cardinal sin; for humanitarians, war crimes; for those inclined towards the protection of human rights, crimes against humanity; for those who seek to defend particular groups, genocide; and for feminists, sexual violence'.[121] With this in mind, it is not uncommon for different civil society groups to try to influence the narrative frames of international criminal trials by, for example, campaigning for international prosecutors to include particular thematically focused charges in their indictments.

[117] S Ford, 'A Social Psychology Model of the Perceived Legitimacy of International Criminal Courts: Implications for the Success of Transitional Justice Mechanisms' (2012) 45 *Vanderbilt Journal of Transnational Law* 405, 459–461; M Milanović, 'Establishing the Facts about Mass Atrocities: Accounting for the Failure of the ICTY to Persuade Target Audiences' (2016) 47 *Georgetown Journal of International Law* 1321, 1343–1344 and 1347–1352.

[118] M Damaška, 'Unacknowledged Presences in International Criminal Justice' (2012) 10 *Journal of International Criminal Justice* 1239, 1240. See similarly, Mégret (n 13) 308–309.

[119] See, in this regard, O Triffterer, 'Prosecution of State for Crimes of State' (1996) 67 *Revue internationale de droit penal* 341, 346 (noting that 'findings of individual responsibility for crimes under international law imply in many cases an *obiter dictum* that a state was engaged in criminal activity'); and Damaška (n 118) 1243 (noting that stigma 'fastens not only upon subjects formally charged and pronounced guilty of such crimes, but also—and not necessarily in lesser measure—upon those who, though uncharged, are identified in a court judgment as having been implicated in the same criminal event').

[120] Damaška (n 118) 1248.

[121] Mégret (n 13) 298. For an overview of different civil society groups connected to the work of the ICC, see generally, M Glasius, *The International Criminal Court: A Global Civil Society Achievement* (Routledge 2006).

Ultimately, of course, it falls to the *judges* of international criminal courts to construct historical narratives within their judgments. Particularly in their final judgments, judges attempt to achieve narrative closure through a rigorous evaluation of the law, facts, and evidence.[122] According to Stiina Löytömäki, for example, judges try to 'impose a normative judgement on the past, appearing to bring moral clarity to the disoriented world'.[123] However, whether narrative closure is achieved in practice will always depend on how judicial narratives are received and understood by different audiences both within and beyond the courtroom.[124]

Although these actors tend to be strongly invested in struggles for historical justice, there are exceptions. Defendants, for example, do not always seek *judicial* validation of their historical interpretation of events. In particular, defendants sometimes deploy strategies of rupture that seek to delegitimise international criminal courts by drawing attention to atrocities allegedly committed by the trial's architects.[125] In such circumstances, defendants effectively renounce the possibility of achieving historical justice within the courtroom in the hope of promoting their preferred version of events amongst the general public beyond it.[126] Similarly, States may be more interested in instrumentalising the narratives that accompany the charges brought against particular individuals for short-term expressive gains—such as legitimating military campaigns against non-state armed groups—rather than the narratives ultimately constructed within the judgments of international criminal courts.[127]

Importantly, actors that participate in struggles for historical justice perform particular roles within international criminal proceedings and possess varying levels of authority, technical ability, and narrative influence.[128] In this vein, those participating in struggles for historical justice may be characterised as 'actors' in a dual sense:[129] first, in the sociological sense of being agents, namely those who enact and, in an important sense, bring about the events that unfold; and second, in the theatrical sense of having prescribed roles to play, albeit pursuant to a script that is more improvisational than in most plays. Put differently, while actors that participate in struggles for historical justice exercise agency to influence the construction of judicial narratives, they do so against a background of contextual constraints. 'Context' here is understood in a broad sense to include not only the set of circumstances *external* to actors, such

[122] I Tallgren, 'The Sensibility and Sense of International Criminal Law' (2002) 13 *European Journal of International Law* 561, 562 (referring to 'the miraculous seal of finality').

[123] Löytömäki (n 72) 18.

[124] J Boyd White, 'Telling Stories in the Law and in Ordinary Life: The *Oresteia* and "Noon Wine"', in J Boyd White, *Heracles' Bow: Essays on Rhetoric and Poetics of the Law* (University of Wisconsin Press 1985) 168, 185.

[125] See, for example, Koskenniemi (n 108) 26–32; and Mégret (n 13) 313–314.

[126] O Kirchheimer, *Political Justice: The Use of Legal Procedure for Political Ends* (Princeton University Press 1961) 337.

[127] See similarly, SMH Nouwen and WG Werner, 'Doing Justice to the Political: The International Criminal Court in Uganda and Sudan: A Rejoinder to Bas Schotel' (2011) 22 *European Journal of International Law* 1161, 1163 ('international criminal law achieves its impact through authoritative invocation, application and enforcement, which can take place outside judgments').

[128] See generally, P Bourdieu, 'The Force of Law: Toward a Sociology of the Juridical Field' (1987) 38 *Hastings Law Journal* 814.

[129] DO Pendas, *The Frankfurt Auschwitz Trial, 1963–1965: Genocide, History, and the Limits of the Law* (CUP 2006) 80. See similarly, Osiel (n 24) 284–285 (noting how the courtroom tends to involve 'no small measure of role-playing and thus is not entirely discontinuous with theatrical performance').

as their prescribed roles within international criminal processes and the influence of other actors and audiences, but also their *internal* context, encompassing their prior experiences and presuppositions.[130]

Consider, for example, the practices of international prosecutors. In terms of their *external* context, prosecutors are constrained by a range of factors including the jurisdictional boundaries of international criminal courts which limit which situations may be investigated and which charges can be brought in any particular case, as well as the level of cooperation afforded by States in terms of funding, facilitating access to evidence, and securing arrests. International prosecutors may also be influenced by other actors such as victims and civil society groups, who may campaign for particular charges to be included in indictments.

At the same time, the practices of international prosecutors are also shaped by their *internal* context. To refer to an actor's internal context is to recognise that each and every actor is situated. As Stanley Fish famously put it, 'we are never not in a situation' and therefore practices are never available 'independently of a set of beliefs'.[131] This means that actors always carry with them assumptions and presuppositions gained through professional training and experience.[132] For example, it is not uncommon for international prosecutors to rely upon knowledge and experience gained through their domestic practices to develop their prosecutorial powers at the international level.[133] Importantly, an interpreter's internal context should not be thought of as fixed; assumptions and presuppositions can develop over time.[134] In this regard, it is notable that international criminal justice has typically been characterised as a juridical

[130] A Bianchi, 'Textual Interpretation and (International) Law Reading: The Myth of (In)determinacy and the Genealogy of Meaning', in PHF Bekker et al (eds), *Making Transnational Law Work in the Global Economy: Essays in Honour of Detlev Vagsts* (CUP 2010) 34, 41. See similarly, R Levi et al, 'International Courts in Atypical Political Environments: The Interplay of Prosecutorial Strategy, Evidence, and Court Authority in International Criminal Law' (2016) 79 *Law and Contemporary Problems* 289, 290–291 (understanding authority within international criminal courts through two broad elements: 'First, the *contextual factors* that shape the authority of international courts, in particular the constituencies they can mobilize, the geopolitical context in which they operate, and their relations with national fields of power; and second, connected to these, the *international legal practices* that these courts and their actors develop') (emphasis in original).

[131] S Fish, *Is There a Text in this Class? The Authority of Interpretive Communities* (Harvard University Press 1980) 276 and 365. See similarly, R Rorty, *Contingency, Irony, and Solidarity* (CUP 1989) 54 (dismissing the idea of 'presuppositionless critical reflection, conducted in no particular language and outside of any particular historical context'); and T Kuhn, *The Structure of Scientific Revolutions* (50th anniversary ed, University of Chicago Press 2012) 113 (noting that 'something like a paradigm is prerequisite to perception itself' and that, therefore, '[w]hat a man sees depends both upon what he looks at and also upon what his previous visual-conceptual experience has taught him to see').

[132] A Bianchi, 'Reflexive Butterfly Catching: Insights from a Situated Catcher', in J Pauwelyn et al (eds), *Informal International Lawmaking* (OUP 2012) 200, 203.

[133] J Hagan and R Levi, 'Crimes of War and the Force of Law' (2005) 83 *Social Forces* 1499.

[134] S Fish, *Doing What Comes Naturally: Change, Rhetoric, and the Practice of Theory in Literary and Legal Studies* (OUP 1989) 146 ('Even though the mind is informed by assumptions that limit what it can even notice, among those is the assumption that one's assumptions are subject to challenge and possible revision under certain circumstances and according to certain procedures when they are set in motion by certain persons'). See also, P Bourdieu and LJD Wacquant, 'The Purpose of Reflexive Sociology', in P Bourdieu and LJD Wacquant, *An Invitation to Reflexive Sociology* (University of Chicago Press 1992) 60, 133–134 (arguing that the internal dispositions of an interpreter will generally become more and more rigid and less and less responsive to challenge over time and referring, by way of illustration, to the process of aging, whereby 'the mental and bodily schemata of a person who ages become more and more rigid, less and less responsive to external solicitations').

field at the crossroads, situated at the confluence of different bodies of law,[135] informed by a variety of legal traditions,[136] and host to social actors from a diversity of professional backgrounds.[137] Andrew Clapham, for example, has observed how the field of international criminal justice tends to be populated by 'a series of tribes with their own customs, totems, traditions and prophets', including the '*pénalistes*', the '*droits de l'hommistes*', and the '*internationalistes*', each influencing the development of the field according to their distinct conceptual frameworks.[138] As a result of this multifaceted hybridity,[139] international criminal courts have often suffered from crises of identity, oscillating between the prioritisation of conflicting normative values.[140]

As this overview indicates, in order to critically examine struggles for historical justice it is important to analyse not only the different actors that participate within international criminal proceedings but also the ways in which their practices are informed by their external and internal context.

B. The Questions

International criminal courts are adjudicative bodies, tasked with determining the criminal responsibility of individuals for their participation in the commission of crimes. As such, the struggles for historical justice waged within them tend to be structured around questions specifically tailored towards the fulfilment of this adjudicative function. In particular, historical contestation within international criminal courts tends to focus on whether particular categories of *crimes* have been committed (the *crime* question) and whether criminal responsibility for their commission may be attributed according to particular categories of *culpability* (the *culpability* question) to particular categories of *persons* (the *prosecutorial targets* question). These questions help to explain the balance that tends to be struck between *specificity* and *contextualisation* within the narratives constructed in the judgments of international criminal courts.

[135] MC Bassiouni, *Introduction to International Criminal Law* (2nd edn, Martinus Nijhoff Publishers 2013) 1.

[136] E van Sliedregt and S Vasiliev, 'Pluralism: A New Framework for International Criminal Justice', in E van Sliedregt and S Vasiliev (eds), *Pluralism in International Criminal Law* (OUP 2014) 3, 30.

[137] P Dixon and C Tenove, 'International Criminal Justice as a Transnational Field: Rules, Authority and Victims' (2013) 7 *International Journal of Transitional Justice* 393, 397; M Swart, 'Is there a Text in this Court? The Purposive Method of Interpretation and the ad hoc Tribunals' (2010) 70 *Heidelberg Journal of International Law* 767, 777.

[138] A Clapham, 'Concluding Remarks: Three Tribes Engage on the Future of International Criminal Law' (2011) 9 *Journal of International Criminal Justice* 689, 689–691. See also, L van den Herik and C Stahn, '"Fragmentation", Diversification and "3D" Legal Pluralism: International Law as the Jack-in-the-Box', in L van den Herik and C Stahn (eds), *The Diversification and Fragmentation of International Criminal Law* (Martinus Nijhoff 2012) 21, 23–4.

[139] PP Soares, 'Tangling Human Rights and International Criminal Law: The Practice of International Tribunals and the Call for Rationalized Legal Pluralism' (2012) 23 *Criminal Law Forum* 161, 162 (referring to international criminal law's 'intrinsic hybridity concerning sources, principles, institutions and actors').

[140] See generally Robinson (n 40); L Grover, 'A Call to Arms: Fundamental Dilemmas Confronting the Interpretation of Crimes in the *Rome Statute of the International Criminal Court*' (2010) 21 *European Journal of International Law* 543, 550–551. See also van Sliedregt and Vasiliev (n 136) 32–34 (preferring the term 'normative pluralism' to 'identity crisis').

In terms of *specificity*, international criminal courts consistently focus on the particular over the structural, directing their gaze towards specific incidents, select individuals, and particular crimes at the expense of examining the structural logics that lurk beneath them.[141] As Zinaida Miller puts it, 'Criminal courts try individuals, not structures. They pursue particular violations, not a situation of structural violence.'[142]

At the same time, the crime and culpability questions examined within international criminal courts often require actors to contest selective aspects of the social contexts in which accused individuals previously operated. Selective *contextualisation* is necessitated by the fact that the crimes adjudicated by international criminal courts tend to be collective in nature—both in terms of their perpetrators and their victims.[143] Although the perpetrators are individually culpable, they generally commit such crimes in support of collective criminal policies. In addition, the victims of the crimes adjudicated by international criminal courts are often targeted based on their actual or perceived membership of particular groups. As such, international criminal trials tend to require a broader optic to adequately represent the collective nature of such crimes and to assess the culpability of individuals in relation to them. As a result, the narrative frames of international criminal courts often extend beyond a narrow focus on the acts and omissions of the accused towards a broader examination of the activities of related organisations and groups over extended periods of time.[144]

Importantly, contestation over the crime, culpability, and prosecutorial targets questions occurs at various junctures within international criminal proceedings, commencing as early as the drafting of statutory frameworks and continuing right up until the moment of judgment. As such, in order to understand how these questions have been resolved in different institutional contexts, it is important to examine the practices of the actors that participate within struggles for historical justice *throughout* international criminal justice processes.

C. The Practices

The historical narratives constructed in the judgments of international criminal courts are the product of two interrelated types of practices—*evidentiary* and *legal*. The nature of the transformations that result from these practices have been characterised by scholars in varying terms. For some, these practices accomplish a process of translation. Pierre Bourdieu, for example, famously argued that in order to bring a case before a court 'a complete retranslation of all of the aspects of the controversy is

[141] R Knox, 'Marxism, International Law, and Political Strategy' (2009) 22 *Leiden Journal of International Law* 413, 430.

[142] Z Miller, 'Anti-Impunity Politics in Post-Genocide Rwanda', in K Engle et al (eds), *Anti-Impunity and the Human Rights Agenda* (CUP 2016) 149, 169.

[143] RD Sloane, 'The Expressive Capacity of International Punishment: The Limits of the National Law Analogy and the Potential of International Criminal Law' (2007) 43 *Stanford Journal of International Law* 39, 56–58; K Campbell, 'Victims and Perpetrators of International Crimes: The Problem of the "Legal Person"' (2011) 2 *International Humanitarian Legal Studies* 325; and M Osiel, 'Choosing Among Alternative Responses to Mass Atrocity: Between the Individual and the Collectivity' *Ethics & International Affairs* (18 September 2015).

[144] Damaška (n 41) 336.

necessary in order ... to institute the controversy *as a lawsuit*, as a juridical problem that can become the object of juridically regulated debate'.[145] For others, the process is one of filtration. According to Larissa van den Herik, for instance, international criminal law 'filters realities through the use of precise definitions and categories of responsibility including concomitant rules of interpretation guiding their application, as well as through the use of the highest evidentiary standards and other strict rules of procedure'.[146]

Whether characterised as translation or filtration, it is through a combination of evidentiary and legal practices that mass atrocity situations are transformed into a legal form, with the result that certain aspects of such conflicts are taken into consideration and other aspects are overlooked.[147]

1. Evidentiary practices

Evidentiary practices concern evidentiary materials—the various forms of information, such as documents, testimony, and tangible objects, that are put before courts to prove or contest the existence of particular alleged facts.[148] In terms of historical narration, evidentiary materials constitute the raw materials with which the past is constructed.

In international criminal courts, evidentiary materials are contested through recourse to rules of procedure and evidence.[149] These rules provide a vocabulary for evidentiary practices, transforming international criminal courts into processes of 'rule-governed storytelling'.[150] Importantly, rules of procedure and evidence are underpinned by the principle of fairness,[151] which has generally been understood to

[145] Bourdieu (n 128) 831–832. See also, J Boyd White, *Justice as Translation: An Essay in Cultural and Legal Criticism* (University of Chicago Press 1990) 235 and 241 (noting how translation always entails 'deficiencies', namely aspects of the meaning of the original that are lost in translation, and 'exuberances', namely aspects of meaning that appear in the translation but were not part of the original, and concluding that with these concepts in mind law may be characterised as 'a kind of translation').

[146] L van den Herik, 'International Criminal Law as a Spotlight and Black Holes as Constituents of Legacy' (2016) 110 *AJIL Unbound* 209, 210. See similarly, L Douglas, 'The Didactic Trial: Filtering History and Memory into the Courtroom' (2006) 14 *European Review* 513, 515–516.

[147] M Heikkilä, *Coping with International Atrocities through Criminal Law: A Study into the Typical Features of International Criminality and the Reflection of these Traits in International Criminal Law* (Åbo Akademi University Press 2013) 70. See also, Wilson (n 42) 8–9 (discussing 'legal exceptionalism', namely the way that '[l]aw's unique conventions, special categories, and exceptional rules impel courts to perceive historical events through a counterintuitive prism, which leads to all manner of unintended consequences and absurd outcomes').

[148] M Klamberg, *Evidence in International Criminal Trials: Confronting Legal Gaps and the Reconstruction of Disputed Events* (Martinus Nijhoff Publishers 2013) 3.

[149] Rules of procedure and evidence may be spread across of a number of different documents of an international criminal court. For example, at the ICC, rules of procedure and evidence can be found in the ICC Statute, the ICC Rules of Procedure and Evidence, and the ICC Regulations of the Court, while guidance is also contained in the ICC Chambers Practice Manual. See generally, Y McDermott, 'The International Criminal Court's Chambers Practice Manual: Towards a Return to Judicial Law Making in International Criminal Procedure?' (2017) 15 *Journal of International Criminal Justice* 873.

[150] P Brooks, 'The Law as Narrative and Rhetoric', in P Brooks and P Gewirtz (eds), *Law's Stories—Narrative and Rhetoric in the Law* (Yale University Press 1996) 14, 20.

[151] On the principle of fairness in international criminal proceedings, see generally Ambos (n 38) 95–97; and Y McDermott, *Fairness in International Criminal Trials* (OUP 2016) Chapter 2.

encompass two components:[152] first, a general component, entailing a duty to ensure the fairness of the proceedings for all participants; and second, a specific component, which stands for the proposition that the right to a fair trial applies to the accused.[153] The general component reflects the fact that the notion of fairness in international criminal proceedings is not confined to the accused, but also extends to the recognition of the interests and procedural rights of other parties to the process.[154] The specific component emphasises that the fair trial rights of the accused must never be subordinated to the interests of other parties to the process.[155] In practice, therefore, the precise conception of fairness embodied in the rules of procedure and evidence of different international criminal courts is always reflective of a particular balance that has been struck between a range of interests including not only the fair trial rights of the accused, but also the interests of prosecutors, victims, witnesses, and States, as well as the unique challenges posed by the institutional contexts in which international criminal courts operate such as the cultural diversity of their proceedings.[156]

Within international criminal courts, evidentiary practices are diverse, spanning the collection, admissibility, presentation, scrutiny, and evaluation of evidentiary materials throughout the international criminal justice process. Each of these practices can have a significant bearing on the historical narratives ultimately constructed within the judgments of international criminal courts.

For instance, only if sufficient evidence is *collected*—whether through State cooperation or other avenues such as new information and communication technologies and social media channels—will it be possible for prosecutors to indict particular individuals and for trial participants to allege and contest the existence of the material facts of a case.[157] Moreover, evidentiary materials may only be relied upon if they

152 See, for example, *Situation in Uganda: Case 01/05* (Decision on Prosecutor's Application for Leave to Appeal dated the 15th Day of March 2006 and to Suspend or Stay Consideration of Leave to Appeal Dated the 11th Day of May 2006, Pre-Trial Chamber) ICC-02/04-01//05-90 (10 July 2006) [24].

153 For a critical discussion of jurisprudence asserting that the right to a fair trial applies principally rather than exclusively to the accused, see generally, McDermott (n 151) Chapter 4.

154 See, for example, *Prosecutor v Duško Tadić* (Decision on the Prosecutor's Motion Requesting Protective Measures for Victims and Witnesses, Trial Chamber) IT-94-I (10 August 1995) [55] 'A fair trial means not only fair treatment to the defendant but also to the prosecution and to the witnesses'); and *Situation in the Democratic Republic of the Congo* (Decision on the Prosecutor's application for leave to appeal the Chamber's decision of 17 January 2006 on the applications for participation in the proceedings of VPRS 1, VPRS 2, VPRS 3, VPRS 4, VPRS 5, and VPRS 6, Pre-Trial Chamber) ICC-01/04-135-tEN (31 March 2006) [38] ('The term "fairness" (*equité*), from the Latin "*equus*", means equilibrium, or balance. As a legal concept, equity, or fairness, "is a direct emanation of the idea of justice". Equity of the proceedings entails equilibrium between the two parties, which assumes both respect for the principle of equality and the principle of adversarial proceedings. In the view of the Chamber, fairness of the proceedings includes respect for the procedural rights of the Prosecutor, the Defence, and the Victims as guaranteed by the relevant statutes (in systems which provide for victim participation in criminal proceedings)').

155 International Bar Association, *Fairness at the International Criminal Court* (August 2011) 20.

156 See similarly, Klamberg (n 148) 48–65; and F Mégret, 'Beyond "Fairness": Understanding the Determinants of International Criminal Procedure' (2009) 14 *UCLA Journal of International Law and Foreign Affairs* 37, 60*ff*.

157 See, for example, Mégret (n 156) 61 ('unlike domestic courts, a significant part of what international criminal tribunals do is mediated by states. Difficulties arise particularly in terms of securing state cooperation and access to evidence'); KA Rodman, 'Justice as a Dialogue Between Law and Politics: Embedding the International Criminal Court within Conflict Management and Peacebuilding' (2014) 12 *Journal of International Criminal Justice* 437, 442–443 ('the prospects for prosecution will depend upon the willingness of external actors to act as "surrogate enforcers" to alter the incentives facing resistant governments in favour of compliance'); and R Cryer et al, *An Introduction to International Criminal Law and Procedure* (3rd

are *admissible*. Although generally liberal and flexible in nature within international criminal courts,[158] principles of admissibility constitute important filters that ensure case records are not overburdened with evidence that lacks relevance and probative value to the case at hand or which is prejudicial to the fairness of the trial.[159]

How evidence is *presented and scrutinised* during international criminal proceedings will also influence the shape of the historical narratives constructed within international criminal judgments. In international criminal courts, prosecution and defence teams tend to develop rival theories of the case that seek to prove or contest the culpability of the accused. In this context, a 'theory of the case' may be understood to refer to 'the overarching story that aligns individual facts and amalgamates them into a coherent whole'.[160] Beyond the prosecution and defence, some international criminal courts have also recognised the possibility for victims to participate in the proceedings. For instance, at the ICC, Article 68(3) of the ICC Statute entitles victims to participate 'at stages of the proceedings determined to be appropriate by the Court' when 'the personal interests of the victims are affected' so long as it is 'in a manner which is not prejudicial to or inconsistent with the rights of the accused and a fair and impartial trial'.[161] Providing opportunities for victims to participate in international criminal proceedings can open up the possibility for an additional rival narrative to emerge in the courtroom as well as create opportunities for evidence to be subjected to an additional layer of scrutiny.[162]

Importantly, a party's theory of the case is not necessarily static and may develop during the course of a trial. In the case of *Slobodan Milošević*, for example, the ICTY Prosecutor's initial thesis was that the accused's specific intent to commit genocide was not accidental but rather 'the culmination of a century-old ideological program to carve a Greater Serbia from the patchwork of minorities in the Balkans'.[163] As the trial developed, however, the Prosecutor's position shifted, particularly under pressure from testimony given by Vojislav Šešelj, who claimed that Milošević had never adopted a policy of creating a Greater Serbia, a policy which had remained confined

edn, CUP 2014) 425 ('procedures that require the suspect or accused to conduct his or her investigation in preparation of a separate case may prove difficult, or even impossible, in international criminal proceedings dependent upon State cooperation').

158 See, for example, Klamberg (n 148) 335 (identifying 'a flexible approach to the admission of evidence unhindered by technical rules').

159 See, in particular, Articles 19–20, Nuremberg Charter; Article 13(a)–(b), Tokyo Charter; Rule 89(C)–(D), ICTY Rules of Procedure and Evidence; Rules 89(C) and 95, ICTR Rules of Procedure and Evidence; Rules 89(C) and 95, SCSL Rules of Procedure and Evidence (omitting any mention of probative value); and Article 69(4) and (7), ICC Statute. For a useful overview of these provisions, see generally, Klamberg (n 148) 344–357 and 395–406.

160 Wilson (n 42) 82.

161 Article 68(3), ICC Statute. See also, Rule 85, ICC Statute (defining 'victims' in general terms to include 'natural persons', who have suffered harm as a result of the commission of any crime within the jurisdiction of the Court, as well as 'organizations or institutions', which have sustained direct harm to any of their property such as schools, hospitals, and historic monuments). For a useful overview of victim participation, see generally, Cryer et al (n 157) 482–499; and S Vasiliev, 'Victim Participation Revisited—What the ICC is Learning about Itself', in C Stahn (ed), *The Law and Practice of the International Criminal Court* (OUP 2015) 1133.

162 Wilson (n 42) 212.

163 Ibid 100.

to his Serbian Radical Party.[164] As Gideon Boas explains, in the end the Prosecutor drew a distinction between 'the actions and intentions of Milošević with regard to the espousal of a Serb-controlled State from which non-Serbs were to be removed' on the one hand, and 'those nationalists like Šešelj, who advocated a Greater Serbia based on an ideological and historical idea that encompassed broad swathes of territory of the former Yugoslavia' on the other.[165]

In developing their rival theories of the case at trial, prosecution and defence teams rely to a greater or lesser extent on different forms of evidence, including documents, multimedia, factual witness testimony, and expert witness testimony. Lawrence Douglas refers to these different evidential forms as 'paradigms of proof' or 'didactic paradigms',[166] understood as methods or tools aimed at 'transforming an unspeakable event into evidence for a trial staged to serve both conventionally juridical and pedagogic ends'.[167]

By offering a platform for the antagonists to put forward their preferred evidentiary materials, international criminal courts provide opportunities for different forms of evidence to be contextualised,[168] as well as subjected to thorough and repeated testing.[169] According to Florian Bieber, for example, international criminal trials provide 'a feedback loop' concerning the evidence related to particular conflicts by subjecting such materials to significant and ongoing scrutiny.[170]

The procedural model applied by an international criminal court can be an important factor in this regard—influencing, for example, the ability of judges to overcome impediments to accurate witness testimony that stem from the multicultural environments in which their proceedings tend to be conducted.[171] Nancy Combs, for example, has suggested that the more relaxed, informal, free-flowing narrative nature of judge-led non-adversarial procedures may be more suited to responding to the needs of witnesses who suffer from *inabilities* to testify accurately—for example as a result of cultural misunderstandings, complications with translation, or memory lapse. By contrast, the zealousness of adversarial questioning, through which advocates are able to vigorously challenge and press witnesses in a manner that if carried out by judges might impair their neutrality, may be more likely to root out fact-finding impediments that stem from witnesses' *unwillingness* to testify accurately.[172]

[164] Ibid 106–107.

[165] G Boas, *The Milošević Trial: Lessons for the Conduct of Complex International Criminal Proceedings* (CUP 2007) 92.

[166] Douglas (n 28) 5–6 and 257.

[167] Ibid 6.

[168] See, for example, F Bieber, 'Do Historians Need a Verdict?', in T Waters (ed), *The Milošević Trial: An Autopsy* (OUP 2014) 349, 353 (providing the example of the testimony given by Vojislav Šešelj at the ICTY in which he provided an insight into the political motivations behind particular comments about Slobodan Milošević made during the BBC documentary, *The Death of Yugoslavia*).

[169] Wilson (n 42) 220.

[170] Bieber (n 168) 353.

[171] See, in this regard, NA Combs, *Fact-Finding Without Facts—The Uncertain Evidentiary Foundations of International Criminal Convictions* (CUP 2010) Chapters 2–5; and T Kelsall, *Culture under Cross-Examination: International Justice and the Special Court for Sierra Leone* (CUP 2009) Chapters 6–7.

[172] Combs (n 171) 303–316. Since it is difficult for courts to determine in advance which types of fact-finding impediments are likely to predominate in any given trial, Nancy Combs suggests that it may be preferable for international criminal courts to adopt a one-size fits all *sui generis* procedural model, entailing a judge-driven direct examination to allow witnesses to effectively convey the information they need to, followed by a partisan cross-examination to deter the danger of perjury. Ibid 318–319.

The methods by which judges *evaluate* evidence as well as the standard of proof that must be satisfied to establish the guilt of the accused can also influence the historical narratives constructed within the judgments of international criminal courts.[173] The standard of proof determines the degree of uncertainty that may remain within judicial findings of fact.[174] Formally, international criminal courts have relied upon a 'beyond-a-reasonable-doubt' standard for the purpose of determining the guilt of an accused,[175] a threshold that requires a high level of certainty to convict an individual,[176] whilst at the same time tolerating severe doubts about the accuracy of acquittals.[177] In practice, however, the evidence deemed sufficient to satisfy the standard of proof has sometimes fluctuated depending on the types of facts at issue. Simon de Smet, for example, has argued that 'when one analyses the type of evidence which is deemed sufficient to enter findings beyond reasonable doubt concerning facts pertaining to the contextual elements of the crimes charged, it is fairly obvious that a lower standard is applied than for facts pertaining directly to the criminal responsibility for the accused'.[178]

Finally, beyond evidentiary materials, a number of doctrines have been recognised by international criminal courts for expediting and improving the consistency of factual findings. These processes are important since they constitute alternative avenues by which facts may filter into international criminal proceedings in particular cases. The doctrine of judicial notice, for example, refers to a 'court's acceptance, for purpose of convenience and without requiring a party's proof, of a well-known and indisputable fact'.[179] In practice, international criminal courts have consistently been under an obligation to take judicial notice of 'facts of common knowledge', namely 'those facts which are not subject to reasonable dispute including, common or universally known facts, such as general facts of history, generally known geographical facts and the

[173] See generally, Klamberg (n 148) Chapter 3.

[174] S De Smet, 'The International Criminal Standard of Proof at the ICC—Beyond Reasonable Doubt or Beyond Reason', in C Stahn (ed), *The Law and Practice of the International Criminal Court* (OUP 2015) 861, 861. For a discussion of the distinction between 'material facts', understood as those facts upon which the charges are premised and which must be established beyond reasonable doubt, and 'evidentiary facts' or 'subsidiary facts', understood as those facts which are used as indirect proof of material facts, see generally, E Fry, 'Legal Recharacterisation and the Materiality of Facts at the International Criminal Court: Which Charges Are Permissible?' (2016) 29 *Leiden Journal of International Law* 577.

[175] See, for example: Rule 87(A), ICTY Rules of Procedure and Evidence; Rule 87(A), ICTR Rules of Procedure and Evidence; Rule 87(A), SCSL Rules of Procedure and Evidence; and Article 66(3), ICC Statute.

[176] Combs (n 171) 344 ('The traditional view of the beyond-a-reasonable-doubt standard conceives of it as a fixed and unchanging standard that reflects a high level of certainty').

[177] De Smet (n 174) 883 (noting that 'the truth-tropic effect of the criminal standard of proof is asymmetrical' and that, therefore, 'standards of proof are not so much tools to create greater accuracy, but rather mechanisms for minimizing expected losses in case the decision turns out to be wrong').

[178] De Smet (n 174) 888. See also, Combs (n 171) 189, 271, and 350–351 (arguing that judges at the ICTR, SCSL, and Special Panels for Serious Crimes in East Timor have often required less certainty to satisfy the 'beyond a reasonable doubt' standard—for example, by neglecting to mention testimonial deficiencies or attributing such flaws to innocent causes that do not impact the credibility of witnesses—with respect to accused individuals who have institutional affiliations that are suggestive of their association with criminal activities). For a critique of the types of fluctuations in the standard of proof identified by Nancy Combs, see generally, BS Lyons, 'Enough is Enough: The Illegitimacy of International Criminal Convictions: A Review Essay of *Fact-Finding Without Facts, The Uncertain Evidentiary Foundations of International Criminal Convictions* by Nancy Amoury Combs' (2011) 13 *Journal of Genocide Research* 287, 302–304.

[179] Klamberg (n 148) 471 (citing Black's Law Dictionary).

laws of nature'.[180] In addition, international criminal courts have generally possessed a discretionary power to take judicial notice of certain 'adjudicated facts' from prior proceedings.[181] Beyond judicial notice, the doctrine of agreed facts enables the prosecution and defence to agree that certain alleged facts are uncontested.[182] However, agreed facts remain subject to the tests of relevance and probative value,[183] and agreements between the parties concerning alleged facts are not binding on international criminal courts, which retain the power to insist on the submission of evidence in practice.[184]

As this snapshot of the evidentiary practices of international criminal courts reveals, it is through contestation over evidentiary materials that the building blocks of the historical narratives constructed within international criminal judgments are established.

2. Legal practices

Legal practices concern legal categories—the jurisdictional requirements, admissibility criteria, and sentencing factors relied upon within international criminal proceedings. Jurisdictional requirements encompass the personal, temporal, territorial, and subject-matter categories, which define the types of persons and crimes that may be prosecuted, the territories and time periods over which crimes must have been committed, the modes of participation by which persons may be linked to crimes, and the grounds upon which criminal responsibility may be excluded. Admissibility criteria are additional conditions that must be satisfied for an investigation or prosecution to proceed—for example, the doctrines of complementarity and gravity at the

180 *Prosecutor v Laurent Semanza* (Decision on the Prosecutor's Motion for Judicial Notice and Presumptions of Facts Pursuant to Rules 94 and 54, Trial Chamber) ICTR-97-20-I (3 November 2000) [23].

181 See, for example, Rule 94(B), ICTY Rules of Procedure and Evidence; Rule 94(B), ICTR Rules of Procedure and Evidence; and Rule 94(B), SCSL Rules of Procedure and Evidence. See also, *Prosecutor v Momčilo Krajišnik* (Decision on Prosecution Motions for Judicial Notice of Adjudicated Facts and for Admission of Written Statements of Witnesses Pursuant to Rule 92bis, Trial Chamber) IT-00-39-PT (28 February 2003) [15] (noting that judicial notice may only be taken of adjudicated facts that: (i) have already been contested at trial and formed part of a judgment that either has not been appealed, falls outside the issues in dispute of an ongoing appeal, or has been finally settled on appeal; (ii) are not the subject of reasonable dispute between the parties to a particular case; and (iii) neither include legal characterisations nor attest to the criminal responsibility of the accused). The ICC contains no equivalent doctrine of judicial notice of adjudicated facts and it remains to be seen whether such a doctrine will be recognised by judges in the interest of expediting cases in practice.

182 See, for example, Rule 65*ter* (H) and (M), ICTY Rules of Procedure and Evidence; Rue 73*bis* (B) (ii), ICTR Rules of Procedure and Evidence; and Rule 69, ICC Rules of Procedure and Evidence. See also, *Prosecutor v Brima et al* (Judgment, Trial Chamber) SCSL-04-16-T (20 June 2007) ('*Brima et al* Trial Judgment') [154] ('There is no provision in the Rules [of the SCSL] pertaining to agreed facts. Nonetheless, it follows from the very nature of adversarial proceedings that the Parties may stipulate to any fact on which they reach consensus').

183 See, for example, *Prosecutor v Vidoje Blagojević and Dragan Jokić* (Judgment, Trial Chamber) IT-02-60-T (17 January 2005) [28]; and *Brima et al* Trial Judgment (n 182) [154].

184 See, for example, Rule 69, ICC Rules of Procedure and Evidence ('a Chamber may consider such alleged fact as being proven, unless the Chamber is of the opinion that a more complete presentation of the alleged facts is required in the interests of justice, in particular the interests of the victims'). See similarly, *Prosecutor v Popović et al* (Judgment: Volume I, Trial Chamber) IT-05-88-T (10 June 2010) [68] ('The Trial Chamber recalls that it is not bound by any agreements reached between the parties, and that it is not obliged to make explicit findings on facts agreed upon by the parties or on undisputed facts; the reference to such facts is by itself indicative that it accepts those facts as true').

ICC. Sentencing factors encompass criteria—including aggravating and mitigating circumstances—relied upon to determine the appropriate sentence of a convicted individual.

A common starting point for thinking about the relationship between historical narration and legal categories is to liken legal categories to narrative grids within which fact patterns must be specifically framed to fit to ensure their legal relevance in any particular case. According to Christiane Wilke, for example, jurisdictional rules 'create and order spaces by determining how and by whom they are governed', whilst also shaping 'the public visibility of violence'.[185] In practice, the denial of jurisdiction facilitates forms of 'legal anaesthesia', excluding the substance of particular claims from judicial consideration and 'muting the claims of victims in the legal arena'.[186] That legal categories perform this restrictive function is undeniable.

Personal jurisdiction, for example, serves to restrict the personal focus of the histories constructed within international criminal courts. For instance, at the Tokyo IMTFE, the personal jurisdiction of the tribunal was restricted to 'the just and prompt trial and punishment of the major war criminals in the Far East',[187] a provision that ensured the construction of a one-sided historical narrative focused on the crimes of the Japanese to the exclusion of Allied personnel.

Subject-matter jurisdiction also influences the narrative focus of the historical narratives constructed in international criminal judgments. The Nuremberg IMT, for example, was unable to make 'a general declaration' that acts committed prior to 1939 constituted crimes against humanity within the meaning of the Nuremberg Charter because 'revolting and horrible as many of these crimes were, it [had] not been satisfactorily proved that they were done in execution of, or in connection with' war crimes or crimes against peace as required by Article 6(c) of the Nuremberg Charter.[188]

Yet, while these examples illustrate how historical narratives are sometimes excluded by or shoe-horned to fit within the restrictive elements of a particular legal category, they occlude the extent to which legal categories are themselves to a certain extent adaptable in the face of novel factual circumstances through the process of legal interpretation.

In international criminal courts, legal categories are interpreted through recourse to what Owen Fiss famously labelled 'disciplining rules'.[189] Although these rules can take a variety of forms depending on the court in question and the type of legal category under examination, in international criminal courts they are generally recognisable in particular conceptions of the principle of legality, the doctrine of sources, and rules of interpretation including those set out in Articles 31–33 of the Vienna Convention

[185] C Wilke, 'High Altitude Legality: Visuality and Jurisdiction in the Adjudication of NATO Air Strikes' (2019) 34 *Canadian Journal of Law and Society* 261, 263–264.

[186] Ibid 264.

[187] Article 1, Tokyo Charter.

[188] *Göring and others*, Nuremberg International Military Tribunal, Judgment, 1 October 1946, *Trial of the Major War Criminals before the International Military Tribunal, Nuremberg, 14 November 1945 1 October 1946: Volume I* (Nuremberg IMT 1947) 171, 254.

[189] See generally, O Fiss, 'Objectivity and Interpretation' (1982) 34 *Stanford Law Review* 739; and OM Fiss, 'Conventionalism' (1985) 58 *Southern California Law Review* 177.

on the Law of Treaties.[190] These disciplining rules provide a vocabulary for legal practices, facilitating the conversion of narrative conflicts into a juridical form.

The principle of legality, for example, may be understood to be comprised of two interrelated branches.[191] The first branch—the prohibition on retroactivity—requires that an individual may only be held criminally responsible and punished for conduct that, at the time it took place, had a *sufficient* legal basis under the applicable law. The second branch—the rule of specificity—requires that the criminal offence be defined with *sufficient* clarity and precision so as to ensure that an individual can freely choose whether to comply with or breach the relevant standard of behaviour. Importantly, what international criminal courts have deemed *sufficient* to satisfy each branch of the principle of legality has not been uniform but subject to variation depending on the methodologies utilised to identify and interpret their applicable law in different institutional contexts.

Similar to evidentiary practices, legal practices are diverse, including *drafting* practices that determine the range and definition of the legal categories included within statutory frameworks,[192] *interpretative* practices that influence the meanings attributed to legal categories in the context of particular cases,[193] *charging* practices that determine the nature of the charges in indictments,[194] and *defensive* practices that determine whether and which grounds for excluding responsibility will be relied upon by the accused in the context of particular cases.[195] Each of these legal practices plays a part in determining the scope and content of the historical narratives constructed within the judgments of international criminal courts.

The statutory frameworks of international criminal courts constitute the primary instruments that international criminal courts are called upon to apply in practice.

[190] See generally, D Akande, 'Sources of International Criminal Law', in A Cassese (ed), *The Oxford Companion to International Criminal Justice* (OUP 2009) 41; J Powderly, 'The Rome Statute and the Attempted Corseting of the Interpretative Judicial Function: Reflections on Sources of Law and Interpretative Technique', in C Stahn (ed), *The Law and Practice of the International Criminal Court* (OUP 2015) 444; and S Vasiliev, 'The Making of International Criminal Law', in C Brölmann and Y Radi (eds), *Research Handbook on the Theory and Practice of International Law-Making* (Edward Elgar 2016) 354.

[191] See similarly, Cryer et al (n 157) 18–21; and WN Ferdinandusse, *Direct Application of International Criminal Law in National Courts* (TMC Asser Press 2006) 223.

[192] See generally, R Cryer, *Prosecuting International Crimes: Selectivity and the International Criminal Law Regime* (CUP 2005).

[193] See generally, M Cupido, 'Facing Facts in International Criminal Law: A Casuistic Model of Judicial Reasoning' (2016) 14 *Journal of International Criminal Justice* 1; and A Grabert, *Dynamic Interpretation in International Criminal Law: Striking a Balance between Stability and Change* (Herbert Utz Verlag 2015).

[194] The Statutes of all modern-day international criminal courts provide that charges must be brought against an accused person, who is entitled to be informed of 'the nature and cause of the charge against him'. The 'nature' of the charge generally refers to its legal characterisation, namely the categories of crime and modes of participation that the prosecutor seeks to establish, whilst the 'cause' of the charge generally refers to the material facts that the prosecutor seeks to rely on for the purpose of satisfying the elements of such categories. See, in this regard, Article 21(4)(a), ICTY Statute; Article 20(4)(a), ICTR Statute; Article 17(4)(a), SCSL Statute; and Article 67(1)(a), ICC Statute (referring to 'the nature, cause *and content* of the charge'; however, the additional reference to the 'content' of the charge is unlikely to add anything substantive that was not already covered by the term 'cause'). On charging practices within international criminal courts, see generally, KJ Heller, 'The Role of the International Prosecutor', in CPR Romano et al (eds), *The Oxford Handbook of International Adjudication* (OUP 2013) 669; and Ford (n 46).

[195] See generally, UNICRI and Association of Defence Counsel Practising Before the ICTY (ADC-ICTY), *Manual on International Criminal Defence: ADC-ICTY Developed Practices Within the Framework of the War Crimes Justice Project* (UNICRI Publisher 2011).

As such, the *drafting* practices that determine the range and definition of the legal categories included within such frameworks are significant to the extent that they typically mark the beginning of the interpretative process within international criminal courts.

In practice, statutory frameworks tend to vary in terms of the level of detail provided regarding the applicable law and interpretative methodology to be relied upon by an international criminal court, as well as the level of precision with which the constituent elements of jurisdictional categories and admissibility conditions are defined. Regardless of their specificity, however, legal categories always require *interpretation* in the context of particular situations and cases for their meaning to be illuminated in practice. The inescapability of interpretation results from a degree of indeterminacy that typically exists on two sometimes overlapping levels:[196] first, with respect to what counts as law; and second, with respect to what the identified law means.

The first level of indeterminacy concerns *uncertainty over the applicable law* of international criminal courts. Even if judges within a particular court agree that they are bound to apply their statutory framework, uncertainty may remain over whether it must also be established that legal categories such as crimes and modes of participation have a legal basis in international law, how such a basis should be identified in practice, as well as whether the statutory framework permits recognition of legal categories not expressly mentioned therein and on what basis.

The second level of indeterminacy concerns *uncertainty over the meanings of the legal categories* identified within the applicable law of international criminal courts. To some extent, a degree of indeterminacy over the meaning of legal categories inevitably results from the general properties of language. As Jan Klabbers explains, 'since there is no necessary correspondence between words and rules or institutions (there is, after all, nothing particularly and inherently ashtray-ish about an ashtray), and since intentions can never be fully communicated (every published author will be familiar with misreadings of their work), those rules and institutions rely on further conventions and acts of interpretation to give them meaning'.[197]

In addition, a degree of indeterminacy also arises from the open-textured and context-independent terms in which legal categories tend to be drafted.[198] Whilst the wording of a particular legal category is typically drafted with a certain event in mind—for example, the Holocaust with respect to the crime of genocide—a more

[196] G Fitzmaurice, 'The Future of Public International Law and of the International Legal System in the Circumstances of Today', in Institut de Droit International, *Livre du Centenaire de l'Institut de Droit International 1873–1973* (1973) 197, 251 (noting that in the international plane there is uncertainty both as to 'what is law' as well as 'what the law is'). These two levels of indeterminacy correspond to the sometimes overlapping interpretative stages of *law-ascertainment* and *content-determination*, on which see generally, J d'Aspremont, 'The Multidimensional Process of Interpretation: Content-Determination and Law-Ascertainment Distinguished', in A Bianchi et al (eds), *International in International Law* (CUP 2015) 111, 116*ff.* (distinguishing between 'law-ascertainment', the function of which is 'to determine whether a given norm qualifies as a legal rule and can claim to be part of the international legal order', and 'content-determination', the function of which is 'to elucidate the content of rules with a view to determining the standard of behaviour or normative guidance provided by them'). See similarly, in the domestic context, R Dworkin, *Law's Empire* (Harvard University Press 1986) 65–68.

[197] J Klabbers, 'The Meaning of Rules' (2006) 20 *International Relations* 295, 297. See similarly, KS Gallant, *The Principle of Legality in International and Comparative Criminal Law* (CUP 2009) 31–33.

[198] Cupido (n 193) 3.

general formulation is usually relied upon to ensure that a broader range of possible fact patterns fall within its scope.[199] As such, when judges adjudicate individual cases, they are required to interpret legal categories with a view to applying them to the specific factual circumstances of the case at hand—a process that requires judges to translate legal categories into more specific definitions and criteria.[200] In this way, the interpretative enterprise may be understood as a complex interplay or oscillation between facts and law,[201] the historical narratives constructed within international criminal judgments depending to a significant degree on how the two are 'fitted to each other'.[202] In practice, this process of going back and forth between facts and law gives rise to a tension between interpreting legal categories restrictively or dynamically in response to the novel factual circumstances of new cases.[203]

Despite the indeterminacy that tends to arise within the interpretive process, the meanings of particular legal categories often become increasingly clear and settled the more they are interpreted in the context of specific situations and particular sets of factual circumstances.[204] With this in mind, as Beth van Schaack explains, international criminal law tends to develop 'asymptotically', with early international criminal cases addressing 'vast open areas in legal doctrine' and later cases addressing 'issues that are more nuanced, involving the resolution of more micro irregularities and the filling in of increasingly smaller gaps'.[205] Importantly, the more settled the meaning of a legal category becomes, the more it is able to guide and restrict the types of facts and narratives that must be established to satisfy its constituent elements in practice.

Charging practices also have a significant influence on the narrative orientation of international criminal courts. Within the jurisdictional parameters of an international criminal court, it is the charges that determine which individuals will be prosecuted, for which crimes, pursuant to which modes of participation, and over which time periods and territories. As ICC Judge Christine Van den Wyngaert explains, 'charges are more than a list of atomic facts and corresponding list of legal elements', but instead 'allege the existence of specific relations between different facts and construct a particular narrative on this basis which, if true, would cover all the legal elements of the charges with which it corresponds'.[206]

199 Klabbers (n 197) 297–298.

200 Cupido (n 193) 3.

201 See generally, Cupido (n 193). See also, FV Kratochwil, *Rules Norms, and Decisions: On the Conditions of Practical and Legal Reasoning in International Relations and Domestic Affairs* (CUP 1989) 240 ('It is precisely this going back and forth between "facts" and norms in which the "artfulness" of legal reasoning (*ars legis*) consists').

202 Kratochwil (n 201) 241.

203 AM Danner, 'When Courts Make Law: How the International Criminal Tribunals Recast the Laws of War' (2006) 59 *Vanderbilt Law Review* 1, 5.

204 See generally, I Venzke, *How Interpretation Makes International Law: On Semantic Change and Normative Twists* (OUP 2012).

205 B van Schaak, '*Crimen Sine Lege*: Judicial Lawmaking at the Intersection of Law and Morals' (2008) 97 *Georgetown Law Journal* 119, 189. See similarly, Akande (n 190) 53 (arguing that judicial decisions 'provide an "off the shelf" assessment of the law which is often the starting point for deciding future cases'); Danner (n 203) 57 (referring to judicial decisions as 'focal points'); and S Darcy, *Judges, Law and War: The Judicial Development of International Humanitarian Law* (CUP 2014) 317 ('The cumulative effect of repeated judicial iteration of norms or standards is such that their legal standing can eventually become impossible to refute').

206 *Prosecutor v Germain Katanga* (Judgment Pursuant to Article 74 of the Statute, Trial Chamber) ICC-01/04-01/07-3436-AnxI (7 March 2014) (minority op Van den Wyngaert) [32].

Charging practices also define the prosecution's theory of the case that the defence must counter.[207] To this end, defence counsel may not only challenge the admissibility or probative value of the prosecution's evidence and identify new exculpatory facts through their own evidence, but also contest the prosecution's interpretation of the elements of the crimes and modes of participation relied upon in the indictment.[208] In addition, defence counsel may also undertake *defensive practices* that seek to establish one or more affirmative grounds for excluding responsibility in an effort to raise a reasonable doubt that the prosecution has met its burden of proof.[209]

Importantly, these different types of legal practices are very much interrelated. For instance, charging and defensive practices are restricted by the jurisdictional parameters of international criminal courts as illuminated through the drafting of statutory frameworks and the interpretations of legal categories rendered by judges in their prior decisions and judgments. In turn, the interpretive practices of judges in particular cases are generally confined to examining the legal categories relied upon as the charges in indictments, subject to the possibility within some courts to legally recharacterise the facts under certain conditions.[210]

As this overview of the legal practices of international criminal courts indicates, it is not only contestation over evidentiary materials that determines the scope and content of the historical narratives constructed within international criminal judgments, but also contestation over the legal categories that influence the scope and content of the fact patterns that must be established by sufficient evidentiary materials to satisfy their constituent elements in particular cases.

IV. Conclusion: The Road Ahead

The field of international criminal justice has been beset by a normative debate amongst scholars and practitioners contesting the scope of the historical inquiries that international criminal courts should be expected to conduct in practice. Taking this debate as its point of departure, this study seeks to shift analytical perspective towards an examination of the struggles for historical justice that inevitably take place within international criminal courts. For this purpose, this study critically examines the scope and content of the historical narratives constructed within the judgments of international criminal courts and identifies whose histories have been made to matter in different institutional contexts. By relying on a framework that distinguishes between the actors involved in struggles for historical justice, the questions that structure such struggles, and the practices through which such struggles are conducted, this study

[207] See generally, UNICRI and ADC-ICTY (n 195) Chapter III.
[208] Ibid 38.
[209] Ibid Chapter II.
[210] International criminal courts have adopted different approaches to the question of how to respond to erroneous legal characterisation of charges. For an overview of the different approaches, see generally, Cryer et al (n 157) 459–460; C-F Stuckenberg, 'Cumulative Charges and Cumulative Convictions', in C Stahn (ed), *The Law and Practice of the International Criminal Court* (OUP 2015) 840, 852–858; and *Prosecutor v Kupreškić et al* (Judgment, Trial Chamber) IT-95-16-T (14 January 2000) [728]–[748].

seeks to illuminate the constructed and legitimating qualities of international criminal judgments.

All studies make choices and this study is no exception. The chapters that follow have been organised according to the different questions that structure struggles for historical justice within international criminal courts—the prosecutorial targets question (*Chapter 3*), the crime question (*Chapter 4*), and the culpability question (*Chapter 5*). However, rather than seeking to comprehensively examine the full range of legal and evidentiary practices identifiable within international criminal courts, each chapter focuses primarily—though not exclusively—on the relationship between *legal categories* and historical narration.[211]

In this vein, *Chapter 3* identifies which categories of persons have been selected for international prosecution by examining the drafting and interpretative practices that have defined the jurisdictional boundaries and admissibility requirements of international criminal courts, the policy criteria developed by international prosecutors to guide their charging practices, and the facilitation and obstruction of prosecutorial evidence collection by States.

In *Chapter 4*, the study identifies which categories of crimes have been adjudicated within international criminal courts by examining the drafting practices that have defined the categories of crime included within statutory frameworks, the interpretative practices that have determined the meanings attributed to such categories in particular cases, and the charging practices that have determined which crime categories to include within indictments.

Chapter 5 then turns to explore which categories of culpability—encompassing modes of participation doctrines, grounds for excluding responsibility, and grounds for mitigating punishment—have been adjudicated within international criminal courts by analysing the interpretative practices that have determined the meanings attributed to such categories in particular cases.

Building on the findings in these chapters, *Chapter 6* conducts a closer examination of those aspects of mass atrocity situations that have tended to be marginalised and excluded from the historical narratives constructed within the judgments of international criminal courts, while *Chapter 7* critically reflects on the expectations of historical finality that have typically accompanied international criminal judgments by illuminating the narrative pluralism that can arise both within and beyond the courtroom.

[211] As such, the presentation, scrutiny, and evaluation of evidentiary materials do not form the focus of the present study. For a detailed examination of the evidentiary foundations of international criminal judgments, see generally, Combs (n 171); NA Combs, 'Grave Crimes and Weak Evidence: A Fact-Finding Evolution in International Criminal Law' (2017) 58 *Harvard International Law Journal* 47; and G Chlevickaitė, B Holá, and C Bijleveld, 'Judicial Witness Assessments at the ICTY, ICTR and ICC' (2020) 18 *Journal of International Criminal Justice* 185.

3
The Prosecutorial Targets Question

The determination of which persons to target for international prosecution inevitably has implications for the orientation of the historical narratives constructed within the judgments of international criminal courts. Such determinations define not only the persons whose criminal responsibility will be adjudicated, but also which social contexts will be examined in the process. It is this 'prosecutorial targets question' that forms the focus of the present chapter.

A pertinent starting point for this discussion is the individualism of international criminal courts. The emergence of international criminal courts in the twentieth century is often considered to have ushered in a paradigm shift within international relations away from assigning (often political) responsibility to States towards assigning criminal responsibility to individuals for episodes of mass violence.[1] This development took the form of a double movement:[2] first, the criminalisation of international law, characterised by an increasing tendency to proscribe criminal acts under international law by imposing obligations directly on individuals without the intermediary of the State; and second, the internationalisation of criminal law, characterised by an increasing tendency to prosecute individuals in international criminal courts above the level of the State.

Significantly, the statutory frameworks of international criminal courts have consistently *restricted* their mandates to the determination of individual criminal responsibility.[3] As the Nuremberg International Military Tribunal (IMT) famously put it, 'crimes against international law are committed by men, not abstract entities and *only* by punishing individuals who commit such crimes can the provisions of international law be enforced'.[4] Ever since this now-infamous pronouncement, a paradigm of individual criminal responsibility has held the field of international criminal justice firmly

[1] A Clapham, 'Issues of Complexity, Complicity and Complementarity: From the Nuremberg Trials to the Dawn of the New International Criminal Court', in P Sands (ed), *From Nuremberg to The Hague: The Future of International Criminal Justice* (CUP 2003) 30, 33.

[2] K Ainley, 'Individual Agency and Responsibility for Atrocity', in R Jeffery (ed), *Confronting Evil in International Relations: Ethical Responses to Problems of Moral Agency* (Palgrave Macmillan 2008) 37, 44.

[3] See, for example, the references to 'natural persons' in: Article 6, ICTY Statute; Article 5, ICTR Statute; and Article 25(1), ICC Statute. Article 9 of the Nuremberg Charter provided that a group or organisation may be declared to be 'a criminal organization'. However, this power did not entail the assignation of responsibility as such, but was a mechanism designed to facilitate the determination of the individual criminal responsibility of members of such organisations. The SCSL Statute appeared to leave open the possibility of prosecuting persons other than individuals, though this never eventuated in practice.

[4] *Göring and others*, Nuremberg International Military Tribunal, Judgment, 1 October 1946, *Trial of the Major War Criminals before the International Military Tribunal, Nuremberg, 14 November 1945–1 October 1946: Volume I* (Nuremberg IMT 1947) 171 ('Nuremberg Judgment') 223 (emphasis added).

Doing Justice to History. Barrie Sander, Oxford University Press (2021). © Barrie Sander.
DOI: 10.1093/oso/9780198846871.003.0003

within its grasp.[5] According to this paradigm, international criminal proceedings constitute 'dramas of individual human reckoning',[6] premised on a cult of individualism that understands the individual as the primary unit of responsibility and punishment.[7]

The paradigm of individual criminal responsibility has traditionally been viewed as one of the strengths of international criminal courts, a mark of progress from purportedly antiquated and primitive notions of collective responsibility that preceded them.[8] For instance, in his role as President of the International Criminal Tribunal for the former Yugoslavia (ICTY), Antonio Cassese famously declared that past experience had demonstrated that 'clinging to feelings of "collective responsibility" easily degenerates into resentment, hatred and frustration and inevitably leads to further violence and new crimes'.[9] Indeed, the initial recognition of individual criminal responsibility at Nuremberg may even be viewed as a riposte to the perceived failings of collective responsibility in the Versailles settlement that followed the First World War.[10]

From a narrative perspective, however, the implications of the individualisation of responsibility for mass atrocities have been twofold.

First, international criminal courts have been precluded from formally determining the responsibility of collective entities for mass atrocities. The result, as Mark Drumbl explains, is that international criminal courts have been mandated to render only 'a very partial print of justice', their narratives of individual criminal responsibility leaving behind 'a retributive shortfall'.[11] Specifically, international criminal courts have risked masking the collective dimensions of responsibility for mass atrocities behind the depoliticised veil of the individuals on trial.[12] According to Frédéric Mégret, for example, 'international criminal justice may occasionally let states and society off the hook too easily and even delay a necessary realization of collective faults'.[13]

Second, the paradigm of individual criminal responsibility has also necessitated a high degree of selectivity concerning which individuals to target for prosecution in practice. Prosecutorial selectivity is inevitable in any criminal justice system.

[5] K Ambos, *Treatise on International Criminal Law: Volume I: Foundations and General Part* (OUP 2013) 103.

[6] G Simpson, *Law, War and Crime: War Crimes Trials and the Reinvention of International Law* (Polity 2007) 54.

[7] LC Backer, 'The Führer Principle of International Law: Individual Responsibility and Collective Punishment' (2003) 21 *Penn State International Law Review* 509, 525.

[8] A Nollkaemper, 'Introduction', in A Nollkaemper and HG van der Wilt (eds), *System Criminality* (CUP 2009) 1, 9.

[9] 'Annual Report of the International Tribunal for the Prosecution of Persons Responsible for Serious Violations of International Humanitarian Law Committed in the Territory of the Former Yugoslavia since 1991' UN Docs A/49/342, S/1994/1007 (1994) [16].

[10] G Simpson, 'Men and Abstract Entities: Individual Responsibility and Collective Guilt in International Criminal Law', in A Nollkaemper and HG van der Wilt (eds), *System Criminality* (CUP 2009) 69, 80.

[11] MA Drumbl, *Atrocity, Punishment, and International Law* (CUP 2007) 153.

[12] GP Fletcher, 'The Storrs Lectures: Liberals and Romantics at War: The Problem of Collective Guilt' (2002) 111 *Yale Law Journal* 1499, 1514.

[13] F Mégret, 'International Criminal Justice: A Critical Research Agenda', in C Schwöbel (ed), *Critical Approaches to International Criminal Law: An Introduction* (Routledge 2014) 17, 29.

However, what distinguishes the field of international criminal justice is the sheer scale of its selectivity given the range of mass atrocity situations that could plausibly be subject to investigation and the large numbers of individuals typically implicated in the commission of crimes within each situation.[14] The high degree of prosecutorial selectivity exhibited by international criminal courts often lends their narratives a broader symbolic resonance. As Ronen Steinke has argued, 'To place a person in the dock in this particular judicial system with its symbolic trials means to *symbolically* place a (political or military) group in the dock'.[15] This symbolism is reinforced by the contextualisation and collectivisation of the accused's conduct that emerges from the definitions of the categories of crime and modes of participation adjudicated by international criminal courts.[16] From this perspective, *who* is on trial within international criminal courts is often closely connected to *what* is on trial.[17] As US Prosecutor Robert Jackson famously emphasised in his opening statement before the Nuremberg IMT, on trial were not only the individual accused, but also—symbolically—the politics and system of Nazism itself.[18] Viewed in this light, the narrative significance of identifying targets for international prosecutions becomes clear, such determinations defining not only which individuals will be called to answer in particular institutional contexts, but also which aspects of the broader systems of criminality with which they are associated will be scrutinised in the process.[19]

Against this background, the present chapter illuminates the actors and practices that have determined how the prosecutorial targets question has been resolved in different institutional contexts. For this purpose, the chapter examines two forms of selectivity within international criminal courts: first, *situational* selectivity, which concerns the mass atrocity situations that have been targeted for investigation (Section I); and second, *case* selectivity, which concerns the individuals that have been targeted for prosecution within each situation (Section II). After revealing the prevailing influence of the political context on the prosecutorial focus of international criminal courts, the chapter turns to examine the different strategies that have been deployed by defendants and their counsel—often in vain—in an effort to counter this hegemonic orientation (Section III). Finally, the chapter closes with some concluding remarks (Section IV).

[14] See similarly, from the perspective of victimhood, S Kendall and S Nouwen, 'Representational Practices at the International Criminal Court: The Gap between Juridified and Abstract Victimhood' (2013) 76 *Law and Contemporary Problems* 235, 241.

[15] R Steinke, *The Politics of International Criminal Justice: German Perspectives from Nuremberg to The Hague* (Hart Publishing 2012) 16 (emphasis added).

[16] BI Bonafè, *The Relationship Between State and Individual Responsibility for International Crimes* (Brill 2009) 188.

[17] S Veitch, 'Judgment and Calling to Account: Truths, Trials and Reconciliations', in A Duff et al (eds), *The Trial on Trial: Volume 2: Judgment and Calling to Account* (Hart Publishing 2006) 155, 165.

[18] 'Second Day, Wednesday 21 November 1945', *Trial of the Major War Criminals before the International Military Tribunal, Nuremberg, 14 November 1945–1 October 1946: Volume II* (Nuremberg IMT 1947) 95, 99 (referring to the defendants as 'living symbols').

[19] H Rousso, *The Haunting Past: History, Memory and Justice in Contemporary France* (R Schoolcraft trans, University of Pennsylvania Press 2002) 56.

I. Situational Selectivity

The field of international criminal justice is characterised by the exceptionalism of international criminal courts.[20] In practice, international criminal courts have been established as ad hoc reactions to a select number of crisis situations.[21] Even the International Criminal Court (ICC) has focused its resources on only a few specific crisis situations, whether ongoing conflicts or recently expired periods of violence.[22] According to Gerry Simpson, situational selectivity renders each international criminal court 'an exercise in partial justice to the extent that it reminds us that the majority of war crimes remain unpunished. If Yugoslavia, why not Somalia, if Rwanda, why not Guatemala?'[23] From a narrative perspective, situational selectivity also orients the focus of the histories constructed within international criminal courts.

Against this background, this section examines the actors and practices that have influenced the establishment and situational focus of international criminal courts in different institutional contexts. The section identifies a consistent pattern whereby situational selectivity predominantly reflects the balance of State interests at particular moments of time.

A. The Nuremberg IMT and Tokyo IMTFE

Beginning with the Nuremberg IMT and Tokyo International Military Tribunal for the Far East (IMTFE), these tribunals may be understood as products of a diversity of Allied interests, which included discrediting and eliminating the leading Japanese and German malefactors, setting an example to act as a deterrent for the future, establishing international law by setting a precedent, and vindicating the Allied cause in the eyes of the public.[24]

At a general level, the Nuremberg and Tokyo tribunals were mechanisms for constructing a new world order.[25] Elizabeth Borgwardt, for example, situates the establishment of the Nuremberg IMT along three intersecting axes:[26] as a particular

[20] R Cryer, *Prosecuting International Crimes: Selectivity and the International Criminal Law Regime* (CUP 2005) 211.

[21] See generally, S Starr, 'Extraordinary Crimes at Ordinary Times: International Justice Beyond Crisis Situations' (2007) 101 *Northwestern Law Review* 1257.

[22] B Sander, 'The ICC's Crisis Mentality and the Limits of Global Justice' *Justice in Conflict* (9 March 2015).

[23] G Simpson, 'War Crimes: A Critical Introduction', in TLH McCormack and GJ Simpson (eds), *The Law of War Crimes: National and International Approaches* (Martinus Nijhoff 1997) 1, 8–9. See also, R DeFalco and F Mégret, 'The Invisibility of Race at the ICC: Lessons from the US Criminal Justice System' 7 *London Review of International Law* (2019) 55, 76 ('ICL has historically ignored certain atrocities, from the Herero Genocide to countless other colonial massacres, including some that occurred in the wake of Nuremberg itself').

[24] ES Kopelman, 'Ideology and International Law: The Dissent of the Indian Justice at the Tokyo War Crimes Trial' (1991) 23 *NYU Journal of International Law and Politics* 373, 380.

[25] See generally, E Borgwardt, 'Re-examining Nuremberg as a New Deal Institution: Politics, Culture and the Limits of Law in Generating Human Rights Norms' (2005) 23 *Berkeley Journal of International Law* 401; and Kopelman (n 24).

[26] Borgwardt (n 25) 411–412.

mechanism within a broader set of denazification programmes that would serve to re-educate and rehabilitate ordinary Germans; as a product of lessons learned from the failures of the post-war settlement that followed the First World War; and as part of a broader set of international institutions including the Bretton Woods system and the United Nations that were designed to empower the United States in post-war global governance.

Equally, however, the establishment of the Nuremberg and Tokyo tribunals were also mechanisms for promoting specific Allied agendas. The Soviets, for example, envisaged the Nuremberg IMT as a means for establishing a legal claim for reparations—deemed necessary for rebuilding the Soviet Union—as well as to expose the horrors of the Nazi regime.[27] According to Francine Hirsch, the Soviets imagined Nuremberg as 'a grand exercise in education and enlightenment, a sort of show trial writ large', a means to 'rally the war-weary Soviet people and provide collective catharsis', and a mechanism that would provide 'the Soviets the opportunity to take their place among the postwar powers and to make clear what they had sacrificed to win the war'.[28] The Americans, by contrast, viewed the Nuremberg IMT as 'a forum to showcase American leadership and the rule of law',[29] while US support for the Tokyo IMTFE was primarily informed by its interest in punishing Japanese aggression.[30]

Viewed from this perspective, the Nuremberg and Tokyo tribunals may be understood as mechanisms to legitimate particular post-war structures of global governance as well as a means to punish the leading perpetrators of crimes committed during the Second World War in alignment with specific Allied political projects.[31]

B. The UN Ad Hoc Tribunals

Whereas the Nuremberg and Tokyo tribunals were established in the midst of cementing a new international institutional landscape, the ICTY and International Criminal Tribunal for Rwanda (ICTR) emerged in response to the failures of those same structures of global governance. Crucially, the Yugoslavia and Rwanda tribunals were only established after human rights experts and civil society groups had managed to generate a 'public relations nightmare' for the United Nations (UN) Security Council by mobilising public shame and outrage towards the international community's inaction in the face of atrocities that had been beamed around the world by the television camera.[32] In this context, establishing the tribunals served the interests of the Security Council by providing both a pretext for military inaction and 'a kind of insurance

[27] F Hirsch, *Soviet Judgment at Nuremberg: A New History of the International Military Tribunal after World War II* (OUP 2020) 4 and 56.

[28] Ibid 9, 27, and 72.

[29] Ibid 42.

[30] N Boister and R Cryer, *The Tokyo International Military Tribunal—A Reappraisal* (OUP 2008) 119.

[31] See similarly, K Bachmann and A Fatić, *The UN International Criminal Tribunals: Transition without Justice?* (Routledge 2015) 3–4; and V Nesiah, 'Doing History with Impunity', in K Engle et al (eds), *Anti-Impunity and the Human Rights Agenda* (CUP 2016) 95, 108.

[32] M Mutua, 'Never Again: Questioning the Yugoslav and Rwanda Tribunals' (1997) 11 *Temple International & Comparative Law Journal* 167, 174.

policy against the risk of being accused of complicity by "posterity"'.[33] According to Gary Bass, for example, the ICTY was 'an act of tokenism by the world community, which was largely unwilling to intervene in ex-Yugoslavia but did not mind creating an institution that would give the *appearance* of moral concern'.[34]

The decisions to establish the ICTY and ICTR were also relatively painless for the Security Council since the tribunals would be temporary in duration and limited to the situations in the former Yugoslavia and Rwanda respectively—conflicts where the political stakes for the international community were relatively low.[35] In the case of the ICTR, for example, the Security Council deliberately restricted the temporal jurisdiction of the tribunal to the calendar year of 1994.[36] As a result, a range of conduct fell beyond the tribunal's jurisdiction, including crimes committed during the Rwandan civil war prior to 1994 and the alleged culpability of foreign actors for assisting them,[37] as well as atrocities committed in the region after 1994 including the dissolution of Hutu refugee camps and massacres against the civilian population in neighbouring Democratic Republic of the Congo (DRC).[38] In other words, the Security Council made sure that the ICTR would focus its attention on the Rwandan genocide committed during the course of 1994.[39]

The establishment of the ICTR was also driven by the initial support of the Rwandan government which already in August 1994 had urged the UN Secretary-General to establish a tribunal similar to the ICTY.[40] Although the Rwandan government would ultimately cast the only dissenting vote on the creation of the ICTR, its initial support reflected expectations that the tribunal could become part of a national project of political and social transformation that would solidify the authority and legitimacy of the government.[41] Despite its withdrawal of support at the moment of the ICTR's establishment, the Rwandan government would eventually cooperate with the tribunal, particularly once it realised that its domestic governance objectives were in fact realisable.

[33] F Mégret, 'The Politics of International Criminal Justice' (2002) 13 *European Journal of International Law* 1261, 1273.

[34] GJ Bass, *Stay the Hand of Vengeance—The Politics of War Crimes Tribunals* (Princeton University Press 2000) 207 (emphasis in original).

[35] Mégret (n 33) 1283.

[36] See Articles 1 and 7, ICTR Statute. The ICTY's temporal jurisdiction, by contrast, was open-ended, commencing on 1 January 1991. See Articles 1 and 8, ICTY Statute.

[37] JE Alvarez, 'Crimes of Hate/Crimes of State: Lessons from Rwanda' (1999) 24 *Yale Journal of International Law* 365, 397 (arguing that this compromise is best understood in terms of the fact that a broader jurisdiction 'could well have led to inquiries that would have embarrassed the UN as a whole or a particular member of the Security Council', referring to France in particular).

[38] Office of the UN High Commissioner for Human Rights, 'Report of the Mapping Exercise documenting the most serious violations of human rights and international humanitarian law committed within the territory of the Democratic Republic of the Congo between March 1993 and June 2003' (August 2010).

[39] The ICTR's temporal jurisdiction was opposed by the Rwandan government, which had argued that it should commence on 1 October 1990, the date when the civil war broke out following the Rwandan Patriotic Front's (RPF) invasion of northern Rwanda, and end on 17 July 1994, when the RPF defeated the Hutu government. See further, L van den Herik, *The Contribution of the Rwandan Tribunal to the Development of International Law* (Martinus Nijhoff Publishers 2005) 81 and 83.

[40] D Shraga and R Zacklin, 'The International Criminal Tribunal for Rwanda' (1996) 7 *European Journal of International Law* 501, 503.

[41] Z Miller, 'Anti-Impunity Politics in Post-Genocide Rwanda', in K Engle et al (eds), *Anti-Impunity and the Human Rights Agenda* (CUP 2016) 149, 162–164.

In a similar vein, the initial impetus for the creation of the Special Court for Sierra Leone (SCSL) was a letter sent by the President of Sierra Leone to the President of the Security Council requesting support from the UN to prosecute 'those members of the rebel Revolutionary United Front (RUF) and their accomplices responsible for committing crimes against the people of Sierra Leone and for the taking of United Nations peacekeepers as hostages'.[42] In the letter, the President of Sierra Leone emphasised both domestic and international interests in establishing a court:[43] domestically, he pointed to the need for a 'strong court in order to bring and maintain peace and security in Sierra Leone and the West African subregion'; internationally, he argued that the nature of the crimes committed by the RUF leadership and their accomplices should be 'of concern to all persons in the world, as they greatly diminish respect for international law and for the most basic human rights'. Responding to the President of Sierra Leone's request, the Security Council adopted Resolution 1315 (2000), which confirmed the domestic and international interests that supported the establishment of an independent special court for Sierra Leone and directed the UN Secretary-General to negotiate an agreement with the government of Sierra Leone to this end.[44]

Beyond this political context, the SCSL was also established against the backdrop of lessons learned from the experiences of the ICTY and ICTR. This institutional context led to the creation of a court that was leaner in terms of resources, financed solely through voluntary donations from UN Member States, as well as more hybrid in nature, as illustrated by its personnel, subject-matter jurisdiction, and location on the territory of Sierra Leone.[45] Importantly, the SCSL's territorial jurisdiction was limited to crimes committed 'in the territory of Sierra Leone', whilst its temporal jurisdiction commenced on 30 November 1996, the date of the signing of the unsuccessful Abidjan Peace Accord, and was left open-ended in light of ongoing hostilities in the country.[46] The government of Sierra Leone had suggested that the temporal jurisdiction should begin in 1991 so that the beginning of the civil war would fall within the Court's remit, but this was rejected by the Secretary-General so as not to impose a 'heavy burden' on the Court.[47] Together, the jurisdictional restrictions and hybrid qualities of the SCSL constituted a symbolic reflection of the confluence of domestic governance and international security interests that led to the Court's establishment.

[42] 'Letter dated 9 August 2000 from the Permanent Representative of Sierra Leone to the United Nations addressed to the President of the Security Council' (Annex) UN Doc S/2000/786 (10 August 2000).

[43] Ibid.

[44] UN Security Council Resolution 1315, UN Doc S/RES/1315 (14 August 2000).

[45] CC Jalloh, 'Special Court for Sierra Leone: Achieving Justice?' (2011) 32 *Michigan Journal of International Law* 395, 402.

[46] Article 1, SCSL Statute.

[47] 'Report of the Secretary-General on the Establishment of a Special Court for Sierra Leone' UN Doc S/2000/915 (4 October 2000) [26]. See, however, WA Schabas, *The UN International Criminal Tribunals: The Former Yugoslavia, Rwanda and Sierra Leone* (CUP 2006) 135 (suggesting that the real reason for the later start-date may have been the discomfort of the Secretary-General's lawyers 'with their possible involvement in pre-Abidjan prosecutions because they did not object to the amnesty provisions included in that peace agreement, in contrast with the position taken two and a half years later at Lomé').

C. The ICC

The dominance of State interests in shaping the situational focus of international criminal courts has also been evident within the practices of the ICC. For many scholars and practitioners, the establishment of the ICC was intended to constitute a 'cosmopolitan moment' for international law,[48] ushering in a new era of international criminal justice that would remedy the situational biases that had undermined the legitimacy of earlier international criminal tribunals. Importantly, in contrast to other international criminal courts, the ICC Prosecutor is not required to select cases within pre-defined situations, but is empowered to determine when and where to initiate investigations in accordance with the ICC Statute.[49] In practice, however, a combination of formal *legal* criteria, including jurisdictional and admissibility requirements, and dynamic *political* factors, including budgetary restrictions, security challenges, and selective State cooperation, have shaped the situational focus of the ICC primarily in accordance with the political context in which the Prosecutor operates. As a result of this interplay between legal and political considerations, the vast majority of the ICC Prosecutor's investigations have concerned situations in Africa and all individuals publicly indicted by the ICC to date have been African.[50]

To explain the ICC's situational focus, *legal criteria* are undoubtedly an important part of the story.[51] As Adam Branch has observed, the ICC Prosecutor typically attributes the Court's Africa focus to 'legal rationales—it is following referrals, pursuing the gravest atrocities and intervening where national judicial systems are weakest'.[52] Less acknowledged, however, are the ways in which the legal limitations of the ICC often reflect and institutionalise asymmetries in power between States beyond the courtroom.

Consider, for example, the jurisdictional limitations of the ICC.[53] In order for the ICC to exercise its jurisdiction, it must first be triggered in one of three ways:[54] first,

48 P Hayden, 'Political Evil, Cosmopolitan Realism, and the Normative Ambivalence of the International Criminal Court', in SC Roach (ed), *Governance, Order, and the International Criminal Court: Between Realpolitik and a Cosmopolitan Court* (OUP 2009) 157, 157.

49 ICC Office of the Prosecutor, 'Policy Paper on Preliminary Examinations' (November 2013) ('ICC OTP Preliminary Examination Policy Paper') [24].

50 To date, the only investigations initiated in situations outside Africa are the situations in Georgia, Bangladesh/Myanmar, and Afghanistan. The ICC Prosecutor's preliminary examinations have been more geographically varied including situations in Asia-Pacific, Latin America and Caribbean, Eastern Europe, and the Western European and Others Group. For a recent overview, see generally, S Wharton and R Grey, 'The Full Picture: Preliminary Examinations at the International Criminal Court' (2019) 56 *Canadian Yearbook of International Law* 1.

51 The ICC Prosecutor has also clarified the general principles upon which preliminary examinations are conducted, namely the principles of independence, impartiality, and objectivity. See, ICC OTP Preliminary Examination Policy Paper (n 49) [25]–[33].

52 A Branch, 'Dominic Ongwen on Trial: The ICC's African Dilemmas' (2017) 11 *International Journal of Transitional Justice* 30, 34.

53 The discussion in this paragraph leaves aside the special jurisdictional requirements for the crime of aggression, over which the ICC will only be able to exercise jurisdiction as of 17 July 2018. See generally, D Akande, 'The International Criminal Court Gets Jurisdiction Over the Crime of Aggression' *EJIL Talk!* (15 December 2017); and A Whiting, 'Crime of Aggression Activated at the ICC: Does it Matter?' *Just Security* (19 December 2017).

54 Articles 13–15, ICC Statute.

by a State Party referring a situation to the Prosecutor; second, by the UN Security Council referring a situation to the Prosecutor; or finally, by the Prosecutor initiating an investigation *proprio motu* into a situation with the authorisation of the Pre-Trial Chamber. In determining whether to initiate an investigation into a situation, the ICC Prosecutor is required to adhere to the temporal,[55] subject-matter,[56] territorial, and personal jurisdictional boundaries of the Court.[57] In the context of referrals by States Parties or the exercise of its *proprio motu* powers, the ICC Prosecutor is only empowered to investigate situations in which the conduct of crimes occurred on the territory of a State Party or a State that has issued an ad hoc declaration pursuant to Article 12(3) of the ICC Statute, or where the persons accused of participating in the commission of crimes are nationals of such States.[58] The ICC Prosecutor can only investigate situations beyond these territorial and personal parameters if acting pursuant to a referral by the Security Council.[59] In practice, the implications of this jurisdictional regime for the situational focus of the ICC have been threefold.

First, since only 123 States are parties to the ICC Statute,[60] the ICC has been unable to exercise (territorial) jurisdiction over a considerable portion of the international community—including three of the five permanent members of the Security Council (the United States, Russia, and China) as well as the vast majority of the Middle East and Asia—other than in very limited circumstances.[61] As a result, several major conflicts that have occurred in the past twenty years—including particularly high-profile conflicts in Syria and Yemen—have almost entirely fallen beyond the reach of the ICC Prosecutor.[62]

Second, by enabling the UN Security Council to refer any situation to the Court, unconfined by territorial or nationality restrictions, Article 13(b) of the ICC Statute has perpetuated the Council's 'legalised hegemony'.[63] When the ICC Prosecutor acts pursuant to such referrals, the Court's situational focus becomes wedded to the privileged interests of the Council's permanent members. Indeed, the practice of the

[55] Articles 11 and 24, ICC Statute. The temporal jurisdiction of the ICC applies from the date of entry into force of the ICC Statute, which for many States is 1 July 2002 onwards. In addition, as the ICC Prosecutor has summarised, temporal jurisdiction may depend on 'the date of entry into force of the Statute for the State Party concerned in the case of a later ratification or accession, the date specified in a Security Council referral, or the date indicated in a declaration lodged pursuant to article 12(3)'. ICC OTP Preliminary Examination Policy Paper (n 49) [37].

[56] Article 5, ICC Statute; and ICC OTP Preliminary Examination Policy Paper (n 49) [38]–[39].

[57] Article 12, ICC Statute; and ICC OTP Preliminary Examination Policy Paper (n 49) [40].

[58] Articles 12(2)–(3), ICC Statute.

[59] Article 13(b), ICC Statute.

[60] 'Rome Statute of the International Criminal Court', *UN Treaty Collection* (status as at 4 May 2020). To date, Burundi and the Philippines are the only States to withdraw from the ICC Statute, their withdrawals taking effect on 27 October 2017 and 17 March 2019 respectively.

[61] The only way for non-State Party nationals to become a target of an ICC investigation is if they commit a crime on the territory of a State Party (Article 12(2)(a)) or if the Security Council refers a situation to the Prosecutor pursuant to Article 13(b). With respect to conflicts on the territory of a non-State Party, the ICC Prosecutor can still investigate nationals of States Parties accused of participating in the commission of crimes on such territories pursuant to Article 12(2).

[62] See, for example, ICC Prosecutor, 'Statement of the Prosecutor of the International Criminal Court, Fatou Bensouda, on the alleged crimes committed by ISIS' (8 April 2015) (concluding that the jurisdictional basis for opening a preliminary examination into the situation concerning ISIS is too narrow at present).

[63] G Simpson, *Great Powers and Outlaw States: Unequal Sovereigns in the International Legal Order* (2nd edn, CUP 2006) 7.

Security Council to date illustrates the partiality of such referrals in line with the interests of its permanent members, with some situations referred (Darfur and Libya), and others overlooked (Iraq and Syria, for example). As a result, States with friends amongst the permanent members of the Council have generally remained beyond the reach of the ICC.[64]

Finally, although many States Parties are likely to have been motivated to ratify the ICC Statute by principled support for the Court, it is also important to acknowledge that several States were very likely subject to political pressures. According to Kamari Clarke, for example, 'many African states joined the ICC treaty system based on the formal and informal pressure of Western states, institutions, and civil society groups ... [some of whom] tied international treaty participation to monetary lending'.[65] In other words, once appropriately contextualised, State consent to the ICC Statute may itself be a reflection of existing inequalities between States beyond the courtroom.

Beyond jurisdictional limitations, other legal criteria—in particular, the doctrines of complementarity, gravity, and the interests of justice—have also influenced the situational orientation of the ICC.[66] However, given the open-textured and notoriously vague nature of these doctrines, the ICC Prosecutor has generally exercised significant discretion in determining whether and when to initiate investigations into situations falling within the jurisdictional parameters of the ICC Statute.[67] Importantly, the Prosecutor has not exercised its discretion in a vacuum, but has had to select which situations to investigate against a background of *political constraints*.[68] Although formally independent, the ICC Prosecutor's lack of any supranational enforcement mechanism has rendered it functionally reliant on States in practice. This dependence reveals itself in at least three ways.

First, the ICC has been deliberately designed by States to be a relatively compact institution with a *limited budget*.[69] Alex Whiting, for example, has observed how the ICC's annual budget, though roughly equivalent to that of the ICTY, is spread across preliminary examinations and investigations pertaining to different situations rather than focused on one geographic area.[70] The ICC's limited resources are at once a reflection of State ambivalence towards the project of international criminal justice and

[64] S Nouwen, 'Legal Equality on Trial: Sovereign and Individuals before the International Criminal Court' (2012) 43 *Netherlands Yearbook of International Law* 151, 167.

[65] KM Clarke, 'Power Politics and its Global Shadows: From Margins to Center' *Blog of James G Stewart* (20 February 2015).

[66] See generally, ICC OTP Preliminary Examination Policy Paper (n 49) [42]–[71].

[67] See similarly, WA Schabas, 'Prosecutorial Discretion v. Judicial Activism at the International Criminal Court' (2008) 6 *Journal of International Criminal Justice* 731, 735; and KJ Heller, 'The Role of the International Prosecutor', in CPR Romano et al (eds), *The Oxford Handbook of International Adjudication* (OUP 2013) 669, 680.

[68] See similarly, WA Schabas, 'Victor's Justice: Selecting "Situations" at the International Criminal Court' (2010) 43 *John Marshall Law Review* 535, 549.

[69] See, in this regard, S Kendall, 'Commodifying Global Justice: Economies of Accountability at the International Criminal Court' (2015) 13 *Journal of International Criminal Justice* 113, 127 ('the ICC's political economy is not singular but multiple: there is the formal economy ..., which is populated by its states parties who make both assessed and voluntary contributions, as well as an informal economy of other agents who fall outside frame').

[70] A Whiting, 'Dynamic Investigative Practice at the International Criminal Court' (2013) 76 *Law and Contemporary Problems* 163, 174–175.

in keeping with the doctrine of complementarity's prioritisation of domestic investigations and prosecutions.[71] In light of its limited budget, the ICC Prosecutor has had to determine which preliminary examinations and investigations to prioritise in practice.

Beyond budgetary restrictions, the ICC Prosecutor has also faced *security challenges* in territories subject to preliminary examination, for example because of ongoing hostilities.[72] Such challenges can inhibit evidence collection as well as complementarity assessments, thereby causing delays to preliminary examinations and the initiation of investigations.

However, most important of all, the ICC Prosecutor is highly dependent on the *cooperation* of other actors, principally States, to collect evidence with respect to particular situations. To borrow the words of Antonio Cassese, the ICC Prosecutor is like 'a giant without arms and legs',[73] heavily reliant on the artificial limbs of external actors to function in practice. As a result, the ICC Prosecutor has generally only been able to make progress with its inquiries and assessments either by forging and nurturing cooperative relationships with States to gain secure access to their territories or by identifying so-called 'surrogate enforcers' that are able to exert pressure on obstructionist States on its behalf.[74]

Operating within these political constraints, the ICC Prosecutor has predominantly aligned its situational focus with the balance of power between States in the international community. This may be illustrated from three perspectives.

First, the ICC Prosecutor has generally moved relatively swiftly to initiate investigations into situations referred to it by States Parties or the Security Council.[75] The almost reflexive speed at which the Prosecutor has sometimes initiated investigations into situations referred by States Parties and the Security Council is not inevitable since it is always for the Prosecutor to determine whether there is a reasonable basis to proceed with an investigation in response to such referrals.[76] Nonetheless, it is easy to understand why the Prosecutor has been able to proceed so promptly in such circumstances because these referrals have typically been accompanied by supporting evidence as well as more forthcoming cooperation, which have helped to expedite the

[71] Ibid 177.

[72] NA Combs, 'Deconstructing the Epistemic Challenges to Mass Atrocity Prosecutions' *Humanity* (11 July 2017).

[73] A Cassese, 'On Current Trends Towards Criminal Procedure and Punishment of Breaches of International Humanitarian Law' (1998) 9 *European Journal of International Law* 2, 13 (referring to the ICTY).

[74] V Peskin, 'An Ideal Becoming Real? The International Criminal Court and the Limits of the Cosmopolitan Vision of Justice', in R Pierik and W Werner (eds), *Cosmopolitanism in Context: Perspectives from International Law and Political Theory* (CUP 2010) 195, 206.

[75] See generally, Wharton and Grey (n 50) 41–43 (providing data on the duration of preliminary examinations) and 52–54 (noting that the length of preliminary examinations tends to be shorter when triggered by referrals by the UN Security Council or States Parties).

[76] ICC OTP Preliminary Examination Policy Paper (n 49) [35] (emphasising that it is ultimately the decision of the ICC Prosecutor whether to initiate an investigation into a situation based on an examination of the factors set out in Article 53(1) of the ICC Statute, regardless of how the jurisdiction of the ICC has been triggered).

process.[77] The result has been to orient the situational focus of the ICC in line with the interests of States Parties and the Security Council.[78]

Second, the ICC Prosecutor has also pursued a policy of actively inviting particular States to make so-called 'self-referrals' of situations on their territories.[79] In 2006, the Prosecutor expressly acknowledged that his Office had been adopting a policy of 'inviting and welcoming voluntary referrals by territorial states as a first step in triggering the jurisdiction of the Court', specifically citing the situations in Uganda and the DRC as examples.[80] Subsequent to these situations, the Central African Republic and Mali also made self-referrals, while Cote d'Ivoire issued an Article 12(3) ad hoc declaration.[81] Uniting these situations—other than their geographic location on the African continent—is their marginality in the eyes of major powers.[82] According to Adam Branch, for example, one of the reasons Africa has become the predominant situational focus for the ICC Prosecutor is 'because it was the only place politically marginal enough that the US would allow the Court to intervene there'.[83] From this perspective, the situational focus of the ICC has been shaped at least partially by the ICC Prosecutor's institutional interest in validating its own profile with situations that are both capable of yielding the (selective) cooperation of self-referring State Parties whilst at the same time avoiding ruffling the feathers of the international community's major powers.[84]

Finally, the ICC Prosecutor has proceeded with contrasting levels of enthusiasm towards initiating investigations into particular situations *proprio motu*. For example, with respect to the electoral violence in Kenya that took place over the relatively limited period of late 2007 into early 2008, the ICC Prosecutor enthusiastically sought the authority of the Pre-Trial Chamber to initiate a formal investigation into the situation as early as late 2009. By contrast, with respect to the prolonged and systematic violence that has devastated Afghanistan for a number of years, the ICC Prosecutor waited a decade before requesting authorisation from the Pre-Trial Chamber in November 2017. The ICC Prosecutor's variable enthusiasm towards these situations is explicable on the basis of the Prosecutor's political context. With respect to Kenya, the Prosecutor intervened as part of a carefully negotiated process with the backing

[77] F Guariglia and E Rogier, 'The Selection of Situations and Cases by the OTP of the ICC', in C Stahn (ed), *The Law and Practice of the International Criminal Court* (OUP 2015) 350, 357 (noting that in the case of a referral by a State Party or the Security Council, 'there is an expectation that the OTP will proceed unless contrary criteria are met' due to evidence and cooperation advantages).

[78] WA Schabas, 'Selecting Situations and Cases', in C Stahn (ed), *The Law and Practice of the International Criminal Court* (OUP 2015) 365, 372.

[79] S Nouwen, *Complementarity in the Line of Fire: The Catalysing Effect of the International Criminal Court in Uganda and Sudan* (CUP 2014) 13 and 350–351.

[80] ICC Office of the Prosecutor, 'Report on the activities performed during the first three years (June 2003–June 2006)' (12 September 2006) 7.

[81] P McAuliffe, 'From Watchdog to Workhorse: Explaining the Emergence of the ICC's Burden-sharing Policy as an Example of Creeping Cosmopolitanism' (2014) 13 *Chinese Journal of International Law* 259, 278–279 ('investigations in Côte d'Ivoire consented to initially by Laurent Gbagbo and later requested by Alassane Ouattara represent a highly convoluted self-referral via Article 12(3), notwithstanding its technical status as a proprio motu investigation').

[82] Schabas (n 68) 548.

[83] Branch (n 52) 34.

[84] As discussed later in this chapter, the price of the ICC Prosecutor's self-referral policy has been the subsequent limitation of prosecutions to only one side of the conflicts in which it has intervened.

of the international community and the major authorities directly involved in the situation.[85] By contrast, in Afghanistan, the Prosecutor consistently pointed to challenges raised by 'security concerns, limited or reluctant cooperation, and verification of information'.[86]

In light of these trends, the ICC Prosecutor's investigatory practices have followed a fairly consistent pattern of proceeding opportunistically in accordance with State interests—whether the major powers of the international community or particular States that have referred situations on their own territory to the Prosecutor.[87]

Somewhat against this trend, however, more recently the ICC Prosecutor successfully secured judicial authorisation to commence an investigation into crimes committed in the conflict between Georgia and Russia in mid-2008,[88] as well as an investigation into crimes committed in the situation in Afghanistan, including allegations that US military and Central Intelligence Agency personnel have committed acts of torture in connection with the conflict.[89] In addition, the ICC Prosecutor also recently concluded that there is a reasonable basis to initiate an investigation into the situation in Palestine—including allegations of war crimes committed by members of the Israel Defense Forces in Gaza and by members of the Israeli authorities in the context of Israel's occupation of the West Bank—albeit subject to first seeking a ruling on the scope of the ICC's territorial jurisdiction in Palestine.[90] These practices are significant since they demonstrate a willingness on the part of the ICC Prosecutor to proceed with investigations into situations against the interests of powerful States or those allied with powerful States.[91]

However, there are three points that put the significance of these recent practices in perspective. First, the long duration of the preliminary examinations into these situations gives reason to believe that the ICC Prosecutor was not eager to initiate these investigations. While the Prosecutor can act strategically with respect to the timing and prioritisation of investigations, the ICC Statute requires an investigation to be initiated if all the pre-conditions have been satisfied. With this in mind, the requests to initiate investigations in Georgia and Afghanistan, together with the recent request for a ruling on the Court's territorial jurisdiction in Palestine, arguably reflect the statutory reality that while nothing prevents the Prosecutor from delaying the start of an

[85] D Bosco, *Rough Justice: The International Criminal Court in a World of Power Politics* (OUP 2014) 160.

[86] ICC Office of the Prosecutor, 'Report on Preliminary Examination Activities 2014' (2 December 2014) [98].

[87] See similarly, Bosco (n 85) 184–187 (identifying a 'pattern of deference' to the interests of the major powers, with the result that the ICC has, for the most part, become little more than 'an instrument in the toolkit of major powers responding to instability and violence in weaker states').

[88] *Situation in Georgia* (Decision on the Prosecutor's Request for Authorization of an Investigation, Pre-Trial Chamber) ICC-01/15-12 (27 January 2016).

[89] *Situation in the Islamic Republic of Afghanistan* (Judgment on the appeal against the decision on the authorisation of an investigation into the situation in the Islamic Republic of Afghanistan, Appeals Chamber) ICC-02/17-138 (5 March 2020).

[90] *Situation in the State of Palestine* (Prosecutor request pursuant to article 19(3) for a ruling on the Court's territorial jurisdiction in Palestine, Office of the Prosecutor) ICC-0118-12 (22 January 2020).

[91] On the importance of 'prosecutorial audacity' vis-à-vis powerful States for the legitimacy of the ICC, see T Dannenbaum, 'Against Modesty at the ICC' *Opinio Juris* (11 April 2020). See, however, T Krever, 'Africa in the Dock: On ICC Bias' *Critical Legal Thinking* (30 October 2016) (arguing that the Georgia investigation 'reproduces a Western narrative of Russian aggression that justifies not intervention in Africa now but NATO's largest build-up of military forces in eastern Europe since the Cold War').

investigation, she cannot delay indefinitely.[92] Second, the focal points of the investigations in Georgia and Afghanistan are unlikely to be Russian or US crimes, but rather South Ossetian and Taliban crimes. In the Georgia situation, for example, the cautious wording of the ICC Prosecutor's request concerning Russian involvement in the commission of crimes attributed to South Ossetian forces gives rise to doubts regarding the likelihood of Russian military personnel being at the forefront of the Prosecutor's investigation.[93] Similarly, if an investigation were to be initiated into the situation in Palestine, it is highly likely that the ICC Prosecutor would prioritise the prosecution of members of Hamas, particularly since, as Kevin Heller has argued, their deliberate rocket attacks on civilians would be 'the easiest to prove in terms of ... legal elements and evidentiary considerations'.[94] Finally, given the delicate political contexts in which these investigations will have to be conducted, it is highly probable that the Prosecutor will be forced to proceed cautiously in moving from the investigation stage towards initiating prosecutions, particularly since State cooperation is unlikely to be forthcoming going forward.[95]

As this snapshot of the situational focus of the ICC demonstrates, despite its universalist aspirations, the ICC has not been able to free itself from the influence of State interests in practice. As Frederick Cowell has argued, 'the distinct problem with a cosmopolitan vision of the ICC is that there remain deep asymmetries of power between states, which means that any utopian project to dilute sovereignty is invariably going to affect some states more than others'.[96] In this vein, similar to other international criminal courts, the situational focus of the ICC has predominantly replicated interstate power imbalances within the political contexts in which it operates.[97]

II. Case Selectivity

Within each of the situations that have been subject to international criminal investigation, international prosecutors have typically been confronted by extremely high numbers of potential prosecutorial targets. In Rwanda, for example, the ICTR Prosecutor was confronted with thousands of individuals for whom there was a reasonable prospect for prosecution and conviction for crimes falling within the jurisdiction of the tribunal.[98] Given the frequently vast numbers of potential indictees

[92] See similarly, A Whiting, 'An ICC Investigation of the U.S. in Afghanistan: What Does it Mean?' *Just Security* (3 November 2017); and M Kersten, 'Why is the International Criminal Court Stepping out of Africa and into Georgia' *Justice in Conflict* (6 February 2016).

[93] *Situation in Georgia* (Corrected Version of 'Request for Authorisation of an Investigation pursuant to Article 15', 16 October 2015, ICC-01/15-4-Corr, Office of the Prosecutor) ICC-01/15-4-Corr2 (17 November 2015) [137]–[141]. See also, N Tsereteli, 'Pre-Trial Chamber of the International Criminal Court Authorizes Initiation of Investigation in Georgia' *EJIL Talk!* (1 February 2016).

[94] KJ Heller, 'The ICC in Palestine: Be Careful What You Wish For' *Justice in Conflict* (2 April 2015).

[95] See, for example, KJ Heller, 'Russia's Short-Sighted Approach to the Georgia Investigation' *Opinio Juris* (13 February 2016); and Whiting (n 92).

[96] F Cowell, 'Inherent Imperialism: Understanding the Legal Roots of Anti-Imperialist Criticism of the International Criminal Court' (2017) 15 *Journal of International Criminal Justice* 667, 681.

[97] See similarly, A Kiyani, Group-Based Differentiation and Local Repression: The Custom and Curse of Selectivity' (2016) 14 *Journal of International Criminal Justice* 939, 948.

[98] A Obote-Odora, 'Case Selection and Prioritization Criteria at the International Criminal Tribunal for Rwanda', in M Bergsmo (ed), *Criteria for Prioritizing and Selecting Core International Crime Cases* (2nd

identifiable within mass atrocity situations and the limited resources available to international criminal courts, the degree of selectivity exercised by international prosecutors in choosing particular cases for investigation and prosecution has tended to be significantly higher than their domestic counterparts.[99] As former ICTY Prosecutor Louise Arbour once put it, the real challenge faced by international prosecutors is 'to choose from many meritorious complaints the appropriate ones for international intervention, rather than to weed out weak or frivolous ones'.[100]

In practice, therefore, international prosecutors have typically conducted 'exemplary' prosecutions of a small number of individuals, with the vast majority of those implicated in mass atrocity situations either deferred to other institutions for prosecution or simply left unprosecuted. For instance, only twenty-four defendants were indicted at the Nuremberg IMT, twenty-eight at the Tokyo IMTFE, 161 at the ICTY, ninety-three at the ICTR, and thirteen at the SCSL.[101] Similarly, to date, the ICC Prosecutor has typically targeted no more than a handful of individuals within each of the situations it has investigated. The practical necessity of selecting only a small number of individuals from the far larger pool of potential indictees has meant that case selectivity has had a considerable impact on the historical narratives constructed by international criminal courts in practice. As Ronen Steinke explains, 'at an international tribunal, each trial is part of one overall historical account; the selection of a tiny fraction of cases from a conflict will inevitably focus the audience on one particular version of that larger "truth"'.[102]

All international criminal courts have entrusted the prosecution with the primary, if not exclusive, authority to determine which cases to select for investigation and prosecution.[103] In practice, however, the exercise of prosecutorial discretion has not been absolute, but constrained by a number of legal criteria, policy criteria, and political factors.

Legal criteria have typically included general principles, including the principles of independence,[104] impartiality,[105] and objectivity,[106] as well as the jurisdictional

edn, TOAEP 2010) 45, 50 (estimating that between 30 and 50 per cent of the population of Rwanda were involved in the killing of Tutsis, or stood by and failed to intervene).

[99] AKA Greenawalt, 'Justice Without Politics: Prosecutorial Discretion and the International Criminal Court' (2007) 39 *NYU Journal of International Law and Politics* 583, 610.

[100] LM Arbour, 'Statement to the Preparatory Commission on the Establishment of an International Criminal Court' (1997) *ICTY Yearbook* 229, 232.

[101] Figures for the Nuremberg IMT and the Tokyo IMTFE are from A Smeulers et al, 'Sixty-Five Years of International Criminal Justice: The Facts and Figures' (2013) 13 *International Criminal Law Review* 7, 19. Figures for the ad hoc tribunals are from the official websites of the tribunals.

[102] Steinke (n 15) 14.

[103] See, for example, Article 14, Nuremberg Charter; Article 8, Tokyo Charter; Article 16(1), ICTY Statute; Article 15(1), ICTR Statute; Article 15(1), SCSL Statute; and Article 54(1), ICC Statute.

[104] See, for example, Article 16(2), ICTY Statute; Article 15(2), ICTR Statute; Article 15(1), SCSL Statute; and Article 42(1), ICC Statute.

[105] See, for example, Article 2(c), ICTY and ICTR Standards of Professional Conduct for Prosecution Counsel (1999); Articles 21(3) and 42(7), ICC Statute. See also, ICC Office of the Prosecutor, 'Policy Paper on Case Selection and Prioritisation' (15 September 2016) ('ICC OTP Policy Paper on Case Selection and Prioritisation') [19]–[20].

[106] Most international criminal courts have evidentiary thresholds that must be met before an indictment is confirmed or an arrest warrant issued. See, for example, Article 19(1), ICTY Statute and Rule 47(B), ICTY Rules of Procedure and Evidence (requiring that a judge of the Trial Chamber be satisfied that there is 'a

parameters and admissibility requirements of the international criminal court in question.[107] However, since these legal criteria have typically left significant room for prosecutorial discretion, international prosecutors have often developed additional policy criteria to guide their case selection practices—albeit with varying levels of transparency.[108] Two policy criteria in particular have proven prominent across several different international criminal courts: the gravity of the crimes allegedly perpetrated by potential indictees; and the degree of responsibility of potential indictees.

With respect to the gravity of crimes, international prosecutors have typically sought to target individuals responsible for *the most serious crimes* within a particular situation.[109] For this purpose, international prosecutors have considered—to varying degrees—a range of factors including the scale, nature, manner of commission, and impact of the crimes, the extent to which particular crimes have been under-prosecuted in the past, and the extent to which crimes committed in different localities have been represented through their prosecutions.[110]

In terms of the degree of responsibility of potential indictees, international prosecutors have typically sought to target individuals who bear *the greatest or most responsibility* for the commission of crimes.[111] For this purpose, international prosecutors have considered—to varying degrees—a range of factors including the seniority of an individual within a particular hierarchy, the extent of an individual's authority, the notoriety and viciousness of their participation, the degree of an individual's participation including their intent, and the existence of a discriminatory motive.[112]

prima facie case' before confirming an indictment); Article 18(1), ICTR Statute and Rule 47(B), ICTR Rules of Procedure and Evidence (requiring that a judge of the Trial Chamber be satisfied that there is 'a *prima facie* case' before confirming an indictment); Article 58(1), ICC Statute (requiring that a Pre-Trial Chamber be satisfied that there are 'reasonable grounds to believe' that the person has committed a crime within the jurisdiction of the Court before issuing a warrant of arrest of a person); and Article 61(5) and (7), ICC Statute (requiring that a Pre-Trial Chamber confirm that the Prosecutor has provided sufficient evidence to establish that there are 'substantial grounds to believe' that the person committed the crime charged). See also, ICC OTP Policy Paper on Case Selection and Prioritisation (n 105) [21]–[23].

107 See, for example, ICC OTP Policy Paper on Case Selection and Prioritisation (n 105) [26]–[33].

108 On the varying degrees of transparency of international criminal prosecutorial decision-making, see generally, Heller (n 67) 681; and L Côté, 'Reflections on the Exercise of Prosecutorial Discretion in International Criminal Law' (2005) 3 *Journal of International Criminal Justice* 162, 171–172.

109 See, in this regard, ICTY–UNICRI, *ICTY Manual on Developed Practices* (UNICRI Publisher 2009) [18] ('the seriousness of the crimes, the number of victims, the duration of the offense and the scope of destruction'); 'Report on the Completion of the Mandate of the International Criminal Tribunal for Rwanda as at 15 November 2015', Enclosure to Letter dated 17 November 2015 from the President of the International Criminal Tribunal for Rwanda addressed to the President of the Security Council, UN Doc S/2015/884 (17 November 2015) ('ICTR Completion Report') [51] ('the nature and gravity of the crime committed'); and ICC Office of the Prosecutor, 'Strategic plan: 2016–2018' (6 July 2015) ('ICC OTP Strategic Plan 2016–2018') [35] ('the most serious crimes of concern to the international community').

110 See, for example, ICTY–UNICRI (n 109) [18]; ICTR Completion Report (n 109) [51]; and ICC OTP Policy Paper on Case Selection and Prioritisation (n 105) [34]–[40] and [45]–[46].

111 See, in this regard, Article 1, Nuremberg Charter ('major war criminals'); Article 1, Tokyo Charter ('major war criminals'); ICTY–UNICRI (n 109) [20] (referring to persons suspected of being 'most responsible'); ICTR Completion Report (n 109) [14] (referring to persons who bear 'the greatest responsibility'); Article 1(1), SCSL Statute ('persons who bear the greatest responsibility'); ICC Office of the Prosecutor, 'Paper on some policy issues before the Office of the Prosecutor' (September 2003) ('ICC OTP Policy Issues Paper') 3 (referring to persons 'who bear most responsibility').

112 See, for example, ICTY–UNICRI (n 109) 18; ICTR Completion Report (n 109) [14]; HB Jallow, 'Prosecutorial Discretion and International Criminal Justice' (2005) 3 *Journal of International Criminal*

Importantly, the interpretation and relative weight given to these policy criteria have typically varied not only *between* different international criminal courts, but also over time *within* international criminal courts. In this regard, a significant factor at play has been the *political context* in which international prosecutors have operated in practice. In particular, international prosecutors have in general been able to bring charges and progress their cases to trial only when their work has been supported by States where the crimes took place or external actors with sufficient influence over such States to compel cooperation.

Against this background, by examining the interaction between legal criteria, policy criteria, and political factors in different institutional contexts, this section explores three categories of case selectivity that have shaped the historical narratives constructed within international criminal courts in practice: first, *factional* selectivity, which concerns the extent to which individuals belonging to particular factions or groups to mass atrocity conflicts have been targeted for prosecution to the marginalisation or complete exclusion of others; second, *functional* selectivity, which concerns the extent to which individuals who played particular types of roles—for example, high-ranking or low-ranking, political or economic—within mass atrocity situations have been targeted for prosecution to the marginalisation or complete exclusion of others; and finally, *procedural* selectivity, which concerns the inability to prosecute particular individuals on technical or procedural grounds, in particular their lack of fitness to stand trial or death prior to arrest, trial, or judgment.

Similar to situational selectivity—albeit with distinct narrative implications—a consistent pattern that emerges from this examination of case selection practices is the predominant influence of the political context in shaping who has been targeted for international prosecution in practice.

A. Factional Selectivity

In mass atrocity situations, it is not uncommon for different factions to be implicated in the commission of crimes. In this context, 'factions' may be understood to refer to the different groups that participate in mass atrocity situations, allegiance to which is typically organised around a particular form of collective identity such as nationality or ethnicity. Yet, while multiple factions typically participate in mass atrocity conflicts, in practice international prosecutors have consistently failed to prosecute individuals belonging to factions aligned with the interests of States on whose cooperation they have been reliant and/or States which are particularly powerful within the international community more generally.[113] This may be illustrated by briefly reviewing the individuals prosecuted in each of the international criminal courts that form the focus of this study.

Justice 145, 152–153; ICC OTP Strategic Plan 2016–2018 (n 109) [34]; and ICC OTP Policy Paper on Case Selection and Prioritisation (n 105) [43].

[113] See similarly, D Zolo, *Victors' Justice: From Nuremberg to Baghdad* (trans MW Weir, Verso 2009) 30; and Kiyani (n 97) 948–951.

1. The Nuremberg IMT and Tokyo IMTFE

Beginning with the Nuremberg IMT and the Tokyo IMTFE, the Allied States responsible for drafting the statutory frameworks of these tribunals ensured that only individuals from the defeated nations would fall within their personal jurisdiction.[114] The one-sided prosecutions that followed raised the spectre of victors' justice and led to narratives oriented against the vanquished.[115] Notable omissions from the historical narratives that resulted from these prosecutions included the saturation bombing of German and Japanese civilian population centres,[116] as well as the atomic bombing of Hiroshima and Nagasaki.[117]

The hypocrisy of these one-sided prosecutions was softened to some extent by the prosecutorial practice of not, in general, charging defendants with acts that had also been committed by Allied forces.[118] A prominent example was the bombing of civilian population centres, which had been practised by both Allied and Axis forces.[119] From a narrative perspective, however, this strategy created a double omission, which risked legitimating particular forms of wartime violence by sending the message that the acts not charged were permissible rather than criminal.[120]

At the Tokyo IMTFE, notable omissions from prosecution also included the Japanese Emperor Hirohito, as well as members of Unit 731, the notorious military unit of the Kwantung Army that used prisoners of war for bacteriological weapons experimentation. With regard to the decision not to prosecute the Japanese Emperor, the dominant school of thought asserts that US General MacArthur ensured the Emperor would not be prosecuted for fear that his prosecution would provoke mass resistance to Allied occupation and destabilise Japan.[121] With respect to the decision not to prosecute members of Unit 731, it seems that the US intervened to ensure their immunity in order to learn from their expertise and advance their own weapons programmes.[122] According to Robert Cryer, the combined effect of these decisions was 'a double imposition of unacceptable selectivity', not only enforcing the law solely against the

114 See, in this regard, Article 1, Nuremberg Charter; and Article 1, Tokyo Charter.

115 See similarly, D Luban, 'The Legacies of Nuremberg', in G Mettraux (ed), *Perspectives on the Nuremberg Trial* (OUP 2008) 638, 659.

116 See, for example, I Henderson, 'The Firebombing of Tokyo and Other Japanese Cities', in Y Tanaka et al (eds), *Beyond Victor's Justice: The Tokyo War Crimes Trial Revisited* (Martinus Nijhoff 2011) 311; Luban (n 115) 659.

117 See, for example, Y Tanaka, 'The Atomic Bombing, the Tokyo Tribunal and the *Shimoda* Case: Lessons for Anti-Nuclear Legal Movements', in Y Tanaka et al (eds), *Beyond Victor's Justice: The Tokyo War Crimes Trial Revisited* (Martinus Nijhoff 2011) 293.

118 Acts of Soviet aggression were, however, overlooked. See, in this regard, R Merkel, 'The Law of the Nuremberg Trial: Valid, Dubious Outdated', in G Mettraux (ed), *Perspectives on the Nuremberg Trial* (OUP 2008) 555, 572; and H Arendt, *Eichmann in Jerusalem: A Report on the Banality of Evil* (revised and enlarged edition, Penguin Books 1994) 255.

119 Cryer (n 20) 206.

120 See, similarly, C Jochnick and R Normand, 'The Legitimation of Violence: A Critical History of the Laws of War' (1994) 35 *Harvard International Law Journal* 49, 89–95.

121 See, for example, Y Otomo, 'The Decision Not to Prosecute the Emperor', in Y Tanaka et al (eds), *Beyond Victor's Justice: The Tokyo War Crimes Trial Revisited* (Martinus Nijhoff 2011) 63, 63–64; and Boister and Cryer (n 30) 65–69.

122 See, for example, T Kei-ichi, 'Reasons for the Failure to Prosecute Unit 731 and its Significance', in Y Tanaka et al (eds), *Beyond Victor's Justice: The Tokyo War Crimes Trial Revisited* (Martinus Nijhoff 2011) 177; and Boister and Cryer (n 30) 63–64.

defeated powers, but also selectively amongst the individuals associated with the defeated powers for reasons of Allied self-interest.[123]

2. The ICTY

At the ICTY, while Prosecutors attempted to shape rather than be shaped by the political landscape in which they operated,[124] it was State pressure that was primarily responsible for their failure to prosecute members of the armed forces of the North Atlantic Treaty Organization (NATO). This became clear in the context of the Prosecutor's decision whether or not to open a full investigation into the bombing campaign conducted by NATO against the Federal Republic of Yugoslavia in 1999.

Having received information from various sources, including civil society groups and the Federal Republic of Yugoslavia, ICTY Prosecutor Louise Arbour took the innovative step of ordering a preliminary report on the question of crimes allegedly committed by NATO during its bombing campaign. Although this decision was a welcome sign of prosecutorial independence, the report that followed, published by Arbour's successor Carla Del Ponte, ultimately left the impression that it had been prepared specifically so that the ICTY Prosecutor could ensure that the issue went away.[125] In particular, the report based its recommendation not to investigate the bombing campaign further at least partially on the assumption that an investigation would be 'unlikely to result in the acquisition of sufficient evidence to substantiate charges against high level accused or against lower accused for particularly heinous offences'.[126] Given that the ICTY Prosecutor had previously initiated investigations against numerous defendants *in spite of* considerable State opposition to hand over evidence, the report's conclusion that it should not investigate the NATO bombing campaign in the face of similar resistance constituted a clear case of double standards.[127] On 2 June 2000, Carla Del Ponte closed the chapter on the issue by informing the UN Security Council that although NATO had made some mistakes during its campaign in Kosovo, it had not deliberately targeted civilians and therefore its personnel would not be subject to a full investigation by the ICTY.[128]

Ultimately, the incident revealed the political limits of the ICTY, which remained contingent on NATO support to function and therefore drew back from attempting to bite the hand that was feeding it. Indeed, in her memoirs, Carla Del Ponte confirmed as much, noting how she quickly arrived at the conclusion that it would be impossible

123 Cryer (n 20) 209.

124 See, for example, Bass (n 34) 243–244 (giving the example of former ICTY Prosecutor Richard Goldstone specifically timing the issuance of three major indictments around the time of the Dayton peace conference in 1995 in order to make it harder for negotiators to undermine the tribunal's efforts by, for example, offering amnesties); and Mégret (n 33) 1278–1279 (giving the example of former ICTY Prosecutor Louise Arbour issuing an indictment against Slobodan Milošević at a time when she had little chance of apprehending him, a strategy which seemed aimed at placing pressure on the international community to assist in such efforts).

125 Cryer (n 20) 218.

126 ICTY Prosecutorial Committee, 'Final Report to the Prosecutor by the Committee Established to Review the NATO Bombing Campaign Against the Federal Republic of Yugoslavia' (8 June 2000) ('ICTY NATO Report') [90].

127 See similarly, Côté (n 108) 182.

128 UN Press Release, 'Prosecutor for International Tribunals Briefs Security Council' *Press Release SC/6870* (2 June 2000).

to investigate NATO in practice, first because NATO and its Member States would not cooperate, and second because such an investigation would render her office incapable of continuing to investigate crimes committed by local forces since the tribunal depended on NATO for security in Bosnia and Herzegovina and Kosovo.[129] As Del Ponte put it, 'it was impossible to go on politically without undermining the rest of the tribunal's work'.[130] As a result, the determination of responsibility for a number of crimes allegedly committed by NATO forces, including the attack on Koriša village alleged to have caused up to eighty-seven civilian deaths as well as the attack on the Djakovica Convoy alleged to have killed up to seventy-five civilians, was omitted from the ICTY's historical record.[131]

With the exception of NATO personnel, Prosecutors at the ICTY were able to bring charges against individuals belonging to all other major factions involved in the conflict in the former Yugoslavia. In practice, the ability of Prosecutors to secure individuals from different factions into custody largely stemmed from an increasingly favourable political environment.[132] In particular, three changes to the political context over time proved pivotal: first, the political transitions to more cooperative governments in Croatia and Serbia, which were increasingly willing to share evidence with the tribunal as well as apprehend suspects;[133] second, the increasing support from European Union (EU) Member States which were willing to link reconstruction aid and the prospects of EU membership to cooperation with the ICTY;[134] and finally, the increasing support received from NATO, which assisted in making arrests pursuant to secret indictments, as well as helping change power realities on the ground through a more interventionist approach to the conflict in the Balkans more generally.[135]

The ability to pursue different factions to the underlying conflict in the former Yugoslavia confronted Prosecutors at the ICTY with the additional challenge of determining whether and how to take into account the relative distribution and gravity of crimes committed by different factions for the purpose of selecting indictees.[136] In practice, the largest number of indictees at the ICTY were ethnically Serbian (68 per cent), followed by smaller numbers of Croatians (21 per cent) Bosniaks (4 per cent), Kosovar Albanians (4 per cent), Macedonians (1 per cent), and those whose ethnicity is unknown (2 per cent).[137] Bearing in mind that several studies have concluded that the vast majority of serious crimes during the Yugoslav conflict were committed by Serb forces,[138] these figures suggest that Prosecutors at the ICTY attempted to ensure

[129] C Del Ponte, *Madame Prosecutor: Confrontations with Humanity's Worst Criminals and the Culture of Impunity* (Other Press 2009) 60.

[130] Ibid 61.

[131] ICTY NATO Report (n 126) [9].

[132] KA Rodman, 'Justice as a Dialogue Between Law and Politics: Embedding the International Criminal Court within Conflict Management and Peacebuilding' (2014) 12 *Journal of International Criminal Justice* 437, 444.

[133] Bachmann and Fatić (n 31) 122 and 125.

[134] J Hagan and R Levi, 'Crimes of War and the Force of law' (2005) 83 *Social Forces* 1499, 1516.

[135] Ibid 1516 and 1518.

[136] Steinke (n 15) 14.

[137] S Ford, 'Fairness and Politics at the ICTY: Evidence from the Indictments' (2013) XXXIX *North Carolina Journal of International Law and Commercial Regulation* 45, 69.

[138] See, for example, Greenawalt (n 99) 647, fn 200 ('Separate assessments by a U.N. Commission of Experts and the CIA estimated that roughly ninety percent of crimes in Bosnia were committed by Serb forces').

that individuals from different factions were prosecuted—even if the relative gravity of the crimes committed by some factions was lower than others—whilst at the same time striving not to lose sight of the relative distribution of the most serious crimes between the factions.[139]

3. The ICTR

At the ICTR, Prosecutors were able to successfully launch investigations and prosecutions against those connected to the former Hutu government. By contrast, not a single member of the Rwandan Patriotic Front (RPF) was targeted for prosecution for crimes allegedly committed during the same period,[140] largely it seems as a result of pressure exerted by the Rwandan government.[141]

The obstructionist tactics of the Rwandan government took a variety of forms. For instance, in response to an Appeals Chamber decision to release Jean-Bosco Barayagwiza because the prosecution had violated the right of the accused to a prompt trial following arrest,[142] the Rwandan government suspended its relations with the tribunal and refused to issue a visa for Prosecutor Carla Del Ponte.[143] Following a plea from the Prosecutor, the Appeals Chamber reinstated the accused's indictment and relations with the tribunal normalised once more.[144] As Nancy Combs has observed, 'few would maintain that Rwanda's hardball tactics did not influence the Appeals Chamber's decision'.[145]

An additional example concerns Carla Del Ponte, who has claimed that she lost her job as Prosecutor as a result of her attempts to pursue investigations against members of the RPF for alleged crimes committed in 1994. Early in her tenure, Del Ponte announced that her office would be investigating the conduct of RPF forces through so-called 'Special Investigations'.[146] When Del Ponte's position as Prosecutor came up for reappointment in 2003, the Rwandan government, which had consistently failed to cooperate with the ICTR's Special Investigations, lobbied hard for the ICTR to have its own chief prosecutor rather than one shared with the ICTY.[147] On 28 August 2003, the

[139] See similarly, Côté (n 108) 176 (describing how prosecutorial reliance on criteria related to whether a potential indictee belonged to or was affiliated with a particular group was 'an open secret').

[140] See, in this regard, 'Preliminary Report of the Independent Commission of Experts established in accordance with Security Council resolution 935 (1994)' UN Doc S/1994/1125 (4 October 1994) [82] (identifying substantial grounds to conclude that 'Tutsi elements' had committed 'mass assassinations, summary executions, breaches of international humanitarian law and crimes against humanity'); and Human Rights Watch, *Justice After Genocide: 20 Years On* (28 March 2014) 11 (noting that the RPF government has even admitted that its forces had carried out killings in 1994, though has also sought to downplay the extent of such crimes, characterising them as isolated revenge killings and claiming that it would bring those responsible to justice).

[141] See also, Human Rights Watch (n 140) 11–12 (noting that, even outside the ICTR, 'fewer than 40 RPF soldiers have been tried for these crimes, and most have received comparatively lenient sentences').

[142] *Prosecutor v Jean Bosco Barayagwiza* (Decision, Appeals Chamber) ICTR-97-19-AR72 (3 November 1999).

[143] NA Combs, *Fact-Finding Without Facts—The Uncertain Evidentiary Foundations of International Criminal Convictions* (CUP 2010) 227.

[144] *Prosecutor v Jean Bosco Barayagwiza* (Decision on Prosecutor's Request for Review or Reconsideration, Appeals Chamber) ICTR-97-19-AR72 (31 March 2000).

[145] Combs (n 143) 227 fn 1014.

[146] L Reydams, 'The ICTR Ten Years On: Back to the Nuremberg Paradigm?' (2005) 3 *Journal of International Criminal Justice* 977, 979.

[147] 'Prosecutor Loses Rwanda Role' *BBC* (28 August 2003).

Security Council voted to remove Del Ponte from her role as ICTR Prosecutor, though retained her services at the ICTY.[148] Although both Rwanda and the Security Council cited management concerns for taking this step, Del Ponte is on record connecting her non-renewal to the Special Investigations.[149]

From a narrative perspective, the factional selectivity of prosecutions at the ICTR generated a one-sided historical narrative in the judgments of the tribunal. According to Richard Wilson, for example, the Kagame regime's sustained campaign of obstructionism led to the construction of 'a hegemonic historical mythology that represents the RPF as noble liberators who led the way to an ethnic reconciliation without reprisals'.[150]

4. The SCSL

At the SCSL, the Prosecutor's indictment strategy has generally been applauded by commentators as 'impressively impartial',[151] and a 'most sincere attempt at balanced prosecution',[152] in light of his decision to indict political and military leaders from different factions to the underlying conflict, encompassing: the rebel Revolutionary United Front (RUF); the Civil Defence Forces (CDF) militia that had fought on the side of the government; rogue elements of the Sierra Leone Army that constituted the Armed Forces Revolutionary Council (AFRC); and former President of Liberia, Charles Taylor.

Nonetheless, a number of important figures were omitted from prosecution at the SCSL. Arguably the most notable exclusion was Sierra Leonean President Ahmed Tejan Kabbah. This omission was particularly conspicuous since pro-Kabbah individuals from the CDF, such as Sam Hinga Norman, had been indicted for atrocities committed by their forces whilst fighting in support of the government. To the extent that individuals such as Norman had been working closely with Kabbah, it is plausible that the President shared some of the responsibility for atrocities committed in support of his regime.[153] According to Chris Mahoney, President Kabbah's omission from prosecution likely stems from the influence he was able to exert over case selection:[154] first, by selecting Desmond de Silva, his former colleague as deputy prosecutor; and second, by seconding police officers to investigate CDF crimes that were allegedly committed under his command as Minister of Defence and Head of State.

Beyond the exclusion of President Kabbah, Presidents Muammar al Ghadaffi of Libya and Blaise Compaoré of Burkina Faso were also not called to account before the SCSL despite their alleged involvement in providing training and logistical support to rebel groups during the conflict.[155] These omissions were specifically raised by defence counsel for Charles Taylor, who alleged that Taylor's prosecution had been

148 UN Security Council Resolution 1503, UN Doc S/RES/1503 (28 August 2003).

149 Reydams (n 146) 979 fn 10 (referring to an interview given by Carla Del Ponte with Hirondelle).

150 RA Wilson, *Writing History in International Criminal Tribunals* (CUP 2011) 48.

151 Schabas (n 67) 750.

152 Cryer (n 20) 229.

153 See similarly, WA Schabas, 'A Synergistic Relationship: The Sierra Leone Truth and Reconciliation Commission and the Special Court for Sierra Leone' (2004) 15 *Criminal Law Forum* 3, 12.

154 C Mahoney, 'Sierra Leone: The Justice v. Reconciliation Archetype?' (2015) *TOAEP Policy Brief Series No. 33*, 2.

155 Jalloh (n 45) 422.

'selective and vindictive in nature' and based on political motives and interests of the US government.[156] In response, the Prosecutor submitted that the evidence against Ghadaffi and Compaoré was less than a tenth of the evidence involving Taylor's assistance to the RUF; moreover, most of that evidence indicated that Ghadaffi and Compaoré had provided the majority of their assistance through Charles Taylor.[157] The SCSL Trial Chamber ultimately dismissed the submissions of the defence on the basis that there was no clear evidence of a discriminatory motive and that, in any case, the evidence indicated that Ghadaffi and Compaoré were not 'similarly situated' to Charles Taylor in terms of the roles they played during the conflict.[158] Whilst the Trial Chamber's analysis is coherent from a formal legal perspective, it remains the case that the omission of Ghadaffi and Compaoré from prosecution clearly shielded their conduct from scrutiny. Moreover, according to Charles Jalloh, it is highly likely that State influence played a part in the SCSL Prosecutor's decision not to prosecute Ghadaffi and Compaoré since 'the political fallout from such actions might, in his judgment, have been too big a burden for the fledgling Sierra Leone tribunal to handle'.[159]

Finally, State influence was also at play in the Prosecutor's failure to investigate or prosecute any peacekeepers before the SCSL. In this regard, Article 1(b) of the SCSL Statute ensured that primary jurisdiction over 'peacekeepers and any related personnel' resided with the sending State.[160] In the event that the sending State was found to be unwilling or unable genuinely to carry out an investigation or prosecution, the SCSL could exercise jurisdiction over such peacekeepers 'if authorized by the Security Council on the proposal of any State'.[161] As William Schabas explains, during the conflict in Sierra Leone, there were several serious and credible charges that peacekeepers, particularly those accredited to the mission of the Economic Community of West African States, had committed crimes.[162] With this in mind, Article 1(b) seems to have been purposefully designed to deter the SCSL Prosecutor from investigating such cases in practice.[163]

5. The ICC

At the ICC, there has been a disjuncture between the rhetoric and practice of the Prosecutor with respect to case selection.[164] Rhetorically, the Prosecutor has resisted

[156] *Prosecutor v Charles Ghankay Taylor* (Judgment, Trial Chamber) SCSL-03-01-T (18 May 2012) [73]–[74].

[157] Ibid [76].

[158] Ibid [81]–[83].

[159] Jalloh (n 45) 423. See also, Mahoney (n 154) 3 (arguing that the US State Department had told the Prosecutor's office to stop such investigations or risk losing funding).

[160] Article 1(b), SCSL Statute.

[161] Article 1(c), SCSL Statute.

[162] Schabas (n 47) 143.

[163] See similarly, Mahoney (n 154) 2 (noting how the provision bestowed *de facto* immunity on mercenaries acting on behalf of Tony Buckingham's British Heritage Group, a mining diamond mining company in the region). Contrast Cryer (n 20) 230 (arguing that the provision was probably unnecessary since 'there have been no allegations that peacekeepers are among those who "bear the greatest responsibility" for crimes in Sierra Leone').

[164] This disjuncture is a particular manifestation of what Leslie Vinjamuri has termed the 'authority paradox' at the ICC, born of seeking to manage the conflicting interests of its different constituencies: on the one hand, the ICC's authority amongst civil society groups 'is intimately wrapped up … in the assumption that justice must be independent from politics'; on the other hand, being structurally dependent on States for cooperation, '[a]ctions that help secure the support of powerful states threaten to alienate civil

attempts to define situations along factional lines, even when States Parties and the Security Council have attempted factional exclusions as part of the terms of their referrals. For instance, in response to the Ugandan government's self-referral, entitled 'Referral of the Situation Concerning the Lord's Resistance Army',[165] the Prosecutor explained that the scope of the referral would be interpreted to encompass '*all* crimes committed in Northern Uganda in the context of the ongoing conflict involving the LRA'.[166] Similarly, despite the inclusion of a jurisdictional carve-out clause to exclude the nationals of non-State Parties from the jurisdictional reach of the ICC in the Security Council's Libya referral,[167] the Prosecutor has since confirmed that her office has a mandate 'to investigate allegations of crimes by *all* actors' and has therefore been investigating allegations of crimes committed by NATO air strikes.[168]

In practice, however, the ICC Prosecutor has predominantly brought charges against individuals in accordance with the interests of States on whose cooperation it has depended.[169] Importantly, State cooperation has generally been contingent on the ability of incumbent governments to instrumentalise cooperation with the ICC for domestic political ends—in particular, to stigmatise and delegitimise domestic opposition groups in circumstances where incumbents are able to minimise the risk of accountability for themselves.[170] While pressure from international actors is an additional factor that may in certain circumstances nudge States in the direction of cooperating with the ICC, in practice such efforts have generally been insufficient to overcome domestic political interests.[171]

This trend has been especially apparent when the Prosecutor has developed charging strategies in response to self-referrals by States Parties—several of which the Prosecutor has actively encouraged. In such circumstances, the Prosecutor has

society'. L Vinjamuri, 'The International Criminal Court and the Paradox of Authority' (2016) 79 *Law and Contemporary Problems* 275, 277.

165 'Referral of the Situation Concerning the Lord's Resistance Army', submitted by the Republic of Uganda (16 December 2003).

166 *Situation in Uganda* (Decision to Convene a Status Conference on the Investigation in the Situation in Uganda in Relation to the Application of Article 53, Pre-Trial Chamber) ICC-02/04-01/05-68 (2 December 2005) [5] (emphasis added). Similar statements have been made with respect to other situations. See, for example, ICC Office of the Prosecutor, 'Statement of ICC Prosecutor at the Commencement of Trial in the Case against Messrs. Laurent Gbagbo and Charles Blé Goudé' (28 January 2016) ('My Office will seek to ensure justice and accountability on all sides. This should be clear; my Office is investigating both sides of the conflict.')

167 UN Security Council Resolution 1970, UN Doc S/RES/1970 (26 February 2011) [6]. See similarly, UN Security Council Resolution 1593, UN Doc S/RES/1593 (31 March 2005) [6] (with respect to the situation in Darfur). For discussion, see generally, R Cryer, 'Sudan, Resolution 1593, and International Criminal Justice' (2006) 19 *Leiden Journal of International Law* 195, 209–214.

168 ICC Office of the Prosecutor, 'Third Report of the Prosecutor of the International Criminal Court to the UN Security Council Pursuant to UNSCR 1970 (2011)' (16 May 2012) [52] (emphasis added). See also, ICC Office of the Prosecutor, 'Fourth Report of the Prosecutor of the International Criminal Court to the UN Security Council Pursuant to UNSCR 1970 (2011)' (7 November 2012) [11]; and ICC Office of the Prosecutor, 'Fifth Report of the Prosecutor of the International Criminal Court to the UN Security Council Pursuant to UNSCR 1970 (2011)' (8 May 2013) [13].

169 F Mégret, 'Is the ICC Focusing Too Much on Non-State Actors?', in MM deGuzman and DM Amann (eds), *Arcs of Global Justice* (OUP 2018) 173, 183.

170 C Hillebrecht and S Straus, 'Who Pursues the Perpetrators? State Cooperation with the ICC' (2017) 39 *Human Rights Quarterly* 162, 167–170.

171 Ibid 163 and 171.

consistently brought charges against individuals aligned with non-State armed groups rather than those affiliated with the incumbent government on the territory where the mass atrocity conflict was and, in some instances, continues to be waged.[172]

In the situation of Uganda, for example, the ICC Prosecutor has focused on allegations of crimes committed by members of the Lord's Resistance Army (LRA) to the neglect of allegations of crimes committed by government forces against Acholi communities.[173] Similarly, in the situation of Côte d'Ivoire, only the deposed regime of Laurent Gbagbo and his supporters have been targeted by the ICC Prosecutor, despite allegations of comparable crimes by those connected to President Alassane Ouattara.[174] The ICC Prosecutor's selective charging strategy with respect to the conflict in the Ituri district of the DRC is also illustrative. In its judgment in *Lubanga*, the ICC Trial Chamber referred to a UN report, which asserted that the crisis in Ituri would not have turned into a situation of mass violence without the involvement of national and foreign actors including the Ugandan and Rwandan armies.[175] Yet, to date, charges have only been directed against the leaders of rival local ethnic militias, neglecting the roles played by political and military figures in Kinshasa, Uganda, and Rwanda.[176] As a consequence, although the judgments that have been delivered concerning the conflict have tended to acknowledge and to a limited extent examine the interventions of this broader array of actors,[177] the narratives of responsibility constructed by the Court have focused solely on individuals belonging to local rebel armed groups.

The ICC Prosecutor's alignment with State power has sometimes been accompanied by a public legal justification that the crimes of the factions prosecuted are relatively graver than those of the factions not (yet) targeted.[178] When the arrest warrants against five members of the Lord's Resistance Army were made public, for example, the ICC Prosecutor explained that they had been targeted because their alleged crimes were 'much more numerous and of much higher gravity' than those allegedly committed by the forces of the Ugandan government.[179]

[172] See generally, Mégret (n 169) 173, 175–179.

[173] See generally, A Branch, 'Against Humanitarian Impunity: Rethinking Responsibility for Displacement and Disaster in Northern Uganda' (2008) 2 *Journal of Intervention and Statebuilding* 151; and Human Rights Watch, *Uprooted and Forgotten: Impunity and Human Rights Abuses in Northern Uganda* (September 2005).

[174] See generally, ST Rosenberg, 'The International Criminal Court in Côte d'Ivoire: Impartiality at Stake?' (2017) 15 *Journal of International Criminal Justice* 471.

[175] *Prosecutor v Thomas Lubanga Dyilo* (Judgment pursuant to Article 74 of the Statute, Trial Chamber) ICC-01/04-01/06-2842 (14 March 2012) [76].

[176] See generally, Human Rights Watch, *Unfinished Business: Closing Gaps in the Selection of ICC Cases* (September 2011) 11–16.

[177] See, for example, *Prosecutor v Germain Katanga* (Judgment Pursuant to Article 74 of the Statute, Trial Chamber) ICC-01/04-01/07 (7 March 2014) Chapter VI.

[178] See, in this regard, ICC OTP Preliminary Examination Policy Paper (n 49) [66] ('The principle of impartiality ... does not mean an "equivalence of blame" between different persons and groups within a situation, or that the Office must necessarily prosecute all sides, in order to balance-off perceptions of bias; instead, it requires the Office to focus its efforts objectively on those most responsible for the most serious crimes within the situation in a consistent manner, irrespective of the States or parties involved or the person(s) or group(s) concerned').

[179] ICC Office of the Prosecutor, 'Statement by the Chief Prosecutor on the Uganda Arrest Warrants' (14 October 2005) 2–3. For critique, see, for example, Schabas (n 67) 747 (arguing that the Prosecutor's analysis of gravity with respect to the LRA neglects the significance that the crimes allegedly committed by the

A more convincing explanation, however, resides in the confluence of interests that typically exists—at least in the short term—between self-referring States and the ICC Prosecutor.[180] For the self-referring State, a referral to the ICC Prosecutor accompanied by selective cooperation to facilitate the prosecution of non-State actors operating on its territory offers the possibility of instrumentalising the stigmatising power of the ICC for its own political ends—in particular, the criminalisation and depoliticisation of the agenda of non-State opposition groups together with the legitimation of the deployment of State violence against them under the banner of law enforcement.[181] In the Central African Republic, for example, former President François Bozizé managed, initially at least, to instrumentalise the ICC to remove one of his political enemies, Jean-Pierre Bemba of the DRC, whilst achieving a measure of legitimacy for his government.[182] Similarly, the government of Mali was content to cooperate with the ICC's efforts to prosecute Ahmad Al Faqi Al Mahdi for the destruction of cultural sites in Timbuktu as part of its broader strategy to reassert control over the north of the country.[183]

At the same time, for the ICC Prosecutor, the selective cooperation received from a self-referring State enables it to pursue some relatively easier cases in an effort to validate its own profile.[184] While it is plausible that this pragmatic approach is part of a grand design to ease the path towards eventual prosecutions against individuals affiliated with incumbent governments at a later stage,[185] in such circumstances the ICC Prosecutor effectively enters into 'a sort of Faustian bargain' according to which targeting State officials in the future is likely to prove difficult if not impossible to achieve in the absence of local or international pressure.[186]

Importantly, the ICC Prosecutor's attempts to pragmatically align itself with the interests of States on whose cooperation it relies have not been limited to the context of self-referrals. For instance, with respect to the Security Council's referral of the situation in Libya, the Prosecutor has primarily sought arrest warrants for individuals aligned with the former Gaddafi regime—notwithstanding evidence of crimes committed by Libyan rebel forces identified by the International Commission of Inquiry

Ugandan People's Defence Force are attributable to a State); and Kiyani (n 97) 956 ('Gravity assessments should point *towards* political power instead of away from it') (emphasis in original).

180 Mégret (n 169) 183–184.

181 See similarly, Branch (n 52) 35; and SMH Nouwen and WG Werner, 'Doing Justice to the Political: The International Criminal Court in Uganda and Sudan' (2010) 21 *European Journal of International Law* 941, 962–963.

182 Hillebrecht and Straus (n 170) 176–177.

183 Ibid 177.

184 Ibid 172 ('facing extensive criticism, Court officials have a strong incentive to secure finished cases rather than open confrontations with states, thereby risking existing cases or engendering more paralysis').

185 See, in this regard, M Kersten, 'In the ICC's Interest: Between "Pragmatism" and "Idealism"?' *Justice in Conflict* (16 July 2013) (referring to a talk given by ICC Deputy Prosecutor James Stewart, in which he concluded as follows: 'The Prosecutor, for example in the case of Cote D'Ivoire, has always made it clear that she intends to look at all sides of the conflict. Sometimes you just can't do everything at once. You have to make a choice between action and paralysis and between pragmatism and ideals. And I think if you choose pragmatic action, you really shouldn't be criticized. But in the end, I suppose history will tell us whether or not the OTP has acted appropriately.')

186 Mégret (n 169) 184.

on Libya.[187] The only public arrest warrant for an individual who fought against Gaddafi forces—Mahmoud Mustafa Busayf al-Werfalli—concerns crimes unconnected with the 2011 uprising.[188] In light of NATO and Security Council support for the Libyan rebels during the civil war in 2011, the chances of ICC prosecutions being launched against such individuals appear to be relatively remote.[189]

By pursuing this pragmatic charging strategy, a particular challenge for the ICC Prosecutor has been the reality that State interests are rarely static, but shift over time.[190] As such, attempts by the Prosecutor to align the focus of its indictments with the balance of power between and within States have not always paid dividends. The ICC Prosecutor's initiation of an investigation *proprio motu* into the situation of Kenya is illustrative in this regard. The Kenyan situation remains the only instance where the ICC Prosecutor has sought to charge individuals belonging to opposing factions to a conflict in parallel. The Prosecutor was able to proceed in this fashion in light of the strong backing it originally received from major powers within the international community, as well as an initial pledge from the Kenyan government that it would cooperate with the investigation.[191] Over time, however, the Kenya cases became mired in controversy, with defence teams claiming that the Prosecutor had initiated prosecutions on an inadequate evidentiary basis,[192] and the Prosecutor alleging that its witnesses had been intimidated and bribed.[193] As the interest of the international community ebbed away and the Kenyan government became increasingly hostile to the ICC Prosecutor's intervention, the Kenya cases eventually collapsed.[194]

As the Kenyan situation illustrates, when faced with opposition from an incumbent government and insufficient external support from the international community, the ICC Prosecutor has been rendered *de facto* powerless. The situation in Sudan offers a further illustration. Although the investigation in Darfur was triggered by a referral from the UN Security Council, the ICC Prosecutor's eventual pursuit of President al-Bashir contradicted the Council's political strategy of engagement rather than confrontation with Khartoum.[195] As Alex de Waal explains, by attempting to prosecute President al-Bashir, 'Moreno Ocampo was demanding that the world reverse the policy of negotiating with the Sudan government and instead adopt a strategy of

[187] 'Full Report of the International Commission of Inquiry to Investigate All Alleged Violations of International Law in Libya' UN Doc A/HRC/19/68 (8 March 2012).

[188] M Kersten, 'Will the International Criminal Court's Latest Target in Libya Be Brought to Justice?' *The Washington Post: Monkey Cage* (31 August 2017).

[189] A Tiemessen, 'The International Criminal Court and the Politics of Prosecutions' (2014) 18 *International Journal of Human Rights* 444, 456.

[190] Whiting (n 70) 183; and Hillebrecht and Straus (n 170) 178–185 (reviewing shifts in State cooperation based on strategic interactions with the ICC in the situations of Côte d'Ivoire, Kenya, and Libya).

[191] Bosco (n 85) 160.

[192] See, for example, 'Exclusive Interview with Steven Kay' *The Hague Trials Kenya* (16 March 2015) (in which defence counsel for Uhuru Kenyatta, Steven Kay, suggests that the ICC Prosecutor's case was 'built on sand . . . without any cement, bricks, anything to hold it up').

[193] See generally, A Whiting, 'The ICC in Kenya: Institutional Promises and Limitations' *Just Security* (15 September 2015).

[194] M Kersten, 'A Missed Trial or a Mistrial? The End of the ICC Cases against Ruto and Sang' *Justice in Conflict* (7 April 2016); T Maliti, 'Judges Unanimously Terminate Charges Against Kenyatta' *International Justice Monitor* (18 March 2015).

[195] Rodman (n 132) 447–450. See also, Bosco (n 85) 142–148 (describing the political build-up and reaction to the ICC Prosecutor's decision to seek an arrest warrant against President al-Bashir).

regime change'.[196] Since such a reversal of policy was not forthcoming, the Security Council has been consistently unresponsive to the Prosecutor's repeated requests for assistance aimed at incentivising the Sudanese government to cooperate with its investigations,[197] a trend which eventually led the Prosecutor to hibernate investigative activities in Darfur.[198]

The pattern that emerges from this overview of the ICC Prosecutor's case selection practices is one of consistent, albeit at times reluctant or forced, alignment with the interests of referring entities—whether self-referring States Parties or the Security Council—or the major powers of the international community in general. As Sarah Nouwen has observed:[199]

> What governments have to offer the Court in terms of cooperation influences the likelihood that people protected by them will be held to account by the ICC. States that have a lot to offer in terms of cooperation when their enemies are prosecuted or that are protected by powerful states can effectively immunise their nationals from the Court's jurisdiction. *Vice versa*, those who are not protected by their governments, indeed, sought by them (for instance rebel movements in Uganda, DRC and CAR) or those governments that lack protection from the hegemonic order (for example, members of the present Sudanese and former Libyan government) are targeted by ICC proceedings. Inequality between states thus also leads to inequality among individuals before the Court.

Notably, the ICC Prosecutor expressly acknowledged these political constraints in its *Policy Paper on Case Selection and Prioritisation*. In a moment of unprecedented transparency, the Prosecutor explained how cases are prioritised both within a given situation and across situations according to, *inter alia*, 'operational conditions', which include the availability of evidence, the level of international cooperation and judicial assistance supporting the Prosecutor's activities, and the potential to secure the arrest and surrender of suspects.[200] Although these factors were referred to in the context of discussing case *prioritisation*, as Alex Whiting has argued, 'it seems likely that the line between prioritization and case selection might blur over time; cases that are de-prioritized because they are not feasible may never get prosecuted, meaning that they will in effect have been de-selected'.[201]

[196] A de Waal, 'Moreno-Ocampo's Coup de Theatre' *African Arguments* (29 July 2008).

[197] See, for example, ICC Office of the Prosecutor, 'Statement to the United Nations Security Council on the Situation in Darfur, pursuant to UNSCR 1593 (2005)' (12 December 2014) [4] (reprimanding the Security Council for failing to adequately assist with the arrest of suspects wanted in relation to the situation in Darfur).

[198] Ibid.

[199] Nouwen (n 64) 171. See similarly, Kiyani (n 97) 955 (noting how the ICC Prosecutor's factional selectivity 'positions the impartial and neutral mechanisms of the Court in service of an oppressive regime, and implicates it in the ahistorical continuation of colonial policies and ethnic strife in the contemporary post-colonial state'); and Branch (n 52) 36 ('it appears that the ICC can carry out prosecutions in the name of global justice only by taking advantage of the existing lines of racial division, global inequality and violence that have defined Africa over the last centuries').

[200] ICC OTP Policy Paper on Case Selection and Prioritisation (n 105) [11], [13], and [51]. See also, ICC OTP Strategic Plan 2016–2018 (n 109) [26] and [28];

[201] AG Whiting, 'Finding Strength within Constraints' *International Criminal Justice Today* (23 November 2016).

Ultimately, from a narrative perspective, factional selectivity in the charging practices of the ICC Prosecutor inevitably leads to imbalanced historical accounts of the mass atrocity situations examined in the judgments of the ICC. In other words, inequality between and within States beyond the courtroom generates factionally selective historical narratives inside it.

B. Functional Selectivity

Individuals implicated in the commission of mass atrocities generally perform a range of different roles and participate to varying degrees. In particular, the profiles of such individuals tend to vary in terms of the extent of their responsibility—ranging from the so-called 'big fish' to the 'small fry'—as well as the nature of their roles—including, for example, political, military, and economic positions. From a narrative perspective, prosecutions of differently situated individuals tend to generate distinct historical perspectives of mass atrocity situations. For instance, whereas the prosecution of a political or military leader may lead to a more detailed assessment of the overarching policies behind mass atrocity situations, the prosecution of a lower-level functionary may generate more detailed insights into the physical perpetration of atrocities in particular localities as well as the emergence of processes of bureaucratisation.[202] In addition, the prosecution of a private businessperson is likely to generate a more detailed examination of crimes that fuel mass atrocities compared to the prosecution of a military leader in charge of an armed group on the battlefield.[203]

In practice, the charging practices of international prosecutors have tended to be *functionally* selective—evincing a clear preference for targeting political and military leaders perceived to bear the highest levels of responsibility for their participation in the commission of crimes.

The preference for prosecuting *leading* figures reflects the view that international criminality often constitutes 'masterminded violence', in which crimes are set in motion by remote 'intellectual' architects and physically perpetrated by an executive machinery.[204] Importantly, this preference has operated subject to an implicit opportunity principle—an openness to targeting mid-lower ranking individuals based on access to evidence and ease of apprehension. In addition, the willingness of international prosecutors to target lower-ranking individuals has tended to be heightened where: the extent of their participation was exceptionally notorious or vicious; they were alleged to have committed specific categories of crimes, such as rape and other forms of sexual violence, which were particularly widespread or systematic within the mass atrocity situation and/or under-prosecuted in the past; and/or the individual's formal position does not reflect the actual extent of their authority within a particular group or organisation. Prosecutions of lower-ranking individuals may also be pursued

[202] JE Alvarez, 'Rush to Closure: Lessons of the Tadić Judgment' (1997–1998) 96 *Michigan Law Review* 2031, 2092.

[203] JG Stewart, 'Atrocity, Commerce and Accountability: The International Criminal Liability of Corporate Actors' (2010) 8 *Journal of International Criminal Justice* 313, 316.

[204] E van Sliedregt, 'The Curious Case of International Criminal Liability' (2012) 10 *Journal of International Criminal Justice* 1171, 1174.

by international prosecutors as a means to develop a better understanding of the mass atrocity situation, including the command structures and roles played by different actors, in anticipation of eventually prosecuting more complex cases involving higher-ranking figures at a later stage.[205]

The preference for prosecuting *political and military* figures reflects the common perception that such actors bear the greatest responsibility for the commission of mass atrocities, particularly in light of the nature and extent of their participation. However, the strength of this prosecutorial focus on political and military actors has tended to marginalise the roles played by other actors in mass atrocity situations, including, perhaps most significantly, individuals who have used their positions within *private business entities* to participate in the commission of crimes.[206]

Private businesspersons may participate in the commission of mass atrocities in a variety of ways.[207] For instance, such individuals may be direct perpetrators, as when a businessperson appropriates property without the consent of the owner in the context of and associated with an armed conflict. Equally, such individuals may become accomplices through the assistance they provide to the principal perpetrators of crimes. Such assistance can take various forms including: the provision of goods (for example, weapons or poisonous substances); the provision of logistical support (for example, construction works); the provision of services (for example, financial or banking services); and/or the procurement and use of resources such as labour or goods that involve the commission of crimes (for example, the use of slave labour within business supply chains).

In practice, the relative neglect of individuals within private business entities appears to stem from a combination of different factors, the relevance of which varies depending on the precise form of their involvement in mass atrocity situations.[208] Relevant factors include: the difficulty of determining when neutral business activities—such as the provision of goods or services—become criminally relevant contributions to the commission of crimes;[209] attribution challenges arising from

[205] See, for example, ICTY–UNICRI (n 109) [16]; and ICC OTP Strategic Plan 2016–2018 (n 109) [34].

[206] See similarly, JG Stewart, 'A Pragmatic Critique of Corporate Criminal Theory: Lessons From The Extremity' (2013) 16 *New Criminal Law Review* 261, 298; J Kyriakakis, 'Justice After War: Economic Actors, Economic Crimes, and the Moral Imperative for Accountability After War', in L May and A Forcehimes (eds), *Morality, Jus Post Bellum, and International Law* (CUP 2012) 113, 132–134; and F Jessberger, 'On the Origins of Individual Criminal Responsibility under International Law for Business Activity' (2010) 8 *Journal of International Criminal Justice* 783, 799–800.

[207] For useful summaries of the different types of involvement of private business entities in international crimes, see generally, International Commission of Jurists, *Report of the Expert Legal Panel on Corporate Complicity in International Crimes: Volume 2: Criminal Law and International Crimes* (International Commission of Jurists 2008) 37–43; W Kaleck and M Saage-Maaß, 'Corporate Accountability for Human Rights Violations Amounting to International Crimes: The Status Quo and its Challenges' (2010) 8 *Journal of International Criminal Justice* 699, 700–709; and H van der Wilt, 'Corporate Criminal Responsibility for International Crimes: Exploring the Possibilities' (2013) 12 *Chinese Journal of International Law* 43, 49–65.

[208] For a useful framework that identifies the different types of involvement of private business actors in the commission of mass atrocities, see generally, E Schmid, 'Distinguishing Types of "Economic Abuses": A Three-Dimensional Model' (2015) 26 *Criminal Law Forum* 225.

[209] See, for example, Schmid (n 208) 246–251; Kaleck and Saage-Maaß (n 207) 720-722; and C Burchard, 'Ancillary and Neutral Business Contributions to "Corporate-Political Core Crime": Initial Enquiries Concerning the Rome Statute' (2010) 8 *Journal of International Criminal Justice* 934.

the remoteness of such actors from the commission of crimes;[210] the perceived lower gravity of the interventions of such actors in comparison to those who orchestrated the crimes;[211] evidentiary and fact-finding obstacles;[212] and the interests of States in working with, rather than against, private business actors for the purpose of rebuilding societies in the aftermath of mass atrocity situations.[213] From a narrative perspective, by neglecting to prosecute private businesspersons, international prosecutors have deprived international criminal courts of the possibility of examining some of the economic dimensions and drivers of mass atrocity situations.

Each of these trends may be demonstrated by reviewing the charging practices of international prosecutors in different institutional contexts.

1. The Nuremberg IMT and Tokyo IMTFE

The Nuremberg and Tokyo Charters each specified that the tribunals had been established for the trial and punishment of '*major* war criminals'.[214] In line with these provisions, the individuals selected for prosecution were predominantly the political and military leaders of Japan and Germany suspected of having orchestrated the commission of crimes during the Second World War.[215] Notably, the omission of prosecutions against private businesspersons in these tribunals resulted from a mixture of State reticence and misfortune.

At the Nuremberg IMT, US Prosecutor Robert Jackson initially made clear his intention to indict individuals 'in the financial, industrial and economic life of Germany'.[216] To this end, US lawyer Frank Shea was instructed to draw up a tentative list of defendants for what became known as the 'economic case'; in his memorandum of 23 July 1945, Shea identified a mixture of former government ministers as well as private industrial and financial leaders.[217] Ultimately, however, the list was narrowed so that only some of the former ministers and one industrialist, Gustav Krupp, were

210 See, for example, E Schmid, 'Distinguishing Types of 'Economic Abuses': A Three-Dimensional Model' (2015) 26 *Criminal Law Forum* 225, 236–238; W Kaleck and M Saage-Maaß, 'Corporate Accountability for Human Rights Violations Amounting to International Crimes: The Status Quo and its Challenges' (2010) 8 *Journal of International Criminal Justice* 699, 722; and F Jessberger and J Geneuss, 'Introduction' (2010) 8 *Journal of International Criminal Justice* 695, 696.

211 See, for example, Stewart (n 203) 317; and Kaleck and Saage-Maaß (n 207) 722.

212 Kaleck and Saage-Maaß (n 207) 722.

213 See, for example, Kaleck and Saage-Maaß (n 207) 718–719; MB Taylor et al, *Overcoming Obstacles to Justice: Improving Access to Judicial Remedies for Business Involvement in Grave Human Rights Abuses* (FAFO 2010) 23–24. See also, LA Payne et al, *Transitional Justice and Corporate Accountability from Below: Deploying Archimedes' Lever* (CUP 2020) 32–38 (discussing the power of the business community to veto accountability efforts for business human rights abuses due to 'economic, social, and political connections with the ruling elite', 'state dependence on the private sector for income, employment, and resources', and 'active and direct lobbying and campaigning efforts').

214 Article 1, Nuremberg Charter (emphasis added); and Article 1, Tokyo Charter (emphasis added).

215 Smeulers et al (n 101) 26 (noting that the possible exception to the focus on the highest-ranking leaders was Julius Streicher, owner of the newspaper *Der Stürmer*). For detailed discussions of the selection of defendants at Nuremberg and Tokyo, see generally, Boister and Cryer (n 30) 49–69; and D Bloxham, *Genocide on Trial: War Crimes Trials and the Formation of Holocaust History and Memory* (OUP 2001) 21–24.

216 RH Jackson, 'Report to the President by Mr. Justice Jackson, June 6, 1945', in RH Jackson, *Report of Robert H. Jackson to the International Conference on Military Tribunals* (US Department of State 1945) 42, 47.

217 FM Shea, 'Tentative Memorandum for Mr. Justice Jackson', 23 July 1945, reproduced in J Bähr et al (eds), *Der Flick-Konzern im Dritten Reich* (Oldenbourg Wissenschaftsverlag GmbH 2008) 880, 883–884.

indicted in practice,[218] with the British reportedly expressing concern that the inclusion of a broader range of economic defendants might be overly complex and lead to embarrassing acquittals.[219] The retention of Gustav Krupp as the only industrialist meant that he was to be the symbol of German private industry at the Nuremberg IMT. That the case was deemed important to the US is evident from the lofty words used by Robert Jackson as part of his failed application to keep the Krupp case alive, dramatically claiming to the tribunal that the Krupps were 'one of the most persistent and influential forces that made this war' and that 'no greater disservice to the future peace of the world could be done than to excuse the entire Krupp family'.[220] However, Gustav Krupp was later deemed unfit for trial due to senile dementia, and a proposal by Robert Jackson to substitute his son, Alfried, was rejected by the tribunal.[221]

Subsequent to the Nuremberg IMT trial, the French and Russians favoured a second international trial of the industrialists but the British and the US were opposed. Robert Jackson, in particular, feared that attacking the industrialists within a second international trial would 'tend to discourage industrial co-operation with our Government in maintaining its defenses in the future while not at all weakening the Soviet position, since they [did] not rely upon private enterprise'.[222] There was also an additional concern that a second international trial might be used by the Soviets to reveal links between pre-war German and American economies in an effort to embarrass the US.[223] This sentiment appeared to be shared by the British, who were concerned that a second international trial of German industrialists could degenerate into 'a wrangle between the capitalist and communist ideologues'.[224] Ultimately, it was the British and the US who prevailed, the idea of a second international trial abandoned in favour of zonal trials conducted by each of the occupying powers.[225] Notably, however, the trials of the industrialists that eventually took place in the US occupied zone of Germany occurred at a time when the US was transforming its policy towards German industry away from its initial goal of disabling the German economy, under the influence of US Treasury Secretary Henry Morgenthau, towards a goal of rehabilitating the German

218 See, for example, Payne et al (n 213) 65–66 (identifying Walter Funk, Hjalmar Schacht and Julius Streicher as the economic actors prosecuted at the Nuremberg IMT); and R Overy, 'The Nuremberg Trials: International Law in the Making', in P Sands (ed), *From Nuremberg to The Hague: The Future of International Criminal Justice* (CUP 2003) 1, 12 ('the unfortunate Schacht and his successor as economics minister, Walther Funk, were made to represent German capitalism').

219 T Taylor, *The Anatomy of the Nuremberg Trials: A Personal Memoir* (Skyhorse Publishing 1993), 86.

220 'Answer of the United States Prosecution on the Motion on Behalf of Defendant Gustav Krupp von Bohlen', 12 November 1945, *Trial of the Major War Criminals before the International Military Tribunal, Nuremberg, 14 November 1945 – 1 October 1946: Volume I* (Nuremberg IMT 1947) 134.

221 For an account of the disagreements between the different prosecutorial teams about whether to indict Gustav or Alfried Krupp, as well as Robert Jackson's failed attempt to substitute Alfried for Gustav, see generally, Bloxham (n 215) 22–24; and Taylor (n 219) 90–94 and 151–164.

222 RH Jackson, 'Memo for the President on American Participation in Further International Trial of Nazi War Criminals', 13 May 1946, reproduced in T Taylor, *Final Report to the Secretary of the Army on the Nuernberg War Crimes Trials Under Control Council Law No. 10* (15 August 1949) 276, 277.

223 Bloxham (n 215) 31.

224 Ibid 30.

225 For recent examinations of these cases, see generally, G Baars, 'Capitalism's Victor's Justice? The Hidden Stories Behind the Prosecution of Industrialists Post-WWII', in KJ Heller and G Simpson (eds), *The Hidden Histories of War Crimes Trials* (OUP 2013) 163, 178–191; H van der Wilt, 'Corporate Criminal Responsibility for International Crimes: Exploring the Possibilities' (2013) 12 *Chinese Journal of International Law* 43, 52–61; and Payne et al (n 213) 66–69.

economy pursuant to what became known as the Truman Doctrine.[226] As Grietje Baars has recently demonstrated, this political landscape seemed to have a profound impact on the trials themselves, which were conducted with a sympathetic eye to the industrialists as prospective allies and 'manipulated to produce outcomes that were materially desirable'.[227]

At the Tokyo IMTFE, although Australia had initially drawn up a list to indict a number of Japanese industrialists, including the managing director of Kawasaki Heavy Industries and the president of the Sumitomo Bank, none made it to the final indictment.[228] The reason for the omission of members of these industrial conglomerates, typically referred to as the *zaibatsu*, is disputed.[229] One explanation is that there was simply a lack of clear evidence of their involvement in crimes against peace. As Boister and Cryer explain, 'while the prosecution considered economic support crucial for waging an aggressive war, it drew a line between those individuals who were responsible for harnessing that support within government, and those who merely provided it from outside of government'.[230] Similarly, Bert Röling, one of the judges of the Tokyo IMTFE, later argued that the Japanese industrialists had not been indicted because they had desired economic rather than military aggression and therefore had no case to answer.[231] On the other hand, others have suggested the omission of the industrialists resulted from their connections with US monopolies,[232] or the fact that the US needed their support and cooperation in the future.[233]

From a narrative perspective, the omission of private businesspersons from prosecution at Nuremberg and Tokyo marginalised their visibility in the historical accounts constructed by the tribunals in their judgments. To the extent that private businesses were mentioned, it was typically only in passing where it related to particular aspects of governmental policy.[234] In practice, discussions of the economic dimensions of the conflict were largely confined to *governmental* economic activities.[235]

[226] See generally, Baars (n 225) 174–178.

[227] Ibid 179–187.

[228] Boister and Cryer (n 30) 62–63 and fn 124 (also noting that the USSR had asked for five suspects to be added to the indictment, three of whom were industrialists).

[229] See generally, G Baars, *Law(yers) Congealing Capitalism: On the (Im)possibility of Restraining Business in Conflict through International Criminal Law* (University College London Doctoral Thesis 2012) 192–198.

[230] Boister and Cryer (n 30) 63.

[231] BVA Röling and A Cassese, *The Tokyo Trial and Beyond: Reflections of a Peacemonger* (Polity Press 1993) 39.

[232] Boister and Cryer (n 30) 63, fn 124.

[233] Röling and Cassese (n 231) 39; Payne et al (n 213) 72–75 (concluding that the global context was one in which 'business was seen as critical to global security rather than a threat to it'). For a recent discussion of the industrialist trials conducted by Allied courts with respect to Japanese defendants, see generally, Baars (n 229) 198–205.

[234] See, for example, Nuremberg Judgment (n 4) 182–183 (discussing how the Nazi regime had 'set about re-organizing the economic life of Germany' in cooperation with the German armament industry and Gustav Krupp in particular) and 243 (documenting how at least 5 million persons had been deported from the occupied territories to Germany 'to serve German industry and agriculture')

[235] See, for example, Nuremberg Judgment (n 4) 307–310 (discussing Hjalmar Schacht's provision of financing for Germany's rearmament programme; Schact was ultimately acquitted) and 320–322 (discussing Fritz Sauckel's systematic exploitation of the labour resources of the occupied territories in his role as Plenipotentiary General for the Utilization of Labor); and *USA and Others v Araki Sadao and Others*, International Military Tribunal for the Far East, Judgment (1 November 1948) reprinted in N Boister and R Cryer (eds), *Documents on the Tokyo International Military Tribunal: Charter, Indictments and Judgments*

2. The UN ad hoc tribunals

Unlike the Nuremberg and Tokyo Charters, the Statutes of the ICTY and ICTR were not expressly limited to the prosecution of high-ranking individuals, although they did refer to prosecuting persons responsible for 'serious' violations.[236] By the time of their closure, however, both tribunals had tried many of the highest-ranking political and military figures responsible for orchestrating the perpetration of crimes during the conflicts in the former Yugoslavia and Rwanda.[237] The preference for prosecuting more senior figures resulted from a combination of prosecutorial policies,[238] a favourable political landscape,[239] and pressure from the Security Council—the latter becoming increasingly interested in catalysing the tribunals' paths towards completion.[240]

At the same time, both the ICTY and ICTR also tried a range of lower- and mid-ranking individuals—primarily as a result of the pragmatic charging strategy that had been adopted in their early years of operation.[241] Prosecutor Richard Goldstone, in particular, initially adopted a 'pyramidal strategy' whereby lower-ranking suspects would be targeted first, before gradually moving up the chain of command to the political and military leaders.[242] Faced with minimal resources and inadequate support from the international community,[243] the opportunistic prosecution of lower-ranking individuals for whom evidence was available and apprehension possible was a strategy that aimed to transform what were essentially virtual tribunals into living realities.[244]

(OUP 2008) 71, pagination paras 49,793–49,795 and 49,801–49,802 (convicting two prominent financial officials in the Japanese regime: Hoshino Naoki and Kaya Okinori).

236 Article 1, ICTY Statute; Article 1, ICTR Statute. See, however, A Cassese, 'The ICTY: A Living and Vital Reality' (2004) 2 *Journal of International Criminal Justice* 585, 587 (arguing that the reference to 'serious' violations indicated that the ICTY was based on the same assumption as the Nuremberg IMT, namely that the focus of its prosecutions should be on the leaders).

237 For a statistical overview of the rank of those convicted at the ICTY and ICTR, see Smeulers et al (n 101) 27.

238 See, for example, ICTY Press Release, 'Statement by the Prosecutor Following the Withdrawal of the Charges Against 14 Accused' *Press Release CC/PIO/314-E* (8 May 1998) (outlining a strategy to focus on 'persons holding higher levels of responsibility' as well as 'those who have been personally responsible for the exceptionally brutal or otherwise extremely serious offences'); and Jallow (n 112) 152 (noting how 'OTP prosecution policy has fortunately been quite consistent over many years in targeting the governmental, political and military *leadership* which planned the genocide') (emphasis in original).

239 Bachmann and Fatić (n 31) 121–123.

240 See, for example, UN Security Council Resolution 1534, UN Doc S/RES/1534 (26 March 2004) [5]; UN Security Council Resolution 1503, UN Doc S/RES/1503 (28 August 2003) Preamble [7]; and UN Press Release, 'Security Council Endorses Proposed Strategy for Transfer to National Courts of Certain Cases Involving Humanitarian Crimes in Former Yugoslavia' *Press Release SC/7461* (23 July 2002).

241 See generally, 'Final Report of Serge Brammertz, Prosecutor of the ICTY, provided to the Security Council under paragraph 6 of Security Council resolution 1534 (2004)' Annex II to UN Doc S/2017/1001 (29 November 2017) [32]–[34] (describing how the Office of the Prosecutor initially pursued 'a combination of bottom-up and top-down investigations', before later shifting towards 'a largely top-down approach' under pressure to meet the deadline for completing investigations and new indictments by the end of 2004).

242 Cassese (n 236) 586 (explaining how this strategy was revealed to the judges of the ICTY in an *in camera* meeting on 20 January 1995).

243 Bachmann and Fatić (n 31) 91–92 and 123–124 (noting the dependency of the ICTY Prosecutor on NGO and media support in directing the focus of its investigations).

244 For instance, Richard Goldstone has stated that one of the reasons he prosecuted Duško Tadić was because he 'was the only accused available ... at a time when the judges, the media, and the international community were clamouring for [the Tribunal] to begin prosecutions' (cited in S Mohamed, 'A Neglected

In contrast to the ICTY and ICTR, the Statute of the SCSL expressly provided that the Court was established to 'prosecute persons *who bear the greatest responsibility* for serious violations of international humanitarian law',[245] a term which was understood to refer to individuals who played a leadership role within the Sierra Leonean conflict.[246] Although the SCSL Appeals Chamber held that this provision only constituted a form of guidance for the Prosecutor rather than a formal jurisdictional limitation,[247] in practice the SCSL Prosecutor indicted thirteen individuals, leading to the conviction of nine perpetrators, all of whom were high-ranking leaders, with the possible exception of Santigie Borbor Kanu who was arguably only mid-ranking.[248]

A common theme that united the charging practices at the UN ad hoc tribunals was their focus on political and military figures.[249] Only the ICTR was host to trials that concerned individuals beyond political and military personnel, including prosecutions against several religious leaders, as well as a small number of private businesspersons. The latter included the owners, directors, and senior employees of the newspaper *Kangura* and the radio station *Radio Télévision Libre des Mille Collines*,[250] which had devoted itself to broadcasting information designed to facilitate the killing of Tutsis during the genocide, as well as Alfred Musema, the director of Gisovu Tea Factory in Kibuye prefecture.[251]

Whilst these prosecutions constituted a rare attempt to illuminate the participation of private businesspersons in the commission of crimes, they reflected only a narrow picture of business involvement in the Rwandan genocide.[252] First, although

Option: The Contributions of State Responsibility for Genocide to Transitional Justice' (2009) 80 *University of Colorado Law Review* 327, 389). See also, Hagan and Levi (n 134) 1510*ff*; and van den Herik (n 39) 65.

245 Article 1, SCSL Statute.

246 See, for example, *Prosecutor v Norman et al* (Decision on the Preliminary Motion on the Lack of Personal Jurisdiction Filed on Behalf of the Accused Fofana, Trial Chamber) SCSL-2004-14-PT (3 March 2004) [40]; 'Letter dated 22 December 2000 from the President of the Security Council to the Secretary-General' UN Doc S/2000/1234 (22 December 2000) [1]. For criticism of the SCSL Prosecutor's hierarchical selectivity, see generally, Human Rights Watch, *Bringing Justice: The Special Court for Sierra Leone: Accomplishments, Shortcomings, and Needed Support* (September 2004) 19–20; and T Kelsall, *Culture under Cross-Examination: International Justice and the Special Court for Sierra Leone* (CUP 2009) 260–261.

247 *Prosecutor v Brima et al* (Judgment, Appeals Chamber) SCSL-2004-16-A (22 February 2008) [282].

248 A Smeulers et al, 'The Selection of Situations by the ICC: An Empirically Based Evaluation of the OTP's Performance' (2015) 15 *International Criminal Law Review* 1, 28.

249 See, in this regard, Ford (n 137) 67 (summarising the profiles of indictees at the ICTY); and 'Report on the Completion of the Mandate of the International Criminal Tribunal for Rwanda as at 15 November 2015' Enclosure to Letter dated 17 November 2015 from the President of the International Criminal Tribunal for Rwanda addressed to the President of the Security Council, UN Doc S/2015/884 (17 November 2015) ('ICTR Final Completion Report') Annex I (summarising the profiles of indictees at the ICTR).

250 See generally, *Nahimana et al v Prosecutor* (Judgment, Appeals Chamber) ICTR-99-52-A (28 November 2007); and *Prosecutor v Georges Ruggiu* (Judgment and Sentence, Trial Chamber) ICTR-97-32-I (1 June 2000). At the time of finalising this study, the Chief Prosecutor of the International Residual Mechanism for Criminal Tribunals (IRMCT) announced the arrest of Félicien Kabuga, long considered a key financier and enabler of the Rwandan genocide, whose case may offer further insight into the economic dimensions of the genocide. See generally, IRMCT Office of the Prosecutor 'Mechanism Fugitive Félicien Kabuga Arrested Today' *Press Release* (16 May 2020); and R Raman, 'What Is Next for Félicien Kabuga? Socratic Connivance and Rupture in International Criminal Trials' *IntLawGrrls* (21 May 2020).

251 See generally, *Prosecutor v Alfred Musema* (Judgment and Sentence, Trial Chamber) ICTR-96-13-A (27 January 2000). See also, *Prosecutor v Gaspard Kanyarukiga* (Judgment and Sentence, Trial Chamber) ICTR-2002-78-T (1 November 2010) (concerning the participation of a businessman in the Nyange Parish Church massacre).

252 See similarly, Baars (n 229) 266; and Payne et al (n 213) 75–79.

these cases concerned the participation of private businesspersons in the commission of crimes in Rwanda, several of the cases did not concern their participation *through* their typical commercial activities or *for the benefit of* their commercial operations.[253]

In addition, all the business-related cases at the ICTR concerned *local* actors, thereby ignoring the involvement of *international* business entities in the Rwanda conflict.[254] For instance, the ICTR was silent on the intervention of international business entities in the supply of arms and ammunition to the Rwandan government despite the use of such weapons for the commission of crimes.[255] In a similar vein, although the SCSL Prosecutor was open to prosecuting local political actors such as Charles Taylor for their involvement in the illicit arms and diamonds trade that fuelled the Sierra Leonean conflict,[256] the broader international networks of individuals implicated in such activities were left untouched.[257]

Also neglected by the UN ad hoc tribunals were the roles played by private security contractors. At the ICTY, for example, the Prosecutor omitted to investigate the alleged involvement of private military contractor, Military Professional Resources Inc (MPRI), in the planning of Operation Storm,[258] which formed the focus of the ICTY case of *Gotovina et al.*[259] In a similar vein, the SCSL Prosecutor failed to investigate Sandline International,[260] which had been contracted to restore ousted President Kabbah's regime to power after it had been toppled in May 1997 and whose shipment

[253] See similarly, van der Wilt (n 225) 67; and H Vest, 'Business Leaders and the Modes of Individual Criminal Responsibility under International Law' (2010) 8 *Journal of International Criminal Justice* 851, 858 and 871.

[254] See, for example, AL Des Forges, *"Leave None to Tell the Story": Genocide in Rwanda* (Human Rights Watch 1999) 988–990 (documenting commercial arms transactions during the Rwandan genocide).

[255] Indeed, arms trading in general received only passing mention in the judgments of the ICTR. See, for example, *Prosecutor v Bagosora et al* (Judgment and Sentence, Trial Chamber) ICTR-98-41-T (18 December 2008) [1963]–[1965] (confirming instances when the Minister of Defence of the Seychelles had provided arms to Bagosora in June 1994); and *Prosecutor v Bizimungu et al* (Judgment and Sentence, Trial Chamber) ICTR-99-50-T (30 September 2011) [1018] (noting that there was not a sufficient basis to conclude that Bizimungu was sent to Zaire on 12 April 1994 to buy weapons and did purchase them).

[256] See, for example, *Taylor* Trial Judgment (n 156) Chapter VIII(F) (discussing the defendant's involvement in the supply of arms and ammunition) and Chapter VIII(G) (discussing the defendant's involvement in diamonds trading).

[257] See, for example, 'Report of the Panel of Experts appointed pursuant to Security Council resolution 1306 (2000), paragraph 19, in relation to Sierra Leone' UN Doc S/2000/1195 (20 December 2000) [129] (identifying evidence that a number of companies may have been illicitly exporting smuggled Sierra Leonean conflict diamonds out of Liberia) and [195], [213], and [253] (identifying evidence of supply lines of weapons sourced from Eastern Europe to the RUF through Burkina Faso and Niger, including the individual arms brokers and intermediaries involved); and Human Rights Watch, *World Report 2004: Human Rights and Armed Conflict* (2004) 280–281 (noting how the RUF was heavily backed with weapons and other support by the government of Charles Taylor in Liberia, with the help of regional allies such as Burkina Faso, as well as arms suppliers such as Ukraine that were willing to sell weapons without asking any questions).

[258] See generally, PW Singer, *Corporate Warriors: The Rise of the Privatized Military Industry* (Cornell University Press 2008) 119–135 (discussing MPRI's involvement in the conflict in the former Yugoslavia).

[259] See, in this regard, *Prosecutor v Gotovina et al* (Transcript, Trial Chamber) IT-06-90-T (6 June 2008) 4438–4439 (in which UN Commander Alain Forand confirmed his view that MPRI had helped plan Operation Storm); and C Lehnhardt, 'Individual Liability of Private Military Personnel under International Criminal Law' (2008) 19 *European Journal of International Law* 1015, 1022–1024 (examining MPRI's potential criminal responsibility for Operation Storm).

[260] At the SCSL, Sandline was only briefly referred to in the *Taylor* judgment regarding its mining activities in the region. *Taylor* Trial Judgment (n 156) [3055], [3059], and [5843].

of arms to Sierra Leone had been held by Britain's Customs and Excise agency to be in violation of a UN arms embargo that had been in place at the time.[261] Whilst these cases may have suffered from evidentiary challenges and fallen beyond the prosecutorial policy of targeting persons who bear the greatest responsibility for crimes, their omission rendered juridically invisible some of the business activities that had fuelled the violence in these conflicts.

3. The ICC

At the ICC, the general policy of the Prosecutor has also been to target those most responsible for the commission of crimes within particular situations, including the leaders of armed groups and heads of State.[262] In the early years of the ICC's operation, the Prosecutor developed a 'consensual division of labour' policy,[263] pursuant to which the ICC would focus on prosecutions of 'the leaders who bear most responsibility for the crimes', whilst encouraging national prosecutions of lower-ranking perpetrators.[264] According to Sarah Nouwen, this policy has been so successfully marketed that 'the international jargon of "the big fish" for the international courts and "the small fry" for national mechanisms is literally being vernacularized'.[265]

More recently, however, the ICC Prosecutor has indicated that due to limitations in investigative possibilities and cooperation challenges, the Prosecutor is open to first investigating and prosecuting a limited number of mid- and high-level perpetrators, as well as lower-level perpetrators where their conduct has been particularly grave and has acquired extensive notoriety, before 'gradually building upwards' to prosecute the most responsible.[266] In fact, on several occasions, the ICC Prosecutor has already demonstrated a willingness to prosecute lower-level individuals for relatively narrow forms of criminality where access to both evidence and the accused has proven attractive—the prosecution of Ahmad Al-Mahdi for the destruction of religious and cultural monuments being a pertinent illustration.[267]

The ICC Prosecutor has also followed the path of its predecessors by consistently targeting political and military figures to the neglect of private businesspersons. However, private businesspersons have not completely escaped the Prosecutor's attention. For example, the ICC Prosecutor recently confirmed her intention to 'give

[261] Singer (n 258) 115; A Buncombe et al, 'Inquiry Finds Sandline Did Breach Arms Embargo' *The Independent* (17 May 1998). The Attorney-General for England and Wales ultimately declined to open criminal proceedings. See 'Sandline Not to Face Prosecution' *BBC* (31 May 1998).

[262] See, for example, XA Aranburu, 'Gravity of Crimes and Responsibility of the Suspect', in M Bergsmo (ed), *Criteria for Prioritizing and Selecting Core International Crime Cases* (2nd edn, Torkel Opsahl Academic EPublisher 2010) 205, 227–228 (calculating that in the first five years of its work, 77 per cent of the accused were high-ranking, 23 per cent mid-ranking, and none at the lowest-ranking level).

[263] ICC Office of the Prosecutor, 'Statement made by Mr. Luis Moreno-Ocampo, Chief Prosecutor' *Ceremony for the Solemn Undertaking of the Chief Prosecutor of the International Criminal Court* (16 June 2003) 3.

[264] ICC OTP Policy Issues Paper (n 111) 3. See similarly, ICC Office of the Prosecutor, 'Prosecutorial Strategy: 2009–2012' (1 February 2010) ('ICC OTP Strategy 2009–2012') [19].

[265] Nouwen (n 79) 344 (specifically referring to examples from Uganda and Sudan).

[266] ICC Office of the Prosecutor, 'Strategic Plan: June 2012–2015' (11 October 2013) [22]; ICC OTP Strategic Plan 2016–2018 (n 109) [34]; and ICC Office of the Prosecutor, 'Strategic Plan: 2019–2021' (17 July 2019) [24].

[267] Whiting (n 201).

particular consideration to prosecuting Rome Statute crimes that are committed by means of, or that result in, *inter alia*, the destruction of the environment, the illegal exploitation of natural resources or the illegal dispossession of land',[268] a focus which several commentators have suggested may provide an opportunity for private business personnel implicated in such crimes to be targeted for prosecution.[269]

In addition, as far back as 2003, then-ICC Prosecutor Luis Moreno-Ocampo expressed his concern that atrocities allegedly committed in the DRC 'may be fuelled by the exploitation of natural resources ... and the arms trade, which are enabled through the international banking system', and stated his belief that 'investigation of the financial aspects of the alleged atrocities will be crucial to prevent future crimes and for the prosecution of crimes already committed'.[270] Later, the Prosecutor announced that his office would 'work together with national investigators and prosecutors in order to determine the contribution, if any, that ... businesses are making to the commission of the crimes in the DRC', specifically referring to the precedents set by the trials of the German industrialists in the aftermath of the Second World War.[271] Moreover, in the context of discussing the investigations being conducted in the Kivu provinces of the DRC, the Prosecutor explained that his mandate was 'to go up the chain of command to those most responsible, to those who ordered *and financed* the violence'.[272] Yet, despite evidence of business involvement in the commission of crimes in the DRC revealed in a range of UN expert reports,[273] to date the ICC Prosecutor's efforts have been limited to encouraging and supporting national prosecutions of private businesspersons through its Law Enforcement Network rather than launching international prosecutions itself.[274] As a result, private businesspersons have been notable only for their absence at the ICC, the resource struggles underpinning mass

[268] ICC OTP Policy Paper on Case Selection and Prioritisation (n 105) [41].

[269] See, for example, T Smith, 'Why the International Criminal Court is Right to Focus on the Environment' *The Conversation* (23 September 2016); and AFP 'ICC Prosecutors Put New Focus on Ecological Harm, Land Grabs' *Justice Info* (15 September 2016).

[270] ICC Office of the Prosecutor, 'Communications Received by the Office of the Prosecutor of the ICC' *Press Release No.pids.009-2003-EN* (16 July 2003) 3–4.

[271] ICC Office of the Prosecutor, 'The Prosecutor on the Co-operation with Congo and other States regarding the situation in Ituri, DRC' *Press Release ICC-OTP-20030926-37* (26 September 2003).

[272] ICC Office of the Prosecutor, 'Keynote Address: Mr Luis Moreno-Ocampo, Prosecutor of the International Criminal Court' *Interdisciplinary Colloquium: Sexual Violence as International Crime: Interdisciplinary Approaches to Evidence* (16 June 2009) 9 (emphasis added). See similarly, ICC OTP Strategy 2009–2012 (n 264) [19].

[273] See generally, 'Report of the Panel of Experts on the Illegal Exploitation of Natural Resources and Other Forms of Wealth of the Democratic Republic of the Congo' UN Doc S/2001/357 (12 April 2001); 'Final Report of the Panel of Experts on the Illegal Exploitation of Natural Resources and Other Forms of Wealth of the Democratic Republic of the Congo' UN Doc S/2002/1146 (16 October 2002); 'Report of the Panel of Experts on the Illegal Exploitation of Natural Resources and Other Forms of Wealth of the Democratic Republic of the Congo' UN Doc S/2003/1027 (23 October 2003); and Office of the UN High Commissioner for Human Rights, 'Report of the Mapping Exercise documenting the most serious violations of human rights and international humanitarian law committed within the territory of the Democratic Republic of the Congo between March 1993 and June 2003' (August 2010).

[274] On the work of the Law Enforcement Network, see generally, R Gallmetzer, 'Prosecuting Persons Doing Business with Armed Groups in Conflict Areas: The Strategy of the Office of the Prosecutor of the International Criminal Court' (2010) 8 *Journal of International Criminal Justice* 947. See also, ICC OTP Strategic Plan 2016–2018 (n 109) [30] (calling for the global community to focus its attention on the connection between international crimes and 'other forms of transnational or organized criminal activity').

atrocity situations receiving a mere passing mention in the background sections to its judgments.[275]

C. Procedural Selectivity

In international criminal courts, it is not possible to prosecute individuals who are unfit to stand trial or have passed away. Since no mechanisms exist for rendering judgments posthumously, in such circumstances international criminal courts are denied the possibility of constructing historical narratives in their judgments. Importantly, this form of selectivity is not limited to defendants that pass away prior to indictment, but also encompasses those who are indicted but die prior to their verdict being rendered.

In practice, selectivity that results from unfitness to stand trial or death prior to verdict is not uncommon at international criminal courts.[276] At the Nuremberg IMT, for example, the most prominent absentees were Hitler, Himmler, and Goebbels who had committed suicide prior to apprehension.[277] In addition, as already discussed, Gustav Krupp's unfitness to stand trial undermined the Prosecution's business case at Nuremberg. At the ICTY, ten individuals were reported deceased prior to being transferred to the tribunal, while a further seven passed away after transfer—a mortality rate of approximately 10 per cent of those indicted.[278] Amongst those who passed away prior to being indicted were Arkan, the leader of the Arkan Tigers, who was murdered in Belgrade in January 2000,[279] as well as Franjo Tudjman, the former President of Croatia.[280] Arguably the most high profile death, however, was Slobodan Milošević, former President of Serbia and the Federal Republic of Yugoslavia, who passed away four years after the commencement of his trial.[281] At the ICTR, four indictees died

[275] See, for example, *Lubanga* Trial Judgment (n 175) [76]. See also, JG Stewart, 'Commerce and Atrocity: The Elephant in the Room' *Blog of James G Stewart* (5 March 2015) (noting that while the ICC has charged various military actors with the war crime of pillaging, it has 'turned a blind eye to the mountain of evidence that foreign companies were responsible for precisely the same war crime in the same region, with far worse consequences for local populations').

[276] For a statistical overview, see generally, Smeulers et al (n 248) 19.

[277] Ibid 36.

[278] 'Key Figures of ICTY Cases' *ICTY Website*, accessible at: https://www.icty.org/en/cases/key-figures-cases (last accessed 2 June 2020).

[279] Smeulers et al (n 248) 36.

[280] See, in this regard, Bachmann and Fatić (n 31) 131 (noting that the decision not to indict President Tudjman appears to have been the result of 'initiatives taken on behalf of the Croatian president by his diplomats', whilst also observing that former ICTY Prosecutor Carla Del Ponte has claimed that she would have indicted Tudjman had he not died in 1999).

[281] According to Marko Hoare, a former research officer in the ICTY's Office of the Prosecutor, a number of senior individuals within the former Yugoslav and Serb leadership—including Velko Kadijević, Blagoje Adzić, Borisav Jović, Branko Kostić, Momir Bulatović, and others—who had initially been included in a draft collective indictment together with Slobodan Milošević for crimes committed in Bosnia, were ultimately excluded and never indicted. Their exclusion resulted from the intervention of former ICTY Prosecutor Carla Del Ponte, whom Hoare suggests was primarily concerned with what was deemed important by the public, which she believed had no significant interest in the prosecution of individuals less notorious than Milošević. See generally, MA Hoare, 'Florence Hartmann's 'Peace and Punishment' *Greater Surbiton: The Perfect is the Enemy of the Good* (10 January 2008).

before or during trial,[282] while at the SCSL, two individuals—Foday Saybana Sankoh, leader of the RUF, and Sam Bockarie, former Battlefield Commander of the RUF—died prior to trial, and another—Sam Hinga Norman, leader of the CDF—passed away during trial. In addition, another indictee—Johnny Paul Koroma, former leader of the AFRC—remains at large though is suspected to have passed away.[283] Finally, at the ICC, a number of cases have been terminated as a result of death, including:[284] Muammar Gaddafi, former Head of State of Libya; Saleh Mohammed Jerbo Jamus, the Sudanese Liberation Army-Unity's Chief of Staff; Raska Lukwiya, Deputy Army Commander of the LRA; and Okot Odhiambo, Deputy Army Commander of the LRA.

Whether from unfitness to stand trial or death, the termination of international criminal proceedings prior to judgment amounts to an 'interrupted performance'.[285] As Mark Drumbl explains, 'When the antagonist dies before the protagonist's pursuit is complete, the script becomes frustrated. The performance reaches an end, but it is an anti-climax.'[286] At the same time, it is important to recognise that the termination of a case may be mitigated in two respects.

First, the judgment is not the only aspect of international criminal proceedings that has historical value. For instance, where a case is terminated after at least part of the trial has been conducted, the proceedings retain expressive significance. According to Timothy Waters, for example, 'the residuum of a terminated trial has uses—the accumulated transcripts, exhibits, briefs, orders, and interim decisions constitute an archive with a meticulously documented provenance that any historian would value'.[287]

Second, judicial narratives relevant to the substance of terminated cases may ultimately be constructed in the judgments of other cases that represent the products of full trials. Christian Nielsen, for example, has revealed how judgments at the ICTY have managed to contribute to the historical record concerning Slobodan Milošević's role in the conflicts in the former Yugoslavia, despite the termination of Milošević's own trial due to his untimely death.[288]

Without diminishing the importance of these mitigating factors, however, the termination of a case prior to judgment remains an obstacle in struggles for historical justice—one that can inhibit the pursuit of judicial validation of particular interpretations of the past.[289]

282 This figure has been calculated on the basis of: ICTR Final Completion Report (n 249) [10]; and IRMCT Office of the Prosecutor, 'Mechanism Prosecutor Serge Brammertz Confirms the Death of Fugitive Augustin Bizimana' *Press Release* (22 May 2020).

283 No Peace Without Justice, *Impact and Legacy Survey for the Special Court for Sierra Leone* (August 2012) 9–10.

284 The ICC still lists Vincent Otti, former deputy-leader of the LRA, as 'at large' even though he is also believed to have passed away in January 2008.

285 Drumbl (n 11) 177.

286 Ibid.

287 TW Waters, 'A Kind of Judgment: Searching for Judicial Narratives After Death' (2010) 42 *George Washington International Law Review* 279, 297.

288 CA Nielsen, 'Can We Salvage a History of the Former Yugoslav Conflicts from the Milošević Trial?', in T Waters (ed), *The Milošević Trial: An Autopsy* (OUP 2014) 326. See also, Steinke (n 15) 21, fn 69 (noting that former ICTY Prosecutor Carla Del Ponte has admitted that the indictment of Jadranko Prlić and five other Bosnian Croats was 'an indictment by proxy' since the highest-level Croat leaders around former President Tudjman had passed away).

289 See similarly, Waters (n 287) 298 ('the particular problem posed by Milošević is the lack of final authority and the consequent search—at least by those convinced that judgment matters—for an alternative').

III. Defence Strategies of Rupture and Rebuttal

Given the predominant alignment of the charging practices of international prosecutors with the balance of power between and within States, defendants and their counsel have sometimes deployed particular strategies in an effort to counter this hegemonic orientation. This section examines two such strategies—those of rupture and rebuttal—and identifies the extent to which they have influenced the orientation of the historical narratives constructed by international criminal courts in their judgments.

A. Strategies of Rupture

Strategies of rupture have sometimes been deployed by defendants and their counsel in an effort to undermine the legitimacy of the trial process by diverting attention away from the acts of the defendant towards atrocities allegedly committed by the States on whose behalf the prosecution is conducted.[290] This strategy was famously developed by French advocate Jacques Vergès, who revealed how a defence could be conducted in the form of an attack on the system represented by the prosecution.[291] Specifically, a strategy of rupture entails the construction of a historical counter-narrative to the prosecution's case, one which does not necessarily exonerate the defendant of wrongdoing, but rather contextualises his or her conduct by drawing attention to atrocities allegedly committed by the trial's architects.[292] By illuminating the atrocities of other actors, the defence attempts to transform the conviction of the defendant into a form of martyrdom, elevating the significance of its own counter-narrative rendered at trial above the narrative ultimately constructed in the court's final judgment.[293] As Vergès put it, the trial is used 'less to acquit the accused than to illuminate his ideas'.[294]

Within international criminal courts, such a strategy was deployed by Slobodan Milošević who notoriously used the courtroom of the ICTY to draw attention to the alleged criminality of the NATO bombing campaign against the Federal Republic of Yugoslavia in 1999 and divert attention from his own alleged wrongdoing. At his initial appearance, for example, Milošević dismissed the trial as an attempt 'to produce

[290] See generally, Simpson (n 6) 98–101; and M Koskenniemi, 'From Impunity to Show Trials' (2002) 6 *Max Planck Yearbook of United Nations Law* 1, 26–32.

[291] Koskenniemi (n 290) 26.

[292] A Branch, *Displacing Human Rights: War and Intervention in Northern Uganda* (OUP 2011) 214.

[293] F Mégret, 'Practices of Stigmatization' (2013) 76 *Law and Contemporary Problems* 287, 312–314; and R Cockayne, 'Hybrids or Mongrels? Internationalized War Crimes Trials as Unsuccessful Degradation Ceremonies' (2005) 4 *Journal of Human Rights* 455, 467–468.

[294] J Vergès, *De La Stratégie Judiciaire* (Les Éditions de Minuit 1968) 104, cited in and translated by R Knox, 'Strategy and Tactics' (2010) 21 *Finnish Yearbook of International Law* 193, 225. See also Koskenniemi (n 290) 16–17 ('When a trial concerns large political events, it will necessarily involve an interpretation of the context which is precisely what is disputed in the individual actions that are the object of the trial'); and Veitch (n 17) 157 ('Trials of this type tend to make visible what ordinarily remains hidden: the terms on which people are called to account and the conditions to which they must submit for the judgment of the courts').

false justification for the war crimes of NATO committed in Yugoslavia',[295] a position that he would continue to advance in subsequent hearings as well as at trial.[296]

What is striking about rupture arguments is how little influence they have tended to have over the narratives ultimately constructed in the judgments of international criminal courts. International criminal courts have consistently and quite understandably rejected any notion of comparative fault in their proceedings—declining to recognise any 'doctrinal device for mitigating the wrongdoing or culpability of the accused in light of the accusers'.[297] As such, when defendants and their counsel have attempted to support their rupture arguments by adducing evidence aimed at illuminating the commission of atrocities by the accused's adversaries, such evidence has generally been robustly rejected. Such efforts have tended to be dismissed as attempts by defence counsel to advance a *tu quoque* ('you also') defence,[298] namely a plea that the commission of atrocities by the adversary should offer a substantive defence for the commission of similar atrocities by the accused.[299] In response to such efforts, international criminal courts have consistently characterised substantive *tu quoque* arguments as 'flawed in principle' and consequently dismissed attempts by the defence to advance them in practice.[300]

Nonetheless, it should be remembered that the primary target audience of the counter-narratives put forward as part of strategies of rupture is not the judges within the courtroom, but the public beyond it.[301] Consequently, the success of such strategies tends not to hinge on their *legal* acceptance, but on their ability to *transmit* counter-narratives to various audiences beyond the courtroom.[302]

B. Strategies of Rebuttal

Whilst strategies of rupture have primarily targeted audiences *beyond* the courtroom, defence counsel have also resorted to other strategies that seek to influence the narratives constructed *within* international criminal judgments. Rather than using atrocities committed by other actors as a means of *rupturing* the legitimacy of the trial process, defence counsel have instead deployed such evidence to *rebut* the prosecution's theory of the case. In particular, such evidence has been relied upon

[295] *Prosecutor v Slobodan Milošević* (Transcript, Trial Chamber) IT-02-54-T (3 July 2001) 4.

[296] G Boas, *The Milošević Trial: Lessons for the Conduct of Complex International Criminal Proceedings* (CUP 2007) 10–11.

[297] M Osiel, *Mass Atrocity, Collective Memory, and the Law* (Transaction Publishers 1997) 123.

[298] See generally, S Yee, 'The *Tu Quoque* Argument as Defence to International Crimes, Prosecution or Punishment' (2004) 3 *Chinese Journal of International Law* 87; MC Bassiouni, *Introduction to International Criminal Law* (2nd edn, Martinus Nijhoff Publishers 2013) 465–470.

[299] *Prosecutor v Kupreškić et al* (Judgment, Trial Chamber) IT-95-16-T (14 January 2000) [515]; and *Prosecutor v Kupreškić et al* (Decision on Evidence of the Good Character of the Accused and the Defence of Tu Quoque, Trial Chamber) IT-95-16 (17 February 1999).

[300] *Kupreškić et al* Decision Tu Quoque (n 299). See similarly, *Kupreškić et al* Trial Judgment (n 299) [515]–[520]; *Prosecutor v Limaj et al* (Judgment, Trial Chamber) IT-03-66-T (30 November 2005) [193]; and *Prosecutor v Milan Martić* (Judgment, Appeals Chamber) IT-95-11-A (8 October 2008) [111].

[301] See similarly, Mégret (n 293) 314; and Cryer (n 20) 202.

[302] O Kirchheimer, *Political Justice: The Use of Legal Procedure for Political Ends* (Princeton University Press 1961) 337.

either to obtain an interpretation of the applicable law that is favourable to the accused or to raise doubts concerning the evidence adduced by the prosecution. To illustrate the extent to which this strategy can influence the narratives constructed by international criminal courts, it is useful to turn to two examples.

The first example concerns the trial of German Admiral Dönitz at the Nuremberg IMT.[303] One of the counts against Dönitz was for 'crimes against persons and property on the high seas'. Dönitz's legal counsel, Otto Kranzbühler, had reason to believe that the prosecution would argue that Dönitz had violated the London Submarine Protocol of 1936 by waging unrestricted submarine warfare through the practice of frequently sinking British and other merchant ships in the Atlantic without warning. Kranzbühler also had reason to believe, however, that the US Navy, under the command of Admiral Nimitz, had routinely engaged in identical practices by sinking Japanese merchant ships without warning. As such, two months prior to start of trial, Kranzbühler requested permission from the tribunal to send an interrogatory to Admiral Nimitz. The prosecution objected on the ground that Kranzbühler was attempting to raise a *tu quoque* defence. However, Kranzbühler dismissed this suggestion, instead arguing that his intention was 'to establish that the American Admiralty in practice interpreted the London Agreement in exactly the same way as the German Admiralty, and thus prove that the German sea war was perfectly legal'.[304] In other words, Kranzbühler sought to rely on the evidence as an interpretative aid, rather than for a *tu quoque* defence.

The tribunal allowed the questionnaire to be sent to Admiral Nimitz. Upon its return, the questionnaire confirmed that it had been customary practice for the US Navy to attack Japanese merchant ships without warning. In its judgment, the tribunal rejected Kranzbühler's argument regarding the legality of unrestricted submarine warfare, finding that Admiral Dönitz *had* violated the London Submarine Protocol of 1936. However, the tribunal also held that, in light of both British and US naval practices, the sentence of Dönitz would not be assessed on the ground of his violations of the international law of submarine warfare.[305]

What this case reveals, therefore, is that it may be possible to adduce evidence concerning atrocities committed by other actors in the conflict if it is relevant to the interpretation of the applicable law. Moreover, even if the defence is unsuccessful in its legal arguments in this regard, such evidence may nonetheless serve to mitigate the sentence of the accused.[306] In the process, the narrative frame of the court may be expanded to illuminate atrocities allegedly committed by other parties to the conflict.

Beyond influencing the applicable law, defence counsel have also deployed evidence of atrocities committed by other actors to cast doubt on evidence adduced by the prosecution.[307] In the case of *Bagosora et al*, for example, the ICTR Prosecutor argued that

[303] This paragraph draws on Telford Taylor's summary of the proceedings: Taylor (n 219) 399–409.
[304] Ibid 400.
[305] Nuremberg Judgment (n 4) 313.
[306] See similarly, Yee (n 298) 109–113; and Wilson (n 150) 162–167.
[307] A further example of this strategy is the unsuccessful attempts made by several defendants at the ICTY to dismiss allegations that Albanians had been systematically expelled from Kosovo by Serbian armed forces by laying the blame on both the Kosovo Liberation Army as well as the airstrikes undertaken by NATO. See, for example, *Prosecutor v Šainović et al* (Judgment, Appeals Chamber) IT-05-87-A (23 January

four military leaders had conspired to commit genocide prior to its commencement in Rwanda in 1994. During the trial, the Prosecutor claimed that its evidence revealed a growing and developing preparedness on the part of the accused to commit genocide from late 1990, which later crystallised into a conspiracy to commit genocide several months or possibly even a year prior to its commencement in April 1994.[308] The prosecution's case was primarily circumstantial, relying on statements made by the accused, their affiliation with clandestine organisations, as well as their role in the preparation of lists and military training of civilians.[309]

In order to undermine the prosecution's conspiracy narrative, the defence sought to advance an alternative explanation for the Rwandan genocide.[310] Rather than the result of a plan or conspiracy by the former Rwandan government or military, the defence argued that the wave of civilian killings had been more spontaneous with primary responsibility lying with the RPF. Specifically, the defence argued that the RPF had shot down President Habyarimana's plane, using it as a pretext for plunging the country into civil war and decisively seizing power. According to the defence, the RPF were aware that the resumption of war would lead to massive civilian casualties, in light of the fear and mistrust that had been generated in the region by the recent assassination of Burundi's first elected Hutu President in October 1993 and the subsequent massacres of tens of thousands of civilians by the Burundian Tutsi-dominated army. As such, the defence submitted that it was the RPF that bore responsibility for triggering the massacres that unfolded in Rwanda, not the so-called Hutu extremists.

The strategy of the defence in *Bagosora et al* is significant for several reasons. First, it is notable that the defence was able to persuade the Trial Chamber to allow it to adduce at least *some* evidence relating to the attack on President Habyarimana's plane, despite the Chamber emphasising that responsibility for the crash was merely 'a collateral issue in the case'.[311] In particular, the defence was successful in convincing the Trial Chamber that evidence pertaining to the fact of the shooting down of the plane was 'undoubtedly a matter of contextual significance' for the events described in the indictment against the accused, even if detailed information concerning the responsibility of any particular person for the attack was not.[312] As such, the case illustrates how the defence may be able to successfully enlarge the narrative frame of an international criminal trial by linking broader contextual evidence to the events set out in the indictment.

2014) [395], [480], [493], and [616]–[626]; and *Prosecutor v Slobodan Milošević* (Transcript, Trial Chamber) IT-02-54-T (14 February 2002) 253.

308 *Bagosora et al* Trial Judgment and Sentence (n 255) [2094].
309 Ibid [2097].
310 Ibid [2092].
311 Ibid [1997].
312 *Prosecutor v Bagosora et al* (Decision on Request for Subpoenas of United Nations Officials, Trial Chamber) ICTR-98-41-T (6 October 2006) [17]. See also, *Prosecutor v Bagosora et al* (Decision on Disclosure of Defence Witness Statements in Possession of the Prosecution Pursuant to Rule 68(A), Trial Chamber) ICTR-98-41-T (8 March 2006) [6]; *Prosecutor v Bagosora et al* (Decision on Ntabukuze Motion for Disclosure of Prosecution Files, Trial Chamber) ICTR-98-41-T (6 October 2006) [3]–[4]; and *Prosecutor v Bagosora et al* (Decision on Request for Cooperation of the Government of France, Trial Chamber) ICTR-98-41-T (6 October 2006) [4]–[6].

Second, it is also possible that the defence's strategy of broadening the narrative frame of the trial contributed to the acquittal of the accused for the charge of conspiracy to commit genocide in the Trial Chamber's judgment. Since the prosecution's case concerning the conspiracy charge had relied on circumstantial evidence, the Trial Chamber could only convict the accused if the crime of conspiracy to commit genocide was 'the only reasonable inference' that could be drawn from the evidence.[313] Yet, by drawing the Trial Chamber's attention to the periodic resumption of hostilities between October 1990 and April 1994 between the RPF and the Rwandan government, the defence had provided 'a context' for the Chamber's assessment of the prosecution's evidence concerning the preparation of lists and the creation of civilian militias and 'raised some doubt as to whether they were at their inception intended for genocidal purposes'.[314] As such, since conspiracy to commit genocide was not the only reasonable inference that could be drawn from its evidence, the Trial Chamber concluded that the prosecution had failed to prove beyond reasonable doubt that the four accused had conspired to commit genocide prior to its commencement on 7 April 1994.[315]

At the same time, it is important to recognise the limits of the defence's strategy. In particular, the strategy had not persuaded the Trial Chamber to engage with the defence's counter-narrative on its merits. For instance, the Chamber declined to express any view on who the perpetrators of the attack on President Habyarimana's plane might have been, an issue that was understandably considered to have no bearing on the criminal responsibility of the accused.[316] Moreover, the Chamber noted that the evidence adduced by the defence concerning atrocities allegedly committed by the RPF had generally been considered irrelevant to the core issues in the case.[317] As such, while it is significant that the Chamber acquitted the four accused of the crime of conspiracy to commit genocide, it is equally the case that the defence failed to obtain an official endorsement of its counter-narrative concerning how the genocide had unfolded or any examination of the atrocities allegedly committed by the RPF. What this case seems to suggest, therefore, is that the most defence counsel can hope for in such circumstances is the destabilisation of the prosecution's narrative, albeit without further securing a firm validation of their own counter-narrative.

IV. Conclusion

Reflecting on situational and case selectivity before international criminal courts, a common pattern emerges—the orientation of international prosecutions against

[313] *Bagosora et al* Trial Judgment and Sentence (n 255) [2110].

[314] Ibid [1995].

[315] Ibid [2113]. The ICTR has acquitted other individuals of conspiracy to commit genocide prior to its commencement. See, for example, *Prosecutor v Juvénal Kajelijeli* (Judgment and Sentence, Trial Chamber) ICTR-98-44A-T (1 December 2003) [449] and [794]–[796]; *Prosecutor v Ndindiliyimana et al* (Judgment and Sentence, Trial Chamber) ICTR-00-56 (17 May 2011) [2069]; and *Prosecutor v Édouard Karemera and Mathieu Ngirumpatse* (Judgment, Appeals Chamber) ICTR-98-44-A (29 September 2014) [731]–[742].

[316] *Bagosora et al* Trial Judgment and Sentence (n 255) [1997].

[317] Ibid [2000]–[2001].

particular individuals in accordance with imbalances of power that exist between and within States. While accident has played a role, particularly where a suspect or defendant has passed away prior to prosecution or judgment, a clear thread running through the charging practices of international prosecutors is the dominant influence of the political context in which they operate. Whilst international prosecutors may strive to emancipate themselves from the interstate world, they are ultimately inescapably dependent on it to function in practice.[318] Whether by means of formally delimiting the jurisdictional requirements by which situations and cases have been defined and selected or by exerting more informal pressure through the obstruction or selective provision of cooperation, the balance of power between and within States beyond the courtroom has had a profound impact on the orientation of international prosecutions within it.

For their part, defendants and their counsel have sometimes deployed strategies of rupture and rebuttal in an effort to counter the hegemonic orientation of international prosecutions; however, whilst such strategies may have had some impact beyond the courtroom, they have generally had limited influence on the narrative orientation of international criminal judgments. As a result, the narratives constructed by international criminal courts generally constitute apologetic historical accounts that tend to accord with the interests of States on whose cooperation international prosecutors have been reliant and/or which are particularly powerful within the international community more generally.[319] In other words, rather than transcending imbalances of power between and within States, the prosecutorial focus of international criminal courts has generally replicated and even reinforced their patterns of domination.[320] As Mégret has succinctly put it, 'rather than speaking truth to power, [international criminal courts] can legitimately be suspected of having spoken a certain truth *of* power'.[321]

[318] See similarly, Kendall (n 69) 132; Rodman (n 132) 440; and J Hoover, 'Moral Practices: Assigning Responsibility in the International Criminal Court' (2013) 76 *Law and Contemporary Problems* 263, 283.

[319] G Simpson, 'International Criminal Justice and the Past', in G Boas et al, *International Criminal Justice: Legitimacy and Coherence* (Edward Elgar 2012) 123, 140.

[320] Nouwen (n 64) 179.

[321] Mégret (n 13) 34 (emphasis in original).

4
The Crime Question

Categories of crime are central to the scope and content of the historical narratives constructed within the judgments of international criminal courts. In practice, these categories perform a dual narrative function, not only defining the specific harms for which accused persons are called to answer, but also influencing which aspects of their social context will be rendered visible in the process. Importantly, regardless of whether an accused person is ultimately held responsible for participating in the commission of a particular crime, the process of determining whether a crime has occurred remains a significant part of the historical function of international criminal courts. As David Luban explains, 'it is the acts of exposing the deeds, categorizing them as crimes, and naming exactly which crime they are that are the central point of the international proceeding'.[1] It is this 'crime question' that forms the focus of the present chapter.

Much ink has been spilled on the question of what is meant by an 'international crime', a term that has been subject to a diversity of taxonomies as well as a range of theories seeking to identify the unifying characteristics shared by every offence with a claim to categorisation within its scope.[2] Without diminishing the importance of those debates, this chapter is concerned with examining the range and definition of crimes which have been adjudicated within the international criminal courts that form the focus of this study, regardless of their precise designation as 'international crimes'.

With few exceptions,[3] the crimes adjudicated by the courts under examination in this study generally share a common structural form, comprised of two components:[4] first, a list of prohibited acts, which are either criminal offences in domestic legal systems (for example, murder or rape) or forms of illegal conduct defined in international rules (for example, the use of prohibited weapons or persecution); and second, a collective or contextual element, which defines the collective dimensions of the crime or the context in which the prohibited acts are committed. From a narrative perspective, this structure is significant, enabling actors to surface and contest both the individual and collective interests protected by these crimes.[5]

[1] D Luban, 'State Criminality and the Ambition of International Criminal Law', in T Isaacs and R Vernon (eds), *Accountability for Collective Wrongdoing* (CUP 2011) 61, 74.

[2] See generally, R O'Keefe, *International Criminal Law* (OUP 2015) Chapter 2; and C Stahn, *A Critical Introduction to International Criminal Law* (CUP 2019) 15–22.

[3] Article 5 of the Statute of the SCSL empowered the Special Court to prosecute persons who had committed certain crimes under Sierra Leonean law, though these were not prosecuted in practice.

[4] See generally, A Cassese et al, *Cassese's International Criminal Law* (3rd edn, OUP 2013) 37–38; K Ambos, *Treatise on International Criminal Law: Volume I: Foundations and General Part* (OUP 2013) 84–86.

[5] Ambos (n 4) 65–67; and C Laverty, 'What Lies Beneath? The Turn to Values in International Criminal Legal Discourse' *EJIL Talk!* (23 April 2018).

Doing Justice to History. Barrie Sander, Oxford University Press (2021). © Barrie Sander.
DOI: 10.1093/oso/9780198846871.003.0004

In practice, determining the range and definition of crimes adjudicated by an international criminal court is not a neutral process, but reflects choices and historical patterns that prioritise certain interests and voices at the expense of others.[6] In other words, the inclusions and exclusions, as well as the meaning, of the crimes adjudicated within international criminal courts are not random, but the outcome of an intense struggle between different actors interacting against a background of contextual constraints.[7]

This chapter examines this struggle by focusing on three junctures in international criminal justice processes: the *drafting* of statutory frameworks; the scope and focus of *charges* brought against accused persons; and the *interpretation* of crime categories in judicial decisions and judgments in light of the arguments advanced by the antagonists within the proceedings. By examining the relative influence of different actors at these junctures in a variety of institutional contexts, this chapter reveals consistencies and discontinuities in the range of crime categories adjudicated within international criminal courts, variability in the strategies and practices that have defined the scope and focus of charges brought against accused persons, and fluidity in the meanings attached to different categories of crime.[8] Through this analysis, the chapter reveals how the scope and content of the historical narratives constructed within international criminal courts are shaped to a significant extent by struggles for control over the selection and definition of categories of crime.

The chapter is structured into five sections. The chapter begins by examining the crimes adjudicated within each of the three sets of international criminal courts that form the focus of this study: the Nuremberg International Military Tribunal (IMT) and Tokyo International Military Tribunal for the Far East (IMTFE) (Section I); the United Nations (UN) ad hoc tribunals (Section II); and the International Criminal Court (ICC) (Section III). Importantly, these sections do not attempt to provide a comprehensive account of every crime adjudicated within these courts, but rather adopt an illustrative approach that seeks to illuminate the dynamics of drafting, charging, and interpretation through which the range and definition of crimes were determined in different institutional contexts. The chapter then turns to identify particular forms of criminality that were rarely prosecuted within these courts despite falling within the scope of their jurisdictional mandates (Section IV). Finally, the chapter concludes by identifying some of the continuities and discontinuities concerning the range and definition of crime categories adjudicated by different international criminal courts and reflects on what such trends reveal about the scope and content of the historical narratives constructed in their judgments (Section V).

[6] See similarly, J Reynolds and S Xavier, '"The Dark Corners of the World": TWAIL and International Criminal Justice' (2016) 14 *Journal of International Criminal Justice* 959, 981; and M Koskenniemi, 'Hersch Lauterpacht and the Development of International Criminal Law' (2004) 2 *Journal of International Criminal Justice* 810, 825.

[7] See similarly, C Schwöbel-Patel, 'The Core Crimes of International Criminal Law' in KJ Heller et al (eds), *The Oxford Handbook of International Criminal Law* (OUP 2020) 768.

[8] See also, B Sander, 'Unveiling the Historical Function of International Criminal Courts: Between Adjudicative and Sociopolitical Justice' (2018) 12 *International Journal of Transitional Justice* 334.

I. The Nuremberg IMT and Tokyo IMTFE

Although the Nuremberg IMT and Tokyo IMTFE were created by distinct processes, comprised of different judges, and governed by separate statutory frameworks, a common thread ran through the drafting, charging, and interpretative practices that determined the range and definition of the crime categories adjudicated by these tribunals. In essence, the overarching theme that pervaded these tribunals was one of control by the Allied powers, whose interests dominated the determination of which crime categories were adjudicated and how they were defined. Importantly, as this section reveals, the implications of Allied domination for the scope and content of the historical narratives constructed within the tribunals' judgments were significant.

A. Drafting Practices

Turning first to drafting practices, the processes that led to the adoption of the Nuremberg and Tokyo Charters were dictated by the interests of the Allied powers emerging from the Second World War. The Nuremberg Charter was drafted by representatives of the United States, Britain, France, and the Soviet Union during fifteen sessions of the International Conference on Military Trials in London in the summer of 1945.[9] The Tokyo Charter, by contrast, was reportedly drafted by Joseph Keenan, who would become the IMTFE's Chief Prosecutor, together with US staff of the International Prosecution Service and General Douglas MacArthur's legal secretary.[10] However, given the similarities of the Tokyo Charter to its Nuremberg counterpart, the latter appears to have had a significant influence over the final text of the former.

The crimes falling within the jurisdictional mandates of the Nuremberg and Tokyo tribunals were elaborated in Article 6 of the Nuremberg Charter and Article 5 of the Tokyo Charter respectively. Although the precise wording of these provisions contained slight variations, both recognised the categories of war crimes, crimes against peace, and crimes against humanity. Reference was also made to conspiracy; however, given the distinct issues surrounding this category, conspiracy will be examined separately in *Chapter 5* of this study in the context of discussing categories of culpability.

1. War crimes

During the drafting of the Nuremberg Charter, the category that proved least contentious was war crimes. With respect to this category, there was general agreement amongst the Allied powers that the terms of the 1907 Hague Convention and 1929 Geneva Convention had become customary international law and, in addition, that the history of prosecuting these acts as crimes in domestic courts had demonstrated

[9] For a narrative account of the London Conference, see generally, T Taylor, *The Anatomy of the Nuremberg Trials: A Personal Memoir* (Skyhorse Publishing 1993) 59–77.

[10] N Boister and R Cryer, *The Tokyo International Military Tribunal—A Reappraisal* (OUP 2008) 25, fn 142.

that they could be treated as crimes under both national and international law.[11] During the drafting of the Tokyo Charter, the US reportedly suggested that the jurisdiction of the IMTFE should be limited to crimes against peace; ultimately, however, war crimes—as well as crimes against humanity—were included at the insistence of the United Kingdom.[12]

In contrast to the ease by which the category of war crimes was included within the subject-matter jurisdictions of the Nuremberg and Tokyo tribunals, the categories of crimes against peace and crimes against humanity proved more divisive, bringing to the fore the varied narrative interests of the Allied powers.

2. Crimes against peace

While it is possible to situate the emergence of crimes against peace in the context of a wider movement of belief that foregrounded the idea of 'peace through law', the inclusion of this crime category in the Nuremberg and Tokyo Charters was very much a product of particular circumstances, a 'historical quirk' that owed more to short-term Allied calculation than a long-term vision of international criminal justice.[13] Primarily, the category of crimes against peace was included in the Nuremberg and Tokyo Charters to satisfy the interests of the US. During the drafting of the Nuremberg Charter, Robert Jackson, the US representative at the London Conference, was keen on vindicating his own and US statesman Henry Stimson's position that the German war had been illegal in its inception and, as such, that the US had been justified in departing from strict rules of neutrality in providing the Allied nations with various forms of aid, including weapons, prior to entering the conflict.[14]

In contrast to the US, other delegations were less enthused by the prospect of including crimes against peace within the Nuremberg Charter. For example, General Nikitchenko, head of the Soviet delegation, made clear that a 'general definition [of crimes against peace] ... would not be agreeable'.[15] As this remark suggests, the Soviets were keen to limit the definition of crimes against peace to aggressive wars started by the European Axis nations. According to Telford Taylor, the Soviet position was likely

[11] KS Gallant, *The Principle of Legality in International and Comparative Criminal Law* (CUP 2009) 69–72 and 77.

[12] Boister and Cryer (n 10) 25.

[13] F Mégret, 'International Criminal Justice as a Peace Project' (2018) 29 *European Journal of International Law* 835, 837–840 and 844. See also, S Moyn, 'From Aggression to Atrocity: Rethinking the History of International Criminal Law', in KJ Heller et al (eds), *The Oxford Handbook of International Criminal Law* (OUP 2020) 341.

[14] 'Minutes of Conference Session of July 24, 1945', reproduced in *Report of Robert H. Jackson to the International Conference on Military Trials* (USA Department of State International Organisation and Conference Series II 1949) 360, 363, and 384; and 'Minutes of Conference Session of July 19, 1945', reproduced in *Jackson Report* ibid 295, 299. For other possible US motivations, see Moyn (n 13) 351 (arguing 'more speculatively, [that] aggression took pride of place because it was regarded as the gateway crime for others and because New Dealers brought an institutional optic to the task of international justice').

[15] 'Minutes of Conference Session of July 25, 1945', reproduced in *Jackson Report* (n 14) 376, 387. See, however, F Hirsch, *Soviet Judgment at Nuremberg: A New History of the International Military Tribunal after World War II* (OUP 2020) 8 and 35 (noting how 'the Soviets had pushed the hardest to try the Nazis ... for the crime of launching what they called a "war of aggression" to begin with' and that it was a Soviet lawyer, Aaron Trainin, 'who coined the term "crime against peace"').

spurred by 'the circumstances of the Soviet government's participation in carving up Poland and the attack against Finland'.[16]

A different set of concerns was raised by the French delegation, which argued that launching a war of aggression was not a crime under international law. Professor Gros, head of the French delegation, conceded that it would be 'morally and politically desirable' for such acts to be criminal,[17] but nonetheless proceeded to voice concerns that the recognition of crimes against peace would amount to '*ex post facto* legislation'.[18] Interestingly, Professor Gros was less opposed to the inclusion of crimes against peace in the Charter per se,[19] than to the arguments put forward by the US and British that the definition of crimes within the Charter should be decisive and binding on the judges,[20] a position which—if accepted—would preclude judicial determination of the question of whether crimes falling within their jurisdiction were crimes under international law.[21]

Ultimately, both Soviet and French concerns were alleviated through compromise. The Soviet concern was allayed by ensuring that only individuals belonging to the European Axis nations fell within the jurisdiction of the Nuremberg IMT. The French concern was assuaged by deliberate ambiguity in the *chapeau* to Article 6 of the Nuremberg Charter, the final text of which could be read to support either the French view that the judges were entitled to determine the legality of the crimes falling within their jurisdiction or the US and British position that the Nuremberg Charter was decisive and binding on the tribunal.[22]

Although defined in similar terms to the Nuremberg Charter,[23] the category of crimes against peace was given an even more prominent position in the Tokyo Charter. Again, US political interests proved pivotal, though in this context the category was included more as a means of punishing Japanese aggression than politically and legally justifying US involvement in the war.[24] The significance attached to crimes against peace is evident from an early policy paper developed by the US government, which specified that investigations with respect to what would ultimately become the Tokyo IMTFE 'should attach importance' to the category.[25] This sentiment was later expressly incorporated into the *chapeau* of Article 5 of the Tokyo Charter, which delimited the powers of the Tokyo tribunal to trying and punishing individuals 'charged with offenses *which include Crimes against Peace*'.[26] According to this wording, defendants before the Tokyo IMTFE were to be charged *at a minimum* with

[16] Taylor (n 9) 66.

[17] 'Minutes of Conference Session of July 19, 1945' (n 14) 297.

[18] 'Minutes of Conference Session of July 23, 1945', reproduced in *Jackson Report* (n 14) 328, 335.

[19] See generally, Gallant (n 11) 81–87.

[20] See, for example, 'Minutes of Conference Session of July 23, 1945' (n 18) 328 (Sir Maxwell Fyfe, the British representative at the London conference) and 329–330 (Robert Jackson, the US representative at the London conference).

[21] 'Minutes of Conference Session of July 25, 1945' (n 15) 378.

[22] See generally, Gallant (n 11) 87–91.

[23] Article 6(b), Nuremberg Charter; Article 5(b), Tokyo Charter.

[24] Boister and Cryer (n 10) 119.

[25] 'Report by the State-War-Navy Coordinating Subcommittee for the Far East' (12 September 1945) in US Department of State, *Foreign Relations of the United States: Diplomatic Papers 1945: Volume VI: The British Commonwealth, The Far East* (US Government Printing Office 1969) 926, 930.

[26] Article 5, Tokyo Charter (emphasis added).

crimes against peace, with additional charges of war crimes and crimes against humanity deemed merely optional.

3. Crimes against humanity

The roots of the concept of crimes against humanity may be traced to the underlying notion of humanity in the Martens Clause of the Hague Peace Conferences and the use of the term in a joint declaration of 1915 issued by the French, British, and Russian governments condemning the Ottoman massacre of Armenians. However, according to a recent study by Kerstin von Lingen, decisive for the emergence of crimes against humanity as a legal category were exiled lawyers within the United Nations (UN) War Crimes Commission during the 1940s, who 'changed the perception of international law into a protector, as they put more weight on the experience of violence and victim's voices than on the earlier approach of protecting states from violence'.[27] At the London Conference, divisions over the category of crimes against humanity centred primarily on its definition. As articulated in Article 6(c) of the Nuremberg Charter, the category was at once both radical and conservative.

In certain respects, the recognition of crimes against humanity constituted a legal innovation, which seemed specifically designed to represent and respond to some of the unprecedented atrocities that had been perpetrated by the Nazis. The innovative nature of the category of crimes against humanity, as defined in the Nuremberg Charter, was reflected in at least four features:[28] first, the category applied to prohibited acts committed against '*any* civilian population', thereby protecting civilians not only from the atrocities of foreign States but also those of their own; second, the category applied to acts committed '*before* and during the war', thereby protecting individuals from atrocities outside of wartime; third, the category applied 'whether or not in violation of domestic law of the country where perpetrated', thereby affirming the supremacy of international over domestic law; and finally, the category recognised 'persecution on political, racial, religious grounds' as a crime despite the lack of clear domestic analogues.

Interestingly, despite these innovative elements, the French delegation, which had been opposed to the recognition of crimes against peace in light of its unprecedented nature, had declined to raise similar concerns during the drafting of the category of crimes against humanity.[29] One explanation may be that the French had vested interests in the recognition of crimes against humanity. According to

[27] K von Lingen, 'Legal Flows: Contributions of Exiled Lawyers to the Concept of "Crimes Against Humanity" During the Second World War' (2020) 17 *Modern Intellectual History* 507, 524–525 (also noting that the role performed by Hersch Lauterpacht in developing the legal category 'was crucial, as he acted as a transmitter between the voices from the periphery toward the real powerful bodies at the Allied Conference').

[28] L Douglas, *The Memory of Judgment: Making Law and History in the Trials of the Holocaust* (Yale University Press 2001) 47. See also, W Schabas, *Unimaginable Atrocities: Justice, Politics, and Rights at the War Crimes Tribunals* (OUP 2012) 58 (referring to the communication of Hersch Lauterpacht to a legal officer in the UK Foreign Office that the category of crimes against humanity was 'clearly an innovation').

[29] Gallant (n 11) 86. See also, 'Minutes of Conference Session of July 24, 1945' (n 14) 360 (where Professor Gros seemed to justify the category of crimes against humanity on the ground that 'for the last century ... [a]ll countries have interfered in affairs of other countries to defend minorities who were persecuted').

Professor Gros, the French people 'just want to show that the Nazis were bandits'.[30] In this vein, Professor Gros emphasised that if Germany had launched a war of aggression but had not committed war crimes or crimes against humanity, there would be no need to set up a court to judge the German government: 'It is what is in the aggression, what comes after the aggression, that makes really the necessity and the right of judging those men.'[31]

Notwithstanding its innovative elements, the drafting of crimes against humanity also included a more conservative element. In particular, Article 6(c) of the Nuremberg Charter provided that the acts relied upon to constitute crimes against humanity must have been committed 'in execution of or in connection with any crime within the jurisdiction of the Tribunal' (the so-called 'war nexus' requirement).[32] If the recognition of the general category of crimes against humanity seemed motivated by a desire to respond to the unprecedented atrocities that had been committed by the Nazis, the inclusion of the war nexus requirement seemed motivated by other concerns. Such concerns were revealed in no uncertain terms by Robert Jackson during the drafting of the Nuremberg Charter:[33]

> [O]rdinarily we do not consider that the acts of a government toward its own citizens warrant our interference. *We have some regrettable circumstances at times in our own country in which minorities are unfairly treated.* We think it is justifiable that we interfere or attempt to bring retribution to individuals or to states only because the concentration camps and the deportations were in pursuance of a common plan or enterprise of making an unjust or illegal war in which we became involved.

As this passage suggests, the war nexus requirement seems to have been a deliberate attempt to restrict the definition of crimes against humanity so as to dodge any allegations of hypocrisy that might have been raised against the Allies as well as to avoid setting a precedent that might one day be applied against the Allies with respect to the treatment of their own nationals.[34] In terms of the narrative implications of the war nexus requirement, Professor Gros cautioned that the element was likely to constitute 'a difficult burden because, even in the Nazi plan against the Jews, there is no apparent aggression against other nations'.[35] As discussed later in this chapter, these words of warning proved to be somewhat prophetic.

30 'Minutes of Conference Session of July 25, 1945' (n 15) 381–382.

31 Ibid 386.

32 There was initially a discrepancy between the English, French, and Russian versions of the Nuremberg Charter which raised doubts as to whether all types of crimes against humanity had to be tied to crimes against peace or war crimes, or simply the sub-category of persecution-based crimes against humanity. On the famous Semicolon Protocol of 6 October 1945, which clarified that *all* crimes against humanity must be linked to crimes against peace or war crimes, see Douglas (n 28) 53–54; and D Bloxham, *Genocide on Trial: War Crimes Trials and the Formation of Holocaust History and Memory* (OUP 2001) 64, fn 27.

33 'Minutes of Conference Session of July 23, 1945' (n 18) 333 (emphasis added).

34 BVA Röling and A Cassese, *The Tokyo Trial and Beyond: Reflections of a Peacemonger* (Polity Press 1993) 55.

35 'Minutes of Conference Session of July 24, 1945' (n 14) 360.

B. Charging Practices

Turning to charging practices, although the prosecutors were tasked with determining the scope and focus of the Nuremberg and Tokyo indictments,[36] in practice they were not expected to act independently of their governments. With respect to the Nuremberg indictment, a Committee of Chief Prosecutors—one for each of the four Allied powers—was responsible for selecting and defining the charges to be brought against the defendants.[37] The Tokyo indictment, by contrast, was compiled by the British chair of the assigned Indictment Sub-Commission, Sir Arthur Comyns-Carr, who is reported to have drawn together recommendations from the eleven Allied nations involved in the drafting process.[38]

Through these processes, the indictments at both tribunals became products of the political contexts in which they were drafted—the process of selecting the charges best characterised as a political negotiation.[39] Cementing the political insularity of the charging processes, it is also notable that neither were the indictments subject to any formal judicial confirmation process,[40] nor does there appear to have been any significant formal input from civil society or victims as to which specific crimes should be charged.[41] Consequently, both the scope and focus of the charges selected for prosecution at Nuremberg and Tokyo very much reflected the priorities of the Allied powers at that time.

1. Scope of charges

In terms of the scope of the charges, the Nuremberg and Tokyo indictments reflected the Allied objective of constructing an extensive historical record of the conflicts under examination.[42]

The Nuremberg indictment consisted of four counts—common plan and conspiracy, crimes against peace, war crimes, and crimes against humanity—concerning twenty-three individuals and six organisations spanning the years 1923 to 1945.[43] As Robert Jackson observed in his opening statement before the Nuremberg IMT, 'Never before in legal history has an effort been made to bring within the scope of a single

[36] Article 14, Nuremberg Charter; and Article 8, Tokyo Charter.

[37] Article 14(a)–(d), Nuremberg Charter.

[38] H Friman et al, 'Charges', in G Sluiter et al (eds), *International Criminal Procedure: Principles and Rules* (OUP 2013) 381, 384; and Boister and Cryer (n 10) 69–70.

[39] MM deGuzman and WA Schabas, 'Initiation of Investigations and Selection of Cases', in Sluiter et al (n 38) 131, 134. See also, Hirsch (n 15) 83 ('The politics of the Indictment were the politics of history. The four wartime Allies understood that in putting together the case against the Nazi elite and their organizations, the prosecutors were also setting out a version of events for posterity').

[40] Friman et al (n 38) 397.

[41] See, for example, Bloxham (n 32) 67 (noting how US Prosecutor Robert Jackson refused a request by Jewish organisations for representation on the prosecution).

[42] J Locke, 'Indictments', in L Reydams et al (eds), *International Prosecutors* (OUP 2012) 604, 614.

[43] 'Indictment (as amended)' (7 June 1946) *Trial of the Major War Criminals before the International Military Tribunal, Nuremberg, 14 November 1945 1 October 1946: Volume I* (Nuremberg IMT 1947) 27 ('Nuremberg Indictment').

litigation the developments of a decade, covering a whole continent, and involving a score of nations, countless individuals, and innumerable events'.[44]

The Tokyo indictment was similarly ambitious in scope, consisting of fifty-five counts divided into three groups—crimes against peace and conspiracies to commit that crime; murder and conspiracies to murder as a result of killings in a war of aggression; and conventional war crimes, crimes against humanity, and conspiracies to commit those crimes—concerning twenty-eight individuals and spanning the years 1928 to 1945.[45]

2. Focus of charges

In terms of the focus of the charges, Allied influence was evident both with respect to the inclusions and exclusions of the Nuremberg and Tokyo indictments.

With respect to the Nuremberg indictment, for example, the Soviet Union was able to insist on charging German defendants with the war crime of killing prisoners of war for the massacre of 11,000 Polish officers, who were alleged to have been executed and buried in the Katyn Forest in September 1941.[46] Since the massacre was rightly believed to have been committed by the Soviets, the inclusion of the charge was a source of considerable controversy.[47] Ultimately, the Nuremberg IMT only briefly examined the issue at trial, allowing the prosecution and defence to call a few witnesses each. The result was largely inconclusive and the judges decided to exclude any mention of the incident from its judgment.[48] The episode illustrates both the dominance of Allied interests in determining the orientation of the charges at the Nuremberg IMT, as well as the independence of the judges in declining to discuss the charges in their judgment.

In terms of controversial charges, the Tokyo indictment fared little better. Particularly contentious was the inclusion of murder charges for killings committed as part of an illegal war.[49] These charges were premised on the provocative view that killings could only be justified if they took place as part of a just war.[50] Had the Tokyo IMT accepted these charges, it would have undermined the fundamental distinction between the legality of going to war (*jus ad bellum*) and the legality of the conduct of a war (*jus in bello*).[51] According to Boister and Cryer, the murder charges were a relic of a suggestion initially put forward by US General MacArthur as a response to the surprise Japanese attack on Pearl Harbour; specifically, MacArthur had pressed

[44] 'Second Day, Wednesday 21 November 1945', *Trial of the Major War Criminals before the International Military Tribunal, Nuremberg, 14 November 1945 1 October 1946: Volume II* (Nuremberg IMT 1947) 95, 100.

[45] *USA and Others v Araki Sadao and Others*, International Military Tribunal for the Far East, Indictment, reprinted in N Boister and R Cryer (eds), *Documents on the Tokyo International Military Tribunal: Charter, Indictments and Judgments* (OUP 2008) 16 ('Tokyo Indictment').

[46] Nuremberg Indictment (n 43) 54 ('In September 1941, 11,000 Polish officers who were prisoners of war were killed in the Katyn Forest near Smolensk').

[47] Schabas (n 28) 153–156.

[48] Ibid 156 (arguing that the episode stands out as an example of international judges deciding not to demean the credibility of their judgment 'by endorsing a lie or simply obscuring the truth in the interests of political convenience').

[49] See generally, Boister and Cryer (n 10) 154–159.

[50] Röling and Cassese (n 34) 56–57.

[51] N Boister, 'The Tokyo Trial', in WA Schabas and N Bernaz (eds), *Routledge Handbook of International Criminal Law* (Routledge 2011) 17, 26.

Washington to charge the defendants with conspiracy to wage aggressive war and then convict them of 'murder for killing US nationals on US soil without declaration of war'.[52] Beyond a tool for appealing to the US audience of the trial, the murder charges were also intended to serve as an expressive device for stripping State officials of the grandeur that tends to accompany holding State positions by painting them as common murderers.[53] Ultimately, however, the Tokyo IMTFE held that it was unnecessary 'to express any opinion upon the validity of the charges of murder' since they were subsumed under the charge of crimes against peace.[54] The episode illustrates both how the US attempted to craft the charges to fit its narrative priorities regardless of any legality concerns,[55] as well as the independence of the judges in finding a way to diplomatically avoid expressing any opinion on the validity of the charges of murder whilst at the same time ensuring their *de facto* exclusion from their judgment.

While the judges of the IMT and IMTFE were able to side-step validating some of the more controversial charges included within the Nuremberg and Tokyo indictments, they were powerless to examine crimes and incidents that had been purposefully *omitted* in accordance with Allied interests.

In the Nuremberg indictment, for example, particularly notable was the failure to include charges concerning the bombing of civilian population centres, which had been practised by both Allied and Axis forces. In the Tokyo indictment, significant omissions included the failure to include charges concerning the biological experiments conducted by Unit 731 of the Kwantung Army in exchange for the US obtaining access to their research, the neglect of crimes committed against Japanese nationals, and the relative inattention devoted to crimes committed by Japanese forces against civilian populations living under the colonial domination of Japan, such as the Koreans or Chinese in Taiwan (Formosa).[56]

Both the Nuremberg and Tokyo indictments also suffered from a major blind spot in terms of sexual and gender-based crimes. Although sexual and gender-based violence (SGBV) had been extremely widespread during the Second World War—and SGBV could potentially have been prosecuted as the war crime of 'ill-treatment' or the crime against humanity of 'other inhumane acts' under Articles 6(b) and (c) of the Nuremberg Charter—the prosecutors at Nuremberg opted not to pursue such charges.[57] Moreover, even though references were made at trial to evidence that demonstrated the rape and sexual abuse of civilian women by German forces,[58] the general

[52] Boister and Cryer (n 10) 157.

[53] Ibid 157–158 (referring to statements made to this effect by lead prosecutor Joseph Keenan as well as Sir Arthur Comyns-Carr).

[54] *USA and Others v Araki Sadao and Others*, International Military Tribunal for the Far East, Judgment (1 November 1948) reprinted in Boister and Cryer (n 45) 71 ('Tokyo Judgment'), pagination paras 48,452–48,453.

[55] R Cryer, *Prosecuting International Crimes: Selectivity and the International Criminal Law Regime* (CUP 2005) 249.

[56] Boister and Cryer (n 10) 61–65 and 203–204; and F Hisakazu, 'The Tokyo Trial: Humanity's Justice v Victors' Justice', in Y Tanaka et al (eds), *Beyond Victor's Justice? The Tokyo War Crimes Trial Revisited* (Martinus Nijhoff Publishers 2011) 3, 14.

[57] See generally, KD Askin, *War Crimes Against Women: Prosecution in International War Crimes Tribunals* (Martinus Nijhoff Publishers 1997) 49–95, 138 and 142.

[58] See, for example, the 'Molotov Note', which documented *inter alia* the systematic violence perpetrated against women by the Nazis: 'Fifty-ninth Day, Thursday 14 February 1946', *Trial of the Major War Criminals before the International Military Tribunal, Nuremberg, 14 November 1945–1 October 1946: Volume VII*

impression generated by the Nuremberg proceedings was one of 'seeming indifference' towards SGBV.[59] Not only did the Nuremberg IMT fail to refer to rape in its final judgment, it also neglected to recognise any notion of gender-based violence.[60]

In contrast to Nuremberg, the Tokyo indictment did include some specific allegations of rape, which was referred to euphemistically as 'inhuman treatment', 'mistreatment', 'ill treatment', and 'failure to respect family honour and rights'.[61] Although no victims of rape were called to testify about such charges, the Tokyo IMTFE was able to conclude on the basis of evidence adduced at trial that during the invasion of the city of Nanking, 'approximately 20,000 cases of rape [had] occurred within the city during the first month of the occupation'.[62] The tribunal also sentenced to death General Matsui, the Commander-in-Chief of the Central China Area Army, for the 'wholesale massacres', including rape, which had been committed by Japanese soldiers under his command during the invasion.[63] According to Susan Brownmiller, were it not for the Tokyo IMTFE, the full extent of the atrocities committed at Nanking 'might have passed out of history then and there, relegated in typical fashion to the dubious area of unsupported wartime rumour'.[64] Nonetheless, omissions with respect to SGBV were also evident at Tokyo, perhaps none more prominent than the failure of the tribunal to address the hundreds of thousands of 'comfort women' from the Korean peninsula and other Japanese occupied territories, who had been systematically sexually enslaved by the Japanese military.[65]

The omission of sexual and gender-based charges at Nuremberg and the inadequate prosecution of such atrocities at Tokyo were the product of a range of factors.[66] First, the exclusion of sexual and gender-based crimes was in line with the desire of the Allies to avoid prosecutions for crimes that they themselves had committed.[67] Second, the omission of sexual and gender-based crimes also reflected the Allied tendency to prioritise crimes committed against their own nationals over those committed against victims of nations not represented at the tribunal, such as Korea from where a significant number of 'comfort women' had originated.[68] Third, the focus of prosecutors on charges against higher-ranking defendants for crimes against peace and their reliance primarily on documentary evidence for this purpose also diminished the attention

(Nuremberg IMT, 1947) 403, 456–457. For other examples, see generally, N Henry, *War and Rape: Law, Memory and Justice* (Routledge 2011), 30–36.

59 Henry (n 58) 34.

60 R Grey, *Prosecuting Sexual and Gender-Based Crimes at the International Criminal Court: Practice, Progress and Potential* (CUP 2019) 76.

61 KD Askin, 'Prosecuting Wartime Rape and Other Gender-Related Crimes under International Law: Extraordinary Advances, Enduring Obstacles' (2003) 21 *Berkeley Journal of International Law* 288, 302.

62 Tokyo Judgment (n 54) pagination para 49,606. See also, ibid pagination paras 49,617 (mention of rapes in China), 49,638 (mention of rapes in Hong Kong), and 49,640 (mention of rapes in Manila).

63 Tokyo Judgment (n 54) pagination paras 49,814–49,816.

64 S Brownmiller, *Against Our Will: Men, Women and Rape* (Penguin Books 1976) 58.

65 The judgment includes only a fleeting reference to the practice. Tokyo Judgment (n 54) pagination para 49,617. See also, Grey (n 60) 77–78 (referring to military archival research, which confirms that the Allies were aware of the system of 'comfort stations').

66 Henry (n 58) 39–52.

67 Cryer (n 55) 206.

68 Henry (n 58) 44–46.

paid to SGBV and resulted in by-passing the personal stories of survivors that could have been illuminated through live testimony.[69] And finally, the omission of sexual and gender-based crimes also resulted from the diminished status of women and SGBV during this period in general, including the characterisation of such violence as a private experience which should not be relayed in a public forum.[70]

C. Interpretative Practices

As the positions adopted by the Nuremberg IMT towards the Katyn massacre and the Tokyo IMTFE towards the murder charges indicate, the judges at these tribunals were not mere instruments of the Allied powers. At the same time, on most of the major interpretative questions that confronted the judges, considerable deference was shown to the wishes of the Allied nations. In particular, the judges—or, at least, a clear majority of them in the case of the Tokyo IMTFE—proved willing to give their judicial seal of approval to the legality of the categories of war crimes, crimes against peace, and crimes against humanity, at times on the basis of extremely tenuous reasoning.[71]

1. War crimes

With respect to the category of war crimes, the Nuremberg IMT simply asserted that the relevant rules laid down in the 1907 Hague Convention and the 1929 Geneva Convention were, by 1939, 'already recognised as War Crimes under international law', adding that the question of whether these provisions entailed individual criminal responsibility was 'too well settled to admit of argument'.[72] The Tokyo IMTFE was similarly succinct, confining itself to noting that 'under the customary rules of war, acknowledged by all civilized nations, all prisoners of war and civilian internees must be given humane treatment' and that the 1929 Geneva Convention 'merely reaffirm[ed] the pre-existing and prescribe[d] detailed provisions for its application'.[73] Although the reasoning of the judges was concise to the point of being almost non-existent and may be critiqued for lacking a coherent or convincing methodology,[74] most commentators consider their conclusions defensible.[75]

[69] Askin (n 57) 142, fn 492; and Henry (n 58) 47–49.

[70] Henry (n 58) 49–52.

[71] See, in this regard, G Mettraux, 'Trial at Nuremberg', in Schabas and Bernaz (n 51) 5, 11 (noting how, in a memorandum dated 10 July 1946, Francis Biddle, the US judge at the Nuremberg IMT, was advised in the following terms: 'It is essential to state the views of the Tribunal as to just what the international law *was*. It is not too cynical to point out that whether it was or was not before your honors spoke, from the period when you do so speak it *is* the law.').

[72] *Göring and others*, Nuremberg International Military Tribunal, Judgment, 1 October 1946, *Trial of the Major War Criminals before the International Military Tribunal, Nuremberg, 14 November 1945–1 October 1946: Volume I* (Nuremberg IMT 1947) 171 ('Nuremberg Judgment') 253.

[73] Tokyo Judgment (n 54) pagination para 49,720. For further analysis of the IMTFE's discussion of the legality of war crimes, see Boister and Cryer (n 10) 180–189.

[74] A Zahar and G Sluiter, *International Criminal Law: A Critical Introduction* (OUP 2008) 82.

[75] See, for example, Boister and Cryer (n 10) 189; and Gallant (n 11) 69–72. See, *contra*, I Bantekas, 'Reflections on Some Sources and Methods of International Criminal and Humanitarian Law' (2006) 6 *International Criminal Law Review* 121, 122–123.

2. Crimes against peace

Far more contentious was the Nuremberg IMT's recognition of the category of crimes against peace. Prior to the commencement of the Nuremberg trial, counsel for the accused filed a pre-trial motion arguing that the category of crimes against peace was 'not as yet valid international law'.[76] In particular, it was argued, the tribunal should confine itself to the identification of instances where acts of aggressive war had been committed, but decline to find the defendants criminally liable for such acts. Rather, based on the tribunal's findings of fact, it would be up to the international community to 'create a new law under which those who *in the future* would be guilty of starting an unjust war would be threatened with punishment by an International Tribunal'.[77] Although the pre-trial motion was refused on the ground that Article 3 of the Nuremberg Charter prohibited challenges to the jurisdiction of the tribunal,[78] the substance of the motion's objections were later confronted in the Nuremberg IMT's final judgment.

In its judgment, the tribunal began by asserting that the law set out in the Nuremberg Charter, including the categorisation of aggressive war as a crime, was 'decisive, and binding upon the Tribunal'.[79] Nonetheless, 'in view of the great importance of the questions of law involved', the judges decided to put forward two additional arguments to buttress the legitimacy of recognising aggressive war as a crime within the tribunal's jurisdiction.[80]

First, the Nuremberg IMT argued that the recognition of crimes against peace in the Nuremberg Charter was in conformity with the demands of substantive justice. For this purpose, the IMT relied on reasoning which conflated the illegality, immorality, and criminality of acts of aggressive war.[81] The IMT argued that since the defendants' designs of invasion and aggression were carried out 'in defiance of all international law' (*illegality*), the defendants 'must have known' that their acts were 'wrong' (*immorality*), and consequently 'far from it being unjust to punish [them], it would be unjust if [their] wrong were allowed to go unpunished' (*criminality*).[82] According to this line of reasoning, even if the criminalisation of aggressive war had been retroactive, it was nonetheless justifiable in light of its conformity with the general tenets of substantive justice.

However, the judges were not content with merely demonstrating that the recognition of crimes against peace by the Allies had been 'demanded by the conscience of the world',[83] and proceeded to argue that the crime category also constituted the expression of international law existing both 'at the time of [the Charter's] creation' as well

[76] 'Motion Adopted By All Defense Counsel', 19 November 1945, *Trial of the Major War Criminals before the International Military Tribunal, Nuremberg, 14 November 1945–1 October 1946: Volume I* (Nuremberg IMT 1947) 168, 168–169.

[77] Ibid 169 (emphasis added).

[78] 'Second Day, Wednesday 21 November 1945', *Trial of the Major War Criminals before the International Military Tribunal, Nuremberg, 14 November 1945–1 October 1946: Volume II* (Nuremberg IMT 1947) 95, 95.

[79] Nuremberg Judgment (n 72) 218.

[80] Ibid 219.

[81] See similarly R Cryer, 'The Philosophy of International Criminal Law', in A Orakhelashvili (ed), *Research Handbook on the Theory and History of International Law* (Edward Elgar 2011) 232, 241.

[82] Nuremberg Judgment (n 72) 219.

[83] Ibid 222.

as 'in 1939'.[84] For this purpose, the tribunal relied on an expansive interpretation of the Kellogg-Briand Pact of 1928 to conclude that resort to a war of aggression was not merely illegal, but also criminal under international law.[85] The IMT began by arguing that the substantive provisions of the Pact rendered war as an instrument of national policy illegal under international law.[86] Next, the IMT confronted the absence of any express reference to criminal liability in the Kellogg-Briand Pact. To overcome this hurdle, the IMT drew attention to the long history of war crimes prosecutions that had been conducted by military tribunals for violations of the rules of the 1907 Hague Convention, which prohibited recourse to certain methods of waging war. The IMT observed that these prosecutions had been carried out despite the fact that the 1907 Hague Convention 'nowhere designates such practices as criminal'.[87] On this basis, the IMT reasoned that if individuals who violated the 1907 Hague Convention could be subject to criminal liability despite the lack of express wording to that effect, so too could those who violated the Kellogg-Briand Pact. This was particularly justifiable, the IMT asserted, since 'those who wage aggressive war are doing that which is equally illegal, and of much greater moment than a breach of one of the rules of the Hague Convention'.[88] Finally, the IMT made reference to a number of unratified treaties and non-binding declarations, which it argued reinforced its interpretation of the Kellogg-Briand Pact.[89]

The reasoning adopted by the IMT to conclude that crimes against peace was an established crime under international law has been described as 'tenuous',[90] 'not very solid',[91] and seeming 'more like rationalisation than proof'.[92] In particular, the absence of State practice in support of individual criminal responsibility for wars of aggression appears to constitute an insurmountable obstacle to the reasoning of the Nuremberg IMT.[93] In fact, it is almost universally accepted that the IMT was forging new ground both in recognising crimes against peace in its judgment, as well as in the reasoning it adopted for the purpose.[94] Despite its novelty, a majority of the Tokyo IMTFE expressed its 'unqualified adherence' to the reasoning adopted by the Nuremberg IMT,[95]

[84] Ibid 218–219.
[85] Ibid 222.
[86] Ibid 220.
[87] Ibid 220–221.
[88] Ibid 221.
[89] Ibid 221–222.
[90] B van Schaak, '*Crimen Sine Lege*: Judicial Lawmaking at the Intersection of Law and Morals' (2008) 97 *Georgetown Law Journal* 119, 129.
[91] JN Shklar, *Legalism—Law Morals, and Political Trials* (Harvard University Press 1964) 179.
[92] Cryer (n 81) 242.
[93] Boister and Cryer (n 10) 118 and 136 ('During the war itself division emerged in the UNWCC between Australia, China, New Zealand, Poland, and Yugoslavia which supported the Czech lead that aggression was criminal, and the US, France, UK, Netherlands, and Greece, which maintained it was not').
[94] See, for example, BVA Röling, 'The Nuremberg and the Tokyo Trials in Retrospect', in G Mettraux (ed), *Perspectives on the Nuremberg Trial* (OUP 2008) 455, 460 ('It is at this moment a practically undisputed thesis that before World War II positive international law did not recognise the crime of aggressive war for which individuals could be punished').
[95] Tokyo Judgment (n 54) pagination paras 48,437–48,439. Despite its claim of unqualified adherence to the judgment of the Nuremberg IMT, the Tokyo IMTFE nonetheless qualified its assertion that the Tokyo Charter was decisive and binding with the observation that the Allied nations could not have acted 'in conflict with recognised international law or rules or principles thereof' and could only have conferred powers on the tribunal 'within the limits of international law'. Ibid pagination para 48,436.

concluding in no uncertain terms that aggressive war was 'a crime at international law long prior to the date of the Declaration of Potsdam'.[96]

The legal validation of the category of crimes against peace by both the Nuremberg and Tokyo tribunals had a profound influence on the historical narratives constructed by these tribunals in practice. The *recognition* of crimes against peace enabled the judges to examine alleged Nazi and Japanese acts of aggression and to determine whether individual defendants could be held criminally responsible for them. The importance of the crime to the narrative focus of the trials was emphasised in the strongest terms by the Nuremberg IMT, which held that to initiate a war of aggression was not only a crime, but also 'the supreme international crime differing only from other war crimes in that it contains within itself the accumulated evil of the whole'.[97] In addition, the *reasoning* adopted by these tribunals, in particular their attempts to identify a basis for crimes against peace in international law as it existed at the time of the relevant acts, enabled the judges to portray those convicted of the crime as rule-breakers—disruptive deviants who had undermined the established international political order by breaching a pre-existing criminal prohibition.

3. Crimes against humanity

Beyond the recognition of crimes against peace and the reasoning adopted for this purpose, its centrality to the historical narratives constructed in the Nuremberg and Tokyo judgments was also cemented by the judicial validation of the war nexus requirement with respect to the category of crimes against humanity.

In its final judgment, the Nuremberg IMT concluded that the war nexus requirement meant that the tribunal was unable to make 'a general declaration that the acts before 1939 were Crimes against Humanity within the meaning of the Charter' because 'revolting and horrible as many of these crimes were, it [had] not been satisfactorily proved that they were done in execution of, or in connection with' war crimes or crimes against peace.[98] As foretold by Professor Gros during the drafting of the Nuremberg Charter, judicial acceptance of the war nexus requirement resulted in narrowing the narrative frame of the IMT's judgment, marginalising the interests and suffering of victims of Nazi atrocities committed prior to the outbreak of war.[99]

The war nexus requirement also seemed to motivate the IMT to conflate crimes against humanity with war crimes when entering convictions against defendants. Beyond the confused, somewhat jumbled, discussion of the two categories in the IMT's judgment,[100] their conflation is also evident from the fact that only two defendants—Julius Streicher and Baldur von Schirach—were convicted of crimes against humanity independently of war crimes.[101] The result of this framing was to focus the narratives

[96] Ibid pagination para 48,440.

[97] Nuremberg Judgment (n 72) 186.

[98] Ibid 254. For a discussion of how the war nexus requirement influenced the narratives put forward by the prosecution during the Nuremberg trial, see generally, Douglas (n 28) 75–77.

[99] L Moffett, 'The Role of Victims in the International Criminal Tribunals of the Second World War' (2012) 12 *International Criminal Law Review* 245, 251.

[100] See, for example, Nuremberg Judgment (n 72) 254–255.

[101] For a detailed examination of the different ways in which these convictions were framed within the different language versions of the Nuremberg Judgment, see generally, G Acquaviva, 'At the Origins of Crimes

constructed by the judgment on the Nazi war effort. As Michael Marrus explains, war was considered to be at the heart of Nazi criminality in the Nuremberg proceedings:[102]

> [E]verything else the Nazis did, including their anti-Jewish campaign, tended to be seen in instrumental terms—as a means to hold the Nazi movement together, eliminate enemies, consolidate power, mobilize support, or carry out robbery or intimidation.

By placing emphasis on the war, the significance of racially motivated persecutions conducted largely independent of the war effort was diminished; the result was an interpretation of the Nazi regime that was, as Martti Koskenniemi has put it, 'predominantly one of aggressive militarists that put its racist and genocidal character in a secondary and at times almost invisible role'.[103]

If the category of crimes against humanity was underutilised at the Nuremberg IMT, the category proved to be of even less importance at Tokyo where the IMTFE rendered no findings concerning crimes against humanity.[104] As Totani explains, in practice the prosecution 'made little conceptual distinction between war crimes and crimes against humanity', a reflection of 'the general understanding among the prosecutors that in the Asia Pacific region, they did not have instances of mass atrocity that required the special use of law pertaining to crimes against humanity'.[105] As such, in its judgment, the judges treated the counts falling under the general heading in the indictment entitled, 'conventional war crimes and crimes against humanity', as *in substance* war crimes.[106]

D. Conclusion

The range and definition of crime categories adjudicated by the Nuremberg and Tokyo tribunals were shaped primarily in accordance with the Allied powers responsible for their establishment. The Allied nations dominated the drafting processes that led to the adoption of the Nuremberg and Tokyo Charters and steered the orientation of the charges brought against the defendants. Although the tribunals were able to avoid validating a few of the most controversial charges that had been included in the indictments, they ultimately proved highly deferential to Allied interests—particularly in their recognition and reasoning concerning the legality

Against Humanity: Clues to a Proper Understanding of the *Nullum Crimen* Principle in the Nuremberg Judgment' (2011) 9 *Journal of International Criminal Justice* 881; and Gallant (n 11) 119–124.

102 MR Marrus, 'History and the Holocaust in the Courtroom', in R Smelser (ed), *Lessons and Legacies V: The Holocaust and Justice* (Northwestern University Press 2002) 215, 218.

103 M Koskenniemi, 'From Impunity to Show Trials' (2002) 6 *Max Planck Yearbook of United Nations Law* 1, 20.

104 Y Totani, 'The Case against the Accused', in Tanaka et al (n 56) 147, 154.

105 Ibid.

106 Ibid.

of crimes against peace and their acceptance of the war nexus requirement with respect to the category of crimes against humanity.

As a result, the historical narratives within the Nuremberg and Tokyo judgments were constructed first and foremost through the prism of crimes against peace—with atrocity crimes, and the Holocaust in particular, relegated to secondary importance.[107] As Robert Jackson proclaimed in his opening statement before the Nuremberg IMT, 'This inquest represents the practical effort of four of the most mighty of nations, with the support of seventeen more, to utilize international law to meet the greatest menace of our times—aggressive war.'[108] Whether purposefully omitted from the indictments or side-lined by the primacy given to crimes against peace in the drafting and interpretation of the Nuremberg and Tokyo Charters, atrocity crimes including SGBV, the bombing of civilian population centres, and a range of acts that amounted to crimes against humanity were either marginalised or completely excluded from view within the Nuremberg and Tokyo judgments. The result was the construction of historical narratives, whose scope and content reflected above all the priorities and balance of power between the Allied nations emerging from the Second World War.

II. The UN Ad Hoc Tribunals

While the overarching theme that characterised the Nuremberg and Tokyo tribunals was one of Allied domination, a more diverse set of factors influenced the range and definition of crime categories adjudicated by the UN ad hoc tribunals. Similar to Nuremberg and Tokyo, States were primarily responsible for delimiting the general categories of crime that fell within the subject-matter jurisdiction of the ad hoc tribunals, albeit with the involvement of the UN Secretary-General and input from civil society groups. By contrast, the scope and focus of indictments were influenced by a broader range of factors including the investigative practices and priorities of prosecutors, judicial oversight, witness testimony, and civil society pressure. In addition, significant room was left for judges to creatively define the meaning of crime categories in the context of individual cases. By examining these practices, this section illuminates the relationship between the range and definition of crime categories adjudicated by the ad hoc tribunals and the scope and content of the historical narratives constructed within their judgments.

A. Drafting Practices

Turning first to drafting practices, although the Statutes of the ad hoc tribunals were drafted in similar terms, they were negotiated pursuant to separate processes.

107 See, in this regard, Moyn (n 13) 350 ('[I]t is not really so surprising that the Holocaust, or even atrocity more generally, remained so marginal. The Holocaust was simply too poorly publicized in the period to be an important causal factor in the framing of postwar justice ... Not that basic information was unavailable or even widely known, but it was lost in the shuffle of other facts and interests given more weight by most audiences.')

108 'Second Day, Wednesday 21 November 1945' (n 78) 99.

The drafting of the Statute of the International Criminal Tribunal for the former Yugoslavia (ICTY) was delegated by the UN Security Council to the Office of the UN Secretary-General.[109] Drawing on suggestions and drafts provided by States, intergovernmental and non-governmental organisations, and individual experts, the UN Secretary-General is reported to have approached the task by endeavouring 'to meet the requirements laid down by the Security Council while remaining within the legal and political mainstream of the international community'.[110] Ultimately, both the report and draft statute that emerged from this process were adopted unanimously by the Security Council without modification.[111]

In contrast to the ICTY, the drafting of the Statute of the International Criminal Tribunal for Rwanda (ICTR) was led by New Zealand and the US, with the assistance of Rwanda, which at the time was a non-permanent member of the Security Council.[112] Although the ICTR Statute was clearly modelled on that of the ICTY, there were some differences that reflected the nature of the Rwandan situation and the distinct process by which the text was finalised.[113]

Just over half a decade later, the SCSL Statute was drafted pursuant to a negotiation between the UN Secretary-General, the Security Council, and Sierra Leone.[114] Again, although the Statute of the Special Court for Sierra Leone (SCSL) was modelled on the Statutes of the ICTY and ICTR, there were some unique aspects which reflected the particularities of the conflict in Sierra Leone and the specific context in which the statutory framework was drafted. Notably, the SCSL Statute was drafted against the background of the emerging jurisprudence of the ICTY and ICTR, as well as the adoption of the ICC Statute.

In terms of the scope and content of the historical narratives constructed within the ad hoc tribunals, the statutory frameworks performed two key functions: first, identifying which general categories of crime fell within the jurisdictional scope of the ad hoc tribunals; and second, recognising certain forms of criminality whose precise status under conventional or customary international law was uncertain at that time.

1. Recognition of general categories of crime

An important function of the Statutes of the ad hoc tribunals was to circumscribe the limits of their subject-matter jurisdiction. To this end, the ICTY and ICTR Statutes recognised three general categories of crime:[115] war crimes, crimes against humanity,

[109] UN Security Council Resolution 808, UN Doc S/RES/808 (22 February 1993) [2].

[110] D Shraga and R Zacklin, 'The International Criminal Tribunal for the Former Yugoslavia' (1994) 5 *European Journal of International Law* 360, 362. For an overview of the submissions made to the Secretary General, see generally, WA Schabas, *The UN International Criminal Tribunals: The Former Yugoslavia, Rwanda and Sierra Leone* (CUP 2006) 21–22.

[111] UN Security Council Resolution 827, UN Doc S/RES/827 (25 May 1993) [1]–[2].

[112] RS Lee, 'The Rwanda Tribunal' (1996) 9 *Leiden Journal of International Law* 37, 41–42.

[113] D Shraga and R Zacklin, 'The International Criminal Tribunal for Rwanda' (1996) 7 *European Journal of International Law* 501, 504.

[114] 'Report of the Secretary-General on the Establishment of a Special Court for Sierra Leone' UN Doc S/2000/915 (4 October 2000) ('UN Secretary-General Report on the SCSL') [5]–[6]. For an overview of the process, see generally, Schabas (n 110) 34–40.

[115] Articles 2–5, ICTY Statute; and Articles 2–4, ICTR Statute. For an overview of the thinking behind the subject-matter jurisdiction of the ICTY and ICTR, see generally, Shraga and Zacklin (n 110) 363–369; and Shraga and Zacklin (n 113) 507–510.

and the crime of genocide. By contrast, the SCSL Statute recognised the categories of war crimes and crimes against humanity, as well as offences relating to the abuse of girls and the wanton destruction of property under Sierra Leonean law.[116] According to the UN Secretary-General, the crime of genocide was purposefully omitted from the SCSL Statute due to a 'lack of evidence that the massive, large-scale killing in Sierra Leone was at any time perpetrated against an identified national, ethnic, racial or religious group with an intent to annihilate the group as such'.[117]

From a narrative perspective, the general categories of crime recognised in the Statutes of the ad hoc tribunals marked a shift of perspective away from the 'aggressive war paradigm', which had dominated the Nuremberg and Tokyo tribunals, towards an 'atrocity paradigm',[118] focused on the adjudication of war crimes,[119] crimes against humanity,[120] and the crime of genocide.[121] As a result of this shift, certain historical questions fell beyond their purview.

[116] Articles 2–5, SCSL Statute.

[117] UN Secretary-General Report on the SCSL (n 114) 13.

[118] L Douglas, 'From IMT to NMT: The Emergence of a Jurisprudence of Atrocity', in KC Priemel and A Stiller (eds), *Reassessing the Nuremberg Military Tribunals: Transitional Justice, Trial Narratives, and Historiography* (Berghahn Books 2012) 276, 285–288 (locating the beginnings of the shift in the Nuremberg Military Tribunals). See also, Mégret (n 13) 842–848.

[119] The category of war crimes was elaborated in distinct terms in each of the Statutes. In the ICTY Statute, the war crimes provisions encompassed the grave breaches of the 1949 Geneva Conventions and a non-exhaustive list of violations of the laws or customs of war. The Statutes of the ICTR and SCSL, by contrast, referred to a non-exhaustive list of serious violations of Article 3 common to the 1949 Geneva Conventions and of Additional Protocol II, as well as—in the Statute of the SCSL—a closed list of three other serious violations of international humanitarian law. These variations primarily reflected the distinctive character of the different atrocity situations, including the fact that the conflicts in Rwanda and Sierra Leone were non-international in character. See Articles 2–3, ICTY Statute; Article 4, ICTR Statute; and Articles 3–4, SCSL Statute.

[120] The category of crimes against humanity was elaborated in distinct terms in each of the Statutes. Article 5 of the ICTY Statute required that the prohibited acts be 'committed in armed conflict, whether international or national in character, and directed against any civilian population'. In practice, this requirement was deemed merely jurisdictional and posed little obstacle since it required nothing more than 'proof that *there was* an armed conflict'. *Prosecutor v Duško Tadić* (Judgment, Appeals Chamber) IT-94-1-A (15 July 1999) ('*Tadić* Appeal Judgment') [251] (emphasis in original). Article 3 of the ICTR Statute, by contrast, required that the prohibited acts be committed 'as part of a widespread or systematic attack against any civilian population on national, political, ethnic, racial or religious grounds'. This definition omitted any armed conflict requirement but added a reference to a discriminatory *animus*. In practice, this requirement was also deemed merely jurisdictional and posed little difficulty to satisfy given the nature of the mass atrocity situation in Rwanda in 1994. *Prosecutor v Jean-Paul Akayesu* (Judgment, Appeals Chamber) ICTR-96-4-A (1 June 2001) [464]. By the time the SCSL Statute was drafted, the jurisprudence of the ad hoc tribunals had settled on defining the contextual element of crimes against humanity under customary international law as the commission of prohibited acts 'as part of a widespread or systematic attack directed against any civilian population'. Taking into account this development, this formulation was included in Article 2 of the Statute of the SCSL. Beyond the contextual element, the acts expressly recognised in the illustrative list of prohibited acts for crimes against humanity in each of the Statutes were based on those elaborated in Article 6(c) of the Nuremberg Charter, with a few additions. In the Statutes of the ICTY and ICTR, the prohibited acts of imprisonment, torture, and rape were added to the list. Seemingly inspired by the language of Article 7 of the ICC Statute, the Statute of the SCSL enumerated the same prohibited acts as those listed in the Statutes of the ICTY and ICTR, but added 'sexual slavery, enforced prostitution, forced pregnancy and any other form of sexual violence', as well as 'ethnic' to the discriminatory grounds of persecution.

[121] The definition of the crime of genocide in Article 2 of the Convention on the Prevention and Punishment of the Crime of Genocide was reproduced *verbatim* in the Statutes of the ICTY and ICTR. See Article 4, ICTY Statute; and Article 2, ICTR Statute.

At the ICTY, for example, the omission of the crime of aggression meant that the question of the legality of the North Atlantic Treaty Organization's (NATO) bombing campaign against the Federal Republic of Yugoslavia in 1999 fell beyond the scope of the tribunal's jurisdiction.[122] The decision not to include the crime of aggression in the ICTY Statute was, of course, taken several years prior to the NATO campaign and was likely driven by uncertainties that existed over the definition of the offence under customary international law as well as the preoccupation of the UN Security Council with the conduct of the war in the former Yugoslavia rather than its causes.[123] Nonetheless, the omission of the category not only denied ICTY prosecutors the possibility of investigating the legality of the NATO campaign, but may even have helped legitimise the controversial proposition that situations of mass atrocity may warrant the waging of wars of aggression.[124]

The omission of the crime of aggression from the Statutes of the ICTR and SCSL is easier to understand given that aggression only addresses interstate uses of force and the underlying conflicts in Rwanda and Sierra Leone were non-international in character (notwithstanding notable influences by external States).[125] Nonetheless, the atrocity-focus of these tribunals also excluded a number of historical questions from examination. At the SCSL, for example, the lack of a legal concept to adjudicate the outbreak of hostilities meant that questions of responsibility for initiating the conflict were not directly addressed by the tribunal.[126] At the ICTR, the question of responsibility for the plane crash that killed Rwandan President Habyarimana, sparking the outbreak of genocide in Rwanda in 1994, also proved to be an awkward legal issue in light of the tribunal's limited jurisdiction. In a recent interview, former Chief Prosecutor of the ICTR and ICTY, Louise Arbour, revealed that she had not been persuaded that the shooting down of the plane constituted a war crime or a crime against humanity, while it would have been difficult to construe it as an act of genocide 'unless it was perpetrated by the leaders of the genocide to act as a trigger for the mass mobilization that followed'.[127] Arbour's perspective was shared by her successor, Carla Del

[122] ICTY Prosecutorial Committee, 'Final Report to the Prosecutor by the Committee Established to Review the NATO Bombing Campaign Against the Federal Republic of Yugoslavia' (8 June 2000) ('ICTY NATO Report') [30]–[34].

[123] Cryer (n 55) 244.

[124] Douglas (n 118) 286.

[125] L van den Herik, *The Contribution of the Rwandan Tribunal to the Development of International Law* (Martinus Nijhoff Publishers 2005) 68–69.

[126] The issue arose tangentially in the case of *Fofana and Kondewa*, in which the Trial Chamber concluded that since the crimes of the defendants had been carried out 'in defending a cause that is palpably just and defendable, ... acting in defence of constitutionality by engaging in a struggle or a fight that was geared towards the restoration of the ousted democratically elected Government of President Kabbah', this constituted a mitigating circumstance in their favour as part of determining their sentence. *Prosecutor v Moinina Fofana and Allieu Kondewa* (Judgment on the Sentencing of Moinina Fofana and Allieu Kondewa, Trial Chamber) SCSL-04-14-T (9 October 2007) [86]. A majority of the Appeals Chamber overturned this finding by re-asserting the well-established distinction between *jus ad bellum* and *jus in bello* and concluding that '[c]onsideration of political motive by a court applying humanitarian law not only contravenes, but would undermine a bedrock principle of that law'. *Prosecutor v Moinina Fofana and Allieu Kondewa* (Judgment, Appeals Chamber) SCSL-04-14-A (28 May 2008) [531].

[127] L Reydams, 'Politics or Pragmatism? The International Criminal Tribunal for Rwanda and the Burying of the Investigation into the Assassination of President Juvénal Habyarimana' (2018) 40 *Human Rights Quarterly* 989, 1006. On the challenges of characterising the shooting down of the plane as a war crime, see generally, P Robinson and G Ghahraman, 'Can Rwandan President Kagame Be Held Responsible at the ICTR for the Killing of President Habyarimana?' (2008) 6 *Journal of International Criminal Justice* 981.

Ponte, who considered the latter type of scenario 'almost too Machiavellian to imagine'.[128] Consequently, the assassination of President Habyarimana remained one of the untold histories of the tribunal.

2. Progressive development of general categories of crime

The Statutes of the ad hoc tribunals were also notable for their progressive development of certain aspects of the crime categories that fell within their subject-matter jurisdiction. A review of the war crimes category within the ICTR and SCSL Statutes is illustrative.

The recognition of war crimes in Article 4 of the ICTR Statute proved particularly controversial at the time. The inclusion of war crimes was one of the reasons that Rwanda ultimately voted against the adoption of the Statute, its concern being that the tribunal would waste its meagre financial and human resources prosecuting war crimes instead of trying 'the crime of crimes, genocide'.[129] In other words, the Rwandan government desired the narrative focus of the tribunal to be on the crime of genocide. In the end, the expectation that the tribunal would focus on the crime of genocide was only reflected by placing genocide first within the list of crimes within the Statute, as well as by expressly referring to genocide in the full name of the tribunal.[130] In addition, whilst Rwanda was bound by Article 3 common to the Geneva Conventions and Additional Protocol II as a matter of treaty law, in 1994 it remained unclear whether such provisions entailed individual criminal responsibility. Notably, the uncertain status of war crimes in non-international armed conflicts led the UN Secretary-General to conclude that the Security Council had '*for the first time* criminalize[d] article 3 of the four Geneva Conventions'.[131] The implication was that the inclusion of war crimes in the ICTR Statute constituted a progressive development of the law that the Security Council had adopted in response to the atrocities committed during the armed conflict in Rwanda.[132]

At the SCSL, progressive developments included the recognition of the war crime of intentionally directing attacks against peacekeepers in Article 4(b) of the SCSL Statute, as well as the inclusion of the war crime of enlisting children under the age of fifteen years into armed forces or groups in Article 4(c) of the SCSL Statute. As regards the former, the UN Secretary-General supported the customary status of the crime on the basis that it constituted merely '*a specification* of a targeted group within the generally protected group of civilians which because of its humanitarian or peacekeeping mission deserves special attention'.[133] As regards the latter, during the drafting of the SCSL Statute the Secretary-General had in fact queried the customary status of the crime of enlistment and suggested that the crime of recruiting and using child

[128] C Del Ponte, *Madame Prosecutor: Confrontations with Humanity's Worst Criminals and the Culture of Impunity* (Other Press 2009) 180.

[129] 'Provisional Verbatim Record of the Three Thousand Four Hundred and Fifty Third Meeting' UN Doc S/PV.3453 (8 November 1994) 15.

[130] van den Herik (n 125) 68; Shraga and Zacklin (n 113) 508.

[131] 'Report of the Secretary-General Pursuant to Paragraph 5 of Security Council Resolution 955 (1994)' UN Doc S/1995/134 (13 February 1995) ('UN Secretary-General Report on the ICTR') [12] (emphasis added).

[132] Cryer (n 55) 267.

[133] UN Secretary-General Report on the SCSL (n 114) [16] (emphasis added).

soldiers instead be limited to the 'abduction and forced recruitment of children under the age of 15 years into armed forces or groups for the purpose of using them to participate actively in hostilities'.[134] However, the Security Council disagreed and drafted Article 4(c) of the SCSL Statute in near-identical terms to Article 8(e)(vii) of the ICC Statute.[135] According to Ilene Cohn, a programme officer with the Office of the UN Special Representative of the Secretary-General for Children and Armed Conflict, the final text of Article 4(c) was heavily influenced by several UN actors and civil society groups—including Amnesty International, Human Rights Watch, and Save the Children (United Kingdom and Sweden)—who successfully lobbied the Security Council to utilise the language of Article 8(e)(vii) of the ICC Statute, which they asserted had codified existing customary international law.[136]

As these examples reveal, the drafters of the Statutes of the ad hoc tribunals were confronted by a tension between the uncertain legal status of particular categories of crime on the one hand and a desire to respond to the atrocities that were alleged to have been committed during the situations under examination on the other. With respect to the categories of war crimes discussed above, the drafters prioritised progressively developing the law in an effort to ensure its continued relevance to modern-day conditions of armed conflict.

B. Charging Practices

Turning to charging practices, primary authority to determine the scope and focus of the charges at the ad hoc tribunals was entrusted to the prosecution,[137] subject to a degree of judicial oversight that varied over time.[138] In contrast to the Nuremberg and Tokyo tribunals, prosecutors at the ad hoc tribunals were under a formal statutory duty to act independently as separate organs of the tribunals,[139] as well as a professional ethical obligation 'to be, and appear to be, consistent, objective, and independent, and avoid all conflicts of interest'.[140] From a narrative perspective, most significant was the fact that prosecutors at the ad hoc tribunals were not restricted to initiating just one case, but were empowered to launch multiple cases, developing a prosecutorial programme whose scope and focus would evolve over time.

1. Scope of charges

In terms of the scope of the charges, it is possible to identify a shift in charging practices at the ad hoc tribunals away from initial attempts to develop near-comprehensive

[134] Ibid [17]–[18].

[135] 'Letter dated 22 December 2000 from the President of the Security Council to the Secretary-General' UN Doc S/2000/1234 (22 December 2000) 2.

[136] I Cohn, 'The Protection of Children and the Quest for Truth and Justice in Sierra Leone' (2001) 55 *Journal of International Affairs* 1, 21.

[137] Article 16(1), ICTY Statute; Article 15(1), ICTR Statute; Article 15(1), SCSL Statute.

[138] See generally, Friman et al (n 38) 397–399 and 415–422.

[139] Article 16(2), ICTY Statute; Article 15(2), ICTR Statute; Article 15(1), SCSL Statute.

[140] Article 2(c), ICTY and ICTR Standards of Professional Conduct for Prosecution Counsel (1999).

charges against defendants towards a more streamlined approach to indictments and a willingness to rely upon negotiated justice where feasible.

The initial charging practices at the ICTY and ICTR were characterised by a prosecutorial preference for broad indictments that extended over long periods of time and broad geographical areas with numerous incidents and large numbers of victims and alleged perpetrators.[141] The practice of overloading indictments appears to have been driven by a desire to ensure that the charges reflected the *full* alleged criminality of defendants in order to construct a more comprehensive historical record.[142]

Illustrative of this approach was the indictment strategy deployed with respect to Slobodan Milošević. In that case, then-ICTY Prosecutor Carla Del Ponte decided to apply for the joinder of the three indictments that had been issued against Milošević concerning crimes that had allegedly been committed in Kosovo, Croatia, and Bosnia and Herzegovina. Del Ponte appeared to be motivated by a desire to construct a comprehensive historical narrative concerning the role played by Milošević over the course of the entire conflict.[143] Del Ponte argued that Milošević had been involved in a single 'transaction' or common scheme to create a 'Greater Serbia' that warranted the joinder of the three indictments.[144] Although the ICTY Trial Chamber initially only permitted the joinder of the Croatia and Bosnia and Herzegovina indictments,[145] the Prosecutor's argument was successful on appeal and all three indictments were eventually joined together to form a single trial.[146] As a result, the final indictment against Milošević comprised sixty-six counts, each encompassing multiple alleged criminal acts and crime scenes, spanning three broad geographical areas over a ten year period.[147] To give an indication of the complexity of the charges in the case, Gillian Higgins has observed that one count of deportation in Kosovo encompassed allegations that the defendant was responsible for this particular crime 'in at least sixty-four different locations within thirteen municipalities, pursuant to eight different forms of conduct'.[148]

In the early 2000s, the extensive charging practices at the ICTY and ICTR fell into disfavour, driven primarily by two factors.

First, prosecutors and judges began to realise that extensive indictments risked generating trials that were both unwieldy and difficult to manage within a reasonable period of time.[149] Indeed, the dangers of the comprehensive approach to charging were surfaced when Slobodan Milošević died prior to a verdict being delivered in his

141 Locke (n 42) 616.

142 ICTY and UNICRI, *ICTY Manual on Developed Practices* (UNICRI Publisher 2009) 36.

143 TW Waters, 'A Kind of Judgment: Searching for Judicial Narratives After Death' (2010) 42 *George Washington International Law Review* 279, 301–302.

144 *Prosecutor v Slobodan Milošević* (Decision on Prosecution's Motion for Joinder, Trial Chamber) IT-99-37-PT, IT-01-50-PT & IT-01-51-PT (13 December 2001) [16] and [42].

145 Ibid [52]–[53].

146 *Prosecutor v Slobodan Milošević* (Decision on Prosecution's Interlocutory Appeal from Refusal to Order Joinder, Appeals Chamber) IT-99-37-AR73, IT-01-50- AR73 & IT-01-51- AR73 (1 February 2002).

147 See generally, G Higgins, 'The Impact of the Size, Scope, and Scale of the *Milošević* Trial and the Development of Rule 73*bis* before the ICTY' (2009) 7 *Northwestern Journal of International Human Rights* 239.

148 Ibid 247.

149 ICTY and UNICRI (n 142) 36.

case.[150] In this context, it is perhaps unsurprising that the SCSL Prosecutor was reportedly 'strongly advised' by ICTY prosecutors 'to focus his indictments rather than follow their tradition of including numerous cumulative charges'.[151]

Second, both judges and the UN Security Council began to reflect on the time span of the ad hoc tribunals. Amidst perceptions that the international community's interest in the ICTY was waning, then-ICTY President Judge Jorda and his colleagues devised the concept of a 'Completion Strategy' in 2000.[152] Several years later, in August 2003, the Security Council adopted Resolution 1503, which called on the ICTY and ICTR to take all possible measures to complete investigations by the end of 2004, all trial work at first instance by the end of 2008, and all work in general in 2010.[153] By endorsing the ICTY's Completion Strategy and urging the ICTR to formalise a detailed strategy modelled on its ICTY counterpart, the Security Council heightened the pressure on prosecutors and judges to ensure that cases were manageable in size.[154] Relatedly, at least partially in response to concerns that had arisen over the extensive indictments at the ICTY and ICTR, the SCSL was established with the expectation that it would dispense justice in a cost-effective and expeditious manner, operating on a fraction of the budget of the other ad hoc tribunals.[155] As a result, the SCSL Prosecutor was left with little choice but to adopt a more disciplined approach to his charging strategy from the outset.[156]

It was in this climate that the charging practices at the ad hoc tribunals began to shift in two significant respects.

First, the practice of developing near-comprehensive indictments at the ICTY and ICTR gradually gave way to a representative charging strategy characterised by an increasing willingness to streamline indictments.[157] In a similar vein, the indictments at the SCSL included fewer than twenty charges each, the SCSL Prosecutor striving from the outset to be representative rather than comprehensive.[158] Significantly, beyond prosecutors reviewing and reducing the number of counts and crimes charged, judges at the ICTY in particular became more active in their management of cases—expediting proceedings by inviting or directing the Prosecutor to further reduce the scope of indictments.[159] In *Karadžić*, for example, the ICTY Trial Chamber relied on

150 Schabas (n 28) 163 ('Arguably, had the charges against him been more focussed, ... at least one set of proceedings might have been completed').

151 T Perriello and M Wierda, *The Special Court for Sierra Leone Under Scrutiny* (ICTJ 2006) 27.

152 F Pocar, 'Completion or Continuation Strategy? Appraising Problems and Possible Developments in Building the Legacy of the ICTY' (2008) 6 *Journal of International Criminal Justice* 655, 657.

153 UN Security Council Resolution 1503, UN Doc S/RES/1503 (28 August 2003) [7].

154 Locke (n 42) 618.

155 A Cassese, *Report on the Special Court for Sierra Leone* (12 December 2006) 65–66 (referring to the SCSL as 'shoestring justice').

156 T Cruvellier, *From the Taylor Trial to a Lasting Legacy: Putting the Special Court Model to the Test* (ICTJ 2009) 19; KJ Heller, 'The Role of the International Prosecutor', in CPR Romano et al (eds), *The Oxford Handbook of International Adjudication* (OUP 2013) 669, 683.

157 'Report on the Completion of the Mandate of the ICTR as at 15 November 2015' Enclosure to UN Doc S/2015/884 (17 November 2015) ('ICTR Final Completion Report') [52]; 'Final Report of Serge Brammertz, Prosecutor of the ICTY, provided to the Security Council under paragraph 6 of Security Council resolution 1534 (2004)' Annex II to UN Doc S/2017/1001 (29 November 2017) ('ICTY Prosecutor Final Completion Report') [74].

158 Cruvellier (n 156) 21.

159 ICTY Prosecutor Final Completion Report (n 157) [75].

Rule 73*bis*(D) to hold that the prosecution was not permitted to present evidence in respect of eight municipalities in their entirety as well as a number of specific individual incidents or crime sites connected to the remaining municipalities, Srebrenica enclave, and Sarajevo siege.[160] The result of these practices was to narrow *the factual scope* of the charges examined by the ad hoc tribunals in their trials and judgments—particularly at the level of specific incidents and crime sites.

Relatedly, at times prosecutors at the ad hoc tribunals also narrowed *the narrative frame* of the charges. Richard Wilson, for example, identifies a shift in prosecutorial strategy at the ICTY away from attempting to construct 'a grand, sweeping metanarrative of history' in the tribunal's early cases towards 'a more conventional crime-based methodology based on documents and fact-witness testimony, an approach with less exalted intellectual ambitions perhaps but also less risk of malfunctioning'.[161] The shift appears to have been triggered by an evolution in prosecutorial understanding concerning the types of evidence and case theory that would prove most persuasive and convincing to the judges.[162] The prosecution's construction of a grand monumental history of the Balkans in the *Milošević* trial, for example, represented an attempt to build an inferential case to prove the specific intent of genocide.[163] When it became clear in the case of *Brđanin* that broad monumental narratives would not generally assist in proving genocidal intent, prosecutors turned to 'a new formula' that entailed bringing together internal and external expert witnesses who 'presented complementary micro-histories and ... composed a narrative arc that gave order and unity to the disparate documents and items of evidence in the case'.[164]

Second, prosecutors at the ICTY and ICTR also began to engage in negotiated justice.[165] The term 'negotiated justice' refers to negotiations between the prosecution and defence concerning the outcome of the proceedings, in most cases resulting in a guilty plea by the defendant and/or the provision of other assistance to the prosecution in exchange for more lenient treatment, for example a recommended reduction in sentence, the withdrawal of some of the charges, and/or a recommended favourable location of imprisonment.[166] In terms of numbers, twenty individuals at the ICTY and eight individuals at the ICTR pleaded guilty in practice, typically pursuant to a plea agreement,[167] while no individuals pleaded guilty at the SCSL.[168] The vast majority were mid- or low-ranking individuals in the political or military hierarchy who had

[160] *Prosecutor v Radovan Karadžić* (Order to the Prosecution under Rule 73bis(D), Trial Chamber) IT-95-5/18-PT (22 July 2009). For additional examples, see Higgins (n 147) 251–257.

[161] RA Wilson, *Writing History in International Criminal Tribunals* (CUP 2011) 109.

[162] Ibid 121.

[163] Ibid 109.

[164] Ibid 219.

[165] On 'negotiated justice', see generally, JI Turner and T Weigend, 'Negotiated Justice', in Sluiter et al (n 38) 1375.

[166] Ibid 1375 and 1384–1386.

[167] Ibid 1383 (these figures exclude the guilty plea of a former ICTR witness who gave false testimony at the tribunal).

[168] Although the SCSL never received any guilty pleas, it is well known that the Prosecutor relied on insider witnesses to assist with the conviction of those subject to prosecution, a practice the Prosecutor referred to as 'dancing with the devil'. For critique, see W Jordash, 'Insiders: The Special Court for Sierra Leone's Dirty Laundry' *JusticeInfo.Net* (30 April 2020).

been charged with fewer counts at a limited number of sites.[169] Several of these individuals were ultimately relied upon to provide insider testimony about higher-ranking suspects, as well as to offer previously unknown insights about particular events and a personal perspective about the conflict more generally.[170]

Negotiated justice affected the historical records rendered by the ad hoc tribunals in a number of ways. First, by foregoing a full trial, the facts alleged by the prosecution and admitted by the defendant were not subject to the scrutiny of the evidentiary rules typically utilised by the ad hoc tribunals.[171] As a result, the factual basis of plea agreements was typically far more succinct than court judgments, merely setting out a brief historical sketch of the defendant's involvement in atrocities.[172] Second, where a plea agreement involved the withdrawal of charges in exchange for a guilty plea, the effect was to edit out either the full factual basis upon which a conviction rested and/or particular legal characterisations of the underlying facts—rendering the historical record incomplete or at least open to question.[173] Finally, although the public acceptance and acknowledgement of responsibility by a defendant was itself an act that formed an important part of the historical record of the ad hoc tribunals, the case of Biljana Plavšić—the 'Serbian Iron Lady', who was deputy to Bosnian Serb leader Radovan Karadžić and later President of the Republika Srpška—revealed how a defendant might offer a tactical guilty plea in order to obtain more lenient treatment, only to later retract the sincerity of their plea upon release from imprisonment.[174]

2. Focus of charges

Turning to the focus of the charges, since space does not permit a comprehensive examination of all of the indictments of the ad hoc tribunals, this section first highlights some of the overarching themes within the indictments before turning to identify some of the factors that help to explain the focus of the charges and how they evolved over time.

a. Thematic focus of charges

Beginning with an overview of the thematic focus of the charges, a number of themes emerge from the indictments of the ad hoc tribunals.

[169] J Meernik, 'What Kind of Bargain Is a Plea?' (2014) 14 *International Criminal Law Review* 200, 207–209; S Ford, 'Fairness and Politics at the ICTY: Evidence from the Indictments' (2013) XXXIX *North Carolina Journal of International Law and Commercial Regulation* 45, 102.

[170] K Bachmann and A Fatić, *The UN International Criminal Tribunals: Transition Without Justice?* (Routledge 2015) 127–129; and JN Clark, 'Plea Bargaining at the ICTY: Guilty Pleas and Reconciliation' (2009) 20 *European Journal of International Law* 415, 424–425.

[171] *Prosecutor v Momir Nikolić* (Sentencing Judgment, Trial Chamber) IT-02-60/1-S (2 December 2003) ('*Momir Nikolić* Trial Sentencing Judgment') [61].

[172] See, for example, *Prosecutor v Biljana Plavšić and Momčilo Krajišnik* (Factual Basis for Plea of Guilt, Trial Chamber) IT-00-39&40-PT (30 September 2002).

[173] *Momir Nikolić* Trial Sentencing Judgment (n 171) [63]. See also, Clark (n 170) 428; and RE Rauxloh, 'Negotiated History: The Historical Record in International Criminal Law and Plea Bargaining' (2010) 10 *International Criminal Law Review* 739, 753.

[174] DU Goldberg, 'Plavšić Retracts War-Crimes Confession' *Bosnian Institute* (4 February 2009).

At the ICTY, almost all of the 161 indictees were charged with war crimes and crimes against humanity, while twenty-two indictees were charged with genocide.[175] According to a study conducted by Leila Sadat, in total ICTY prosecutors charged 939 counts of war crimes (56.9 per cent of all indicted offences), 670 counts of crimes against humanity (40.6 per cent), and forty counts of genocide (2.4 per cent).[176] The high number of war crimes counts enabled prosecutors to illuminate a range of violations committed by different sides to the conflict, including attacks on civilians and civilian objects,[177] the maintenance of camps in which physical abuse and inhuman treatment were pervasive,[178] acts of violence the primary purpose of which was to spread terror among the civilian population,[179] and the taking of hostages.[180]

Although important to the historical narratives construted within the ICTY, the war crimes counts failed to fully capture the discriminatory dimensions of the conflict in the former Yugoslavia. These dimensions were addressed primarily through the category of crimes against humanity and, less frequently, the crime of genocide. In practice, prosecutors at the ICTY confined charges of genocide to specific local contexts,[181] with fewer than 1 per cent resulting in convictions.[182] By contrast, the nationwide campaigns pursued by States in the territory of the former Yugoslavia were predominantly understoood through the lens of ethnic cleansing,[183] namely 'a purposeful policy designed by one ethnic or religious group to remove by violent and terror-inspiring means the civilian population of another ethnic or religious group from certain geographic areas'.[184] This is evident not only from the fact that seventy-one indictees were charged with the forcible transfer or deportation of civilians, often involving thousands of people,[185] but also from the importance that came to be placed on charges of persecution as a crime against humanity.[186] According to William Fenrick, a former legal advisor to the Office of the Prosecutor, 'just as genocide [became] the offence which represents what happened in Rwanda during 1994 so the

[175] Ford (n 169) 74–75 (calculating that 159 indictees were charged with at least one war crime, 142 indictees were charged with at least one crime against humanity, and only 22 indictees were charged with genocide).

[176] LN Sadat, 'Crimes Against Humanity in the Modern Age' (2013) 107 *American Journal of International Law* 334, 342–343.

[177] See, for example, *Prosecutor v Pavle Strugar* (Judgment, Trial Chamber) IT-01-42-T (31 January 2005) ('*Strugar* Trial Judgment') [277]–[289].

[178] See, for example, *Prosecutor v Delalić et al* (Judgment, Appeals Chamber) IT-96-21-A (20 February 2001) (concerning events at a detention facility in the village of Čelebići in central Bosnia and Herzegovina).

[179] See, for example, *Prosecutor v Stanislav Galić* (Judgment, Appeals Chamber) IT-98-29-A ICTY Appeals Chamber (30 November 2006) ('*Galić* Appeal Judgment') [79]–[109].

[180] See, for example, *Prosecutor v Radovan Karadžić* (Judgment, Trial Chamber) IT-95-5/18-T (24 March 2016) [5852]–[5994].

[181] WA Schabas, 'Was Genocide Committed in Bosnia and Herzegovina? First Judgments of the International Criminal Tribunal for the Former Yugoslavia' (2001) 25 *Fordham International Law Journal* 23, 42–43.

[182] Sadat (n 176) 344.

[183] C Tournaye, 'Genocidal Intent Before the ICTY' (2003) 52 *International and Comparative Law Quarterly* 447, 447.

[184] 'Final Report of the Commission of Experts Established Pursuant to Security Council Resolution 780 (1994)' UN Doc S/1994/674 (27 May 1994) ('Former Yugoslavia Commission of Experts Final Report') [130].

[185] Ford (n 169) 85.

[186] Sadat (n 176) 344.

crime against humanity of persecution [came] to typify what happened in the territory of the former Yugoslavia'.[187]

Finally, ICTY prosecutors also made particular efforts to bring charges of rape and other forms of sexual violence. In total, seventy-eight individuals were charged with sexual violence crimes, leading to thirty-two convictions.[188] These charges included a landmark thematic prosecution in *Kunarac et al*, which focused on sexual violence crimes committed by male Serb forces against Muslim and Croat women in Foča, Bosnia and Herzegovina.[189]

At the ICTR, prosecutors primarily brought charges of genocide and crimes against humanity, with far fewer war crimes charges. According to Leila Sadat's study, in total ICTR prosecutors charged 282 counts of crimes against humanity (44.4 per cent of all indicted offences), 254 counts of genocide (40 per cent), and 99 counts of war crimes (15.6 per cent).[190] In contrast to the ICTY, prosecutors at the ICTR sought to establish a nationwide genocidal campaign in Rwanda. To this end, ICTR prosecutors brought charges that enabled the tribunal to examine the diversity of means by which the genocidal campaign across Rwanda was perpetrated,[191] including the use of roadblocks to identify, kill, or rape Tutsis,[192] large-scale massacres at places of refuge such as churches,[193] and the use of the news media to incite the population to commit acts of violence against the Tutsi population and those sympathetic to them.[194] The prosecution of sexual violence was also described as a 'major priority' for the Office of the Prosecutor.[195] In total, fifty-two individuals were charged with sexual violence crimes, leading to thirteen convictions.[196]

At the SCSL, the prosecution charged 105 counts of war crimes (57.7 per cent of all indicted offences) and seventy-seven counts of crimes against humanity (42.3 per cent).[197] In all four cases that went to trial, the Prosecutor brought charges of murder as a crime against humanity, as well as the war crimes of murder, acts of terrorism, pillage, and recruiting and using child soldiers. In three out of the four cases that went to trial, the Prosecutor brought charges of enslavement as a crime against humanity,

187 WJ Fenrick, 'The Crime Against Humanity of Persecution in the Jurisprudence of the ICTY' (2001) 32 *Netherlands Yearbook of International Law* 81, 89.

188 'In Numbers' *ICTY Website*, accessible at: https://www.icty.org/en/features/crimes-sexual-violence/in-numbers (last accessed 2 June 2020) (numbers accurate as of September 2016).

189 *Prosecutor v Kunarac et al* (Judgment, Trial Chamber) IT-96-23-T & IT-96-23/1-T (22 February 2001); *Prosecutor v Kunarac et al* (Judgment, Appeals Chamber) IT-96-23 & IT-96-23/1-A (12 June 2002).

190 Sadat (n 176) 347.

191 ICTR Final Completion Report (n 157) [55].

192 See, for example, *Prosecutor v Nyiramasuhuko et al* (Judgment, Appeals Chamber) ICTR-98-42-A (14 December 2015) [1389]–[1504].

193 See, for example, *Prosecutor v Athanase Seromba* (Judgment, Appeals Chamber) ICTR-2001-66-A (12 March 2008) (concerning the deaths of at least 1,500 Tutsi refugees who had sought refuge in Nyange church before a decision was taken to destroy it).

194 See, for example, *Nahimana et al v Prosecutor* (Judgment, Appeals Chamber) ICTR-99-52-A (28 November 2007) ('*Nahimana et al* Appeal Judgment').

195 ICTR Final Completion Report (n 157) [56].

196 ICTR Office of the Prosecutor, 'Best Practices Manual for the Investigation and Prosecution of Sexual Violence Crimes in Post-Conflict Regions: Lessons Learned from the Office of the Prosecutor for the International Criminal Tribunal for Rwanda' (30 January 2014) [10]–[11] (although the Manual states that 13 individuals have been convicted, it is important to note that as of May 2020, the review of Augustin Ngirabatware's appeal judgment remains pending).

197 Sadat (n 176) 349–350.

rape and other forms of sexual violence as a crime against humanity, as well as the war crimes of collective punishment and outrages upon personal dignity. Other notable charges included the war crimes of violence to life, health and physical or mental well-being of persons involving mutilation or cruel treatment, as well as the war crime of intentionally directing attacks against peacekeepers.[198] Despite the inclusion of domestic crimes in the Statute of the SCSL, the Prosecutor declined to include violations of domestic law in the indictments, describing such charges as 'a legal mine field' that would have led to complicated jurisdictional challenges.[199]

Beyond these tribunal-specific practices, a trend that pervaded the ad hoc tribunals was a prosecutorial propensity to illuminate how different types of violence and crimes *intersected*. For example, prosecutors at the ad hoc tribunals brought innovative charges that recognised how sexual and gender-based crimes intersected with other acts prohibited under the categories of genocide, crimes against humanity, and war crimes.[200] This practice of 'intersectionality' was often relied upon to illuminate the different ends to which SGBV had been instrumentalised in particular mass atrocity contexts.[201] Significantly, judges at the ad hoc tribunals proved receptive to this practice. In *Akayesu*, for example, the ICTR Trial Chamber acknowledged that rape and other forms of sexual volence could constitute a means of committing genocide, for example by constituting a form of serious bodily or mental harm that results in the phyiscal and biological destruction of Tutsi women, their families, and their communities.[202] At the ICTY, judges concluded that rape and other forms of sexual violence may constitute the crime against humanity of persecution,[203] as well as the war crime of torture.[204] And in *Sesay et al*, the SCSL Trial Chamber confirmed that various forms of SGBV, including rape, sexual slavery, forced marriages, and outrages on personal dignity, when committed against a civilian population with the specific intent to terrorise, could amount to an act of terror.[205]

There were at least three narrative consequences of intersectional analyses of SGBV.[206] First, an intersectional understanding of SGBV raised the prominence of

[198] For an overview of the cases at the SCSL, see generally, SCSL, 'Eleventh and Final Report of the President of the Special Court for Sierra Leone' (December 2013) 11–17.

[199] War Crimes Studies Center, *Interim Report on the Special Court for Sierra Leone* (War Crimes Studies Center April 2005) 7 (citing an interview conducted with the SCSL Prosecutor).

[200] Grey (n 60) 80–82 (noting that the strategy of intersectional charging of sexual and gender-based crimes proved controversial among tribunal prosecutors).

[201] The term 'intersectionality' is drawn from the work of Valerie Oosterveld. See generally, V Oosterveld, 'Evaluating the Special Court for Sierra Leone's Gender Jurisprudence', in CC Jalloh (ed), *The Sierra Leone Special Court and its Legacy: The Impact for Africa and International Criminal Law* (CUP 2014) 234, 254–255; and V Oosterveld, 'The Gender Jurisprudence of the Special Court for Sierra Leone: Progress in the Revolutionary United Front Judgments' (2011) 44 *Cornell International Law Journal* 49, 72–74.

[202] *Prosecutor v Jean-Paul Akayesu* (Judgment, Trial Chamber) ICTR-96-4-T (2 September 1998) ('*Akayesu* Trial Judgment') [731]–[732].

[203] *Prosecutor v Radoslav Brđanin* (Judgment, Trial Chamber) IT-99-36-T (1 September 2004) ('*Brđanin* Trial Judgment') [1010]–[1013]. See similarly, *Prosecutor v Bagosora et al* (Judgment and Sentence, Trial Chamber) ICTR-98-41-T (18 December 2008) ('*Bagosora et al* Trial Judgment') [2210]–[2212].

[204] *Prosecutor v Delalić et al* (Judgment, Trial Chamber) IT-96-21-T (16 November 1998) ('*Delalić et al* Trial Judgment') [494]–[496].

[205] *Prosecutor v Sesay et al* (Judgment, Trial Chamber) SCSL-04-15-T (2 March 2009) ('*Sesay et al* Trial Judgment') [1352]. The war crime of acts of terrorism was enunciated in Article 3(d), SCSL Statute.

[206] Oosterveld (2014) (n 201) 255; and Oosterveld (2011) (n 201) 73–74, fn 182.

such crimes in the judgments of the tribunals, signalling a retreat from the silence that had traditionally accompanied such offences. Second, intersectional analyses enabled a more precise determination of the nature of the harm caused to victims by particular acts of SGBV.[207] And finally, the contextualisation inherent in intersectional analyses enabled a more nuanced understanding of SGBV, in particular by illuminating their instrumentalisation for different ends, including genocide, persecution, torture, and terror.

b. Explaining the focus of charges

Turning to examine the different factors that influenced the focus of the charges at the ad hoc tribunals, it is possible to identify a number of elements at play.

At a general level, the focus of the charges depended on the availability of and access to relevant evidence. Initially, evidence collection at the ad hoc tribunals was guided by prior efforts to map atrocties that had been conducted by UN-sponsored Commissions of Experts,[208] civil society groups,[209] and journalists.[210] As the work of the tribunals evolved over time, access to evidence typically fluctuated according to the degree and form of cooperation received from the States whose territories formed the focus of investigations—a variable that itself typically depended on prosecutorial strategies to develop alliances with compliance partners, the degree of external pressure applied by other States, and changes in the domestic political landscape within the territories under examination.[211]

At a more granular level, the focus of the charges at the ad hoc tribunals may be understood to be the product of a more diverse set of factors. In order to illustrate the

[207] See, however, R Arnold, 'The Judicial Contribution of the Special Court for Sierra Leone to the Prosecution of Terrorism', in CC Jalloh (ed), *The Sierra Leone Special Court and its Legacy: The Impact for Africa and International Criminal Law* (CUP 2014) 260, 286 (cautioning that intersectional analyses of SGBV should be ancillary or concurrent, not prevailing, in order to ensure that individual incidents of such violence are not 'swallowed' up in the collectivity of victims addressed in prosecutions of other prohibited acts such as the war crime of terrorism).

[208] Former Yugoslavia Commission of Experts Final Report (n 184); and 'Preliminary Report of the Independent Commission of Experts established in accordance with Security Council resolution 935 (1994)' UN Doc S/1994/1125 (4 October 1994).

[209] See, for example, C Del Ponte, 'Investigation and Prosecution of Large-scale Crimes at the International Level: The Experience of the ICTY' (2006) 4 *Journal of International Criminal Justice* 539, 543 (confirming that investigations at the ICTY included 'reviewing open source material, NGO reports, [and] identifying and conducting interviews of victims'); and P van Tuyl, *Effective, Efficient, and Fair? An Inquiry into the Investigative Practices of the Office of the Prosecutor at the Special Court for Sierra Leone* (War Crimes Studies Center 2008) 7 (confirming that SCSL Prosecutor Crane had sought the input of civil society groups and local human rights advocates).

[210] See, for example, Bachmann and Fatić (n 170) 91–92 and 123–124 (explaining how the ICTY Prosecutor's indictment strategy was influenced by its pursuit of public and media support in light of its limited resources, which led to a focus on crimes that had been highlighted in the media that were likely to garner public support for the institution).

[211] See, for example, R Levi et al, 'International Courts in Atypical Political Environments: The Interplay of Prosecutorial Strategy, Evidence, and Court Authority in International Criminal Law' (2016) 79 *Law and Contemporary Problems* 289, 301–308 (revealing how prosecutors at the ICTY 'needed to build alliances across potential compliance partners—diplomats, police forces, and militaries—to secure state cooperation and to cope with a changing geopolitical context towards domestic courts in Bosnia and Herzegovina'); and Bachmann and Fatić (n 170) 121–122 (pointing to the significance of governmental transitions in Serbia and Croatia in terms of access to evidence at the ICTY).

different influences at play, the fluctuating record of the ICTR concerning the prosecution of sexual violence crimes offers a useful case-study.

During his two-year tenure from November 1994 to September 1996, Prosecutor Richard Goldstone failed to develop a comprehensive prosecutorial strategy concerning sexual violence crimes.[212] Challenges experienced during his tenure included a lack of specialist training for investigators, a lack of political will amongst those leading the investigations, and a lack of diversity on the investigative teams which were predominantly male and from outside Rwanda.[213] As a result, Goldstone failed to include sexual violence crimes in many of the early indictments at the ICTR.[214]

A turning point for the prosecution of sexual violence crimes occurred during the trial of *Akayesu* in 1997 when one of the prosecution witnesses spontaneously revealed how her daughter had been raped, and another witness described her own personal experience of rape during the genocide.[215] At the encouragement and questioning of the judges of the Trial Chamber, both witnesses proceeded to elaborate additional details about sexual violence during the Rwandan genocide.[216] After the close of their testimony, a coalition of civil society groups—the Coalition for Women's Human Rights in Conflict Situations—applied to to the Trial Chamber to submit an *amicus curiae* brief with the aim of convincing the Chamber to invite the Prosecutor to amend the indictment to include charges of rape and other forms of sexual violence.[217] While it appears that no decision as to the admissibility of the brief was rendered by the Trial Chamber,[218] ICTR prosecutors sought leave to amend the indictment to include three new counts of sexual violence in light of the testimony concerning sexual violence that had arisen at trial, conceding that the Coalition's brief had been 'a factor' though only to the extent that it had served as a reminder of the importance of the issue of sexual violence.[219] Taking due note of the fair trial rights of the accused, the Trial Chamber granted the motion.[220] Louise Arbour, who had succeeded Richard Goldstone as Chief Prosecutor for both the ICTR and ICTY in October 1996—during the course of the *Akayesu* trial—went on to amend the indictments in a number of other cases to include charges of rape and other forms of sexual violence, and put into action the Sexual Assault Team which had been established at the end of Goldstone's tenure.[221]

However, the heightened focus on charges of rape and other forms of sexual violence that emerged during Arbour's tenure was short-lived and ultimately scaled back upon the appointment of her successor, Carla Del Ponte, in September 1999. A number of Del Ponte's strategic decisions have been the focus of significant criticism from experts

[212] B Nowrojee, '"Your Justice is Too Slow" Will the ICTR Fail Rwanda's Rape Victims?' *United Nations Research Institute for Social Development Occasional Paper Series 10* (November 2005) 9.

[213] Ibid.

[214] Ibid.

[215] *Akayesu* Trial Judgment (n 202) [417].

[216] B van Schaak, 'Engendering Genocide: The Akayesu Case before the International Criminal Tribunal for Rwanda' (2008) *Santa Clara University School of Law* 6–7.

[217] S Williams and H Woolaver, 'The Role of the *Amicus Curiae* before International Criminal Tribunals' (2006) 6 *International Criminal Law Review* 151, 174.

[218] For an account of what happened to the *amicus curiae* brief, see van Schaak (n 216) 8–9, fn 19.

[219] Ibid 9.

[220] *Prosecutor v Jean-Paul Akayesu* (Leave to Amend the Indictment, ICTR Office of the Prosecution) ICTR-96-4-T (17 June 1997).

[221] Nowrojee (n 212) 10.

in the field, including:[222] her decision to disband the Sexual Assault Team in 2000; her failure to bring sexual violence charges even where evidence existed to do so; and her lack of commitment to adequately develop the evidence in cases where charges of rape and other forms of sexual violence had already been included.

In the case of *Ntagerura et al*, for example, victim-witnesses began giving evidence at trial about sexual violence that they had experienced in Cyangugu. Again, the Coalition for Women's Human Rights in Conflict Situations filed an *amicus curiae* motion before the tribunal, calling upon the Trial Chamber to invite the prosecution to amend the indictment to include sexual violence charges. On this occasion, the prosecution opposed the Coalition's motion and it was ultimately rejected by the Trial Chamber on the grounds that the issue raised was not a live issue in the case and that 'the Prosecutor has indicated that she intends to file a new indictment against the Accused Bagambiki and Imanishimwe alleging acts constituting rape'.[223] However, the latter action was ultimately never implemented. Rather, as Binaifer Nowrojee explains, 'the proportion of new indictments including sexual violence charges dropped from 100 per cent in 1999–2000 to 35 per cent in 2001–2002' and 'by Del Ponte's final year, none of the new indictments contained rape charges'.[224]

By 2003, when the final Chief Prosecutor of the ICTR, Hassan Jallow, had taken office, many in the Office of the Prosecution were beginning to recognise their poor record concerning the investigation and prosecution of sexual violence crimes.[225] In response, Prosecutor Jallow adopted a number of measures in an effort to improve the conviction record for such crimes and identify lessons that could be learned from past investigative and prosecutorial practices.[226] Ultimately, however, Jallow's ability to remedy the ICTR's record regarding the investigation and prosecution of sexual violence crimes was restricted by completion strategy pressures, which meant that the Prosecutor had to work with files already in existence and focus upon improving the prosecution of charges in existing indictments.[227]

The ICTR's fluctuating charging record with respect to sexual violence crimes provides a useful window into the multiplicity of factors that influenced the focus of charges at the ad hoc tribunals over time. While the investigative practices and priorities of the prosecution were arguably the most influential factors, sporadic witness testimony, civil society activism, the exercise of judicial discretion, and State pressure all played a part in shaping the charging record in practice. Ultimately, it was the precise interplay between these different variables over time that influenced not only the focus of charges but also the orientation of the historical narratives constructed within the ad hoc tribunals in practice.

[222] Ibid.

[223] *Prosecutor v Ntagerura et al* (Decision on the Application to File an Amicus Curiae Brief According to Rule 74 of the Rules of Procedure and Evidence Filed on Behalf of the NGO Coalition for Women's Human Rights in Conflict Situations, Trial Chamber) ICTR-94-46-T (24 May 2001) [20]. For a full account of this episode, see Nowrojee (n 212) 14–17.

[224] Nowrojee (n 212) 10.

[225] L Bianchi, 'Challenging Impunity for Crimes of Sexual Violence: The Efforts of Prosecutor Jallow to Set the Record Straight', in CC Jalloh and ABM Marong (eds), *Promoting Accountability under International Law for Gross Human Rights Violations in Africa* (Brill 2015) 355, 359.

[226] Ibid 355–356.

[227] Ibid 359–360.

C. Interpretative Practices

Similar to the drafters of their Statutes, the judges of the ad hoc tribunals were faced with a tension between a set of general categories of crime whose scope and content had remained relatively static for decades and a set of factual circumstances that reflected the evolving nature of atrocities and conflicts that had emerged in the second half of the twentieth century. In confronting this tension, the judges received minimal guidance from their Statutes, which had been drafted in laconic terms,[228] setting out little more than a brief list of general categories of crime and omitting any express statement concerning the applicable law as distinct from the tribunals' subject-matter jurisdiction.[229] The laissez-faire approach of the drafters is understandable when it is remembered that the mandates of the tribunals were tightly focused on the situations in the former Yugoslavia, Rwanda, and Sierra Leone, which generally posed little threat to the nationals of the States involved in their enactment.[230]

By drafting the Statutes in such terse terms, the drafters delegated significant authority and discretion to the judges to clarify the meaning of crime categories in the context of individual cases.[231] According to Zahar and Sluiter, for example, the concise nature of their Statutes ensured that judges would be forced to live the lives of

[228] See, for example, PM Wald, 'International Criminal Courts: Some Kudos and Concerns' (2006) 150 *Proceedings of the American Philosophical Society* 241, 244 ('it was a shock to me to judge in a system that basically had no precedent or statutory base to rely upon as to what the law was'); and D Hunt, 'The International Criminal Court: High Hopes, "Creative Ambiguity" and an Unfortunate Mistrust in International Judges' (2004) 2 *Journal of International Criminal Justice* 56, 58 ('There was no Moses to produce on slabs of stone a code of commandments which were intended to be all-encompassing for all time').

[229] O'Keefe (n 2) 493 and 520. A degree of guidance concerning the applicable law was provided by the UN Secretary-General. With respect to the ICTY, the Secretary-General confirmed—in a report that was expressly 'endorsed' by the Security Council at the time of the tribunal's establishment—that 'the application of the principle *nullum crimen sine lege* requires that the international tribunal should apply rules of international humanitarian law which are *beyond any doubt part of customary law* so that the problem of adherence of some but not all States to specific conventions does not arise'. 'Report of the Secretary-General Pursuant to Paragraph 5 of Security Council Resolution 808 (1993)' UN Doc S/25704 (3 May 1993) ('UN Secretary-General Report on the ICTY') [34] (emphasis added). With respect to the ICTR, the Secretary-General confirmed—in a report released a few months after the adoption of the Statute of the ICTR—that the Security Council had adopted 'a more expansive approach to the choice of applicable law' in the ICTR Statute, deciding to include within its subject-matter jurisdiction 'international instruments regardless of whether they were considered part of customary international law or whether they have customarily entailed the individual criminal responsibility of the perpetrator of the crime'. UN Secretary-General Report on the ICTR (n 131) [12]. With respect to the SCSL, in his initial presentation of a draft Statute to the Security Council, the Secretary-General noted that '[i]n recognition of the principle of legality, in particular *nullum crimen sine lege*, and the prohibition on retroactive criminal legislation, the international crimes enumerated, are crimes considered to have had the character of customary international law at the time of the alleged commission of the crime'. UN Secretary-General Report on the SCSL (n 114) [12]. See also, Rule 72*bis*, SCSL Rules of Procedure and Evidence, introduced in 2004, which clarified the applicable law of the SCSL.

[230] This was even the case with respect to the SCSL, which was established by an agreement between the UN and Sierra Leone. Although members of the Sierra Leonean government fell within the personal jurisdiction of the tribunal, the predominant assumption amongst most of the Sierra Leonean government was that the SCSL had been established to prosecute the RUF leaders and the overthrown junta. See generally, Cryer (n 55) 234–238.

[231] See, in this regard, AM Danner, 'When Courts Make Law: How the International Criminal Tribunals Recast the Laws of War' (2006) 59 *Vanderbilt Law Review* 1, 4–5 and 41*ff* (arguing that the Security Council had tacitly delegated lawmaking authority to the judges of the ad hoc tribunals).

'hunter-gatherers in a legal wilderness', left with little choice but to 'track down and synthesize for themselves the law to apply to the facts'.[232] Over time, four themes emerged within the jurisprudence of the ad hoc tribunals in terms of their understanding of their applicable law and approach to interpretation.

First, the ad hoc tribunals recognised the sources of public international law as their applicable law, with customary international law constituting the most prominent source relied upon as a basis for the categories of crimes that fell within their subject-matter jurisdiction.[233] To identify customary international law, the ad hoc tribunals generally relied upon a flexible and inconsistent methodology—often resorting to slim, selective, and sometimes irrelevant evidence for the purpose.[234] By adopting a relaxed approach to the identification of customary international law, the ad hoc tribunals engaged in what Robert Cryer has termed 'presentational positivism'—an attempt to legitimise acts of judicial lawmaking by utilising a notionally positivist vocabulary.[235] According to former ICTY Judge Patricia Wald, for example, if judicial creativity was to become 'the mantra' of the ad hoc tribunals, the process of identifying and articulating the law 'had to be performed in a ... carefully crafted way'.[236]

Second, although reference was sometimes made to the rules of interpretation set out in Articles 31 and 32 of the Vienna Convention on the Law of Treaties, the ad hoc tribunals relied upon a diversity of interpretative methodologies in practice. According to Leena Grover, for example, neither did a prevailing hermeneutic emerge, nor were any of the interpretative principles relied upon—including literal, logical, contextual, purposive, effective, or progressive interpretation, to name a few—authoritatively defined or consistently applied in the jurisprudence of the ad hoc tribunals.[237]

Third, although the ad hoc tribunals often proclaimed adherence to the principle of legality in their recognition and interpretation of crime categories, in practice they relied upon a flexible conception of the principle that permitted the progressive adaptation of crime categories to changing social conditions so long as the adaptation was 'sufficiently foreseeable' and 'sufficiently accessible' at the time of commission and fell

[232] Zahar and Sluiter (n 74) 80.

[233] See, for example, *Galić* Appeal Judgment (n 179) [85]; and *Sesay et al* Trial Judgment (n 205) [48]. The ICTR, however, proved more willing to rely on applicable treaty law. See, for example, *Prosecutor v Clément Kayishema and Obed Ruzindana* (Judgment, Trial Chamber) ICTR-95-1-T (21 May 1999) ('*Kayishema and Ruzindana* Trial Judgment') [156].

[234] See generally, N Arajärvi, *The Changing Nature of Customary International Law: Methods of Interpreting the Concept of Custom in International Criminal Tribunals* (Routledge 2014) 75*ff*.

[235] R Cryer, 'International Criminal Tribunals and the Sources of International Law: Antonio Cassese's Contribution to the Canon' (2012) 10 *Journal of International Criminal Justice* 1045, 1048. See similarly, S Darcy, *Judges, Law and War: The Judicial Development of International Humanitarian Law* (CUP 2014) 319 ('a vehicle for expansive judicial lawmaking'); J Powderly, 'Judicial Interpretation at the Ad Hoc Tribunals: Method from Chaos?', in S Darcy and J Powderly (eds), *Judicial Creativity at the International Criminal Tribunals* (OUP 2010) 17, 31 ('a springboard for judicial creativity'); W Schabas, 'Customary Law or "Judge-Made" Law: Judicial Creativity at the UN Criminal Tribunals', in J Doria et al (eds), *The Legal Regime of the ICC: Essays in Honour of Prof. I.P. Blishchenko* (Brill 2009) 77, 100 ('a convenient license for judicial lawmaking'); Zahar and Sluiter (n 74) 99 ('an aspiration to fill gaps in the law—to legislate from the bench—is often the only method discernible in the tribunals' efforts to prove the existence of a rule of customary law').

[236] P Wald, 'Note from the Bench', in Darcy and Powderly (n 235) xxxv, xxxvi.

[237] L Grover, *Interpreting Crimes in the Rome Statute of the International Criminal Court* (CUP 2014) 63.

within 'the reasonable limits of acceptable clarification'.[238] This conception of the principle of legality provided judges with significant leeway to render progressive interpretations of the crime categories that fell within their subject-matter jurisdiction.[239]

Finally, although the ad hoc tribunals formally characterised judicial decisions as merely a 'subsidiary means for the determination of rules of law',[240] as their case law developed, detailed examinations of sources of law declined in favour of increasingly dense cross-referencing to earlier decisions. As Sergey Vasiliev explains, 'over time their decision-making became ever more precedent-driven, self-referential, and enclosed vis-à-vis the nominal sources'.[241] In this way, initially novel interpretations of crime categories could emerge to become 'content-laden reference points'.[242] When sufficiently endorsed in subsequent cases, these reference points became almost impossible to ignore.

In general, therefore, by relying upon a flexible approach to their applicable law, a diversity of interpretative methodologies, and a relaxed conception of the principle of legality, judges at the ad hoc tribunals were able to progressively identify and develop the meaning of crime categories in light of the factual circumstances of the situations in the former Yugoslavia, Rwanda, and Sierra Leone. In addition, over time, initial acts of judicial creativity often matured to become authoritative reference points that were relied upon in future cases under the gravitational pull of internal interpretative integration.

Importantly, the propensity to dynamically and creatively develop the law was visible across each of the general categories of crime that fell within the jurisdictional mandates of the ad hoc tribunals—often with significant implications for the historical narratives constructed in their judgments.[243]

[238] See, for example, *Prosecutor v Milutinović et al* (Decision on Dragoljub Ojdanić's Motion Challenging Jurisdiction—Joint Criminal Enterprise, Appeals Chamber) IT-99-37-AR72 (21 May 2003) [10] and [37]–[38]; and *Prosecutor v Sesay et al* (Judgment, Appeals Chamber) SCSL-04-15-A (26 October 2009) [888]. For detailed discussions of this aspect of the principle of legality, see generally, Grover (n 237) 170–174; Gallant (n 11) 359–366; and WN Ferdinandusse, *Direct Application of International Criminal Law in National Courts* (TMC Asser Press 2006) 236–248.

[239] For critique, see, for example, Grover (n 237) 171 ('the concept of reasonable foreseeability is not sufficiently robust') Darcy (n 235) 62 ('With reasonableness often being in the eye of the beholder, the charge of creating new law and acting as a legislator has been made by several of the judges serving at the ad hoc tribunals'); Gallant (n 11) 364 ('The doctrine of foreseeability . . . may swallow the principle of legality whole'); and D Robinson, 'Legality and Other Contradictory Commitments: Some Thoughts About How We Think' (2009) *ASIL Proceedings* 104, 104 ('In light of past trends of ambitious interpretation in ICL, does a "foreseeable innovation" test *exclude* anything?') (emphasis in original).

[240] *Prosecutor v Kupreškić et al* (Judgment, Trial Chamber) IT-95-16-T (14 January 2000) ('*Kupreškić et al* Trial Judgment') [540].

[241] S Vasiliev, 'The Making of International Criminal Law', in C Brölmann and Y Radi (eds), *Research Handbook on the Theory and Practice of International Law-Making* (Edward Elgar 2016) 354, 385.

[242] I Venzke, 'Between Power and Persuasion: On International Institutions' Authority in Making Law' (2013) 4 *Transnational Legal Theory* 353, 368. See similarly, Danner (n 231) 57 ('focal points'); and D Akande, 'Sources of International Criminal Law', in A Cassese (ed), *The Oxford Companion to International Criminal Justice* (OUP 2009) 41, 53 ('an "off the shelf" assessment of the law which is often the starting point for decision future cases').

[243] The account of the jurisprudence of the ad hoc tribunals in this section is illustrative—additional examples appear in Chapter 7 of this study in the context of examining historical narrative pluralism within international criminal courts.

1. War crimes

The development of the category of war crimes is illustrative of the dynamic approach adopted by the ad hoc tribunals more generally. If proof were needed that war crimes law had become radically out-dated, the complexity of the conflicts that took place in the former Yugoslavia in the early 1990s provided ample evidence. As the ICTY Appeals Chamber observed, 'the conflicts in the former Yugoslavia could have been characterised as both internal and international, or alternatively, as an internal conflict alongside an international one, or as an internal conflict that had become internationalised because of external support, or as an international conflict that had subsequently been replaced by one or more internal conflicts, or some combination thereof'.[244] In this context, judges at the ICTY were confronted by two challenges: first, the predominant position in the early 1990s amongst scholars and experts, including the International Committee of the Red Cross, was that war crimes did not apply to non-international armed conflicts;[245] and second, the war crimes law applicable to international armed conflicts had generally been formulated with traditional interstate wars in mind rather than the internationalised conflicts that characterised certain aspects of the Yugoslav war.

It was in this climate that judges at the ICTY engineered a tectonic shift in the law of war crimes, first by identifying the existence of war crimes within non-international armed conflicts under customary international law, and second by expanding the circumstances where seemingly non-international armed conflicts could transform to become international armed conflicts.

a. Non-international armed conflicts

In its *Decision on Jurisdiction* in the case of *Tadić*, the ICTY Appeals Chamber significantly diminshed the distinction between international and non-international armed conflicts. The judges began by relying on literal, contextual, and unidimesnional victim-focused teleological interpretative methodologies to conclude that Article 3 of the ICTY Statute constituted a residual clause 'designed to ensure that no serious violation of international humanitarian law is taken away from the jurisdiction of the International Tribunal'.[246] The judges then advanced a number of moralising sentiments concerning the incongruity of confining war crimes to international armed conflicts in light of elementary considerations of humanity, common sense, and the humanitarian imperative to protect human beings, in combination with relatively slim evidence of State practice and *opinio juris*, to conclude that that customary international law imposes criminal liability for serious violations of Article 3 common to the Geneva Conventions as well as certain fundamental principles and rules regarding the means and methods of combat in non-international armed conflicts.[247]

244 See, for example, *Prosecutor v Duško Tadić* (Decision on the Defence Motion for Interlocutory Appeal on Jurisdiction, Appeals Chamber) IT-94-I-AR72 (2 October 1995) ('*Tadić* Appeal Decision on Jurisdiction') [72].

245 See, for example, *Tadić* Appeal Decision on Jurisdiction (n 244) (sep op Li) [9]; and Former Yugoslavia Commission of Experts Final Report (n 184) [52].

246 *Tadić* Appeal Decision on Jurisdiction (n 244) [91].

247 Ibid [86]–[137]. On the innovative nature of the decision, see A Cassese, 'The International Criminal Tribunal for the Former Yugoslavia and the Implementation of International Humanitarian Law', in L Condorelli et al (eds), *The United Nations and International Humanitarian Law* (Editions Pedone 1996) 230,

From a narrative perspective, the decision in *Tadić* not only ensured that the narrative frame of the ICTY extended to conflicts in the former Yugoslavia that were non-international in character, but also paved the way for the ad hoc tribunals more generally to respond to the increasingly privatised nature of warfare, setting the foundations for judges in future cases to identitfy a range of war crimes applicable to non-international armed conflicts under customary international law.[248]

Two examples from the jurisprudence of the SCSL are illustrative of the flexible approach to the identification of a customary basis for war crimes in non-international armed conflicts utilised by judges at the ad hoc tribunals in practice.[249] In *Sesay et al*, the SCSL Trial Chamber concluded that the war crime of intentionally directing attacks against peacekeepers was not a new crime under customary international law, but merely '*a particularisation* of the general and fundamental prohibition in international humanitarian law against attacks on civilians and civilian objects'.[250] Although the Trial Chamber conducted a review of State practice and *opinio juris*, since much of the evidence relied upon concerned the condemnation rather than express criminalisaton of intentional attacks directed against peacekeepers, the Trial Chamber's primary argument seems to have been that the crime constituted a specification of the targeted group within the existing offence of attacks on civilians.[251] Similarly, in *Norman et al*, a majority of the SCSL Appeals Chamber relied primarily upon evidence that demonstrated the *illegality* of the crime of enlisting children below the age of fifteen into armed forces or groups, to conclude that child recruitment—a term encompassing both the crimes of enlistment and conscription—was *criminal* under customary international law prior to November 1996 when the SCSL's temporal jurisdiction commenced.[252]

In each of these cases, the flexible and relaxed approach to the identification of crime categories under customary international law enabled an expansion of the historical narrative frame of the SCSL to include not only examinations of attacks against peacekeepers and the practice of enlisting child soldiers into armed forces or groups but also the criminal responsibility of individuals for such acts.

233 ('some of the views expressed in the Decision could be considered "innovative". By using these terms, I mean to say no more than that these views go beyond what some, more traditional, commentators may consider to be the current state of international humanitarian law').

[248] MP Scharf, *Customary International Law in Times of Fundamental Change: Recognizing Grotian Moments* (CUP 2013) 148–156 (characterising the *Tadić* decision as a 'Grotian Moment' in international law because of how significantly and quickly it transformed the law of war crimes); and T Hoffmann, 'The Gentle Humanizer of Humanitarian Law—Antonio Cassese and the Creation of the Customary Law of Non-International Armed Conflict' *SSRN* (15 December 2009) (summarising the transformative effect of the *Tadić* decision on the law of war crimes).

[249] For an example from the jurisprudence of the ICTY, see *Galić* Appeal Judgment (n 179) [86]–[98] (concluding, by majority, that acts or threats of violence the primary purpose of which is to spread terror among the civilian population were not only prohibited under customary international law, but also entailed individual criminal responsibility).

[250] *Sesay et al* Trial Judgment (n 205) [215] (emphasis added).

[251] S Wharton, 'The Evolution of International Criminal Law: Prosecuting "New" Crimes before the Special Court for Sierra Leone' (2011) 11 *International Criminal Law Review* 217, 235.

[252] *Prosecutor v Norman et al* (Decision on Preliminary Motion Based on Lack of Jurisdiction (Child Recruitment), Appeals Chamber) SCSL-2004-14-AR72(E) (31 May 2004) [30]–[53]. For critique, see ibid (diss op Robertson) [20] and [32]–[33].

b. Internationalised armed conflicts

In its judgment in the case of *Tadić*, the ICTY Appeals Chamber expanded the scope of application of the grave breaches regime under the 1949 Geneva Conventions by developing a relaxed understanding of when a seemingly non-international armed conflict could be considered internationalised as a result of the participation of another State.

Relying upon a number of decisions rendered by domestic and international courts, the relevance of which has been disputed,[253] the Appeals Chamber concluded that a conflict between a State and armed forces, militias, or paramilitary units can be international if another State exercises 'overall control' over the organised armed group.[254] In order to satisfy the overall control test, evidence was required of State involvement in 'organizing, coordinating or planning the military actions of the military group, in addition to financing, training and equipping or providing operational support to that group.'[255]

Beyond elaborating the overall control test, the Appeals Chamber also clarified the categories of protected persons who could fall victim to grave breaches in situations where a non-international armed conflict had become internationalised. An important provision in this context is Article 4(1) of Geneva Convention IV, which defines 'protected persons' as those 'in the hands of a Party to the conflict or Occupying Power *of which they are not nationals*'.[256] Relying upon a unidimensional victim-focused telelogical interpretation of this provision, the Appeals Chamber concluded that the decisive factor for defining 'proteted persons' was 'allegiance' to a party to the conflict and added that, in the context of present-day internationalised armed conflict, 'ethnicity may become determinative of national allegiance'.[257]

From a narrative perspective, these findings not only extended the application of the grave breaches regime to conflicts that previously may have been characterised as non-international in character, but also instigated detailed examinations of the precise relationships that existed between non-State armed groups and States in different conflict situations within the former Yugoslavia.[258]

2. Crimes against humanity

Beyond 'humanizing' international humanitarian law through its jurisprudence on war crimes,[259] the ad hoc tribunals also adapted and modernised crimes against

[253] M Milanović, 'State Responsibility for Genocide' (2006) 17 *European Journal of International law* 553, 586–588.

[254] *Tadić* Appeal Judgment (n 120) [137]. For an overview of critiques that have been directed against the Appeals Chamber's approach, see Darcy (n 235) 89–96.

[255] *Tadić* Appeal Judgment (n 120) [137].

[256] Article 4(1), Geneva Convention Relative to the Protection of Civilian Persons in Time of War, signed on 12 August 1949, entered into force on 21 October 1950, 75 UNTS 287 (emphasis added).

[257] *Tadić* Appeal Judgment (n 120) [166].

[258] See, for example, ibid [146]–[162] (concluding that the Army of Republika Srpska (VRS) acted under the overall control of the Federal Republic of Yugoslavia in the Bosnian conflict in 1992); and *Prosecutor v Prlić et al* (Judgment: Volume 3 of 6, Trial Chamber) IT-04-74-T (29 May 2013) [545]–[567] (concluding, by majority, that the Croatian Defence Council acted under the overall control of the Croatian authorities and the Army of the Republic of Croatia).

[259] T Meron, 'The Humanization of Humanitarian Law' (2000) 94 *American Journal of International Law* 239, 243.

humanity, a category whose interpretation had been somewhat in flux prior to the establishment of the tribunals,[260] but which emerged in their jurisprudence to become 'a "gentle civilizer" of modern forms of violence'.[261]

a. The contextual element

Traditionally, the category of crimes against humanity was characterised as a crime committed pursuant to a State policy.[262] However, the situations in the former Yugoslavia, Rwanda, and Sierra Leone each experienced atrocities committed by members of non-State armed groups. As such, the question of which kinds of non-State entities fell within the scope of crimes against humanity, as well as the criteria such entities had to fulfil, became of significant narrative importance.[263] Since prosecutors failed to bring charges against members of the Rwandan Patriotic Front, this question did not arise before the ICTR. However, in a number of cases involving non-state actors at the ICTY and SCSL, these tribunals gradually broadened the types of collective entities on whose behalf crimes against humanity could be carried out.

In *Tadić*, for example, the ICTY Trial Chamber acknowledged that the traditional conception of crimes against humanity was 'not only that a policy must be present but that the policy must be that of a State, as was the case in Nazi Germany'.[264] This conception was premised on the idea that only States had the necessary institutions, personnel, and resources to carry out crimes against humanity in practice. While this may have been true at the time of the Second World War, the Trial Chamber asserted that the recent events in the former Yugoslavia had demonstrated that 'this is no longer the case'.[265] Against this background, the Trial Chamber relied upon Article 18 of the International Law Commission's (ILC) Draft Code of Crimes against the Peace and Security of Mankind and the commentaries that accompanied its final and earlier drafts,[266] as well as a single US civil law case concerning the liability of non-State actors for genocide, to conclude that the customary international law definition of crimes against humanity had evolved by the time of the situation in the former Yugoslavia 'to take into account forces which, although not those of the legitimate government, have *de facto* control over, or are able to move freely within, defined territory'.[267] The Trial Chamber also took note of the prosecution's argument that crimes against humanity could be committed 'by a terrorist group or organization', an assertion that

[260] The definitional uncertainty concerning crimes against humanity was reflected in the drafting of the category's contextual element which differed between each of the Statutes of the ad hoc tribunals. See (n 120) and accompanying text.

[261] Stahn (n 2) 59.

[262] See generally, WA Schabas, 'State Policy as an Element of International Crimes' (2008) 98 *Journal of Criminal Law & Criminology* 953, 960–965.

[263] See generally, T Rodenhäuser, 'Beyond State Crimes: Non-State Entities and Crimes against Humanity' (2014) 27 *Leiden Journal of International Law* 913; K Ambos, *Treatise on International Criminal Law: Volume II: The Crimes and Sentencing* (OUP 2014) 72–75; and D Robinson, 'Essence of Crimes against Humanity Raised by Challenges at ICC' *EJIL Talk!* (27 September 2011).

[264] *Prosecutor v Duško Tadić* (Judgment, Trial Chamber) IT-94-I-T (7 May 1997) [654].

[265] Ibid.

[266] Ibid [655] (Article 18 of the Draft Code of Crimes against the Peace and Security of Mankind (1996) referred to prohibited acts 'instigated or directed by a Government or by any organization or group').

[267] Ibid [654].

went unchallenged by the defence and was held to conform with recent statements regarding crimes against humanity.[268]

In *Limaj*, the ICTY Trial Chamber conceded that 'due to structural factors and organizational and military capabilities' an attack comprising crimes against humanity 'will most often be committed at the behest of a State'.[269] Nonetheless, the Trial Chamber relied on the findings in *Tadić* to conclude that the attack requirement of crimes against humanity could be satisfied by the Kosovo Liberation Army (KLA) given its *de facto* control over parts of Kosovo during the relevant timeframe.[270] This conclusion was drawn notwithstanding the characterisation of the KLA as 'a non-state actor with extremely limited resources, personnel and organisation', [271] 'a guerrilla force engaged in limited combat',[272] and 'a small, though rapidly expanding, insurgent force'.[273]

Finally, in *Brima et al*, the SCSL Trial Chamber examined crimes against humanity allegedly committed by members of the Armed Forces Revolutionary Council (AFRC). In this context, the Chamber noted that despite being faced with 'the challenge of more limited resources and poorer organisational capacity', the AFRC was very much capable of launching attacks against the civilian population.[274] Notably, the SCSL did not expressly require proof of *de facto* control over territory to find the non-State actor capable of carrying out crimes against humanity; rather, the decisive requirement was that the armed group had the functional capacity to commit widespread or systematic attacks directed against a civilian population.[275]

Taken together, these cases illustrate the propensity of judges at the ICTY and SCSL to progressively develop the meaning of the category of crimes against humanity under customary international law—often on the basis of minimal evidence of State practice or *opinio juris*—in order to ensure the category's continued relevance to the factual circumstances of the situations in the former Yugoslavia and Sierra Leone.[276]

b. Prohibited acts

Beyond the contextual element, the ad hoc tribunals also relied upon a diversity of interpretative techniques to progressively develop the prohibited acts recognised within the category of crimes against humanity. Three technqiues are illustrative in this regard.

First, certain forms of violence were recognised as particularised versions of more general prohibited acts.[277] In *Sesay et al*, for example, the SCSL Trial Chamber

268 Ibid.

269 *Prosecutor v Limaj et al* (Judgment, Trial Chamber) IT-03-66-T (30 November 2005) [191].

270 Ibid [213]–[214].

271 Ibid [191].

272 Ibid [195].

273 Ibid.

274 *Prosecutor v Brima et al* (Judgment, Trial Chamber) SCSL-04-16-T (20 June 2007) [226] and [233]–[239].

275 Rodenhäuser (n 263) 920.

276 See similarly, C Kreß, 'On the Outer Limits of Crimes against Humanity: The Concept of Organization within the Policy Requirement: Some Reflections on the March 2010 ICC *Kenya* Decision' (2010) 23 *Leiden Journal of International Law* 855, 870.

277 Wharton (n 251) 235–239.

confirmed that the prohibited act of sexual slavery—expressly recognised in Article 2(g) of the Statute of the SCSL—constituted 'a particularised form of slavery or enslavement' and noted that 'acts which could be classified as sexual slavery have been prosecuted as enslavement in the past'.[278] According to the Chamber, the prohibition of more particularised offences such as sexual slavery was 'designed to draw attention to serious crimes that have been historically overlooked and to recognise the particular nature of sexual violence that has been used, often with impunity, as a tactic of war to humiliate, dominate and instil fear in victims, their families and communities during armed conflict'.[279]

Second, the prohibited act of 'persecution' provided a conduit for the recognition of a broad range of violent acts which, either separately or combined, constituted 'the gross or blatant denial, on discriminatory grounds, of a fundamental right, laid down in international customary or treaty law, reaching the same level of gravity as the other acts prohibited [as crimes against humanity]'.[280] Importantly, since the underlying acts of persecution did not have to amount to crimes under international law and their gravity could be assessed in combination, persecution provided an important category for the recognition of a diversity of harmful acts.[281] Examples of acts recognised to constitute persecution when committed with the requisite discriminatory intent included not only the prohibited acts already listed in the statutory definitions of crimes against humanity, but also a range of conduct amounting to severe deprivations of political, social, or economic rights.[282] In *Nahimana et al*, for example, the ICTR Appeals Chamber concluded that hate speeches made after 6 April 1994, accompanied by calls for genocide against the Tutsi group and taking place in the context of a massive campaign of persecution directed at the Tutsi population of Rwanda, including acts of violence (killings, torture and ill-treatment, rape) and the destruction of property, themselves amounted to underlying acts of persecution.[283]

Finally, various forms of violence were also recognised within the catch-all residual category of 'other inhumane acts'.[284] According to the ICTY Trial Chamber, the residual category was important because '[h]owever much care were taken in establishing all the various forms of infliction, one would never be able to catch up with the imagination of future torturers who wished to satisfy their bestial instincts'.[285] In practice, the jurisprudence of the ad hoc tribunals clarified that only acts or omissions of 'similar seriousness' to the other prohibited acts of crimes against humanity and which 'caused serious mental or physical suffering or injury or constituted a serious

278 *Sesay et al* Trial Judgment (n 205) [155].

279 Ibid [156].

280 *Kupreškić et al* Trial Judgment (n 240) [621].

281 *Prosecutor v Kvočka et al* (Judgment, Appeals Chamber) IT-98-30/1-A (28 February 2005) [323]; and *Nahimana et al* Appeal Judgment (n 194) [987].

282 See, for example, *Prosecutor v Kvočka et al* (Judgment, Trial Chamber) IT-98-30/1-T (2 November 2001) ('*Kvočka et al* Trial Judgment') [186]; *Prosecutor v Simon Bikindi* (Judgment, Trial Chamber) ICTR-01-72-T (2 December 2008) [392].

283 *Nahimana et al* Appeal Judgment (n 194) [988].

284 Wharton (n 251) 230–233.

285 *Prosecutor v Tihomir Blaškić* (Judgment, Trial Chamber) IT-95-14-T (3 March 2000) [237] (referring to the Commentary to Geneva Convention IV).

attack of human dignity' may be recognised under the residual clause.[286] Examples of 'other inhumane acts' recognised in the jurisprudence of the ad hoc tribunals included 'mutilation and other types of severe bodily harm, beatings and other acts of violence, serious physical and mental injury, forcible transfer, inhumane and degrading treatment, forced prostitution, and forced disappearance'.[287] In *Akayesu*, for instance, the ICTR Trial Chamber found that forced undressing of women and marching them in public and forcing women to perform exercises naked fell within the scope of the residual category.[288]

Through these techniques, the ad hoc tribunals were able to expand the range of violent acts that they could examine and condemn, and for which they could determine individual criminal responsibility, within the narratives constructed in their judgments.

3. The crime of genocide

The crime of genocide is defined in Article 2 of the Convention on the Prevention and Punishment of the Crime of Genocide (Genocide Convention) as the commission of any of a closed list of prohibited acts with 'intent to destroy, in whole or in part, a national, ethnical, racial or religious group, as such'.[289] This definition was reproduced *verbatim* in the Statutes of the ICTY and ICTR.[290] Yet, while the general definition of the crime of genocide was well-established by the time of the creation of the ad hoc tribunals, the precise meaning of its constituent elements was less clear due to a dearth of existing jurisprudence concerning the category. In practice, four aspects of the interpretation of the crime of genocide by the ICTY and ICTR proved particularly significant for the historical narratives constructed in their judgments.

a. Protected groups

One of the distinguishing features of the crime of genocide is that it seeks to protect the rights of certain protected groups to exist and to contribute to human diversity.[291] However, not all groups fall within the crime's scope: Article 2 of the Genocide Convention is expressly limited to the protection of 'national, ethnical, racial or religious' groups. Since these groups were not subject to further elaboration either in the Genocide Convention or the Statutes of the ICTY and ICTR, it was left to the judges of the ad hoc tribunals to determine whether a group falling within the scope of the definition of genocide had been targeted for destruction. The issue rose to the fore primarily at the ICTR where the tribunal examined whether Rwanda's Tutsi population constituted a protected group within the meaning of the crime of genocide. This question was of significant narrative importance since only if the Tutsi population

[286] *Prosecutor v Mitar Vasiljević* (Judgment, Appeals Chamber) IT-98-32-A (25 February 2004) [165]. See similarly, *Bagosora et al* Trial Judgment (n 203) [2218].

[287] *Kvočka et al* Trial Judgment (n 282) [208].

[288] *Akayesu* Trial Judgment (n 202) [697].

[289] Article 2, 1948, Convention on the Prevention and Punishment of the Crime of Genocide, adopted 9 December 1948, entered into force 12 January 1951, 78 UNTS 277.

[290] Article 4, ICTY Statute; Article 2, ICTR Statute.

[291] See, for example, *Akayesu* Trial Judgment (n 202) [469]; and UN General Assembly Resolution 96(I), UN Doc A/RES/96(I) (11 December 1946). The crime of genocide has also been recognised as protecting *individual* legal interests. See, for example, Ambos (n 263) 4–5.

constituted a protected group could the tribunal conclude that genocide had occurred in Rwanda in 1994.

Underpinning this question was a tension between two competing demands. On the one hand, the Genocide Convention is generally considered to provide a closed list of protected groups, a fact which seems to suggest a need to identify some degree of objective basis for the existence of such groups and to ensure the exclusion of more 'mobile groups' such as those based on political or economic commitments.[292] On the other hand, the structure of the crime of genocide focuses on the perpetrator's state of mind and as such no objective basis may exist for the distinctions put forward by perpetrators, which will often be more imagined than real.[293] Steer too far towards the objective approach and judges risked replicating the epistemological assumptions of the perpetrators by seeking 'to essentialise the complex reality of society by reducing and simplifying "complex phenomena into a more manageable, schematised form" '.[294] Steer too far towards the subjective approach and judges risked expanding the scope of protection of the Genocide Convention to any group fabricated by the perceptions of the perpetrators.[295]

Although the ICTR initially adopted a predominantly objective understanding of the protected groups, the jurisprudence eventually shifted towards a combined subjective-objective approach.[296] Importantly, in articulating the objective side of the equation, the judges acknowledged that no general or internationally accepted definition existed for each of the protected groups, referring instead to the objective particulars of a given social or historical context.[297] With respect to the subjective side of the equation, the judges referred to the self-identification of a particular group by victims, as well as the subjective perceptions of the perpetrators.[298] Applying this approach, the ICTR was able to recognise the Tutsi population as a separate ethnic group because they were treated as such in official classifications and identified themselves as distinct.[299]

[292] *Prosecutor v Georges Anderson Nderubumwe Rutaganda* (Judgment and Sentence, Trial Chamber) ICTR-96-3-T (6 December 1999) [57]; and *Prosecutor v Alfred Musema* (Judgment and Sentence, Trial Chamber) ICTR-96-13-A (27 January 2000) [162].

[293] R Cryer et al, *An Introduction to International Criminal Law and Procedure* (3rd edn, CUP 2014) 214 ('it may be that with racism there is not always an objective basis: perceptions may be based on imagined distinctions rather than genuine ones').

[294] N Eltringham, *Accounting for Horror: Post-Genocide Debates in Rwanda* (Pluto Press 2004) 32–33 (reference omitted).

[295] Cryer et al (n 293) 214.

[296] See, for example, *Prosecutor v Laurent Semanza* (Judgment and Sentence, Trial Chamber) ICTR-97-20-T (15 May 2003) ('*Semanza* Trial Judgment') [317].

[297] See, for example, ibid ('by reference to the *objective* particulars of a given social or historical context') (emphasis in original); and *Prosecutor v Ignace Bagilishema* (Judgment, Trial Chamber) ICTR-95-1A-T (7 June 2001) [65] ('the concepts of national, ethnical, racial, and religious enjoy no generally or internationally accepted definitions ... [and] must be assessed in the light of a particular political, social, historical, and cultural context').

[298] See, for example, *Kayishema and Ruzindana* Trial Judgment (n 233) [98]; and *Semanza* ICTR Trial Judgment (n 296) 317.

[299] *Kayishema and Ruzindana* Trial Judgment (n 233) [522]–[526]. However, in some cases, judges simply referred to the Tutsi population as a protected group without further specification. See, for example, *Prosecutor v Karemera et al* (Decision on Motions for Reconsideration, Appeals Chamber) ICTR-98-44-AR73(C) (1 December 2006) [25].

b. Inferring specific intent

Beyond the protected group element, a further distinguishing feature of the crime of genocide is the requirement to prove a specific intent to destroy a protected group in whole or in part. Importantly, the jurisprudence of the ICTY and ICTR consistently found that the specific intent element requires proof that an individual acted 'with the goal of destroying all or part of a group'.[300] In practice, however, peering into the minds of individuals to identify specific intent proved complicated due to the absence of documents directly evidencing such intent with respect to incidents in the former Yugoslavia and Rwanda.[301] As such, the ICTY and ICTR generally inferred the specific intent of defendants from the cicumstances, adopting a two-stage analysis for this purpose.

The first stage involved determining whether it was possible to establish the existence of a collective genocidal context, either at the national and/or more localised level. For this purpose, the existence of a specific intent to destroy was generally inferred from a range of facts and circumstances, including 'the general context, the perpetration of other culpable acts systematically directed against the same group, the scale of atrocities committed, the systematic targeting of victims on account of their membership in a particular group, the repetition of destructive and discriminatory acts, or the existence of a plan or policy'.[302]

The second stage involved determining whether it was possible to infer a specific intent to destroy on the part of individual defendants from their acts, utterances, and/or position in combination with the collective genocidal context.[303] For this purpose, the tribunals tended to examine the effect of the accused's conduct on the collective context, the accused's knowledge of the collective context, including awareness of the extent and consequences of the crimes committed, and/or the accused's position in relation to the collective context.[304]

In terms of the historical narratives constructed by the ICTY and ICTR, this bipartite approach to inferring genocidal intent proved significant. In particular, it enabled the ad hoc tribunals to establish the existence of collective genocidal contexts even in situations where the individuals on trial were ultimately found not to possess

[300] *Prosecutor v Radislav Krstić* (Judgment, Trial Chamber) IT-98-33-T (2 August 2001) ('*Krstić* Trial Judgment') [571]. See similarly, *Akayesu* Trial Judgment (n 202) [498].

[301] *Prosecutor v Radovan Karadžić* (Judgment (Rule *98bis*), Appeals Chamber) IT-95/18-AR98bis.1 (11 July 2013) [80]; and *Prosecutor v Sylvestre Gacumbitsi* (Judgment, Appeals Chamber) ICTR-2001-64-A (17 July 2006) [40].

[302] *Prosecutor v Zdravko Tolimir* (Judgment, Appeals Chamber) IT-05-88/2-A (8 April 2015) ('*Tolimir* Appeal Judgment') [246]. See similarly, at the ICTR: *Prosecutor v Ndindiliyimana et al* (Judgment and Sentence, Trial Chamber) ICTR-00-56 (17 May 2011) [2073].

[303] For examples where the ICTR relied on a combination of the national genocidal context in Rwanda in conjunction with the personal conduct of accused to infer genocidal intent, see, for example, *Akayesu* Trial Judgment (n 202) [112]–[126] and [729]–[733]; and *Kayishema and Ruzindana* Trial Judgment (n 233) [273]–[312] and [528]–[540]. For examples where the ICTY relied on a combination of a more localised genocidal context in conjunction with the personal conduct of accused to infer genocidal intent, see, for example, *Prosecutor v Popović et al* (Judgment Volume I, Trial Chamber) IT-05-88-T (10 June 2010) ('*Popović et al* Trial Judgment Volume I') [863], [1180], and [1318]; *Prosecutor v Zdravko Tolimir* (Judgment, Trial Chamber) IT-05-88/2-T (12 December 2012) [750]–[782], [1157], and [1172].

[304] M Cupido, 'The Contextual Embedding of Genocide: A Casuistic Analysis of the Interplay between Law and Facts' (2014) 15 *Melbourne Journal of International Law* 1, 20–22.

genocidal intent themselves.[305] In addition, the breadth of the contextual circumstances examined, the relative weight placed on an individual's conduct and the contextual circumstances, as well as the precise relationship drawn between the two for the purpose of inferring genocidal intent, tended to vary in practice.[306] In the early cases of the ICTR, for example, Trial Chambers generally began by establishing the existence of genocide at the national level and then placed significant weight on the nationwide genocidal context as evidence from which to infer the genocidal intent of the accused.[307] By contrast, in later judgments, the ICTR shifted its focus away from the national genocidal context towards establishing genocide in more localised contexts and began to place greater weight on the conduct of the accused for the purpose of inferring genocidal intent.[308] As this shift indicates, the precise focus of the ICTR's narrative frame was prone to fluctuation across different cases depending upon the precise methodology utilised to infer genocidal intent.

c. Type of destruction

A third question that fell to be examined by the judges concerned the type of destruction envisaged within the intent to destroy element of the crime of genocide. At an abstract level, this question was resolved by the ICTY Trial Chamber in *Krstić*, which found that 'customary international law limits the definition of genocide to those acts seeking the *physical or biological* destruction of all or part of the group'.[309] However, in determining whether this definition was satisfied on the facts of particular cases, the jurisprudence of the ICTY narrowed the distinction between genocide and other forms of violence—including, in particular, the practice of ethnic cleansing—by demonstrating an openness to placing reliance on non-physically destructive acts—such as forcible transfer—as evidence from which to infer an intent to destroy.[310]

This issue proved particularly important to the historical narratives constructed by the ICTY with respect to the Srebrenica massacres. In *Krstić*, for example, the ICTY Appeals Chamber confirmed that the Trial Chamber had been entitled to rely on the forcible transfer of Bosnian Muslim women, children, and the elderly from Srebrenica as an indicator in support of its finding that some members of the Bosnian Serb Army intended to destroy the Bosnian Muslims in Srebrenica.[311] The tribunal argued that the transfer 'completed the removal of all Bosnian Muslims from Srebrenica, thereby

[305] See, for example, *Popović et al* Trial Judgment Volume I (n 303) [863] and [1414]–[1415] (concluding that one of the accused, Nikolić, did not possess the requisite genocidal intent, despite the existence of a general genocidal context. Instead, the Trial Chamber convicted Nikolić of aiding and abetting genocide).

[306] See, in this regard, Cupido (n 304) 28–29 (identifying a sliding scale of contextual embedding of the crime of genocide in international criminal courts).

[307] See similarly, Cupido (n 304) 19; and van den Herik (n 125) 121–122.

[308] See similarly, Cupido (n 304) 20; and van den Herik (n 125) 105.

[309] *Krstić* Trial Judgment (n 300) 580 (emphasis added).

[310] See generally, Cupido (n 304) 15–18. See also, *Tolimir* Appeal Judgment (n 302) [208]–[212] (further loosening the distinction between genocide and forcible transfer by concluding that the suffering of the women, children, and elderly forcibly transferred from Srebrenica—considered holistically in conjunction with other factors and evidence—amounted to serious mental harm within the meaning of the *actus reus* of the crime of genocide).

[311] *Prosecutor v Radislav Krstić* (Judgment, Appeals Chamber) IT-98-33-A (19 April 2004) ('*Krstić* ICTY Appeal Judgment') [33]. See similarly, *Popović et al* Trial Judgment Volume I (n 303) [862]; and *Tolimir* Appeal Judgment (n 302) [254].

eliminating even the residual possibility that the Muslim community in the area could reconstitute itself'.[312] The Appeals Chamber also argued that the decision not to kill them may be explained by 'the Bosnian Serbs' sensitivity to public opinion', adding that, in any event, it need not be proven that the perpetrator chose 'the most efficient method to accomplish his objective of destroying the targeted part'.[313]

The Appeals Chamber's findings have proven controversial with some commentators, who argue that an inference of genocidal intent was not the *only* reasonable inference that could have been drawn from the record and that therefore the tribunal should have limited its characterisation of the Srebrenica atrocities to crimes against humanity and war crimes.[314] From a narrative perspective, the result was to extend the scope of application of the crime of genocide to a situation that did not involve the indiscriminate approach to physical destruction that had characterised other recognised instances of genocide.

d. Localised genocide

Beyond broadening the notion of intent to destroy, the ICTY further expanded the scope of the crime of genocide by clarifying the threshold that must be satisfied to prove an intent to destroy a protected group 'in part'. In *Krstić*, the ICTY Appeals Chamber clarified that the part 'must be a *substantial* part of that group' and 'must be *significant* enough to have an impact on the group as a whole'.[315] To determine whether the targeted part was sufficiently substantial, the Appeals Chamber elaborated a range of quantitative and qualitative guidelines, emphasising in particular that if a specific part of the group were 'emblematic of the overall group' or 'essential to its survival', such facts may support a finding that the part is substantial.[316]

Applied to the facts of the case, the Appeals Chamber concluded that the Bosnian Muslims of Srebrenica or the Bosnian Muslims of Eastern Bosnia was sufficiently substantial to satisfy these guidelines.[317] Although the Muslim inhabitants of Srebrenica constituted only a small percentage (2.9 per cent) of the overall Muslim population of Bosnia and Herzegovina, the substantiality criterion was satisfied due to its 'immense strategic importance' to the Bosnian Serb leadership, its 'prominence' amongst the Bosnian Muslims and the international community which rendered the fate of the Bosnian Muslims of Srebrenica 'emblematic of that of all Bosnian Muslims', and the fact that the ambit of the authority of the Bosnian Serb forces in question was limited to the Srebrenica area.[318]

By accepting that 2.9 per cent of a protected group was suffiient to constitute a part of a group within the meaning of the crime of genocide in light of its strategic

[312] *Krstić* Appeal Judgment (n 311) [31].
[313] Ibid [32].
[314] See, for example, Zahar and Sluiter (n 74) 177 (characterising the massacres as crimes against humanity and war crimes); KG Southwick, 'Srebrenica as Genocide? The *Krstić* Decision and the Language of the Unspeakable' (2005) 8 *Yale Human Rights & Development Law Journal* 188, 221–222 (characterising the Srebrenica massacres as crimes against humanity); and Schabas (n 181) 47 (characterising the Srebrenica massacres as crimes against humanity).
[315] *Krstić* Appeal Judgment (n 311) [8]–[12] (emphasis added).
[316] Ibid [12].
[317] Ibid [15].
[318] Ibid [15]–[17].

importance, the ICTY reduced the crime's overall quantitive threshold,[319] extending the reach of the crime beyond other recognised instances of genocide, such as the Holocaust or the massacre of Rwanda's Tutsi population.

D. Conclusion

The range and definition of crime categories adjudicated by the ad hoc tribunals—and the scope and content of the historical narratives constructed through recourse to those categories within their judgments—were the product of a complex interplay of factors.

The general categories of crime included within the jurisdictional mandates of the ad hoc tribunals reflected the interests of their creators in responding to the atrocities that had been committed during the situations in the former Yugoslavia, Rwanda, and Sierra Leone. From a narrative perspective, the Statutes of the ad hoc tribunals marked a shift away from the aggressive war paradigm that had dominated the Nuremberg IMT and Tokyo IMTFE towards an atrocity paradigm focused on the prosecution of war crimes, crimes against humanity and the crime of genocide.

Operating within this atrocity paradigm, prosecutors at the ad hoc tribunals were mandated to bring multiple indictments, developing a series of cases whose scope and focus fluctuated over time. The scope of indictments shifted from a comprehensive to a representative charging strategy, characterised by more streamlined indictments and an openness to negotiated justice. The focus of indictments fluctuated not only in response to the availability and accessibility of evidence, but also under the influence of the investigative strategies and priorities of prosecutors, as well as State pressure, judicial oversight, civil society activism, and witness testimony.

Perhaps most important of all to the scope and content of the historical narratives constructed in the judgments of the ad hoc tribunals were the interpretative practices of the judges. Whereas the engines of legal innovation at the Nuremberg and Tokyo tribunals had been the Allied States, at the ad hoc tribunals it was the judges who would emerge as the drivers of legal creativity. By relying on a flexible approach to custom, a diversity of interpretative techniques, and a relaxed conception of the principle of legality, the ad hoc tribunals were able to progressively develop the meaning of both the contextual/collective elements and prohibited acts of the crime categories that fell within the scope of their jurisdictional mandates—taking care to clothe their humanising advancement of the law in a positivist garb.[320] As Antonio Cassese candidly acknowledged, 'there is much opportunity for courts to be innovative and create new law, as long as, of course, one offers convincing reasoning, one relies upon general principles, and one applies, or, if you prefer, one *manipulates* those principles in a proper and well-balanced way'.[321]

[319] C Kreß, 'The Crime of Genocide under International Law' (2006) 6 *International Criminal Law Review* 461, 491.

[320] This turn of phrase is drawn from Cryer (n 81) 246. See similarly, van Schaak (n 90) 172.

[321] Darcy (n 235) 50 (emphasis added).

The result was the construction of historical narratives that incorporated forms of criminality, whose scope and content were progressively developed by the ad hoc tribunals to reflect the modern-day conditions of mass atrocities. The categories of war crimes and crimes against humanity, for example, were adapted to the privatisation of contemporary violence, while the crime of genocide was expanded to encompass local contexts where the distinction with crimes against humanity became increasingly narrow. Similarly, the prohibited acts recognised within each of the general crime categories were modernised to reflect not only more diverse forms of criminality, but also the ways in which different forms of violence intersect.

At the same time, it is also notable that many of the ad hoc tribunals' most innovative interpretative acts—including, for example, their recognition of war crimes in non-international armed conflicts—were in alignment with the interests of the most powerful States in the international community.[322] Moreover, as Shane Darcy has observed, the ad hoc tribunals 'not only overlooked the conduct of their creators, but . . . also tended to focus on areas of the law that do not excessively impinge on their interests'.[323] In particular, as further discussed later in this chapter, less judicial attention was devoted to the law governing the conduct of hostilities in armed conflict, an area in which powerful States arguably have more at stake.[324]

Viewed from this perspective, just as the judges of the Nuremberg and Tokyo IMTs fulfilled the expectations of their creators by validating several of the more innovative aspects of the Nuremberg and Tokyo Charters, so the judges of the ad hoc tribunals may be understood to have fulfilled the expectations of their creators by progressively developing the meaning of the crime categories within their jurisdictional mandates in an effort to ensure that the atrocities committed in the situations in the former Yugoslavia, Rwanda, and Sierra Leone did not go unpunished, whilst at the same time generally steering clear of areas of law that might have encroached upon the interests of more powerful States in the international community.[325]

III. The ICC

In contrast to other international criminal courts, the ICC is a permanent international court with primarily prospective and potentially worldwide jurisdiction. Similar to its predecessors, States held the primary authority for determining which general categories of crime to include within the ICC's subject-matter jurisdiction. However, the negotiation of the ICC Statute benefitted from far broader State participation than other statutory frameworks, as well as an unprecedented degree of input

[322] See, for example, Danner (n 231) 45 ('The decisions reached by the ICTY in *Tadić* largely reflect the positions taken by powerful countries—particularly the United States—in the negotiations of the 1949 and 1974-77 Geneva Conventions').

[323] Darcy (n 235) 326.

[324] Ibid; Danner (n 231) 44.

[325] See similarly, Danner (n 231) 48–49 (exploring the hypothesis that the ICTY was 'a quite sophisticated agent—one that understood the tacit message of the Security Council and stayed within the boundaries desired by the principal's key members'). For a notable exception to this trend, see Darcy (n 235) 260–263 (discussing decisions at the ICTY asserting the unlawfulness of reprisals against civilians in armed conflict and the negative reaction to such decisions by powerful States such as the UK).

from civil society groups and the emerging jurisprudence of the ad hoc tribunals. The outcome of the drafting process was a detailed statutory framework, which, in conjunction with the guidance provided by the Elements of Crimes, left less space for judicial creativity compared to the ad hoc tribunals. As such, while the interpretative practices of judges remain an important influence over the meaning of the crimes adjudicated by the ICC, it has been the charging practices of the ICC Prosecutor which have proven most significant in shaping the range and definition of crime categories—and, consequently, the scope and content of the historical narratives—contested within the ICC in practice.

A. Drafting Practices

The drafting of the ICC Statute was the outcome of a delicate consensus-building negotiation process.[326] The process can be traced back to the work of the International Law Commission, which, at the request of the UN General Assembly, produced a Draft Statute for an International Criminal Court in 1994 and a Draft Code of Crimes Against the Peace and Security of Mankind in 1996.[327] According to William Schabas, these documents played 'a seminal role' in the preparation of the ICC Statute.[328] The finalisation of the ICC Statute was also preceded by the work of an Ad Hoc Committee on the Establishment of an International Criminal Court, convened by the UN General Assembly in 1994,[329] as well as a Preparatory Committee (PrepCom), convened by the UN General Assembly from 1995 until 1998.[330] As Cherif Bassiouni has observed, the work of these committees ensured that the delegates who participated at the Rome Conference where the ICC Statute was finalised 'did not begin negotiating with a blank slate'.[331] The five-week Rome Conference itself involved the negotiation of a wealth of controversies, ranging from the definition of crimes to technical aspects of criminal procedure. The negotiations culminated in the adoption of the ICC Statute by a vote of 120 to 7, with twenty-one abstentions.[332]

Beyond adopting the ICC Statute, the State participants at Rome also agreed that a Preparatory Commission should draft an 'Elements of Crimes' document containing detailed definitions of each of the crimes falling within the jurisdiction of the ICC.[333] This was included primarily to appease those States—in particular, the US—who

[326] See generally, WA Schabas, *An Introduction to the International Criminal Court* (4th edn, CUP 2011) Chapter 1; and MC Bassiouni, 'Negotiating the Treaty of Rome on the Establishment of an International Criminal Court' (1999) 32 *Cornell International Law Journal* 443.

[327] See, in this regard, Draft Statute for an International Criminal Court, in *Report of the International Law Commission on the Work of its Forty-Sixth Session*, UN GAOR 49th Session, Supp No 10, UN Doc A/49/10 (1994); and Draft Code of Crimes against the Peace and Security of Mankind, in *Report of the International Law Commission on the Work of its Forty-Eighth Session*, UN GAOR 51st Session, Supp No 10, UN Doc A/51/10 (1996).

[328] Schabas (n 326) 11.

[329] UN General Assembly Resolution 49/53, UN Doc A/RES/49/53 (9 December 1994).

[330] UN General Assembly Resolution 50/46, UN Doc A/RES/50/46 (11 December 1995).

[331] Bassiouni (n 326) 455.

[332] Cryer et al (n 293) 149.

[333] Final Act of the United Nations Diplomatic Conference of Plenipotentiaries on the Establishment of an International Criminal Court, Annex I, Resolution F, para 5(b), in *UN Diplomatic Conference of*

insisted on definitional precision with respect to the content of the crimes.[334] As a compromise, Article 9 of the ICC Statute provides that the Elements of Crimes 'shall assist the Court on the interpretation and application' of the crimes, serving merely as a guide rather than binding the Court.[335] In any case, according to Kirsch and Oosterveld, by the end of the fifth session of the Preparatory Commission in June 2000, 'many of the States that had originally questioned whether Elements of Crimes were necessary had accepted their usefulness'.[336] The Elements of Crimes were eventually adopted by consensus by the Preparatory Commission on 30 June 2000 and subsequently endorsed in September 2002 by the Assembly of States Parties.[337]

As with other international criminal courts, the ultimate authority for adopting the ICC Statute resided with States. However, there were a number of characteristics that distinguished the drafting of the ICC Statute.

First, State participation was far broader, with over 160 States sending delegates to the Rome Conference.[338] Since the interests of States were not uniform, in practice a number of different caucuses formed, including, for example, the Like-Minded Group, a coalition that had emerged at the Ad Hoc Committee and PrepCom meetings and ultimately grew to over sixty States by the time of the Rome Conference.[339] Interestingly, according to Marlies Glasius, there was a notable absence of a North-South divide at the Rome Conference, the main division being between 'a majority of states in favour of a strong, independent Court and a minority trying to curtail its powers'.[340] In light of competing State interests, the ICC Statute is to some extent a reflection of the political compromises deemed necessary in order to satisfy the conflicting demands of States.

Second, although States were the dominant actors at the Rome Conference, possessing ultimate authority to accept or reject the text of the ICC Statute, their negotiations took place against the backdrop of a significant civil society presence. 236 civil society groups were accredited to participate at Rome, all but a few of which were members of the Coalition for an International Criminal Court—a network initially established in response to the PrepCom in 1995, which grew to over 800 members by the beginning of the Rome Conference.[341] Civil society groups contributed in several ways to the final outcome of the ICC Statute, including through lobbying State representatives, producing expert research and position papers, monitoring and reporting

Plenipotentiaries on the Establishment of an International Criminal Court: Rome 15 June–17 July 1998, Official Records, Volume I, Final Documents (UN 2002) 71, 72.

[334] P Kirsch and V Oosterveld, 'The Preparatory Commission for the International Criminal Court' (2002) 25 *Fordham International Law Journal* 563, 569.
[335] Article 9, ICC Statute.
[336] Kirsch and Oosterveld (n 334) 570.
[337] Schabas (n 326) 98.
[338] Ibid 18.
[339] See generally, M Glasius, *The International Criminal Court: A Global Civil Society Achievement* (Routledge 2006) 22–26.
[340] Ibid 24.
[341] On the structure and composition of civil society groups at the Rome Conference, see generally, Z Pearson, 'Non-Governmental Organizations and the International Criminal Court: Changing Landscapes of International Law' (2006) 39 *Cornell International Law Journal* 243, 255–271; Glasius (n 339) 26–37.

on the progress of negotiations, and raising awareness to a wider public audience.[342] Importantly, however, while civil society groups were permitted to attend open plenary and formal meetings, receive official documents, make available their materials to delegates, and address opening and closing sessions to a limited extent,[343] they did not have speaking rights or access to informal meetings.[344] As such, their formal status within the negotiations was very much secondary to that of States, even if their contribution at Rome has been characterised by some as heralding a 'new diplomacy'.[345]

Finally, the drafters of the ICC Statute also benefitted from the emerging jurisprudence of the ICTY and ICTR, which provided an important point of reference during the drafting process. As Danner explains, 'delegates at the Rome Conference demonstrated familiarity with the Tribunals' cases, bringing copies of key decisions with their materials for the negotiations'.[346]

In terms of the scope and content of the historical narratives constructed at the ICC, the ICC Statute—in conjunction with the guidance provided by the Elements of Crimes—performs two key functions: first, identifying which general categories of crime fall within the scope of its subject-matter jurisdiction; and second, defining the elements of the crimes.

1. Recognition of general categories of crimes

The ICC Statute identifies four general categories of crime: the crime of genocide, crimes against humanity, war crimes, and the crime of aggression.[347] Despite the inclusion of the crime of aggression, the ICC Statute is further evidence of a narrative shift away from the focus on aggression that dominated the Nuremberg and Tokyo tribunals towards a humanitarian concern for atrocities committed during episodes of mass violence.[348] This is evident from the history of the crime of aggression's inclusion in the ICC Statute, as well as the restrictive conditions that must be satisfied for the ICC to exercise jurisdiction over the crime in practice.

After lengthy negotiations, both in the build-up to and during the Rome Conference, it was agreed that the crime of aggression would be included within the jurisdiction of the ICC Statute, but that the Court would only be able to exercise jurisdiction over the crime once agreement had been reached on its definition and the precise conditions under which jurisdiction could be exercised. Following further negotiations, amendments to the ICC Statute were adopted by consensus at the Kampala Review Conference in 2010, resulting in the elaboration of a definition of the crime (Article 8*bis*) and the conditions for the Court to exercise jurisdiction (Articles 15*bis* and 15*ter*).[349]

342 On the functions of civil society groups at the Rome Conference, see generally, Pearson (n 341) 271–281; Glasius (n 339) 37–44; Grey (n 60) 99–121.

343 UN General Assembly Resolution 52/160, UN Doc A/RES/52/160 (15 December 1997) [9].

344 Pearson (n 341) 258.

345 C Fehl, 'Explaining the International Criminal Court: A Practice Test for Rationalist and Constructivist Approaches', in SC Roach (ed), *Governance, Order, and the International Criminal Court: Between Realpolitik and a Cosmopolitan Court* (OUP 2009) 75, 95.

346 Danner (n 231) 35.

347 Article 5(1), ICC Statute.

348 See (n 118) and accompanying text.

349 See generally, ICC Assembly of States Parties, Review Conference, Resolution RC/Res.6 (11 June 2010) Annex I.

Although the jurisdiction of the ICC over the crime of aggression was activated by the Assembly of States Parties as of 17 July 2018,[350] the conditions for the Court's exercise of jurisdiction are highly restrictive. With respect to situations referred to the ICC Prosecutor by a State Party or investigations initiated by the ICC Prosecutor *proprio motu*, the Court may only exercise its jurisdiction where a crime of aggression:[351] (i) occurred on the territory of a State Party that has accepted the aggression amendments pursuant to Article 121(5) of the ICC Statute; *and* (ii) was committed by nationals of an alleged aggressor State Party that has accepted the aggression amendments; *and* (iii) the alleged aggressor State has not opted out pursuant to Article 15*bis* of the ICC Statute. In other words, the Court cannot exercise jurisdiction over the crime of aggression when committed by a national or on the territory of a State that is not party to the ICC Statute, a State Party that has not ratified the aggression amendments, or a State Party that has ratified the aggression amendments but opted out of the aggression jurisdictional regime. In these circumstances, exercise of jurisdiction over the crime of aggression is tied to the prospect of a referral by the Security Council.[352] Given these limitations, the likelihood of an aggression prosecution at the ICC is exceedingly slim.[353] As of 12 May 2020, only 39 States had ratified the aggression amendments,[354] while the prospect of a Security Council referral appears improbable given its existing record. In practice, therefore, the narrative focus of the ICC is likely to remain directed towards the general categories of genocide, crimes against humanity, and war crimes.[355]

Beyond controversies over the crime of aggression, negotiations both prior to and during the Rome Conference also discussed a number of transnational crimes, including the crimes of terrorism and drug trafficking, which were ultimately omitted from the ICC Statute due to a lack of State support.[356] Reasons officially voiced for excluding these crimes included concerns about the treaty-based character of the crimes, the danger of overburdening the ICC, and the capacity of States to effectively respond to these crimes through international cooperation agreements.[357] Equally,

[350] ICC Assembly of States Parties, Review Conference, Resolution ICC-ASP/16/Res.5 (14 December 2017) [1].

[351] See, in this regard, ICC Assembly of States Parties, Review Conference, Resolution RC/Res.6 (11 June 2010) Annex I, Article 15*bis*(4)–(5); Article 121(5), ICC Statute; and ICC Assembly of States Parties, Review Conference, Resolution ICC-ASP/16/Res.5 (14 December 2017) [2]. For a discussion of some of the uncertainties surrounding how these provisions apply to the crime of aggression, see Cryer et al (n 293) 323–324; and D Akande, 'The International Criminal Court Gets Jurisdiction Over the Crime of Aggression' *EJIL Talk!* (15 December 2017).

[352] ICC Assembly of States Parties, Review Conference, Resolution RC/Res.6 (11 June 2010) Annex I, Article 15*bis* and Article 15*ter*.

[353] A Whiting, 'Crime of Aggression Activated at the ICC: Does it Matter?' *Just Security* (19 December 2017).

[354] 'Amendments on the crime of aggression to the Rome Statute of the International Criminal Court' *UN Treaty Collection* (status as at 12 May 2020).

[355] See, for example, Mégret (n 13) 856 (observing that the inclusion of the crime of aggression may owe more to 'a nostalgia for a simpler, starker world than a real willingness to engage the complexities of the current international system as it is'); and KJ Heller, 'Who Is Afraid of the Crime of Aggression?' *Amsterdam Law School Research Paper No 2019-49* (2019).

[356] See generally, H von Hebel and D Robinson, 'Crimes Within the Jurisdiction of the Court', in RS Lee (ed), *The International Criminal Court: The Making of the Rome Statute: Issues, Negotiations, and Results* (Kluwer Law International 1999) 79, 85–87; Stahn (n 2) 107.

[357] von Hebel and Robinson (n 356) 86.

however, it is notable that the omission of at least some of these crimes was in alignment with the interests of powerful States. According to Christine Schwöbel-Patel, for example, 'whilst the criminalisation of war-lords tends to localise conflict, the money flows of drug-lords and financiers tends to expose global capital flows which benefit the richer states'.[358] From this perspective, the omission of transnational crimes such as drug trafficking has helped steer the narrative focus of the ICC away from areas of law that might have intruded on the interests of powerful States.

2. Defining the general categories of crimes

Beyond delimiting the general categories of crime, the ICC Statute, in conjunction with the guidance elaborated in the Elements of Crime, also serves the important function of defining them. As several commentators have observed, the materials relied upon during the drafting of the ICC Statute reveal an intention to define the crimes in accordance with existing custom or to crystallise emerging custom, subject to compromises deemed necessary to build consensus.[359] While it is beyond the scope of this book to comprehensively detail the drafting decisions adopted for each general category of crime,[360] it is pertinent to examine a few examples that illustrate not only the diversity of influences that shaped the subject-matter jurisdiction of the ICC, but also the unique blend of progressive and restrictive elements that emerged from the drafting process.

Some of the more progressive elements of the ICC Statute reflected the receptivity of the drafters to the then-emerging jurisprudence of the ad hoc tribunals. The seminal *Decision on Jurisdiction* rendered by the ICTY Appeals Chamber in *Tadić*, for example, informed the elaboration of war crimes applicable in non-international armed conflicts within Article 8 of the ICC Statute, perhaps even constituting the tipping point for their inclusion.[361] With respect to other progressive aspects of the ICC's subject-matter jurisdiction, the influence of civil society was also palpable. For instance, civil society groups played an instrumental role in the inclusion of the war crimes of conscripting or enlisting children under the age of fifteen years or using them to participate actively in hostilities,[362] a significant development since the customary status of the crime of enlistment in particular was uncertain at the time.[363] Civil society groups also proved influential in expanding the list of sexual and gender-based crimes elaborated within the general categories of war crimes and crimes against humanity, the final version of which includes certain forms of reproductive violence, such as forced pregnancy and enforced sterilisation, as well as gender as a ground of persecution.[364]

[358] Schwöbel-Patel (n 7) 787.

[359] L Grover, 'A Call to Arms: Fundamental Dilemmas Confronting the Interpretation of Crimes in the Rome Statute of the International Criminal Court' (2010) 21 *European Journal of International Criminal Law* 543, 567; Schabas (n 326) 92.

[360] See generally, Cryer (n 55) Chapter 5; and von Hebel and Robinson (n 356).

[361] Darcy (n 235) 284; and Danner (n 231) 35–36.

[362] MA Drumbl, 'The Effects of the *Lubanga* Case on Understanding and Preventing Child Soldiering' (2012) 15 *Yearbook of International Humanitarian Law* 87, 149.

[363] See, in this regard, von Hebel and Robinson (n 356) 117 ('The United States in particular took the view that [Article 8(2)(b)(xxvi)] did not reflect customary international law and was more a human rights provision than a criminal law provision').

[364] See generally, Grey (n 60) 105–114.

In line with the negotiated nature of the ICC Statute, however, the more progressive dimensions of the statutory framework were only accepted subject to certain restrictions, which reflect the difficult compromises forged during the drafting process. For instance, although Article 8 of the ICC Statute includes war crimes applicable in non-international armed conflicts, the list is narrower than those recognised as applicable in international armed conflicts, initially omitting any provisions concerning the use of prohibited weapons,[365] or deliberate starvation,[366] as well as excluding, *inter alia*, a number of prohibited methods of warfare, including the use of human shields, attacks contrary to the principle of proportionality, direct attacks on civilian objects, and direct attacks on undefended buildings. The definition of the crime of conscripting, enlisting, or using child soldiers was also restrictively defined to satisfy the interests of certain States. In particular, although a number of civil society groups had lobbied for the crime to prohibit the recruitment and use of children under the age of *eighteen*, opposition to this proposal, particularly from the US whose army permits seventeen-year-olds to enlist,[367] led to the final text only prohibiting the recruitment and use of children under the age of *fifteen*.[368]

Similarly, the SGBV provisions within the ICC Statute were also subject to compromise. For instance, although the crime of forced pregnancy was included in the ICC Statute as a war crime and a crime against humanity with strong support from civil society groups such as the Women's Caucus for Gender Justice, concerns about the crime's relationship to abortion raised by the Holy See, several States with large Muslim and Catholic populations, and a number of 'pro-life' civil society groups, led to a compromise definition, which requires that a woman be forcibly made pregnant *and* unlawfully confined.[369] In a similar vein, gender-based persecution also generated significant controversy at Rome, with a number of conservative and religious States and civil society groups raising concerns that its inclusion might compel them to recognise rights based on sexual orientation.[370] Ultimately, gender was retained as a ground of persecution amidst lobbying by the Women's Caucus for Gender Justice, but subject to a provision that defines 'gender' ambiguously to refer to 'the two sexes, male and female, within the context of society'—the notion of 'two sexes' pointing towards a restrictive biologically determined definition of gender in contrast to the reference

[365] In 2010, three paragraphs were added to Article 8(2)(e), which correspond to the weapons prohibited in international armed conflicts in Article 8(2)(xvii) to (xix). In 2017, the list of weapons was further extended to include the employment of weapons using biological agents or toxins, weapons injuring with undetectable X-ray fragments, and laser weapons designed to cause permanent blindness in both international and non-international armed conflicts. ICC Assembly of States Parties, Review Conference, Resolution ICC-ASP/16/Res.4 (14 December 2017).

[366] See, in this regard, 'Swiss initiative: intentional starvation of civilians in civil wars is now a war crime' *Swiss Federal Department of Foreign Affairs* (6 December 2019) (confirming the adoption of an amendment to the ICC Statute to include the war crime of intentional starvation of civilians in non-international armed conflicts). For discussion, see KJ Heller, 'The Rome Statute's Flawed Amendment Regime—Starvation in NIAC Edition' *Opinio Juris* (7 December 2019).

[367] K Austin, 'Small Victories: Children's Rights under the International Criminal Court' 5 *Human Rights Tribunal* (1998).

[368] See Article 8(2)(b)(xxvi) and Article 8(2)(e)(vii), ICC Statute.

[369] See generally, Grey (n 60) 107–111.

[370] See generally, ibid 39–43 and 112–113 (and accompanying references).

to 'within the context of society' which seems to imply a broader socially constructed notion of gender.[371]

The result of these omissions and definitional compromises has been to potentially restrict the types of violence that fall within the scope of the ICC's subject-matter jurisdiction. With respect to definitional compromises in particular, however, it is important to remember that the statutory framework only marks the beginning of the interpretative process, with the precise meaning of different crime categories ultimately dependent on how they are interpreted in the context of particular cases.

B. Charging Practices

Turning to charging practices, it is the ICC Prosecutor who is tasked with selecting which crimes to charge in particular cases, [372] subject to judicial oversight concerning whether the relevant evidentiary standard has been met at different stages of a case.[373] Similar to prosecutors at the ad hoc tribunals, the ICC Prosecutor is required to act independently of instructions from external sources,[374] as well as refrain from participating in any matter in which their impartiality might reasonably be doubted on any ground.[375] The ICC Prosecutor has also emphasised that the principle of impartiality requires the application of consistent methods and criteria regardless of the States, parties, persons, or groups concerned,[376] and that the exercise of prosecutorial discretion must be 'information and evidence-driven' so as to ensure that there is sufficient information and evidence to reasonably justify the selection of a case for investigation and prosecution.[377]

From a narrative perspective, of particular importance is the fact that the ICC Prosecutor is empowered to initiate multiple cases within each of the situations under investigation. To this end, the ICC Prosecutor has outlined a policy of aiming 'to ensure, jointly with the relevant national jurisdictions, that the most serious crimes committed in each situation do not go unpunished'.[378] However, given resource limitations and the challenge of managing preliminary examinations and investigations into multiple situations, the ICC Prosecutor has generally targeted no more than a handful of individuals for prosecution within each situation under investigation—a far narrower approach compared to prosecutors at the ICTY and ICTR. In practice, the narrower selection of cases within each situation under investigation at the ICC has served to heighten the narrative significance of the scope and focus of the charges for which individuals have been prosecuted.

[371] Article 7(3), ICC Statute.
[372] Rule 121(3), ICC Rules of Procedure and Evidence.
[373] Articles 58(1)(a), 61(7), and 66(3), ICC Statute.
[374] Article 42(1), ICC Statute. See also, ICC Office of the Prosecutor, 'Policy Paper on Case Selection and Prioritisation' (15 September 2016) ('ICC OTP Policy Paper on Case Selection and Prioritisation') [17]–[18].
[375] Articles 21(3) and 42(7), ICC Statute.
[376] ICC OTP Policy Paper on Case Selection and Prioritisation (n 374) [19]–[20].
[377] Ibid [21]–[23].
[378] Ibid [45].

1. Scope of charges

In terms of the scope of the charges, the official policy relied upon by the Office of the Prosecution at the ICC has remained relatively consistent over time. During the tenure of former ICC Prosecutor Luis Moreno Ocampo, the Office of the Prosecution made clear its intention to present 'expeditious and focused cases',[379] selecting a limited number of incidents that 'provide a sample that is reflective of the gravest incidents and the main types of victimization'.[380] Since Fatou Bensouda took over as ICC Prosecutor, the Office of the Prosecution has maintained that it 'will continue to conduct focused prosecutions in which we present the relevant evidence in a clear and efficient way'.[381] In accordance with this policy, the Office of the Prosecution has confirmed that 'the charges chosen will constitute, whenever possible, a representative sample of the main types of victimisation and of the communities which have been affected by the crimes in that situation'.[382] Most recently, in its *2019–2021 Strategic Plan*, the Office of the Prosecution indicated its intention to narrow the scope of cases even further, clarifying that going forward it would give increased consideration to the possibility of bringing 'narrower but stronger cases' that focus on 'key aspects of victimisation, particular incidents, areas, time periods, or a single accused'.[383]

Yet, notwithstanding the rhetoric emanating from the Office of the Prosecution, in practice the scope of charges brought by the ICC Prosecutor has varied considerably between cases. In particular, it is possible to identify three different types of charging practices adopted by the ICC Prosecutor to date.

First, both the current and former ICC Prosecutor have brought charges focused narrowly on *particular crimes*. In *Lubanga*, for example, ICC Prosecutor Moreno-Ocampo limited the charges to the war crimes of conscripting, enlisting, and using child soldiers from July 2002 to December 2003 in Ituri, Democratic Republic of Congo.[384] Similarly, in *Al Mahdi*, ICC Prosecutor Bensouda limited the charges to the war crime of intentionally directing attacks against buildings dedicated to religion and historic monuments between approximately 20 June and 11 July 2012 in Timbuktu, Mali.[385]

Second, both the current and former ICC Prosecutor have sometimes focused prosecutions on *a small number of incidents*. In *Katanga and Ngudjolo*, for example,

[379] ICC Office of the Prosecutor, 'Report on the activities performed during the first three years (June 2003–June 2006)' (12 September 2006) [3].

[380] ICC Office of the Prosecutor, 'Prosecutorial Strategy: 2009–2012' (1 February 2010) [20]. See similarly, Regulation 34(2), ICC Regulations of the Office of the Prosecution.

[381] ICC Office of the Prosecutor, 'Strategic Plan: June 2012–2015' (11 October 2013) [51].

[382] ICC OTP Policy Paper on Case Selection and Prioritisation (n 374) [45].

[383] ICC Office of the Prosecutor, 'Strategic Plan 2019–2021' (17 July 2019) [24].

[384] *Prosecutor v Thomas Lubanga Dyilo* (Decision on the Confirmation of Charges, Pre-Trial Chamber) ICC-01/04-01/06-803-tEN (29 January 2007) ('*Lubanga* DCC') [9]–[12].

[385] *Prosecutor v Ahmad Al Faqi Al Mahdi* (Decision on the Confirmation of Charges against Ahmad Al Faqi Al Mahdi, Pre-Trial Chamber) ICC-01/12-01/15 (24 March 2016) ('*Al Mahdi* DCC'). See also, *Prosecutor v Mahmoud Mustafa Busayf Al-Werfalli* (Warrant of Arrest, Pre-Trial Chamber) ICC-01/11-01/17-2 (15 August 2017) (concerning the charge of the war crime of murder for the killing of 33 people in seven separate incidents, which allegedly occurred in Benghazi, Libya between 2016 and 2017); and *Prosecutor v Mahmoud Mustafa Busayf Al-Werfalli* (Second Warrant of Arrest, Pre-Trial Chamber) ICC-01/11-01/17-13 (4 July 2018) (concerning the charge of the war crime of murder for an additional mass killing, which allegedly occurred in Benghazi, Libya in January 2018).

ICC Prosecutor Moreno-Ocampo brought thirteen counts of war crimes and crimes against humanity, all of which focused on a single attack on Bogoro village in Ituri on 24 February 2003.[386] The charges brought by ICC Prosecutor Bensouda in *Gbagbo* and *Blé Goudé* with respect to the situation in Côte d'Ivoire provide a more recent illustration. In *Gbagbo*, the accused faced four charges of committing the crimes against humanity of murder, rape, other inhumane acts, and persecution in relation to four incidents,[387] while in *Blé Goudé*, the accused faced the same charges in relation to five sets of incidents.[388] In both cases, the charges focused exclusively on incidents in Abidjan, notwithstanding the fact that the ICC Prosecutor—in earlier applications before the Court—had initially relied on allegations of crimes committed by pro-Gbagbo forces in localities in the western part of Côte d'Ivoire.[389]

Finally, in a few cases, both the current and former ICC Prosecutor have brought *more extensive charges*. In *Ahmad Harun and Ali Kushayb*, for example, ICC Prosecutor Moreno-Ocampo secured the issuance of arrest warrants for charges covering thirteen crimes, divided into fifty-one counts, which related to indiscriminate attacks that targeted civilians and rebels from the Fur, Masalit, and Zaghawa groups in Darfur, Sudan between August 2003 and March 2004.[390] More recently, upon the capture of Dominic Ongwen in early 2015, ICC Prosecutor Bensouda expanded the charges initially elaborated in the arrest warrant both in terms of crimes and geographical scope. In its decision on the confirmation of charges, the Pre-Trial Chamber confirmed seventy counts of crimes against humanity and war crimes against the accused, divided into six parts:[391] the first four parts encompass armed attacks in the Pajule, Odek, Lukodi, and Adok IDP camps (counts 1–49); the fifth part concerns sexual and gender-based crimes directly and indirectly committed by the accused (counts 50–68); and the final part concerns the crimes of conscription and use in hostilities of children under the age of fifteen (counts 69–70).

[386] *Prosecutor v Germain Katanga and Mathieu Ngudjolo Chui* (Decision on Confirmation of Charges, Pre-Trial Chamber) ICC-01/04-01/07-717 (30 September 2008) [573]–[581] (confirming 10 of the 13 counts). See also, *Prosecutor v Abdallah Banda Abakaer Nourain and Saleh Mohammed Jerbo Jamus* (Corrigendum of the 'Decision on the Confirmation of Charges', Pre-Trial Chamber) ICC-02/05-03/09 (7 March 2011) ('*Banda and Jerbo* DCC') (confirming the charges of three war crimes committed during an attack carried out on 29 September 2007 against an African Union peacekeeping mission in North Darfur, Sudan).

[387] *Prosecutor v Laurent Gbagbo* (Decision on the Confirmation of Charges Against Laurent Gbagbo, Pre-Trial Chamber) ICC-02/11-01/11 (12 June 2014) ('*Gbagbo* DCC') [267]–[278] (confirming the charges against the accused).

[388] *Prosecutor v Charles Blé Goudé* (Decision on the Confirmation of Charges Against Charles Blé Goudé, Pre-Trial Chamber) ICC-02/11-02/11-186 (11 December 2014) ('*Blé Goudé* DCC') [183]–[194] (confirming the charges against the accused).

[389] Human Rights Watch, *Making Justice Count: Lessons from the ICC's Work in Côte d'Ivoire* (August 2015) 38–39.

[390] *Prosecutor v Ahmad Muhammad Harun and Ali Muhammad Al Abd-Al-Rahman* (Warrant of Arrest for Ahmad Harun, Pre-Trial Chamber) ICC-02-05-01/07-2 (27 April 2007); *Prosecutor v Ahmad Muhammad Harun and Ali Muhammad Al Abd-Al-Rahman* (Warrant of Arrest for Ali Kushayb, Pre-Trial Chamber) ICC-02-05-01/07-3-Corr (27 April 2007).

[391] *Prosecutor v Dominic Ongwen* (Decision on the Confirmation of Charges Against Dominic Ongwen, Pre-Trial Chamber) ICC-02/04-01/15-422-Red (23 March 2016) ('*Ongwen* DCC').

2. Focus of charges

With respect to the focus of the charges, almost all crimes charged to date have been war crimes or crimes against humanity, with only one individual—former Sudanese President Al Bashir—subject to an arrest warrant which includes counts of genocide.[392] Within the general category of war crimes, the most common charges at the arrest warrant phase have been murder, torture, cruel treatment, attacks against the civilian population, pillage, and rape. Within the general category of crimes against humanity, the most frequent charges at the arrest warrant phase have been murder, torture, rape, deportation or forcible transfer, persecution on political grounds, and other inhumane acts.

An important policy of the ICC Prosecutor has been to 'pay particular attention to crimes that have been traditionally under-prosecuted'.[393] To date, this policy has been implemented in two ways: first, the ICC Prosecutor has brought thematic prosecutions oriented exclusively or predominantly around themes of traditionally under-prosecuted forms of criminality, including crimes against or affecting children,[394] sexual and gender-based crimes,[395] attacks against protected objects,[396] and attacks against a peacekeeping mission;[397] and second, the ICC Prosecutor has also made specific efforts to include charges of crimes against or affecting children,[398] as well as sexual and gender-based crimes,[399] within its cases more generally whenever relevant evidence has been identified. Particularly notable in this regard—given the dearth of prosecutions in the past—have been charges encompassing: sexual violence against men;[400] sexual violence against child soldiers;[401] forced marriage;[402] forced pregnancy;[403] gender-based

[392] See *Prosecutor v Omar Hassan Ahmad Al Bashir* (Second Decision on the Prosecution's Application for a Warrant of Arrest, Pre-Trial Chamber) ICC-02/05-01/09-94 (12 July 2010) ('*Al Bashir* Second Arrest Warrant Decision').

[393] ICC OTP Policy Paper on Case Selection and Prioritisation (n 374) [46].

[394] See, for example, *Lubanga* DCC (n 384).

[395] See, for example, *Prosecutor v Al Hassan Ag Abdoul Aziz Ag Mohamed Ag Mohmoud* (Decision on the Prosecutor's Application for the Issuance of a Warrant of Arrest for Al Hassan Ag Abdoul Aziz Ag Mohamed Ag Mohmoud, Pre-Trial Chamber) ICC-01/12-01/18-Red2-tENG (22 May 2018) ('*Al Hassan* Arrest Warrant Decision').

[396] See, for example, *Al Mahdi* DCC (n 385).

[397] See, for example, *Banda and Jerbo* DCC (n 386).

[398] Examples of charges of conscripting, enlisting and/or using child soldiers include the cases against: Kony, Otti, and Ongwen (*Situation in Uganda*); and Lubanga, Katanga, Ngudjolo, and Ntaganda (*Situation in the Democratic Republic of the Congo*).

[399] See, for example, Grey (n 60) 253 (noting that, as of 17 July 2018, sexual and gender-based crimes 'account for almost half of all crimes charged at the ICC', specifically '85 out of 173 charges (49.13 per cent) in requests for arrest warrants/summons to appear and 50 of 110 charges (45.45 per cent) in charging documents').

[400] Examples include the cases against Bemba (rape of male civilians), Ntaganda (rape of male civilians and civilians being forced to rape one another), Muthaura et al (genital mutilation of men), and Mbarushimana and Mudacumura (genital mutilation of men's genitals, rape of male civilians, and forcing male civilians to rape other female victims).

[401] *Prosecutor v Bosco Ntaganda* (Decision Pursuant to Article 61(7)(a) and (b) of the Rome Statute on the Charges of the Prosecutor Against Bosco Ntaganda, Pre-Trial Chamber) ICC-01/04-02/06-309 (9 June 2014) ('*Ntaganda* DCC') [76].

[402] *Ongwen* DCC (n 391) [87]–[95].

[403] Ibid [96]–[101]; and *Al Hassan* Arrest Warrant Decision (n 395).

persecution;[404] and sexual violence as an act of genocide through causing serious bodily or mental harm.[405] Looking to the future, the ICC Prosecutor has also committed to give particular consideration to crimes committed by means of, or that result in 'the destruction of the environment, the illegal exploitation of natural resources or the illegal dispossession of land',[406] as well as to examine the feasibility of opening an investigation into 'migrant-related crimes' in Libya.[407]

Following the path pursued by prosecutors at the ad hoc tribunals, the ICC Prosecutor has also seen fit to illuminate how different types of violence intersect within its charging practices. In this regard, despite some early decisions which indicated a degree of judicial reticence towards intersectional analyses of crimes,[408] judges at the ICC have now begun to allow the practice. For instance, in its 2010 *Al Bashir* Arrest Warrant decision, the Pre-Trial Chamber concluded that acts of rape, torture, and forcible displacement could be legally characterised as both crimes against humanity and genocide.[409] More recently, in *Bemba*, the ICC Trial Chamber also recognised that 'convictions for multiple offences are permissible where those offences have materially distinct elements, i.e. each requires proof of a fact not required by the others'.[410] According to the Trial Chamber, adopting this approach ensures that 'an accused is convicted only for distinct offenses and, at the same time, that the convictions entered fully reflect his or her culpability and criminal conduct'.[411]

Importantly, in order for charges to proceed to trial at the ICC, the ICC Prosecutor must first obtain confirmation of the charges from the Pre-Trial Chamber. In its *2016–2018 Strategic Plan*, the Office of the Prosecution revealed that its success rate with respect to confirmations of charges had been increasing, with 85.83 per cent of charges confirmed in the period June 2012–2015 compared to 62.5 per cent in the period 2003–June 2012.[412] At the same time, these statistics mask other developments that suggest the ICC Prosecutor is struggling to present convincing cases in practice.[413] In cases that have moved beyond the confirmation of charges phase, the ICC Prosecutor has withdrawn charges with respect to two defendants due to insufficient evidence

404 *Prosecutor v Callixte Mbarushimana* (Decision on the Prosecutor's Application for a Warrant of Arrest against Callixte Mbarushimana, Pre-Trial Chamber) ICC-01/04/01/10-1-US (28 September 2010); *Al Hassan* Arrest Warrant Decision (n 395).

405 *Al Bashir* Second Arrest Warrant Decision (n 392).

406 ICC OTP Policy Paper on Case Selection and Prioritisation (n 374) [41].

407 ICC Office of the Prosecutor, 'Statement of ICC Prosecutor to the UNSC on the Situation in Libya' (8 May 2017) [29].

408 See, for example, *Prosecutor v Jean-Pierre Bemba Gombo* (Decision Pursuant to Article 61(7)(a) and (b) of the Rome Statute on the Charges of the Prosecutor Against Jean-Pierre Bemba Gombo, Pre-Trial Chamber) ICC-01/05-01/08 (15 June 2009) ('*Bemba* DCC') [199]–[205]; *Prosecutor v Jean-Pierre Bemba Gombo* (Decision on the Prosecutor's Application for Leave to Appeal the 'Decision Pursuant to Article 61(7)(a) and (b) of the Rome Statute on the Charges of the Prosecutor Against Jean-Pierre Bemba Gombo', Pre-Trial Chamber) ICC-01/05-01/08-532 (18 September 2009) [56].

409 *Al Bashir* Second Arrest Warrant Decision (n 392) [25]–[31].

410 *Prosecutor v Jean-Pierre Bemba Gombo* (Judgment Pursuant to Article 74 of the Statute, Trial Chamber) ICC-01/05-01/08-3343 (21 March 2016) ('*Bemba* Trial Judgment') [748]. See similarly, *Prosecutor v Germain Katanga* (Judgment Pursuant to Article 74 of the Statute, Trial Chamber) ICC-01/04-01/07 (7 March 2014) ('*Katanga* Trial Judgment') [1695].

411 *Bemba* Trial Judgment (n 410) 748.

412 ICC Office of the Prosecutor, 'Strategic Plan: 2016–2018' (6 July 2015) [15].

413 See, in this regard, ICC Office of the Prosecutor, 'Strategic Plan 2019–2021' (17 July 2019) [5] (observing 'a period of mixed performance in court').

(*Muthaura* and *Kenyatta*). In the cases that have proceeded to trial, the ICC Prosecutor has secured four core crimes convictions (*Lubanga*, *Katanga*, *Al Mahdi* (guilty plea), and *Ntaganda* (subject to appeal)), while two have led to acquittals (*Ngudjolo* and *Bemba*) and charges against two other defendants have been vacated (*Ruto* and *Sang*). Most recently, the Trial Chamber in *Gbagbo and Blé Goudé*, by majority, acquitted the defendants from all charges of crimes against humanity on the basis that the ICC Prosecutor had failed to submit sufficient evidence to demonstrate several core constitutive elements of the crimes charged.[414]

In terms of the historical narratives constructed at the ICC, these trends concerning the scope and focus of the charges have proven significant.

First, the predominantly focused nature of the ICC Prosecutor's charging strategy means that the narrative frame in individual cases tends to be concentrated on a narrow selection of crimes and incidents. In line with this approach, the Office of the Prosecution has expressly confirmed that 'the Office's mandate does not include production of comprehensive historical records for a given conflict'.[415]

Second, the willingness of the ICC Prosecutor to adopt a thematic approach to prosecutions, focusing charges in a given case exclusively or predominantly on a specific theme of criminality, tends to facilitate the construction of thematic historical narratives—for example, narratives focused narrowly on the recruitment and use of child soldiers in *Lubanga* or the protection of cultural property in *Al Mahdi*. The thematic focus in each of these cases has received significant criticism from civil society groups in light of other charges—particularly sexual and gender-based crimes—that could potentially have been brought.[416] In *Lubanga*, for example, while the omission of charges concerning sexual and gender-based crimes did not prevent a certain amount of SGBV evidence emerging at trial—both through witness testimony facilitated by questioning from the prosecution and judges, as well as in the prosecution's opening and closing arguments—not only was such evidence limited by the lack of specific charges concerning such crimes, but also the historical narratives constructed by the majority of the Trial Chamber in its judgment were understandably confined to recognising such evidence without more fully examining or relying upon it to support the conviction of the defendant.[417]

Third, the willingness of the ICC Prosecutor to engage in intersectional analyses of crimes has generated opportunities for more precise examinations of the nature of the harm caused to victims and more nuanced understandings of the interrelationship between different types of violence.

414 'ICC Trial Chamber I acquits Laurent Gbagbo and Charles Blé Goudé from all charges' *ICC Press Release* (15 January 2019). The ICC Prosecutor is appealing the decision. See *Prosecutor v Laurent Gbagbo and Charles Blé Goudé* (Corrected Version of 'Prosecution Notice of Appeal', September 16, 2019, ICC-02/11-01/15-1270, Office of the Prosecutor) ICC-01/11-01/15-1270-Corr (17 September 2019).

415 ICC Office of the Prosecutor, 'Prosecutorial Strategy: 2009–2012' (1 February 2010) [20].

416 See, for example, Women's Initiatives for Gender Justice, 'Letter to ICC Prosecutor' (August 2006) (expressing 'grave concern' at the absence of charges for gender-based crimes in *Lubanga*); and FIDH, 'Mali: The Hearing of Al Mahdi before the ICC is a Victory, but Charges Must Be Expanded' (30 September 2005) (insisting that the ICC Prosecutor consider credible allegations of Al Mahdi's criminal responsibility for additional crimes committed against civilians, including rape, sexual slavery, and forced marriage).

417 For discussion of the trial and judgment, see generally, Grey (n 60) 133–140.

Fourth, the record of the ICC Prosecutor in terms of unconfirmed, withdrawn, and vacated charges has resulted in the historical narratives that formed the focus of contestation within a number of cases remaining untold or incomplete before the ICC.

And finally, a recent development that has emerged at least partially as a result of the focused charging strategy of the ICC Prosecutor is the prospect of additional criminal proceedings being brought at the domestic level against individuals who have already been tried and convicted at the ICC. In April 2016, the Presidency of the ICC issued a decision approving a request by the Democratic Republic of the Congo (DRC) to prosecute Germain Katanga before the High Military Court in Kinshasa for war crimes and crimes against humanity, which the DRC had assured the Court are unrelated to the crimes for which Katanga had already been convicted and acquitted by the ICC with respect to the attack on the village of Bogoro in Ituri.[418] The *Katanga* decision raises the prospect of individuals being prosecuted by both the ICC and domestic courts for different crimes, with a plurality of historical narratives concerning the conduct of particular individuals being constructed by different courts at the international and domestic levels.

3. Explaining the scope and focus of charges

The scope and focus of the charges brought before the ICC are the product of a range of different factors. At a general level, the charges have been significantly influenced by the institutional design of the ICC. In contrast to the ad hoc tribunals, the ICC Prosecutor has had to manage a jurisdictional mandate that extends far beyond the confines of a single mass atrocity situation. In addition, the ICC Prosecutor has had to determine the scope and focus of the charges against a background of political constraints, including a restricted budget, fluctuating security concerns, and dependency on State cooperation to conduct effective investigations. In the latter regard, cases in the situations in the Central African Republic and Kenya concerning offences against the administration of justice related to intentionally corruptly influencing witnesses underscore the challenges faced by the ICC in ensuring the integrity of its investigations and trials.[419] Taken together, these institutional and political constraints provide an important context for understanding the narrower scope and more focused approach to charging at the ICC.

At a more granular level, the precise scope and focus of charges in particular cases may be understood to reflect a more diverse set of factors. In order to illustrate the different influences at play, the fluctuating record of the ICC concerning the prosecution of sexual and gender-based crimes provides a useful case-study.

Arguably the most important factor that has influenced the inclusion of sexual and gender-based crimes within charging documents, as well as their confirmation by Pre-Trial Chambers, has been the shifting investigative strategy and priorities of the ICC Prosecutor.

[418] *Prosecutor v Germain Katanga* (Decision Pursuant to Article 108(1) of the Rome Statute, ICC Presidency) ICC-01/04-01/07-3679 (7 April 2016). For discussion, see P Labuda, 'The Flipside of Complementarity: Double Jeopardy at the International Criminal Court' (2019) 17 *Journal of International Criminal Justice* 369.

[419] See, in particular, *Prosecutor v Jean-Pierre Bemba Gombo et al* ICC-01/05-01/13; *Prosecutor v Walter Osapiri Barasa* ICC-01/09-0113; *Prosecutor v Paul Gicheru and Philip Kipkoech Bett* ICC-01/09-01/15.

Under Luis Moreno-Ocampo, the Office of the Prosecution adopted a policy of 'focused investigations', pursuant to which a very limited number of incidents were selected so as to allow the Prosecutor to carry out short investigations, limit the number of persons put at risk, and propose expeditious trials.[420] In practice, two dimensions of this strategy were particularly significant in shaping the scope and focus of charges at the ICC.

First, seemingly driven by a sense of urgency to prove itself as a young institution,[421] the Office of the Prosecution under Moreno-Ocampo initially prioritised the objective of expeditiously presenting cases before the Court rather than ensuring that charges represented the different forms of criminality for which defendants were allegedly responsible. According to first-hand interviews with former ICC staff conducted by Katy Glassborow, in its early investigations the Office of the Prosecution would begin by developing a case hypothesis in the abstract on the basis of open-source information, after which investigators were told 'which alleged perpetrators and particular incidents—such as specific attacks on villages, mass killings or forced transfer of civilians—to focus on'.[422] According to those interviewed, since investigators would arrive in a target State already focused on gathering evidence with respect to 'a particular set of crimes, committed in specific locations and on specific dates', this meant that other atrocities would be overlooked.[423]

In pursuing this approach, the investigation of sexual and gender-based crimes does not appear to have been a major priority. For instance, charges encompassing sexual and gender-based crimes were only included in the case of *Kony et al* after investigators happened to uncover relevant evidence whilst pursuing other leads.[424] Moreover, in the case of *Lubanga*, investigators were instructed 'to drop a year and a half of investigative work and focus solely on the use of child soldiers', notwithstanding the fact that incidents of sexual and gender-based crimes had already been identified.[425] According to the ICC Prosecutor, the decision to focus on the crime of recruiting and using child soldiers 'was triggered by the possible imminent release of Thomas Lubanga Dyilo, who had been under arrest in the DRC for appoximately one year before he was transferred to the Court'.[426] According to a former ICC investigator, however, the decision to maintain such limited charges in *Lubanga* was at least partially driven by Moreno-Ocampo's concern that 'the first ICC trial could not fail' and his belief that omitting other possible charges would help 'to organise a good trial'.[427] As Rosemary Grey explains, such an attitude reflects 'the historical tendency to overlook

420 ICC Office of the Prosecutor, 'Prosecutorial Strategy: 2009–2012' (1 February 2010) [20].

421 K Glassborow, 'ICC Investigative Strategy Under Fire' *Institute for War & Peace Reporting* (27 October 2008).

422 Ibid.

423 Ibid. For judicial criticism of this approach, see *Prosecutor v Callixte Mbarushimana* (Decision on the Confirmation of Charges, Pre-Trial Chamber) ICC-01/04-01/10-465-Red (16 December 2011) ('*Mbarushimana* DCC') [51].

424 Glassborow (n 421).

425 Ibid.

426 ICC Office of the Prosecutor, 'Report on the activities performed during the first three years (June 2003–June 2006)' (12 September 2006) [3].

427 Glassborow (n 421).

or trivialise sexual violence crimes in international criminal law, or assume that these crimes are too difficult to investigate'.[428]

Second, Moreno-Ocampo also seemed to concentrate first and foremost on using 'the shadow of the court' to deter crimes—prioritising the message a case might send over the forensic work required to establish sufficient evidence to secure a conviction.[429] For instance, in his desire to move swiftly, Moreno-Ocampo adopted a phased approach to investigations—securing only enough evidence to satisfy the evidentiary threshold of a particular pre-trial proceeding in the hope of improving the case with additional evidence in time to meet the higher evidentiary threshold for the next stage of the proceedings.[430] Moreno-Ocampo also declined to establish a significant field presence in several States under investigation so as to reduce the exposure of staff and witnesses to risk, with the result that heightened reliance was placed on open-source material.[431] For example, in *Mbarushimana*—a case in which the Prosecutor failed to obtain confirmation of any of the charges—Moreno-Ocampo failed to rely on any insider or crime base witnesses to support over half of the charges, instead relying entirely on indirect evidence provided by civil society groups and international organisations.[432] Ultimately, these investigative practices contributed towards Moreno-Ocampo's weak record of obtaining confirmation of sexual and gender-based charges, with Pre-Trial Chambers declining to confirm sixteen of thirty-two charges for sexual and gender-based crimes during his time in office.[433]

Under ICC Prosecutor Fatou Bensouda, the Office of the Prosecution has shifted strategy towards 'in-depth, open-ended investigations while maintaining focus to avoid over-expanding the investigations at the expense of efficiency'.[434] This new strategy entails a number of different components: first, the expansion and diversification of evidence collection, including increased field presence and country knowledge; second, the application of multiple case hypotheses throughout the investigation; and

[428] Grey (n 60) 252. For judicial criticism of the ICC Prosecutor's approach to the issue of sexual violence during the *Lubanga* trial, see *Prosecutor v Thomas Lubanga Dyilo* (Judgment Pursuant to Article 74 of the Statute, Trial Chamber) ICC-01/04-01/06-2842 (14 March 2012) ('*Lubanga* Trial Judgment') [60].

[429] J Verini, 'The Prosecutor and the President' *The New York Times* (22 June 2016) (attributing the phrase 'the shadow of the court' to Moreno-Ocampo).

[430] N Hayes, '*La Lutte Continue*: Investigating and Prosecuting Sexual Violence at the ICC', in C Stahn (ed), *The Law and Practice of the International Criminal Court* (OUP 2015) 801, 817–818. For judicial criticism of this approach, see *Prosecutor v Muthaura et al* (Decision on the Confirmation of Charges Pursuant to Article 61(7)(a) and (b) of the Rome Statute, Pre-Trial Chamber) ICC-01/09-02/11 (23 January 2012) ('*Muthaura et al* DCC') (diss op Kaul) [52].

[431] See, in this regard, ICC Office of the Prosecutor, 'Strategic Plan: June 2012–2015' (11 October 2013) [42]; and C de Vos, 'Investigating from Afar: The ICC's Evidence Problem' (2013) 26 *Leiden Journal of International Law* 1009, 1016–1019. For judicial criticism of the ICC Prosecutor's limited field presence and over-reliance on civil society groups and press articles, see *Prosecutor v Laurent Gbagbo* (Decision Adjourning the Hearing on the Confirmation of Charges Pursuant to Article 61(7)(c)(i) of the Rome Statute, Pre-Trial Chamber) ICC-02/11-01/11 (3 June 2013) ('*Gbagbo* Adjournment Decision') [35]; *Prosecutor v Mathieu Ngudjolo Chui* (Judgment Pursuant to Article 74 of the Statute, Trial Chamber) ICC-01/04-02/12-3-tENG (18 December 2012) [118]. For judicial criticism of the ICC Prosecutor's lack of oversight of intermediaries, see *Lubanga* Trial Judgment (n 428) [482]–[483].

[432] Hayes (n 430) 822.

[433] Women's Initiative for Gender Justice, *Gender Report Card on the International Criminal Court 2014 Anniversary Edition* (December 2014) 112.

[434] ICC Office of the Prosecutor, 'Strategic Plan: June 2012–2015' (11 October 2013) [23]; ICC Office of the Prosecutor, 'Strategic Plan: 2016–2018' (6 July 2015) [34].

third, the aim of presenting cases at the confirmation hearing that are 'as trial ready as possible'.[435]

In addition, the Office of the Prosecution has also more comprehensively institutionalised a commitment to the investigation and prosecution of sexual and gender-based crimes by including it as a strategic goal within its Strategic Plans,[436] adopting the 2014 *Policy Paper on Sexual and Gender-Based Crimes*,[437] requiring team leaders to elaborate the steps adopted to investigate sexual and gender-based crimes in their investigative plans or to justify to the Office of the Prosecution why such steps have not been taken,[438] establishing a more formalised evidence review process,[439] and appointing advisors with particular legal expertise on issues related to SGBV as well as more general issue-areas such as international humanitarian law.[440]

Taken together, these reforms appear to be at least partially responsible for the more consistent inclusion of sexual and gender-based crimes within charging documents, as well as the increase in the number of charges confirmed at the confirmation stage of proceedings.[441] In particuar, during Fatou Bensouda's time as ICC Prosecutor, all charges for sexual and gender-based crimes have been confirmed by Pre-Trial Chambers in the cases of *Ntaganda*,[442] *Gbagbo*,[443] *Blé Goudé*,[444] and *Ongwen*.[445] At the same time, the limitation of the charges in *Al Mahdi* to the destruction of cultural property indicates that the Office of the Prosecution retains a propensity to focus narrowly on charges for which it already has trial-ready evidence to the exclusion of other charges—including sexual and gender-based crimes—for which significant evidence also emerged.[446] Moreover, the recent acquittal of Laurent Gbagbo and Charles Blé Goudé on the basis that there was no case to answer—without the defence even having to rebut the prosecution's evidence—suggests that the Office of the Prosecution under Fatou Bensouda's leadership still needs further reflection on how it resources and conducts investigations, the type of evidence it requires to prove its cases, and how it develops and presents its case theories in practice.[447] While acquittals do not necessarily follow from inadequacies in the Office of the Prosecution—and are in fact integral to the credibility and fairness of the ICC—it is extremely rare for a 'no case to answer' motion to result in an acquittal at the end of the prosecution's presentation of evidence, an indication that greater efforts are required on the part of the ICC Prosecutor

[435] ICC Office of the Prosecutor, 'Strategic Plan: June 2012–2015' (11 October 2013) [23].
[436] Ibid Goal 3; ICC Office of the Prosecutor, 'Strategic Plan: 2016–2018' (6 July 2015) Goal 2.
[437] ICC Office of the Prosecutor, 'Policy Paper on Sexual and Gender-Based Crimes' (June 2014).
[438] Grey (n 60) 262–263.
[439] Ibid 263.
[440] Ibid 264 (referring to the appointment of Catharine MacKinnon (2008–2012), Brigid Inder (2012–2016), and Patricia Sellers (since 2017) as Gender Advisors, as well as the appointment of Tim McCormack (since 2010) as Advisor on International Humanitarian Law).
[441] ICC Office of the Prosecutor, 'Strategic Plan: 2016–2018' (6 July 2015) [15]–[16].
[442] *Ntaganda* DCC (n 401).
[443] *Gbagbo* DCC (n 387).
[444] *Blé Goudé* DCC (n 388).
[445] *Ongwen* DCC (n 391).
[446] P Clark, *Distant Justice: The Impact of the International Criminal Court on African Politics* (CUP 2018) 295.
[447] See generally, Y McDermott, 'Gbagbo's Acquittal Isn't Bad for the ICC. But Problems Around Evidence Remain' *The Conversation* (24 January 2019); P Labuda, 'The ICC's "Evidence Problem": The Future of International Criminal Investigations After the Gbagbo Acquittal' *Völkerrechtsblog* (18 January 2019).

to ensure that only cases supported by adequate evidence and a coherent case theory are prosecuted in practice.[448]

Beyond the investigative strategy and priorities of the ICC Prosecutor, the judges have also influenced the ICC's charging record concerning sexual and gender-based crimes, not only by clarifying the meaning of different categories of crime, but also by providing an oversight function concerning the charges in particular cases.

In *Lubanga*, for example, the Trial Chamber strongly deprecated the ICC Prosecutor for advancing extensive submissions concerning sexual violence in his opening and closing arguments, as well as contending that sexual violence should be an aggravating factor in sentencing, having failed to apply to include sexual violence or sexual slavery charges at any stage during the proceedings, including in the original charges.[449] This stinging critique appears to have been heeded by the Office of the Prosecution, which has not repeated the mistake of attempting to make extensive allegations of sexual and gender-based crimes at trial without first advancing relevant charges at the pre-trial stage.[450]

More recently, in *Bemba*, a majority of the Appeals Chamber clarified the degree of specificity required within the charges for criminal acts to be included in a conviction decision of the Trial Chamber. The majority explained that the conviction of the defendant had exceeded the scope of the confirmed charges with respect to certain criminal acts of rape, murder, and pillage that had been added by the ICC Prosecutor by means of disclosure and inclusion in auxiliary documents after the confirmation of charges decision without formally amending the charges.[451] The majority explained that it was not sufficient that the criminal acts in question fell within the scope of the categories of crime set out in the charging document and the operative part of the confirmation decision—each of which elaborated the temporal and geographical frame of certain categories of crime, followed by a non-exhaustive list of specific criminal acts, prefaced by the phrase 'including, but not limited to'.[452] The majority accepted that adding specific criminal acts after confirmation would not 'in all circumstances' require an amendment to the charges, but somewhat regrettably left this question open for resolution in future cases.[453] Whether regarded as 'a naïve and pointless act of formalism',[454] or a position with 'a strong legal and fair trial basis',[455] the relative rigidity of the majority's approach is likely to present significant challenges to the

[448] See generally, D Guilfoyle, 'Part II—This is not fine: The International Criminal Court in Trouble' *EJIL:Talk!* (22 March 2019); and R Goldstone, 'Acquittals by the International Criminal Court' *EJIL:Talk!* (18 January 2019).

[449] *Prosecutor v Thomas Lubanga Dyilo* (Decision on Sentence Pursuant to Article 76 of the Statute, Trial Chamber) ICC-01/04-01/06 (10 July 2012) [60].

[450] Grey (n 60) 262.

[451] *Prosecutor v Jean-Pierre Bemba Gombo* (Judgment on the Appeal of Mr Jean-Pierre Bemba Gombo against Trial Chamber III's 'Judgment pursuant to Article 74 of the Statute', Appeals Chamber) ICC-01/05-01/08-3636-Red (8 June 2018) [114]–[115].

[452] Ibid [115].

[453] Ibid [107]–[111] and [115].

[454] A Whiting, 'Appeals Judges Turn the ICC on its Head with Bemba Decision' *Just Security* (14 June 2018); J Powderly and N Hayes, 'The Bemba Appeal: A Fragmented Appeals Chamber Destabilises the Law and Practice of the ICC' *PhD Studies in Human Rights* (26 June 2018).

[455] Amnesty International, 'Bemba Appeals Judgment Highlights the Challenges of Charging Sexual Violence Crimes' *Human Rights in International Justice* (3 October 2018).

ICC Prosecutor's investigation and prosecution of sexual and gender-based crimes—evidence of which often emerges late in investigations and sometimes even at trial.[456]

In addition to judicial oversight, civil society groups and victims' legal representatives can also exert influence over the charging practices of the ICC Prosecutor. In this context, it is useful to distinguish between influence within the proceedings of a particular case and influence on the charging practices of the ICC Prosecutor more generally. During the trial of Thomas Lubanga, for example, the Victims' Legal Representatives exerted formal pressure by requesting the judges to consider revising the legal characterisation of the facts pursuant to Regulation 55 of the Regulations of the Court to include charges of sexual slavery as a crime against humanity and war crime, and cruel and/or inhuman treatment as a war crime.[457] Notably, the Prosecutor objected to the re-characterisation, arguing *inter alia* that the Victims' Legal Representatives were attempting to incorporate new facts and circumstances into the subject-matter of the trial beyond those described in the charges, thereby violating Article 74(2) of the ICC Statute and circumventing the amendment procedures set out in Article 61(9) of the ICC Statute.[458] The Appeals Chamber agreed with the Prosecutor, dismissing the motion on the ground that a legal re-characterisation of facts under Regulation 55 must not exceed the facts and circumstances described in the charges.[459] Yet, while this formal pressure proved unsuccessful in the context of the *Lubanga* case itself, Fatou Bensouda has acknowledged that the widespread criticism put forward by the Victims' Legal Representatives, as well as the external pressure exerted by civil society groups, influenced the charging practices of the Office of the Prosecution going forward, in particular by increasing the attention paid to sexual and gender-based crimes in investigations and charging decisions.[460]

The ICC's fluctuating charging record concerning sexual and gender-based crimes provides a useful illustration of the different factors that can influence the scope and focus of charges over time. Beyond the institutional design and operational context of the ICC—including budgetary constraints, security concerns, and pressure from States—it is the investigative practices and priorities of the prosecution that are arguably the most influential factors in shaping the scope and focus of charges at the ICC. At the same time, judges, victims' legal representatives, and civil society groups also play important roles in influencing the ICC's charging record in practice. Ultimately,

[456] S SáCouto, 'The Impact of the Appeals Chamber Decision in Bemba: Impunity for Sexual and Gender-based Crimes?' *International Justice Monitor* (22 June 2018).

[457] *Prosecutor v Thomas Lubanga Dyilo* (Judgment on the Appeals of Mr Lubanga Dyilo and the Prosecutor against the Decision of Trial Chamber I of 14 July 2009 entitled 'Decision giving notice to the parties and participants that the legal characterization of the facts may be subject to change in accordance with Regulation 55(2) of the Regulations of the Court', Appeals Chamber) ICC-01/04-01/06-2205 (8 December 2009) [4].

[458] Ibid [53]–[56].

[459] Ibid [89]–[95].

[460] F Bensouda, 'Gender Justice and the ICC' (2014) 16 *International Feminist Journal of Politics* 538, 540. Beyond exerting pressure on the ICC Prosecutor, civil society groups may also influence charging practices by acting as a source of information, whether through mapping atrocities in a particular conflict or serving as intermediaries that facilitate contact with witnesses, victims, and affected communities. See generally, D Clancy, '"They Told Us We Would Be Part of History": Reflections on the Civil Society Intermediary Experience in the Great Lakes Region' in C de Vos et al (eds), *Contested Justice: The Politics and Practice of International Criminal Court Interventions* (CUP 2015) 219.

similar to the ad hoc tribunals, it is the precise interplay between these different elements over time that shapes not only the scope and focus of charges but also the orientation of the historical narratives constructed within the ICC in practice.

C. Interpretative Practices

In contrast to the statutory frameworks of other international criminal courts, the ICC Statute—particularly when read together with the Elements of Crimes—is akin to a detailed domestic criminal code. The adoption of such a detailed framework is considered by most commentators to be reflective of at least one of two concerns amongst the State drafters:[461] first, a principled concern to safeguard defendants from the arbitrary application of the criminal law;[462] and second, a more opportunistic concern to curtail the creative capacity of judges to progressively develop the law in light of the fact that the ICC might, in the future, exercise jurisdiction over their own nationals.[463] In the latter regard, the detailed nature of the ICC Statute has invited accusations that the statutory framework reflects a high degree of distrust amongst States in the international judiciary,[464] including a 'fear of the "Cassese approach", namely judges overdoing it, becoming dangerous by, say, producing judgments that were innovative'.[465]

That the drafters sought to restrict the interpretative freedom of judges at the ICC may also be inferred from the ICC Statute's detailed elaboration of the applicable law, the principle of legality, and accompanying rules of interpretation.

The applicable law is identified in Article 21 of the ICC Statute, which elaborates a hierarchy of sources.[466] Pursuant to Article 21(1)(a), judges are required to apply 'in the first place' the ICC Statute, the Elements of Crimes, and the Rules of Procedure and Evidence.[467] Interpreting this provision, the Trial Chamber in *Bemba* has confirmed that 'the Statute always prevails over the Elements of Crimes and the Rules'.[468] Reflecting on the status of the Elements of Crimes, the Trial Chamber also concluded that 'the Elements of Crimes should be applied subject to any conflict with the provisions of the Statute'.[469] The jurisprudence of the ICC has also held that recourse to

461 See, for example, J Powderly, 'The Rome Statute and the Attempted Corseting of the Interpretative Judicial Function: Reflections on Sources of Law and Interpretative Technique', in Stahn (n 430) 444, 444–445 and 453–454; Grover (n 359) 552.

462 See, for example, D Robinson, 'The Identity Crisis of International Criminal Law' (2008) 21 *Leiden Journal of International Law* 925, 958–959.

463 See, for example, Powderly (n 461) 478; Darcy (n 235) 286; and Cryer (n 55) 236–237.

464 See, for example, Hunt (n 228) 61 ('the Statute evinces a deep suspicion of the Court's judges'); and A Cassese, 'The Statute of the International Criminal Court: Some Preliminary Reflections' (1999) 10 *European Journal of International Law* 144, 163 ('the Statute seems to evince a certain mistrust in the Judges').

465 HV Stuart and M Simons, *The Prosecutor and the Judge: Benjamin Ferencz and Antonio Cassese, Interviews and Writings* (Pallas Publications 2009) 52 (referring to the words of Antonio Cassese as part of an interview). See similarly, Grover (n 237) 13.

466 See, for example, *Katanga* Trial Judgment (n 410) 38; and *Bemba* Trial Judgment (n 410) [66].

467 Article 21(1)(a), ICC Statute.

468 *Bemba* Trial Judgment (n 410) [66].

469 Ibid [68]. Contrast: *Prosecutor v Omar Hassan Ahmad Al Bashir* (Decision on the Prosecution's Application for a Warrant of Arrest against Omar Hassan Ahmad Al Bashir, Pre-Trial Chamber) ICC-02/05-01/09-3 (4 March 2009) ('*Al Bashir* First Arrest Warrant Decision') [128] (concluding that the Elements must be applied unless there is an 'irreconcilable contradiction' between its provisions and the ICC Statute);

the other 'subsidiary sources of law' elaborated in Article 21(1) is possible only where there is 'a lacuna in the provisions of the Statute, the Elements of Crimes and the Rules'.[470] Accordingly, the Court may apply other applicable treaties and customary international law (Article 21(1)(b)) and, failing that, general principles of law derived from national laws (Article 21(1)(c)), only in the event that the Statute, the Elements of Crimes, and the Rules leave a gap that cannot be remedied through recourse to the rules on treaty interpretation provided for in the Vienna Convention on the Law of Treaties.[471]

Accompanying the ICC's applicable law, the ICC Statute also codifies the principle of legality's prohibition on retroactivity. In particular, Article 22(1) provides that '[a] person shall not be criminally responsible under this Statute unless the conduct in question constitutes, at the time it takes place, a crime within the jurisdiction of the Court'.[472] This provision is complemented by a number of related rules of interpretation.[473] Specifically, Article 22(2) provides that the definitions of crimes must be strictly construed, not extended by analogy and, in case of ambiguity, interpreted in favour of the person being investigated, prosecuted, or convicted.[474] In addition, Article 24(2) provides that '[i]n the event of a change in the law applicable to a given case prior to a final judgment, the law more favourable to the person being investigated, prosecuted or convicted shall apply'.[475] Finally, Article 21(3) of the ICC Statute requires that the application and interpretation of the applicable law 'must be consistent with internationally recognized human rights, and be without any adverse distinction founded on grounds such as gender . . . , age, race, colour, language, religion or belief, political or other opinion, national, ethnic or social origin, wealth, birth or other status'.[476]

Reflecting on the principle of legality as enshrined in Article 22 of the Statute, the Trial Chamber in *Katanga* has confirmed that recourse to a victim-focused teleological method of interpretation, underpinned by the need to end impunity for the

and ibid (sep and partly diss op Ušacka) [17]–[18] (concluding that the Elements of Crimes are not binding and, pursuant to Article 9(1) of the ICC Statute are merely intended to provide assistance to the Court in the interpretation and application of categories of crime).

470 *Katanga* Trial Judgment (n 410) [39]; and *Bemba* Trial Judgment (n 410) [69].

471 For discussion of the application of the Vienna Convention on the Law of Treaties to the practice of interpreting the ICC Statute and Elements of Crimes, see *Katanga* Trial Judgment (n 410) [43]–[49]; and *Bemba* Trial Judgment (n 410) [75]–[81].

472 Article 22(1), ICC Statute.

473 For discussion of the application of the principle of legality to the interpretation of the ICC Statute, see generally *Katanga* Trial Judgment (n 410) [50]–[57]; and *Bemba* Trial Judgment (n 410) [82]–[84].

474 Article 22(2), ICC Statute. See, in this regard, *Bemba* Trial Judgment (n 410) [83] (clarifying that 'the bar on the use of analogy does not prevent the Chamber from resorting to other sources of law whenever necessary to determine the precise content of the definition of a specific criminal conduct'); and *Katanga* Trial Judgment (n 410) [53] (clarifying that the principle *in dubio pro reo* is applicable only 'in case of ambiguity' and should therefore be relied upon 'only after an unsuccessful attempt at interpretation effected in good faith and in accordance with the General Rule of the Vienna Convention or in accordance with article 32 of the Convention').

475 Article 24(2), ICC Statute.

476 Article 21(3), ICC Statute. See, in this regard, *Katanga* Trial Judgment (n 410) [50]; and *Bemba* Trial Judgment (n 410) [82]. For discussion of the ambiguity of this provision, see generally, A Grabert, *Dynamic Interpretation in International Criminal Law: Striking a Balance between Stability and Change* (Herbert Utz Verlag 2015) 139–141; and Powderly (n 461) 484–489.

perpetrators of crimes, 'could be considered antithetical to the principle of legality' and as such 'can under no circumstance be used to create a body of law extraneous to the terms of the treaty or incompatible with a purely literal reading of its text'.[477] At the same time, the Trial Chamber also asserted that 'the object and purpose of the Statute must always be borne in mind and fully considered during the interpretation of its provisions as they are one of the components which make it possible to establish its definitive meaning'.[478]

Finally, Article 21(2) of the ICC Statute provides that the Court 'may apply principles and rules law as interpreted in its previous decisions'.[479] In *Bemba*, the Trial Chamber confirmed that although it is at the Chamber's discretion, following its prior case law—particularly findings of the Appeals Chamber—is 'desirable in the interests of expeditiousness, procedural economy, and legal certainty'.[480] In this vein, similar to the ad hoc tribunals, as increasing numbers of interpretative decisions accumulate at the ICC, one can expect that judges will become more restrained in their interpretative practices under the pull of internal integration.

Despite the drafters' best efforts to reign in judicial creativity through the ICC Statute's detailed elaboration of the applicable law, the principle of legality, and accompanying rules of interpretation,[481] in practice whether the Court has rendered a more or less progressive interpretation of a particular crime category has tended to depend upon how these interpretative rules have been understood and applied in the context of particular cases.

1. Restrictive interpretative practices

On a number of occasions, the ICC has rendered relatively restrictive interpretations of the crime categories within its jurisdiction. In *Bemba*, for example, the Pre-Trial Chamber adopted a restrictive interpretation of the offence of 'other forms of sexual violence' as a crime against humanity, concluding that factual allegations relating to individuals being forced to undress in public in order to humiliate them did not constitute a form of sexual violence of comparable gravity to the other crimes set forth in Article 7(1)(g) of the ICC Statute.[482] This finding not only contradicts the drafting history of the Rome Statute and Elements of Crimes,[483] but also contrasts with the findings of the ICTR Trial Chamber in *Akayesu*, which had previously concluded that sexual violence encompassed acts of forced nudity for the purposes of humiliation.[484] In *Muthaura et al*, the Pre-Trial Chamber rendered a further restrictive interpretation

[477] *Katanga* Trial Judgment (n 410) [54]–[55].

[478] Ibid [55].

[479] Article 21(2), ICC Statute.

[480] *Bemba* Trial Judgment (n 410) [74].

[481] For an overview of the rules of interpretation applied by the ICC, see generally *Katanga* Trial Judgment (n 410) [43]–[57]; and *Bemba* Trial Judgment (n 410) [75]–[86].

[482] *Prosecutor v Jean-Pierre Bemba Gombo* (Decision on the Prosecutor's Application for a Warrant of Arrest against Jean-Pierre Bemba Gombo, Pre-Trial Chamber) ICC-01/05-01/08-14-tENG (10 June 2008) [39]–[40].

[483] V Oosterveld, 'Gender-Sensitive Justice and the International Criminal Tribunal for Rwanda: Lessons Learned for the International Criminal Court' (2005) 12 *New England Journal of International and Comparative Law* 119, 124.

[484] *Akayesu* Trial Judgment (n 202) [688].

of the offence of 'other forms of sexual violence', concluding that acts of forcible circumcision and penile amputation of men of Luo ethnicity were not of a 'sexual nature',[485] a finding that neglected the impact of such acts on the sexual lives and sexual identity of the victims.[486]

The ICC has also rendered a number of restrictive decisions concerning the meaning of the policy element of crimes against humanity.[487] In *Mbarushimana*, for example, a majority of the Pre-Trial Chamber declined to infer the existence of a policy despite findings of fact that there had been repeated patterns of attacks by the Democratic Forces for the Liberation of Rwanda and orders issued to commit crimes.[488] The reluctance of the Pre-Trial Chamber to confirm the existence of a policy seems to have been based at least partially on the fact that the motive behind the attacks was retaliatory, rather than aimed at creating a humanitarian catastrophe as had been alleged by the ICC Prosecutor.[489] Yet, as Judge Sanji Mmasenono Monageng explains in her dissenting opinion, the motive behind the attacks is irrelevant to the question of whether a policy can be established: 'While the evidence discussed by the Majority does show that retaliation was a motive to attack, this evidence does not contradict the view that the order was to attack civilians'.[490]

In *Gbagbo*, a majority of the Pre-Trial Chamber decided to adjourn the confirmation hearing and request the Prosecutor to provide further evidence of '[h]ow, when and by whom the alleged policy/plan to attack the "pro-Ouattara civilian population" was adopted, including specific information about meetings at which this policy/plan was allegedly adopted as well as how the existence and content of this policy/plan was communicated or made known to members of the "pro-Gbagbo forces" once it was adopted'.[491] As Darryl Robinson observes, the majority's approach appeared to reflect 'a formalized, bureaucratic conception of the policy element', seemingly requiring the formal adoption of a policy rather than adhering to the more flexible conception of the policy element intended by the drafters of the ICC Statute—namely, a policy that could be implicit rather than formal.[492]

2. Progressive interpretative practices

On other occasions, the Court has rendered relatively progressive interpretations of the crime categories falling within its jurisdiction. For instance, the Court has sometimes endorsed the dynamic interpretation of crime categories rendered by other international courts and tribunals, the jurisprudence of which the ICC has concluded may be relied upon for assistance for the purpose of identifying customary

485 *Muthaura et al* DCC (n 430) 266.
486 Grey (n 60) 293–294.
487 See generally, D Robinson, 'Crimes Against Humanity: A Better Policy on "Policy"', in Stahn (n 430) 705; and L Sadat, 'Crimes Against Humanity in the Modern Age' (2013) 107 *American Journal of International Law* 334.
488 See, for example, *Mbarushimana* DCC (n 423) [144] and [149].
489 Ibid [253]–[254].
490 *Mbarushimana* DCC (n 423) (diss op Monageng) [17].
491 *Gbagbo* Adjournment Decision (n 431) 44.
492 Robinson (n 487) 709 and 717. More recently the Trial Chambers in *Katanga* and *Bemba* have applied more flexible understandings of the policy element. See *Katanga* Trial Judgment (n 410) [1109]–[1110]; *Bemba* Trial Judgment (n 410) [159]–[160].

international law, as well as interpreting the ICC Statute pursuant to Article 31 of the Vienna Convention on the Law of Treaties.[493]

The ICC Trial Chamber in *Lubanga*, for example, followed the jurisprudence of the ad hoc tribunals in its identification of indicators for determining whether an armed group is 'organised' and violence 'protracted' for the purpose of establishing the existence of a non-international armed conflict,[494] as well as its adoption of the 'overall control' test for determining when a non-international armed conflict may be internationalised due to the involvement of an armed group acting on behalf of another State.[495] A further example is the case of *Al Bashir*, in which a majority of the ICC Pre-Trial Chamber endorsed the findings of the International Court of Justice—itself following the jurisprudence of the ad hoc tribunals—in concluding that the specific intent required by the crime of genocide must be to destroy at least a 'substantive' part of a protected group and may be confined to a geographically limited area.[496] Finally, drawing on the jurisprudence of the SCSL and the Extraordinary Chambers in the Courts of Cambodia, the Pre-Trial Chamber in *Ongwen* recognised forced marriage as an 'other inhumane act',[497] taking care to elaborate its distinctive nature 'in terms of conduct, ensuing harm, and protected interests'.[498] In each of these cases, the ICC was able to enlarge the Court's narrative frame, whether to examine the possible internationalisation of conflicts in *Lubanga*, acts of genocide in *Al Bashir*, or instances of forced marriage in *Ongwen*.

Beyond consolidating the expansive findings of the ad hoc tribunals, the ICC has also developed its own dynamic interpretations of the elements of different crime categories within its jurisdiction.

In *Ntaganda*, for example, the ICC Appeals Chamber confirmed that rape and sexual slavery of child soldiers by members of their own armed group constitute war crimes—deviating from a ruling by the SCSL which had concluded that the 'law of international armed conflict was never intended to criminalise acts of violence committed by one member of an armed group against another, such conduct remaining first and foremost the province of the criminal law of the State of the armed group concerned and human rights law'.[499] In contrast to the SCSL, the ICC Appeals Chamber upheld the view that international humanitarian law does not contain a general rule that categorically excludes the idea of 'intra-party protection',[500] concluding that 'any

[493] *Bemba* Trial Judgment (n 410) [71]–[72] and [78]; *Katanga* Trial Judgment (n 410) [47]; and *Lubanga* Trial Judgment (n 428) [603].

[494] *Lubanga* Trial Judgment (n 428) [535]–[538]. See, however, *Katanga* Trial Judgment (n 410) [1185] (requiring that 'organised armed groups' must have 'a sufficient degree of organisation to enable them to carry out protracted armed violence *and to implement the provisions of humanitarian law applicable to that type of conflict*', the latter requirement seemingly more restrictive than prior jurisprudence) (emphasis added).

[495] *Lubanga* Trial Judgment (n 428) [541].

[496] *Al Bashir* First Arrest Warrant Decision (n 469) [146].

[497] *Ongwen* DCC (n 391) [87]–[95].

[498] Ibid [92].

[499] *Sesay et al* Trial Judgment (n 205) [1453].

[500] S Sivakumaran, *The Law of Non-International Armed Conflict* (OUP 2012) 246–249. See similarly, Cryer et al (n 293) 283, fn 142; and T Rodenhäuser, 'Squaring the Circle? Prosecuting Sexual Violence against Child Soldiers by their "Own Forces"' (2016) 14 *Journal of International Criminal Justice* 171, 188–191.

undue expansion of the reach of the law of war crimes can be effectively prevented by a rigorous application of the nexus requirement'.[501] By adopting this perspective, the Appeals Chamber was able to expand the narrative frame of the case to encompass intra-party war crimes.

In *Ongwen*, the Pre-Trial Chamber rendered a dynamic interpretation of forced pregnancy as a crime against humanity, concluding that the offence does not depend on the perpetrator's involvement in the woman's conception, but 'only required that the perpetrator knows that the woman is pregnant and that she has been made pregnant forcibly'.[502] According to the Pre-Trial Chamber, this interpretation follows from the fact that 'the essence of the crime of forced pregnancy is in unlawfully placing the victim in a position in which she cannot choose whether to continue the pregnancy'.[503] By foregrounding the notion of reproductive autonomy in this way, the Pre-Trial Chamber broadened the range of circumstances in relation to which the crime could be charged.[504]

In a series of decisions, the ICC has also adopted a broad interpretation of the types of entities that may be behind a 'widespread or systematic attack directed against any civilian population' for the purpose of satisfying the contextual element of crimes against humanity. The pertinent provision in this regard is Article 7(2)(a) of the ICC Statute, which defines an 'attack directed against any civilian population' as a course of conduct involving the multiple commission of prohibited acts against any civilian population, pursuant to or in furtherance of 'a State or organizational policy' to commit such attack.

According to a majority of the Pre-Trial Chamber in the *Kenya Authorization Decision*, the defining criterion of what constitutes an 'organizational policy' for the purpose of Article 7(2)(a) is not 'the formal nature of a group and the level of its organization' but its 'capability to perform acts which infringe on basic human values'.[505] The Pre-Trial Chamber supported this capacity-based interpretation by referring to the Commentary to the ILC's 1991 Draft Code of Crimes against the Peace and Security of Mankind, which provides that its draft article on crimes against humanity 'does not rule out the possibility that private individuals with *de facto* power or organized in criminal gangs or groups might also commit the kind of systematic or mass violations of human rights covered by the article'.[506] The majority also argued that 'had the drafters of the Statute intended to exclude non-State actors from the term "organization", they would not have included this term in article 7(2)(a) of the Statute'.[507]

[501] *Prosecutor v Bosco Ntaganda* (Judgment on the appeal of Mr Ntaganda against the 'Second decision on the Defence's challenge to the jurisdiction of the Court in respect of Counts 6 and 9', Appeals Chamber) ICC-01/04-02/06 OA5 (15 June 2017) [63] and [68].

[502] *Ongwen* DCC (n 391) [99]–[100].

[503] Ibid.

[504] Grey (n 60) 284.

[505] *Situation in the Republic of Kenya* (Decision Pursuant to Article 15 of the Rome Statute on the Authorization of an Investigation into the Situation in the Republic of Kenya, Pre-Trial Chamber) ICC-01/09-19 (31 March 2010) ('*Kenya* Authorization Decision') [90] and [93] (elaborating a non-exhaustive list of characteristics that could be taken into account on a case-by-case basis to determine whether this threshold had been met). Judge Kaul dissented, arguing that to fall within the scope of the term 'organizational policy', a non-State actor must at the very least be 'state-like', understood as partaking of 'some characteristics of a State' so that it may be said to possess 'quasi-State abilities'. Ibid (diss op Kaul) [51] and [66].

[506] *Kenya* Authorization Decision (n 505) [91].

[507] Ibid [92].

Neither argument seems to be decisive, the majority failing to elaborate why the Draft Code was relevant to the interpretation of the ICC Statute or how the latter argument helped determine precisely *which* non-State actors fall within the term 'organizational' under Article 7(2)(a) of the ICC Statute.[508]

In *Katanga*, the ICC Trial Chamber relied on the interpretative methodology outlined in Article 31(1) of the Vienna Convention on the Law of Treaties to define an organisation as any private entity consisting of a group of persons which possesses 'a set of structures or mechanisms, whatever those may be, that are sufficiently efficient to ensure the coordination necessary to carry out an attack directed against a civilian population'.[509] According to the Trial Chamber, such organisations need not be endowed with a well-developed, centralised or hierarchical structure or possess quasi-State characteristics.[510] This definition retains the capacity-oriented approach towards the definition of an organisation, but links it to the other components of the contextual element in Article 7 of the ICC Statute.[511]

Although the Trial Chamber in *Katanga* and the majority of the Pre-Trial Chamber in the *Kenya* case adopted slightly varying approaches to the definition of an organisation, both are premised on a capacity-based conception that broadens the types of non-state actors that fall within the scope of protection afforded by the category of crimes against humanity.

D. Conclusion

The categories of crime adjudicated by the ICC—and the scope and content of the historical narratives constructed through recourse to them—are the product of a diversity of factors. The range and definition of the crime categories included within the ICC Statute reflect the compromises reached between the States responsible for establishing the ICC. Importantly, these compromises were negotiated under the influence of a significant civil society presence and against the background of the emerging jurisprudence of the ad hoc tribunals. At the level of general categories of crime, notwithstanding the crime of aggression amendments, the ICC Statute continues the shift away from the aggressive war paradigm of the Nuremberg and Tokyo tribunals towards an atrocity paradigm focused on the prosecution of war crimes, crimes against humanity, and the crime of genocide. At the level of the definition of these crimes, the ICC Statute includes both progressive and restrictive elements—a reflection of the delicate consensus-building negotiating process that preceded its finalisation.

Significantly, the detailed elaboration of crime categories in the ICC Statute and the Elements of Crimes—which, in certain respects, consolidated some of the more expansive interpretations enunciated by the ad hoc tribunals—has in practice left less

508 Kreß (n 276) 858–859.

509 *Katanga* Trial Judgment (n 410) [1119].

510 Ibid [1117]–[1122].

511 See similarly, Rodenhäuser (n 263) 923. See similarly, *Bemba* Trial Judgment (n 410) [158]. In *Bemba*, Judge Kuniko Ozaki rendered a Separate Opinion, in which she offered further guidance on how the term 'organizational policy' should be understood, relying on the definition of 'organized criminal group' in Article 2(a) of the UN Convention against Transnational Organized Crime. Ibid (sep op Ozaki [24]–[32]).

leeway or need for judges at the ICC to progressively develop the meaning of such categories in their case law. In other words, whereas judicial creativity proved to be one of the dominant factors in shaping the scope and content of the historical narratives constructed in the judgments of the ad hoc tribunals, the influence of the interpretative practices of the judges has been far less pronounced at the ICC.

Rather, it has been the charging practices of the ICC Prosecutor that have proven to be particularly influential in determining the orientation of the historical narratives constructed at the ICC. In practice, a number of factors have proven significant in shaping the scope and focus of the charges at the ICC. One constant has been the need for the ICC Prosecutor to operate in an institutional context that requires limited resources to be spread across multiple preliminary examinations and investigations concerning a range of different situations and in political environments that are often characterised by challenging security concerns and State obstruction. In addition, the scope and focus of the charges at the ICC have also tended to fluctuate according to the evolving investigative strategies and priorities of the ICC Prosecutor, the oversight provided by judges, and the influence of victims' legal representatives and civil society groups.

In terms of historical narration, the result has primarily been twofold: first, the ICC Prosecutor's charging record has been characterised by a number of unconfirmed, withdrawn, and vacated charges, with the consequence that the historical narratives contested in some cases never culminated in a judgment; and second, within the judgments that have been rendered to date, the prevailing trend has been the production of relatively narrow historical narratives centred on a limited number of incidents and particular themes of criminality.

IV. Marginalised Forms of Criminality

Stepping back from the particularities of the international criminal courts examined in this study, it is possible to identify several forms of criminality that have tended to be marginalised despite falling within their subject-matter jurisdiction. Without intending to be exhaustive,[512] this section highlights three forms of marginalised criminality: sexual violence against men and boys; environmental harms; and war crimes concerning the conduct of hostilities.

A. Sexual Violence Against Men and Boys

Although increasing efforts have been devoted to the prosecution of sexual and gender-based crimes within international criminal courts, sexual violence against men and boys has rarely been prosecuted in practice.[513] At the ICTR, for example,

[512] For other marginalised forms of criminality, see, for example, Stahn (n 2) 105–116.

[513] See generally, V Oosterveld, 'Sexual Violence Directed Against Men and Boys in Armed Conflict or Mass Atrocity: Addressing a Gendered Harm in International Criminal Tribunals' (2014) 10 *Journal of International Law and International Relations* 107; S Sivakumaran, 'Sexual Violence Against Men in Armed Conflict' (2007) 18 *European Journal of International Law* 253; and Grey (n 60) 88–93 and 255–258. In

sexual violence against men and boys was almost uniformly omitted from indictments,[514] while at the SCSL, experiences of male sexual violence were only recognised in the judgment of *Sesay et al.*[515] Other international criminal courts have fared slightly better. The ICTY, for example, examined various forms of male sexual violence, particularly in the context of cases concerning detention centres.[516] In addition, male sexual violence has also been charged in a number of cases at the ICC.[517] However, even at the ICTY and ICC, it is possible to identify a number of missed opportunities to recognise male sexual violence. In *Brđanin*, for example, the ICTY Trial Chamber considered that evidence of an elderly man who had been forced under threat to rape a female prisoner amounted to a violation only against the female prisoner.[518] In *Ongwen*, an unsuccessful request by the victims' legal representatives for leave to present the testimony of three men who claimed to have been sexually abused by the forces of the Lord's Resistance Army has raised questions concerning the adequacy of the steps taken by the ICC Prosecutor to investigate male sexual violence in that case.[519]

A number of explanations may account for the marginalisation of experiences of male sexual violence within international criminal courts. Relevant factors include a dearth of in-depth reporting on male sexual violence; barriers that exist for men and boys to understand and reveal their sexual victimisation; inadequate sensitivity and understanding on the part of investigators, lawyers, and judges concerning male sexual violence; and the lack of express legal recognition of certain forms of sexual violence that are typically directed against men and boys.[520] As a result, while sexual violence against men and boys has not been completely invisible within international criminal courts, it has remained vulnerable to inadequate investigation, omission from indictments, and unpredictability in terms of whether and how such experiences are explained by prosecutors and understood by judges in practice.[521]

B. Environmental Harms

International criminal courts have sometimes received critical scrutiny for marginalising the economic, social, and cultural dimensions of mass atrocity

addition to male sexual violence, little attention has also been paid to the gendered nature of both sexual and non-sexual crimes within international criminal courts. See generally, Grey (n 60) 95–98 and 258–259.

[514] Grey (n 60) 91.
[515] *Sesay et al* Trial Judgment (n 205) [1194], [1205], [1207]–[1208], [1210], [1304], [1307]–[1308], and [1347].
[516] See, for example, *Prosecutor v Ranko Češić* (Sentencing Judgment, Trial Chamber) IT-95-10/1-S (11 March 2004) [13]–[14] and [33]; and *Delalić et al* Trial Judgment (n 204) [1035]–[1040] and [1060*ff*.].
[517] See, for example, *Ntaganda* DCC (n 401) [52]; and *Bemba* DCC (n 408) [171].
[518] *Brđanin* Trial Judgment (n 203) [516].
[519] *Prosecutor v Dominic Ongwen* (Decision on the Legal Representatives for Victims Requests to Present Evidence and Views and Concerns and Related Requests, Trial Chamber) ICC-02/04-01/15 (6 March 2018). For discussion, see generally R Grey et al, 'Evidence of Sexual Violence Against Men and Boys Rejected in the Ongwen Case' *Human Rights in International Justice* (10 April 2018).
[520] See generally, Oosterveld (n 513) (identifying a 'factual gap', 'social gap', and 'legal gaps').
[521] Grey (n 60) 89 and 93.

situations.[522] In practice, modest efforts have in fact been made to surface these themes within international criminal courts.[523] In particular, certain economic, social, and cultural dimensions of crimes have not only proven relevant to the contextual/collective elements of crimes, but also fallen within the scope of prohibited acts, including:[524] property-related offences such as pillage and attacks on religious, educational, historical, or cultural buildings;[525] collective punishment;[526] slavery-related crimes such as enslavement and forced marriage;[527] prohibited movement of persons offences such as forcible transfer;[528] and discrimination-based crimes such as persecution and genocide.[529]

While it is important not to overstate the extent to which international criminal courts have been able to draw attention to the economic, social, and cultural dimensions of conflicts,[530] their case law reveals that these dimensions have not been completely obscured in practice. At the same time, however, one area that has received significantly less attention is environmental harm.[531] For example, although the

[522] See, for example, the literature reviewed in E Schmid, *Taking Economic, Social and Cultural Rights Seriously in International Criminal Law* (CUP 2015) Chapter 2.

[523] See generally, ibid; and L van den Herik, 'Economic, Social, and Cultural Rights: International Criminal Law's Blind Spot?', in E Riedel et al (eds), *Economic, Social and Cultural Rights in International Law: Contemporary Issues and Challenges* (OUP 2014) 343.

[524] This list builds on Stahn (n 2) 113.

[525] See, for example, Nuremberg Judgment (n 72) 133–134 (economic exploitation of occupied territories) and 238–243 (pillage of public and private property); *Prosecutor v Dario Kordić and Mario Čerkez* (Judgment, Appeals Chamber) IT-95-14/2-A (17 December 2004) [85] and [92] (destruction of educational buildings); *Strugar* Trial Judgment (n 177) [446] (attacking old town of Dubrovnik as protected cultural property); *Prosecutor v Charles Ghankay Taylor* (Judgment, Trial Chamber) SCSL-03-01-T (18 May 2012) [684], [716], [772], [778], and [6959] (destruction of civilian property by burning homes in Sierra Leone), [1957] (money), [1958] (food), and [1962] (property from shops); *Katanga* Trial Judgment (n 410) (destruction of property and pillaging); and *Prosecutor v Ahmad Al Faqi Al Mahdi* (Judgment and Sentence, Trial Chamber) ICC-01/12-01/15-171 (27 September 2016) (intentionally directing attacks against religious and historic buildings in Timbuktu, Mali).

[526] See, for example, *Prosecutor v Moinina Fofana and Allieu Kondewa* (Judgment, Trial Chamber) SCSL-04-14-T (2 August 2007) [176]–[181] (burning of homes and the pillage of food, livestock, and medical drugs).

[527] See, for example, Nuremberg Judgment (n 72) 243–247 (slave labour policy); Tokyo Judgment (n 54) (enslavement); *Prosecutor v Milorad Krnojelac* (Judgment, Trial Chamber) IT-97-25-T (15 March 2000) [353] (forced labour); *Ongwen* DCC (n 391) [87*ff*] (forced marriage).

[528] See, for example, *Prosecutor v Momčilo Krajišnik* (Judgment, Trial Chamber) IT-00-39-T (27 September 2006) [729] (discriminatory dismissals from employment and cutting off water or electricity); *Popović et al* Trial Judgment Volume I (n 303) 920 (intentional deprivation of food, water, shelter, and humanitarian relief); *Ntaganda* DCC (n 401) [64]–[68] (forcible transfer of population and displacement of civilians).

[529] See, for example, Nuremberg Judgment (n 72) 247–249 and 254; *Kupreškić et al* Trial Judgment (n 240) [631] (destruction of homes and property of Bosnian Muslims); *Prosecutor v Dario Kordić and Mario Čerkez* (Judgment, Trial Chamber) IT-95-14/2-T (26 February 2001) [206]–[207] (destruction of religious and educational institutions of Bosnian Muslims); *Akayesu* Trial Judgment (n 202) [503] (causing serious bodily or mental harm as genocide) and [506] (lack of proper housing, clothing, hygiene, excessive work, physical exertion relevant to deliberately inflicting on the group conditions of life calculated to bring about its physical destruction); *Al Bashir* Second Arrest Warrant Decision (n 392) [34] and [38] (indirect forms of killing as part of genocide and crimes against humanity).

[530] See, for example, Schmid (n 522) 326–331 (discussing limitations of international criminal law in remedying violations of economic, social, and cultural rights).

[531] Stahn (n 2) 108–110; MA Drumbl, 'Waging War Against the World: The Need to Move from War Crimes to Environmental Crimes' (1998) 22 *Fordham International Law Journal* 122; and L Prosperi and J Terrosi, 'Embracing the "Human Factor": Is There New Impetus at the ICC for Conceiving and Prioritizing

conflict in Rwanda was witness to the poaching of endangered species, land-mining of national parks, and devastation of agricultural lands, these issues received minimal attention in the proceedings before the ICTR.[532] In addition, whilst the Nuremberg IMT was willing to characterise the exploitation of the territories occupied by Germany as 'a systematic "plunder of public or private property"',[533] more recent international criminal courts have consistently overlooked the application of pillage charges to the systematic extraction and exploitation of natural resources. Charles Taylor's conviction for aiding and abetting pillage, for example, was confined to traditional looting of personal property rather than the systemic exploitation of diamonds and other natural resources that was at the heart of the conflict in Sierra Leone.[534] With this in mind, while it is notable that the ICC Prosecutor has recently signalled her intention to give particular consideration to environmental harms,[535] the extent to which this policy will be translated into concrete actions remains to be seen.[536]

In terms of accounting for the limited engagement of international criminal courts with environmental harms, relevant factors include the limits of substantive international criminal law in responding to such harms, difficulties encountered in the collection of evidence of environmental damage, and the challenge of connecting particular incidents of environmental damage to responsible individuals.[537] As a result of these factors, the capacity of international criminal courts to respond to environmental harms is likely to remain narrow.

C. War Crimes Concerning the Conduct of Hostilities

A final area of marginalisation concerns violations of rules of international humanitarian law concerning the conduct of hostilities, which have rarely formed the basis of war crimes charges before international criminal courts.[538] The dearth of such charges stems from a range of factors including the selective criminalisation by treaty of violations of rules concerning the conduct of hostilities, evidentiary challenges, and uncertainties and complexities over the application of the rules governing the conduct of hostilities in armed conflicts.[539]

International Environmental Harms as Crimes Against Humanity?' (2017) 15 *Journal of International Criminal Justice* 509.

532 Drumbl (n 531) 145–146.
533 Nuremberg Judgment (n 72) 239.
534 L van den Herik and D Dam de Jong, 'Revitalizing the Antique War Crime of Pillage: The Potential and Pitfalls of Using International Criminal Law to Address Illegal Resource Exploitation During Armed Conflict' (2011) 15 *Criminal Law Forum* 237, 266–269.
535 ICC OTP Policy Paper on Case Selection and Prioritisation (n 374) [41].
536 For a critical discussion, see ET Cusato, 'Beyond Symbolism: Problems and Prospects with Prosecuting Environmental Destruction before the ICC' (2017) 15 *Journal of International Criminal Justice* 491.
537 Ibid 494–503.
538 See, similarly, P Gaeta, 'Serious Violations of the Law on the Conduct of Hostilities: A Neglected Class of War Crimes?', in F Pocar et al (eds) *War Crimes and the Conduct of Hostilities: Challenges to Adjudication and Investigation* (Edward Elgar 2013) 20, 21–22; and C Ponti, 'The Crime of Indiscriminate Attack and Unlawful Conventional Weapons: The Legacy of the ICTY Jurisprudence' (2015) 6 *Journal of International Humanitarian Legal Studies* 118, 120.
539 For discussion of these ambiguities, see generally, Gaeta (n 538) 26–30; and Ponti (n 538) 145.

Concerns regarding these rules were expressly identified in the report of the Committee appointed by the ICTY Prosecutor to conduct a preliminary review of the NATO bombing campaign against the Federal Republic of Yugoslavia.[540] With respect to the principle of proportionality, for example, the Committee noted that the principle was easier to formulate in the abstract than to apply to particular circumstances because it is difficult to weigh 'the value of innocent human lives as opposed to capturing a particular military objective'—an assessment that is likely to vary depending on 'the background and values of the decision maker'.[541] The ambiguities that exist within the rules governing the conduct of hostilities are unsurprising. As Payam Akhavan explains, such ambiguities are driven by States—particularly powerful ones—that 'want to have loopholes that do not curtail their power to use armed force'.[542]

Beyond challenges pertaining to rule application, evidence of civilian casualties resulting from NATO airstrikes also tended to be explained away by the Committee. As Christiane Wilke observes, since crimes within the jurisdiction of the ICTY required intent, 'these cases hinged on the committee's review of what the pilots saw, could have seen, or should have seen before they released the bombs'.[543] In making such assessments, the Committee not only placed significant reliance on NATO's own descriptions and evaluations of the strikes, but also consistently characterised the presence of civilians in targeted areas as 'unexpected' and 'surprising', whilst deferring to the use and availability of high-end technologies as sufficient evidence that NATO took adequate precautions.[544]

More recently, in its request for authorisation of an investigation into the situation of Afghanistan, the ICC Office of the Prosecutor determined that information concerning a large number of operations attributed to international forces that resulted in incidental loss of civilian life and harm to civilians—including the 2015 airstrike on the Kunduz Trauma Centre operated by *Médecins Sans Frontières* by US armed forces—did 'not provide a reasonable basis to believe that the military forces *intended* the civilian population as such, or individual civilians not taking direct part in hostilities, to be the object of the attack'.[545] Specifically, the Office of the Prosecutor concluded that many of these incidents concerned situations in which 'members of anti-government armed groups appear to have conducted operations in close proximity to civilians' or 'apparently sought to use civilians as human shields', or were incidents where 'civilians appear to have been mistakenly identified and targeted as fighters'.[546] As Wilke argues, these assessments reveal how high-tech violence operationalised through airstrikes is

540 See generally, ICTY NATO Report (n 122).

541 Ibid [48] and [50].

542 P Akhavan, 'The Dilemmas of Jurisprudence' (1998) 13 *American University International Law Review* 1518, 1520. See similarly, C Wilke, 'Asymmetric Legality: The Invisibility of High-Tech Violence in Afghanistan' *Public Seminar* (2 May 2019) (referring to the 'asymmetries and blinds spots built into the structure of international law').

543 C Wilke, 'High Altitude Legality: Visuality and Jurisdiction in the Adjudication of NATO Air Strikes' (2019) 34 *Canadian Journal of Law and Society* 261, 271.

544 Ibid.

545 *Situation in the Islamic Republic of Afghanistan* (Public redacted version of 'Request for authorisation of an investigation pursuant to article 15', 20 November 2017, ICC-0217-7-Conf-Exp, Office of the Prosecutor) ICC-02/17-7-Red (20 November 2017) [257] (emphasis added).

546 Ibid [258].

often 'shielded by the requirement of "intent" because the larger distance between the authors of the violence and its victims allows for claims of "errors"', such technologies effectively enabling 'both the attack and the legal excuse'.[547]

From a narrative perspective, the result of prosecutorial reticence to bring war crimes charges relating to the conduct of hostilities is to steer the focus of the narratives constructed by international criminal courts away from questions involving seemingly complex examinations of battleground decision-making concerning the propriety of particular objectives and means of warfare, except for the clearest cases of attacks directed against civilians or civilian objects.[548]

V. Conclusion

This chapter has examined the relationship between the range and definition of the crime categories adjudicated by international criminal courts and the scope and content of the historical narratives constructed in their judgments. Reflecting on the trends identified in this chapter both within and across different international criminal courts, a number of continuities and discontinuities are identifiable.

In terms of the *general categories of crimes* included within the jurisdictional mandates of the courts examined in this chapter, the range of such categories has generally reflected the balance of power between the States involved in the drafting of each court's respective statutory framework. The primacy given to the category of crimes against peace in the Nuremberg and Tokyo Charters, for example, appears to have been driven by US political interests, which viewed the crime as a means of validating its foreign policy during the Second World War and punishing acts of Japanese and Nazi aggression.

The shift to an atrocity paradigm focused on the prosecution of war crimes, crimes against humanity, and the crime of genocide at the ad hoc tribunals and the ICC, by contrast, reflects the contemporary humanitarian imperative of powerful States—together with the humanitarian ethos of the human rights movement—to respond to atrocities committed during episodes of mass violence rather than resolving questions of responsibility for their outbreak. According to Mégret, for example, within the modern-era of international criminal justice 'the marginalization of aggression is a symptom of a deeper phenomenon that one might describe as *ad bellum* capitulation before the pragmatic, humanitarian imperative'.[549] As a result, the historical narratives constructed in contemporary international criminal courts have focused on crimes committed *during* mass atrocity situations to the neglect of examining questions of responsibility for the *initiation* of periods of mass violence.

Within the boundaries of the subject-matter jurisdiction of international criminal courts, *the scope and focus of the charges* have been determined by international

547 Wilke (n 542).

548 At the ICTY, for example, serious violations of the principle of proportionality have never been charged as a distinct war crime, instead constituting mere evidence of attacks directed against civilians or civilian objects. Ponti (n 538) 145.

549 Mégret (n 13) 856.

prosecutors under the fluctuating influence of States, judges, civil society groups, victims, and witnesses. At Nuremberg and Tokyo, for example, the extensive scope of the indictments as well as their focus were determined in accordance with the interests of the Allied States. While the judges of the Nuremberg and Tokyo tribunals were able to omit or evade consideration of some of the more controversial charges—such as the charge concerning the Katyn Forest massacre in the Nuremberg indictment and the murder charges in the Tokyo indictment—they were powerless to examine the crimes and incidents that had been purposefully excluded as a result of Allied interests.

The scope and focus of the charges at the ad hoc tribunals and the ICC, by contrast, were influenced by a broader set of factors. In terms of scope, prosecutors at the ad hoc tribunals gradually shifted away from a comprehensive towards a more representative charging strategy, as well as an openness to negotiated forms of justice, in light of lessons learned from earlier cases and pressures from judges and States to ensure the efficient completion of their mandates. At the ICC, the Prosecutor has predominantly brought charges that are much narrower in scope, a trend that primarily reflects the institutional need to distribute limited resources across multiple atrocity situations. As a result, the historical narratives constructed in the judgments of the ICC to date have tended to focus on specific themes of criminality and/or a limited number of incidents.

The focus of the charges at the ad hoc tribunals and the ICC has also been the product of a diversity of factors. At a general level, the focus of the charges has reflected the availability and accessibility of evidence, which have often hinged on fluctuating security concerns on the territories under investigation as well as the degree and form of coopertion received from States to conduct effective investigations. At a more granular level, this chapter examined the fluctating records of the ICTR and the ICC concerning the prosecution of sexual and gender-based crimes to illuminate the influence of the shifting investigative strategies and priorities of different international prosecutors, as well as the variable impact of judicial oversight, pressure from victim legal representatives and civil society groups, and witness testimony. These case studies have revealed how the precise orientation of historical contestation within the ad hoc tribunals and the ICC has been shaped by the micro-practices of a broad range of actors in practice.

The scope and content of the historical narratives constructed in the judgments of international criminal courts have also been influenced by the interpretative practices of judges that have shaped *the definition and meaning of the crime categories* falling within the scope of their mandates. In particular, the chapter revealed how judges have generally been confronted by a tension between interpreting crime categories *dynamically* in order to respond to novel factual circumstances in the interest of protecting victims and society on the one hand, and interpreting crime categories *restrictively* in the interest of safeguarding the accused against the retroactive imposition of the criminal law on the other. According to the *dynamic* approach, the need to adequately represent novel atrocities warrants the progressive development of the meaning of crime categories, even if doing so risks undermining protections designed to safeguard the accused. According to the *restrictive* approach, the need to protect the rights of the accused warrants the assimilation of unprecedented factual circumstances into existing crime categories, even if doing so inadequately represents the unique nature and gravity of the atrocities that have taken place. In other words, judges have generally been confronted by a tension between the warring interests of legal *flexibility* and *stability* in the face of changing factual circumstances.[550]

At Nuremberg and Tokyo, the judges of the IMT and IMTFE generally deferred to the wishes of the Allied States, adhering to a dynamic interpretative approach in giving a judicial seal of approval to the legality of the novel categories of crimes against peace and crimes against humanity and a restrictive interpretative approach in accepting the validity of the war nexus requirement. The result was the production of historical narratives that prioritised the punitive concerns of the Allied States.

At the ad hoc tribunals, the judges relied upon a relaxed conception of the principle of legality, a diversity of interpretative techniques, and a flexible approach to customary international law to progressively develop the meaning of both the contextual/collective elements and prohibited acts of the crime categories falling within their subject-matter jurisdiction. The result was to expand the range of factual circumstances that fell within the scope of the categories of war crimes, crimes against humanity, and the crime of genocide—modernising these categories to reflect not only the privatisation of contemporary violence, but also its diverse and intersecting forms.

At the ICC, by contrast, the detailed elaboration of crime categories in the ICC Statute, together with the elaboration of their elements in the Elements of Crimes, has left less leeway or need for judges to progressively develop the meaning of such categories in their case law. In practice, judges have generally adhered to a stricter conception of legality, pursuant to which progressive interpretations of crime categories have become less frequent and less extreme.

Although the substantive focus of international criminal courts has fluctuated over time, the final section of this chapter identified a number of forms of criminality that have consistently received marginal attention in their judgments despite falling within the scope of their subject-matter jurisdiction—in particular, sexual violence against men and boys, environmental harms, and war crimes concerning the conduct of hostilities. The relative neglect of these forms of criminality is the product of a diversity of factors, including inadequacies in the sensitivity and understanding of investigators, lawyers, and judges, difficulties encountered in evidence collection, and uncertainties and ambiguities in the law. As a result, incidents involving marginalised forms of violence often amount to untold histories within the judgments of international criminal courts.

[550] Danner (n 231) 5 (identifying 'the contradictory demands of rule stability and flexibility in the face of changing conditions'); and R Teitel, *Transitional Justice* (OUP 2000) 11*ff* (identifying 'a tension between the rule of law in transition as backward-looking and forward-looking, as settled versus dynamic').

5
The Culpability Question

While identifying whether or not crimes have been committed is undoubtedly an important function of international criminal courts, their primary adjudicative task is to determine whether or not responsibility for such crimes may be attributed to the accused under prosecution. In practice, this culpability question has been complicated by the fact that the vast majority of offences adjudicated by international criminal courts constitute manifestations of 'system criminality', a term that speaks to two dimensions of such crimes and the environments in which they tend to be carried out.[1] First, system crimes generally involve the *collective* participation of large numbers of individuals in their perpetration. In contrast to the interpersonal violence predominantly adjudicated within domestic systems, mass violence tends to require the interaction of significant numbers of individuals cooperating and coordinating through formal or informal networks and multi-layered decision-making structures.[2] Second, system crimes tend to be underpinned by *systemic* authorisation or enablement. In other words, mass atrocities are often perpetrated in 'climates of moral degeneracy',[3] in which criminal activity serves and is empowered by the system in which it is embedded—where the system typically takes the form of a collective entity, such as a State, organised armed group, or corporation.[4]

The collective and systemic features of system crimes raise vexing questions for international criminal courts tasked with determining when and how criminal responsibility for their commission may be attributed to individuals. According to George Fletcher, 'attribution' captures the idea of 'bringing home the crime to the offender and holding the offender responsible for the crime'.[5] Although different criminal law systems approach questions of attribution in distinctive ways,[6] within international criminal courts reference has typically been made to the principle of personal culpability.[7] In this context, the principle of personal culpability may be understood to comprise two components, one pertaining to the attribution of criminal responsibility per

[1] A Smeulers, 'Punishing the Enemies of All Mankind' (2008) 21 *Leiden Journal of International Law* 971, 976–981; and E van Sliedregt, *Individual Criminal Responsibility in International Law* (OUP 2012) 20–22.

[2] C Stahn, *A Critical Introduction to International Criminal Law* (CUP 2019) 127.

[3] GP Fletcher, 'The Storrs Lectures: Liberals and Romantics at War: The Problem of Collective Guilt' (2002) 111 *Yale Law Journal* 1499, 1541.

[4] A Nollkaemper, 'Introduction', in A Nollkaemper and HG van der Wilt (eds), *System Criminality* (CUP 2009) 1, 16–19.

[5] GP Fletcher, *Basic Concepts of Criminal Law* (OUP 1998) 81.

[6] See generally, GP Fletcher, *The Grammar of Criminal Law: American, Comparative, and International: Volume One: Foundations* (OUP 2007) 43–46 and 49–55 (distinguishing bipartite and tripartite perspectives).

[7] See, for example, *Göring and others*, Nuremberg Tribunal, Trial of the Major War Criminals before the International Military Tribunal, Nuremberg, 14 November 1945–1 October 1946 (Nuremberg IMT 1947) Volume I, 171–341 ('Nuremberg Judgment') 256; and *Prosecutor v Duško Tadić* (Judgment, Appeals Chamber) IT-94-1-A (15 July 1999) ('*Tadić* Appeal Judgment') [186].

Doing Justice to History. Barrie Sander, Oxford University Press (2021). © Barrie Sander.
DOI: 10.1093/oso/9780198846871.003.0005

se, and the other pertaining to the calibration of criminal punishment.[8] With respect to criminal responsibility, the principle permits attribution only where an individual has in some way participated in the commission of a crime and made a blameworthy moral choice to do so. With respect to criminal punishment, the principle requires a proportionate sentence that does not exceed the degree of an individual's personal guilt. Of course, the devil is in the detail and contestation has arisen concerning which forms of participation are sufficient to establish responsibility, what types of moral choices are blameworthy, and what is meant by proportionality, both within and across different institutional contexts. Nonetheless, at its core, the principle of personal culpability is animated by a concern for ensuring that criminal responsibility is attributed to individuals and their punishment calibrated in ways that respect individual agency.[9] According to Darryl Robinson, for example, the principle of personal culpability requires that the attribution of criminal responsibility always be accompanied by plausible and convincing 'deontological justifications',[10] which explain how attribution adheres to the criminal law's 'underlying deontic commitment ... to treat persons as moral agents, possessed of dignity and capable of directing their behaviour by reason'.[11]

In the context of adjudicating individual criminal responsibility for various forms of system criminality, adhering to the principle of personal culpability confronts international criminal courts with the complex task of reflecting on the different ways in which the collective and systemic characteristics of mass atrocity situations may expand and diminish individual agency, thereby altering the normative expectations that may reasonably be placed on individuals in particular societal contexts.[12] In the field of social science, it is well established that the collective and systemic features of system crimes and the environments in which they tend to be carried out may *expand* individual agency by enabling individuals to achieve a heightened degree of violence and harm that would otherwise be unattainable acting alone, as well as *diminish* individual agency through the subjection of individuals to different types of situational pressures.[13] According to this relational understanding of human agency,[14]

[8] See generally, G Werle and B Burghardt, 'Establishing Degrees of Responsibility: Modes of Participation in Article 25 of the ICC Statute', in E van Sliedregt and S Vasiliev (eds), *Pluralism in International Criminal Law* (OUP 2014) 301, 304.

[9] D Robinson, 'A Cosmopolitan Liberal Account of International Criminal Law' (2013) 26 *Leiden Journal of International Law* 127, 140 ('Once we decide to punish and stigmatize individuals for crimes, we are obliged to determine what we are punishing them *for*. This inevitably brings the question of individual agency—to identify the actions and contributions for which that individual is to be held responsible.')

[10] D Robinson, 'How Command Responsibility Got So Complicated: A Culpability Contradiction, Its Obfuscation, and a Simple Solution' (2012) 13 *Melbourne Journal of International Law* 1, 24.

[11] Robinson (n 9) 131. See similarly, in the domestic criminal context, A Ashworth and J Horder, *Principles of Criminal Law* (7th edn, OUP 2013) 23.

[12] See similarly, Robinson (n 9) 140–142.

[13] KJ Fisher, *Moral Accountability and International Criminal Law: Holding Agents of Atrocity Accountable to the World* (Routledge 2012) 77–78.

[14] See generally, D Foster, 'Rethinking the Subjectivity of Perpetrators of Political Violence', in A Smeulers (ed), *Collective Violence and International Criminal Justice: An Interdisciplinary Approach* (Intersentia 2010) 39 (outlining a 'relational model' for the genesis of system criminality that 'retain[s] some measure of agency (people are not merely passive victims, acted upon by external forces) while simultaneously grasping the collective, organizational and ideological nature of political violence'); and A Norrie, *Crime, Reason and History: A Critical Introduction to Criminal Law* (2nd edn, CUP 2001) 172 (recognising the 'duality of human life, as both individual and social').

whilst individuals are rarely reducible to the contexts in which they operate, nor are their actions intelligible without them.[15] With this in mind, a central question for international criminal courts has been to determine the extent to which the collective and systemic features of mass atrocity situations should be deemed *legally relevant* for the purpose of attributing criminal responsibility for system crimes to individuals in particular cases.

In this chapter, I explore how international criminal courts have addressed this culpability question through recourse to two types of categories: first, *modes of participation doctrines*, which enable international criminal courts to connect individuals to the commission of particular crimes; and second, *grounds for excluding responsibility and desert-based mitigating factors in sentencing*, which enable international criminal courts to exclude or reduce the culpability of individuals. These culpability categories perform an important narrative function within international criminal courts, defining not only the types of behaviour that can connect and disconnect individuals to and from the commission of crimes, but also which aspects of their social contexts are relevant for rendering their behaviour intelligible for this purpose.

Similar to categories of crime, determining the range and definition of culpability categories adjudicated by an international criminal court is not a neutral process, but the outcome of an intense struggle between different actors vying for control over their recognition and meaning. Although this struggle occurs at different junctures in the international criminal justice process—including the drafting of statutory frameworks, the scope and focus of the charges brought against the accused, and the scope and focus of grounds for excluding responsibility or desert-based mitigating factors raised by defendants in particular cases—the present chapter focuses on the *interpretation* of culpability categories in the decisions and judgments of international criminal courts.

By examining the judicial interpretation of modes of participation doctrines on the one hand, and grounds for excluding responsibility and mitigating punishment on the other, this chapter reveals how the scope and content of the historical narratives constructed within international criminal courts have been shaped to a significant extent by struggles for control over the recognition and meaning of categories of culpability in different institutional contexts. On an institutional level, the chapter reveals how *understandings of individual agency* given expression in the formulation of modes of participation doctrines, grounds for excluding responsibility, and desert-based

[15] See similarly, A Smeulers and F Grünfeld, *International Crimes and Other Gross Human Rights Violations: A Multi- and Interdisciplinary Textbook* (Martinus Nijhoff Publishers 2011) 317 (noting how individuals are not 'passive automatons or unwilling products of their environments', but 'continuously interact with their environment and thus shape the environment just like the environment shapes them'); MA Drumbl, *Reimagining Child Soldiers in International Law and Policy* (OUP 2012) 98–99 (outlining 'a model of circumscribed action', in which actors exercise bounded discretion that 'varies according to *an ever fluctuating admixture of disposition and situation*') (emphasis in original); Z Bohrer, 'Is the Prosecution of War Crimes Just and Effective? Rethinking the Lessons from Sociology and Psychology' (2012) 33 *Michigan Journal of International Law* 749, 762 (noting how 'the more accepted position in the fields of sociology and psychology views behavior as a product of both rationality (and dissuadable behavior) and sociological and psychological conditions'); and S Mohamed, 'Deviance, Aspiration, and the Stories We Tell: Reconciling Mass Atrocity and the Criminal Law' (2015) 124 *Yale Law Journal* 1628, 1681 (proposing 'to understand agency and choice as a spectrum rather than as extremes').

mitigating factors, have varied according to the judicial context. On a doctrinal level, the chapter reveals a tendency on the part of international criminal courts to *selectively contextualise* the behaviour of the accused individuals on trial when determining their culpability, placing greater emphasis on how the collective and systemic character of system criminality may expand—rather than diminish—individual agency. Ultimately, the chapter illuminates the implications of these insights not only for the culpability of the accused individuals on trial, but also the scope and content of the historical narratives constructed by international criminal courts within their judgments.

The chapter is divided into three sections. The chapter begins by examining a selection of modes of participation doctrines through which international criminal courts have determined whether or not to attribute criminal responsibility to individuals alleged to have masterminded system crimes (Section I). The chapter then turns to examine a selection of grounds for excluding responsibility and desert-based mitigating factors through which international criminal courts have determined whether or not to exclude or mitigate the culpability of individuals in light of the situational pressures of the social contexts in which they operated (Section II). Finally, the chapter concludes by reflecting on the historical narrative implications of the different understandings of individual agency given expression through the recognition and definition of categories of culpability in different institutional contexts (Section III).

I. Modes of Participation Doctrines

For the purpose of determining the criminal responsibility of individuals for system crimes, international criminal courts have generally treated the identification of crimes and modes of participation as separate legal questions. The principal exception to this crime/participation model concerns inchoate offences—such as conspiracy—where, in essence, participation *is* the crime and vice versa.[16] Whether free-standing or not, in practice modes of participation doctrines generally perform a dual narrative function within the judgments of international criminal courts.[17]

First, modes of participation doctrines are *linking devices*,[18] defining not only *whether* but also *how* individuals may be connected to particular crimes.[19] In particular, each mode of participation doctrine constructs a particular narrative about the

[16] A Zahar and G Sluiter, *International Criminal Law: A Critical Introduction* (OUP 2008) 220 (explaining that for inchoate crimes, 'responsibility *is* the crime, and vice versa') (emphasis in original). See similarly, in the domestic context, Ashworth and Horder (n 11) 6.

[17] On the narrative significance of modes of participation doctrines, see generally, N Jain, *Perpetrators and Accessories in International Criminal Law: Individual Modes of Responsibility for Collective Crimes* (Hart Publishing 2014) 7–8; and AM Danner and J Martinez, 'Guilty Associations: Joint Criminal Enterprise, Command Responsibility, and the Development of International Criminal Law' (2005) 93 *California Law Review* 75, 167.

[18] JD Ohlin, 'Second-Order Linking Principles: Combining Vertical and Horizontal Modes of Liability' (2012) 25 *Leiden Journal of International Law* 771, 772.

[19] Jain (n 17) 7–8; and H van der Wilt, 'Srebrenica: On Joint Criminal Enterprise, Aiding and Abetting and Command Responsibility' (2015) 62 *Netherlands International Law Review* 229, 239.

role and function of an individual within a given collective context and may also provide meaningful indicators of an individual's degree of culpability for the crime.[20]

Second, modes of participation doctrines portray *the organisational dynamics and collective decision-making structures* through which system crimes are executed.[21] By describing the collective environments within which accused persons were operating, modes of participation doctrines depict the social phenomena of system crimes in particular ways, highlighting certain characteristics of their organisation and affecting how the collective context is represented.[22]

Within the jurisprudence of international criminal courts, a range of modes of participation doctrines have been recognised in an effort to reflect the diverse roles and functions undertaken by individuals within mass atrocity situations. Different doctrines enable distinct narratives to be constructed about the contributions of individuals to system crimes as well as the collective contexts within which they were operating.[23]

In order to explore the historical narrative significance of the individual and collective dimensions of modes of participation across different institutional contexts, this section examines a selection of modes that have been relied upon to attribute criminal responsibility to individuals alleged to have been the masterminds or central figures in the commission of system crimes.[24] To this end, this section begins by examining the narrative salience of different models of participation within criminal law theory (subsection A), as well as the conceptual challenges of attributing criminal responsibility to the alleged masterminds of system crimes (subsection B). The section then proceeds to examine the inchoate crime of *conspiracy* at the Nuremberg IMT and Tokyo IMTFE (subsection C), the doctrine of *joint criminal enterprise* at the UN ad hoc tribunals (subsection D), and different forms of *perpetration* at the ICC (subsection E). The section concludes by reflecting on the historical narrative significance of the variable formulations of modes of participation doctrines adopted in different institutional contexts (subsection F).

A. The Narrative Salience of Different Models of Participation

In order to illuminate the narrative salience of modes of participation doctrines in practice, it is useful at the outset to briefly review two basic *models* of participation that

[20] D Guilfoyle, 'Responsibility for Collective Atrocities: Fair Labelling and Approaches to Commission in International Criminal Law' (2011) 64 *Current Legal Problems* 255, 260 and 268; Werle and Burghardt (n 8) 312 and 318; and JD Ohlin, 'Co-Perpetration: German *Dogmatik* or German Invasion?', in C Stahn (ed), *The Law and Practice of the International Criminal Court* (OUP 2015) 517, 531.

[21] M Osiel, 'Choosing Among Alternative Responses to Mass Atrocity: Between the Individual and the Collectivity' *Ethics & International Affairs* (18 September 2015).

[22] M Heikkilä, *Coping with International Atrocities through Criminal Law: A Study into the Typical Features of International Criminality and the Reflection of these Traits in International Criminal Law* (Åbo Akademi University Press 2013) 230, 236, and 259–260.

[23] For a useful typology of modes of participation doctrines, see generally, Heikkilä (n 22) 188*ff*.

[24] See, in this regard, E van Sliedregt, 'The Curious Case of International Criminal Liability' (2012) 10 *Journal of International Criminal Justice* 1171, 1174; and Jain (n 17) 141.

tend to be distinguished as a matter of criminal law theory: the unitary model; and the differentiated model.

According to the *unitary* model, each individual who contributes to the carrying out of a crime is regarded as a 'perpetrator' or 'principal' to the crime;[25] in their purest form, unitary systems define only a minimum threshold of individual criminal responsibility and refrain from further distinguishing different modes of participation.[26] As such, responsibility in a unitary model is 'autonomous', with each person who causally contributes to the crime being individually responsible for his or her own conduct.[27]

The *differentiated* model, by contrast, distinguishes between the 'perpetrator' or 'principal' who physically commits a crime, stands in the centre of its commission, or controls its commission by means of their predominant influence, and the 'accomplice' or 'secondary party' who assists or prompts its commission.[28] Under this model, the responsibility of accomplices is 'derivative' or dependent on the responsibility of the principal to the crime, the precise nature of the dependence varying according to the domestic system in question.[29]

Within differentiated models, the precise borderline between principals and accomplices varies depending on the domestic system. According to Elies van Sliedregt, a useful distinction may be drawn in this regard between 'naturalistic' and 'normative' approaches.[30] The naturalistic approach is 'bottom-up', beginning with the identification of the individual who most immediately and directly causes the crime and then proceeding to examine the middle and upper levels of participation. According to this approach, 'the principal is the one who most immediately causes the *actus reus*/the offence and the accessory is the one who contributes to causing the *actus reus*'.[31] By contrast, the normative approach is 'top-down', beginning with the identification of the individual who stands at the centre of the commission of the crime, for example a senior leader, and then proceeding to examine the smaller fish in the lower ranks of a military unit. According to this approach, 'the principal is the one who is "most responsible" in the sense of having decisive influence on the commission of the crime, without necessarily physically committing it'.[32]

[25] According to Elies van Sliedregt, this model has been adopted, at least to some degree, in Austria, Brazil, Denmark, Germany (but only in relation to particular types of offences), Italy, Norway, and Sweden. van Sliedregt (n 1) 66, fn 18.

[26] Werle and Burghardt (n 8) 302–303.

[27] van Sliedregt (n 1) 65–66 and 69.

[28] According to Sarah Finnin, this model has been adopted by 'the majority of European countries (such as Spain, Germany, France and Switzerland), several Latin American countries, and (with certain peculiarities …) countries which belong to the common law tradition such as the United States and England'. S Finnin, *Elements of Accessorial Modes of Liability: Articles 25(3)(b) and (c) of the Rome Statute of the International Criminal Court* (Martinus Nijhoff Publishers 2012) 13.

[29] van Sliedregt (n 1) 66–69; H Olásolo, *The Criminal Responsibility of Senior Political and Military Leaders as Principals to International Crimes* (Hart Publishing 2009) 14–16; and A Eser, 'Individual Criminal Responsibility', in A Cassese et al (eds), *The Rome Statute of the International Criminal Court* (OUP 2002) 767, 783.

[30] van Sliedregt (n 1) 71–73.

[31] Ibid 71–72.

[32] Ibid 72.

Drawing on the recent work of Miles Jackson, three further kinds of differentiation may be made between differentiated models:[33] first, 'doctrinal differentiation', whereby the criminal law distinguishes between different participants in wrongdoing through the recognition of different modes of participation doctrines; second, 'differentiation in the attribution of responsibility', whereby the criminal law distinguishes between different participants in wrongdoing at the stage of conviction; and finally, 'differentiation in the consequences of responsibility', whereby the criminal law distinguishes between different participants in wrongdoing at the sentencing stage of proceedings. Not all differentiated systems of criminal law differentiate at each of the three stages. For instance, some domestic criminal systems doctrinally differentiate between participants, but nonetheless treat principals and accomplices as formally equivalent at the conviction and sentencing stage of proceedings such that accomplices are held responsible and sentenced for the principal's crime rather than for their contributions to the crime.[34] Equally, some legal systems afford discretion to judges to take into account an accomplice's lower degree of participation at the sentencing stage even though accomplices are held responsible for the crimes of principals.[35]

In practice, the distinction between unitary and differentiated participation models has been fading in domestic criminal systems.[36] For instance, judges in some unitary systems still doctrinally differentiate modes of participation for the purpose of describing an accused's participation in the crime,[37] while the adoption of a normative approach to perpetration in some differentiated systems has resulted in a broadening of the scope of autonomous conceptions of principal responsibility.[38] Moreover, it should be remembered that in all legal systems, the sentence should reflect the culpability of the defendant. With this in mind, Mikaela Heikkilä has noted that the different models arguably 'only vary in relation to at what stage of the proceedings the evaluation of the scope of the contribution to the crime has to be done and how explicitly it has to be articulated in the form of legal labels'.[39]

Despite some contestation,[40] the vast majority of international criminal scholars argue that that some form of differentiated model of participation is preferable in the international criminal context because it facilitates greater precision in identifying the roles and contributions of individuals with respect to system crimes.[41] As Jens Ohlin has argued, to insist on more precise labelling is to recognise 'that labels matter, that the legal categories that attach to conduct and agents have real meaning and significance' and that 'defendants have a right to insist that these labels are accurate and

[33] M Jackson, *Complicity in International Law* (OUP 2015) 22–26.
[34] Ibid 22–23.
[35] Ibid 25.
[36] van Sliedregt (n 1) 73.
[37] A Cassese et al, *Cassese's International Criminal Law* (3rd edn, OUP 2013) 162.
[38] van Sliedregt (n 1) 73.
[39] Heikkilä (n 22) 180.
[40] James Stewart, in particular, has emerged as a strong advocate for a unitary model of participation in international criminal law. See generally, JG Stewart, 'The End of "Modes of Liability" for International Crimes' (2012) 25 *Leiden Journal of International Law* 165; and JG Stewart, 'Ten Reasons for Adopting a Universal Concept of Participation in Atrocity', in van Sliedregt and Vasiliev (n 8) 320, 334–335.
[41] See, for example, Jackson (n 33) 18; and C Meloni, 'Fragmentation of the Notion of Co-Perpetration in International Criminal Law?', in L van den Herik and C Stahn (eds), *The Diversification and Fragmentation of International Criminal Law* (Martinus Nijhoff Publishers 2012) 481, 501.

carefully capture their relative culpability and the nature of their conduct'.[42] As such, whilst views differ as to how differentiation should be achieved in practice,[43] most commentators agree that some form of differentiation is preferable in the interest of carefully distinguishing the roles and contributions of individuals whose association with system crimes tends to vary considerably.[44]

For present purposes, the elaboration of different models of participation serves to illuminate the different narrative functions that modes of participation may potentially perform in practice. Whereas under unitary models, the function of modes tends to be confined to defining the outer limits of criminal responsibility, under differentiated models, modes also identify the precise role performed by individuals within these limits and sometimes also weigh the degree of their culpability.[45] By illuminating the different narrative functions of modes of participation, the different models of participation can serve as useful points of reference when examining the approaches adopted by international criminal courts in their jurisprudence.

B. Conceptual Challenges of Attributing Responsibility for Masterminded Violence

As discussed at the outset of this chapter, system crimes have a number of collective and systemic features that distinguish them from most domestic offences. In practice, these qualities have confronted international criminal courts with at least two conceptual challenges when formulating modes of participation doctrines through which responsibility may be attributed to the masterminds of such crimes.

First, international criminal courts have been confronted by the challenge that the degree of culpability for system criminality generally depends less on physical proximity and more on an individual's structural relationship to the crime.[46] Whereas those most responsible for domestic offences tend to be the physical perpetrators, the individuals who physically perpetrate the underlying prohibited acts of system crimes typically constitute only a small part of the collective and systemic endeavours that characterise such crimes. For system crimes, it is more often the individuals who occupy central positions within the collective or contextual dimensions of such crimes who are most responsible for their occurrence.[47] Indeed, system criminality is commonly referred to as 'masterminded violence' for the very reason that such crimes are often initiated or enabled by remote 'intellectual' perpetrators and physically perpetrated by an executive machinery.[48] As Neha Jain explains, the central figure within

[42] Ohlin (n 20) 531.

[43] Compare, for example, van Sliedregt (n 1) 80 ('Making clear who masterminded crimes by referring to him/her as the "principal" who "commits" crimes is important in communicating to victims and the international community as a whole, who was the "real" culprit'); and Guilfoyle (n 20) 281 (preferring to refer to the masterminds as accessories who are 'aggregators of responsibility' rather than principals).

[44] See similarly, Werle and Burghardt (n 8) 311; H Vest, 'Problems of Participation—Unitarian, Differentiated Approach, or Something Else?' (2014) 12 *Journal of International Criminal Justice* 295, 302.

[45] Werle and Burghardt (n 8) 302.

[46] Stahn (n 2) 128.

[47] Jain (n 17) 141; and M Osiel, *Making Sense of Mass Atrocity* (CUP 2009) 85.

[48] van Sliedregt (n 24) 1174.

system crimes 'is the person who sets this entire machinery in motion and utilises it in order to achieve the criminal result he intends, or knows will occur'.[49] This perspective reflects the view that individuals who are able to marshal and exploit the authority, power, and influence of collective entities to create environments conducive to the commission of crimes generally cause more aggregate harm than those responsible for physically committing the underlying prohibited acts of system crimes. According to this view, focusing narrowly on the behaviour of individuals in isolation from their collective context risks missing the larger harm to which an individual may have contributed. As Robert Sloane has argued, '[t]he cloak of collective authority poses a heightened danger, and its manipulation and abuse by elites should be penalized accordingly'.[50]

Since the masterminds of system crimes tend to be geographically remote from the physical execution of such crimes, international criminal courts have been confronted by the challenge of linking such individuals to system crimes whilst at the same time reflecting the centrality of their role in their commission. Specifically, this has required the formulation of modes of participation doctrines that strive to account for the normative weight of the conduct of masterminds despite their physical remoteness, describe the causal link between the conduct of masterminds and the physical perpetrators of the crime, and represent the parallel nature of the culpability of individuals participating at different levels in relation to the crime.[51]

The application of traditional modes of participation doctrines has generally been deemed inadequate for this purpose because of their failure to reflect the central role played by senior leaders in the commission of system crimes.[52] According to the Appeals Chamber of the International Criminal Tribunal for the former Yugoslavia (ICTY) in *Tadić*, for example, 'to hold criminally liable as a perpetrator only the person who materially performs the criminal act would disregard the role as co-perpetrators of all those who in some way made it possible for the perpetrator physically to carry out that criminal act', whilst 'to hold the latter liable only as aidors and abettors might understate the degree of their criminal responsibility'.[53] With this

[49] Jain (n 17) 142. See, famously, *The Attorney General of the Government of Israel v Eichmann* (Judgment, District Court of Jerusalem) Criminal Case No 40/61 (11 December 1961) [197] ('[I]n general, the degree of responsibility increases as we draw further away from the man who uses the fatal instrument with his own hands and reach the higher ranks of command, the "counsellors" in the language of our Law'). See, however, Stahn (n 2) 129 (explaining how in some organisations the degree of culpability may be 'less dependent on hierarchy' and more on 'the role that the individual shared').

[50] R Sloane, 'The Expressive Capacity of International Punishment: The Limits of the National Law Analogy and the Potential of International Criminal Law' (2007) 43 *Stanford Journal of International Law* 39, 60. See also, HC Kelman, 'The Policy Context of International Crimes', in Nollkaemper and van der Wilt (n 4) 26, 26–29 (distinguishing 'crimes of authority', which tend to be committed by higher ranked individuals who formulate the general policies that create environments conducive to the commission of mass atrocities, and 'crimes of obedience', which tend to be committed by mid-lower ranked individuals in conformity with authority structures).

[51] E van Sliedregt, 'Perpetration and Participation in Article 25(3)', in Stahn (n 20) 499, 514–515.

[52] See similarly, Osiel (n 47) 85 ('Our customary legal categories ... get the moral valences entirely wrong—almost backward in fact. To employ the doctrine of complicity is to employ a deceptive device ... insofar as it both understates the top leaders' true role and, in focusing on their mere "knowing contribution" to subordinates' wrongs, does not clear distinguish this role from that of many others who will escape prosecution').

[53] *Tadić* Appeal Judgment (n 7) [192].

in mind, the challenge for international criminal courts has been not only to formulate modes of participation that enable criminal responsibility to be attributed to the masterminds of system crimes but to do so in ways that accurately reflect the nature and extent of the individual's role and contribution in relation to such offences.[54]

Second, since the collective and organisational structures through which system crimes have been carried out have not been uniform, international criminal courts have been confronted by the additional challenge of formulating modes of participation doctrines that are sufficiently flexible to accommodate such diversity. In practice, system crimes have been committed through a range of organisational structures, including vertically structured hierarchies, horizontally structured networks, or some combination of the two, often of varying sizes and degrees of cohesion.[55] As Mark Osiel explains:[56]

> There is, of course, both a vertical and lateral dimension to the social dynamics between those involved in state-sponsored mass atrocity. On the one hand, instructions are generally given from top to bottom and information conveyed from bottom to top. On the other hand, those at the same level in the hierarchy—and beyond its formal boundaries—often have to cooperate to implement such instructions. Still more important, those involved often display considerable initiative in implementing criminal policies beyond the terms of superiors' directives. Interaction among interested parties is thus simultaneously organized and spontaneous, vertical and horizontal.

With this in mind, international criminal courts have faced the thorny challenge of formulating a conceptual repertoire adequate to the task of mapping and matching the organisational variability by which system crimes have been implemented in practice.

Taken together, these challenges have confronted international criminal courts with the task of formulating a range of modes of participation doctrines that seek not only to connect masterminds to system crimes, but also to accurately convey the weight of their contributions in light of the collective and systemic contexts in which they operated. According to Kai Ambos, for example, attribution for system crimes has tended to require 'a mixed system of individual-collective responsibility in which the overall act or criminal situation (*Gesamttat*) and the criminal enterprise or organisation which controls this situation take centre stage and serve as the points of reference for imputation'.[57] Importantly, the modes of participation doctrines identified and interpreted by international criminal courts in practice have varied in terms of how the collective contexts in which system crimes occur have been represented and relied upon for the purpose of determining and articulating the criminal responsibility of individuals for such crimes. Against this background, the remainder of this section conducts a comparative analysis of the varying relationship between the individual and collective dimensions of modes of participation doctrines in different institutional contexts

[54] Osiel (n 47) 86–87.
[55] Heikkilä (n 22) 234–243.
[56] Osiel (n 47) 25–26.
[57] K Ambos, *Treatise on International Criminal Law: Volume I: Foundations and General Part* (OUP 2013) 177.

and reveals how the judicial interpretation of such doctrines has influenced the scope and content of the historical narratives constructed in the judgments of international criminal courts in practice.

C. Conspiracy at the Nuremberg IMT and Tokyo IMTFE

A number of modes of participation doctrines were incorporated within the Nuremberg and Tokyo Charters, albeit somewhat scattered across their texts. The concept of conspiracy was included in the Charters as both an inchoate crime and a mode of participation doctrine; the focus of this section is the former. Viewed with particular scepticism by the French and Russian delegations, who were concerned it might lead to endless confusion,[58] a diluted version of a proposal to incorporate the conspiracy concept, initially spearheaded by the United States, was eventually agreed upon.[59]

It is generally accepted that the Nuremberg and Tokyo Charters and tribunals adhered to a unitary model of attribution in terms of conviction and sentencing, declining to strictly distinguish between principal and accessorial liability or to suggest that the degree of an individual's culpability depended on the mode of participation charged.[60] Pursuant to this model, any form of support or assistance to the crime was simply characterised as a punishable form of contribution in the commission of the crime.[61] Notwithstanding this approach to attribution, the concept of conspiracy was intended to provide a useful doctrinal device for attributing criminal responsibility to senior leaders in a way that would reflect the collective and systemic dynamics by which the atrocities under examination had been organised, whilst addressing concerns that had arisen regarding a potential shortage of direct evidence connecting the leaders to the violent acts in question.[62]

In practice, ambiguities in the drafting of the Nuremberg and Tokyo Charters left prosecutors considerable leeway to interpret the boundaries of the concept of conspiracy in their indictments. At Nuremberg, the prosecution put forward a grand conspiracy charge spanning over twenty-five years from the formation of the Nazi Party

[58] BF Smith, *Reaching Judgment at Nuremberg: The Untold Story of How the Nazi War Criminals Were Judged* (Basic Books 1977) 51. See, however, F Hirsch, *Soviet Judgment at Nuremberg: A New History of the International Military Tribunal after World War II* (OUP 2020) 8 (noting how Soviet lawyer, Aron Trainin, 'brought Soviet ideas about criminal responsibility and complicity into the international discussion about war crimes well in advance of the Allied victory').

[59] For a detailed account of the drafting process of the concept of conspiracy in the Nuremberg and Tokyo Charters, see generally, S Darcy, *Collective Responsibility and Accountability under International Law* (Transnational Publishers 2007) 198–216; and L Yanev, 'A Janus-Faced Concept: Nuremberg's Law on Conspiracy *Vis-à-vis* the Notion of Joint Criminal Enterprise' (2015) 26 *Criminal Law Forum* 419, 426*ff*.

[60] LN Sadat and JM Jolly, 'Seven Canons of ICC Treaty Interpretation: Making Sense of Article 25's Rorschach Blot' (2014) 27 *Leiden Journal of International Law* 755, 771.

[61] Olásolo (n 29) 20–21.

[62] See, for example, JA Bush, 'The Prehistory of Corporations and Conspiracy in International Criminal Law: What Nuremberg Really Said' (2009) 109 *Columbia Law Review* 1094, 1137 ('a procedural device to ensure successful prosecution of the most notorious German war criminals'); and N Boister and R Cryer, *The Tokyo International Military Tribunal—A Reappraisal* (OUP 2008) 221 ('served the ideological rationale of construing Japanese "militarism" to fit the conspiratorial model that applied well to the Nazis' and 'allowed the prosecution to allege an agreement but to prove it through circumstantial evidence').

in 1919 until the end of the war in 1945 and argued, in essence, that 'any significant participation in the affairs of the Nazi Party or Government [amounted to] evidence of a participation in a conspiracy that is in itself criminal'.[63] The Tokyo indictment included a range of conspiracy charges, including a broad conspiracy, spanning eighteen years in length, the alleged objective of which was that Japan should secure military, naval, political, and economic domination over East Asia, the Pacific and Indian Oceans, and all countries and islands within or bordering them, through wars of aggression against any States that might oppose that purpose.[64] The Tokyo prosecution also alleged a conspiracy over the same period between Germany, Italy, and Japan, the objective of which was to secure by means of mutual assistance 'domination of the whole world, each having special domination in its own sphere'.[65] Finally, the Tokyo indictment also included conspiracy charges concerning the murder of soldiers, civilians, and prisoners of war, as well as the commission of war crimes.[66]

In their judgments, the Nuremberg and Tokyo tribunals neglected to examine the legal basis of the concept of conspiracy—either as an inchoate crime or a mode of participation. As such, the judicial recognition of the concept left the tribunals open to similar critiques that had been levelled against their acceptance of the category of crimes against peace. Conspiracy was a concept without precedent at the international level, a fact that proved fatal to any claim of customary status.[67] Its status as a general principle of law was also contestable. At Tokyo, Judge Pal denied that conspiracy as an inchoate crime could be recognised as a general principle of law because 'nations have not as yet considered the conditions of international life ripe enough for the transposition of principles of criminality into rules of law in international life',[68] while Judge Webb declared that 'it would be nothing short of judicial legislation for this Tribunal to declare that there is a crime of naked conspiracy for the safety of the international order'.[69] Most scholars have also concluded that the recognition of conspiracy by domestic legal systems was insufficiently widespread to have attained the status of a general principle of law during the relevant period.[70] Similar to other innovative

[63] Nuremberg Judgment (n 7) 224–225.

[64] *USA and Others v Araki Sadao and Others*, International Military Tribunal for the Far East, Indictment, reprinted in N Boister and R Cryer (eds), *Documents on the Tokyo International Military Tribunal: Charter, Indictments and Judgments* (OUP 2008) 16 ('Tokyo Indictment') 18 (Count 1). In order to guard against the possibility of acquittal on Count 1, Counts 2 to 4 broke down the grand conspiracy into its constituent parts. Ibid 18–19 (Counts 2 to 4).

[65] Tokyo Indictment (n 64) 19 (Count 5).

[66] Tokyo Indictment (n 64) 27–32 (Counts 37, 38, 44, and 53).

[67] Boister and Cryer (n 62) 220 and 226.

[68] *USA and Others v Araki Sadao and Others* (Judgment of Justice Pal, International Military Tribunal for the Far East) (1 November 1948), reprinted in Boister and Cryer (n 64) 809 ('Judgment of Justice Pal') pagination paras 1003–1004.

[69] *USA and Others v Araki Sadao and Others* (sep op of the President of the Tribunal, Sir William Flood Webb, International Military Tribunal for the Far East) (1 November 1948), reprinted in Boister and Cryer (n 64) 629, pagination paras 8–9. Justice Webb did, however, consider conspiracy as a mode of participation to be 'a universal rule of criminal responsibility' despite its lack of recognition in every domestic legal system. Ibid pagination para 9.

[70] See, for example, R Cryer, *Prosecuting International Crimes: Selectivity and the International Criminal Law Regime* (CUP 2005) 309. See, however, KJ Heller *The Nuremberg Military Tribunals and the Origins of International Criminal Law* (OUP 2011) 277–278 ('pre-war German criminal law ... had long accepted the idea that the mere agreement to commit certain kinds of violent acts was criminal').

aspects of the Nuremberg and Tokyo Charters, therefore, the judicial acceptance of conspiracy reflected a willingness to recognise a novel legal concept, in this instance one aimed at ensuring the accountability of the senior leaders of Nazi and Japanese aggression, at the expense of safeguarding the accused from the retroactive imposition of the criminal law.[71]

If the Nuremberg and Tokyo tribunals were united in their neglect of the legal basis of the concept of conspiracy, they nonetheless diverged in defining the concept's boundaries.

In the Nuremberg judgment, the International Military Tribunal (IMT) adopted a relatively cautious approach towards the concept of conspiracy. In terms of scope of application, the tribunal concluded that conspiracy as an inchoate crime was applicable only to crimes against peace and decided to address the crimes of conspiracy and aggression together—effectively collapsing the former into the latter.[72] In terms of definition, the tribunal clarified that a conspiracy must have a clearly outlined criminal purpose (in this case to commit crimes against peace), not be too far removed from the moment of its execution (in this case post-November 1937 was deemed sufficient in terms of temporal proximity), and be based on a concrete plan (as opposed to mere political affirmations such as those expressed in *Mein Kampf*).[73] To be considered a party to the conspiracy, the prosecution had to demonstrate that an accused 'with knowledge of [Hitler's] aims, gave him their cooperation'.[74] Although the formula of knowing cooperation may appear broad, in practice the IMT required direct participation in the preparation of acts of aggression at the highest level, in particular through direct contact with Hitler, and strict proof of knowledge, refusing to infer it from the circumstances.[75]

By strengthening the required connection between the behaviour of the accused and the conspiracy for which they were charged, the IMT dismissed the prosecution's narrative of a single master conspiracy and confined its conspiracy convictions to eight individuals who formed part of Hitler's inner circle. Although the IMT's restraint was laudable from the perspective of taking the agency of the accused seriously, it has nonetheless been suggested that the tribunal's approach may have been over-cautious in places, particularly in its refusal to infer knowledge of the Nazi plans of aggressive war.[76] In other words, by defining conspiracy in rigid terms, the judges risked understating the agency of some of the accused.[77]

71 According to Boister and Cryer, the offences of 'planning and preparing' and accessorial liability for substantive offences would also have enabled the conviction of Japan's leaders, but lacked the expressive qualities of the conspiracy concept. Boister and Cryer (n 62) 221.

72 Nuremberg Judgment (n 7) 224 and 226.

73 Ibid 225.

74 Ibid 226.

75 N Boister, 'The Application of Collective and Comprehensive Criminal Responsibility for Aggression at the Tokyo International Military Tribunal: The Measure of the Crime of Aggression?' (2010) 8 *Journal of International Criminal Justice* 425, 428.

76 See, for example, JR Amenge Okoth, *The Crime of Conspiracy in International Criminal Law* (Springer 2014) 91–93.

77 See, however, HL Stimson, 'The Nuremberg Trial: Landmark in Law', in G Mettraux (ed), *Perspectives on the Nuremberg Trial* (OUP 2008) 617, 624 ('In this first great international trial, however, it is perhaps as well that the Tribunal has very rigidly interpreted both the law and the evidence.... It is far better that a [defendant such as] Schacht should go free than that a judge should compromise his conscience').

In the Tokyo judgment, by contrast, the majority relied upon a significantly more expansive notion of conspiracy. Similar to Nuremberg, the majority confined conspiracy as an inchoate crime exclusively to crimes against peace.[78] Yet, while dismissing the most grandiose conspiracy allegations that had been put forward by the prosecution,[79] the majority confirmed the existence of a grand conspiracy to wage wars of aggression pertaining to East Asia, the Western and Southwestern Pacific Ocean, the Indian Ocean, and certain islands within them—ultimately acquitting just two of the twenty-five accused on this count.[80] For this purpose, the majority took a far more elastic view of conspiracy as an inchoate crime compared to the standards that had been applied at Nuremberg. For instance, the majority failed to identify any express agreement, instead relying on the emergence of a looser design around the expansionist ideas of Okawa (one of the original accused who had been discharged from the trial on account of his mental condition), and appeared to infer agreement from a concurrence of wills based on concurrent actions.[81] In addition, individual participation in the conspiracy was inferred from an extremely broad range of factors, including:[82] presence at meetings where the conspiracy was discussed; occupying a prominent official position; participating in schemes to overthrow the opposition; and spreading propaganda and inciting the Japanese people.[83] Similarly, in terms of the mental element of conspiracy, an accused's knowledge of the aggressive aims of the conspiracy was also liberally inferred from a wide range of factors, including the accused's position, participation in official decisions, public statements, and private correspondence.[84]

By loosening the required connection between the behaviour of the accused and the conspiracy for which they were charged, the majority constructed a narrative that seemed to inflate the agency of the accused and their degree of collaboration in an effort to ensure convictions. By liberally inferring both participation and knowledge from a range of vaguely defined facts and relationships, the majority was able to pass over deep divisions that had existed between the accused during their time in the Japanese government and military.[85] In this way, conspiracy became an elastic device to overcome the complexity, fluidity, and lack of transparency of the decision-making processes of the Japanese government and military.[86] The result was the construction

[78] *USA and Others v Araki Sadao and Others* (Judgment, International Military Tribunal for the Far East, Judgment) (1 November 1948) reprinted in Boister and Cryer (n 64) 71 ('Tokyo Judgment') pagination paras 48,449–48,451.

[79] See, in particular, Tokyo Judgment (n 78) pagination paras 49,763 (concluding that the conspirators had never 'seriously resolved to attempt to secure the domination of North and South America') and 49,770 (concluding that the alleged Axis conspiracy for global domination was not supported by sufficient evidence).

[80] Tokyo Judgment (n 78) pagination paras 49,769.

[81] Boister and Cryer (n 62) 218.

[82] Tokyo Judgment (n 78) pagination paras 49,773–49,851.

[83] Participation ranged from being 'one of the leaders' to merely 'taking part' in the conspiracy, although the precise degree of participation did not impact on sentencing. Boister and Cryer (n 62) 219.

[84] Boister and Cryer (n 62) 219–220. Boister and Cryer note that the accused also had to possess a special intention to support the aims of the conspiracy, a requirement that could be inferred from the majority's decision to acquit defendant Matsui of the conspiracy charge despite the fact that he 'must have been aware of the purposes and policies of the conspirators'. See, Tokyo Judgment (n 78) pagination para 49,814.

[85] Boister (n 75) 431; and AM Danner, 'Beyond the Geneva Conventions: Lessons from the Tokyo Tribunal in Prosecuting War and Terrorism' (2005) 46 *Virginia Journal of International Law* 83, 115.

[86] Boister (n 75) 431.

of a narrative that presented 'a series of discrete events spanning more than a decade, and marked by a combination of foresight, accident and surprise, as a linear historical progression with a calculated object'.[87] By significantly attenuating the link between the conduct of the accused and the conspiracy for which they were charged, the majority constructed a narrative that has since been dismissed as 'much closer to propaganda than to serious historical analysis'.[88]

D. Joint Criminal Enterprise at the UN Ad Hoc Tribunals

Although the Statutes of the United Nations (UN) ad hoc tribunals incorporated a range of modes of participation doctrines, the doctrine of joint criminal enterprise (JCE) was not expressly mentioned, its recognition entirely judge-driven. In its landmark judgment in *Tadić*, the ICTY Appeals Chamber concluded that JCE fell within the scope of its jurisdiction by relying on a victim-focused understanding of the object and purpose of the ICTY Statute in combination with placing emphasis on the importance of adequately reflecting the collective character of many of the crimes under adjudication.[89] Although the precise nature of JCE was initially contested, the jurisprudence of the ad hoc tribunals gradually cemented the view that the doctrine should be understood as a form of commission.[90] In practice, however, the ad hoc tribunals generally declined to differentiate between modes when entering convictions, instead holding individuals responsible for the underlying crimes regardless of their mode of participation.[91] Nonetheless, within the jurisprudence of the ICTY and the International Criminal Tribunal for Rwanda (ICTR) in particular, a gravity-based hierarchy between modes of participation doctrine gradually emerged, pursuant to which aiding and abetting came to be viewed as a form of 'lesser liability' that generally warranted a lower sentence in comparison to JCE liability.[92]

Within their jurisprudence, the ad hoc tribunals interpreted the objective elements of JCE liability as requiring:[93] a plurality of persons; the existence of a common plan, design, or purpose, which amounts to or involves the commission of a crime provided for in the Statute; and participation of the accused in the furtherance of the common plan, amounting to a significant contribution to the crimes in question. In practice, three categories of JCE were recognised and differentiated according to their

[87] Jain (n 17) 26.

[88] JW Dower, *Embracing Defeat: Japan in the Wake of World War II* (WW Norton & Company / New Press 1999), 463, cited in Danner (n 85) 118. See also, Judgment of Justice Pal (n 68) pagination paras 353 and 987 (dismissing the conspiracy narrative as 'preposterous').

[89] *Tadić* Appeal Judgment (n 7) [187]–[193]. For a critical discussion of this reasoning, see generally, Jain (n 17) 29–32.

[90] van Sliedregt (n 24) 1175–1178.

[91] Jackson (n 33) 86–87.

[92] Werle and Burghardt (n 8) 309–310. See, however, *Prosecutor v Charles Ghankay Taylor* (Judgment, Appeals Chamber) SCSL-03-01-A (26 September 2013) [670] ('there is no hierarchy or distinction for sentencing purposes between forms of criminal participation').

[93] *Tadić* Appeal Judgment (n 7) [227]. See also, *Prosecutor v Prlić et al* (Judgment: Volume 1 of 6, Trial Chamber) IT-04-74-T (29 May 2013) ('*Prlić et al* Trial Judgment Vol 1') [212]; and *Prosecutor v Zdravko Tolimir* (Judgment, Trial Chamber) IT-05-88/2-T (12 December 2012) ('*Tolimir* Trial Judgment') [889]–[894].

circumstances and required mental elements:[94] JCE I—the 'basic' form—encompassed participants acting pursuant to a common design and sharing a common intention to commit a crime; JCE II—the 'systemic' form—concerned the existence of an organised system of ill-treatment, such as a detention camp, and participants who were aware of the nature of the system and intended to further the criminal purpose of the system; and JCE III—the 'extended' form—assigned criminal liability to participants in a basic JCE I or a systemic JCE II for crimes committed outside the original common plan or system where it was foreseeable that such crimes might be committed and the accused willingly assumed the risk that they would occur.

The doctrine of JCE was initially developed by the ad hoc tribunals in the context of small-scale enterprises concerning cases of mob violence and detention camp personnel. A distinguishing feature of these cases was that the physical perpetrators and the accused were all members of the joint criminal enterprise. Although not completely free of controversy,[95] smaller-scale JCEs where the accused were familiar with other members of the enterprise, present at the scene of the crime, and very closely involved in the objective elements of the crime, raised relatively few concerns both in terms of their status under customary international law and their adherence with the principle of personal culpability.[96] Even in their small-scale form, however, the customary basis of extended form JCEs was uncertain at best,[97] while the doctrine's imprecise foreseeability standard led several commentators to suggest that JCE III would only adhere to the principle of personal culpability if it were characterised as a form of accessorial liability that accorded with the accused's lower degree of culpability relative to those who committed the crimes outside the original plan or system with intent.[98]

Despite the small-scale beginnings of the JCE doctrine, the ad hoc tribunals were soon confronted with cases concerning higher-ranking military and political leaders. These cases were characterised by a higher number of crime sites, the involvement of larger numbers of individuals and institutions, and the geographical and structural remoteness of the accused from the physical perpetrators of the crimes.[99] In practice, two types of leadership-level JCEs were recognised in the jurisprudence of the ad hoc tribunals.[100] The first type was defined by a common purpose limited to the

[94] *Tadić* Appeal Judgment (n 7) [195*ff*]. See also, *Prlić et al* Trial Judgment Vol 1 (n 93) [213]–[221]; and *Tolimir* Trial Judgment (n 93) [895]–[898].

[95] See generally, Olásolo (n 29) 182*ff*; and Jain (n 17) 28*ff*.

[96] For a defence of the customary international law basis of the different categories of JCEs, see generally, *Tadić* Appeal Judgment (n 7) [194]–[226]; and *Prosecutor v Vlastimir Đorđević* (Judgment, Appeals Chamber) IT-05-87/1-A (27 January 2014) ('*Đorđević* Appeal Judgment') [27]–[53]. For a defence of the adherence of the different categories of JCEs with the principle of personal culpability, see generally, Cassese et al (n 37) 163*ff*.

[97] See, for example, JD Ohlin, 'Joint Intentions to Commit International Crimes' (2011) 11 *Chicago Journal of International Law* 693, 706*ff* (discussing the 'shaky foundation of JCE III'). Contrast: S SaCouto, LN Sadat, and PV Sellers, 'Collective Criminality and Sexual Violence: Fixing a Failed Approach' (2020) 33 *Leiden Journal of International Law* 207, 230–233 (arguing in favour of JCE III's basis in customary international law).

[98] See, for example, Guilfoyle (n 20) 273; and Ambos (n 57) 162.

[99] S Ford, 'Fairness and Politics at the ICTY: Evidence from the Indictments' (2013) XXXIX *North Carolina Journal of International Law and Commercial Regulation* 45, 82.

[100] van Sliedregt (n 24) 1179.

commission of a particular type of crime in a particular region with respect to a certain group of people. Examples included: 'a plan involving a plurality of persons to murder the able-bodied Bosnian Muslim men from Srebrenica in July 1995';[101] and a JCE whose common purpose consisted of 'killing Tutsis in Butare'.[102] The second type of leadership-level JCE was defined in broader terms to encompass higher-level political objectives, the commission of more than one type of crime, and/or a wider geographical area. Examples included: 'a common plan by the leadership of the FRY and Serbia, including politicians, military figures, and the police leadership … to modify the ethnic balance in Kosovo by waging a campaign of terror against the Kosovo Albanian civilian population';[103] and a JCE whose common purpose consisted of 'the destruction of the Tutsi population in Rwanda'.[104]

The structure of these leadership-level JCEs was distinct from those that had originally been conceptualised in *Tadić*. In particular, the doctrine of JCE evolved in at least five respects in an effort to better reflect and respond to the collective dynamics that characterised leadership-level cases.

1. Loosening the link between JCE members and remote physical perpetrators

First, the ad hoc tribunals loosened the link required between JCE members at the leadership level and the remote physical perpetrators at the execution level. As originally formulated, JCE seemed ill-equipped for leadership-level cases since the doctrine appeared to require not only the existence of a common plan, design, or purpose, but also that the crimes had been perpetrated by one or more members of the common enterprise.[105] In the context of leadership-level cases, this formulation of the doctrine would have required the prosecution to demonstrate the existence of extremely vast JCEs encompassing senior military and political leaders who designed the common criminal plan, mid-level superiors who operationally prepared its implementation, and low-level subordinates who physically perpetrated the crimes.[106] Not only would it have been difficult and unrealistic to prove the existence of such vast all-encompassing enterprises, but also the application of the doctrine in this way would have risked becoming an umbrella to 'just convict everyone',[107] deferring more refined distinctions between the culpability of different types of accused to sentencing.[108]

Responding to this challenge, the ICTY Appeals Chamber in *Brđanin* determined that what mattered was 'not whether the person who carried out the *actus reus* of a particular crime is a member of the JCE, but *whether the crime in question forms part*

[101] *Prosecutor v Popović et al* (Judgment: Volume I, Trial Chamber) IT-05-88-T (10 June 2010) ('*Popović et al* Trial Judgment Vol I') [1072].

[102] *Prosecutor v Bizimungu et al* (Judgment and Sentence, Trial Chamber) ICTR-99-50-T (30 September 2011) [1947].

[103] *Prosecutor v Vlastimir Đorđević* (Public Judgment with Confidential Annex: Volume I of II, Trial Chamber) IT-05-87/1-T (23 February 2011) [2007].

[104] *Édouard Karemera and Mathieu Ngirumpatse v Prosecutor* (Judgment, Appeals Chamber) ICTR-98-44-A (29 September 2014) [137].

[105] A Cassese, 'The Proper Limits of Individual Responsibility under the Doctrine of Joint Criminal Enterprise' (2007) 5 *Journal of International Criminal Justice* 109, 125–126.

[106] Olásolo (n 29) 230.

[107] ME Badar, '"Just Convict Everyone!"—Joint Perpetration: From *Tadić* to *Stakić* and Back Again' (2006) 6 *International Criminal Law Review* 293, 302.

[108] Guilfoyle (n 20) 264–265.

of the common purpose'.[109] In order to hold a JCE member responsible for crimes committed by non-members, it would be necessary to demonstrate 'that the crime can be imputed to one member of the joint criminal enterprise, and that this member—when *using* a principal perpetrator—*acted in accordance with the common plan*'.[110] Whether a sufficiently strong factual link existed between a JCE member and the crimes committed by non-members was a question to be assessed on a case-by-case basis. In practice, however, the factual link requirement was generally satisfied by evidence that JCE members possessed positions of authority and *de facto* powers that enabled them either to order the crimes in question or to control institutions to which the direct perpetrators either belonged or acted in concert with.[111]

From a narrative perspective, the factual link requirement between leadership-level JCE members and the crimes of remote physical perpetrators enabled the ad hoc tribunals to avoid constructing vast and unrealistic enterprises comprised of individuals structurally and geographically removed from each other.[112] Instead, the ad hoc tribunals were free to focus on identifying the common plan and shared intent elements of the JCE doctrine entirely at the leadership level. In addition, the factual link requirement also ensured that remote physical perpetrators would not be held responsible for all the crimes committed in furtherance of the JCE.[113]

At the same time, however, where the strength of the factual link between the crimes of non-JCE members and the relevant JCE member was weaker than indirect perpetration—for example, where a JCE member merely instigated, ordered, or encouraged non-JCE members to commit crimes—the conviction of JCE members for the commission of the crimes in question raised concerns in terms of the principle of personal culpability.[114] As Judge Meron argued in his separate opinion in *Brđanin*, where a JCE member uses a non-JCE member to carry out a crime in furtherance of a common purpose, it would be more coherent in terms of the principle of personal culpability for all other JCE members to be liable via the JCE 'under the same mode of liability that attaches to this JCE member'.[115] According to Meron, such an approach would have the dual advantage of ensuring that JCE members were only held responsible for crimes that further the common purpose to the same extent as the relevant

[109] *Prosecutor v Radoslav Brđanin* (Judgment, Appeals Chamber) IT-99-36-A (3 April 2007) ('*Brđanin* Appeal Judgment') [410] (emphasis added).

[110] Ibid [413] (emphasis added).

[111] See, for example, *Đorđević* Appeal Judgment (n 96) [171] (noting that 'the acts of the physical perpetrators were the direct consequence of the orders and directions of . . . JCE members'); *Prosecutor v Šainović et al* (Judgment, Appeals Chamber) IT-05-87-A (23 January 2014) ('*Šainović et al* Appeal Judgment') [1258] (noting that it was sufficient that the evidence demonstrated that various JCE members had held 'prominent positions' and wielded 'significant power' over the VJ and/or the MUP in Kosovo and that the physical perpetrators had been members of the VJ and/or MUP); and *Prosecutor v Milan Martić* (Judgment, Appeals Chamber) IT-95-11-A (8 October 2008) ('*Martić* Appeal Judgment') [195] (concluding that the accused was responsible for killings perpetrated in Lipovača by Serb paramilitary forces based on the fact that such forces were 'at least acting in concert with' the Yugoslav People's Army, which was under the control of a number of other members of the JCE).

[112] See similarly, M Cupido, 'Pluralism in Theories of Liability: Joint Criminal Enterprise versus Joint Perpetration', in van Sliedregt and Vasiliev (n 8) 128, 136.

[113] See, similarly, *Brđanin* Appeal Judgment (n 109) (dec van den Wyngaert) [5]–[6].

[114] See, for example, van Sliedregt (n 1) 164–165; and C Farhang, 'Point of No Return: Joint Criminal Enterprise in *Brđanin*' (2010) 23 *Leiden Journal of International Law* 137, 156–157.

[115] *Brđanin* Appeal Judgment (n 109) (sep op Meron) [6].

delegating JCE member, whilst at the same time compelling a clearer and more precise identification of the link between JCE members and non-JCE members to the benefit of the historical record.[116] Notwithstanding the merits of this approach, it was expressly rejected by the Appeals Chamber in *Šainović*, leaving somewhat of a gap in the conceptual coherence of the leadership-level doctrine of JCE.[117]

2. The 'joint action' requirement

Turning to the horizontal relationship between leadership-level JCE members, the ad hoc tribunals recognised that the identification of a common purpose alone is not always sufficient to determine the existence of an enterprise because different and independent groups may share identical objectives merely by coincidence.[118] With this in mind, the ICTY Trial Chamber in *Krajišnik* emphasised the importance of demonstrating that JCE members 'act together, or in concert with each other, in the implementation of a common objective'.[119] According to the Trial Chamber, it was the identification of 'links forged in pursuit of a common objective' that transformed individuals into members of a criminal enterprise—their reliance on each other's contributions, as well as the acts of remote physical perpetrators used by them to commit crimes, enabling the achievement of criminal objectives on a scale that they could not otherwise have attained.[120]

Over time, this 'joint action' requirement emerged as the central doctrinal element for identifying the horizontal links that bound members of leadership-level JCEs together. In practice, the ad hoc tribunals relied on a range of factual circumstances to demonstrate that JCE members worked together at the leadership level in the implementation of a common objective.[121] On the basis of an extensive review of the relevant jurisprudence, Marjolein Cupido has divided these factual circumstances into three categories:[122] first, the nature of the crimes and the context in which they were committed; second, the relations and connections between participants in the JCE; and finally, the active and passive contributions of the JCE members in light of their knowledge of the violent context.

Significantly, for the purpose of assessing the joint action requirement, the ad hoc tribunals began to accord increasing importance to the role played by institutions, taking into account not only the *personal* relationships between individual JCE members, but also the *institutional* relationships between relevant political and military organisations.[123] In particular, considerable attention was devoted to the positions and roles that JCE members held within implicated political and military institutions as well as the lines of authority, communication, and control that existed both within and between such institutions.[124] This approach was complemented by a judicial tendency

[116] Ibid [7]. For a critique of Judge Meron's proposal, see Farhang (n 114) 159–161.
[117] *Šainović et al* Appeal Judgment (n 111) [1260]–[1263].
[118] *Prosecutor v Momčilo Krajišnik* (Judgment, Trial Chamber) IT-00-39-T (27 September 2006) ('*Krajišnik* Trial Judgment') [884].
[119] Ibid [884].
[120] Ibid [1082].
[121] See, for example, ibid [1081]–[1082].
[122] Cupido (n 112) 137–143.
[123] Ibid 140.
[124] Ibid 150.

to assess whether an accused had significantly contributed to the crimes charged by relying on an accused's *institutional* participation in furtherance of the common plan.[125] In *Krajišnik*, for example, the ICTY Trial Chamber found that the accused's significant contribution consisted of helping to establish and perpetuate the SDS party in Republika Srpska and State structures that were instrumental to the commission of crimes, as well as deploying his political skills both locally and internationally to facilitate the implementation of the common plan.[126] On appeal, the Appeals Chamber confirmed that 'the fact that it was not criminal to be involved in the setting up of SDS is irrelevant: ... the participation of an accused in the JCE need not involve the commission of a crime, what is important is that it furthers the execution of the common objective or purpose involving the commission of crimes'.[127]

From a narrative perspective, the joint action requirement focused greater attention on the collective dimensions of system criminality.[128] In terms of personal culpability, however, the assessment of the criminal responsibility of the accused in light of their position and participation in criminal institutions served to attenuate the link between the accused and the crimes for which they were charged.[129] This was particularly pronounced where the common plan was defined in especially broad terms that encompassed overarching political objectives,[130] as well as where the extended form of JCE was relied upon to attribute responsibility to leadership-level JCE members for crimes committed outside the common purpose.[131] In these types of situations, the link between JCE members and the crimes for which they were ultimately convicted was loosened to an extent that sometimes made it difficult to track the precise contours of their personal fault.[132]

3. Fluid JCEs

Beyond adopting an increasingly institutional perspective towards defining the vertical and horizontal links and relationships related to leadership-level JCEs, the ad hoc tribunals also accepted that common plans could be fluid in their criminal means. In *Krajišnik*, the ICTY Appeals Chamber found that 'the criminal means of realising the

[125] Ibid 156.

[126] *Krajišnik* Trial Judgment (n 118) [1120].

[127] *Prosecutor v Momčilo Krajišnik* (Judgment, Appeals Chamber) IT-00-39-A (17 March 2009) ('*Krajišnik* Appeal Judgment') [218].

[128] BI Bonafè, *The Relationship Between State and Individual Responsibility for International Crimes* (Brill 2009) 185.

[129] H van der Wilt, 'Joint Criminal Enterprise and Functional Perpetration', in Nollkaemper and van der Wilt (n 4) 158, 175.

[130] See, for example, *Šainović et al* Appeal Judgment (n 111) (diss op Tuzmukhamedov) [35]–[36] (arguing that the ICTY Trial Chamber had failed to explain how defendant Šainović, as a political co-ordinator, had made a significant contribution to the crimes for which he was convicted, beyond resorting to 'nebulous concepts of Šainović's authority at the time').

[131] See, for example, *Martić* Appeal Judgment (n 111) [183]–[187], [194]–[196], and [202]–[206] (finding the accused guilty pursuant to JCE III of a range of crimes including persecution as a crime against humanity and murder as a war crime and crime against humanity that occurred during the course of the implementation of the common plan to forcibly displace the non-Serb population).

[132] See, in this regard Cupido (n 112) 156–157 (suggesting that, in order for the doctrine of JCE to correspond more closely with the personal fault of JCE members in leadership-level cases, it would be preferable if JCE were relied upon to establish responsibility for participation in a criminal organisation, rather than as a tool for attributing criminal responsibility for the crimes *per se*).

common objective of the JCE can evolve over time'.[133] More specifically, the Appeals Chamber held that 'a JCE can come to embrace expanded criminal means, as long as the evidence shows that the JCE members agreed on this expansion of means'.[134]

In practice, the requirements to prove the existence of an expanded JCE were threefold:[135] first, it needed to be ascertained that leading members of the JCE were informed of the crimes; second, it needed to be determined that they did nothing to prevent their recurrence and persisted in the implementation of the expansion of the common objective; and finally, confirmation was required concerning when the expanded crimes became incorporated into the common objective. Importantly, it was not necessary to show that the JCE members expressly agreed to the expansion of criminal means; the agreement could materialise extemporaneously and be inferred from the circumstances.[136]

On the facts of *Krajišnik*, the Trial Chamber found that whereas in the early stages of the Bosnian-Serb campaign the common objective of the basic form JCE was discriminatory deportation and forced transfer, it soon evolved to encompass an expanded set of crimes including murders, extermination, and other forms of persecution.[137] On appeal, the Appeals Chamber quashed the defendant's conviction for the expanded crimes, concluding that the Trial Chamber had failed to specify when leading JCE members had become aware of the commission of the expanded crimes, at which particular point in time the expanded crimes had become part of the common crime, and whether the JCE members possessed the requisite intent with respect to them.[138]

From a narrative perspective, the recognition that a common objective could be 'fluid in its criminal means' reflected the reality that plans can evolve over time.[139] This was particularly important in leadership-level JCE cases where the implementation of the common plan could extend over a long period of time.[140] Nonetheless, in terms of the personal culpability of the accused, the notion of fluidity risked blurring the distinction between JCE I and JCE III.[141] In particular, uncertainty persisted over how to identify leading members of the JCE and whether the accused's contribution towards the expanded crimes also needed to be significant. In addition, the more broadly an expanded JCE was defined, the easier it would become to develop a case that additional crimes outside the expanded common plan occurred as a natural and foreseeable consequence of the fluid common plan.

4. Specific intent crimes and extended form JCEs

A further development in JCE doctrine concerned the application of extended form JCEs to specific intent crimes such as the crime of genocide and persecution as a crime against humanity. In *Brđanin*, the ICTY Appeals Chamber held that a JCE member

133 *Krajišnik* Appeal Judgment (n 127) [163].
134 Ibid.
135 Ibid [171].
136 Ibid [163].
137 *Krajišnik* Trial Judgment (n 118) [1095]–[1118].
138 *Krajišnik* Appeal Judgment (n 127) [172]–[178].
139 *Krajišnik* Trial Judgment (n 118) [1098].
140 van der Wilt (n 129) 174–175.
141 See similarly, Jain (n 17) 53–54; and van Sliedregt (n 1) 137.

may be held responsible for specific intent crimes that fell outside the common plan provided that it was reasonably foreseeable to the accused that such crimes would be committed with the requisite specific intent; significantly, however, the accused need not share the specific intent.[142] Despite significant criticism,[143] this position was consistently upheld in the jurisprudence of the ICTY and ICTR.[144]

The breadth of this position may be illustrated by the case of *Martić*, in which the ICTY Appeals Chamber confirmed the conviction of the accused for, *inter alia*, the crime of persecution as a crime against humanity in relation to killings perpetrated in Lipovača by Serb paramilitary forces with intent to discriminate on the basis of Croat ethnicity.[145] Even though this crime fell outside the common purpose, the accused was held criminally responsible for it on the basis that it was a natural and foreseeable consequence of the implementation of the common purpose of the JCE. In this regard, it bears emphasising that the Serb paramilitary forces who perpetrated the crime were only linked to the accused because they were acting in concert with the Yugoslav People's Army, which was found to be under the control of a number of other members of the JCE.[146] As such, the accused was held criminally responsible for the crime of persecution despite the crime not falling within the common purpose of the JCE, the perpetrators of the crime being non-JCE members whose only link to the JCE was acting in concert with forces controlled by other JCE members, and without the accused himself sharing the specific discriminatory intent of the crime.

From a narrative perspective, the application of JCE III to specific intent crimes reflected the notion that individuals operating within larger enterprises will often have different levels of knowledge and aspirations even if they have agreed to pursue a common objective.[147] In addition, the application of JCE III to sexual and gender-based crimes of specific intent has been welcomed by some commentators for capturing the reality of how such crimes unfold in mass atrocity contexts: in particular, rather than isolated and purely opportunistic crimes, JCE III has enabled judges to demonstrate how sexual and gender-based crimes, including those requiring specific intent, can be a foreseeable consequence of common plans to commit other crimes.[148]

In terms of personal culpability, however, it is questionable whether an accused should be held responsible as a principal perpetrator of a specific intent crime where he or she lacks specific intent. As several commentators have observed, such a position risks undermining the gravity and stigma of the crime in question.[149] Moreover, as

[142] *Prosecutor v Radoslav Brđanin* (Decision on Interlocutory Appeal, Appeals Chamber) IT-99-36-A (19 March 2004) [6] and [9].

[143] See, for example, Ambos (n 57) 176; Cassese et al (n 37) 172–173; and van Sliedregt (n 1) 139.

[144] See, for example, *Đorđević* Appeal Judgment (n 96) [73]–[84]; and *André Rwamakuba v The Prosecutor* (Decision on Interlocutory Appeal Regarding Application of Joint Criminal Enterprise to the Crime of Genocide, Appeals Chamber) ICTR-98-44-AR72.4 (22 October 2004) [31]. See, *contra*, *Prosecutor v Charles Ghankay Taylor* (Judgment, Trial Chamber) SCSL-03-01-T (18 May 2012) [468] ('The Trial Chamber ... finds that the Accused may not be held liable under the third form of JCE for specific intent crimes such as terrorism.')

[145] *Martić* Appeal Judgment (n 111) [194]–[196].

[146] Ibid [180] and [194]–[196].

[147] H van der Wilt, 'The Spider and the System', in T Waters (ed), *The Milošević Trial: An Autopsy* (OUP 2014) 484, 486.

[148] SaCouto, Sadat, and Sellers (n 97) 214 and 235.

[149] See, for example, Cassese et al (n 37) 172–173; van Sliedregt (n 1) 172; and *Šainović et al* Appeal Judgment (n 111) (partially diss op and dec Liu) [12]–[15].

Antonio Cassese argued, it is questionable whether specific intent crimes can ever be objectively foreseeable in the sense of being sufficiently 'connected to or in line with the agreed-upon offence of the foundational JCE I'.[150] For Cassese, the causal connection between the agreed-upon crime and the extended crime was 'too tenuous', such that to hold the accused responsible for the extended crime would be 'inconsistent with the principle of personal culpability'.[151] Instead, a secondary form of liability such as aiding and abetting would be more appropriate in such circumstances.[152]

5. Expanded common plan requirement

A final development in JCE doctrine took place solely in the context of cases at the Special Court for Sierra Leone (SCSL) where the Appeals Chamber expanded the definition of the common plan requirement beyond plans that necessarily amount to or involve the commission of crimes to encompass plans that merely 'contemplate' the commission of crimes.[153] According to this expanded definition, JCE members could be held criminally responsible for the commission of crimes pursuant to a basic form JCE where they shared a non-criminal objective, such as gaining and exercising political power over the territory of Sierra Leone, and each foresaw the possibility that crimes may be committed in achieving the objective. This broadening of the common plan requirement was problematic on at least two grounds.

First, the expanded definition of the common plan requirement blurred the distinction between the law on the use of force (*jus ad bellum*) and the law applicable in armed conflict (*jus in bello*). As Jordash and Martin explain, 'in a bloody civil war awash with crimes, the contemplation nexus—that is the thinking about or being aware of the commission of crimes—is automatically satisfied and impossible to disprove'.[154] In other words, given its potential to lead to all combatants of an armed force being held criminally responsible as soon as crimes being committed are merely contemplated, the expanded definition effectively criminalises the waging of armed conflicts.[155] In this vein, ICTY Judge Afanđe emphasised the importance of clearly distinguishing JCE liability from 'Joint Warfare Enterprise' liability, the latter encompassing a plurality of persons making contributions to a common plan with the intent to further not a criminal purpose, but rather 'a legal "warfare purpose" which is common to them'.[156]

Second, the expanded definition of the common plan requirement also blurred the distinction between basic and extended form JCEs, with the result of stretching the

[150] Cassese et al (n 37) 172–173.

[151] Ibid. See similarly, van Sliedregt (n 1) 173; and *Šainović et al* Appeal Judgment (n 111) (partially diss op and dec Liu) [17]–[18].

[152] Cassese et al (n 37) 172–173. See similarly, van Sliedregt (n 1) 172; and *Šainović et al* Appeal Judgment (n 111) (partially diss op and dec Liu) [19].

[153] *Prosecutor v Brima et al* (Judgment, Appeals Chamber) SCSL-04-16-A (22 February 2008) ('*Brima et al* Appeal Judgment') [80]; *Prosecutor v Sesay et al* (Judgment, Appeals Chamber) SCSL-04-15-A (26 October 2009) ('*Sesay et al* Appeal Judgment') [296].

[154] W Jordash and S Martin, 'How the Approach to JCE in *Taylor* and the RUF Case Undermined the Demands of Justice at the Special Court for Sierra Leone', in CC Jalloh (ed), *The Sierra Leone Special Court and its Legacy: The Impact for Africa and International Criminal Law* (CUP 2014) 96, 110–111.

[155] SM Meisenberg, 'Joint Criminal Enterprise at the Special Court for Sierra Leone', in Jalloh (n 154) 69, 89–91.

[156] *Prosecutor v Jovica Stanišić and Franko Simatović* (Judgment, Appeals Chamber) IT-03-69-A (9 December 2015) ('*Stanišić and Simatović* Appeal Judgment') (diss op Afanđe) [13].

limits of JCE III liability.[157] In *Sesay et al*, for example, the SCSL Appeals Chamber confirmed that Augustine Gbao was a participant in a JCE based on the fact that he shared the common plan to control parts of the territory of Sierra Leone and contemplated the commission of crimes.[158] By virtue of that conclusion, the Appeals Chamber found that Gbao was responsible for 'all crimes that he either intended, or were naturally foreseeable would be committed by members of the JCE or persons under their control'.[159] As Judge Fisher observed in her partially dissenting and concurring opinion, in reaching this conclusion the majority's reasoning was 'not only circular, but dangerous':[160] first, the Appeals Chamber failed to explain how Gbao was a 'participant' in the JCE despite lacking the shared intent for all the crimes falling within the common plan;[161] and second, by holding Gbao responsible for crimes within the common plan that he did not intend and that were only reasonably foreseeable to him, the Appeals Chamber collapsed the distinction between JCE I and JCE III.[162] As a result, Judge Fisher concluded that 'Gbao stands convicted of committing crimes which he did not intend, to which he did not significantly contribute, and which were not a reasonably foreseeable consequence of the crimes he did intend'.[163]

6. Conclusion

The doctrine of JCE has been described as a 'jack of all trades'.[164] In its small-scale form, JCE was utilised to represent the collaborative character of system criminality at the local level, identifying horizontal links between individuals involved in mob violence and systems of ill-treatment such as detention camps. In its leadership-level form, JCE morphed into a doctrine that sought to represent both the horizontal links that exist between high- and mid-ranking leaders of mass atrocity situations, together with their vertical links to remote physical perpetrators at the execution level. Establishing these links enabled the ad hoc tribunals to reflect the diversity of relationships forged between individuals implicated in system crimes,[165] as well as to portray the range of collective and institutional dynamics by which system crimes were carried out.[166]

Reflecting on the judicial development of JCE in leadership-level cases, the doctrine's evolution seems to have been driven primarily by a victim-oriented impulse to ensure that political and military leaders could be held criminally responsible as principal perpetrators for system crimes rather than as 'mere' aidors and abettors. Forging this path, however, raised concerns both in terms of the doctrine's basis in customary international law and its adherence to the principle of personal culpability.

In terms of *legality*, the ICTY Appeals Chamber in *Brđanin* based its loosening of the required factual link between leadership-level JCE members and the crimes committed by remote physical perpetrators on just two cases—the *Justice* case and the

[157] Jain (n 17) 67.
[158] *Sesay et al* Appeal Judgment (n 153) [486].
[159] Ibid [492].
[160] Ibid (partially diss and concurring op Fisher) [18].
[161] Ibid [18] and [24]–[25].
[162] Ibid [17] and [19].
[163] Ibid [45].
[164] van der Wilt (n 129) 160.
[165] Osiel (n 47) 56.
[166] Bonafè (n 128) 178–180.

RuSHA case. Seemingly aware of the thin support for its formulation of the vertical dimensions of leadership-level JCEs, the Appeals Chamber argued that these cases were relied upon as 'a valid source of *the contours* of joint criminal enterprise liability in customary international law'.[167] Yet, as several commentators have observed, excessive reliance on these two cases was both *inappropriate*, given that the indictments in these cases charged the accused as accessories as well as principals and the judgments failed to clearly distinguish between different modes of participation,[168] and *inadequate*, given that two cases hardly seem adequate to establish a basis in customary international law.[169] With this in mind, the establishment of a leadership-level JCE doctrine seems to offer a clear example of what Elies van Sliedregt has termed 'a result-oriented approach towards adjudication where judges redevelop and transform theories of liability to make them fit the facts and a certain (senior) class of defendants'.[170]

In terms of *culpability*, the ad hoc tribunals made important efforts to adhere to the principle of personal culpability by establishing a number of doctrinal safeguards within the leadership-level JCE doctrine, including the requirement to identify a sufficiently strong vertical link between at least one JCE member and the crimes of remote physical perpetrators, as well as the development of a horizontal 'joint action' requirement between JCE members. Nonetheless, two sets of culpability concerns with the JCE doctrine remained unresolved in the jurisprudence of the ad hoc tribunals.

First, JCE encompasses such a broad range of participation that concerns persisted over the doctrine's failure to sufficiently differentiate between different degrees of culpability in the attribution of criminal responsibility.[171] Jens Ohlin, for example, has argued that the breadth of the JCE doctrine came 'close in spirit to a unitary approach to perpetration whereby all members causally responsible for the crime were labelled as perpetrators, regardless of their level of participation'.[172] Lack of differentiation within the JCE doctrines included a failure to differentiate between: the different categories of the JCE doctrine, with the requirements for JCE II and especially JCE III being less stringent than JCE I and more akin to aiding and abetting but still resulting in a conviction for their members as principal perpetrators;[173] the different types of vertical relationships that may exist between JCE members and the crimes of remote physical perpetrators, ranging from merely ordering the commission of a crime to indirectly controlling the physical perpetrators through a hierarchical organisation; and the different degrees of contribution within a particular enterprise above the 'significant' contribution threshold, thereby passing over the internal deliberative structure of collective enterprises, which can be of relevance to the proper allocation of criminal blame.[174]

[167] *Brđanin* Appeal Judgment (n 109) [415] (emphasis added).
[168] Jain (n 17) 52; and Olásolo (n 29) 209–213 and 231.
[169] van Sliedregt (n 1) 163.
[170] van Sliedregt (n 24) 1186.
[171] See, for example, van Sliedregt (n 1) 142; and D Robinson, 'The Identity Crisis of International Criminal Law' (2008) 21 *Leiden Journal of International Law* 925, 940.
[172] Ohlin (n 20) 519.
[173] Jain (n 17) 209–210.
[174] JD Ohlin, 'Three Conceptual Problems with the Doctrine of Joint Criminal Enterprise' (2007) 5 *Journal of International Criminal Justice* 69, 85–88.

A common response to this first set of concerns has been to contend that further differentiation in the culpability of JCE members could be accounted for at the sentencing stage of proceedings. However, this response is inadequate for two reasons: first, an accused's sentence is calibrated according to a multitude of factors, the primary factor generally being the gravity of the crime, such that it may be difficult to ensure sentencing decisions are able to effectively respond to any excesses of the JCE doctrine;[175] and second, postponing a more precise calibration of an individual's culpability until the sentencing stage may not be able to compensate for the stigma of the criminal label pursuant to which JCE members were equally convicted.[176]

Beyond inadequate differentiation within the doctrine of JCE, a second set of concerns claimed that the link between leadership-level JCE members and the crimes for which they were held responsible was sometimes overly attenuated, especially in cases where: a common plan had been defined in particularly broad terms; a common plan had been identified that merely *involved* the commission of crimes rather than amounting to a crime itself; a common plan had been identified that merely *contemplated* the commission of crimes; or recourse had been made to the extended form of JCE. According to Harman van der Wilt, for example, the risk arose that the doctrine of JCE would 'degenerate into a smokescreen that obscures the possible frail connection between the accused and the specific crimes for which they stand trial'.[177] This risk manifested most clearly in the jurisprudence of the SCSL, in which the acceptance of common plans that merely contemplated the commission of crimes effectively transformed the doctrine of joint *criminal* enterprise into a doctrine of joint *warfare* enterprise,[178] blurring the boundary between international criminality and legitimate policy decisions that were accompanied by the mere foreseeable possibility of criminal activities.[179]

E. Perpetration at the ICC

The Statute of the International Criminal Court (ICC) includes an elaborate framework of modes of participation doctrines divided between Article 25, which provides for individual criminal responsibility, and Article 28, which concerns the responsibility of commanders and other superiors. This section focuses on Article 25(3), a provision that has been described as 'a consensus provision'[180] and 'a doctrinal compromise',[181] the outcome of intense negotiations between experts from different legal systems who had to work hard to understand each other's legal traditions.[182]

[175] Danner and Martinez (n 17) 141–142.

[176] M Damaška, 'What Is the Point of International Criminal Justice?' (2008) 83 *Chicago-Kent Law Review* 329, 353.

[177] H van der Wilt, 'Joint Criminal Enterprise: Possibilities and Limitations' (2007) 5 *Journal of International Criminal Justice* 91, 101.

[178] *Stanišić and Simatović* Appeal Judgment (n 156) (diss op Afanđe) [13].

[179] Damaška (n 176) 353.

[180] Sadat and Jolly (n 60) 775.

[181] Vest (n 44) 300.

[182] P Saland, 'International Criminal Law Principles', in RS Lee (ed), *The International Criminal Court: The Making of the Rome Statute: Issues, Negotiations, Results* (Kluwer 1999) 189, 198.

Article 25(3) doctrinally differentiates between a range of modes of participation doctrines. Moreover, although the wording of Article 25(3) suggests that it does not differentiate among participants in the attribution of responsibility—instead, specifying that any person who fulfils one of the modes 'shall be criminally responsible and liable for punishment *for a crime* within the jurisdiction of the Court'—in practice, the Court has referred to the mode of participation in the dispositions of its judgments.[183]

The jurisprudence of the ICC has also cemented the view that Article 25(3) distinguishes between liability as a perpetrator (where an individual is held criminally responsible for committing a crime under Article 25(3)(a)) and liability as an accessory (where an individual is held criminally responsible for contributing to the commission of a crime by another person or persons under Article 25(3)(b)–(d)).[184] According to the Appeals Chamber in *Lubanga*, this distinction is not merely terminological because '*generally speaking* and *all other things being equal*, a person who is found to commit a crime him- or herself bears more blameworthiness than a person who contributes to the crime of another person or persons'.[185] Although the notion that Article 25(3) elaborates a hierarchy of blameworthiness has proven controversial,[186] it is notable that the Appeals Chamber employed the phrases 'generally speaking' and 'all other things being equal', which suggests the recognition of only a *tentative* hierarchy.[187] As the Appeals Chamber subsequently clarified in *Bemba et al*, while the difference between committing a crime and contributing to the crime of others 'would *normally* reflect itself in a different degree of participation and/or intent', in practice 'this does *not* mean that the principal perpetrator of a crime/offence *necessarily* deserves a higher sentence than the accessory to that crime/offence', a determination that 'ultimately depends upon all the variable circumstances of each individual case'.[188]

To distinguish between principals and accessories, the ICC has consistently relied upon the 'control over the crime' theory.[189] According to this theory, principals are not limited to those who physically carry out the objective elements of the crime, but also include 'those who, in spite of being removed from the scene of the

[183] See, for example, *Prosecutor v Thomas Lubanga Dyilo* (Judgment Pursuant to Article 74 of the Statute, Trial Chamber) ICC-01/04-01/06-2842 (14 March 2012) ('*Lubanga* Trial Judgment') [1358] (finding the accused guilty 'within the meaning of Articles 8(2)(e)(vii) and 25(3)(a) of the Statute'); and *Prosecutor v Germain Katanga* (Judgment Pursuant to Article 74 of the Statute, Trial Chamber) ICC-01/04-01/07 (7 March 2014) ('*Katanga* Trial Judgment') Disposition (finding the accused guilty 'under article 25(3)(d) of the Statute, as an accessory to the crimes committed on 24 February 2003').

[184] *Prosecutor v Thomas Lubanga Dyilo* (Judgment on the Appeal of Mr Thomas Lubanga Dyilo Against his Conviction, Appeals Chamber) ICC-01/04-01/06-3121-Red (1 December 2014) ('*Lubanga* Appeal Judgment') [462].

[185] Ibid [462] (emphasis added).

[186] For critique and opposing views, see, for example, *Katanga* Trial Judgment (n 183) [1384]–[1387]; *Lubanga* Trial Judgment (n 183) (sep op Fulford) [6]–[9]; *Prosecutor v Mathieu Ngudjolo Chui* (Judgment, Trial Chamber) ICC-01/04-02/12-3-tENG (18 December 2012) ('*Ngudjolo* Trial Judgment') (concurring op Van den Wyngaert) [22]–[30]; M Aksenova, 'The Modes of Liability at the ICC: The Labels that Don't Always Stick' (2015) 15 *International Criminal Law Review* 629, 653–663; and van Sliedregt (n 1) 85–86.

[187] See generally, Vest (n 44) 301–309.

[188] *Prosecutor v Jean-Pierre Bemba Gombo et al* (Judgment on the Appeals of the Prosecutor, Mr Jean-Pierre Gombo, Mr Fidèle Babala Wandu and Mr Narcisse Arido against the Decision of Trial Chamber VII entitled 'Decision on Sentence pursuant to Article 76 of the Statute', Appeals Chamber) ICC-01/05-01/13-2276-Red (8 March 2018) [60].

[189] *Lubanga* Appeal Judgment (n 184) [469].

crime, control or mastermind its commission because they decide whether and how the offence will be committed'.[190] The judicial recognition of the control theory has been based primarily on a systematic interpretation of the ICC Statute, entailing an examination of the interaction between the different modes of participation set out in Article 25(3) and their distinctive characteristics.[191] The control theory has not, however, found favour with all judges and commentators.[192] In fact, as Sadat and Jolly explain, Article 25(3) has become somewhat akin to 'a legal Rorschach blot, taking on a different meaning depending upon the underlying legal training, tradition, and even policy-orientation of those seeking to interpret it'.[193] This conclusion is supported by the movement of the ICC's jurisprudence away from attempting to demonstrate that the control theory is widely recognised in domestic legal systems towards a more open acknowledgement that the judges have been guided by only a narrow selection of domestic systems as part of what appears to be an effort to develop an ICC-specific *Dogmatik*, 'an attempt to reason from first principles the nature of co-perpetration and collective action in the context of atrocity'.[194] In *Lubanga*, for example, the Appeals Chamber explained that by applying the control theory it was 'not proposing to apply a particular legal doctrine or theory *as a source of law*', but rather seeking guidance from approaches developed in particular domestic jurisdictions 'in order to reach a coherent and persuasive interpretation of the Court's legal texts'.[195]

In practice, the judicial acceptance of the control theory has had significant implications for the scope and content of the historical narratives constructed by the ICC, in particular resulting in a prosecutorial preference for charging individuals with forms of principal liability under Article 25(3)(a) in an effort to portray their centrality to the commission of the crimes under examination.[196] Against this background, this section examines two forms of principal liability—direct co-perpetration and indirect co-perpetration—that have proven particularly salient within the existing jurisprudence of the ICC.

[190] *Prosecutor v Thomas Lubanga Dyilo* (Decision on the Confirmation of Charges, Pre-Trial Chamber) ICC-01/04-01/06-803-tEN (29 January 2007) ('*Lubanga* DCC') [330].

[191] See, for example, *Lubanga* Appeal Judgment (n 184) [462]–[463]. See also, van Sliedregt (n 1) 86 (concluding that the concept of 'control of the crime' was incorporated into Article 25(3)(a) '*by exclusion* of other theories of liability') (emphasis in original).

[192] See, for example, *Lubanga* Trial Judgment (n 183) (sep op Fulford); *Ngudjolo* Trial Judgment (n 186) (concurring op Van den Wyngaert); L Yanev and T Kooijmans, 'Divided Minds in the *Lubanga* Trial Judgment: A Case Against the Joint Control Theory' (2013) 13 *International Criminal Law Review* 789; and Sadat and Jolly (n 60).

[193] Sadat and Jolly (n 60) 756 (referring to the psychological 'Rorschach inkblot test' in which individuals are given a series of cards containing inkblots and asked what they see on each card, the theory being that each person will impose their own meaning on the images, thereby revealing a character trait or something about their thoughts).

[194] Ohlin (n 20) 525.

[195] *Lubanga* Appeal Judgment (n 184) [470] (emphasis added). See also, *Katanga* Trial Judgment (n 183) [1395].

[196] See, for example, Women's Initiative for Gender Justice, 'A Review of the International Criminal Court's Current Jurisprudence and Practice: Modes of Liability' *Expert Paper* (November 2013) 30 (noting that, as of November 2013, '75% of the individuals indicted by the ICC have been charged and/or confirmed pursuant to one of the modes of liability set forth in Article 25(3)(a)').

1. Direct co-perpetration

Direct co-perpetration is well established in the jurisprudence of the ICC. As the Pre-Trial Chamber in *Lubanga* has explained, the concept of co-perpetration is originally rooted in the idea that 'when the sum of co-ordinated individual contributions of a plurality of persons results in the realisation of all the objective elements of a crime, any person making a contribution can be held vicariously responsible for the contributions of all the others and, as a result, can be considered as a principal to the whole crime'.[197] In accordance with the control theory that has been held to underpin Article 25(3)(a), the ICC has confirmed that direct co-perpetration encompasses five elements:[198] (i) an agreement or common plan existed between the accused and one or more persons; (ii) coordinated essential contributions by each co-perpetrator resulting in the realisation of the objective elements of the crime; (iii) the accused possessed the requisite mental element of the crime in question; (iv) the accused and the other co-perpetrators were mutually aware and mutually accepted that implementing the common plan will result in the commission of the crime; and (v) the accused was aware of the factual circumstances enabling him or her to jointly control the crime. In practice, two elements have proven particularly important in determining the scope of direct co-perpetration and its role in shaping the scope and content of narratives that may be constructed through recourse to the doctrine: the common plan requirement; and the essential contribution requirement.

a. The common plan requirement

Co-perpetration is premised on the existence of an agreement or common plan between two or more persons. It is the common plan that 'ties the co-perpetrators together and ... justifies the reciprocal imputation of their respective acts'.[199] Within its jurisprudence, the ICC has confirmed that while the common plan does not need to be specifically directed at the commission of a crime, it must include 'a critical element of criminality'.[200] Contestation has arisen, however, over what this means in practice.

According to the Pre-Trial Chamber in *Lubanga*, for example, it sufficed to demonstrate that the co-perpetrators had agreed to start the implementation of the common plan to achieve a non-criminal goal and to only commit the crime if certain conditions were satisfied, *or* that the co-perpetrators were aware of the risk that implementing the common plan to achieve a non-criminal goal will result in the commission of the crime and accept such an outcome.[201] This finding appeared to endorse a *dolus eventualis* standard regarding the criminality of the common plan, pursuant to which it would be sufficient for there to exist a risk that crimes will occur during the execution of a non-criminal plan.[202] This conclusion was complemented by the Pre-Trial Chamber's

197 *Lubanga* DCC (n 190) [326].

198 See generally, ibid [342]–[367]; *Lubanga* Appeal Judgment (n 184) [434]–[455].

199 *Lubanga* Appeal Judgment (n 184) [445]. See similarly, *Lubanga* Trial Judgment (n 183) [981]. See also, P Bradfield, 'Alternative Charges and Modes of Liability in the Latest CAR Case at the ICC—Trouble Ahead?' *EJIL: Talk!* (21 January 2020) (discussing the paucity of the Pre-Trial Chamber's decision on the confirmation of charges against Alfred Yekatom and Patrice Ngaïsonna, in particular its failure to engage with the 'common plan' requirement).

200 *Lubanga* Appeal Judgment (n 184) [451].

201 *Lubanga* DCC (n 190) [344].

202 Ohlin (n 20) 536.

findings with regard to the mutual awareness and acceptance requirement, with respect to which the judges distinguished between two scenarios:[203] first, if there was a *substantial* risk of bringing about the crime, namely if it was likely that 'it will occur in the ordinary course of events', the mutual acceptance by the co-perpetrators could be inferred from their awareness of 'the substantial likelihood' that implementing the common plan would result in the commission of the crime and the decision by the co-perpetrators to implement the plan despite such awareness; and second, if there was merely a *low* risk of bringing about the crime, the co-perpetrators must have 'clearly or expressly' accepted the idea that implementing the common plan would result in the commission of the crime. Here again, the Pre-Trial Chamber seemed to endorse a *dolus eventualis* standard, encompassing situations where the accused 'does not purposely or knowingly produce the result, though he is aware of the possibility that the result will occur'.[204]

Taken together, the standards elaborated by the Pre-Trial Chamber had the effect of considerably expanding the scope of behaviour deemed to fall within the concept of co-perpetration. According to Kai Ambos, for example, these standards allowed for the possibility of predominantly non-criminal plans, which was problematic since if the common plan does not contain 'a more or less concrete crime' then 'there is nothing (agreed) which could be mutually attributed'.[205] In other words, by loosening the link between the common plan and the crimes charged, the foundation for mutual attribution between co-perpetrators was undermined. The result was similar to the expanded definition of the common plan requirement recognised by the SCSL with respect to the doctrine of JCE, which encompassed crimes merely contemplated by JCE members.

In light of these concerns, the Appeals Chamber in *Lubanga* subsequently clarified that the 'critical element of criminality' requirement should be understood more restrictively to mean that 'it was *virtually certain* that the implementation of the common plan led to the commission of the crimes at issue'.[206] While the 'virtually certain' standard arguably remains lower than that utilised by the ICTY and ICTR in the context of the basic form of JCE, it would appear to be sufficiently high to meet the concern that there must be a more or less concrete crime that can be considered as an agreed part of the common plan. Moreover, although concerns have been raised that the 'virtually certain' standard may be too restrictive to reflect the way sexual violence crimes tend to unfold in mass atrocity situations,[207] the Trial Chamber in *Ntaganda* recently demonstrated how a careful examination of the circumstances prevailing at a particular moment in time in a specific locality can lead to the conclusion that crimes of rape and sexual slavery—in that instance, those against children under the age of 15 within an armed group—were not simply a risk that the (indirect) co-perpetrators accepted, but crimes that were virtually certain.[208]

[203] *Lubanga* DCC (n 190) [363]–[364].
[204] Ohlin (n 20) 533.
[205] Ambos (n 57) 152.
[206] *Lubanga* Appeal Judgment (n 184) [451] (emphasis added).
[207] See, for example, SaCouto, Sadat, and Sellers (n 97) 239, fn 263.
[208] *Prosecutor v Bosco Ntaganda* (Judgment, ICC Trial Chamber) ICC-01/04-02/06-2359 (8 July 2019) ('*Ntaganda* Trial Judgment') [787]–[797] and [811].

b. The essential contribution requirement

Beyond the common plan requirement, contestation has also arisen over the definition of 'essential contribution'. In *Lubanga*, the Pre-Trial Chamber explained that when the objective elements of an offence are carried out by a plurality of persons acting within the framework of a common plan, 'only those to whom *essential* tasks have been assigned—and who, consequently have the power to frustrate the commission of the crime by not performing their tasks—can be said to have joint control over the crime'.[209] In its judgment in *Lubanga*, the Trial Chamber explained that according to this approach, '[n]one of the participants exercises, individually, control over the crime as a whole but, instead, the control over the crime falls in the hands of a collective as such'.[210] In other words, the essential contribution requirement requires a form of *negative* control over the crime, according to which each co-perpetrator cannot determine whether the crime *will* be committed but only whether it will *not*.[211]

By defining the essential contribution requirement in negative terms, the ICC has had to engage in hypothetical evaluations, ones in which the Court is required to posit 'the existence of an alternate world, without the defendant's contribution, and assess how the criminal plan would have progressed in his absence'.[212] Engaging in this kind of counterfactual analysis has been criticised by scholars and judges alike.[213] According to Judge Fulford, for example, 'an *ex post facto* assessment as to whether an individual made an essential contribution ... will often be unrealistic and artificial' since it will 'largely be a matter of guesswork as to the real consequence for the particular crime if the accused is (hypothetically) removed from the equation'.[214] Similarly, Judge van den Wyngaert has expressed concern that the essential contribution requirement 'compels Chambers to engage in artificial, speculative exercises about whether a crime would still have been committed if one of the accused had not made exactly the same contribution'.[215]

Although these critiques would suggest that the essential contribution requirement is difficult to apply, in practice the requirement has arguably facilitated an expansive understanding of co-perpetration.

First, to satisfy the essential contribution requirement, the ICC has confirmed that the prosecution does not need to demonstrate that the accused physically perpetrated any of the elements of the crimes or that the accused was present at the crime scene.[216] In other words, the essential character of an accused's contribution is not restricted to its performance at the execution stage of the crime, but can also be made at its planning or preparation stage, including when the common plan was conceived.[217] According to the Trial Chamber in *Lubanga*, for example, it is 'unnecessary for the prosecution to establish a *direct* or *physical* link between the

[209] *Lubanga* DCC (n 190) [347] (emphasis added).
[210] *Lubanga* Trial Judgment (n 183) [994].
[211] Yanev and Kooijmans (n 192) 795–796.
[212] Ohlin (n 20) 528–529.
[213] See, for example, ibid 529 (arguing that the essential contribution requirement 'demands a trans-modal definition of the crime that crosses possible worlds').
[214] *Lubanga* Trial Judgment (n 183) (sep op Fulford) [17].
[215] *Ngudjolo* Trial Judgment (n 186) (concurring op Van den Wyngaert) [42].
[216] *Lubanga* Appeal Judgment (n 184) [466].
[217] Ibid [465] and [469].

accused's contribution and the commission of the crime';[218] rather, it is sufficient for a co-perpetrator to 'assist in formulating the relevant strategy or plan, become involved in directing or controlling other participants or determine the roles of those involved in the offence'.[219] Yet, as Ohlin, van Sliedregt, and Weigend observe, if all these preparatory contributions, which may be remote in time and place from the commission of the crime, are deemed 'essential' and therefore sufficient to establish perpetratorship, 'then one must ask what remains for mere accessorial liability as an instigator or an aider and abettor'.[220]

Second, the negative framing of the essential contribution has sometimes led the Court to infer the essentiality of an accused's contribution from a range of indicators concerning the accused's position in a hierarchy and his dereliction of duties inherent in that position.[221] In other words, the Court has sometimes applied a standard of 'control through potential prevention'—a standard that is not only difficult to reconcile with the active imagery associated with individuals who 'commit' crimes,[222] but also casts the net of perpetrator liability extremely broadly by inferring the essentiality of an accused's contribution primarily from his high-ranking position in an organisational hierarchy.[223] With this in mind, some scholars have suggested that the ICC may benefit from examining a broader cluster of factors, including both subjective and objective elements, as a means of ensuring that an accused played a sufficiently 'central' role in the commission of a crime to warrant the label 'co-perpetrator'.[224]

Finally, in its initial jurisprudence, the ICC characterised the link between the essential contribution requirement and the crime for which an accused had been charged in relatively weak terms. According to the Pre-Trial Chamber in *Lubanga*, for example, in order to establish joint control over a crime, it was sufficient to demonstrate that the accused had an 'essential overall co-ordinating role which ... gave him the power to frustrate the implementation of *the plan* if he refused to play his part'.[225] By focusing on an accused's essential contribution to the common plan, the Pre-Trial Chamber loosened the link between the charged crime and the contribution of the accused. As Judge van den Wyngaert subsequently explained in her concurring opinion in *Ngudjolo*, 'the focus of attention has shifted away from how the conduct of the accused is related to the commission of a *crime* to what role he/she played in the execution of the common *plan*'. This is problematic where the mental element is linked to a contribution towards a broadly defined common plan because 'the connection to

218 *Lubanga* Trial Judgment (n 183) [1004] (emphasis in original).

219 Ibid [1004]. See also, *Prosecutor v Germain Katanga and Mathieu Ngudjolo Chui* (Decision on Confirmation of Charges, Pre-Trial Chamber) ICC-01/04-01/07-717 (30 September 2008) ('*Katanga and Ngudjolo* DCC') [526].

220 JD Ohlin et al, 'Assessing the Control Theory' (2013) 26 *Leiden Journal of International Law* (2013) 725, 732.

221 A Gil Gil and E Maculan, 'Current Trends in the Definition of "Perpetrator" by the International Criminal Court: From the Decision on the Confirmation of Charges in the *Lubanga* case to the *Katanga* Judgment' (2015) 28 *Leiden Journal of International Law* 349, 357.

222 T Weigend, 'Intent, Mistake of Law, and Co-Perpetration in the *Lubanga* Decision on Confirmation of Charges' (2008) 6 *Journal of International Criminal Justice* 471, 487.

223 Gil Gil and Maculan (n 221) 357.

224 See generally, Ohlin et al (n 220) 730–734.

225 *Lubanga* DCC (n 190) 398 (emphasis added).

the crime might be almost entirely lost' and 'we come dangerously close to treating the mode of responsibility as a crime in itself'.[226]

Given this concern, it is notable that the Appeals Chamber in *Lubanga* subsequently clarified that the common plan serves merely as a framework by which to assess whether the accused made 'an essential contribution with the resulting power to frustrate *the commission of the crime*'.[227] According to the Appeals Chamber, 'what is required is a normative assessment of the role of the accused person in the specific circumstances of the case … [entailing] an evaluation of whether the accused had control over the crime, *by virtue of his or her essential contribution to it* [i.e. the crime] and the resulting power to frustrate its commission'.[228] In this way, the Appeal Chamber re-established the link between the essential contribution of the accused and the crimes charged.[229]

2. Indirect co-perpetration

Beyond direct co-perpetration, Article 25(3)(a) also refers to the commission of a crime 'through another person, regardless of whether that other person is criminally responsible'. By these terms, the ICC Statute incorporates the doctrine of indirect perpetration, a mode of participation described by the Pre-Trial Chamber in *Lubanga* as 'the most typical manifestation of the concept of control over the crime'.[230]

Indirect perpetration encompasses two scenarios:[231] first, cases in which an individual commits a crime through innocent agents, who are not considered to be culpable for their actions; and second, cases in which an individual commits a crime through culpable agents, thereby giving rise to a form of parallel liability at both the leadership and execution levels. The latter scenario is reminiscent of the German law concept of the '*Hintermann*' (or 'man in the background'), encompassing situations where the mastermind of an operation who controls the will of those who directly commit a crime is characterised as the principal rather than an accessory.[232]

In *Katanga*, the Trial Chamber identified three elements that must be satisfied to hold an individual criminally responsible as an indirect perpetrator:[233] (i) the accused exerted control over the crime whose material elements were brought about by one or more persons; (ii) the accused fulfilled the mental elements prescribed by Article 30 of the ICC Statute and the mental elements specific to the crime at issue; and (iii) the accused was aware of the factual circumstances which allowed him or her to exert control over the crime. Although control over the crime may take various forms, the Trial Chamber emphasised that the most common means by which such control tends to be exerted in mass atrocity contexts is 'control over an organisation' (*Organisationsh errschaft*).[234] In order to demonstrate an individual's control over an organisation, two

226 *Ngudjolo* Trial Judgment (n 186) (concurring op Van den Wyngaert) [34]–[35].
227 *Lubanga* Appeal Judgment (n 184) [469] (emphasis added).
228 Ibid [473] (emphasis added).
229 See similarly, Aksenova (n 186) 637.
230 *Lubanga* DCC (n 190) [339].
231 *Katanga* Trial Judgment (n 183) [1398].
232 Ambos (n 57) 154.
233 *Katanga* Trial Judgment (n 183) [1399]–[1400] and [1416].
234 Ibid [1401] and [1403].

criteria must be examined:[235] the first concerns the nature of the organisation; and the second concerns the control exerted by the accused over the organisation.

With respect to the first criterion, the organisation must be based on hierarchical relations between superiors and subordinates and composed of sufficient subordinates to guarantee their 'functional automatism' such that 'the superior knows that if a member of the organisation refuses to comply, another will usually be available to step in and somehow ensure the execution of the orders issued'.[236] It is this key feature of the organisation that ensures the superior's control over the crime, the 'mechanisation' of the organisation ensuring that the execution of a crime will not be compromised by any particular subordinate's failure to comply with an order.[237] As the Trial Chamber in *Katanga* explained, '[c]ontrol over the crime ensues, therefore, from the nature of the organisation and its structural dynamics ... [which] operates autonomously'.[238] Automatic compliance with the superior's orders may be guaranteed by the replaceability or interchangeability of potential physical perpetrators who are members of the organisation.[239] From this perspective, the membership of the organisation constitutes 'a mere gear in a giant machine' that the leader's control over the apparatus enables him to utilise to produce the criminal result automatically.[240]

With respect to the second criterion, the liability of an indirect perpetrator rests on his exertion of 'control and genuine authority over the organisation'.[241] This means that the indirect perpetrator must have used at least part of the apparatus of power in such a way as 'to steer it intentionally towards the commission of a crime, without leaving one of the subordinates at liberty to decide whether the crime is to be executed'.[242]

Taking these criteria together, the Trial Chamber in *Katanga* emphasised that they serve to ensure that individuals wielding control over the apparatus of power are 'unquestionably those in the organisation who conceived the crime, oversaw its preparation at different hierarchical levels, and controlled its performance and execution'.[243] In other words, only those who control 'effectively and undisturbed' at least part of an apparatus of power can be held criminally responsible as indirect perpetrators.[244] It is in this sense that an indirect perpetrator does not merely order the commission of a crime, 'but through his control over the organisation, essentially decides whether and how the crime would be committed'.[245]

Within the jurisprudence of the ICC, indirect perpetration has also been combined with co-perpetration to form 'indirect co-perpetration'. The ICC has supported this combination based on a textual interpretation of the ICC Statute, in particular by arguing that the 'or' in the phrase 'jointly with another, or through another person' in

235 Ibid [1407].
236 Ibid [1408].
237 *Katanga and Ngudjolo* DCC (n 219) [516].
238 *Katanga* Trial Judgment (n 183) [1409].
239 Ibid [1408].
240 *Katanga and Ngudjolo* DCC (n 219) [515].
241 *Katanga* Trial Judgment (n 183) [1411].
242 Ibid.
243 Ibid [1412].
244 Ibid.
245 *Katanga and Ngudjolo* DCC (n 219) [518].

Article 25(3)(a) amounts to an 'inclusive disjunctive', understood to mean 'either one or the other, and possibly both'.[246]

In *Blé Goudé*, the Pre-Trial Chamber explained how indirect co-perpetration:

> combines the commission of a crime 'jointly with another' (in which each of a plurality of persons has the capacity to frustrate the commission of the crime in the way it is realised by not performing his or her coordinated contributive acts within the framework of an agreement among them) with the commission of a crime 'through another person' (in which a person commits the crime by subjugating another person's will, rather than personally and directly executing the objective elements of the crime).[247]

In practice, two different forms of indirect co-perpetration have been recognised within the jurisprudence of the ICC: first, cases of co-perpetration through a single organisational apparatus of power jointly controlled by the accused; and second, cases of co-perpetration through multiple vertical organisations, each of which are under the control of separate accused.

The first factual scenario was confronted by the ICC in the case of *Muthaura et al*, in which the Pre-Trial Chamber concluded that Mr Muthaura and Mr Kenyatta had gained control over a hierarchically structured organisation, referred to as the Mungiki, for the time and for the purposes of committing crimes in or around Nakuru and Naivasha.[248] In other words, this case concerned what some have referred to as the 'junta model' of indirect co-perpetration whereby the accused were alleged to have joint control over a single organisation.[249]

The second factual scenario was examined by the ICC in *Katanga and Ngudjolo*, in which a Pre-Trial Chamber concluded that there were substantial grounds to believe that Mr Katanga had control over a hierarchically organised group called the FRPI and Mr Ngudjolo Chui had control over a hierarchically organised group called the FNI organisation.[250] The Pre-Trial Chamber also found that there were substantial grounds to believe that the two accused had agreed on a common plan to 'wipe out' Bogoro by directing an attack against the civilian population, killing and murdering the predominantly Hema population and destroying their properties.[251]

A key feature of the *Katanga and Ngudjolo* case was that, due to ethnic loyalties, members of each organisation distrusted each other and would only accept orders

[246] Ibid [491]. See similarly, *Prosecutor v Ruto et al* (Decision on the Confirmation of Charges Pursuant to Article 61(7)(a) and (b) of the Rome Statute, Pre-Trial Chamber) ICC-01/09-01/11-373 (23 January 2012) ('*Ruto et al* DCC') [315]; and *Prosecutor v Laurent Gbagbo* (Decision on the Confirmation of Charges Against Laurent Gbagbo, Pre-Trial Chamber) ICC-02/11-01/11 (12 June 2014) [233]–[234].

[247] *Prosecutor v Dominic Ongwen* (Decision on the Confirmation of Charges Against Dominic Ongwen, Pre-Trial Chamber) ICC-02/04-01/15-422-Red (23 March 2016) ('*Ongwen* DCC') [39].

[248] *Prosecutor v Muthaura et al* (Decision on the Confirmation of Charges Pursuant to Article 61(7)(a) and (b) of the Rome Statute, Pre-Trial Chamber) ICC-01/09-02/11 (23 January 2012) ('*Muthaura et al* DCC') [408]. See also, *Ntaganda* Trial Judgment (n 208) [772].

[249] Ohlin et al (n 220) 736.

[250] *Katanga and Ngudjolo* DCC (n 219) [540]–[547].

[251] Ibid [548]–[549]. The Pre-Trial Chamber also found substantial grounds to believe that the pillaging of Bogoro village and, by majority, the rape and sexual slavery of civilian women would inevitably result from the implementation of the plan. Ibid [550]–[551].

from leaders sharing their own ethnicity; in other words, the FRPI soldiers would only obey orders issued by FRPI commanders and, similarly, FNI soldiers would only obey orders issued by FNI commanders.[252] Based on evidence concerning the coordination and participation of the two accused in the implementation of the common plan, as well as their status as the highest commanders of the Ngiti and Lendu combatants, respectively, the Pre-Trial Chamber concluded that there were substantial grounds to believe that the two accused 'had joint control over the implementation of the plan, insofar as their essential overall coordinating roles gave to them, and only to them, the power to frustrate the implementation of the plan'.[253] In other words, the Pre-Trial Chamber found that 'without [the accused's] agreement on the common plan and their participation in its implementation, the crimes would not have been committed as planned'.[254] Although these findings were not ultimately upheld at trial, the case serves as a useful illustration of the second variant of indirect co-perpetration.

From a narrative perspective, indirect co-perpetration seeks to represent complex forms of collective violence, enabling the attribution of criminal responsibility to accused individuals who are remote from the physical perpetrators of the crimes along both horizontal and vertical axes.[255] In addition, indirect co-perpetration by means of an organisation seeks to represent both the reduced autonomy of direct perpetrators in institutional contexts within mass atrocity situations as well as the heightened agency of those in higher-ranking positions who are able to steer organisational apparatuses towards criminal ends.[256] By focusing on the institutional aspects of mass atrocity situations, indirect co-perpetration by means of an organisation also facilitates judicial consideration of the collective dimensions of system criminality.[257] In practice, however, the doctrine has raised a number of concerns.

First, concerns have been raised about the legal basis of the doctrine of indirect co-perpetration by means of an organisation. Judge van den Wyngaert, for example, has queried how commission 'through another *person*' could be read to mean through an *organisation*, particularly as there is no evidence that the drafters of the ICC Statute intended such a meaning.[258] Judge van den Wyngaert has been similarly unconvinced by the argument that co-perpetration and indirect perpetration could be combined by virtue of interpreting the 'or' in the phrase 'jointly with another, or through another person' in Article 25(3)(a) as an 'inclusive disjunctive', a concept she found 'totally foreign to ordinary language . . . and confusing'.[259] While Judge van den Wyngaert was not opposed to the junta model of indirect co-perpetration.[260] such a scenario was to be contrasted with that confronted in the case of *Katanga and Ngudjolo* where the two accused each allegedly had control over separate sets of subordinates and agreed to join forces to carry out a criminal action. According to Judge van den Wyngaert,

[252] Ibid [493], [519], and [560].
[253] Ibid [561].
[254] Ibid [560].
[255] Ohlin et al (n 220) 735.
[256] Ambos (n 57) 157 and 159.
[257] van der Wilt (n 129) 179.
[258] *Ngudjolo* Trial Judgment (n 186) (concurring op Van den Wyngaert) [52] and [57].
[259] Ibid [60] and fn 76.
[260] Ibid [62]. See similarly, van Sliedregt (n 51) 510.

to convict the accused pursuant to indirect co-perpetration under this latter scenario would constitute 'a radical expansion' of Article 25(3)(a) amounting to 'a totally new mode of liability', one which makes it possible to hold the accused responsible for the conduct of the physical perpetrator of a crime 'even though he/she neither exercised any direct influence or authority over this person, nor shared any intent with him or her'.[261]

Perhaps in light of some of these concerns, the Trial Chamber in *Katanga* emphasised that perpetration by means of an organisation was not 'an essential constituent element of commission by an intermediary', but merely one means by which control over a crime committed through another person could be established.[262] According to this approach, the organisation merely represents the 'through' element, connecting the indirect perpetrator with the physical perpetrator.[263] As regards the concerns raised by Judge van den Wyngaert regarding the combination of co-perpetration and indirect perpetration, if it is accepted that it is the common plan between the leaders that is central to their joint responsibility, there would appear to be no reason to limit the form that each co-perpetrator's contribution to such a plan may take. As Thomas Weigend explains, 'a common plan can take many forms, and one of them is bringing together the human agents each co-perpetrator has under his control'.[264]

Second, concerns have arisen regarding the rigidity of the doctrine of indirect co-perpetration by means of an organisation. In particular, since the theory of control over an organisation was originally designed with highly structured and hierarchical bureaucratic dictatorships in mind, it has been suggested that the concept may be insufficiently flexible to accommodate some of the more complex and decentralised organisational forms by which system crimes are carried out in modern conflicts.[265] Mark Osiel, for example, suggests that tightly structured and hierarchical organisational apparatuses of power rarely constitute the medium of modern-day mass atrocities, which tend to be characterised by more informal networks of power in which the lower echelons have room to act spontaneously and commit crimes of opportunity in response to a climate of permissibility.[266] Moreover, in many mass atrocity contexts, it may be difficult to demonstrate that the physical perpetrators were fungible. In smaller organisations, for example, there may be insufficient numbers of subordinates to demonstrate their automatic replaceability. As such, the fungibility of physical perpetrators may not be the most pertinent form of control within modern settings of collective violence.[267]

In *Katanga*, for example, the Trial Chamber relied upon a relatively restrictive understanding of perpetration by means of an organisation—emphasising, in particular, the need to demonstrate the existence of 'an organised and hierarchical apparatus of power, characterised by near-automatic obedience to the orders it hands down' and

[261] *Ngudjolo* Trial Judgment (n 186) (concurring op Van den Wyngaert) [61].
[262] *Katanga* Trial Judgment (n 183) [1406].
[263] See similarly, T Weigend, 'Indirect Perpetration', in Stahn (n 20) 538, 551; and Ohlin et al (n 220) 738.
[264] Weigend (n 263) 555. See similarly, Olásolo (n 29) 329–330.
[265] See, for example, van Sliedregt (n 51) 514 (arguing that the Pre-Trial Chamber in *Katanga and Ngudjolo* was 'blinded by the beauty of *Dogmatik* and lost sight of the African reality').
[266] Osiel (n 47) 99–104. See similarly, Jain (n 17) 194.
[267] Osiel (n 47) 101–102.

requiring that the accused wielding control over the apparatus of power must have 'conceived the crime, oversaw its preparation at different hierarchical levels, and controlled its performance and execution'.[268] On the facts of the case, the Trial Chamber found that although the Ngiti combatants of Walendu-Bindi *collectivité* were organised in a single militia which constituted an organisation for the purposes of crimes against humanity under Article 7(2) of the ICC Statute, the evidence was insufficient either to determine the precise nature of the subordinate-superior relationships between commanders of different camps of the militia and their men, or to establish a centralised command within the militia that would have enabled it to conclude that the Ngiti militia constituted an organised apparatus of power.[269] In addition, the evidence did not support the conclusion that the accused wielded sufficient control over the militia: apart from the accused's powers to receive, store, and distribute weapons and ammunition, it was not proven that he was able to issue and ensure execution of orders or to impose disciplinary sanctions against commanders.[270]

The conclusions of the Trial Chamber in *Katanga* illustrate the difficulties that may arise in applying the concept of indirect perpetration by means of an organisation to modern-day conflicts. Equally, however, it is notable that the Trial Chamber was keen to emphasise that the concept of indirect perpetration by means of an organisation was 'not … inconsistent with the very varied manifestations of modern-day group criminality wherever it arises'.[271] Whilst acknowledging that proving the existence of an 'organised and hierarchical apparatus of power' presents both factual and legal challenges, the Trial Chamber stressed that the types of organisation it had in mind were not limited to bureaucracies akin to those of the German Third Reich that lie at the root of the theory.[272] In this regard, it is significant that a range of Pre-Trial Chambers at the ICC have begun to identify alternative methods of securing automatic compliance with orders beyond the fungibility of subordinates. Such methods include intensive, strict, and violent training regimes,[273] mechanisms of payment that rewarded individuals for committing crimes and mechanisms of punishment that sanctioned individuals for failing to execute crimes,[274] and requirements for direct perpetrators to swear an oath of loyalty to the organisation as a means of instilling fear, as well as deploying disciplinary measures including sanctions and killings for disloyalty.[275]

These developments suggest that it is not implausible that the concept of indirect co-perpetration by means of an organisation could be applied to less rigidly hierarchical contemporary networks of criminality in the future.[276] In *Ntaganda*, for example,

[268] *Katanga* Trial Judgment (n 183) [1410] and [1412]. Concerns have also been raised that this standard is likely to serve as a high bar for cases involving sexual violence charges because 'sexual violence—even when widespread—often occurs because it is tolerated and permitted rather than explicitly ordered or planned'. SaCouto, Sadat, and Sellers (n 97) 228–229.

[269] Jain (n 17) 195.

[270] *Katanga* Trial Judgment (n 183) [1419]–[1420].

[271] Ibid [1410].

[272] Ibid.

[273] *Katanga and Ngudjolo* DCC (n 219) [813]–[819].

[274] *Ruto et al* DCC (n 246) [320]–[323] and [324]–[326].

[275] *Muthaura et al* DCC (n 248) [208]–[213] and [408].

[276] H van der Wilt, 'The Continuous Quest for Proper Modes of Criminal Responsibility' (2009) 7 *Journal of International Criminal Justice* 307, 312; C Stahn, 'Justice Delivered or Justice Denied? The Legacy of the *Katanga* Judgment' (2014) 12 *Journal of International Criminal Justice* 809, 824.

amongst other factors, the Trial Chamber relied upon the violent conditions of living, training, and service imposed on soldiers of the UPC/FPLC armed group, in combination with the high number of persons within the military structure, to conclude that 'the will of the individual soldiers was irrelevant for the execution of a given order'.[277]

While a more flexible notion of perpetration by means of an organisation enlarges the concept's scope of application, it is also important to recognise that a more elastic understanding of the doctrine risks broadening the scope of an accused's criminal responsibility beyond their personal culpability.[278] As Judge van den Wyngaert has cautioned, 'by dehumanising the relationship between the indirect perpetrator and the physical perpetrator, the control over an organisation concept dilutes the level of personal influence that the indirect perpetrator must exercise over the person through whom he or she commits a crime'.[279]

3. Conclusion

By basing its understanding of principal liability on the control over the crime theory, the ICC has tied the criminal responsibility of the masterminds of system crimes to objective factors such as control and essential contribution. In general, the control theory is more favourable towards leadership-level accused than the broadest articulations of JCE—avoiding, in particular, the expansive notions of principal liability reflected in the extended form of JCE and the SCSL's stretched understanding of the common plan requirement.

Nonetheless, over time, the jurisprudence of the ICC has begun to loosen the control theory in ways that are reminiscent of the development of leadership-level JCEs: first, by combining co-perpetration and indirect perpetration, the ICC has sought to articulate a doctrine that is representationally equipped to reflect the links between leadership-level masterminds both horizontally with each other and vertically with geographically remote physical perpetrators; second, by recognising perpetration by means of an organisation, the ICC has increasingly focused on the institutional rather than personal relationships between leadership-level accused and remote physical perpetrators; and finally, by recognising alternative methods of securing automatic compliance with orders within an organisation beyond the fungibility of subordinates, the ICC has broadened the scope of hierarchical relationships that fall within the scope of perpetration by means of an organisation.

These developments demonstrate a propensity amongst judges at the ICC to mould the law to fit the facts before them, betraying a similar result-oriented approach to the formulation of modes of participation as the ad hoc tribunals.[280] At the same time, however, it is important to emphasise that control over the crime remains a theory that focuses on hierarchical relationships of domination and subordination at the expense of more decentralised forms of authority—a perspective that serves to limit the diversity of social relationships and forms of principal liability that fall within its scope.[281]

[277] *Ntaganda* Trial Judgment (n 208) [817]–[819].
[278] van Sliedregt (n 1) 170.
[279] *Ngudjolo* Trial Judgment (n 186) (concurring op Van den Wyngaert) [53].
[280] van Sliedregt (n 51) 516.
[281] Stahn (n 2) 136.

F. Conclusion

Within the jurisprudence of international criminal courts, the judicial recognition and interpretation of modes of participation doctrines—whether free-standing or as part of inchoate crimes—represent attempts to identify the criminal responsibility of individuals in light of the collective and systemic qualities of system crimes and the environments in which such crimes tend to be carried out. In performing this adjudicative function, modes of participation doctrine not only articulate particular conceptions of individual agency but also render particular portrayals of the organisational dynamics of system criminality.

In practice, international criminal courts have demonstrated relatively little restraint in creatively identifying a legal basis for the recognition and development of various modes of participation doctrines. In particular, judges have often shown a propensity to rely on doctrines rooted in specific domestic legal systems, in combination with a willingness to redevelop them to fit the unique characteristics of mass atrocity contexts. As Elies van Sliedregt explains, the result has been the emergence of doctrines that 'have no precise equivalent in domestic law and ... in that sense qualify as truly *sui generis*'.[282] Confronted by a choice between dynamically identifying and interpreting modes of participation doctrines to fit the factual circumstances of contemporary atrocity situations or shoehorning the fact patterns of particular cases into descriptively unconvincing doctrines, international criminal courts have generally favoured the former approach.[283]

Yet, while international criminal courts have generally sought to develop doctrines that reflect how the collective and systemic characteristics of system crimes may expand individual agency, they have varied—at times considerably—in defining *how* such characteristics should be relied upon for the purpose of attributing criminal responsibility to the masterminds of such crimes. In particular, this section has demonstrated how modes of participation doctrines have tended to vary in two interrelated respects: first, in terms of the strength of the connection between the accused and the crimes for which they are held responsible; and second, in terms of the range of different degrees of participation for which particular doctrines have imposed the same culpability label on the accused. In general, the looser the required connection between the accused and the crimes, and the broader the range of different degrees of participation encompassed within particular doctrines, the easier international criminal courts have found it to ensure the accountability of senior leaders within contexts of mass violence, but at the expense of respecting their individual agency or

[282] van Sliedregt (n 24) 1185.

[283] On this tension, see generally, Guilfoyle (n 20) 266 ('The choice of theory is not consequence free. An obvious risk is that if you have a legal theory that maps poorly against the facts that can be proved by the prosecutor, then as a court or prosecutor you may either distort the facts to fit the "straightjacket" of the theory or "one moulds the doctrine ... to fit reality". The first has risks for fair labelling and the second has risks for the stability, predictability, and fairness of criminal law.'); and van der Wilt (n 129) 166 (identifying 'a lasting dilemma' between conforming to the basic tenets of a mode of participation doctrine, with the risk of jettisoning its narrative function, or moulding the doctrine to fit the changing factual circumstances of particular cases, with the risk of jeopardising legal integrity).

accurately portraying the institutional dynamics of the environments within which they operated.[284]

II. Grounds Excluding Responsibility and Mitigating Punishment

The concept of individual criminal responsibility is premised on the assumption that individuals have sufficient agency to make meaningful choices. In the criminal law context, agency may be understood to refer to the possession of certain capacities:[285] first, capacities of *volition*, pursuant to which it is only fair to hold responsible individuals who had a fair opportunity to act otherwise; and second, capacities of *cognition*, pursuant to which it is only fair to hold responsible individuals who had the capacity to comprehend what they were doing. Domestic legal systems generally recognise—albeit to different degrees—that the level of volition and cognition of human behaviour may vary depending on the individual in question and the social environment in which they were operating.[286] Similarly, international criminal courts have recognised a number of grounds for excluding criminal responsibility and desert-based factors for mitigating punishment through which judges determine which aspects of an individual's conduct, disposition, or social context may either eliminate or reduce their culpability.

Rather than exhaustively reviewing all grounds for excluding responsibility and desert-based mitigating factors, this section focuses on a particular subset, namely those that eliminate or reduce the culpability of an individual based on the situational pressures of the social environments in which mass atrocities are carried out. In practice, these grounds and factors perform an important narrative function within the judgments of international criminal courts, not only reflecting particular conceptions of individual agency by defining when the connection between the accused and a crime may be eliminated or mitigated, but also influencing which aspects of an individual's social context are relevant and irrelevant—and thereby rendered visible or invisible—for the purpose of determining their culpability.

This section unfolds as follows. The section begins by examining the narrative salience of different types of defences within criminal law theory (subsection A), as well as reviewing the different types of situational pressures encountered in mass atrocity contexts (subsection B). The section then proceeds to examine the extent to which an

[284] See similarly, Stewart (2012) (n 40) 167 ('the development of modes of liability in international criminal justice reflects a persistent tension between these two competing extremes: functional attempts at ensuring accountability of senior masterminds of mass violence versus the very real threat of illiberal excess'); and Robinson (n 171) 931 (identifying the risk that an accused may be instrumentalised 'as an object in a didactic exercise rather than respecting autonomy and fairness').

[285] See, similarly, Heikkilä (n 22) 88; Norrie (n 14) 10–11; and N Lacey, 'In Search of the Responsible Subject: History, Philosophy and Social Sciences in Criminal Law Theory' (2001) 64 *Modern Law Review* 350, 353. On the cultural contingency of capacity-based conceptions of responsibility, see, for example, T Kelsall, *Culture Under Cross-Examination: International Justice and the Special Court for Sierra Leone* (CUP 2009) 9–10; and Osiel (n 47) 8.

[286] See similarly, Ashworth and Horder (n 11) 23; J Hoover, 'Reconstructing Responsibility and Moral Agency in World Politics' (2012) 4 *International Theory* 233, 241–242; and Bohrer (n 15) 760.

individual's responsibility may be excluded or their sentence mitigated as a result of *enhanced coercion* to act in a wrongful manner or *diminished cognition* of wrongdoing (subsection C). The section concludes by reflecting on the narrative significance of the restrictive approach adopted by international criminal courts towards grounds for excluding responsibility and mitigating punishment across different institutional contexts (subsection D).

A. The Narrative Salience of Different Types of Defences

In criminal law theory, grounds for excluding responsibility and factors for mitigating punishment are typically discussed under the rubric of 'defences'. In general, criminal law theory distinguishes between different types of defences according to the distinct narrative functions they play with respect to the culpability of the accused.

First, a distinction may be drawn between *substantive* and *procedural* defences. Substantive defences concern specific features of an individual's conduct that render it lawful or specific features of an individual's disposition or social context that negate or mitigate their blameworthiness. Understood in their broadest sense, substantive defences may also encompass so-called 'failure of proof defences', pursuant to which the defence negates a definitional element of the crime.[287] Procedural defences, by contrast, tend to be non-exculpatory and based on the limits of the court's jurisdiction or right to try the accused. Procedural defences exempt the accused from criminal prosecution based on public policy considerations rather than justifying or excusing their conduct.

Second, within the category of substantive defences, a distinction may be drawn between *justifications* and *excuses*.[288] Claims of justification concern the rightness or legal permissibility of an act that nominally violates a criminal legal norm.[289] If generally impermissible conduct is justified, the act is one that society tolerates, approves, or even encourages the individual to undertake. As such, the underlying rationale of justificatory defences is 'a balancing of competing interests and a judgment in favour of the superior interest'.[290] Claims of excuse, by contrast, speak not to the rightness of the act but to the personal culpability of the actor.[291] As such, excuses do not negate the wrongfulness of the conduct, but merely negate the blameworthiness of the individual.[292] The underlying rationale of excusatory defences, therefore, is a judgment that due to personal or situational factors it would be unfair to blame the individual for their wrongful conduct.[293] This also points to a further distinction between two different types of excuse:[294] first, excuses where the mental state of the accused is

[287] Ambos (n 57) 307; and I Bantekas, 'Defenses in International Criminal Law', in D McGoldrick et al (eds), *The Permanent International Criminal Court: Legal and Policy Issues* (Hart Publishing 2004) 263, 263–264.

[288] Ambos (n 57) 304–307; and van Sliedregt (n 1) 215–217.

[289] GP Fletcher, 'The Right and the Reasonable' (1985) 98 *Harvard Law Review* 949, 954.

[290] Ambos (n 57) 305 (relying on George Fletcher).

[291] Fletcher (n 289) 954.

[292] Ibid 958; HLA Hart, *Punishment and Responsibility: Essays in the Philosophy of Law* (2nd edn, OUP 2008) 13–14; and PH Robinson, *Criminal Law Defences* (West Group 1984) 100–101.

[293] Heikkilä (n 22) 264–265.

[294] A Cassese, *International Criminal Law* (2nd edn, OUP 2008) 262–263.

diminished to such an extent that he or she is not possessed of individual autonomy and cannot be blamed for his or her conduct; and second, excuses where the accused is fully possessed of individual autonomy but nonetheless is not blameworthy on account of external circumstances, which either lead to enhanced coercion of the accused towards wrongdoing or a diminution in the accused's cognition of wrongdoing.

Finally, a distinction may be drawn between defences in terms of their *legal consequences*.[295] *Full defences* exclude the criminal responsibility of the individual entirely, resulting in an acquittal, whereas *partial defences* only mitigate the culpability of the individual, still resulting in a conviction. Whilst in some domestic criminal law systems, partial defences may result in conviction for a lesser offence, this practice has not been followed in the field of international criminal law. Instead, partial defences take the form of desert-based mitigating circumstances, resulting in a reduction in the punishment imposed on the accused at sentencing.[296] Importantly, as Hart explains, whilst on a purely utilitarian level such mitigating circumstances ensure that punishment does not cause more suffering than that generated by the crime, they can also serve a narrative function by reflecting the fact that 'the situation or mental state of the convicted criminal is such that he was exposed to an unusual or specially great temptation, or his ability to control his actions is thought to have been impaired or weakened otherwise than by his own action, so that conformity to the law which he has broken was a matter of special difficulty for him as compared with normal persons normally placed'.[297]

For present purposes, illuminating the distinctions between different types of defences is useful for revealing the different narrative functions that defences can potentially perform in practice. For example, by making explicit the distinction between a justification and an excuse, a criminal court has the flexibility to deny the culpability of the accused whilst maintaining the wrongfulness of their conduct.[298] Moreover, the recognition of full and partial defences enables courts to specify gradations of individual culpability, with the potential to formulate 'a scale of exculpation'.[299] By illuminating these narrative functions, the different types of defences outlined here can serve as useful points of reference when examining the approaches adopted by international criminal courts in their jurisprudence.

B. Situational Pressures Within Mass Atrocity Contexts

Over the course of the past century, a rich literature in the field of social science has emerged surfacing important insights about how situational pressures may diminish

295 Ambos (n 57) 303-304.

296 On 'desert-based mitigating factors', see D Husak, 'Partial Defenses', in D Husak, *The Philosophy of Criminal Law: Selected Essays* (OUP 2010) 311, 313 (referring to such mitigating factors as those pursuant to which the defendant '*deserves* a lesser punishment') (emphasis in original); and Ambos (n 57) 303 (adopting Husak's terminology in the context of international criminal law).

297 Hart (n 292) 15.

298 G-J Knoops, *Defenses in Contemporary International Criminal Law* (2nd edn, Martinus Nijhoff Publishers 2008) 25.

299 Heikkilä (n 22) 266.

the agency of individuals operating within mass atrocity contexts. In broad terms, a distinction may be drawn between collective pressures on individuals operating within groups and systemic pressures on individuals operating within authority structures.

In terms of *collective* pressures, groups may diminish the agency of individuals in light of their social psychological effects on human behaviour.[300] Examples of effects that may lead to a diffusion of responsibility include: *de-individuation*, which refers to the state of lessened self-awareness, reduced concern for self-evaluation, and weakened restraints against prohibited behaviour brought about by the anonymity of individuals within collectives and the subjugation of their individuality to group identity;[301] *conformism*, which concerns the ways in which the propensity of individuals to check their perceptions and judgments against those of others (informational needs) and to adjust their perceptions and judgments in an effort to gain social acceptance (normative needs) may lead individuals to yield to the perceptions, judgments, and actions of a group;[302] and *cognitive dissonance*, which refers to conflicting knowledge, opinions, or beliefs about the environment, oneself, or one's behaviour that individuals are motivated to reduce in collective contexts by changing and rationalising their beliefs and actions in line with those of the group.[303]

Turning to *systemic* pressures, while one should guard against reducing all atrocity situations to a single psychological profile,[304] it is well established that mass atrocities are often carried out in 'climates of moral degradation',[305] such that participation in the commission of system crimes often conforms to rather than deviates from the social norms prevailing in the relevant time and place.[306] In such contexts, it is often abstention from violence and criminal conduct that are considered deviant. As such, in contrast to the perpetrators of ordinary domestic crimes, whose actions deviate from ruling social norms and values, many of the perpetrators of system crimes—particularly mid-lower ranked individuals—perform acts that despite being considered unlawful by the international community are deemed both legitimate and within the parameters of social acceptability of their communities at the time.[307] In other words, many—though by no means all—perpetrators of system crimes commit

300 For more extensive summaries of some of the major works in this area, see generally, Smeulers and Grünfeld (n 15) Part Three; P Zimbardo, *The Lucifer Effect: Understanding How Good People Turn Evil* (Random House 2007) Chapter 12; and J Waller, *Becoming Evil: How Ordinary People Commit Genocide and Mass Killing* (OUP 2002) Part I. See also, CR Browning, *Ordinary Men: Reserve Police Battalion 101 and the Final Solution in Poland* (Harper Perennial 1998) (a historical study of German Reserve Police Battalion 101 during the Second World War, which points to a range of situational pressures exerted by the group to explain the habitual conformity of battalion members to their violent assignments).

301 See, for example, Smeulers and Grünfeld (n 15) 207–208.

302 See, for example, ibid 245–248.

303 See, for example, Smeulers and Grünfeld (n 15) 252–254.

304 See, in this regard, MA Drumbl, *Atrocity, Punishment, and International Law* (CUP 2007) 26 (distinguishing top-down mass atrocities using targeted covert operations, mass atrocities in which megalomaniacal leaders encourage and reward violence through broad bureaucratic networks of agents and informants, and mass atrocities where conflict entrepreneurs encouraged violence and large numbers of ordinary people responded to the call) and 34 (distinguishing situations of genocide and crimes against humanity from war crimes).

305 Fletcher (n 3) 1541.

306 See, for example, Smeulers (n 1) 978–981.

307 See, for example, Mohamed (n 15) 1634.

'crimes of obedience', namely 'crimes that take place, not in opposition to the authorities, but under explicit instructions from the authorities to engage in [such] acts, or in an environment in which such acts are implicitly sponsored, expected, or at least tolerated by the authorities'.[308] In such contexts, we are faced with what Alette Smeulers has referred to as 'norm-abiding criminals', namely those who obey authority, hierarchical structures, and the social norms of their society, and 'law-abiding criminals', who additionally obey the law that supports their criminal endeavours.[309]

The propensity for ordinary individuals to commit heinous acts when operating in climates of inverted morality has been supported by a number of social psychological studies,[310] including Stanley Milgram's obedience to authority experiments,[311] as well as Philip Zimbardo's Stanford prison experiment.[312] Milgram identified a number of factors to explain the willingness of so many participants in his experiments to obey an authority figure who had instructed them to perform acts that conflicted with their personal conscience—specifically, the infliction of gradually increasing levels of electric shocks on a subject ostensibly as part of an exercise concerned with the effect that punishment would have on learning. These included tendencies for individuals to become so immersed in the narrow technical aspects of their task that they lost sight of its broader consequences, to divest themselves of responsibility by attributing all responsibility to the authority figure, and to view their behaviour in a larger context that they believed to be benevolent and useful to society.[313] In a similar vein, Zimbardo identified a number of situational features within his mock prison experiment that influenced the behaviour of the participants. These included the power of the prison rules to shape the reality inside the prison, the influence of the roles allocated to the participants on their behaviour, a willingness to 'explain away' personal responsibility for damage caused by role-based actions, the ability of the uniforms to promote anonymity and reduce personal accountability, and the influence of the prison's ecology of dehumanisation.[314] Although both experiments revealed the significance of situational pressures on human behaviour, it is important to recognise that no single variation of Milgram's experiment managed to secure 100 per cent obedience, nor did situational factors operate in a uniform manner on the participants in Zimbardo's prison experiment. As such, these studies suggest that whilst situational pressures are a significant determinant of human behaviour, they cannot provide a complete explanation of it.[315]

[308] Kelman (n 50) 27.

[309] Smeulers (n 1) 979.

[310] For an overview of the most recent studies, see generally, A Luft, 'Dehumanization and the Normalization of Violence: It's Not What You Think' *Items* (21 May 2019).

[311] S Milgram, *Obedience to Authority: An Experimental View* (Tavistock Publications 1974). For useful overviews and relevant critiques of Milgram's study as well as replications of the experiment and other similar subsequent studies, see generally, Smeulers and Grünfeld (n 15) 211–232; Zimbardo (n 300) 266–281; and Waller (n 300) 102–111.

[312] Zimbardo (n 300). A useful overview of Zimbardo's experiment appears in Smeulers and Grünfeld (n 15) 232–239.

[313] Milgram (n 311) 7–10 and 143–152.

[314] Zimbardo (n 300) 212–224.

[315] See similarly, Smeulers and Grünfeld (n 15) 220–221 and 232; and D Luban, *Legal Ethics and Human Dignity* (CUP 2007) 247 and 281–285.

To acknowledge the influence of situational pressures on human behaviour is to recognise that human agency may be understood as a *spectrum*, with individuals experiencing more or less severe situational pressures depending upon the social context within which they operate. In this vein, more recent studies have drawn on the insights from a range of psychological and empirical studies to develop explanatory models of how individuals become perpetrators of mass atrocities.[316] James Waller, for example, has identified three sets of proximate influences that impact on individuals in mass atrocity situations.[317] First, Waller identifies a set of cultural models, the tacit knowledge structures and constituent elements of an individual's worldview, which shape how perpetrators of system crimes interpret the social world and make judgments.[318] These include the nurturing of collectivistic values of obedience and conformity to groups, the inculcation of a strong authority orientation within hierarchical vertical relationships, and the perpetuation and legitimation of desires for social dominance. Second, Waller points to a set of mechanisms that may obliterate any common ground between perpetrators and victims.[319] These include the ratcheting up of 'us-them thinking' to intensify antagonism between different groups, the promotion of a range of practices to morally disengage perpetrators from the reprehensible nature of their conduct by portraying it as socially worthy and dehumanising the victims, and exploiting the human propensity to blame the victims for their suffering as a form of rationalisation of the perpetrators' conduct. Finally, Waller identifies a range of processes by which morality is inverted such that perpetrators are enveloped in a social context that promotes and rewards the commission of atrocities.[320] These include professional socialisation techniques such as encouraging the merger of an individual with the role that has been allocated to him, the promotion of identification with groups by diffusing responsibility through bureaucratic organisation into cells and columns, as well as routinisation and deindividuation of bureaucratic tasks, and nurturing conformity to peer pressure and a social definition of kinship within groups.

In broad terms, what emerges from this literature is the insight that the collective and systemic qualities of system crimes may diminish the agency of individuals, with many experiencing *enhanced coercion* to act in a wrongful manner and/or *diminished cognition* of the wrongfulness of their actions in such environments. This raises the question of the extent to which the social contexts in which accused individuals were operating have been deemed legally relevant by international criminal courts for the purpose of determining their criminal responsibility for system crimes.

[316] See, for example, Smeulers and Grünfeld (n 15) 303–318; JE Waller, 'The Ordinariness of Extraordinary Evil: The Making of Perpetrators of Collective Violence', in A Smeulers (ed), *Collective Violence and International Criminal Justice: An interdisciplinary approach* (Intersentia 2010) 19; Foster (n 14); and Kelman (n 50) 34-40.

[317] Waller (n 316) 23–35.

[318] Ibid 26–28.

[319] Ibid 28–31.

[320] Ibid 31–35.

C. Defences in Practice

In general, international criminal courts have adopted a restrictive approach to defences, identifying only a narrow range of grounds for excluding responsibility and mitigating punishment with stringent definitional elements. As Roger O'Keefe recently observed, '[t]he discourse of international criminal law has historically shown a preference for inculpation over exculpation, with shibboleths like "the fight against impunity" almost presupposing the guilt of those accused, formally or in the court of popular opinion, of international crimes'.[321] In practice, it has been more common for accused persons to challenge the basis for conviction, rather than asserting an affirmative defence to justify or excuse their behaviour.[322] This is at least partially a result of the focus of international prosecutors on targeting senior leaders who influenced the environments in which system crimes were carried out—rendering reliance on coercive and cognitive factors by the accused more difficult.[323] Nonetheless, the recognition, rejection, and definition of grounds for excluding responsibility and mitigating punishment have had an important influence on the narratives constructed by international criminal courts in a number of cases.

Against this background, this section examines the extent to which international criminal courts have taken into account the social contexts of mass atrocity situations for the purpose of excluding or mitigating the culpability of individuals through their recognition, rejection, and definition of two different types of defences: first, through determining the extent to which an individual's culpability may be excluded or mitigated as a result of physical or psychological *coercion* to act in a wrongful manner; and second, through determining the extent to which an individual's criminal responsibility may be excluded or mitigated as a result of diminished *cognition* of wrongdoing.

1. Coercion

The coercive environments that often characterise mass atrocity contexts raise the question of the extent to which international criminal courts have taken coercive factors into account when assessing an individual's culpability. In general, coercion has been examined by international criminal courts in two ways: first, through the ground for excluding responsibility of duress; and second, through the recognition of a number of coercion-related factors in sentencing.

a. Duress as a ground for excluding responsibility

Duress as a ground for excluding responsibility concerns situations where an accused's act was wrongful, but a claim is raised that their capacity for moral choice was eradicated by an imminent threat of severe and irreparable physical harm.[324] In practice,

[321] R O'Keefe, *International Criminal Law* (OUP 2015) 224.
[322] Stahn (n 2) 147.
[323] Ibid 147.
[324] On the notion of 'moral choice', see generally, Y Dinstein, *The Defence of 'Obedience to Superior Orders' in International Law* (AW Sijthoff-Leyden 1965) 148–156.

reliance on duress within international criminal courts has been limited by its restrictive definitional elements.

First, international criminal courts have consistently confirmed that the defence of duress requires an accused to demonstrate exposure to 'an immediate threat of severe and irreparable harm to life or limb'.[325] The ICTY Trial Chamber in *Erdemović*, for example, required proof of 'a danger of death or serious bodily harm', which must be 'clear and present' or 'imminent, real, and inevitable'.[326] Article 31(d) of the ICC Statute elaborates a similar formulation requiring that the crime must have been caused by 'a threat of imminent death or of continuing or imminent serious bodily harm', and also clarifies that this threat may originate from another person or other circumstances beyond the accused's control and may be targeted against the accused or another person.[327]

In practice, the imminent threat requirement has restricted the scope of duress considerably. For example, in its confirmation of charges decision in *Ongwen*, the ICC Pre-Trial Chamber rejected the defence's reliance on duress as a ground for excluding the criminal responsibility of the accused—a former child soldier who had been abducted by the Lord's Resistance Army (LRA) at a young age and grown up to allegedly commit crimes as an adult—partially on the ground that the threat alleged by the accused, namely the possibility of later disciplinary measures, was not imminent.[328] As the Pre-Trial Chamber emphasised, 'Duress is not regulated in the [ICC] Statute in a way that would provide blanket immunity to members of criminal organisations which have brutal systems of ensuring discipline as soon as they can establish that their membership was not voluntary'.[329] By adopting a restrictive lens of imminence, the judges ensured their attention would be directed towards the *immediate situation* in which the accused operated rather than the *broader coercive environment* of the LRA.

Second, international criminal courts have also confirmed that the situation of duress must not have been self-induced by the accused.[330] In practice, this requirement has also been interpreted restrictively.

In *Ongwen*, for example, the defence attempted to depict the accused's path to wrongdoing as a *narrative of inevitability*,[331] involving an individual who had simply been 'surviving in an environment which enslaved him'.[332] Abducted by the LRA as a young child and forced to witness and perform unspeakable acts, Ongwen had been

325 *Prosecutor v Dražen Erdemović* (Judgment, Appeals Chamber) IT-96-22-A (7 October 1997) ('*Erdemović* Appeal Judgment') (sep and diss op Cassese) [16].

326 *Prosecutor v Dražen Erdemović* (Sentencing Judgment, Trial Chamber) IT-96-22-T (29 November 1996) ('*Erdemović* Sentencing Judgment') [18].

327 See, in this regard, *Ongwen* DCC (n 247) [152]–[153].

328 Ibid [153].

329 Ibid.

330 *Erdemović* Appeal Judgment (n 325) (sep and diss op Cassese) [16]; Article 31(1)(d), ICC Statute (specifying that the threat must have arisen from 'other persons' or 'other circumstances beyond that person's control').

331 On narratives of inevitability and narratives of choice, see RE Brooks, 'Law in the Heart of Darkness: Atrocity & Duress' (2003) 43 *Virginia Journal of International Law* 861, 881–882.

332 *Prosecutor v Dominic Ongwen* (Further Redacted Version of "Defence Brief for the Confirmation of Charges Hearing", filed on 18 January 2016, Defence for Dominic Ongwen) ICC-02/04-01/15-404-Red2 (3 March 2016) [56].

psychologically broken down and disconnected from the social construct of normal society in northern Uganda.[333] Subjected to systematic indoctrination, instinct and survival became part of Ongwen's daily experience, such that he 'could not be said to have had any control over the ruthless environment in which he found himself at the age of 9.5'.[334]

In response, the ICC Pre-Trial Chamber rejected the defence's reliance on duress partially on the basis that the accused's stay in the LRA could not be said to have been beyond his control. According to the Pre-Trial Chamber, escapes from the LRA were not rare and Ongwen 'could have chosen not to rise in hierarchy and expose himself to increasingly higher responsibility to implement LRA policies'.[335] Instead, the evidence demonstrated that Ongwen 'shared the ideology of the LRA, including its brutal and perverted policy with respect to civilians it considered as supporting the government'.[336]

By interpreting duress in this way, the Pre-Trial Chamber examined the agency of the accused through the de-contextualised lens of the accused's immediate situation rather than adopting a longer-term view that accounted for the social-psychological coercive effects that the accused's upbringing may have had on his agency.[337] As a result, the Pre-Trial Chamber viewed Ongwen's path to wrongdoing as a *narrative of choice*, involving a moral agent who had genuine opportunities to act otherwise than he did notwithstanding his devastating upbringing. As Mark Drumbl observes, 'Whereas the defence sought to link Ongwen's conduct as an adult to his experiences as a child, the Pre-Trial Chamber only examined his agency as an adult—as if he had never been a child, let alone a child in the LRA. In rejecting the duress submissions in *Ongwen*, the Pre-Trial Chamber elided Ongwen's status as a former child soldier. It's as if he lost that status, or ceded it.'[338]

Finally, international criminal courts have also set stringent standards concerning the types of measures an accused may take in response to an imminent threat. At the ICTY, for example, a majority of the Appeals Chamber in *Erdemović* concluded that duress 'does *not* afford a complete defence to a soldier charged with a crime against humanity and/or a war crime involving *the killing of innocent human beings*'.[339] After concluding that neither a rule of customary international law nor a general principle of law had emerged concerning the availability or non-availability of duress as a defence to the killing of innocent individuals,[340] Judges McDonald and Vohrah of the majority adopted an expressly policy-oriented perspective, asserting that 'the law should not be the product or slave of logic or intellectual hair-splitting, but must serve broader normative purposes in light of its social, political and economic role'.[341] In accordance with a victim-oriented purposive understanding of international humanitarian

[333] Ibid [42]–[46].
[334] Ibid [54]–[56].
[335] *Ongwen* DCC (n 247) [154].
[336] Ibid.
[337] See, in this regard, Bohrer (n 15) 815–817 (advocating for the recognition of a 'brainwashing' or 'coercive-indoctrination defense').
[338] MA Drumbl, 'Victims who Victimise' (2016) 4 *London Review of International Law* 217, 242.
[339] *Erdemović* Appeal Judgment (n 325) [19] (emphasis added).
[340] *Erdemović* Appeal Judgment (n 325) (joint sep op McDonald and Vohrah) [55] and [72].
[341] Ibid [75].

law as a body of rules that entails the protection of the weak and vulnerable in situations where their lives and security are endangered, Judges McDonald and Vohrah advanced 'an absolute moral postulate' that an ordinary soldier may reasonably be expected to die rather than kill innocent civilians in any circumstances.[342] According to Judges McDonald and Vohrah, the law could still recognise the human frailty of a soldier who had killed innocent persons under the threat of death by mitigating their punishment. In determining what the law 'expects' of an individual, the majority judges found that it would be superficial to look solely at whether or not an individual was convicted; rather, the law employs mitigation of punishment 'as a far more sophisticated and flexible tool for the purpose of doing justice in an individual case'.[343] Indeed, Judges McDonald and Vohrah even argued that in appropriate cases, 'the offender may receive no punishment at all'.[344]

The ICC, by contrast, recognises duress as a potential ground for excluding responsibility for all crimes in the jurisdiction of the Court, including those that involve the killing of innocent persons. At the same time, however, Article 31(d) of the ICC Statute incorporates two requirements concerning the accused's response to the imminent threat that restrict the scope of application of duress as a ground for excluding responsibility: first, the accused must have acted 'necessarily and reasonably' to avoid the threat, a term which appears to implicitly require that the reaction of the accused not cause greater harm than the one sought to be avoided;[345] and second, the accused must not have intended to cause a greater harm than the one sought to be avoided, a subjective element which requires that the objective balancing of interests also be reflected in the accused's mind.[346]

The ICC Statute's definition of duress elides the distinction made by comparative criminal law theorists between *necessity* (a justification, which serves to negate the wrongfulness of the accused's conduct where an individual chooses the lesser of two evils) and *duress* (an excuse, which serves to exempt individuals from culpability without, however, negating the wrongfulness of their conduct, in situations where, giving due consideration to human frailty, it would not be reasonable to expect them to resist an imminent threat).[347] By incorporating justificatory elements into the definition of duress, the ICC Statute narrows its scope of application—effectively requiring that the act performed, on balance, be the right thing to do under the circumstances. The Pre-Trial Chamber's confirmation of charges decision in *Ongwen* illustrates the difficulties of satisfying the necessity and reasonableness requirement for the types of criminality that tend to be adjudicated before the ICC. According to the Pre-Trial Chamber, even if, *arguendo*, Ongwen could not have avoided accepting forced wives, 'he could have avoided raping them, or, at the very least, he could have reduced the brutality of the sexual abuse'.[348] Similarly, the Pre-Trial Chamber found that even if,

[342] Ibid [75], [80] and [83]–[84].
[343] *Erdemović* Appeal Judgment (n 325) (joint sep op McDonald and Vohrah) [85].
[344] Ibid.
[345] G Werle and F Jeßberger, *Principles of International Criminal Law* (3rd edn, OUP 2014) 241; and Ambos (n 57) 359.
[346] Werle and Jeßberger (n 345) 243; and Ambos (n 57) 360.
[347] See, for example, Ambos (n 57) 347 and 356; and van Sliedregt (n 1) 242–244 and 259.
[348] *Ongwen* DCC (n 247) [155].

arguendo, Ongwen could not have avoided participating as commander in the attacks on civilians in internally displaced persons camps, 'he should have been able to take some action to reduce harm to civilians'.[349]

b. Coercion-based mitigating factors

Beyond the formal recognition of duress as a ground for excluding responsibility, the impact of coercion on individual agency may also be taken into consideration at the sentencing stage of proceedings. In general, sentencing has not been subject to detailed regulation in the statutory frameworks of international criminal courts, which have tended to leave broad discretion to the judges to determine the extent to which different factors should be taken into account in the context of particular cases.[350] The recognition of coercion as a mitigating factor for system crimes has received increasing scholarly support in recent years—a position that can be traced back at least as far as the work of Hannah Arendt, who argued that when dealing with cases of 'personal responsibility under dictatorship', the system within which an accused individual operated 'cannot be left out of account altogether' and should appear in the form of mitigating circumstances.[351] In practice, however, international criminal courts have been reluctant to recognise mitigating factors that address the coercive context of the accused.[352]

Duress, for example, has been successfully relied upon as a mitigating factor in only a small number of cases. Isolated examples include the case of *Erdemović*, where the ICTY Trial Chamber accepted that the evidence revealed 'the extremity of the situation faced by the accused', namely 'to kill or be killed',[353] and the case of *Rutaganira*, where the ICTR Trial Chamber accepted that the accused faced a real danger to his own life and to the lives of his immediate family had he objected to the killings that were taking place in his *secteur*.[354] In general, however, reliance on duress as a mitigating factor has tended to be rejected on evidential grounds.[355]

349 Ibid.

350 See generally, Ambos (n 57) 267–283.

351 H Arendt, 'Personal Responsibility Under Dictatorship', in J Kohn (ed), *Hannah Arendt: Responsibility and Judgment* (Schocken Books 2003) 17, 32. See, more recently, Fletcher (n 3) 1539; L May, *Crimes Against Humanity: A Normative Account* (CUP 2005) 176; Bohrer (n 15) 809–811; and Ambos (n 57) 87.

352 See similarly, Heikkilä (n 22) 355 ('all in all, international sentencing does not support the idea that the collective crime commission context dilutes responsibility'); and A Smeulers and B Holá, 'ICTY and the Culpability of Different Types of Perpetrators of International Crimes', in A Smeulers (ed), *Collective Violence and International Criminal Justice: An Interdisciplinary Approach* (Intersentia 2010) 175, 190 ('to a very limited extent and only in some cases the ICTY judges seem to acknowledge in their sentencing narrative the societal dynamics of international crimes and extraordinary nature of circumstances when such crimes are committed').

353 *Erdemović* Sentencing Judgment (n 326) [17].

354 *Prosecutor v Vincent Rutaganira* (Judgment and Sentence, Trial Chamber) ICTR-95-1C-T (14 March 2005) ('*Rutaganira* Trial Judgment') [159]–[162] and [170].

355 See, for example, *Prosecutor v Darko Mrđa* (Judgment, Trial Chamber) IT-02-59 (31 March 2004) ('*Mrđa* Trial Judgment') [66]; *Prosecutor v Miroslav Bralo* (Sentencing Judgment, Trial Chamber) IT-95-17-S (7 December 2005) ('*Bralo* Sentencing Judgment') [49]–[56]; *Prosecutor v Bizimungu et al* (Judgment and Sentence, Trial Chamber) ICTR-99-50-T (30 September 2011) [2018]; *Prosecutor v Sesay et al* (Sentencing Judgment, Trial Chamber) SCSL-04-15-T, SCSL (8 April 2009) ('*Sesay et al* Sentencing Judgment') [259]; and *Prosecutor v Brima et al* (Sentencing Judgment, Trial Chamber) SCSL-04-16-T (19 July 2007) ('*Brima et al* Sentencing Judgment') [122].

The *general hostile environment* in which an accused was operating has also been recognised as a mitigating factor only on rare occasions. In *Tadić*, for example, the ICTY Trial Chamber took into account the fact that 'the virulent propaganda that stoked the passions of the citizenry' in Prijedor had been 'endemic and contributed to the crimes committed in the conflict' when assessing the appropriate sentence for the accused.[356] Similarly, in *Rugambarara*, the ICTR Trial Chamber considered as a mitigating factor the fact that the environment of 'renewed political intolerance, interethnic tensions and an influx of refugees into the Bicumbi *commune* ... could have made it difficult for Rugambarara to exercise his full authority'.[357] In general, however, reliance on the coercive context in which an accused was operating as a mitigating factor has tended to find little favour within the sentencing decisions of international criminal courts.[358]

An accused's *prior good character* has occasionally been relied upon as a mitigating factor in recognition of the fact that the accused's change of character during a mass atrocity situation may be partially attributable to the coercive circumstances of the conflict rather than solely a consequence of the accused's disposition.[359] In *Ntawukulilyayo*, for example, the ICTR Trial Chamber referred to the accused's life prior to the conflict as a teacher, a member of parliament, and serving in local government, during which time he devoted part of his professional career to easing ethnic tensions in Rwanda. The Chamber noted that while such evidence does not exonerate or excuse the accused's participation in the massacre on Kabuye hill, 'it implies that his participation in the killings may have resulted from external pressures to demonstrate his allegiance to the government rather than from extremism or ethnic hatred'.[360]

Nonetheless, *Ntawukulilyayo* remains a relatively isolated example,[361] with international criminal courts generally concluding that evidence of an accused's prior good

[356] *Prosecutor v Duško Tadić* (Sentencing Judgment, Trial Chamber) IT-94-1-T (14 July 1997) ('*Tadić* Sentencing Judgment') [72]. For similar lines of inquiry, see, for example, *Prosecutor v Delalić et al* (Judgment, Trial Chamber) IT-96-21-T (16 November 1998) [1245], [1248], and [1283]–[1284]; *Prosecutor v Zlatko Aleksovski* (Judgment, Trial Chamber) IT-95-14//1-T (25 June 1999) [235]; *Prosecutor v Enver Hadžihasanović and Amir Kubura* (Judgment, Trial Chamber) IT-01-47-T (15 March 2006) [2081]; and *Prosecutor v Moinina Fofana and Allieu Kondewa* (Judgment on the Sentencing of Moinina Fofana and Allieu Kondewa, Trial Chamber) SCSL-04-14-T (9 October 2007) ('*Fofana and Kondewa* Sentencing Judgment') [66].

[357] *Prosecutor v Juvénal Rugambarara* (Sentencing Judgment, Trial Chamber) ICTR-00-59-T (16 November 2007) ('*Rugambarara* Sentencing Judgment') [47].

[358] See, for example, *Sesay et al* Sentencing Judgment (n 355) [220] and [250] (refusing to consider the fact that two of the accused had been forcibly recruited as a factor in mitigation—instead concluding that each accused 'could well have chosen another path'); *Prosecutor v Tihomir Blaškić* (Judgment, Appeals Chamber) IT-95-14-A (29 July 2004) [711] (refusing to consider the chaotic context of armed conflict as a mitigating factor); *Prosecutor v Clément Kayishema and Obed Ruzindana* (Judgment (Reasons), Appeals Chamber) ICTR-95-1-A (1 June 2001) [365] (noting, with approval, that the Trial Chamber had given little weight to the accused's assertions that he was 'overwhelmed by the events and the mob or "crowd psychology" that existed in Rwanda in 1994'); and *Prosecutor v Prlić et al* (Judgment: Volume 4 of 6, Trial Chamber) IT-04-74-T (29 May 2013) [1346] and [1360] (refusing to consider the 'difficult' or 'testing' circumstances in which two of the accused had operated as a mitigating factor in light of the gravity of crimes for which they were convicted, including the fact that most of the crimes were committed over a period of several months, and the fact that the accused did not make serious efforts to end the crimes).

[359] See similarly, Smeulers and Holá (n 352) 189–190.

[360] *Prosecutor v Dominique Ntawukulilyayo* (Judgment and Sentence, Trial Chamber) ICTR-05-82-T (3 August 2010) [474].

[361] See, however, *Prosecutor v Elizaphan and Gérard Ntakirutimana* (Judgment and Sentence, Trial Chamber) ICTR-96-10-T & ICTR-96-17-T (21 February 2003) [895] (concluding that 'Elizaphan

character carries little weight in the determination of their sentence, particularly in light of the gravity of the crimes.[362] In some cases, international criminal courts have even relied upon an accused's prior good character as an aggravating factor, in particular where the accused was well educated prior to the conflict.[363] In *Lubanga*, for example, the ICC Trial Chamber declared as a 'relevant factor' the fact that the accused was 'clearly an intelligent and well-educated individual, who would have understood the seriousness of the crimes of which he has been found guilty'.[364]

An accused's *provision of assistance to potential victims* has also been recognised as a mitigating factor by international criminal courts in several cases,[365] though only occasionally has this factor been accorded significant weight or provided a vehicle for illuminating the coercive pressures in which an accused was operating.

The Nuremberg IMT, for example, referred to the benevolent acts of certain accused as one of the few recognised mitigating factors in its judgment and the accused in question received sentences for terms of years rather than life imprisonment or the death penalty.[366] For instance, the Nuremberg IMT mitigated Albert Speer's sentence in light of his establishment of blocked industries which kept many labourers in their homes as well as his opposition to Hitler's scorched earth programme 'by deliberately sabotaging it at considerable personal risk'.[367]

More recently, the ICTR Trial Chamber in *Ndindiliyimana et al* relied upon evidence of measures taken by Ndindiliyimana to save the lives of Tutsi civilians as a mitigating factor of 'considerable weight', noting that such measures were 'not well

Ntakirutimana was essentially a person of good moral character until the events of April to July 1994 during which he was *swept along with many Rwandans into criminal conduct*') (emphasis added).

[362] See, for example, at the ICTY, *Prosecutor v Milan Babić* (Judgment on Sentencing Appeal, Appeals Chamber) IT-03-72-A (18 July 2005) [50]; *Popović et al* Trial Judgment Vol I (n 101) [2156], [2161], [2167], [2175], [2193], [2201], and [2209]; and *Prosecutor v Ivica Rajić* (Sentencing Judgment, Trial Chamber) IT-95-12-S (8 May 2006) [162]. See similarly, at the ICTR, *Anatole Ntabukuze v The Prosecutor* (Judgment, Appeals Chamber) ICTR-98-41A-A (8 May 2012) [296]; *Prosecutor v Jean-Baptiste Gatete* (Judgment and Sentence, Trial Chamber) ICTR-2000-61-T (31 March 2011) ('*Gatete* Trial Judgment') [681]; *Prosecutor v Jean de Dieu Kamuhanda* (Judgment, Trial Chamber) ICTR-95-54A-T (22 January 2004) [757]–[758]; and *Prosecutor v Ephrem Setako* (Judgment and Sentence, Trial Chamber) ICTR-04-81-T (25 February 2010) [506]. See similarly, at the ICC, *Prosecutor v Germain Katanga* (Decision on Sentence Pursuant to Article 76 of the Statute, Trial Chamber) ICC-01/04-01/07 (23 May 2014) [88].

[363] See generally, Mohamed (n 15) 1658–1662; and B Holá et al, 'International Sentencing Facts and Figures: Sentencing Practice at the ICTY and ICTR' (2011) 9 *Journal of International Criminal Justice* 411, at 435 (finding that, as of June 2010, prior education was mentioned in 7 per cent of ICTY cases and 12.5 per cent of ICTR cases as an aggravating factor).

[364] *Prosecutor v Thomas Lubanga Dyilo* (Decision on Sentence Pursuant to Article 76 of the Statute, Trial Chamber) ICC-01/04-01/06 (10 July 2012) [56]. See similarly, at the ICTY, *Prosecutor v Radoslav Brđanin* (Judgment, Trial Chamber) IT-99-36-T (1 September 2004) [1114]; *Tadić* Sentencing Judgment (n 356) [59]; and *Krajišnik* Trial Judgment (n 118) [1157] and [1160]. See similarly, at the ICTR, *Prosecutor v Emmanuel Rukundo* (Judgment, Trial Chamber) ICTR-2001-70-T (27 February 2009) [600]; *Prosecutor v Jean de Dieu Kamuhanda* (Judgment, Trial Chamber) ICTR-95-54A-T (22 January 2004) [764]; *Prosecutor v François Karera* (Judgment and Sentence, Trial Chamber) ICTR-01-74-T (7 December 2007) [581]; and *Prosecutor v Ndindiliyimana et al* (Judgment and Sentence, Trial Chamber) ICTR-00-56 (17 May 2011) ('*Ndindiliyimana et al* Trial Judgment') [2182].

[365] See generally, J Galbraith, 'The Good Deeds of International Criminal Defendants' (2012) 25 *Leiden Journal of International Law* 799; and Holá et al (n 363) 433 (finding that, as of June 2010, assistance to victims was mentioned in 38 per cent of ICTY cases and 42.5 per cent of ICTR cases as a mitigating factor).

[366] See, for example, Nuremberg Judgment (n 7) 333 (Speer) and 335 (Von Neurath).

[367] Ibid 333.

received by the population and by some hostile politicians'—an indication that the accused had been acting in defiance of his coercive context.[368] Similarly, in *Popović et al*, the ICTY Trial Chamber relied upon evidence that Pandurević had opened the corridor at Balijkovica and enabled the safe passage of thousands of Bosnian Muslim men as a mitigating factor of 'significant weight'.[369] Reflecting on the fact that the accused had taken this decision against the orders of his superiors and with knowledge that it might put him in jeopardy, the Trial Chamber observed that the accused's action stood out as 'an instance of courage and humanity in a period typified by human weakness, cruelty, and depravity'.[370]

In general, however, evidence of assistance to potential victims has either been referred to as a mitigating factor without elaboration as to its weight,[371] or has been accorded little or no weight at all—whether because of the gravity and heinousness of the crimes in which the accused participated,[372] or because the assistance was selectively rendered to those already known to the accused or who shared similar characteristics with the accused.[373]

Finally, *the rank, authority, and influence of an accused* has also been relied upon by international criminal courts for the purpose of determining the appropriate sentence. According to the Trial Chamber in *Krstić*, for example, in the context of sentencing 'a distinction is to be made between the individuals who allowed themselves to be drawn into a maelstrom of violence, even reluctantly, and those who initiated or aggravated it and thereby more substantially contributed to the overall harm'.[374] In this vein, international criminal courts have often seen fit to rely on evidence that individuals abused their superior position, authority, or influence as an aggravating factor.[375] In doing so, judges have recognised that a person who has authority over a large group of people has a heightened ability to inflict greater damage by means of the group than

[368] *Ndindiliyimana et al* Trial Judgment (n 364) [2189] and [2234]–[2239]. The defendant Ndindiliyimana was ultimately acquitted on appeal. *Ndindiliyimana et al v The Prosecutor* (Judgment, Appeals Chamber) ICTR-00-56-A (11 February 2014).

[369] *Popović et al* Trial Judgment Vol I (n 101) [2222]. See also, *Prosecutor v Sikirica et al* (Sentencing Judgment, Trial Chamber) IT-95-8-S (13 November 2001) [229] (noting that Kolundžija's efforts to ease the harsh conditions in the Keraterm camp for many of its detainees warranted 'a significant reduction in his sentence').

[370] *Popović et al* Trial Judgment Vol I (n 101) [2219].

[371] See, for example, *Prosecutor v Radislav Krstić* (Judgment, Appeals Chamber) IT-98-33-A (19 April 2004) [273]; *Prosecutor v Predrag Banović* (Sentencing Judgment, Trial Chamber) IT-02-65/1-S (28 October 2003) [83]; *Prosecutor v Blagojević and Jokić* (Judgment, Appeals Chamber) IT-02-60-A (9 May 2007) [342]; *Prosecutor v Kupreškić et al* (Judgment, Appeals Chamber) IT-95-16-A (23 October 2001) [430]; *Rutaganira* Trial Judgment (n 354) 155; *Rugambarara* Sentencing Judgment (n 357) [37]; *Prosecutor v Joseph Serugendo* (Judgment and Sentence, Trial Chamber) ICTR-2005-84-I (12 June 2006) [68]–[69]; and *Prosecutor v Joseph Nzabirinda* (Sentencing Judgment, Trial Chamber) ICTR-2001-77-T (23 February 2007) [77].

[372] See, for example, *Prosecutor v Milan Lukić and Sredoje Lukić* (Judgment, Trial Chamber) IT-98-32/1-T (20 July 2009) [1092]; *Prosecutor v Kunarac et al* (Judgment, Appeals Chamber) IT-96-23 & IT-96-23/1-A (12 June 2002) [408]; and *Krajišnik* Trial Judgment (n 118) [1163].

[373] See, for example, *Prosecutor v Kvočka et al* (Judgment, Appeals Chamber) IT-98-30/1-A (28 February 2005) [693]; *Simon Bikindi v The Prosecutor* (Judgment, Appeals Chamber) ICTR-01-72-A (18 March 2010) [163]; and *Prosecutor v Yussuf Munyakazi* (Judgment and Sentence, Trial Chamber) ICTR-97-36A-T (5 July 2010) [520].

[374] *Prosecutor v Radislav Krstić* (Judgment, Trial Chamber) IT-98-33-T (2 August 2001) [711].

[375] See generally, Mohamed (n 15) 1662–1665; and Holá et al (n 363) 433 (finding that, as of June 2010, abuse of superior position, authority, or influence was mentioned in 58 per cent of ICTY cases and 77.5 per cent of ICTR cases as an aggravating factor making it the most popular aggravating factor in both tribunals).

he or she would be able to inflict alone and that by serving as an example for others to act similarly, the criminal behaviour of such persons is likely to entail more serious effects.[376] As Saira Mohamed has observed, by consistently accepting abuse of superior position or influence as an aggravating factor at least partially based on their exhortative effects on the wider community, international criminal courts have offered 'a vision of ordinary people succumbing to social pressures'.[377]

However, only rarely has this vision been upheld when considering whether an accused's *subordinate* position should constitute a factor in mitigation. In *Tadić*, for example, the ICTY Appeals Chamber held that it was important for sentences 'to reflect the relative significance of the role of the Appellant in the broader context of the conflict in the former Yugoslavia'.[378] On this basis, the Appeals Chamber held that although the accused's criminal conduct had been 'incontestably heinous', nonetheless 'his level in the command structure, when compared to that of his superiors, i.e. commanders, or the very architects of the strategy of ethnic cleansing, was low'.[379] Relying on this finding, judges in other cases concluded that those who had held less authoritative positions relative to the general conflict were not only less influential in setting in motion the coercive contexts in which they operated,[380] but also potentially subjected to greater coercive pressures.[381]

In general, however, the fact that an accused held a less influential role relative to the wider conflict has tended to be trumped by other factors, including: the cruelty, sadism, or zeal with which the accused participated in the criminal activity;[382] the gravity of the crimes in which the accused participated;[383] or the high degree of influence possessed by accused persons at the local level in which they operated.[384] In *Aleksovski*, for example, the Appeals Chamber found that the Trial Chamber had placed too much emphasis on the accused's relatively limited participation, rather than focusing on the accused's authority as prison warden and the gravity of the crimes in which he had participated.[385] In this vein, the Appeals Chamber concluded that while the accused

[376] See, for example, *Krajišnik* Trial Judgment (n 118) [1156]; *Gatete* Trial Judgment (n 362) [678]; *Fofana and Kondewa* Sentencing Judgment (n 356) [59]–[62]; and *Prosecutor v Thomas Lubanga Dyilo* (Judgment on the Appeals of the Prosecutor and Mr Thomas Lubanga Dyilo against 'Decision on Sentence pursuant to Article 76 of the Statute', Appeals Chamber) ICC-01/04-01/06-3122 (1 December 2014) [80]–[85].

[377] Mohamed (n 15) 1665.

[378] *Prosecutor v Duško Tadić* (Judgment in Sentencing Appeals, Appeals Chamber) IT-94–1-A and IT-94-1-A*bis* (26 January 2000) [55].

[379] Ibid [56].

[380] See, for example, *Prosecutor v Limaj et al* (Judgment, Trial Chamber) IT-03-66-T (30 November 2005) [732]; *Prosecutor v Ljube Boškoski and Johan Tarčulovski* (Judgment, Trial Chamber) IT-04-82-T (10 July 2008) [594]; and *Prosecutor v Stevan Todorović* (Sentencing Judgment, Trial Chamber) IT-95-9/1-S (31 July 2001) [62].

[381] See, for example, *Prosecutor v Kvočka et al* (Judgment, Trial Chamber) IT-98-30/1-T (2 November 2001) [732].

[382] See, for example, Holá et al (n 363) 431 and 438 (demonstrating empirically that the enthusiasm and cruelty of less influential perpetrators has played a role in aggravating their sentences at the ICTY and ICTR despite their minor role within the overall conflict).

[383] See, for example, *Prosecutor v Delalić et al* (Judgment, Appeals Chamber) IT-96-21-A (20 February 2001) [847] and [850].

[384] See, for example, *Prosecutor v Mladen Naletilić and Vinko Martinović* (Judgment, Trial Chamber) IT-98-34-T (31 March 2003) [751]; and *Prosecutor v Zlatko Aleksovski* (Judgment, Appeal Chamber) IT-95-14//1-A (24 March 2000) ('*Aleksovski* Appeal Judgment') [183]–[184].

[385] *Aleksovski* Appeal Judgment (n 384) [183].

may have had a secondary role compared to others indicted, greater weight should have been placed on the fact that 'he was nonetheless the commander of the prison and as such the authority who could have prevented crimes in the prison and certainly should not have involved himself in them'.[386] While it makes sense to refer to the authority and influence of accused persons at the local level, it is not clear why this perspective justifies effectively ignoring the fact that such individuals were operating in coercive circumstances primarily brought about by those operating above them.

In general, therefore, the picture that emerges from the jurisprudence of international criminal courts is one in which judges have been open to revealing how ordinary people may be acculturated into committing heinous crimes through their recognition of abuse of the influence wielded by accused persons—however localised—as an aggravating factor, whilst resisting attempts to recognise coercive pressures placed on accused persons from above as a factor in mitigation.[387]

2. Cognition

Beyond revealing how mass atrocity situations may enhance coercion towards wrongdoing, studies in the field of social science have also illuminated how individuals in mass atrocity environments may place trust in what they perceive to be legitimate authority structures, such that their awareness of wrongdoing may be dramatically diminished or even eradicated.[388] Despite such findings, international criminal courts have proven extremely reluctant to take account of errors and misperceptions of individuals concerning the wrongdoing of their actions when assessing their culpability.

In general, international criminal courts have rejected consideration of cognition-based defences by strictly adhering to the principle that ignorance of the law is no excuse (*error iuris nocet* or *ignorantia iuris neminem excusat*).[389] The rationale behind this principle is twofold:[390] first, to prevent variation in the applicability of the criminal law according to the degree of knowledge of the law possessed by different individuals in society; and second, to guard against incentivising individuals to break the law by simply proving that they were unaware of relevant legal provisions after the fact. Complementing this principle, the statutory frameworks of international criminal courts have also tended to reject obedience to superior orders as a ground for excluding responsibility.[391] In addition, while obedience to superior orders has generally

[386] Ibid [184].

[387] See similarly, B Hola, 'Sentencing at the ICTY: Doing Justice to Complex Realities of International Crimes?' *Humanity* (4 July 2017).

[388] See, for example, A Smeulers and W Werner, 'The Banality of Evil on Trial', in C Stahn and L van den Herik (eds), *Future Perspectives on International Criminal Justice* (TMC Asser Press 2010) 24, 41; and MJ Osiel, 'Obeying Orders: Atrocity, Military Discipline, and the Law of War' (1998) 86 *California Law Review* 939, 1013–1017.

[389] See, for example, *Prosecutor v Radovan Karadžić* (Decision on Appeal from Denial of Judgment of Acquittal for Hostage-Taking, Appeals Chamber) IT-95-5/18-AR73.0 (11 December 2012) [22]; *Prosecutor v Brima et al* (Judgment, Trial Chamber) SCSL-04-16-T (20 June 2007) [732]; *Brima et al* Appeal Judgment (n 153) [296]. See also, Article 32(2), ICC Statute ('A mistake of law as to whether a particular type of conduct is a crime within the jurisdiction of the Court shall not be a ground for excluding criminal responsibility'); and *Lubanga* DCC (n 190) [305]. See generally, Ambos (n 57) 366–376; and Cassese et al (n 37) 219–222.

[390] Cassese et al (n 37) 220.

[391] See, for example, Article 8, Nuremberg Charter; Article 6, Tokyo Charter; Article 7(4), ICTY Statute; Article 6(4), ICTR Statute; Article 6(4), SCSL Statute.

been accepted as a factor that may potentially be relied upon in mitigation, international criminal courts have predominantly declined to do so in practice.[392]

The ICC Statute adopts a slightly more receptive approach to cognition-based defences in two respects. First, Article 32(2) of the ICC Statute recognises that a mistake of law may be a ground for excluding criminal responsibility 'if it negates the mental element required by such a crime'. This provision is understood by most scholars to constitute a mistake of legal element defence, according to which individuals who misunderstand the definition of a legal element of an offence cannot be said to have acted knowingly with respect to that element.[393] Scholars disagree, however, as to whether the defence is broad or narrow in scope. Kevin Heller, for example, argues that the defence has a potentially broad scope since 'nearly every war crime and crime against humanity in the Rome Statute contains at least one legal element'.[394] Most commentators, however, reject the possibility that the defence will succeed in practice, typically based on the belief that one of two restrictions are implicit in the ICC Statute:[395] first, that mistakes of legal elements may be denied where they were unreasonable or avoidable; or alternatively, that mistakes of legal elements may be denied where the accused had a layperson's understanding of the significance of the incriminating conduct described by a particular set of facts. Notably, in the case of *Lubanga*, the ICC Pre-Trial Chamber confirmed that for a plea of mistake of law to succeed under Article 32(2), the accused must demonstrate that he was 'unaware of a normative objective element of the crime as a result of not realising its social significance (its everyday meaning)'.[396]

Second, Article 33(1) of the ICC Statute provides that obedience to an order of a government or a superior (whether military or civilian) may be a ground for excluding responsibility where the person was under a legal obligation to obey the order in question, the person did not know that the order was unlawful, and the order was not manifestly unlawful. By requiring that an individual lack knowledge that an order was unlawful, this ground for excluding responsibility amounts to an exception to the *error iuris nocet* principle set out in Article 32(2).[397] However, the exception is narrow since Article 33(2) establishes by legislative fiat that orders to commit genocide or crimes against humanity are always manifestly unlawful, thereby limiting the application of the defence to war crimes and the crime of aggression.[398] In line with other

[392] See, for example, Nuremberg Judgment (n 7) 291 and 325; *Mrđa* Trial Judgment (n 355) 67; *Bralo* Sentencing Judgment (n 355) [55]; *Prosecutor v Bagosora et al* (Judgment and Sentence, Trial Chamber) ICTR-98-41-T (18 December 2008) [2274]; *Sesay et al* Sentencing Judgment (n 355) [262]; and *Brima et al* Sentencing Judgment (n 355) [122].

[393] See, for example, R Cryer et al, *An Introduction to International Criminal Law and Procedure* (3rd edn, CUP 2014) 410; Cassese et al (n 37) 222; Ambos (n 57) 373; KJ Heller, 'Mistake of Legal Element, the Common Law, and Article 32 of the Rome Statute' (2008) 6 *Journal of International Criminal Justice* 419, 424–429; and A Eser, 'Mental Elements—Mistake of Fact and Mistake of Law', in A Cassese et al, *The Rome Statute of the International Criminal Court* (OUP 2002) 889, 941.

[394] Heller (n 393) 430.

[395] For a useful overview and critique of these arguments, see generally, van Sliedregt (n 1) 283–285; and Heller (n 393) 436–442.

[396] *Lubanga* DCC (n 190) [316]. For a critique of this formulation in the decision, see Weigend (n 222) 474–476.

[397] See similarly, Cryer et al (n 393) 413; Ambos (n 57) 383; and A van Verseveld, *Mistake of Law: Excusing Perpetrators of International Crimes* (TMC Asser Press 2012) 96.

[398] See similarly, Stahn (n 2) 156.

statutory frameworks, even if a full defence is rejected on the facts of a particular case, the ICC may still consider an accused's obedience to superior orders as a factor in mitigation.[399]

Notwithstanding the slightly less restrictive approach to cognition-based defences in the ICC Statute, international criminal courts have predominantly adhered to a narrow psychological conception of culpability, according to which criminal guilt is synonymous with intent and knowledge to commit the material elements of a crime, rather than a broader normative conception of culpability, according to which criminal guilt also requires awareness of the wrongfulness of one's actions.[400] Following this approach, international criminal courts have generally relied upon a conclusive assumption that individuals could not reasonably have been unaware of the wrongfulness of their conduct or the manifest illegality of their superior orders to commit crimes falling within their jurisdiction. As a result, judges have typically neglected to reflect on how the social contexts in which accused persons were operating may have affected their cognitive capacities and, in particular, failed to assess the evidence concerning whether any alleged ignorance on the part of such individuals was in fact genuine and reasonable in the circumstances of a particular case.[401]

In the *Civil Defence Forces (CDF)* case at the SCSL, for example, the Trial Chamber concluded that Allieu Kondewa, a high priest in charge of initiations and head of all initiators in the CDF militia, 'knew or had reason to know' that a particular child soldier recruit 'was under fifteen years of age, and too young to be enlisted for military service'.[402] Left unexamined by the Trial Chamber, however, was the question of whether Kondewa was aware of the wrongfulness of enlisting children into an armed group. According to Tim Kelsall, various dimensions of the local cultural context in Sierra Leone at the very least raise questions as to whether it was reasonable to expect that someone of Kondewa's background would know or should know the wrongfulness of enlisting children.[403]

In his study, Kelsall paints a picture of childhood in southern Sierra Leone as one characterised by hardship and suffering, often involving secret society initiation and learning the role of 'client' in patron-client relationships.[404] Kelsall argues that in southern Sierra Leone 'child soldiering, while hardly a welcome development, is not necessarily aberrant, showing strong continuities with pre-war forms of social organisation'.[405] More specifically, Kelsall distinguishes between the abduction and forced recruitment conducted by the Revolutionary United Front which 'doubtless transgressed the line of local norms' on the one hand, and initiation into the CDF militia

399 Rule 145(2)(a)(i), ICC Rules of Procedure and Evidence.

400 G Vanacore, 'Legality, Culpability and *Dogmatik*: A Dialogue between the ECtHR, Comparative and International Criminal Law' (2005) 15 *International Criminal Law Review* 823, 851–852. On the distinction between psychological and normative conceptions of culpability, see generally, Ambos (n 57) 366–368; van Sliedregt (n 1) 276–280; and Eser (n 393) 903–904.

401 MJ Osiel, *Mass Atrocity, Ordinary Evil, and Hannah Arendt: Criminal Consciousness in Argentina's Dirty War* (Yale University Press 2001) 145.

402 *Prosecutor v Moinina Fofana and Allieu Kondewa* (Judgment, Trial Chamber) SCSL-04-14-T (2 August 2007) [971].

403 Kelsall (n 285) 170.

404 Ibid 151–155.

405 Ibid 154.

which was probably viewed by local chiefdoms as 'a natural response to insecurity' on the other.[406] Relying on this distinction, Kelsall takes issue with the SCSL's obliviousness to the local cultural context in which the accused had operated:[407]

> [The judges] ignored the fact that conceptions of children in rural Sierra Leone differ greatly to those preferred by the international community; that military operations were allegedly planned from a base deep in the countryside, surrounded by hostile rebel forces and a national army who habitually used child soldiers themselves; and that … under a Sierra Leonean military forces act, recruitment was legal at any age with parental consent.

Given this local context, Kelsall queries the appropriateness of holding individuals criminally responsible for transgressing legal norms of the international community that bear little or no relation to 'local ideologies of childhood and the empirical realities of wartime Sierra Leone'.[408] While Kelsall does not support the practice of enlisting child soldiers, he questions whether individual criminal responsibility is the most humane method to reform such practices in light of local cultural realities.[409]

Kelsall's critique reveals the implications of the SCSL's failure to examine whether the accused was aware that he had transgressed the crime of enlisting child soldiers. Had the SCSL directed its attention to this question, it could have constructed a more nuanced narrative of the accused's cognitive capacities in light of the local cultural context in which he had operated and a more precise determination of the accused's individual culpability based on the evidence rather than a conclusive decontextualised assumption. As Kelsall argues, 'At the very least, Kondewa's knowledge should have been proved, not assumed'.[410]

With these considerations in mind, a growing number scholars have argued that international criminal courts should recognise a general mistake of law defence, one which would excuse the criminal responsibility of individuals if it could be demonstrated that they acted without consciousness of wrongdoing and that their ignorance of the law was unavoidable or reasonable.[411] Such accounts tend to emphasise how the embeddedness of individuals within particular social and cultural contexts may

[406] Ibid. See similarly, Drumbl (n 15) 64 (noting that 'many children joined the CDF on their own out of patriotism to support the democratically-elected Sierra Leonean government, protect their families and communities, or punish the rebels').

[407] Kelsall (n 285) 158.

[408] Ibid 169.

[409] Ibid 170 ('I am not, let me be clear, endorsing Kondewa's actions. Only the most fanatical of cultural relativists would argue that equipping very young persons to fight in wars is a good thing. Yet only an equally unyielding universalist, I contend, could believe that locking up men for acts they did not know were wrong should be the solution, or that making examples of such men would be the most humane way to reform the practices of a culture. … Kondewa, there are reasons to think, was convicted on this charge without regard to moral guilt. … [H]e was held accountable not to the norms of his own culture, but to those of a society thousands of miles away.')

[410] Ibid.

[411] See, for example, Eser (n 393) 945; Ambos (n 57) 375–376; van Verseveld (n 397) 97. See also, with regard to superior orders, Osiel (n 388) 1017; and A Smeulers, 'Why Serious International Crimes Might Not Seem "Manifestly Unlawful" to Low-level Perpetrators: A Social-Psychological Approach to Superior Orders' (2019) 17 *Journal of International Criminal Justice* 105.

sometimes have the effect of blinding them to the wrongfulness of acts that amount to crimes. In such circumstances, rather than holding individuals culpable for failing to live up to aspirational standards of behaviour, international criminal law should excuse them provided that their mistake of law was unavoidable or reasonable in the circumstances.

Had such a defence been advanced by Kondewa and been deemed permissible by the SCSL, the judges could have explored whether Kondewa's alleged mistake of law was genuine and unavoidable/reasonable based on the evidence. Importantly, even if the SCSL had concluded that Kondewa's ignorance of the law was avoidable or unreasonable, such an assessment would still have enabled the judges to more precisely define the standard of reasonableness expected of individuals in the particular social context in which the accused had operated, as well as specify more precisely the accused's culpability, encompassing not only the fact that he had fulfilled the elements of the crime definition but also that he had made an avoidable/unreasonable mistake of law.[412] To date, however, international criminal courts have generally declined to conduct these types of assessments. As a result, once international criminal courts establish that an accused person has participated in the commission of a crime, the effects of the surrounding circumstances on the cognitive capacities of accused individuals have tended to be excluded from view.[413]

D. Conclusion

Defences—whether in the form of grounds for excluding responsibility or mitigating punishment—present judges with opportunities to reflect on the extent to which an individual's social context may exclude or mitigate their culpability. By determining the range, scope, and definition of coercion-based and cognition-based defences, international criminal courts render judgments concerning what behaviour is considered *reasonable* in light of the situational pressures confronted by accused individuals in mass atrocity contexts.[414] In essence, international criminal courts

412 van Verseveld (n 397) 47.

413 See, in this regard, Knoops (n 298) 144 (noting that 'the defense of mistake of law could interrelate with certain specific social-cultural phenomena, insofar as they shed light on the culpability of the accused. Within the context of the defense of mistake of law, several criteria could be relevant, such as the personal background of the accused, his position within society and, in particular, within a military or political organization as well as the question whether the values protected by the rules allegedly breached form part and parcel of the specific society of the accused.')

414 See similarly, *Erdemović* Appeal Judgment (n 325) (sep and diss op Cassese) [47] ('Law is based on what society can reasonably expect of its members'); and T Weigend, 'Kill or Be Killed: Another Look at *Erdemović*' (2012) 10 *Journal of International Criminal Justice* 1219, 1234 ('The general standard, applied differently by legislatures in various legal systems, is whether the imposition on the actor is such that even a normal, reasonable person would be inducted to commit a (serious) crime'). Importantly, a range of different types of reasonableness standards are identifiable as a matter of criminal law theory. See, for example, Mohamed (n 15) 1668–1676 (distinguishing ordinary and aspirational reasonableness); Brooks (n 331) 869–873 (distinguishing strong and weak reasonableness); and D Luban, 'The Legacies of Nuremberg' (1987) 54 *Social Research* 779, 817, fn 73 (distinguishing statistical and normative reasonableness); KJ Heller, 'Beyond the Reasonable Man? A Sympathetic but Critical Assessment of the Use of Subjective Standards of Reasonable in Self-Defense and Provocation Cases' (1998) 26 *American Journal of Criminal Law* 1, 8–9, 56, 66–68, 80–82 (distinguishing objective, subjective, mixed, and particularised standards of reasonableness); and van Sliedregt (n 1) 219–220.

distinguish—even if only implicitly—between situational pressures that are deemed to be *resistible temptations*, that is pressures which accused persons could reasonably have been expected to resist and are therefore legally irrelevant to assessing their culpability, and situational pressures that are *exculpatory or to some extent mitigating*, that is pressures which accused persons could not reasonably have been expected to have fully resisted and are therefore legally relevant to assessing their culpability.[415] Significantly, where situational pressures are deemed *legally irrelevant* to assessing the culpability of accused persons, they tend to be marginalised or excluded from the historical narratives constructed in the judgments of international criminal courts.

Viewed from this perspective, it is notable that international criminal courts have generally adopted a highly restrictive approach to defences—identifying only a narrow and tightly defined range of situational pressures on the basis of which the culpability of accused persons may be excluded or in some way mitigated. By adopting such a restrictive approach, international criminal courts have conveyed the message that most situational pressures encountered in mass atrocity situations could reasonably have been resisted by accused persons. As a result, the historical narratives constructed by international criminal courts tend to decontextualise the behaviour of the accused, excluding or at the very least marginalising those aspects of the accused's social context which have implicitly been deemed merely *explanatory* of their behaviour as opposed to *exculpatory or to some extent mitigating*.

Importantly, the purpose of this section has not been to determine whether the line between the *explanatory* context and the *exculpatory or mitigating* context has been drawn in a convincing manner, but more modestly to illuminate how the line—and consequently the narratives constructed by international criminal courts—has hinged on the recognition, rejection, and definition of grounds for excluding responsibility and mitigating punishment within international criminal courts in practice.

III. Conclusion

In his landmark text, *Ways of Seeing*, acclaimed art critic John Berger explains how '[i]n the age of pictorial reproduction the meaning of paintings is no longer attached to them; their meaning becomes transmittable ... making it possible, even inevitable that an image will be used for many different purposes'.[416] By way of illustration, Berger refers to Sandro Botticelli's famous painting, *Venus and Mars*, and shows how the reproduction of the image of Venus in isolation from the rest of painting could transform its meaning. By zooming in on a particular detail and extracting it from the whole, the meaning of the image is modified: 'An allegorical figure becomes a portrait of a girl'.[417]

In a similar vein, this chapter has revealed how international criminal courts have selectively contextualised the behaviour of accused individuals for the purpose of

[415] Luban (n 414) 817 (distinguishing between 'resistible temptation' and 'excuse'). In the domestic sphere, some scholars have critiqued the selectivity of the criminal law for arbitrarily giving legal significance to particular aspects of an individual's social context, whilst ignoring others for the purpose of assessing their culpability. See, for example, Norrie (n 14) 173, 223–224, 229.

[416] J Berger, *Ways of Seeing* (BBC and Penguin Books 1972) 24.

[417] Ibid 25.

determining their culpability. In practice, this selective contextualisation has been conducted through culpability categories derived from particular domestic legal systems and progressively interpreted to fit particular judicial understandings of how human agency is affected by the collective and systemic qualities that typify system crimes.

Through modes of participation doctrines, international criminal courts have sought to represent the ways in which the collective and systemic qualities of system crimes may *expand* individual agency. Specifically, international criminal courts have relied upon a range of modes of participation doctrines in an effort to contextualise the behaviour of those alleged to have masterminded the commission of system crimes, in particular by linking their behaviour to the collective and organisational structures by which such crimes were carried out. Importantly, the precise judicial understanding of the relationship between individual agency and the collective and systemic qualities of system crimes has not been uniform, but subject to variation both within and between different institutions. In practice, variations have generally been given expression through the strength of the link required between accused persons and the crimes for which they were allegedly responsible as well as the range of different degrees of participation for which particular modes of participation doctrines have imposed the same culpability label on individuals.

With respect to defences, international criminal courts have revealed a certain degree of discomfort in representing the ways in which the collective and systemic contexts of mass atrocity situations may *diminish* individual agency. Specifically, international criminal courts have recognised only a narrow range of tightly defined coercion-based and cognition-based grounds for excluding responsibility and mitigating punishment through which the culpability of accused persons may be excluded or to some extent mitigated in light of the situational pressures encountered in mass atrocity contexts. By attaching only very limited weight to the coercive and cognitive effects of mass atrocity environments on the agency of accused persons, international criminal courts have predominantly conveyed the message that most situational pressures encountered in mass atrocity situations could reasonably have been resisted by accused persons. The result has been to exclude or at the very least marginalise those aspects of an accused's social context which have implicitly been deemed merely *explanatory* of their behaviour—and therefore legally irrelevant—as opposed to *exculpatory or to some extent mitigating*.

The picture that emerges from this chapter, therefore, is one in which the historical narratives constructed by international criminal courts tend to demonstrate significantly more concern for identifying links between individuals and system crimes than in trying to understand how individuals may be acculturated into violence and hatred by situational pressures stemming from the collective and systemic qualities of the mass atrocity environments in which they operated.

6
Beyond the Purview of International Criminal Judgments

With their gaze fastened on the task of determining the personal culpability of individuals, international criminal courts have inevitably been selective in their construction of history. As the preceding chapters have revealed, while international criminal courts have acknowledged that context and culpability are to some extent intertwined, there is a limit to the contextualisation that judges have deemed legally relevant to the task of determining the criminal responsibility of individuals in practice. As a result, various aspects of mass atrocity environments tend to be eclipsed or at the very least marginalised within the narratives constructed by international criminal courts in their judgments.[1]

Taking these observations as its point of departure, this chapter examines three dimensions of mass atrocity contexts that have been diminished within or excluded from the narratives constructed by international criminal courts across different institutional contexts: first, the structural and slow forms of violence that often exist prior to, during, and after the outbreak of mass atrocities (Section I); second, the interventions of international actors, including the policies and practices of colonial powers, international financial institutions, and international peacekeeping forces (Section II); and finally, the roles performed by bystander communities and resisters during episodes of mass violence (Section III).

By examining these different dimensions of mass atrocity contexts, the intention is neither to belittle the behaviour of the accused persons convicted by international criminal courts, nor to suggest that these contextual factors should have an exonerating or mitigating effect on the culpability of such individuals. Rather, this chapter more modestly seeks to illuminate the limits of the historical narratives constructed by international criminal courts, whose capacity to contextualise is significantly restricted by their adherence to a paradigm of individual criminal responsibility.

I. Structural and Slow Violence

In his landmark study on violence and peace, Johan Galtung referred to structural violence as a concept that encompasses social injustices such as entrenched poverty,

[1] M Damaška, 'What is the Point of International Criminal Justice?' (2008) 83 *Chicago-Kent Law Review* 329, 336 ('Another impediment to satisfactory judicial historiography is that judges cannot sufficiently disentangle themselves from the webs of legal relevancy. Even when its limits are considerably enlarged, as they are by the definition of international crimes, matters important to a full historical account still remain legally irrelevant.')

Doing Justice to History. Barrie Sander, Oxford University Press (2021). © Barrie Sander.
DOI: 10.1093/oso/9780198846871.003.0006

unequal economic opportunities, and systematic social deprivation that occur without 'a clear subject-action-object relation'.[2] In such situations, violence is 'built into the structure and shows up as unequal power and consequently as unequal life chances'.[3] Although not a sufficient cause for the outbreak mass atrocities, the inequalities associated with structural violence are often 'a predisposing factor for conflict'.[4]

Structural violence can take many forms.[5] Frances Stewart, for example, has identified four categories of structural violence: political participation; economic assets; incomes and employment; and social aspects.[6] The existence of structural violence in these forms can generate grievances within society that fuel exploitative violence. In practice, it is often the particular form of structural violence that determines the likelihood of violent conflict, with horizontal inequalities—namely, those aligned with groups along cultural, religious, geographical, or class lines—more likely to lead to the onset of direct violence.[7] When inequalities are defined along group lines, they may be instrumentalised by leaders to generate a sense of group identity, which in turn can lead to the mobilisation of group members through appeals to underlying grievances about real or perceived forms of structural violence.[8]

Importantly, structural violence does not inevitably lead to the outbreak of mass atrocities. There are many States that have experienced periods of prolonged and extreme structural violence that have not descended into episodes of mass violence. However, in those States that *have* experienced episodes of mass violence, very often deeply embedded inequalities have pre-existed the onset of conflict. As Rami Mani explains, while the precise causal relation between structural violence and mass atrocity situations is disputed, 'often, although by no means always, underlying or proximate causes of conflicts appear to centre on contentions about distributive justice: unequal access to, distribution of, and opportunities for political power and socio-economic resources'.[9]

Closely related to structural violence is Rob Nixon's notion of 'slow violence', which refers to 'a violence that occurs gradually and out of sight, a violence of delayed destruction that is dispersed across time and space, … a violence that is neither spectacular nor instantaneous, but rather incremental and accretive, its calamitous repercussions playing out across a range of temporal scales'.[10] Similar to structural

[2] J Galtung, 'Violence, Peace, and Peace Research' (1969) 6 *Journal of Peace Research* 167, 171.

[3] Ibid 171.

[4] R Mani, *Beyond Retribution: Seeking Justice in the Shadows of War* (Polity Press 2002) 129. See similarly, AG Kiyani, 'International Crime and the Politics of Criminal Theory: Voices and Conduct of Exclusion' (2015) 48 *NYU Journal of International Law & Politics* 129, 189–200.

[5] There is a tendency in transitional justice literature to limit discussions of structural causes of violence to economic factors to the exclusion of political factors. In fact, structural violence encompasses both economic *and* political harms. For further discussion, see generally, E Schmid and A Nolan, '"Do No Harm"? Exploring the Scope of Economic and Social Rights in Transitional Justice' (2014) 8 *International Journal of Transitional Justice* 362, 371–374.

[6] F Stewart, 'The Root Causes of Conflicts: Some Conclusions' *QEH Working Paper Series: Working Paper Number 16* (1998) 12–14.

[7] See, for example, P Gready and S Robins, 'From Transitional to Transformative Justice: A New Agenda for Practice' (2014) 8 *International Journal of Transitional Justice* 339, 347; and F Stewart, 'Root Causes of Violent Conflict in Developing Countries' (2002) 324 *British Medical Journal* 342, 343.

[8] Mani (n 4) 128.

[9] Ibid 127.

[10] R Nixon, *Slow Violence and the Environmentalism of the Poor* (Harvard University Press 2011) 2.

violence, the concept of slow violence broadens the field of what constitutes violence towards concerns about social justice, hidden agency, and forms of violence that are difficult to perceive.[11] Yet, in contrast to the somewhat static nature of the concept of structural violence, the notion of slow violence seeks 'to foreground questions of time, movement, and change, however gradual' and to emphasise 'the representational challenges and imaginative dilemmas posed not just by imperceptible violence but by imperceptible change whereby violence is decoupled from its original causes by the workings of time'.[12]

Both structural and slow forms of violence stand in contrast to the spectacular and immediate forms of violence that dominate the historical narratives of international criminal courts.[13] In practice, international criminal courts comprehend violence through the narrow vocabulary of specific criminal law violations, their gaze fastened towards the adjudication of particular crimes committed by identifiable individuals at the expense of illuminating the structural logics that lurk beneath.[14] Adopting an individualised frame of interpretation,[15] international criminal courts generally devote little attention to structural and slow forms of violence,[16] either excluding or marginalising issues as diverse as land distribution, extreme poverty, demographics, systemic discrimination, political instability, social marginalisation, environmental degradation, and widespread economic injustice, many of which may be brought

[11] Ibid 10.

[12] Ibid 11.

[13] See similarly, Kiyani (n 4) 183*ff* (noting how international criminal law 'continues to enforce a very narrow set of human rights priorities', encompassing 'incidences of spectacular, not structural, violence'); I Kalpouzos and I Mann, 'Banal Crimes Against Humanity: The Case of Asylum Seekers in Greece' (2015) 16 *Melbourne Journal of International Law* 1, 1–4 (referring to less visible categories of crimes encompassing 'normalised occurrences', 'banal acts', and 'structural human rights violations rooted in global social-economic inequality'); KM Clarke, '"We Ask For Justice, You Give Us Law": The Rule of Law, Economic Markets and the Reconfiguration of Victimhood', in C de Vos et al (eds), *Contested Justice: The Politics and Practice of the International Criminal Court* (CUP 2015) 272, 274–277 (referring to the 'legal encapsulation' of victimhood whereby the victim is 'reduced to someone who suffered physical violence against his/her individual body, not structural forms of victimhood caused by the very conditions of economic or political disenfranchisement at the heart of the new justice discourse'); R DeFalco and F Mégret, 'The Invisibility of Race at the ICC: Lessons from the US Criminal Justice System' (2019) 7 *London Review of International Law* 55, 82 ('Diffuse processes of producing harm over time, most available to especially powerful actors, are . . . assumed—often incorrectly—to fall outside the purview of ICL').

[14] R Knox, 'Marxism, International Law, and Political Strategy' (2009) 22 *Leiden Journal of International Law* 413, 430–431; and T Krever, 'International Criminal Law: An Ideology Critique' (2013) 26 *Leiden Journal of International Law* 701, 722.

[15] On frames of interpretation in international criminal trials, see generally, M Koskenniemi, 'From Impunity to Show Trials' (2002) 6 *Max Planck Yearbook of United Nations Law* 1, 11–19.

[16] See, for example, *Prosecutor v Delalić et al* (Judgment, Trial Chamber) IT-96-21-T (16 November 1998) ('*Delalić et al* Trial Judgment') [89] ('the Trial Chamber does not seek to identify causal factors, nor through history explain why the conflict with which we are concerned occurred. It would indeed do no justice to the victims of this conflict to attempt to explain their suffering by proffering historical "root causes" which somehow inexorably led to the violence which engulfed them'); and *Prosecutor v Clément Kayishema and Obed Ruzindana* (Judgment, Trial Chamber) ICTR-95-1-T (21 May 1999) ('*Kayishema and Ruzindana* Trial Judgment') [32] ('The Trial Chamber is of the opinion that an attempt to explain the causal links between the history of Rwanda and the suffering endured by this nation in 1994 is not appropriate in this forum and may be futile. It is impossible to simplify all the ingredients that serve as a basis for killings on such a scale.') On the perils of the discourse of root causes in the human rights context, see generally, S Marks, 'Human Rights and Root Causes' (2011) 74 *Modern Law Review* 57.

about by the normal operation of the global economy.[17] As Zinaida Miller argues, by directing attention and resources towards high-level criminal prosecutions, international criminal courts risk establishing and cementing 'a hierarchy of harms in which the spectacular violence pursued in international courtrooms is dubbed the most serious while the horrific indignities and suffering of daily life in a poor country or conflict zone are naturalized as largely inescapable and unchangeable'.[18]

The narratives constructed by the Special Court for Sierra Leone (SCSL) concerning the situation in Sierra Leone are illustrative.[19] With respect to the mass violence that devastated Sierra Leone during the course of the 1990s and early 2000s, a substantial body of commentary has identified structural and slow forms of violence as significant contributing factors.[20] Care International, for example, suggests that evidence concerning the root causes of the conflict in Sierra Leone 'points towards issues like corruption, poverty, and bad governance, and the corresponding need for food security, justice, and the creation of democratic mechanisms capable of protecting the rights of ordinary citizens'.[21] A report by Human Rights Watch based on interviews with former combatants in West Africa also illuminates a clear link between economic deprivation and mass violence, specifically identifying how crippling poverty, unemployment, and marginalisation, as well as corruption and exploitation by political leaders caused many to turn to war as a means for survival.[22] These reports also find support in the work of the Sierra Leone Truth and Reconciliation Commission (TRC), which identifies how decades of unsound governance provided 'a context conducive for the interplay of poverty, marginalisation, greed and grievances that caused and sustained the conflict'.[23] More recently, the empirical work of Paul Richards reveals how a majority

[17] See similarly, I Tallgren, 'The Sensibility and Sense of International Criminal Law' (2002) 13 *European Journal of International Law* 561, 593–595; P Allott, *The Health of Nations: Society and Law Beyond the State* (CUP 2002) 37 and 67 R Nagy, 'Transitional Justice as Global Project: Critical Reflections' (2008) 29 *Third World Quarterly* 275, 276, 279, and 284–286; KM Clarke, *Fictions of Justice: The International Criminal Court and the Challenge of Legal Pluralism in Sub-Saharan Africa* (CUP 2009) 46–48, 53–55, and 237; A Branch, *Displacing Human Rights: War and Intervention in Northern Uganda* (OUP 2011) 213; B Leebaw, *Judging State-Sponsored Violence, Imagining Political Change* (CUP 2011) 181; and F Mégret, 'International Criminal Justice: A Critical Research Agenda', in C Schwöbel (ed), *Critical Approaches to International Criminal Law: An Introduction* (Routledge 2014) 17, 30.

[18] Z Miller, 'Anti-Impunity Politics in Post-Genocide Rwanda', in K Engle et al (eds), *Anti-Impunity and the Human Rights Agenda* (CUP 2016) 149, 169. See similarly, F Mégret, 'Three Dangers for the International Criminal Court: A Critical Look at a Consensual Project' (2001) XII *Finnish Yearbook of International Law* 193, 204.

[19] For other illustrations, see, for example: Z Miller, 'Effects of Invisibility: In Search of the "Economic" in Transitional Justice' (2008) 2 *International Journal of Transitional Justice* 266, 282–284 (critiquing the failure of Rwanda's post-genocide transitional justice mechanisms to address issues of structural violence, such as resource inequities and land-based grievances); and M Mamdani, *Saviours and Survivors: Darfur, Politics, and the War on Terror* (HSRC Press 2009) 271–273 (critiquing the ICC Prosecutor's depiction of the conflict in Darfur, Sudan).

[20] For a useful overview of the relevant literature, see generally, D Keen, 'Greedy Elites, Dwindling Resources, Alienated Youths The Anatomy of Protracted Violence in Sierra Leone' (2003) 6 *International Politics and Society* 67.

[21] Care International, *Food Security: Rights Based Approach Project, Peace and Rights Days Analysis Report* (April–May 2002) cited in Keen (n 20) 69.

[22] Human Rights Watch, *Youth, Poverty and Blood: The Lethal Legacy of West Africa's Regional Warriors* (March 2005) 15–16 and 18–21.

[23] Sierra Leone Truth and Reconciliation Commission, *Witness to Truth: Report of the Sierra Leone Truth & Reconciliation Commission: Volume Three A* (2004) Chapter Two [2].

of combatants, at least amongst rebel groups, were recruited from impoverished rural areas in Sierra Leone and that the causes of the conflict can be rooted in abuses associated with rural custom, including labour exploitation and lack of freedom of opportunity for many youths drawn from former slave classes.[24]

At the SCSL, however, structural and slow forms of violence generally received at most a passing mention in the background sections of judgments.[25] To the extent that the SCSL *did* concern itself with the structural drivers of the Sierra Leonean conflict, the judges tended to focus narrowly on the role played by diamonds. In the case of *Sesay et al*, for example, the SCSL Trial Chamber found that high-ranking members of the Armed Forces Revolutionary Council (AFRC) and Revolutionary United Front (RUF) shared a common plan 'to take any action necessary to gain and exercise political power and control over the territory of Sierra Leone, *in particular the diamond mining areas*'[26] and referred to diamond seizures and trading throughout its judgment.[27] In addition, in the case of *Taylor*, the SCSL Trial Chamber devoted an entire sub-chapter to the relationship between the accused and diamonds,[28] concluding that 'there was a continuous supply by the AFRC/RUF of diamonds mined from areas in Sierra Leone to the Accused, often in exchange for arms and ammunition'.[29]

The focus of the SCSL on diamonds aligns with the views of those who consider them to be at the root of the conflict, a position that has typically been accompanied by the belief that the RUF initiated the conflict with the backing of external actors to gain control of diamond resources.[30] Indeed, David Crane, the SCSL

[24] P Richards, 'To Fight or to Farm? Agrarian Dimensions of the Mano River Conflicts (Liberia and Sierra Leone)' (2005) 104 *African Affairs* 571, 574–586.

[25] See, for example, *Prosecutor v Brima et al* (Judgment, Trial Chamber) SCSL-04-16-T (20 June 2007) ('*Brima et al* Trial Judgment') [155] (referring to 'economic decline'); *Prosecutor v Sesay et al* (Judgment, Trial Chamber) SCSL-04-15-T (2 March 2009) ('*Sesay et al* Trial Judgment') [8]–[9] (linking the creation of the Revolutionary United Front with 'economic decline throughout the 1980s, largely attributable to rampant corruption'); and *Prosecutor v Charles Ghankay Taylor* (Judgment, Trial Chamber) SCSL-03-01-T (18 May 2012) ('*Taylor* Trial Judgment') [20] (linking the creation of the Revolutionary United Front with disenchantment with 'political and economic decadence').

[26] *Sesay et al* Trial Judgment (n 25) [1985] (emphasis added), upheld on appeal: *Prosecutor v Sesay et al* (Judgment, Appeals Chamber) SCSL-04-15-A (26 October 2009) [305]. See also, *Sesay et al* Trial Judgment (n 25) [1722] ('By instilling fear in and committing crimes against civilians who were forced to work at the diamond mines, the AFRC/RUF also intended to retain control over this critical resource, *which remained a constant military objective of both sides*') (emphasis added) and [1727] ('control over the diamond mines in Kono and Kenema Districts was *crucial for the war effort of all armed groups in the Sierra Leone conflict*, due to potential revenue to be raised from the sale of diamonds to finance the purchase of arms, ammunition and other logistics') (emphasis added).

[27] See, for example, *Sesay et al* Trial Judgment (n 25) [1088]–[1095], [1118]–[1121], and [1321]–[1330] (concerning forced mining of diamonds at Tongo Field and Cyborg Pit), [1240]–[1259] (concerning forced mining of diamonds in Kono District), and [1415], [1432]–[1433], and [1485]–[1486] (concerning forced mining of diamonds in Kailahun District).

[28] *Taylor* Trial Judgment (n 25) [5843]–[6149].

[29] Ibid [6140].

[30] See, for example, B Crosette, 'Singling Out Sierra Leone, U.N. Council Sets Gem Ban' *New York Times* (6 July 2000) (referring to Sierra Leone's ambassador to the UN, who had stated: 'The root of the conflict is and remains diamonds, diamonds and diamonds'); and Sierra Leone Truth and Reconciliation Commission, *Witness to Truth: Report of the Sierra Leone Truth & Reconciliation Commission: Volume Three B* (2004) Chapter One [7] (noting, and ultimately contesting, the widely held belief in the West that 'the conflict in Sierra Leone was initiated and perpetuated because of diamonds' and that 'the RUF, backed by Charles Taylor and the NPFL, initiated an armed rebellion in Sierra Leone to gain control of its diamond resources').

Prosecutor, once publicly declared that the conflict in Sierra Leone occurred for reasons of 'pure greed', the primary aim being 'to control a commodity, and that commodity was diamonds'.[31]

Yet, while most commentators share the view that diamonds played *a* part in fuelling the war in Sierra Leone, many have also qualified such assertions. For instance, many commentators argue that a blinkered focus on diamonds tends to obscure the complexities of the underlying conflict, in particular the role played by a number of the other structural factors outlined earlier.[32] According to David Keen, for example, 'In the fashionable emphasis on *greed* as a key cause of civil wars, it is easy to forget—or even dismiss as self-serving propaganda—underlying *grievances*'.[33] In this vein, the narrative that the conflict was largely the result of a restricted set of external actors, including Liberia's Charles Taylor and Libya's Muammar Gaddafi, has been disputed as a tactic for narrowing responsibility for the conflict at the expense of recognising not only the multiple internal causes of the war,[34] but also wider structural processes rooted in the operation of the global economy.

In this light, it is notable that the SCSL Trial Chamber in the case of *Taylor* expressly rejected the prosecution's argument that the accused had participated in a joint criminal enterprise with the RUF to terrorise the civilian population of Sierra Leone in order to forcibly control the population and territory of Sierra Leone and pillage its resources including, most notably, diamonds.[35] According to the Trial Chamber, the relationship between these parties was better characterised as 'the expression of converging and synergistic interests',[36] Taylor and the RUF engaging with each other as 'military allies and trading partners' rather than parties to a joint criminal enterprise.[37] As William Schabas explains, by rejecting the narrative that the Sierra Leonean conflict was caused primarily by a narrow set of external actors, the Trial Chamber's judgment is in closer alignment with the perspective that the conflict was the result of a more diverse set of structural factors.[38] Yet, consistent with other international criminal courts, the Trial Chamber failed to shed any light on what these factors might be, the structural causes of the conflict being too remote to be of legal relevance to the determination of individual criminal responsibility.

[31] International Crisis Group, 'The Special Court for Sierra Leone: Promises and Pitfalls of a "New Model"' *ICJ Africa Briefing* (4 August 2003) 14 (referring to a statement by David Crane during an interview with the Public Broadcasting Services on 10 January 2003).

[32] See, for example, Keen (n 20) 67–68 (summarising how diamonds fuelled the conflict) and 68–70 (summarising the structural causes of the conflict); and Sierra Leone Truth and Reconciliation Commission, *Witness to Truth: Report of the Sierra Leone Truth & Reconciliation Commission: Volume Three B* (2004) Chapter One [207] ('The exploitation of minerals and in particular diamonds did not cause the conflict but rather fuelled it.')

[33] Keen (n 20) 69 (emphasis in original).

[34] See, for example, WA Schabas, 'A Synergistic Relationship: The Sierra Leone Truth and Reconciliation Commission and the Special Court for Sierra Leone' (2004) 15 *Criminal Law Forum* 3, 11–12; Keen (n 20) 86; and International Crisis Group (n 31) 14.

[35] *Taylor* Trial Judgment (n 25) [6894] and [6900].

[36] Ibid [6895].

[37] Ibid [6899].

[38] See similarly, WA Schabas, 'Charles Taylor Judgment Suggests a More Modest Level of Participation in the Sierra Leone Conflict' *PhD Studies in Human Rights Blog* (28 April 2012).

As the example of the SCSL reveals, the paradigm of individual criminal responsibility not only reduces the visibility of structural and slow violence,[39] but also renders legally irrelevant questions concerning the relationship between structural and slow forms of violence and the outbreak of mass atrocities.[40] As a result, international criminal courts tend to offer highly restricted perspectives of mass atrocity situations—the conditions of possibility for system criminality consistently falling beyond their purview.

II. International Interventions

The historical narratives constructed by international criminal courts have also tended to neglect, or at the very least marginalise, the extent to which international actors and institutions intervened within mass atrocity contexts. In particular, the narratives constructed by international criminal courts have generally focused narrowly on the behaviour of local actors, depicting mass atrocity situations primarily in ethnic or nationalist terms through the prism of local apparatuses of power, whilst ignoring the role that international actors and institutions have played in shaping the structure of political, social, economic, and cultural life in societies afflicted by mass violence.[41]

Earlier in this study, mention was already made of the dearth of international prosecutions targeting international business entities and persons—the result of a combination of factors, including the restriction of the personal jurisdictional mandates of international criminal courts to individuals, attribution challenges arising from the remoteness of business persons from the commission of crimes, and the perceived lower gravity of international corporate interventions compared to those of political and military actors operating at the local level of conflict situations. The links between mass violence and business networks are well known. According to James Stewart, for example, 'As a consequence of the illegal trade in minerals, metals, timber, and natural resources, armed conflicts in which participants are able to draw upon easily accessible natural resource wealth are often more bloody, financially costly, and intractable than other forms of armed violence'.[42] With this in mind, the failure of international

[39] See, for example, SMH Nouwen, '"As You Set out for Ithaka": Practical, Epistemological, Ethical, and Existential Questions about Socio-Legal Empirical Research in Conflict' (2014) 27 *Leiden Journal of International Law* 227, 254–255 ('In northern Uganda, [international criminal law] sees killings by the LRA; it does not see a thousand people a week dying in camps for internally displaced persons. International criminal law sees LRA leader Joseph Kony, but not the black fly-borne parasite or vitamin B6 deficiency that may be the cause of children dying of a "mysterious disease" without scientific name that has victimized more than 3,000 children in northern Uganda.')

[40] See, for example, V Nesiah, 'The Trials of History: Losing Justice in the Monstrous and the Banal', in R Buchanan and P Zumbansen (eds), *Law in Transition: Human Rights, Development and Transitional Justice* (Hart Publishing 2014) 289, 305 ('the transitional justice field's approach to historical crimes ... have often rendered systemic factors such as economic and racial structures as mere footnotes of history, rather than shining a light on them as enabling conditions of human rights abuse').

[41] On the exclusion of the interventions of 'the international' in conflict narratives, see generally, A Orford, 'Locating the International: Military and Monetary Interventions after the Cold War' (1997) 38 *Harvard International Law Journal* 443.

[42] JG Stewart, *Corporate War Crimes: Prosecuting the Pillage of Natural Resources* (Open Society Justice Initiative 2011) 9. On the 'resource curse', see generally, J Kyriakakis, 'Justice After War: Economic Actors, Economic Crimes, and the Moral Imperative for Accountability After War', in L May and A Forcehimes (eds), *Morality, Jus Post Bellum, and International Law* (CUP 2012) 113, 121–122; and L van den Herik

prosecutors to address international corporate interventions has ensured that the historical narratives constructed within international criminal judgments only provide a partial picture of episodes of mass violence.

In this section, three other forms of international intervention that have tended to be marginalised by international criminal courts are examined, namely the policies and practices of colonial powers, international financial institutions, and international peacekeeping forces.

A. Colonial Powers

The situational focus of international criminal courts has historically ignored colonial massacres. According to DeFalco and Mégret, for example, 'The history of international criminal justice is littered with such silences, and what they made possible, from massacres in Algeria to Biafra.'[43] In addition, the interventions of colonial powers in the decades prior to the onset of violence in societies that *have* been examined by international criminal courts have generally received only a passing mention in international criminal judgments due to their perceived remoteness to the determination of the responsibility of the local actors under prosecution.[44] Judicial reticence to examine colonial interventions within conflict-affected societies complements the historical reluctance of Western powers to countenance the notion of colonialism within the concept of international crimes.[45] Yet, as Michelle Burgis-Kasthala argues, a deep appreciation of a society's colonial history is important 'not simply as an artefact of the past, but as an ongoing aspect of the present and the future.'[46]

With respect to the Rwandan genocide, for example, colonial interventions are generally considered to have exacerbated the split between Tutsis and Hutus and ensured that 'the important feeling of belonging to a social group was fueled by ethnic, indeed racial, hatred.'[47] Indeed, while it is generally acknowledged that inequalities and differentiation between Hutus and Tutsis existed prior to colonial rule, several

and D Dam-De Jong, 'Revitalizing the Antique War Crime of Pillage: The Potential and Pitfalls of Using International Criminal Law to Address Illegal Resource Exploitation During Armed Conflict' (2011) 15 *Criminal Law Forum* 237, 240–244.

43 DeFalco and Mégret (n 13) 76.

44 See, for example, *Prosecutor v Thomas Lubanga Dyilo* (Judgment Pursuant to Article 74 of the Statute, Trial Chamber) ICC-01/04-01/06-2842 (14 March 2012) [70] ('The two expert witnesses addressed the DRC's colonial past in considerable detail. Regardless of whether the origins of the conflict the Chamber is concerned with are to be found in that history, it is essentially too remote to be of direct relevance to the present charges.')

45 C Stahn, *A Critical Introduction to International Criminal Law* (CUP 2019) 114–115 (discussing the resistance by Western powers to International Law Commission Special Rapporteur Doudou Thiam's defence of a broader definition of the concept of international crimes to include colonialism).

46 M Burgis-Kasthala, 'Scholarship as Dialogue? TWAIL and the Politics of Methodology' (2016) 14 *Journal of International Criminal Justice* 921, 936.

47 A Destexhe, *Rwanda and Genocide in the Twentieth Century* (Alison Marschner trans 1995) 41, cited in JE Alvarez, 'Crimes of States/Crimes of Hate: Lessons from Rwanda' (1999) 24 *Yale Journal of International Law* 365, 388. For a useful overview of the scholarly literature concerning the different definitions of 'the Hutu' and 'the Tutsi', see P Uvin, 'Reading the Rwandan Genocide' (2001) 3 *International Studies Review* 75, 76–79.

commentators have argued that the colonial regimes in Rwanda served to enhance these differences through the import of 'race science' first by the Germans and later the Belgians.[48] Interestingly, in its judgments, the International Criminal Tribunal for Rwanda (ICTR) *did* examine some of the interventions by colonial actors that may have contributed to a climate conducive to genocide in Rwanda. For example, some Trial Chambers expressly identified colonial policies that helped exacerbate distinctions between Hutus and Tutsis, most notably the Belgian imposition of identity cards for Rwandans, which made reference to ethnic background.[49] However, not only have such references been relatively rare,[50] they have also consistently been advanced for the sole purpose of proving that the Tutsis were a protected group according to the definition of the crime of genocide, rather than as a means of scrutinising the practices of colonial powers and holding them to account for their discriminatory policies.[51]

To take a different example, in Sierra Leone, the British imperial leadership pursued what was described by the Sierra Leone TRC as 'a social engineering strategy that was deeply divisive in its nature and impact'.[52] For instance, in line with their tradition of indirect rule, the British increased the powers of traditional rulers across Sierra Leone, who became known as Paramount Chiefs.[53] Many of these powers, which included forced labour, land allocations, and the punishment of dissenters, were retained long into the post-colonial period and served to generate deeply entrenched grievances amongst many Sierra Leoneans.[54] In particular, as Paul Richards explains, the rights of Paramount Chiefs to demand community labour, in combination with local marriage rules, meant that many young men were forced to provide labour within their villages as punishment for interfering with the wives of chiefs.[55] The forced division of labour that resulted from these practices meant that social solidarity within the country crumbled, leaving many youths ripe for recruitment by rebel militias.[56] Yet, despite the connection between these interventions and the violence that erupted in Sierra Leone, the narratives constructed within the judgments of the SCSL generally commenced

[48] See, for example, H Musahara and C Huggins, 'Land Reform, Land Scarcity and Post-Conflict Reconstruction: A Case Study of Rwanda', in C Huggins and J Clover (eds), *From the Ground Up: Land Rights, Conflict and Peace in Sub-Saharan Africa* (Institute for Security Studies 2005) 269, 294–296; and Alvarez (n 47) 388–389.

[49] See, for example, *Prosecutor v Jean-Paul Akayesu* (Judgment, Trial Chamber) ICTR-96-4-T (2 September 1998) ('*Akayesu* Trial Judgment') [81]–[85], [170]–[172], and [702]–[703]; and *Kayishema and Ruzindana* Trial Judgment (n 16) [34]–[36] and [523]–[524].

[50] See similarly, L van den Herik, *The Contribution of the Rwandan Tribunal to the Development of International Law* (Martinus Nijhoff Publishers 2005) 18.

[51] An exception is the judgment of *Nahimana*, in which the Trial Chamber refers to the 'ethnic prejudice that resulted from the differential distribution of social and political privileges along ethnic lines, fostered by and during colonial rule' in order to correct a statement in the prosecution's indictment that claimed that the revolution of 1959 had marked the beginning of ethnic clashes between the Hutu and Tutsi in Rwanda. See *Prosecutor v Nahimana et al* (Judgment and Sentence, Trial Chamber) ICTR-99-52-T (3 December 2003) [105]–[109].

[52] Sierra Leone Truth and Reconciliation Commission, *Witness to Truth: Report of the Sierra Leone Truth & Reconciliation Commission: Volume Three A* (2004) Chapter One [10].

[53] Ibid [19]; Keen (n 20) 70–72.

[54] Sierra Leone Truth and Reconciliation Commission, *Witness to Truth: Report of the Sierra Leone Truth & Reconciliation Commission: Volume Three A* (2004) Chapter One [19]; Keen (n 20) 70–72.

[55] Richards (n 24) 584–585.

[56] Ibid 585.

with Sierra Leonean independence from colonial rule,[57] neglecting any mention of how colonial practices helped establish the structures that contributed to the outbreak of war.

B. International Financial Institutions

A further category of interventions that tend to be overlooked within the narratives of international criminal courts are those of international financial institutions, which have often played an important role in shaping the political, social, and economic structures of States prior to, during, and in the aftermath of episodes of mass violence.[58]

The judgments of the International Criminal Tribunal for the former Yugoslavia (ICTY), for example, omit any mention of the systemic political-economic reforms instigated by the International Monetary Fund (IMF) from the late 1970s through to the early 1990s.[59] Yet, according to a range of studies, these policies hold significant explanatory value in terms of understanding the conflict that erupted in the former Yugoslavia in the 1990s. Susan Woodward, for example, argues that the Yugoslav conflict is best understood as resulting from 'the politics of transforming a socialist society to a market economy and democracy' rather than underlying historical animosities or a desire to return to a pre-communist past.[60] Similarly, Michel Chossudovsky suggests that the breakup of the Yugoslav federation 'bears a direct relation to the programme of macro-economic restructuring imposed on the Belgrade government by its external creditors'.[61] Critical to these accounts of the Yugoslav conflict is the interconnection between externally driven economic stabilisation programmes and domestic political reforms.[62] In essence, these commentators argue that the programme of economic reform and macroeconomic stabilisation instigated by the IMF in the former Yugoslavia unleashed an intense political struggle that resulted in a breakdown in domestic order, the rise of nationalism, and ultimately political disintegration.[63]

Faced with economic decline and a foreign debt crisis in the early 1980s, the Yugoslav government turned to the IMF, which conditioned its assistance on a range of domestic economic reforms designed to enable the country to better service its debt.[64] These conditions entailed a macroeconomic stabilisation programme of radical

[57] See, for example, *Brima et al* Trial Judgment (n 25) [155]; *Sesay et al* Trial Judgment (n 25) [7]; and *Taylor* Trial Judgment (n 25) [20].

[58] A Anghie and B Chimni, 'Third World Approaches to International Law and Individual Responsibility in Internal Conflicts' (2003) 2 *Chinese Journal of International Law* 77, 90; A Orford, 'Locating the International: Military and Monetary Interventions after the Cold War' (1997) 38 *Harvard International Law Journal* 443, 459.

[59] The principal text that expounds this thesis is SL Woodward, *Balkan Tragedy: Chaos and Dissolution After the Cold War* (The Brookings Institution 1995). See also, Orford (n 58) 451–459.; and Krever (n 14) 715–720.

[60] Woodward (n 59) 15.

[61] M Chossudovsky, 'Dismantling Former Yugoslavia: Recolonising Bosnia' (1996) 31 *Economic and Political Weekly* 521, 521.

[62] Woodward (n 59) 50 and 383–384

[63] Ibid 50.

[64] Ibid 48–49.

austerity that included cuts to governmental expenditure (for example, abandoning food subsidies and freezing all new investment for infrastructure and social services), the prohibition of all imports not critical to production (including consumer goods), trade and price liberalisation, and the promotion of exports.[65] These early macroeconomic reforms were later expanded to include currency deregulation, the capping of wages, and privatisation.[66] Later IMF programmes also conditioned new credits on various constitutional and institutional reforms, including a strengthened federal administration as well as the amendment of the central bank's voting rules from consensus to majority.[67] The aim was to shift political and economic authority away from republican governments and banks towards the federal government and the National Bank.[68]

Despite these efforts at recentralisation, by the end of 1989 the legitimacy and functioning of the federal Yugoslav government was increasingly being challenged by republican nationalist elements and sharpened inter-republican conflict.[69] Under increasing pressure from the IMF, a 'shock therapy' stabilisation programme was instituted with the aim of removing 'political barriers to a market economy'.[70] Despite a reduction in inflation and improvement in trade balance during the first six months of the programme, the economic situation ultimately took a turn for the worse with a sharp acceleration in prices, a fall in exports, the currency becoming overvalued, and the policy of real interest rates and heavy taxation leading to massive insolvency of firms.[71]

Analysing the relationship between the IMF and the disintegration of the former Yugoslavia, Anne Orford argues that IMF policies 'arguably fuelled the nationalist dynamic by rapidly restructuring republican and federal levels of government, by implementing policies with divisive social consequences, and by advocating the removal of mechanisms that provided some state support to individuals who would suffer under unrestrained economic liberalism'.[72] For Orford, the IMF's programme of structural adjustment, stabilisation, and later shock therapy contributed in at least four ways to conditions that fuelled the republican nationalist dynamic that ultimately led to mass violence.[73]

First, early IMF austerity policies led to an increasing sense of insecurity and social instability for the people of the former Yugoslavia, with rising unemployment, higher prices for staple goods such as food and fuel, and falling real incomes.[74] Second, constitutional and institutional reforms, motivated by IMF-driven economic policies, abolished mechanisms that had been designed for the protection of minority rights

[65] Ibid 49–51.
[66] Orford (n 58) 453.
[67] Woodward (n 59) 82.
[68] Ibid.
[69] Orford (n 58) 454.
[70] Woodward (n 59) 115.
[71] Ibid 128–129.
[72] Orford (n 58) 455. See similarly, M Darrow, *Between Light and Shadow: The World Bank, the International Monetary Fund, and International Human Rights Law* (Hart Publishing 2006) 107–110.
[73] Orford (n 58) 455–459.
[74] Ibid 456.

within the political system, such as the distribution of government positions according to nationality and state expenditures on cultural rights.[75]

Third, the IMF's structural adjustment policies decreased the legitimacy and power of the federal Yugoslav government, whose functions were radically reduced to a narrow focus on maintaining law and order. As Woodward argues, economic reforms required by foreign creditors in the former Yugoslavia essentially asked for 'political suicide', reducing the federal government's capacity to govern at precisely the moment when demand for governmental protection and support was heightened.[76] The result was a rise in nationalism, which re-emerged to provide a sense of community in the absence of a more effective federal government.[77] Finally, the speed with which economic restructuring and shock therapy were carried out also contributed to the rapid process of political disintegration within the former Yugoslavia.[78] The prioritisation of rapid economic reform failed to recognise the need to dedicate time and energy to selling the programme politically and building a governing capacity, with the result that a conflict emerged between 'the conditions necessary to ensure peace and those deemed necessary for economic liberalisation'.[79]

In elaborating these arguments, Orford is careful to recognise that IMF policies were not the *sole* cause of the conflict in the former Yugoslavia and that similar programmes have been implemented in other contexts without leading to violence on the scale witnessed in the former Yugoslavia.[80] Nevertheless, Orford is also emphatic that international financial institutions 'must take account of and responsibility for the reception of the norms and culture they impose', particularly in contexts such as the former Yugoslavia where 'conditions and processes required or supported by international institutions, when combined with local responses, led to violence'.[81] In this regard, it is interesting to observe that the asserted negative implications of IMF intervention are far from unique to the former Yugoslavia and have also been raised by scholars with respect to other conflicts that have been the subject of international criminal adjudication.

For instance, several commentators have suggested that the road to genocide in Rwanda was accelerated by the collapse of the international coffee market and the imposition of macroeconomic reforms by international financial institutions, including trade liberalisation, currency devaluation, the privatisation of State enterprises, the introduction of higher fees for health and education, and the removal of agricultural subsidies.[82] Michel Chossudovsky, for example, attributes much of Rwanda's political disintegration to the impact of IMF-sponsored currency devaluations and austerity measures which he identifies as important factors that contributed to the

[75] Ibid 456–457.

[76] Woodward (n 59) 17.

[77] Orford (n 58) 457–458.

[78] Ibid 458–459.

[79] Ibid 459.

[80] Ibid. See similarly, Krever (n 14) 719.

[81] Orford (n 58) 459.

[82] See, for example, IA Kamola, 'Coffee and Genocide: A Political Economy of Violence in Rwanda' (2008) 99 *Transition* 54, 67; R Andersen, 'How Multilateral Development Assistance Triggered the Conflict in Rwanda' (2000) 21 *Third World Quarterly* 441, 447–449; and M Chossudovsky, 'Economic Genocide in Rwanda' (1996) 31 *Economic and Political Weekly* 938, 939.

impoverishment of the Rwandan population, destroying economic activity, fuelling unemployment, and creating a situation of famine and social despair.[83] Similarly, Isaac Kamola argues that it is possible to understand the Rwandan genocide 'simultaneously both as a particular historic event *and* a symptom of the often violent transformation from colonial to neoliberal modes of accumulation'.[84]

A similar picture emerges from the account of David Keen with respect to the conflict in Sierra Leone.[85] Specifically, Keen suggests that while the causes of the violence in Sierra Leone are varied, the pattern of structural adjustment encouraged by international financial institutions directly fed underlying grievances within Sierra Leonean society that fuelled the conflict.[86] For instance, privatisation of diamond mining and the import-export trade of fisheries, agricultural marketing, and banking failed to bring about an efficient and competitive market; rather, such policies facilitated local elites in creating monopolistic informal economies, whilst starving the State of markets that could be effectively taxed.[87] In addition, repeated devaluations led to a rise in inflation, which proved particularly harmful for farmers whose input prices increased sharply.[88] Harsh austerity measures, implemented to attract further support from the IMF, led to a major reduction in food and petrol subsidies, inciting resentment amongst local communities who were unable to access basic needs.[89] Meanwhile, the government implemented cuts to health and education funding, reducing the social services that it was able to render and generating further resentment amongst the socially excluded.[90] Cuts in the State wage bill also fuelled corruption within the State sector, particularly amongst local chiefs who in turn became more economically exploitative of the local communities they governed.[91] In light of these effects, Keen concludes that while often promoted as an ostensible solution to economic hardship, the policies of international financial institutions were 'part of the problem' in the Sierra Leonean context.[92]

Although there are several scholars who support these positions, it is important to note that these views are far from universally shared. For instance, with respect to the former Yugoslavia, it has been suggested that the negative outcomes of austerity programmes were 'the result of domestic policy choices taken in response to external capital market constraints and were not fundamentally affected by IMF involvement'.[93]

[83] Chossudovsky (n 82) 941.
[84] Kamola (n 82) 70 (emphasis added).
[85] See generally, D Keen, 'Liberalization and Conflict' (2005) 26 *International Political Science Review* 73; and Keen (n 20) 75–76.
[86] Keen (n 85) 74–75.
[87] Ibid 75–77.
[88] Ibid 77.
[89] Ibid.
[90] Ibid 78–79.
[91] Ibid 79–80.
[92] Ibid 73–74. Keen also observes how a willingness to push through structural adjustment policies enabled the government of Sierra Leone to portray itself as a 'model' government, which in turn led foreign governments to raise very little protest about human rights abuses committed during the civil war from 1992 to 1996, prioritising the promotion of liberalisation over compliance with human rights standards. Ibid 81–84.
[93] L Tyson et al, 'Conditionality and Adjustment in Hungary and Yugoslavia', in JC Brada et al (eds), *Economic Adjustment and Reform in Eastern Europe and the Soviet Union: Essays in Honor of Franklyn D. Holzman* (Duke University Press 1988) 72, 105.

Similarly, with respect to Rwanda, Peter Uvin argues that the structural adjustment programme negotiated with the IMF and the World Bank did not cause Rwanda's economic crisis and was merely irrelevant to its resolution: first, because Rwanda only partially implemented the programme; and second, because Rwanda was enmeshed in crises beyond the programme's control such as the ongoing civil war and democratic transition.[94]

Moreover, even amongst those who argue that the interventions of international financial institutions *did* contribute to the descent of certain States into episodes of mass violence, such accounts tend to be qualified in important ways. David Keen, for example, qualifies his account of Sierra Leone by emphasising the need to remember that structural adjustment was introduced in the midst of an already-existing economic crisis, with the prices of exports falling and foreign debt radically rising.[95] Similarly, in his account of the impact of the structural adjustment programme in Rwanda, Andy Storey observes how Rwanda's economy had already been extensively liberalised prior to the adoption of the programme, the implementation of the programme proceeded unevenly, and perhaps most fundamentally that 'with or without adjustment, the Rwandan economy would have been in crisis at this time'.[96] In the latter regard, Storey emphasises the impact of structural political and economic factors, such as chronic land shortages and rapid population growth.[97]

Given these important qualifications, what emerges most vividly from this literature is the failure of international financial institutions to take adequate account of the political effects that their structural adjustment programmes were likely to generate.[98] With respect to Rwanda, for example, David Woodward suggests that even if the adjustment programme did not contribute directly to the genocide in 1994, 'such a reckless disregard for social and political sensitivities in such a conspicuously sensitive situation would unquestionably have increased the risk of creating or compounding a potentially explosive situation'.[99] In other words, the interventions of international financial institutions have generally formed a significant part of the context of mass atrocity conflicts.[100] Yet, in light of their limited mandates, international criminal courts have tended to exclude or marginalise their interventions.[101] In its judgment in the case of *Duško Tadić*, for example, the ICTY Trial Chamber devoted, in somewhat exemplary fashion, a mere one paragraph to the economic crisis that preceded the Yugoslav conflict, omitting any mention of the role played by international financial institutions.[102] Such interventions are considered too remote from the acts and

94 P Uvin, *Aiding Violence: The Development Enterprise in Rwanda* (Kumarian Press 1998) 57–59.

95 Keen (n 85) 75.

96 A Storey, 'Economics and Ethnic Conflict: Structural Adjustment in Rwanda' (1999) 17 *Development Policy Review* 43, 49.

97 Ibid 49–50.

98 See similarly, Darrow (n 72) 111; and Storey (n 96) 57.

99 D Woodward, *The IMF, the World Bank and Economic Policy in Rwanda: Economic, Social and Political Implications* (1996) 24 cited in Darrow (n 72) 111.

100 Orford (n 58) 459.

101 See similarly, Krever (n 14) 718; and G Baars, 'Law(yers) Congealing Capitalism: On the (Im)possibility of Restraining Business in Conflict through International Criminal Law' *Doctoral Thesis* (University College London 2012) 258–259.

102 *Prosecutor v Duško Tadić* (Judgment, Trial Chamber) IT-94-1-T (7 May 1997) [70]. See similarly, *Delalić et al* Trial Judgment (n 16) [96] (referring to 'the escalation of a serious economic crisis');

omissions of the accused individuals on trial to fall within the purview of international criminal courts.

C. International Peacekeeping Forces

A further category of interventions that have remained at the periphery of the narratives constructed by international criminal courts are those of international peacekeeping forces. To the extent that peacekeepers *have* been mentioned in international criminal judgments, they have tended to be depicted in reductionist terms either as victims of crimes or helpless bystanders to atrocities.[103] Yet, the behaviour of peacekeeping forces, together with the entities responsible for their mandates, have been subject to increasing attention in recent years—their interventions often constituting an important dimension of the context in which mass atrocities have occurred.

For example, the conduct of Dutch peacekeeping troops (Dutchbat), who formed part of the UN Protection Force during the Srebrenica massacre in July 1995, has come under heightened scrutiny in recent years.[104] A report commissioned by the Dutch government held the Netherlands partially to blame for Dutchbat's failure to protect the civilian population of Srebrenica,[105] two judgments of the Dutch Supreme Court held the Netherlands legally responsible for the removal of a Dutchbat electrician, Rizo Mustafić, and the family members of a Dutchbat interpreter, Hasan Nuhanović, from the compound protected by Dutchbat,[106] and most recently a judgment of the Dutch Supreme Court held the Netherlands liable for not affording the male refugees who had been sheltering in Dutchbat's compound the choice of remaining there, thereby depriving them of a 10 per cent chance of avoiding execution by the Bosnian Serbs.[107] The United Nations (UN) itself has

and *Prosecutor v Radislav Krstić* (Judgment, Trial Chamber) IT-98-33-T (2 August 2001) ('*Krstić* Trial Judgment') [9] (referring to 'economic woes').

[103] See generally, M O'Brien, 'Prosecutorial Discretion as an Obstacle to Prosecution of United Nations Peacekeepers by the International Criminal Court: The Big Fish/Small Fish Debate and the Gravity Threshold' (2012) 10 *Journal of International Criminal Justice* 525.

[104] To date, no criminal prosecutions of Dutch peacekeepers have been pursued in relation to the Srebrenica situation. See generally, S van den Berg, 'Netherlands Court Backs Decision Not to Prosecute Dutchbat Soldiers over Srebrenica Deaths' *International Justice Tribune* (4 May 2015); and A Morris, 'Dutch Court Decides Not to Prosecute Srebrenica Commander' *JURIST* (29 April 2015).

[105] The publication of the report led to the resignation of the Prime Minister of the Netherlands, Wim Kok. See NIOD Institute for War, Holocaust and Genocide Studies, *Srebrenica, a 'safe' area—Reconstruction, background, consequences and analyses of the fall of a safe area* (2002); and Letter of the Dutch Prime Minister offering the resignation of the cabinet of the Netherlands, 16 April 2002, *Tweede Kamer* (House of Representatives of the Netherlands), Session 2001–2002, *Kamerstuk* (Parliamentary Paper) 28334, No 1.

[106] *The Netherlands v Nuhanović* (Judgment, Supreme Court of the Netherlands) Case No 12/03324 (6 September 2013); and *The Netherlands v Mustafić-Mujić* (Judgment, Supreme Court of the Netherlands) Case No 12/03329 (6 September 2013). For discussion of these cases, see generally, N Higgins, 'The Responsibility of the Netherlands for the Actions of Dutchbat: An Analysis of Nuhanović and Mustafić' (2014) 14 *International Criminal Law Review* 641.

[107] *Mothers of Srebrenica Association et al v The Netherlands* (Judgment, Supreme Court of the Netherlands) Case No 17/04567 (19 July 2019). For discussion, see generally, C Ryngaert and O Spijkers,

managed to avoid formal legal accountability, though only by asserting immunity from suit.[108]

In contrast to this climate of scrutiny, the narratives constructed in the judgments of the ICTY paint a different picture of the role performed by Dutchbat in the former Yugoslavia. In its judgment in the case of *Radislav Krstić*, for example, the ICTY Trial Chamber referred to the conduct of Dutchbat during this period only in general terms, typically as witnesses to atrocities,[109] or as powerless bystanders to the events that unfolded.[110] In light of its limited mandate, the Trial Chamber did not venture to examine the broader responsibilities of the international community for leaving such an ill-equipped peacekeeping force to protect the Bosnian enclaves.[111]

Beyond the situation in the former Yugoslavia, the failures of the international peacekeeping force in Rwanda have also been subject to significant scrutiny in the years following the Rwandan genocide in 1994—one commentator even describing the episode as a 'case study of international negligence'.[112] Both in the lead-up to the outbreak of genocide as well as during its commission, various States, as well as the UN, were heavily criticised for their inaction and incompetence in responding to what many have characterised as an entirely preventable genocide.[113]

For instance, repeated warnings in advance of the genocide, including a crucial cable sent on 11 January 1994 by General Romeo Dallaire of the UN Assistance Mission in Rwanda (UNAMIR) concerning the possibility of a plan to exterminate Tutsis, continually fell on deaf ears.[114] Moreover, during the period when atrocities were committed, UNAMIR was severely under-equipped, lacking the capacity, resources, and mandate to effectively respond to the mass violence in Rwanda.[115] The inadequacy of UNAMIR was in stark contrast to the European troops who were deployed in the early

'The End of the Road: State Liability for Acts of UN Peacekeeping Contingents After the Dutch Supreme Court's Judgment in *Mothers of Srebrenica* (2019)' (2019) 66 *Netherlands International Law Review* 537.

[108] See generally, *Stichting Mothers of Srebrenica and Others v The Netherlands* (Decision, European Court of Human Rights) App No 65542/12 (11 June 2013). For discussion, see generally, MI Papa, 'The *Mothers of Srebrenica* Case before the European Court of Human Rights: United Nations Immunity versus Right of Access to a Court' (2016) 14 *Journal of International Criminal Justice* 893.

[109] See, for example, *Krstić* Trial Judgment (n 102) [45] (referring to a Dutchbat medical officer who witnessed the rape of a young woman by two Serb soldiers) and [58] (referring to Dutchbat troops witnessing signs that the Bosnian Serbs were executing some of the Bosnian Muslim men in Srebrenica).

[110] See, for example, *Krstić* Trial Judgment (n 102) [50] (referring to failed attempts by Dutchbat soldiers to escort the buses carrying the Bosnian Muslim civilians out of the UN compound at Potočari since 'they were stopped along the way and their vehicles were stolen at gunpoint') and [364] (referring to Bosnian Muslim men aboard buses 'begging the UN to do something').

[111] See similarly, Mégret (n 18) 234–235 (describing the responsibility of the international community as one which 'often reached perilous heights of negligence and which, in some cases, bordered on complicity as when . . . a Dutch lieutenant-colonel had drinks with Mladić as he emptied Srebrenica of its population').

[112] P Gourevitch, *We Wish to Inform You that Tomorrow We Will Be Killed with Our Families* (Picador 1998) 326.

[113] For a useful summary of the principal critiques, see generally Alvarez (n 47) 390–392, 396–398, and 440–443.

[114] 'Report of the Independent Inquiry into the actions of the United Nations during the 1994 genocide in Rwanda' S/1999/1257 (16 December 1999) ('Independent Inquiry into UN in Rwanda Report') 33–34.

[115] Ibid 31–32 (critiquing the limited mandate of UNAMIR), 39–41 (critiquing the inadequate resources and logistics of UNAMIR), 43–44 (critiquing the lack of political will to give UNAMIR the personnel and resources necessary to prevent the genocide), and 48 (critiquing organisational problems within UNAMIR).

stages of genocide for the sole purpose of evacuating their own citizens.[116] Indeed, in a telling expression of where the priorities of the international community lay during this period, General Dallaire was sent an explicit cable by the UN Department of Peacekeeping Operations, which stated that while every effort should be made to maintain neutrality and impartiality, an exception could be made if essential for the evacuation of foreign nationals.[117] The Organisation of African Unity's International Panel of Eminent Personalities would later condemn this policy as a 'flagrant double standard'.[118]

As the atrocities began to unfold, UNAMIR failed to protect leading politicians, civilians, as well as its own national staff, in spite of assurances and expectations that such protection would be guaranteed.[119] Moreover, UNAMIR was brought to near disintegration when Belgium unilaterally decided to withdraw its troops following the killing of ten Belgian peacekeepers and then campaigned for the withdrawal of the entire mission.[120] The subsequent decision on 21 April 1994 to reduce UNAMIR to a force of merely 450 troops has been described as the Security Council's 'most shameful hour'.[121] Beyond depleting the capacity of UNAMIR, Alison Des Forges has argued that such international indifference convinced many Rwandans that the genocidal government would succeed:[122] 'Those who hesitated at first now yielded to fear or opportunism and carried the slaughter throughout Rwanda.' Moreover, a UN Independent Inquiry found evidence to suggest that when UNAMIR began to withdraw from areas under its protection, in certain instances 'the trust placed in UNAMIR by civilians left them in a situation of greater risk when the UN troops withdrew than they would have been otherwise'.[123] Such evidence demonstrates how well-intentioned international interventions, when poorly executed, can worsen an already-existing crisis situation.[124]

France has also come under particular scrutiny for its deployment of troops during this period in *Opération Turquoise*, a military operation that has been viewed by several commentators as a cynical scheme on the part of the French government to protect and evacuate those responsible for the genocide.[125] For instance, notwithstanding the fact that the French operation was ultimately credited with rescuing at least 10,000 Tutsis in western Rwanda,[126] Philip Gourevitch argues that 'the signal achievement of the *Opération Turquoise* was to permit the slaughter of Tutsis to continue for an extra

[116] S Power, 'Bystanders to Genocide: Why the United States Let the Rwandan Tragedy Happen' *The Atlantic* (1 September 2001).

[117] Ibid.

[118] Organisation of African Unity International Panel of Eminent Personalities, *Rwanda: The Preventable Genocide* (2000) ('OAU International Panel of Eminent Personalities Rwanda Report') [15.7].

[119] Independent Inquiry into UN in Rwanda Report (n 114) 44–46.

[120] Ibid 36–37.

[121] S Power, 'Accessory to Murder' *New York Times* (11 February 2001). See also, Independent Inquiry into UN in Rwanda Report (n 114) 37 (referring to how the Security Council's decision causes 'widespread bitterness in Rwanda').

[122] AL Des Forges, 'Shame: Rationalizing Western Apathy on Rwanda' *Foreign Policy* (May/June 2001).

[123] Independent Inquiry into UN in Rwanda Report (n 114) 45.

[124] Uvin (n 47) 92.

[125] See, for example, Human Rights Watch, *Justice After Genocide: 20 Years On* (28 March 2014) 16–17; and OAU International Panel of Eminent Personalities Rwanda Report (n 118) [15.62]–[15.66].

[126] Ibid [15.68]; and Gourevitch (n 112) 158.

month, and to secure safe passage for the genocidal command to cross, with a lot of its weaponry, into Zaire'.[127] The result was to expand the remit of the conflict and to destabilise the entire Great Lakes Region.[128]

As this brief summary reveals, both States and the UN have received a great deal of criticism for their actions and inactions during the Rwandan genocide. Indeed, such has been the intensity of the scrutiny that a number of world leaders, including former US President Bill Clinton, former UN Secretary General Kofi Annan, and former Belgian Prime Minister Guy Verhofstadt, have publicly acknowledged and apologised for their failure to halt the genocide in Rwanda.[129]

Despite the significant scrutiny that surrounds the role of the international community's peacekeeping operations both prior to and during the Rwandan genocide,[130] the judgments of the ICTR narrate a different story, one in which the acts and omissions of peacekeepers were either excluded from view or reduced to the roles of witnesses or victims.

In its judgment in *Akayesu*, for example, the ICTR Trial Chamber relied on the testimony of UNAMIR's General Dallaire solely for his insights as a witness to the atrocities committed by local actors, rather than for his thoughts concerning the lack of will of the international community to prevent the violence.[131] During the trial, Dallaire had been summoned as a witness for the defence team in an effort to argue that if the UN was not able to prevent the genocide, how could the defendant have been expected to.[132] During his testimony, Dallaire described the inaction of the international community as 'an unimaginable exercise in frustration', specifically referring to his memo of 11 January 1994 warning of impending massacres, characterising UNAMIR as 'an emasculated force with no resources', and arguing that the genocide could have been prevented had UNAMIR been better equipped.[133] Yet, in its judgment, although the Trial Chamber made passing reference to the warnings and requests issued by Dallaire that were either ignored or rejected,[134] as well as the reductions made to UNAMIR's peacekeeping force by the Security Council,[135] Dallaire's biting critique of the UN and international community was notable only for its absence. In this way, the judges

[127] Gourevitch (n 112) 160–161. See similarly, OAU International Panel of Eminent Personalities Rwanda Report (n 118) [15.68]–[15.80]. By contrast, a parliamentary committee on French military involvement in Rwanda concluded that although successive French governments had made 'errors of judgment', nonetheless 'France in no way incited, encourage, aided or supported those who orchestrated the genocide and began it in the days that followed the assassination'. CR Whitney, 'Panel Finds French Errors in Judgment on Rwanda' *New York Times* (20 December 1998).

[128] OAU International Panel of Eminent Personalities Rwanda Report (n 118) [15.85].

[129] Human Rights Watch (n 125) 17.

[130] See, in this regard, OAU International Panel of Eminent Personalities Rwanda Report (n 118) [9.1] (concluding that while the international community may not have known that genocide was systematically being planned, it nonetheless knew 'that something terrible was under way in Rwanda, that serious plans were afoot for even more appalling deeds, that these went far beyond routine thuggery, and that the world nevertheless stood by and did nothing').

[131] *Akayesu* Trial Judgment (n 49) [115], [121], and [122].

[132] Ibid [31].

[133] L Santoro, 'Rwanda Massacres Were Avoidable, General Says' *The Christian Science Monitor* (27 February 1998).

[134] *Akayesu* Trial Judgment (n 49) [105] and [126].

[135] Ibid [108]. See similarly, *Prosecutor v Ndindiliyimana et al* (Judgment and Sentence, Trial Chamber) ICTR-00-56 (17 May 2011) ('*Ndindiliyimana et al* Trial Judgment') [206].

appear to have adhered to the lengthy statement made by a UN legal representative at the beginning of Dallaire's testimony to the effect that scrutiny of the UN's decision-making processes should be considered strictly beyond the ICTR's jurisdiction unless directly pertinent to the individual criminal responsibility of the accused.[136]

Having initially been depicted as witnesses in *Akayesu*, members of UNAMIR were later depicted as victims in other judgments. For instance, in its judgment in *Bagosora et al*, the ICTR Trial Chamber examined the killing of ten Belgian peacekeepers that had prompted the withdrawal of the Belgian contingent of UNAMIR.[137] Whilst noting that the depletion of the UNAMIR force removed 'a major obstacle to the pursuit of the massacres', the incident was examined solely from the perspective of determining whether the accused were responsible for the killings and whether the deaths had been part of a plan to weaken UNAMIR so as to facilitate the massacre of Tutsi civilians.[138] As such, the Trial Chamber focused narrowly on UNAMIR's victim status, to the exclusion of scrutinising the decision of Belgium to unilaterally withdraw its troops as a result of the attack.

As these examples demonstrate, the focus of international criminal courts on determining the criminal responsibility of accused individuals has tended to occlude scrutiny of the practices of international peacekeeping forces, their behaviour either completely excluded from view or reduced to the role of witnesses or victims.

III. Bystanders and Resisters

The historical narratives constructed by international criminal courts have also tended to neglect the roles performed by bystanders and resisters during episodes of mass violence.

Mass atrocities are often committed in environments where large numbers of individuals acquiesce in the violence around them, many benefitting ideologically, politically, and/or materially from its commission, without bloodying their own hands.[139] According to Iris Young, such individuals 'dwell within the social system that enables the crimes and supply the system with at least passive support'.[140] By engaging in a mass self-deception that the atrocities unfolding around them are acceptable, bystanders evacuate 'any space of popular organization and critical accountability, leaving isolated and ineffectual the few of their fellow members who were inclined to think and criticize'.[141]

[136] Mégret (n 18) 234.

[137] *Prosecutor v Bagosora et al* (Judgment and Sentence, Trial Chamber) ICTR-98-41-T (18 December 2008) ('*Bagosora et al* Trial Judgment') [754]–[796]. See also, *Prosecutor v Théoneste Bagosora and Anatole Nsengiyumva* (Judgment, Appeals Chamber) ICTR-98-41-A (14 December 2011) [607]–[630] (for the discussion of this incident on appeal, in which the Trial Chamber's findings were partially overturned).

[138] *Bagosora et al* Trial Judgment (n 137) [754] and [783]. See also, *Ndindiliyimana et al* Trial Judgment (n 135) [1852]–[1888].

[139] MA Drumbl, *Atrocity, Punishment, and International Law* (CUP 2007) 25; and LE Fletcher, 'From Indifference to Engagement: Bystanders and International Criminal Justice' (2005) 26 *Michigan Journal of International Law* 1013, 1027.

[140] IM Young, *Responsibility for Justice* (OUP 2011) 86.

[141] Ibid 87.

In practice, political leaders who contribute to the outbreak of episodes of mass violence often count on popular support, both to help them achieve power and to look the other way once atrocities have begun.[142] According to Jelena Subotić, senior leaders in mass atrocity contexts have often built their policies on 'a societal receptivity to violent claims that were broadly accepted, normalized, and routinized in society and gave criminal policies a patina of legitimacy'.[143] In such contexts, 'doing nothing' may in fact constitute 'doing something', the inaction of large numbers of individuals serving as a form of silent condonation of the atrocities unfolding around them.[144]

Within the judgments of international criminal courts, bystanders are effectively invisible.[145] Subject to limited exceptions—for example, where an individual's position of authority and physical presence at or very near to a crime scene,[146] or an individual's failure to discharge a legal duty where he or she had the ability to intervene,[147] assisted, encouraged, or lent moral support to the perpetration of a crime and had a substantial effect on its realisation—the inaction and passivity of individuals has generally been insufficiently substantial to fall within the scope of individual criminal responsibility.[148]

In addition, despite the significance of bystander passivity in enabling the formation of a climate of societal permissibility for the commission of crimes, their contributions have generally been deemed too remote to be of legal relevance to the culpability of the individuals on trial. In practice, therefore, bystanders have often been reduced to the role of 'inert props' in the narratives constructed by international criminal courts, a 'nameless populace' that neutrally observed the atrocities unfolding around them.[149] In particular, no effort has been made either to unravel the variety and complexity of bystander relationships to the individuals on trial, or to differentiate the range of roles that bystanders may have played with respect to the violence under examination.[150]

Beyond failing to identify and distinguish the diversity of roles performed by bystanders within mass atrocity situations, international criminal courts have also implicitly lumped together those who simply stood by and allowed the atrocities around them to unfold with those who resisted the violence and attempted to rescue potential victims. Within the judgments of international criminal courts, only limited dimensions of resistance and rescue have tended to be invoked in practice: first, acts of resistance alleged to amount to the commission of a crime; second, acts of assistance

142 Fletcher (n 139) 1026.

143 J Subotic, 'Expanding the Scope of Post-Conflict Justice: Individual, State and Societal Responsibility for Mass Atrocity' (2001) 48 *Journal of Peace Research* 157, 160.

144 LE Fletcher, 'Facing Up to the Past: Bystanders and Transitional Justice' (2007) 20 *Harvard Human Rights Journal* 47, 47.

145 Subotic (n 143) 160; Fletcher (n 139) 1029; K Ainley, 'Excesses of Responsibility: The Limits of Law and the Possibilities of Politics' (2011) 25 *Ethics & International Affairs* 407, 422.

146 See, for example, *Prosecutor v Radoslav Brđanin* (Judgment, Appeals Chamber) IT-99-36-A (3 April 2007) [273]; and *Grégoire Ndahimana v The Prosecutor* (Judgment, Appeals Chamber) ICTR-01-68-A (16 December 2013 [147].

147 *Prosecutor v Mile Mrkšić and Veselin Šljivančanin* (Judgment, Appeals Chamber) IT-95-13/1-A (5 May 2009) [49] and [146].

148 Drumbl (n 139) 25; Fletcher (n 139) 1027, 1030–1031, and 1061; Mégret (n 18) 237.

149 Fletcher (n 139) 1062–1069 (analysing the treatment of bystanders in the ICTY Trial Chamber judgment of *Simić*) and 1078.

150 Ibid 1073–1078.

provided to potential victims relied on by convicted individuals as a factor in mitigation of their sentence;[151] and finally, acts of resistance undertaken by the accused or similarly situated individuals, which help judges establish the agency of accused persons within mass atrocity environments.[152]

Although not insignificant, each of these dimensions offers only a limited insight into the theme of resistance within mass atrocity environments. The first dimension focuses narrowly on identifying and condemning criminal acts of resistance. The second dimension concerns the exceptional and isolated acts of resistance of convicted individuals to the neglect of the broader range of actors who undertake acts of resistance within atrocity-affected communities.

The third dimension focuses on acts of resistance that help to demonstrate that an accused person had agency to act otherwise within a given context. According to Bronwyn Leebaw, by requiring individuals to conform with international legal rules, the normative framework of international criminal law typically demands disobedience to domestic authorities that order or authorise system crimes.[153] This demand for disobedience is most clearly given expression in the limited and restrictively defined grounds for excluding and mitigating responsibility recognised by international criminal law.[154] Article 33 of the Statute of the International Crimianl Court (ICC), for example, is premised on the idea that individuals should resist and disobey manifestly unlawful orders to commit crimes.[155] Bearing in mind the collective and systemic pressures that typically characterise mass atrocity contexts, accounts of disobedience and resistance—whether undertaken by the accused or a similarly situated individual—are sometimes invoked by judges as evidence of the possibility that 'even those who have been subjected to extraordinary coercion, those who have endured shattering trauma, and those subjected to desensitization should remain capable of . . . exercising individual agency'.[156] In *Akayesu*, for example, the ICTR Trial Chamber referred to instances where the accused had acted to prevent violence taking place in the commune of Taba prior to 18 April 1994 as evidence of his capacity for disobeying orders thereafter.[157] In a similar vein, in *Ongwen*, the ICC Pre-Trial Chamber made reference to the fact that 'escapes from the LRA were not rare' as evidence to demonstrate that the accused 'could have chosen not to rise in hierarchy and expose himself to increasingly higher responsibility to implement LRA policies'.[158] Although important, these acts of disobedience and resistance are generally relied upon by judges for the narrow purpose of highlighting the *failure* of accused persons to resist,[159] rather than as a means

[151] See, in this regard, B Holá et al, 'International Sentencing Facts and Figures: Sentencing Practice at the ICTY and ICTR' (2011) 9 *Journal of International Criminal Justice* 411, 433 (finding that, as of June 2010, assistance to victims was mentioned in 38 per cent of ICTY cases and 42.5 per cent of ICTR cases as a mitigating factor).

[152] B Leebaw, 'Justice and the Faithless: The Demand for Disobedience in International Criminal Law' (2018) 24 *European Journal of International Relations* 344, 357.

[153] Ibid 345.

[154] Ibid 351–355.

[155] Article 33, ICC Statute.

[156] Leebaw (n 152) 362.

[157] *Akayesu* Trial Judgment (n 49) [183]–[193].

[158] *Prosecutor v Dominic Ongwen* (Decision on the Confirmation of Charges Against Dominic Ongwen, Pre-Trial Chamber) ICC-02/04-01/15-422-Red (23 March 2016) [154].

[159] On failures to resist, see generally, Leebaw (n 17) 147–156.

for reflecting on and seeking to understand positive attempts to resist in mass atrocity contexts.[160]

Acts of rescue and resistance have a unique meaning in mass atrocity contexts. As Ron Dudai explains, such acts tend to have a heightened practical and symbolic value because rescuers act against the mainstream of their society, defiantly resisting the atrocities around them and affirming the idea of humanity in response to its denunciation by perpetrators of system crimes.[161] In practice, the general neglect of acts of resistance by international criminal courts serves to occlude consideration of the different types of rescue and resistance identifiable in mass atrocity contexts.

Iris Young, for example, makes a distinction between private and political acts of resistance.[162] Examples of private resistance include stories of an artisan who preferred having his independence destroyed and becoming a worker in a factory rather than entering the Nazi Party, and academics who renounced their careers rather than swear by Hitler's name.[163] For resistance to be political, by contrast, it has to be public, specifically aimed at instigating collective action against particular events and initiatives.[164] One example recounted by Hannah Arendt in her study of the *Eichmann* trial concerned the Scholls, a brother and sister at Munich University, who had distributed leaflets referring to Hitler as a 'mass murderer'.[165] A more notorious example is the story of the open resistance of the Danish people and their government in ferrying thousands of Jewish people to safety in Sweden, directly sabotaging the plans of the Nazis.[166]

Bronwyn Leebaw proposes three further distinctions of resistance:[167] first, between violent and non-violent political acts of resistance, the former demanding scrutiny so as to avoid sanitising or glorifying the violence committed in the name of resistance; second, between privileged and non-privileged resistance, the former referring to individuals who occupied elite positions and either abandoned them or made use of them to protest against the regime; and finally, between acts that were successful and those that failed. In addition, Ron Dudai distinguishes between different degrees of altruistic behaviour, including those who acted in a purely humanitarian manner, those who carried out acts of rescue for money or other benefits, those who were selective in who they rescued, and those who carried out both acts of rescue *and* acts of atrocity.[168]

[160] Leebaw (n 152) 357. See similarly, R Dudai, '"Rescues for Humanity": Rescuers, Mass Atrocities, and Transitional Justice' (2012) 34 *Human Rights Quarterly* 1, 31–35.

[161] Dudai (n 160) 6-8.

[162] Young (n 140) 88–91. See also, B Leebaw, 'Lost, Forgotten, or Buried? Transitional Justice, Agency, and the Memory of Resistance' (2013) 2 *Politica & Società* 237, 256*ff* (distinguishing individual acts of disobedience and organised collective resistance).

[163] H Arendt, *Eichmann in Jerusalem: A Report on the Banality of Evil* (revised and enlarged edition, Penguin Books 1994) 104.

[164] Young (n 140) 89.

[165] Arendt (n 163) 104.

[166] Ibid 171–175.

[167] Leebaw (n 17) 156–168. See also, Leebaw (n 152) 357*ff* (distinguishing principled, escape, fatal, and gray zone disobedience); and B Leebaw, 'If Only More Such Stories Could Have Been Told: Ways of Remembering Resistance' (2019) 15 *Law, Culture and the Humanities* 448 (distinguishing between heroic, exemplary, and anti-heroic resistance).

[168] Dudai (n 160) 32.

Despite the dangers inherent in acting against the tide of societal expectations, numerous acts of rescue have been documented within different mass atrocity situations.[169] For instance, by the end of 2018, Yad Vashem, the Israeli Holocaust Remembrance Authority, had recognised 27,362 rescuers as part of its *Righteous Among The Nations* project.[170] Yet, although acts of rescue and resistance during periods of mass atrocity have been gaining increasing prominence, the narratives of international criminal courts tend to portray a world inhabited by criminal deviants and helpless victims, myopically neglecting the actions of those who attempted to prevent harm.[171] The reason for this neglect resides in the paradigm of individual criminal responsibility, which focuses the attention of international criminal courts on promoting *obedience* to the rules and principles of international criminal law, rather than examining in any detail the potential moral value of *disobedience* in the face of episodes of mass violence.[172]

To the extent that international criminal proceedings *have* served a broader role in illuminating acts of rescue and resistance, it has generally been both incidental and accidental. For example, Ron Dudai recently recounted the story of how Refik Hodžić, an ICTY outreach officer and filmmaker, spotted a footnote concerning acts of resistance within an expert report that had been commissioned by the ICTY Office of the Prosecution as part of the case against Drago Nikolić.[173] The footnote referred to the prosecution of two Serbs by wartime Serb authorities because they had tried to help four young Bosniaks flee the Srebrenica massacre. Inspired by the attempted acts of rescue recounted in the footnote, Hodžić went on a journey to identify the relatives of the Bosniaks, their captors, and the Serb rescuers, turning the story into a documentary film, entitled *Statement 710399*.

This example illustrates both the value and limitations of international criminal courts as documenters of resistance. On the one hand, the story may never have come to light without the efforts of the ICTY prosecutors in gathering considerable volumes of information as part of their case against the defendant. On the other hand, the story was only unearthed tangentially to the main trial, confined to a footnote of an expert report, and it took the personal efforts of an outreach officer to bring the details of the story to light.

[169] For useful mapping of various documentation initiatives concerning the Holocaust, Rwanda, and Bosnia, see generally, ibid 12–20.

[170] Yad Vashem, 'The Righteous Among The Nations, About the Righteous: Statistics' accessible at the following link: https://www.yadvashem.org/righteous/statistics.html (last accessed 7 February 2020).

[171] Leebaw (n 162) 249–250; and Dudai (n 160) 9–10.

[172] Leebaw (n 162) 245, 251, and 257; and Dudai (n 160) 6–8.

[173] The theme of resistance has formed a more prominent part of international criminal *trials* within certain domestic criminal courts. In such contexts, however, the danger arises that prosecutors may put forward 'myths of heroic agency' as part of a strategy to divert attention from more widespread forms of complicity and collaboration amongst the wider population. Dudai (n 160) 36–38. For instance, it is widely acknowledged that one of the aims of the French trial of Klaus Barbie was to celebrate the French nation's struggle against the Nazis and thereby 'atone for the collaborationist history of the Vichy Regime'. G Simpson, *Law, War & Crime—War Crimes Trials and the Reinvention of International Law* (Polity Press 2007) 90. According to Bronwyn Leebaw, such cases may problematically function 'to mythologize a triumphalist view of history in such a way as to obfuscate ordinary experiences of suffering and the human costs of violence'. Leebaw (n 162) 247.

IV. Conclusion

This chapter has examined different dimensions of mass atrocity contexts that have consistently been marginalised within or excluded from the historical narratives constructed by international criminal courts. As noted at the outset, highlighting these blind spots is neither to belittle the acts of violence orchestrated by individuals convicted by international criminal courts, nor to suggest that such factors should necessarily have an exculpatory or mitigating effect on individual culpability. Rather, illuminating these blind spots more modestly reveals three *risks* that arise from the narrow historical perspective adopted by international criminal courts in their judgments.

First, the limited visibility devoted to bystanders and resisters within the judgments of international criminal courts risks occluding the complexities associated with moral and political agency within mass atrocity situations in favour of a reductive victim-perpetrator framework that portrays a world populated by helpless victims and criminal deviants.[174] By overlooking the diversity of roles performed by bystanders in mass atrocity situations, international criminal courts may serve as an opportunity for bystanders to deny or evade any critical self-examination of their implication in mass violence and provide an alibi to relieve themselves from responsibility.[175] By marginalising themes of resistance, international criminal courts offer only limited space for critically reflecting on how individuals might cultivate the critical capacity to resist passivity, conformism, and authority structures within mass atrocity contexts,[176] or for understanding and addressing the dilemmas of agency experienced within what Primo Levi famously referred to as the 'grey zone' of human relationships within mass atrocity environments, which cannot be reduced to a simple victim-perpetrator binary.[177] While confronting themes of passivity and resistance is not without challenges in transitional justice contexts,[178] their neglect risks overlooking the widespread acquiescence that characterises mass atrocity situations, as well as the possibilities and ambiguities of agency and solidarity associated with the distinctive logics of mass violence.[179]

Second, by focusing on the behaviour of accused individuals, together with the immediate collective contexts within which they operated, international criminal courts risk depicting such individuals in uniform terms as the *causes* of mass violence, whilst diverting attention from how they are also the *symptoms* of more widely dispersed structures.[180] As Mégret explains, 'the whole international criminal justice enterprise

[174] Leebaw (n 162) 251.

[175] Koskenniemi (n 15) 14; and Fletcher (n 139) 1080.

[176] Leebaw (n 162) 262; and Leebaw (n 152) 345–351.

[177] P Levi, *The Drowned and the Saved* (R Rosenthal trans, Abacus 1988) 23. See also, E Baines, 'Complex Political Perpetrators: Reflections on Dominic Ongwen' (2009) 47 *Journal of Modern African Studies* 169; and MA Drumbl, 'Victims who Victimise' (2016) 4 *London Review of International Law* 217.

[178] Leebaw (n 152) 351; Leebaw (n 167) 451.

[179] Leebaw (n 152) 357; Leebaw (n 167) 449.

[180] See similarly, P Kirby, 'Refusing to be a Man?: Men's Responsibility for War Rape and the Problem of Social Structures in Feminist and Gender Theory' (2012) 16 *Men and Masculinities* 93, 109; and E Dauphinee, 'War Crimes and the Ruin of Law' (2008) 37 *Millennium: Journal of International Studies* 49, 55.

is founded on a hyperbolization of individual agency, which simultaneously denies the element of societal-embeddedness, state-mandatedness and international-structure responsiveness of international crimes'.[181] As a result, international criminal judgments risk being understood as locating an explanation for episodes of mass violence in the choices of individual perpetrators,[182] who may end up symbolically shouldering a greater portion of blame than they are strictly responsible for.[183]

Finally, beyond diverting attention, international criminal courts also risk legitimating more remote contributions to episodes of mass violence that fall beyond the historical perspective of their judgments. According to Gerry Simpson, for example:[184]

> By emphasising individual agency, courts reproduce a dominant account of the international system in which its crimes (hundreds of thousands of preventable deaths every month) are understood as accidents or by-products of international political economy or sovereignty or the free trade in machetes, while its accidents (the system occasionally results in periods of madness (Taylor in Liberia)) or singular political acts (the Hariri assassination in Lebanon) are understood as 'crimes'.

In other words, international criminal courts risk absolving and helping to entrench the systemic processes and actors that they marginalise or exclude.[185] By portraying themselves as neutral arbiters of international criminal rules and procedures, international criminal courts may inadvertently operate ideologically to naturalise, validate, and build consensus in the existing international political order.[186]

Importantly, surfacing these risks is *not* to suggest that international criminal courts should *necessarily* broaden their narrative frames to account for more diffuse, attritive, or structural injustices. As Sarah Nouwen emphasises, 'there are more ways to see the world than through the lens of international criminal law'.[187] Rather, this

[181] F Mégret, 'What Sort of Global Justice is "International Criminal Justice"?' (2015) 13 *Journal of International Criminal Justice* 77, 86.

[182] M Mamdani, 'Beyond Nuremberg: The Historical Significance of the Post-apartheid Transition in South Africa' (2015) 43 *Politics & Society* 61, 81.

[183] Mégret (n 181) 89–90; L Douglas, 'Perpetrator Proceedings and Didactic Trials', in A Duff et al (eds), *The Trial on Trial: Volume 2: Judgment and Calling to Account* (Hart Publishing 2006) 191, 200; Nesiah (n 40) 297. In this respect, international criminal law is little different from domestic criminal law. See, for example, D Garland, *Punishment and Modern Society: A Study in Social Theory* (OUP 1990) 118; A Norrie, *Crime, Reason and History: A Critical Introduction to Criminal Law* (2nd edn, CUP 2001) 211; and S Veitch, 'Judgment and Calling to Account: Truths, Trials and Reconciliations', in Duff et al (n 183) 155, 170.

[184] G Simpson, 'Linear Law: The History of International Criminal Law', in Schwöbel (n 17) 159, 170.

[185] See, for example, MA Drumbl, 'Pluralizing International Criminal Justice' (2005) 103 *Michigan Law Review* 1295, 1313; DS Koller, 'The Faith of the International Criminal Lawyer' (2008) 40 *New York University Journal of International Law and Politics* 1019, 1067; Miller (n 19) 288; J Hoover, 'Moral Practices: Assigning Responsibility in the International Criminal Court' (2013) 76 *Law and Contemporary Problems* 263, 280; S Nouwen, '"As You Set out for Ithaka": Practical, Epistemological, Ethical, and Existential Questions about Socio-Legal Empirical Research in Conflict' (2014) 27 *Leiden Journal of International Law* 227, 255; G Baars, 'Making ICL History: On the Need to Move Beyond Pre-fab Critiques of ICL', in Schwöbel (n 17) 196, 209; C Gevers, 'International Criminal Law and Individualism: An African Perspective', in Schwöbel (n 17) 221, 233; K Engle et al, 'Introduction', in Engle et al (n 18) 1, 8; V Nesiah, 'Doing History with Impunity', in Engle et al (n 18) 95, 113.

[186] T Krever, 'Unveiling (and Veiling) Politics in International Criminal Trials', in Schwöbel (n 17) 117, 128.

[187] Nouwen (n 185) 255.

chapter more modestly seeks to call attention to the limits of international criminal courts—whether in terms of their neglect of structural and slow forms of violence, their under-appreciation of international interventions, or their reductive understanding of agency in mass atrocity environments—and to emphasise that the narratives constructed in international criminal judgments are somewhat inevitably incomplete absent attention being devoted to wider injustices.

7

Historical Narrative Pluralism Within and Beyond International Criminal Courts

The rhetoric that tends to accompany the operation of international criminal courts often emphasises their capacity to render consistent and authoritative historical narratives about the mass atrocity situations that fall within their purview.[1] For example, Larry Johnson, one of the drafters of the Statute of the International Criminal Tribunal for the former Yugoslavia (ICTY), argues that one of the tribunal's major contributions has been 'to uncover the facts, find the truth, ... and refute those who deny that such atrocities ever occurred'.[2] Similarly, former President of the International Criminal Tribunal for Rwanda (ICTR), Judge Byron, suggests that 'among the most basic and most important of the Tribunal's achievements has been the accumulation of an indisputable historical record'.[3]

In contrast to these aspirations towards narrative consistency and closure, this chapter illuminates the historical narrative pluralism that can arise both within and beyond the international criminal courtroom. In particular, the chapter demonstrates how the historical narratives constructed within international criminal judgments are neither static nor final, but subject to a process of ongoing contestation and evolution over time.[4] To this end, the chapter proceeds in three parts. The chapter begins by examining narrative pluralism *within* the courtroom (Section II). Specifically, two types of narrative pluralism are identified: first, *inter-court* narrative pluralism, which arises when different courts examine the same mass atrocity situation from different perspectives; and second, *intra-court* narrative pluralism, which emerges when narratives constructed within an international criminal judgment are revisited in later cases adjudicated by the same court. The chapter then turns to examine narrative pluralism *beyond* the courtroom (Section III). In particular, it is contended that even where international criminal courts manage to achieve inter-court and intra-court narrative consistency, in practice a range of social psychological and practical factors tend to generate a gap between the intended meaning of such narratives and their public or social meaning amongst different audiences. Finally, the chapter concludes by reflecting on some of the implications that follow from the identification of historical narrative pluralism both within and beyond international criminal courts (Section IV).

[1] This chapter is an adapted version of B Sander, 'History on Trial: Historical Narrative Pluralism Within and Beyond International Criminal Courts' (2018) 67 *International and Comparative Law Quarterly* 547.

[2] LD Johnson, 'Ten Years Later: Reflections on the Drafting' (2004) 2 *Journal of International Criminal Justice* 368, 378.

[3] 'Judge Denis Byron's Address to the UN General Assembly' *ICTR Newsletter* (October 2008) 1.

[4] See similarly, D Buss, 'Expert Witnesses and International War Crimes Trial: Making Sense of Large-Scale Violence in Rwanda', in D Zarkov and M Glasius (eds), *Narrative of Justice in and out of the Courtroom: Former Yugoslavia and Beyond* (Springer 2014) 23, 43.

Doing Justice to History. Barrie Sander, Oxford University Press (2021). © Barrie Sander.
DOI: 10.1093/oso/9780198846871.003.0007

I. Narrative Pluralism *Within* the Courtroom

Compared to the narratives put forward by the prosecution, defence, and, in some contexts, victim participants during international criminal trials, the historical narratives constructed within international criminal judgments have often been accompanied by an expectation of finality and closure. Michael Marrus, for example, argues that 'while judgments of courts are fixed, ... historiography moves'.[5] Similarly, the ancestral maxim, *res judicata pro veritate habetur*, stands for the proposition that an adjudicated matter is to be regarded as the truth.[6] Indeed, international criminal courts have a number of doctrines in their armoury that *can* help solidify consensus and prevent further challenges to particular facts within the courtroom. Through the doctrine of judicial notice, for example, the ICTR Appeals Chamber in *Karemera et al* was able to establish the fact that genocide had occurred in Rwanda in 1994 as a fact of common knowledge.[7]

In practice, however, judicially constructed narratives are often less final and uniform than is generally assumed.[8] Most obviously, the narratives rendered within trial judgments may be subject to alteration on appeal. Additionally, judgments may not be unanimous, dissenting opinions of individual judges constituting a further potential source of narrative pluralism.[9] In the case of *Šešelj*, for example, the conclusion of the ICTY Trial Chamber's majority that there was no widespread or systematic attack on civilians across large areas of Bosnia-Herzegovina and Croatia was directly countered by Judge Lattanzi in dissent, who argued that 'no trier of fact could reasonably reach' such a conclusion based on the evidence.[10] This section seeks to move beyond these

[5] M Marrus, 'History and the Holocaust in the Courtroom', in F Brayard (ed), *Le Génocide des Juifs entre procès et historie* (CNRS 2000) 45 cited in L Douglas, 'Perpetrator Proceedings and Didactic Trials', in A Duff et al (eds), *The Trial on Trial: Volume 2: Judgment and Calling to Account* (Hart Publishing 2006) 191, 198.

[6] C Fournet, *The Crime of Destruction and the Law of Genocide: Their Impact on Collective Memory* (Ashgate 2007) xxxii.

[7] *Prosecutor v Karemera et al* (Decision on Prosecutor's Interlocutory Appeal of Decision on Judicial Notice, Appeals Chamber) ICTR-98-44-AR73(C) (16 June 2006) [33]–[38]. The decision was criticised by scholars for its potential to undermine the fair trial rights of the accused, in particular in light of the willingness of the ICTR to infer the genocidal intent of an accused in part from proof of a nationwide genocidal campaign. See, for example, KJ Heller, '*Prosecutor v Karemera, Ngirumpatse & Nzirorera.* Case No. ICTR-98-44-AR73(C). Decision on Prosecutor's Interlocutory Appeal of Decision on Judicial Notice' (2007) 101 *American Journal of International Law* 157, 161–162; and NHB Jørgensen, 'Genocide as a Fact of Common Knowledge' (2007) 56 *International and Comparative Law Quarterly* 885, 895. See, however, *Prosecutor v Karemera et al* (Decision on Motions for Reconsideration, Appeals Chamber) ICTR-98-44-AR73(C) (1 December 2006) [16] (emphasising that 'the taking of judicial notice of genocide does not, in itself, go to alleged conduct or acts of the Applicants as charged in the indictment').

[8] See similarly, L Douglas, 'Perpetrator Proceedings and Didactic Trials', in A Duff et al (eds), *The Trial on Trial: Volume 2: Judgment and Calling to Account* (Hart Publishing 2006) 191, 198 ('it does not follow that the picture of history presented in any specific trial is fixed by the fact that a trial court must render an unequivocal verdict').

[9] For analysis of judicial dissent in the international criminal context, see generally, H Mistry, 'The Paradox of Dissent: Judicial Dissent and the Projects of International Criminal Justice' (2015) 13 *Journal of International Criminal Justice* 449; N Jain, 'Radical Dissents in International Criminal Trials' (2017) 28 *European Journal of International Law* 1163; and G Simpson, *Law, War & Crime—War Crimes Trials and the Reinvention of International Law* (Polity Press 2007) 92–101.

[10] *Prosecutor v Vojislav Šešelj* (Judgment, Trial Chamber) IT-03-67-PT (31 March 2016) [192]–[193]; and ibid (partially diss op Lattanzi) [39].

well-documented forms of narrative pluralism to illuminate the ways in which the historical narratives constructed within international criminal judgments may be revisited and contested by other courts (*inter-court narrative pluralism*), as well as other cases adjudicated by the same court (*intra-court narrative pluralism*).

A. Inter-Court Narrative Pluralism

At the broadest level, narrative pluralism may emerge between the judgments of different courts that have been mandated to examine the same mass atrocity situation. Lawrence Douglas, for example, argues that 'attention must be paid to ways in which specific trials revisit and revise their juridical precursors, and in so doing participate in, and contribute to, an evolving juridical understanding of traumatic history'.[11]

A clear illustration of inter-court narrative pluralism may be revealed by contrasting the judgment of the District Court of Jerusalem in the case of Adolf Eichmann with the judgment of the International Military Tribunal (IMT). Although both judgments examined Nazi atrocities committed during the Second World War, the narratives constructed within them diverged in two important respects.

First, the Nuremberg and Eichmann judgments accorded differing degrees of space to the voices of the victims of Nazi atrocities. During the Nuremberg trial, US Prosecutor Robert Jackson had relied primarily on documentary evidence, a strategy driven both by fear and circumstance.[12] In terms of fear, although survivor testimony may have served to humanise the narratives emanating from the IMT,[13] Jackson was concerned that such evidence would lack credibility as a means for establishing a historical record and could too easily be dismissed as propaganda.[14] In terms of circumstance, the Nazis' fanatical commitment to meticulous record-keeping constituted a convenient mountain of evidence for Jackson to rely on,[15] there being no better material to prove the crimes of the Nazis than their own words drawn from their own archives.[16] As a result, both at trial and in the judgment of the IMT, the voices of victims were largely overlooked.[17] By contrast, the voices of victims were placed at the centre of the Eichmann trial. As Israeli Prosecutor Gideon Hausner explained, 'I knew we

[11] Douglas (n 8) 199.

[12] See NA Combs, *Fact-Finding Without Facts—The Uncertain Evidentiary Foundations of International Criminal Convictions* (CUP 2010) 11; E Stover, *The Witnesses: War Crimes and the Promise of Justice in The Hague* (University of Pennsylvania Press 2005) 18; and L Douglas, *The Memory of Judgment: Making Law and History in the Trials of the Holocaust* (Yale University Press 2001) 16.

[13] See Stover (n 12) 19 (noting that 'eyewitness and survivor testimony would humanize the plight of Nazi victims'); and Douglas (n 12) 17–18 (noting that William J Donovan, Jackson's first deputy, argued in favour of building the case of the prosecution around eyewitness testimony so as to give the trial 'an affirmative human aspect').

[14] RH Jackson, *The Nürnberg Case* (Alfred A Knopf 1947) 10.

[15] See, for example, A Tusa and J Tusa, *The Nuremberg Trial* (1983) 100–101, cited in Combs (n 12) 11 (noting that the Nazis 'had a mania for writing things down. It is an amazing psychological phenomenon that not one of these men could have a minor political conversation without recording it').

[16] See, for example, S Landsman, 'The *Eichmann* Case and the Invention of the Witness-Driven Atrocity Trial' (2012-2013) 51 *Columbia Journal of Transnational Law* 69, 73.

[17] See, for example, ibid 77; L Moffett, 'The Role of Victims in the International Criminal Tribunals of the Second World War' (2012) 12 *International Criminal Law Review* 245, 249; and Stover (n 12) 18.

needed more than a conviction; we needed a living record of a gigantic human and national disaster.'[18] For Hausner, only victim testimony would be able to 'reach the hearts of men' and it was therefore imperative to give their voices a prominent place in the trial.[19] As a result, the experiences of victims became a significant feature of not only the Prosecutor's narrative at trial but also the judgment of the District Court of Jerusalem.[20]

Second, the Nuremberg and Eichmann judgments constructed contrasting narratives about the Holocaust. As recounted earlier in this study, Article 6(c) of the Nuremberg Charter provided that for the enumerated prohibited acts to constitute crimes against humanity, they must have been committed 'in execution of or in connection with any crime within the jurisdiction of the Tribunal'.[21] In practice, this war nexus requirement had the effect of diminishing the attention directed towards the racist and genocidal dimensions of the Nazi regime conducted largely independently of the regime's war effort within the historical narratives constructed in the IMT's judgment.[22]

By contrast, relying on the Nazis and Nazi Collaborators (Punishment) Law pursuant to which Adolf Eichmann had been charged, the District Court of Jerusalem was able to render a narrative that placed the Holocaust front and centre of its judgment, taking care to distinguish between crimes against the Jewish people and crimes against humanity.[23] According to the District Court, Nazi policy had evolved over time, with the beginning of the war against the Soviet Union in June 1941 marking a shift in policy towards 'the third and final stage in the persecution of the Jews within the area of German influence, namely the stage of total extermination'.[24] Reflecting on the acts in which Eichmann had been involved, the Court drew a distinction between acts of persecution committed prior to August 1941 which had *not* been linked to a policy of physical extermination and were therefore characterised as crimes against humanity, and acts committed after August 1941 which *were* linked to such a policy and were therefore characterised as crimes against the Jewish people.[25]

The judgments of the IMT and District Court of Jerusalem offer a clear illustration of how judicially constructed narratives can evolve over time, varying according to the jurisdictional and evidentiary choices and limitations in particular institutional contexts. Taken together, the judgments reflect what Shoshana Felman has termed the 'cross-legal nature' of certain trials, understood as 'a trial's reference to another trial, of which it recapitulates the memory, the themes, the legal questions of the arguments,

[18] G Hausner, *Justice in Jerusalem* (Harper & Row 1966) 291–292.

[19] Ibid.

[20] See, for example, *The Attorney General of the Government of Israel v Eichmann* (Judgment, District Court of Jerusalem) Criminal Case No 40/61 (11 December 1961) ('*Eichmann* Judgment') [129]–[130] (recounting evidence of survivors concerning living conditions in the Nazi camps and ghettos).

[21] See generally, Chapter 4 of the present study.

[22] See similarly, MR Marrus, 'History and the Holocaust in the Courtroom', in R Smelser (ed), *Lessons and Legacies V: The Holocaust and Justice* (Northwestern University Press 2002) 215, 218; and M Koskenniemi, 'From Impunity to Show Trials' (2002) 6 *Max Planck Yearbook of United Nations Law* 1, 20.

[23] See generally, WA Schabas, 'The Contribution of the Eichmann Trial to International Law' (2013) 26 *Leiden Journal of International Law* 667, 670–676.

[24] *Eichmann* Judgment (n 20) [79].

[25] See, in particular, *Eichmann* Judgment (n 20) [182]–[199].

and whose legal structure it repeats or reenacts—unwittingly or by deliberate design'.[26] From this perspective, the Eichmann judgment may be understood as 'the deliberate historical reopening' of the Nuremberg judgment,[27] ultimately leading to the production of narrative pluralism and distinct perspectives concerning the atrocities perpetrated by the Nazi regime during the Second World War.

B. Intra-Court Narrative Pluralism

Beyond inter-court narrative pluralism, it is also possible for historical narratives concerning the same events to deviate within different cases adjudicated by the same international criminal court. Reflecting the fact that episodes of mass atrocity often take place over longer periods of time and span across broader areas of territory than domestic crimes, several of the international criminal courts examined in this study were mandated to render a collection of judgments concerning a particular conflict situation.[28] In such circumstances, although it is possible that an overarching narrative may emerge within the various judgments rendered by the court, it is also likely that a plurality of contrasting interpretations will arise with respect to at least some of the events examined. As Lawrence Douglas observes, '[a]s [the] prosecutorial programme unfolds—as prosecutors, judges, and other legal actors master the learning curve of complex crimes—atrocity trials typically come to frame a richer, more nuanced treatment of the larger historical complex'.[29] Against this background, this section identifies examples of intra-court narrative pluralism that have arisen as a result of the evidentiary, charging, and legal practices of the different actors that participate within international criminal proceedings.

1. Evidence-driven narrative pluralism

The historical narratives constructed within international criminal judgments have sometimes evolved over time as a result of discrepancies concerning the evidence that has been put before them and the scrutiny to which it has been subjected in different cases. This may be illustrated by examining the evolution of the ICTR's findings concerning whether the Rwandan genocide had been planned in advance by Hutu extremists prior to its commencement in April 1994.[30]

In its early judgments, several ICTR Trial Chambers concluded in fairly unambiguous terms that the Rwandan genocide *had* been planned in advance. For instance, in its judgment in the case of *Akayesu*, the Trial Chamber concluded that the genocide 'appears to have been meticulously organized', upholding the view of expert witness

[26] S Felman, *The Juridical Unconscious: Trials and Traumas in the Twentieth Century* (Harvard University Press 2002) 61.

[27] Ibid 62.

[28] R Steinke, *The Politics of International Criminal Justice: German Perspectives from Nuremberg to The Hague* (Hart Publishing 2012) 13.

[29] L Douglas, 'Truth and Justice in Atrocity Trials', in WA Schabas (ed), *The Cambridge Companion to International Criminal Law* (CUP 2016) 34, 46.

[30] For further discussions pertaining to this issue, see generally, K Bachmann and A Fatić, *The UN International Criminal Tribunals: Transition Without Justice?* (Routledge 2015) 247–251; and Buss (n 4).

Alison Des Forges who had referred to 'centrally organized and supervised massacres'.[31] To reach this conclusion, the Trial Chamber relied on a range of evidence, including 'the existence of lists of Tutsi to be eliminated', 'the arms caches in Kigali which Major-General Dallaire mentioned and regarding whose destruction he had sought the UN's authorization in vain', 'the training of militiamen by the Rwandan Armed Forces', as well as 'the psychological preparation of the population to attack the Tutsi'.[32] In *Kayishema*, the Trial Chamber was even more explicit, expressly concluding that 'there indeed was a genocidal plan in place prior to the downing of the President's airplane in April 1994'.[33]

Despite the confident tone of these early pronouncements, later judgments of the Trial Chamber cast doubt on these findings, subjecting the planned nature of the genocide to increasing amounts of scrutiny. In *Bagosora et al*, for example, the ICTR Prosecutor submitted that four military leaders had conspired to commit genocide prior to its commencement in Rwanda in 1994. In its judgment, the ICTR Trial Chamber accepted that it '*cannot exclude* that there were in fact plans prior to 6 April to commit genocide in Rwanda'.[34] In particular, there were 'certain indications' in the evidence of a prior plan or conspiracy to perpetrate genocide, including a campaign to covertly arm and train civilian militiamen, efforts to put in place a 'civil defence' system made up of 'resistance' groups, and the creation of lists primarily aimed at identifying suspected accomplices of the Rwandan Patriotic Front (RPF) and opponents to the Habyarimana regime.[35] Yet, whilst acknowledging that these preparations were 'completely consistent with a plan to commit genocide', the Trial Chamber added that they were also 'consistent with preparations for a political or military power struggle'.[36] Importantly, the Prosecution's case on this charge had been primarily circumstantial so the Trial Chamber could only convict the accused if conspiracy to commit genocide was the only reasonable inference that could be drawn from the evidence.[37] Since the evidence suggested more than one reasonable inference, the Trial Chamber concluded that the prosecution had failed to prove beyond reasonable doubt that the four

[31] *Prosecutor v Jean-Paul Akayesu* (Judgment, Trial Chamber) ICTR-96-4-T (2 September 1998) ('*Akayesu* Trial Judgment') [126]. See similarly, *Prosecutor v Clément Kayishema and Obed Ruzindana* (Judgment, Trial Chamber) ICTR-95-1-T (21 May 1999) ('*Kayishema and Ruzindana* Trial Judgment') [289]; and *Prosecutor v Nahimana et al* (Judgment and Sentence, Trial Chamber) ICTR-99-52-T (3 December 2003) [118]. For further information on the views of expert witness Alison Des Forges concerning the planned nature of the Rwandan genocide, see generally, Human Rights Watch, *The Rwandan Genocide: How It Was Prepared* (April 2006).

[32] *Akayesu* Trial Judgment (n 31) [126].

[33] *Kayishema and Ruzindana* Trial Judgment (n 31) [528].

[34] *Prosecutor v Bagosora et al* (Judgment and Sentence, Trial Chamber) ICTR-98-41-T (18 December 2008) ('*Bagosora et al* Trial Judgment') [2107] (emphasis added). See similarly, *Prosecutor v Ndindiliyimana et al* (Judgment and Sentence, Trial Chamber) ICTR-00-56 (17 May 2011) ('*Ndindiliyimana et al* Trial Judgment') [2066] ('the Chamber cannot rule out the possibility of the existence of plans to commit genocide').

[35] *Bagosora et al* Trial Judgment (n 34) [2107]–[2109].

[36] Ibid [2110]. See similarly, *Ndindiliyimana et al* Trial Judgment (n 34) [2068] ('while certain elements proved by the Prosecution could collectively be suggestive of a conspiracy to commit genocide, they are also consistent with . . . a political and military power struggle against the RPF').

[37] *Bagosora et al* Trial Judgment (n 34) [2110].

accused had conspired to commit genocide prior to its commencement on 7 April 1994.[38]

This aspect of the case is significant not only for its legal verdict, but also for the Trial Chamber's attempt to limit the historical significance of its findings. The Chamber emphasised that the question under examination was not the broader issue of 'whether there was a plan or conspiracy to commit genocide in Rwanda', but rather a more limited inquiry into whether the prosecution had proven beyond reasonable doubt that the four accused had conspired amongst themselves or with others to commit genocide before it unfolded on 7 April 1994.[39] Moreover, the Chamber explained how its task had been restricted by 'exacting standards of proof and procedure, the specific evidence on the record before it and its primary focus on the actions of the four accused in this trial'.[40] As such, although 'a firm foundation' for the crime of conspiracy to commit genocide could not be constructed from the 'fractured bricks' of evidence that had been put before the tribunal in this case, it remained conceivable that 'newly discovered information, subsequent trials or history' might demonstrate a conspiracy involving the accused to commit genocide,[41] and it was also possible that 'some [other] military or civilian authorities did intend these preparations as part of a plan to commit genocide'.[42]

What emerges from the case of *Bagosora et al*, therefore, is a notable reticence on the part of the Trial Chamber—in marked contrast to the tribunal's earlier judgments—to provide historical narrative closure on the issue of whether the genocide was planned in advance. As Doris Buss explains, the judgment in *Bagosora et al* 'reveals a court that was both more knowledgeable about Rwanda while less confident in its ability to know the causes and contexts of the 1994 genocide'.[43]

The evidence-driven narrative pluralism that emerged at the ICTR is far from an isolated example. At the ICTY, for instance, judges in the cases of *Tadić* and *Perisić* reached divergent factual findings concerning the relationship between the Bosnian Serb Army (the VRS) and the Yugoslav Army (the VJ).[44] In *Tadić*, the Appeals Chamber found, in the context of determining the classification of the armed conflict, that 'the VRS and the VJ did not, after May 1992, comprise two separate armies in any genuine sense', but rather 'the renamed Bosnian Serb army still comprised one army under the command of the General Staff of the VJ in Belgrade'.[45] By contrast, in *Perisić*,

[38] Ibid [2113]. The ICTR has acquitted other individuals of conspiracy to commit genocide prior to its commencement. See, for example, *Prosecutor v Juvénal Kajelijeli* (Judgment and Sentence, Trial Chamber) ICTR-98-44A-T (1 December 2003) [449] and [794]–[796]; *Ndindiliyimana et al* Trial Judgment (n 34) [2069]; and *Prosecutor v Édouard Karemera and Mathieu Ngirumpatse* (Judgment, Appeals Chamber) ICTR-98-44-A (29 September 2014) [731]–[742].

[39] *Bagosora et al* Trial Judgment (n 34) [2092].

[40] Ibid [2112]. See similarly, F Gaynor, 'Uneasy Partners—Evidence, Truth and History in International Trials' (2012) 10 *Journal of International Criminal Justice* 1257, 1272 (observing how 'a conscientious historian, analysing the same evidence, might well conclude that it was more probable than not that there had been a high-level conspiracy to commit genocide in Rwanda before it unfolded').

[41] *Bagosora et al* Trial Judgment (n 34) [2112].

[42] Ibid [2111].

[43] Buss (n 4) 24.

[44] See generally, MJ Ventura, 'Specific Direction à la Perišić, the Taylor Appeal Judgment and What It Could Mean for the ICTY Appeals Chamber in Šainović et al.—Part I' *Spreading the Jam* (8 January 2014).

[45] *Prosecutor v Duško Tadić* (Judgment, Appeals Chamber) IT-94-1-A (15 July 1999) [151]–[152].

the Appeals Chamber concluded, in the context of determining whether the requirements for aiding and abetting had been satisfied, that 'the VRS and the VJ [were] separate and independent military entities'.[46]

Similarly, in the cases of *Milutinović et al.* and *Đorđević*, two Trial Chambers at the ICTY reached divergent conclusions regarding a joint criminal enterprise (JCE) that had been orchestrated by the Serbian leadership in Kosovo.[47] In each case, the Trial Chambers identified the existence of a JCE in extremely similar terms. In *Milutinović et al*, the Trial Chamber identified a JCE whose common purpose was 'to ensure continued control by the FRY and Serbian authorities over Kosovo' by forcibly displacing the Kosovo Albanian population both within and outside Kosovo through 'a widespread *and* systematic campaign of terror and violence'.[48] Since the JCE members were aware that it would be unrealistic to displace *all* Kosovo Albanians from Kosovo, the common purpose was 'to displace a number of them sufficient to tip the demographic balance more toward ethnic equality and in order to cow the Kosovo Albanians into submission'.[49] In *Đorđević*, the Trial Chamber identified a common plan 'to modify the ethnic balance in Kosovo by waging a campaign of terror against the Kosovo Albanian civilian population, a plan which included murders, deportations, forcible transfers and the destruction of religious and culturally significant property'.[50]

Despite their similarity, the Trial Chambers reached varying conclusions regarding the membership of the JCEs. Whereas the Trial Chamber in *Milutinović et al* concluded that Ojdanić and Lazarević, who were defendants in that case, were not members of the JCE,[51] the Trial Chamber in *Đorđević* expressly included Ojdanić and Lazarević within its list of JCE members.[52] On appeal in the case of *Đorđević*, the accused questioned the discrepancy between the two cases, contending that 'no reasonable trial chamber could have concluded that Ojdanić and Lazarević were members of the JCE', especially bearing in mind that there was 'no more evidence before the Trial Chamber in Đorđević's trial than was before the Trial Chamber in *Milutinović et al*'.[53]

In response, the Appeals Chamber dismissed the accused's argument by explaining its general position that 'findings of criminal responsibility made in a case before the

[46] *Prosecutor v Momčilo Perišić* (Judgment, Appeals Chamber) IT-04-81-A (28 February 2013) [46].

[47] For a similar example in the jurisprudence of the ICTR, see MA Drumbl, 'The Curious Criminality of Mass Atrocity: Diverse Actors, Multiple Truths, and Plural Responses', in E van Sliedregt and S Vasiliev (eds), *Pluralism in International Criminal Law* (OUP 2014) 68, 97–99 (discussing divergent findings in the ICTR cases related to the Nyange parish church massacre).

[48] *Prosecutor v Milutinović et al* (Judgement: Volume 3 of 4, Trial Chamber) IT-05-87-T (26 February 2009) ('*Milutinović et al* Trial Judgment') [95].

[49] Ibid [95]. The Trial Chamber's analysis and findings as regards the common purpose of the JCE were upheld on appeal. *Prosecutor v Šainović et al* (Judgment, Appeals Chamber) IT-05-87-A (23 January 2014) [604] and [664].

[50] *Prosecutor v Vlastimir Đorđević* (Public Judgement with Confidential Annex: Volume I of II, Trial Chamber) IT-05-87/1-T (23 February 2011) ('*Đorđević* Trial Judgement') [2126]. The Trial Chamber's analysis and findings as regards the common purpose of the JCE were upheld on appeal. See *Prosecutor v Vlastimir Đorđević* (Judgment, Appeals Chamber) IT-05-87/1-A (27 January 2014) ('*Đorđević* Appeal Judgement') [139]–[141] and [158].

[51] *Milutinović et al* Trial Judgment (n 48) [618] (regarding Ojdanić) and [919] (regarding Lazarević).

[52] *Đorđević* Trial Judgement (n 50) [2127] and [2211].

[53] *Đorđević* Appeal Judgement (n 50) [135].

Tribunal are binding only for the individual accused in that specific case'.[54] With this in mind, the Appeals Chamber elaborated as follows:[55]

> [Whereas] in the *Milutinović et al.* case the Trial Chamber was required to scrutinise the *actus reus* and *mens rea* of each JCE member who was accused in that case in order to reach a conclusion beyond a reasonable doubt on their individual criminal responsibility . . . , in the present case, findings concerning those individuals are only relevant to the analysis aimed at establishing that Đorđević acted in concert with a plurality of persons and shared the common purpose to further the JCE, in order to make a finding beyond a reasonable doubt regarding his individual criminal responsibility only.

In addition, the Appeals Chamber noted that, in making factual findings, judges rely 'solely and exclusively on the evidence adduced in the particular case' and, as such, 'it is entirely acceptable that on the basis of two different case records, judges arrive at different conclusions, even if they concern the same events'.[56] In this way, the Appeals Chamber confirmed that not only was evidence-driven narrative pluralism between different cases concerning similar events possible, it was also justifiable.

2. Charge-driven narrative pluralism

Beyond evidence-driven narrative pluralism, divergent narratives may also arise within the judgments of different cases as a result of prosecutorial decisions concerning the scope and content of charges, as well as judicial decisions concerning their oversight of indictments.

Turning first to prosecutorial discretion, international prosecutors are under no obligation to charge different defendants consistently with respect to the same factual incidents in different cases. As Mark Osiel explains, 'the same period of events, people, and facts [can be] grouped differently (i.e., into differently defined enterprises) from one indictment to the next', subject only to the limits of what the evidence permits.[57] As such, where defendants are tried separately in relation to the same factual incidents, the potential always exists for inconsistencies to arise in prosecutorial charging practices. A range of factors might account for such inconsistencies, including new evidence coming to light in the preparation of cases brought at a later period in time, as well as incentives to bring a narrower range of charges in particular cases as a result of completion strategies.[58] Where cases concern the same factual incidents, differences in prosecutorial charging practices can lead to narrative pluralism concerning those incidents. The potential for charge-driven narrative pluralism may be illustrated by contrasting the ICTY Prosecutor's charging strategy with respect to genocide

[54] Ibid [142].
[55] Ibid.
[56] Ibid [143].
[57] M Osiel, *Making Sense of Mass Atrocity* (CUP 2009) 75.
[58] See, in this regard, S Ford, 'The Complexity of International Criminal Trials is Necessary' (2015) 48 *George Washington International Law Review* 151, 193–194 (arguing, based on an empirical study, that adopting a symbolic charging strategy would have reduced trial complexity of the 10 most complex cases at the ICTY by around 27 per cent).

allegations in Bosnia in the case of Slobodan Milošević on the one hand and the case of Jovica Stanišić and Franko Simatović on the other.[59]

In *Milošević*, ICTY Prosecutor Carla Del Ponte successfully applied for the joinder of three indictments that had been issued against the accused concerning alleged serious violations of international humanitarian law in Kosovo, Croatia, and Bosnia and Herzegovina.[60] The indictment promised to paint a picture of how Belgrade—not only Milošević but also several other individuals and institutions of the Serbian administration—was implicated in a criminal scheme whose scope spanned from Croatia, through Bosnia, to Kosovo. For present purposes, of prime interest are the charges of genocide brought against Milošević in the Bosnia Indictment. By the time of the Trial Chamber's Rule 98*bis* decision, the genocide charges against Milošević concerned the Bosnian territories of Brčko, Prijedor, Sanski Most, Srebrenica, Bijeljina, Kotor Varos, Kljuc, and Bosanski Novi.[61] The ICTY Prosecutor submitted that the accused had participated in a JCE, whose common objective consisted of 'the destruction of the Bosnian Muslim group in that part of the territory of Bosnia and Herzegovina intended to be included in the Serbian state'.[62] This JCE begged the question as to how precisely Milošević was linked to the Bosnian Serb leadership. The missing link between Belgrade and the crimes committed by Serb paramilitaries in Bosnia was the Serb Security Service operated by Stanišić and Simatović.[63] In other words, Stanišić and Simatović were alleged to have been 'the essential go-betweens' connecting Milošević with the Bosnian Serb leadership, 'not only indispensable to the factual projection of Milošević's power but also an irreducible link in the legal argument'.[64]

In light of Milošević's death prior to judgment, the ICTY was unable to render a final verdict concerning Milošević's precise role and responsibility with respect to the Bosnian genocide charges. In its Rule 98*bis* decision, which concerned a motion for acquittal that had been requested by the defendant's *amici curiae* and relied upon an extremely low standard of review,[65] the Trial Chamber preserved all counts against Milošević, although Judge Kwon dissented on the charge of genocide pursuant to the basic form of JCE, concluding that he could not agree with the majority that 'there is

59 This example was brought to my attention by F Hartmann, 'Abdicated Legacy: The Prosecution's Use of Evidence from Milošević', in T Waters (ed), *The Milošević Trial: An Autopsy* (OUP 2014) 465.

60 See *Prosecutor v Slobodan Milošević* (Decision on Prosecution's Interlocutory Appeal from Refusal to Order Joinder, Appeals Chamber) IT-99-37-AR73, IT-01-50- AR73 & IT-01-51- AR73 (1 February 2002).

61 *Prosecutor v Slobodan Milošević* (Decision on Motion for Judgment of Acquittal, Trial Chamber) IT-02-54-T (16 June 2004) ('*Milošević* Decision on Motion for Judgment of Acquittal') [138].

62 Ibid [140].

63 Bachmann and Fatić (n 30) 223. See similarly, Hartmann (n 59) 472 (claiming that a significant part of the Prosecutor's strategy to prove that Milošević had participated in the JCE entailed demonstrating how Stanišić and Simatović had served as 'channels of communication between and among the core members of the JCE in Belgrade, and had controlled and directed Serbia's covert special forces in some of the most brutal campaigns against non-Serb civilians').

64 H van der Wilt, 'The Spider and the System', in T Waters (ed), *The Milošević Trial: An Autopsy* (OUP 2014) 484, 487.

65 For a detailed summary of the standard of review applied in Rule 98*bis* decisions, see *Milošević* Decision on Motion for Judgment of Acquittal (n 61) [13] ('Where there is some evidence, but it is such that, *taken at its highest*, a Trial Chamber could not convict on it, the Motion [to acquit the defendant on those charges] is to be allowed') (emphasis added).

sufficient evidence upon which a Trial Chamber could find beyond reasonable doubt that the Accused had the *dolus specialis* required for genocide';[66] by contrast, Judge Kwon agreed with the majority with respect to the other theories of liability that had been alleged by the prosecution, including genocide pursuant to the extended form of JCE.[67] Nonetheless, neither the trial nor the Rule 98*bis* decision provided any clear answers concerning Milošević's links to the Bosnian Serb leadership or whether the genocide charges would have been upheld at judgment.

Given the alleged importance of the role played by Stanišić and Simatović as a conduit between Milošević and the Bosnian Serb leadership with respect to genocide, one might have expected the case against Stanišić and Simatović to have provided further clarity on this relationship. After all, as Florence Hartmann argues, '[i]f Milošević was able to foresee the risk of genocide, as the charges against him implied, logically so did Stanišić and Simatović, who were informing him of everything that occurred in the field'.[68] In practice, however, no genocide charges were brought by the ICTY Prosecutor against the accused in *Stanišić and Simatović*. As such, the Prosecutor's narrative differed substantially compared to *Milošević*, 'now treating the Srebrenica genocide as a *parallel* criminal plan developed separately from the overarching *Milošević* JCE and with a separate and specific intent—in this case, a genocidal one—not shared by Stanišić and Simatović'.[69]

The precise rationale behind the ICTY Prosecutor's altered narrative of Serbian involvement in the Srebrenica genocide is unclear. According to Hartmann, the change in strategy may have reflected a desire not to conflict with the narrative rendered by the International Court of Justice in the *Bosnian Genocide* case, as well as an attempt to simplify its case against *Karadžić* by avoiding any suggestion that Karadžić's authority was sometimes eclipsed by Belgrade.[70] It is also possible that the ICTY Prosecutor determined that there was insufficient evidence to convincingly advance the genocide charges against Stanišić and Simatović. In this regard, it is notable that the Trial Chamber's judgment in Stanišić and Simatović ultimately rejected allegations that the defendants had provided 'channels of communication' between, *inter alia*, Belgrade and the Bosnian Serb leadership.[71]

Regardless of its precise rationale, the variation in the ICTY Prosecutor's charging strategy illustrates the potential for inconsistencies to arise concerning how JCEs concerning the same events are understood at the ad hoc tribunals. In the present example, narrative pluralism did not fully emerge since Milošević's death meant that no judgment was ultimately rendered concerning the genocide allegations. Nonetheless, the Prosecutor's decision not to charge Stanišić and Simatović with genocide at the very least casts doubt on its earlier genocide allegations against Milošević, providing

66 Ibid (diss op Kwon) [1].
67 Ibid [2].
68 Hartmann (n 59) 472.
69 Ibid 474 (emphasis added).
70 Ibid 479–481.
71 *Prosecutor v Jovica Stanišić and Franko Simatović* (Judgment, Trial Chamber) IT-03-69-T (30 May 2013) [2290]–[2304]. The judgment of the Trial Chamber was quashed by the Appeals Chamber, which ordered a re-trial of the defendants. See generally, *Prosecutor v Jovica Stanišić and Franko Simatović* (Judgment, Appeals Chamber) IT-03-69-A (9 December 2015).

a further illustration of how a narrative can twist and turn during the course of a tribunal's lifetime.[72]

Beyond prosecutorial discretion concerning the scope and content of charges, narrative pluralism may also emerge as a result of the exercise of judicial oversight powers concerning alleged defects in the form of indictments, as well as requests to amend or add charges to indictments.[73] These powers are significant since their exercise can potentially lead to the dismissal or omission of charges from indictments in order to safeguard the fair trial rights of the accused.

With respect to defects in the form of indictments, for example, the jurisprudence of the ad hoc tribunals clarified that '[a]n indictment which fails to duly set forth the specific material facts underpinning the charges against the accused is defective'.[74] In some instances, a vague or imprecise indictment may be cured of its defects if the Prosecutor has provided the accused with 'timely, clear and consistent information detailing the factual basis underpinning the charges against him'.[75] However, where a failure to provide the accused with sufficient notice of the legal and factual reasons for the charges was found to have violated the individual's right to a fair trial, no conviction could result.[76] As these tests indicate, whether an indictment was defective depended on both the actions taken by the prosecution to ensure that the fair trial rights of the accused were not prejudiced, as well as the predilections of the judges in determining whether the relevant tests had been satisfied on the facts of particular cases.

The narrative pluralism that may result from the decisions of prosecutors and judges concerning defects in the form of indictments may be illustrated by comparing how allegations of sexual violence directed against men and boys were received in the cases of *Taylor* and *Sesay et al* at the Special Court for Sierra Leone (SCSL). In *Taylor*, the indictment failed to provide the accused with any notice that he was charged with any form of sexual violence other than rape, abduction, or sexual slavery of women and girls.[77] Nonetheless, the SCSL Prosecutor pleaded for the Trial Chamber to consider evidence of sexual violence against male victims. In response, the Trial Chamber found that neither had the Prosecutor been able to point to any references in the charging documents capable of providing timely, clear, and consistent notice to the accused of such allegations, nor were the service of witness statements sufficient for this purpose.[78] As such, the Trial Chamber declined to consider evidence of sexual violence against male victims in its judgment.[79] By contrast, in *Sesay et al*, although

[72] See, in this regard, van der Wilt (n 64) 488 (observing how 'the major blow to the structural cohesion of the JCE [originally alleged in *Milošević*] has been administered by the Prosecution itself, which, by eliding the indispensable links between Milošević and the acts of genocide, has caused the whole JCE to fall apart').

[73] See generally, H Friman et al, 'Charges', in G Sluiter et al (eds), *International Criminal Procedure: Principles and Rules* (OUP 2013) 381, 415–422; and J Locke, 'Indictments', in L Reydams et al (eds), *International Prosecutors* (OUP 2012) 604, 642–645.

[74] *Nahimana et al v Prosecutor* (Judgment, Appeals Chamber) ICTR-99-52-A (28 November 2007) ('*Nahimana et al* Appeal Judgment') [322]. See similarly, *Prosecutor v Kvočka et al* (Judgment, Appeals Chamber) IT-98-30/1-A (28 February 2005) [33]; and *Prosecutor v Moinina Fofana and Allieu Kondewa* (Judgment, Appeals Chamber) SCSL-04-14-A (28 May 2008) [443].

[75] *Nahimana et al* Appeal Judgment (n 74) [325].

[76] Ibid [326].

[77] *Prosecutor v Charles Ghankay Taylor* (Judgment, Trial Chamber) SCSL-03-01-T (18 May 2012) ('*Taylor* Trial Judgment') [124].

[78] Ibid [129]–[131].

[79] Ibid [134].

the indictment was similarly restricted to sexual violence against women and girls, the Trial Chamber found that the prosecution's disclosure—prior to the start of the prosecution's case—of a number of witness statements, in which allegation of sexual violence against male victims had been raised, constituted adequate notice of such allegations, thereby curing the defect in the indictment.[80] This finding enabled the Trial Chamber to document a number of instances of sexual violence directed against male victims in its judgment.[81]

3. Law-driven narrative pluralism

A final avenue by which narrative pluralism has emerged between different international criminal judgments is through the judicial adoption of divergent interpretations of substantive legal categories. In practice, law-driven narrative pluralism has arisen both with respect to the contextual elements of system crimes as well as their underlying prohibited acts.

a. Contextual elements

A clear illustration of law-driven narrative pluralism concerning the contextual element of a system crime occurred at the ICTR with respect to the war crimes nexus requirement. Beyond identifying the existence of an armed conflict, a successful war crimes prosecution requires the establishment of a *nexus* between the conduct of the accused and the armed conflict in question.[82] The nexus requirement serves the dual function of distinguishing war crimes from other crimes under international law on the one hand, and from ordinary domestic crimes with no association to the armed conflict on the other.[83]

Early in its case law, the ICTR had little difficulty identifying the existence of a non-international armed conflict between the Hutu-controlled Rwandan Armed Forces (RAF) and the Tutsi-controlled RPF for at least the duration of the genocide that occurred in Rwanda in 1994.[84] Far more challenging was the task of establishing a nexus between the alleged crimes of the accused on trial and the armed conflict. The central issue confronted by the tribunal in this regard was whether crimes committed against civilians, typically in the context of genocide, could be characterised as closely related

[80] *Prosecutor v Sesay et al* (Judgment, Trial Chamber) SCSL-04-15-T (2 March 2009) ('*Sesay et al* Trial Judgment') [1302]–[1309].

[81] See, in this regard, V Oosterveld, 'Evaluating the Special Court for Sierra Leone's Gender Jurisprudence', in CC Jalloh (ed), *The Sierra Leone Special Court and its Legacy: The Impact for Africa and International Criminal Law* (CUP 2014) 234, 256–257.

[82] For detailed discussions of the 'nexus' requirement, see generally, K Ambos, *Treatise on International Criminal Law: Volume II: The Crimes and Sentencing* (OUP 2014) 140–144; R Cryer et al, *An Introduction to International Criminal Law and Procedure* (3rd edn, CUP 2014) 281–282; A Cassese et al, *Cassese's International Criminal Law* (3rd edn, OUP 2013) 77–79; and G Mettraux, *International Crimes and the Ad Hoc Tribunals* (OUP 2006) 38–47.

[83] Ambos (n 82) 140–141.

[84] See, for example, *Akayesu* Trial Judgment (n 31) [621] and [627] (concluding that the different threshold requirements for the existence of an armed conflict under common Article 3 of the Geneva Conventions of 1949 and Additional Protocol II had both been fulfilled with respect to the conflict between the RPF and the Rwandan governmental forces). For a critical discussion, see generally, S Darcy, *Judges, Law and War: The Judicial Development of International Humanitarian Law* (CUP 2014) 109–110; and L van den Herik, *The Contribution of the Rwandan Tribunal to the Development of International Law* (Martinus Nijhoff Publishers 2005) 216–220 and 226–227.

to the non-international armed conflict in Rwanda.[85] As Larissa van den Herik explains, this question 'goes to the heart of the qualification of what happened in Rwanda in 1994 and how the genocide and armed conflict are interrelated',[86] bringing within the narrative frame of the tribunal the further questions of whether the genocide originated in the civil war, and whether, once it had begun, the genocide was part of the civil war or a separate event.[87] Over time, the ICTR's approach to the nexus requirement evolved, with attendant consequences for its depiction of the relationship between the armed conflict and genocide.

Initially, Trial Chambers at the ICTR adopted a stringent approach to the nexus requirement.[88] The strictness of the tribunal's approach was evident in two respects.

First, the Trial Chamber in *Akayesu* required a nexus not only between the crime and the conflict, but also between *the accused* and a party to the conflict. In what became known as the 'public agent test',[89] the Trial Chamber required the ICTR Prosecutor to prove that the accused 'was either a member of the armed forces under the military command of either of the belligerent parties, or that he was legitimately mandated and expected, as a public official or agent or person otherwise holding public authority or de facto representing the Government, to support or fulfil the war efforts'.[90]

Second, the Trial Chamber in *Kayishema and Ruzindana* asserted that although the armed conflict 'had been used as a pretext to unleash an official policy of genocide', such a pretext was insufficient to establish a nexus between the genocidal acts of the accused and the armed conflict between the RAF and RPF.[91] As the Trial Chamber argued, 'men, women and children were killed not as a result of the military operations between the [RAF] and the RPF but because of the policy of extermination of the Tutsi, pursued by the official authorities of Rwanda'.[92] Whilst these crimes were carried out '*during* the armed conflict', they were committed 'as part of a distinct policy of genocide; they were committed *parallel to*, and not as a result of, the armed conflict'.[93] This approach echoed the conclusions reached by the Trial Chamber in *Akayesu*, which had found that although the genocide 'was probably facilitated by the conflict, in the

85 A Cassese, 'The Nexus Requirement for War Crimes' (2012) 10 *Journal of International Criminal Justice* 1395, 1407. On the 'closely related to' nexus standard, see *Prosecutor v Duško Tadić* (Decision on the Defence Motion for Interlocutory Appeal on Jurisdiction, Appeals Chamber) IT-94-I-AR72 (2 October 1995) [70]; and *Prosecutor v Georges Anderson Nderubumwe Rutaganda* (Judgment and Sentence, Trial Chamber) ICTR-96-3-T (6 December 1999) ('*Rutaganda* Trial Judgment') [104]. For further elaboration of the nexus requirement, see *Prosecutor v Kunarac et al* (Judgment, Appeals Chamber) IT-96-23 & IT-96-23/1-A (12 June 2002) [57]-[59].

86 L van den Herik, 'A Quest for Jurisdiction and an Appropriate Definition of Crime: Mpambara before the Dutch Courts' (2009) 7 *Journal of International Criminal Justice* 1117, 1125.

87 van den Herik (n 84) 228–229.

88 See similarly, Cassese (n 85) 1407 ('initially tepid approach'); H van der Wilt, 'War Crimes and the Requirement of a Nexus with an Armed Conflict' (2012) 10 *Journal of International Criminal Justice* 1113, 1119 ('Initially, trial chambers of the ICTR . . . were quite reluctant to accept a nexus between crimes and the armed conflict'); and van den Herik (n 84) 235 ('high threshold set by the ICTR Chambers').

89 Cassese (n 85) 1408.

90 *Akayesu* Trial Judgment (n 31) [640]. See similarly, *Rutaganda* Trial Judgment (n 85) [98]; and *Prosecutor v Alfred Musema* (Judgment and Sentence, Trial Chamber) ICTR-96-13-A (27 January 2000) ('*Musema* Trial Judgment') [264]–[275] and [280].

91 *Kayishema and Ruzindana* Trial Judgment (n 31) [603].

92 Ibid [619].

93 Ibid [621] (emphasis added).

sense that the fighting against the RPF forces was used as a pretext for the propaganda inciting genocide against the Tutsi', occurred 'concomitantly' with the conflict, and once underway 'became one of the stakes in the conflict' nonetheless the genocide 'was, evidently fundamentally different from the conflict'.[94] As Antonio Cassese later observed, 'the logic here seems to suggest that the "pretext" negates any true *causal* relationship between the conflict and the genocide'.[95]

The stringency of the nexus requirement in the ICTR's early case law led to a series of acquittals for war crimes and a historical narrative in which the genocide and civil war in Rwanda were clearly distinguished.[96] However, this strict approach would soon give way to a more expansive application of the nexus requirement.

First, the Appeals Chamber in *Akayesu* dismissed the public agent test that had been applied by the Trial Chamber. Upon reviewing its Statute, Article 3 common to the Geneva Conventions, and the case law of the ICTY, the Appeals Chamber found no indication that individual criminal responsibility for war crimes was restricted to a particular class of perpetrators.[97] As the Appeals Chamber explained, while 'in most cases, the perpetrator of the crime will probably have a special relationship with one party to the conflict ... such a special relationship is not a condition precedent to the application of common Article 3 and, hence of Article 4 of the Statute'.[98] The Chamber added that this conclusion was reinforced by the object and purpose of Article 3 common to the Geneva Conventions, which had been adopted primarily to ensure the protection of victims.[99]

Second, both Trial and Appeals Chambers gradually began to conflate the genocide and the armed conflict for the purpose of satisfying the nexus requirement. For instance, as part of its analysis to establish a nexus, the Trial Chamber in *Bagosora et al* expressly relied upon the fact that the armed conflict between the RAF and the RPF had 'both created the situation and provided a pretext for the extensive killings and other abuses of members of the civilian population in Rwanda'.[100] Other indicia relied upon by the Trial Chamber to establish the nexus included the substantial influence of military personnel in the manner in which the killings and other crimes had been executed, as well as the fact that the pretext for the killings at roadblocks had been to identify RPF infiltrators.[101] Consequently, defendants were convicted for genocidal acts under the labels of *both* genocide *and* war crimes.[102]

The more lenient application of the nexus requirement facilitated convictions for war crimes, as well as the construction of a historical narrative in which the civil war

[94] *Akayesu* Trial Judgment (n 31) [127]–[128].

[95] Cassese (n 85) 1410 (emphasis in original).

[96] See, for example, *Akayesu* Trial Judgment (n 31) [640]–[644]; *Kayishema and Ruzindana* Trial Judgment (n 31) [598]–[624]; *Musema* Trial Judgment (n 90) [973]–[975]; and *Rutaganda* Trial Judgment (n 85) 442–445.

[97] *Prosecutor v Jean-Paul Akayesu* (Judgment, Appeals Chamber) ICTR-96-4-A (1 June 2001) [433]–[439].

[98] Ibid [444].

[99] Ibid [440]–[444].

[100] *Bagosora et al* Trial Judgment (n 34) [2232]. See similarly, *Prosecutor v Théoneste Bagosora and Anatole Nsengiyumva* (Judgment, Appeals Chamber) ICTR-98-41-A (14 December 2011) [405]; and *Ndindiliyimana et al* Trial Judgment (n 34) [266].

[101] *Bagosora et al* Trial Judgment (n 34) [2233]–[2235].

[102] Ibid [2228]–[2257].

and genocide were more closely intertwined. This turn in the jurisprudence also led to a divide in international criminal scholarship.

In support of the turn, Antonio Cassese claimed that the more lenient nexus requirement was more in line with the purpose of the law of war crimes to protect innocent people at times of armed conflict and also avoids 'the absurd outcome' that the planners of the genocide in Rwanda would avoid individual criminal responsibility for war crimes simply because they had 'used propaganda to incite civilians to engage in an "official policy" of genocide'.[103]

Conversely, scholars such as Harman van der Wilt drew attention to the risk that lumping together genocide and war crimes in the Rwandan context 'might inadvertently add fuel to the *génocidaires* who had adduced the war as a pretext to kill Tutsis randomly'.[104] Similarly, Larissa van den Herik warned that the emphasis of the lenient approach on the pretext of the perpetrators rather than their actual knowledge and intentions may unintentionally echo the Rwandan government's propaganda during the genocide, according to which all Tutsis were characterised as enemies.[105] For van den Herik, only where individual Tutsis were selected for their suspected links with the RPF should the nexus requirement have been regarded as satisfied;[106] reliance on the notion that the armed conflict provided a general pretext for the genocide should have been deemed insufficient since it placed undue reliance on government propaganda and failed to establish 'a *real* link to the armed conflict'.[107]

As this debate indicates, how the nexus requirement was interpreted affected both the likelihood of war crimes convictions and the type of narrative that was constructed about the relationship between the armed conflict and genocide in Rwanda. At the ICTR, in keeping with its victim-focused jurisprudence elsewhere, the judges gradually opted for a more lenient approach to the nexus requirement, resulting in a narrative in which the distinction between the armed conflict and genocide in Rwanda became increasingly blurred.[108]

b. Prohibited acts

Law-driven narrative pluralism may also emerge with respect to the prohibited acts of system crimes. This has often occurred when judges have surfaced different values or rights underlying particular crimes.[109] The evolution of the definition of *rape* at the ICTR from one that emphasised *coercion* and the context in which physical acts of a

[103] Cassese (n 85) 1410–1411.

[104] van der Wilt (n 88) 1122.

[105] van den Herik (n 84) 239.

[106] Ibid 256–257 (referring to the ICTR case of *Ntagerura et al* as an example of a tribunal that applied this approach).

[107] Ibid 257.

[108] Ibid 257 (arguing that the more lenient approach to the nexus requirement 'fails to observe that the Tutsi within Rwanda cannot necessarily be equated with the RPF' and that 'it may be argued that the Rwanda Armed Forces (RAF) had two "war fronts", one against the RPF and the other against the Tutsi population in Rwanda').

[109] See generally, C Laverty, 'What Lies Beneath? The Turn to Values in International Criminal Legal Discourse' *EJIL Talk!* (23 April 2018).

sexual nature took place to one that emphasised *lack of consent* and the mental state of the victim and perpetrator is illustrative.[110]

Faced with a situation in which rape was undefined in conventional or customary international law, the ICTR Trial Chamber in *Akayesu* initially analogised the crime of rape with torture under the Convention Against Torture, which elaborated a conceptual definition focused on the framework of State-sanctioned violence rather than cataloguing specific acts of torture.[111] Following this approach, the Trial Chamber defined rape as 'a physical invasion of a sexual nature, committed on a person under circumstances which are coercive'.[112] The Chamber confirmed that the coercive circumstances need not be evidenced by a show of physical force; they could be created by intimidation, threats, duress, extortion, or desperation, and may also be inherent in the circumstances (for example, an armed conflict or the military presence of an armed group).[113]

Given the brevity of the Trial Chamber's reasoning, the overriding impression is that the judges sought to carve out a definition of rape according to their predilections of how the offence should be understood in light of the particular social circumstances in which system crimes tend to be committed. Indeed, Navanethem Pillay, one of the judges in the *Akayesu* Trial Chamber, later explained in an academic capacity that the conceptual coercion-focused definition of rape adopted in the case had been influenced by the testimony of one of the witnesses at trial which had led her to re-examine traditional definitions of rape in light of 'women's experience of sexual violence, and its consequences during armed conflict'.[114]

Subsequently, in *Gacumbitsi*, the ICTR Appeals Chamber endorsed a more mechanical definition of rape that had initially been elaborated in the ICTY case of *Kunarac et al.* The definition of rape endorsed in *Gacumbitsi* placed lack of consent at the centre of both the physical and mental elements of the crime—requiring sexual penetration without the consent of the victim as well as knowledge of non-consent on the part of the accused.[115] The shift to a consent-based definition of rape was tempered to some extent by the Appeals Chamber's acknowledgement that lack of consent on the part of the victim could be demonstrated 'by proving the existence of coercive circumstances under which meaningful consent is not possible' and could be inferred 'from the background circumstances, such as an ongoing genocide campaign or the

[110] See generally, CA MacKinnon, 'Defining Rape Internationally: A Comment on *Akayesu*' (2006) 44 *Columbia Journal of Transnational Law* 940; W Schomburg and I Peterson, 'Genuine Consent to Sexual Violence Under International Criminal Law' (2007) 101 *American Journal of International Law* 121; N Hayes, 'Creating a Definition of Rape in International Law: The Contribution of the International Criminal Tribunals', in S Darcy and J Powderly (eds), *Judicial Creativity at the International Criminal Tribunals* (OUP 2010) 129; P Weiner, 'The Evolving Jurisprudence of the Crime of Rape in International Criminal Law' (2013) 54 *Boston College Law Review* 1207; A Adams, 'The Legacy of the International Criminals of the Former Yugoslavia and Rwanda and Their Contribution to the Crime of Rape' (2018) 29 *European Journal of International Law* 749.

[111] *Akayesu* Trial Judgment (n 31) [596]–[597]. For an overview of the critical literature concerning the Trial Chamber's reasoning, see generally, Hayes (n 110) 135–136.

[112] *Akayesu* Trial Judgment (n 31) [598].

[113] Ibid [688].

[114] N Pillay, 'Equal Justice for Women: A Personal Journey' (2008) 50 *Arizona Law Review* 657, 666–667.

[115] *Prosecutor v Sylvestre Gacumbitsi* (Judgment, Appeals Chamber) ICTR-2001-64-A (17 July 2006) [151].

detention of the victim'.[116] Similarly, the accused's knowledge of non-consent could be demonstrated by establishing that the individual was aware, or had reason to be aware, of 'the coercive circumstances that undermined the possibility of genuine consent'.[117] The Appeals Chamber also clarified that '[u]nder certain circumstances, the accused might raise reasonable doubt by introducing evidence that the victim specifically consented', but added that pursuant to Rule 96(ii) of the ICTR Rules of Procedure and Evidence, such evidence would be inadmissible if the victim had been subjected to, threatened with, or had reason to fear violence, duress, detention, or psychological oppression or reasonably believed that if the victim did not submit, another might be so subjected, threatened, or put to fear.[118] The mechanical consent-focused definition of rape ultimately emerged to become the established reference point in the jurisprudence of the ad hoc tribunals.[119]

The varying emphasis on coercion or lack of consent as the defining characteristic of rape was significant in terms of the narratives constructed in relation to the offence. As Catherine MacKinnon has argued:[120]

> [C]onceptually speaking, emphasis on non-consent as definitive of rape views the crime fundamentally as a deprivation of sexual freedom, a denial of individual self-acting. Emphasis on coercion as definitive, on the other hand, sees rape fundamentally as a crime on inequality, whether of physical or other force, status, or relation. Where coercion definitions of rape see power—domination and violence—nonconsent definitions envision love or passion gone wrong. Consent definitions accordingly have proof of rape turn on victim and perpetrator mental state: who wanted what, who knew what when. This crime basically occurs in individual psychic space. Coercion definitions by distinction turn on proof of physical acts, surrounding context, or exploitation of relative position: who did what to whom and sometimes why. This crime basically takes place on the material plane. Accordingly, while consent definitions tend to frame the same events as individuals engaged in atomistic one-at-a- time interactions, coercion definitions are the more expressly social, contextual, and collective in the sense of being group-based.

Given the coercive circumstances in which system crimes typically occur, several commentators have suggested that a coercion-focused definition of rape is better suited to the factual circumstances of mass atrocity situations.[121] According to Niamh Hayes, for example, 'it seems crass and counterintuitive even to discuss questions of consent in such [coercive] circumstances, to say nothing of entering into a legal analysis of whether lack of consent has been proven beyond a reasonable doubt'.[122]

[116] Ibid [155].
[117] Ibid [157].
[118] Ibid [156].
[119] See similarly, Darcy (n 84) 182; and Hayes (n 110) 148.
[120] MacKinnon (n 110) 941.
[121] See, in this regard, Schomburg and Peterson (n 110) 128–131.
[122] Hayes (n 110) 151. See similarly, Schomburg and Peterson (n 110) 140 ('In international law, understood in this limited, though extraordinarily important context, crimes of rape and other forms of sexual violence, constituting part of the listed core crimes, per se occur in coercive circumstances that make genuine consent impossible').

Moreover, it is notable that the turn towards the inclusion of non-consent as an element of the crime of rape at times led to the exposure of victims to painful questioning regarding whether particular acts were committed against their will, notwithstanding the fact that the coercive circumstances in which the acts were committed rendered such questions both inappropriate and unnecessary.[123] It is perhaps with these insights in mind that, whilst non-consent formally remained an element of the crime of rape, the Appeals Chamber in *Gacumbitsi* sought to ensure that such ill-conceived lines of questioning would be avoided by emphasising that non-consent could be inferred from the coercive circumstances in which system crimes are typically committed.[124]

A further illustration of how the evolving interpretation of particular prohibited acts can result in the foregrounding of different harms and experiences in the narratives of international criminal judgments concerns a line of cases at the SCSL, which conceptualised the practice of *forced marriage* in no less than three different ways.[125]

First, in *Brima et al*, a majority of the Trial Chamber dismissed charges of forced marriage on the basis that the evidence put forward by the prosecution was 'completely subsumed' by the crime of sexual slavery.[126] According to the majority, 'there is no lacuna in the law which would necessitate a separate crime of "forced marriage" as an "other inhumane act" '.[127] In particular, the majority found that none of the victims of sexual slavery had provided evidence that 'the mere fact that a rebel had declared her to be his wife had caused her any particular trauma, whether physical or mental'.[128] In addition, the majority added that 'had there been such evidence, it would not by itself have amounted to a crime against humanity, since it would not have been of similar gravity' to other prohibited acts of crimes against humanity.[129] The subsumption of the evidence of forced marriages within the crime of sexual slavery affected how such 'marriages' were characterised and understood. First, the majority's approach implicitly characterised the evidence of forced marriages as predominantly sexual in

[123] See, for example, the questioning of Witness 95 in *Kunarac*, who, despite being selected for rape more than 150 times in a period of 40 days, was still questioned by the Prosecutor as to whether such acts had been undertaken against her will. For a fuller account, see A-M de Brouwer, *Supranational Criminal Prosecution of Sexual Violence: The ICC and the Practice of the ICTY and the ICTR* (Intersentia 2005) 122–123 (concluding that such questioning is not without consequence: 'Victims will only perceive the Tribunals and the Court as legitimate if rape is defined in conformity with the reality of the crime. Including consent in the definition of rape is just a tool to silence them; they will not come forward, and justice will not be done to victims of sexual violence.')

[124] For a critical discussion, see generally, Hayes (n 110) 149–153; Schomburg and Peterson (n 110) 140; and MacKinnon (n 110) 954–958.

[125] The following paragraphs are adapted from B Sander, 'The Method is the Message: Law, Narrative Authority and Historical Contestation in International Criminal Courts' (2018) 19 *Melbourne Journal of International Law* 299, 321–326. See also, Oosterveld (n 81) 251–252. For a broader account, elaborating on approaches adopted in Rule 98*bis* decisions and by the Prosecutor in his trial briefs, see generally, S Thompson, 'Forced Marriage at the Special Court for Sierra Leone: Questions of Jurisdiction, Legality, Specificity, and Consistency', in Jalloh (n 81) 215, 223–232.

[126] *Prosecutor v Brima et al* (Judgment, Trial Chamber) SCSL-04-16-T (20 June 2007) ('*Brima et al* Trial Judgment') [713].

[127] Ibid.

[128] Ibid [710].

[129] Ibid.

nature.[130] Secondly, the majority's approach characterised the relationship of the perpetrators to their 'wives' as one of 'ownership'.[131]

On appeal, the Appeals Chamber adopted a different approach, reversing the Trial Chamber's majority judgment on the basis that 'no tribunal could reasonably have found that forced marriage was subsumed in the crime against humanity of sexual slavery'.[132] To reach this conclusion, the Appeals Chamber contended that forced marriage was neither a predominantly sexual crime nor merely the exercise of an ownership interest by the perpetrators over their victims.[133] For the Appeals Chamber, forced marriage entailed the imposition of 'a forced conjugal association upon the victims', pursuant to which women and girls were systematically abducted from their homes and communities by Armed Forces Revolutionary Council (AFRC) troops and compelled to serve as 'conjugal partners' to AFRC soldiers.[134] This relationship entailed the performance of 'conjugal duties' by the victims, including regular sexual intercourse, forced domestic labour, forced pregnancy, and caring for and bringing up children of the 'marriage'. In return, the rebel 'husband' was expected 'to provide food, clothing and protection to his "wife", including protection from rape by other men, acts he did not perform when he used a female for sexual purposes only'.[135] In a further distinction from the crime of sexual slavery, forced marriage implied 'a relationship of exclusivity between the "husband" and "wife", which could lead to disciplinary consequences for breach of this exclusive arrangement'.[136] In terms of the particular harms caused by the crime of forced marriage, the Appeals Chamber pointed to both the social stigmatisation suffered by the 'wives' and children born from such associations, including ostracisation from their communities, as well as the physical injury and psychological trauma related to becoming and living as a 'wife'.[137]

In light of these observations, the Appeals Chamber had little difficulty in concluding that acts of 'forced marriage' were of similar gravity to other enumerated crimes against humanity sufficient to constitute the crime against humanity of 'other inhumane acts'.[138] The final definition of the crime of forced marriage ultimately confirmed by the Chamber referred to a situation in which 'the perpetrator through his words or conduct, or those of someone for whose actions he is responsible, compels a person by force, threat of force, or coercion to serve as a conjugal partner resulting in severe suffering, or physical, mental or psychological injury to the victim'.[139]

[130] See also *Prosecutor v Brima et al* (Judgment, Appeals Chamber) SCSL-04-16-A (22 February 2008) ('*Brima et al* Appeal Judgment') [188].

[131] *Brima et al* Trial Judgment (n 126) [711].

[132] *Brima et al* Appeal Judgment (n 130) [195].

[133] Ibid [190]–[195].

[134] Ibid [190].

[135] Ibid.

[136] Ibid [195].

[137] Ibid [199]–[200].

[138] Ibid [202] (the Appeals Chamber declined to enter a conviction for forced marriage, concluding that the acts in question were encompassed in the conviction for outrages upon personal dignity, and deeming the recognition that such conduct is criminal and that it constitutes an 'other inhumane act' sufficient to convey 'society's disapproval of the forceful abduction and use of women and girls as forced conjugal partners as part of a widespread or systematic attack against the civilian population').

[139] Ibid [196].

The Appeals Chamber's findings were subsequently applied by the Trial Chamber in *Sesay et al*, which convicted all three accused of forced marriage as an 'other inhumane act'.[140] The Trial Chamber referred to forced marriage in terms of 'women and girls being forced into "marriages" and being forced to perform a number of conjugal duties under coercion by their "husbands"'.[141] The Trial Chamber also reiterated the social stigma and physical and psychological harm caused by the practice,[142] as well as confirming that the crime was not subsumed by the crime of sexual slavery because of its distinct elements of 'a forced conjugal association based on exclusivity between the perpetrator and victim'.[143]

A final approach to the practice of forced marriage was adopted by the Trial Chamber in *Taylor*. Even though Charles Taylor had not been charged with forced marriage as an inhumane act, the Trial Chamber decided to elaborate its thoughts on the issue in light of the extensive evidence of the practice that had been adduced by the prosecution under charges related to sexual violence.[144] The Trial Chamber explained that it did not consider the nomenclature of 'marriage' to be a useful label to describe the experiences of the victims who had suffered such practices, preferring instead the descriptor 'conjugal slavery'.[145] The Trial Chamber argued that conjugal slavery entailed forced conjugal relations involving the imposition of sexual and non-sexual acts and placed particular emphasis on the power of ownership exercised by the perpetrators over their 'bush wives'.[146] The Chamber concluded that conjugal slavery was not a new crime, preferring instead to examine the sexual violence aspects of the practice under the crime against humanity of sexual slavery, and the forced labour aspects of the practice under the crime against humanity of enslavement.[147]

The SCSL's jurisprudence on forced marriage reveals how legal categories can be adapted in line with judicial predilections in response to the novel circumstances of a particular case. Significantly, the divergent interpretative approaches of the judges at the SCSL led to divergent conceptualisations of forced marriage and different harms being foregrounded in the narratives constructed in their judgments. Whereas the subsumption of forced marriage within the crimes of sexual slavery and enslavement tended to emphasise the constituent criminal components of the practice (in particular, sexual violence and forced labour), it was only the recognition of forced marriage as a separate crime that foregrounded the trauma and stigma suffered by victims as a result of the forced conferral of the status of 'marriage'.

Interestingly, in the aftermath of these judgments, a number of scholars have expressly relied upon narrative considerations to argue in favour of recognising forced marriage as a distinct crime. According to Valerie Oosterveld, for example, since the act of naming is an important expressive tool, the recognition of forced marriage

140 *Sesay et al* Trial Judgment (n 80) [678].
141 Ibid [164].
142 Ibid [1296].
143 Ibid [2307].
144 *Taylor* Trial Judgment (n 77) [422].
145 Ibid [426]–[428].
146 Ibid [427].
147 See, for example, ibid [1095]–[1098] (evidence of sexual violence aspects of conjugal slavery considered within charges of sexual slavery) and [1824]–[1830] (evidence of forced labour aspects of conjugal slavery considered within charges of enslavement).

as a distinct prohibited act within crimes against humanity has the potential to 'authoritatively transform a previously legally unacknowledged experience' into an acknowledged wrong, as well as help legitimise experiences of victims and identify such experiences as crimes.[148] Equally, for Michael Scharf, the recognition of forced marriage as a separate crime could help to communicate that the practice is 'far more than just the sum of its parts', not only demeaning and distorting the institution of marriage itself, but also causing victims to suffer from being 'indefinably and inexorably bound, "married" to the men who victimize them'.[149]

It remains to be seen which—if any—of the SCSL's conceptualisations of forced marriage will resonate with audiences beyond the courtroom. With respect to communities within Sierra Leone, however, it is notable that although the SCSL referred in general terms to the stigmatisation suffered by individual victims of forced marriage in their communities, the Court tended to neglect the specifically familial nature of marriage in Sierra Leone and the familial nature of the harm that was suffered as a result of such practices. As Tim Kelsall argues, the SCSL tended to be preoccupied with the compulsion of the *individual* victim into marriage, whereas '[i]t was the fact that the *family* had not given its consent that made this a transgressive act in local eyes, not that the "wife" was a non-consenting partner'.[150] Moreover, whereas the SCSL illuminated the different types of harm suffered by the individual victims, from a local perspective forced marriage was seen as 'an offence against the family' and the remedies were generally 'restorative, not retributive'.[151]

II. Narrative Pluralism *Beyond* the Courtroom

Even when international criminal courts manage to achieve inter-court and intra-court narrative consistency, the possibility remains for narrative pluralism *beyond* the courtroom. Narrative pluralism beyond the courtroom refers to the gap between the *intended* meaning of the historical narratives constructed within international criminal judgments and their *public* or *social* meaning within different audiences.[152] In practice, the 'social relay' of judicially constructed narratives will typically vary depending on a range of factors, many of which are beyond the control of international

[148] Oosterveld (n 81) 250.

[149] MP Scharf, 'Forced Marriage as a Separate Crime against Humanity', in Jalloh (n 81) 193, 193.

[150] T Kelsall, *Culture under Cross-Examination: International Justice and the Special Court for Sierra Leone* (CUP 2009) 253 (emphasis added). See also, *Sesay et al* Trial Judgment (n 80) [1469] ('The Chamber observes, however, that *parental and family consent* to the so-called marriages of these sexually enslaved and abused women was conspicuously absent') (emphasis added).

[151] Kelsall (n 150) 253.

[152] See similarly, RD Sloane, 'The Expressive Capacity of International Punishment: The Limits of the National Law Analogy and the Potential of International Criminal Law' (2007) 43 *Stanford Journal of International Law* 39, 84 ('The expressive dimensions of punishment depend on its ability to convey the right meaning against the background of social norms, which vary significantly between the states, societies, cultures, and other constituencies that comprise the international community'); and DM Amann, 'Group Mentality, Expressivism, and Genocide' (2002) 2 *International Criminal Law Review* 93, 118 (focusing 'not on the intended meaning of a deed, but rather on the meaning that is understood by hearers, the public or social meaning').

criminal judges.[153] As James Boyd White famously observed, 'whatever it may purport *to say*, what a judgment shall come *to mean* is a matter for the parties and their audience to address and decide'.[154] Against this background, this section examines two sets of factors that have proven particularly influential in generating and maintaining narrative pluralism beyond the courtroom in practice.

A. Social Psychological Factors

First, the reception of narratives constructed within international criminal judgments will typically vary based on a range of *social psychological factors*.[155] One of the most important insights of social psychology is that human decision-making is not fundamentally rational, but driven by a range of motivational and cognitive biases that influence how we perceive the world and ourselves.[156] *Motivational biases* occur when human reasoning is influenced by a desire to achieve a particular result.[157] For example, according to self-defensive reasoning, individuals tend to be motivated to dismiss information that threatens their sense of self.[158] *Cognitive biases* occur when human reasoning fails to live up to the rational ideal even where an individual's sole motivation is accuracy in decision-making.[159] For instance, according to cognitive dissonance theory, when confronted with conflicting knowledge, opinions, or beliefs about the environment, oneself, or one's behaviour, humans tend to reduce the dissonance, as well as actively avoid situations and individuals that would likely increase it.[160] Similarly, pursuant to confirmation bias theory, humans tend to seek, interpret, and remember information in ways that are partial to existing beliefs and expectations.[161] Confirmation bias can lead to a number of effects including:[162] a propensity

[153] F Mégret, 'Practices of Stigmatization' (2013) 76 *Law and Contemporary Problems* 287, 311. See also, C Stahn, 'Between "Faith" and "Facts": By What Standards Should We Assess International Criminal Justice?' (2012) 25 *Leiden Journal of International Law* (2012) 251, at 273 ('The acceptance and internalization of facts are processes that are shaped by other factors, such as media, inter-ethnic contact, or local politics'); and JN Clark, 'The Impact Question: The ICTY and the Restoration and Maintenance of Peace', in B Swart et al (eds), *The Legacy of the International Criminal Tribunal for the Former Yugoslavia* (OUP 2011) 55, 79 ('attitudes and behaviours are shaped and affected less by the work of a distant and poorly-understood tribunal than by a variety of far more immediate factors, including the media, levels of inter-ethnic contact, and whether a person has had positive experiences with members of other ethnic groups').

[154] J Boyd White, 'Telling Stories in the Law and in Ordinary Life: The *Oresteia* and "Noon Wine"', in J Boyd White, *Heracles' Bow: Essays on Rhetoric and Poetics of the Law* (University of Wisconsin Press 1985) 168, 185 (emphasis added).

[155] See generally, S Ford, 'A Social Psychology Model of the Perceived Legitimacy of International Criminal Courts: Implications for the Success of Transitional Justice Mechanisms' (2012) 45 *Vanderbilt Journal of Transnational Law* 405; M Milanović, 'Establishing the Facts about Mass Atrocities: Accounting for the Failure of the ICTY to Persuade Target Audiences' (2016) 47 *Georgetown Journal of International Law* 1321; and M Milanović, 'Courting Failure: When Are International Criminal Courts Likely to Be Believed by Local Audiences?', in KJ Heller et al (eds), *The Oxford Handbook of International Criminal Law* (OUP 2020) 261.

[156] Ford (n 155) 419.

[157] Ibid 419–420.

[158] Ibid 423.

[159] Ibid 419.

[160] L Festinger, *A Theory of Cognitive Dissonance* (reprint edn [1957] Stanford University Press 1962) 3.

[161] Ford (n 155) 434.

[162] Ibid 436–437.

to attach greater weight to information acquired earlier in time (the primacy effect); a tendency for exposure to evidence that conflicts with one's beliefs to strengthen those beliefs (attitude polarisation); and a propensity for a pre-existing belief to persist even after evidence supporting that belief has been comprehensively undermined (belief perseverance). Finally, pursuant to the theory of ingroup-outgroup bias, membership in a group can generate favouritism towards one's group (ingroup positivity) and dismissal or rejection of other groups (outgroup negativity).[163] Group biases tend to be particularly intense when the group is classified or demarcated according to status or identity and in such a way as to provoke strong emotions.[164]

These social psychological factors have significant value in explaining why narratives constructed within international criminal judgments are often subject to diverse and conflicting interpretations amongst local audiences beyond the courtroom. In the aftermath of episodes of mass violence, it is not uncommon for local groups to maintain strong connections with particular factions to the underlying conflict.[165] Moreover, in many cases, these local groups will possess deeply entrenched internal narratives about the conflict, typically encompassing not only an evasion of responsibility for any crimes committed by the faction with which they identify, but also a cloak of collective victimhood whereby each group views itself as the principal victim of wrongs committed by other groups during the conflict.[166]

Two implications generally follow from this state of affairs. First, members of local communities torn apart by conflict are likely to interpret the historical narratives constructed within international criminal judgments against the background of their communal attachments and self-serving narratives of collective victimhood.[167] As such, the reception of judicially constructed narratives amongst local audiences will typically be subject to confirmation bias, including the tendency to prioritise information about the conflict received prior to the delivery of an international criminal judgment as well as the preservation of their already entrenched beliefs.[168]

Second, local audiences are also likely to view the individuals prosecuted by international criminal courts less in their individual capacity than as symbols for the political and ideological programmes they developed and as representatives of the communities and State to which they belong.[169] In these circumstances, the determination of the criminal responsibility of an individual in an international criminal judgment will often be interpreted by local audiences as a verdict on the responsibility of the community and group to which that individual belongs.[170] As a result, the

[163] Milanović (2016) (n 155) 1340–1341.

[164] Ibid 1341.

[165] Ford (n 155) 459. On the reluctance and resistance of individuals convicted by international criminal courts to consider judicial narratives as legitimate and complete accounts of the past, see generally, M Rauschenbach, 'Individuals Accused of International Crimes as Delegitimized Agents of Truth' (2018) 28 *International Criminal Justice Review* 291.

[166] Ford (n 155) 459–461; Milanović (2016) (n 155) 1343–1344 and 1347–1352; Stover (n 12) 143; M Ignatieff, 'Articles of Faith' (1996) 25 *Index on Censorship* 110, 116.

[167] LE Fletcher and HM Weinstein, 'Violence and Social Repair: Rethinking the Contribution of Justice to Reconciliation' (2002) 24 *Human Rights Quarterly* 573, 588.

[168] Milanović (2016) (n 155) 1343–1344 and 1347–1352; Stover (n 12) 1343.

[169] Koskenniemi (n 22) 16.

[170] F Mégret, 'What Sort of Global Justice Is "International Criminal Justice"?' (2015) 13 *Journal of International Criminal Justice* 77, 90.

conviction of an individual will often cause cognitive dissonance amongst members of that individual's faction, who will view the conviction as an attack on their social identity and reject both the court's attribution of responsibility to the individual as well as the broader historical narrative set out in the judgment.[171]

Of course, mass atrocity situations and their aftermath are far from uniform and in practice the intensity of motivational and cognitive biases will vary depending on the context in question.[172] In this regard, it is apposite to also consider a range of practical factors that have influenced how judicially constructed narratives have been received within audiences beyond the courtroom.

B. Practical Factors

In terms of practical factors that influence narrative reception, it is important to recognise that in some instances judicially constructed narratives fail to reach their target audiences at all.[173] In other instances, narratives constructed within international criminal judgments are first filtered through international and/or local carrier groups before reaching local communities.[174]

For the general public, international criminal proceedings can be alienating experiences. As Richard Wilson has observed, international criminals trials have a tendency to seem 'overly complex, excessively technical, and obsessed with minor procedural details'.[175] This perspective tallies with the views of journalists, such as Rebecca West, who famously characterised the IMT at Nuremberg as 'a citadel of boredom'.[176] The complexity of trial proceedings can alienate local communities as well as those directly participating in the trial as victims or witnesses, who may feel overwhelmed by the intricacies of criminal law procedure.[177] Feelings of alienation can also be exacerbated by the complexity and general inaccessibility of international criminal judgments.[178] One need only point to the trial judgment in the case against Charles Taylor

[171] This has been confirmed by a range of empirical studies. See, for example, Ford (n 155) 426–433 (explaining the effect of cognitive dissonance on Serbians with respect to indictments and convictions at the ICTY); JN Clark, 'The ICTY and Reconciliation in Croatia: A Case Study of Vukovar' (2012) 10 *Journal of International Criminal Justice* 397, 414 (qualitative empirical study in Croatia); Clark (n 153) 77 (qualitative empirical study in Bosnia-Herzegovina); and LE Fletcher and HM Weinstein, 'A World Unto Itself? The Application of International Justice in the Former Yugoslavia', in E Stover and HM Weinstein (eds), *My Neighbour, My Enemy: Justice and Community in the Aftermath of Mass Atrocity* (CUP 2004) 29, 44 (qualitative empirical study of 32 judges and prosecutors with primary or appellate jurisdiction for national war crimes trials in three areas of Bosnia-Herzegovina). See also, Milanović (2016) (n 155).

[172] See, in this regard, Ford (n 155) 463–475 (arguing that in some contexts the accumulation of evidence by international criminal courts can contribute to 'tipping points' that will lead individuals to revise their initial beliefs).

[173] Clark (n 153) 76.

[174] N Henry, *War and Rape: Law, Memory and Justice* (Routledge 2011) 119–122.

[175] RA Wilson, *Writing History in International Criminal Tribunals* (CUP 2011) 11.

[176] R West, *A Train of Powder* (Viking Press 1955) 3.

[177] See similarly, G Frankenberg, 'Human Rights and the Belief in a Just World' (2014) 12 *I-CON* 35, 55 (noting, in the field of human rights, that '[u]nless they're able to command a modicum of legal training or a pathologically robust psyche or both, claimants will hardly be able to avoid feeling dispossessed of what had once been their conflict—a feeling that may very well be described as alienation').

[178] See, for example, Clark (n 171) 409 (noting that 'not everyone has access to the internet' and 'ordinary people cannot be expected to read long and complex legal documents').

at the SCSL,[179] which runs to 2,500 pages, to appreciate the improbability that such judgments will be read by members of the general public.[180]

As a result, carrier groups have often played a significant role in influencing the social relay of narratives constructed within international criminal judgments.[181] For several international criminal courts, the importance of carrier groups has often been heightened by their geographical, cultural, and linguistic remoteness from local audiences.[182] In such circumstances, national politicians and local media outlets have often proven particularly influential in shaping how judicially constructed narratives are received by local audiences in practice.[183]

A clear illustration of this tendency is identifiable in the reactions of several high-ranking politicians and local media outlets to the initial convictions of Croatian Generals Ante Gotovina and Mladen Markač for their involvement in Operation Storm during the Balkans war.[184] At the time the convictions were rendered by the ICTY Trial Chamber, then Prime Minister Jadranka Kosor, as well as President Ivo Jasipović, each addressed a large crowd of Croatians at the annual celebrations of *the Dan Pobjede, Zahvalnosti i Hrvatskih Branitelja* (Day of Victory, Thanksgiving and the Croatian Defenders). The Prime Minister expressly celebrated Gotovina and Markač, whilst the President declared that Operation Storm was the 'crown of the struggle for a free Croatia'.[185] Local media coverage of the convictions was similar, with one military history magazine containing only pro-Gotovina and anti-ICTY articles, including one that claimed that Operation Storm was 'a liberating operation and not a criminal enterprise'.[186] As Janine Clarke has argued, these examples 'strongly attest to the fact that Croatia's politicians have played a major role in shaping popular attitudes towards the ICTY and its judgments'.[187]

179 *Taylor* Trial Judgment (n 77).

180 See similarly, Gaynor (n 40) 1274–1275 (noting that 'length is not necessarily undesirable in a document describing massive criminal activity', but adding that '[w]hat matters to the public, it appears, is . . . clarity and readability').

181 See generally, M Milanović (2016) (n 155) 1330–1336.

182 See, for example, JN Clark, 'From Negative to Positive Peace: The Case of Bosnia and Hercegovina' (2009) 8 *Journal of Human Rights* 360, 374 ('As a Tribunal that is geographically removed from the former Yugoslavia, that does not operate in the local languages of Bosnian/Croatian/Serbian, and that leans towards the unfamiliar adversarial common law system, the ICTY was always going to struggle to reach out to and engage local people').

183 See, for example, E Ramulić, 'Victims' Perspectives', in RH Steinberg (ed), *Assessing the Legacy of the ICTY* (Martinus Nijhoff Publishers 2011) 103, 105; R Hodžić, 'A Long Road Yet to Reconciliation: The Impact of the ICTY on Reconciliation and Victims' Perceptions of Criminal Justice', in RH Steinberg (ed), *Assessing the Legacy of the ICTY* (Martinus Nijhoff Publishers 2011) 115, 117; and M Klarin, 'The Impact of the ICTY Trials on Public Opinion in the Former Yugoslavia' (2009) 7 *Journal of International Criminal Justice* 89, 90. For a discussion of the narrow contexts in which the decisions of international criminal courts have triggered changes in and of media frames about the conflicts which formed the background of their decisions, see generally, K Bachmann et al, 'Like Dust before the Wind, or, the Winds of Change? The Influence of International Criminal Tribunals on Narratives and Media Frames' (2019) 13 *International Journal of Transitional Justice* 368.

184 For discussion of Croatian reactions to the subsequent acquittal of the Generals on appeal, see Clark (n 171) 419–420.

185 Ibid 417.

186 Ibid 418.

187 Ibid 417. See similarly, Ford (n 155) 432 (referring to an 'echo chamber' effect, whereby the initial negative perceptions of the ICTY by the general Croat population are 'reflected back by associates and elites').

Importantly, these practical factors will also affect the intensity of motivational and cognitive biases in the aftermath of mass atrocity situations. According to Marko Milanović, for example, the primary factor that influences the intensity of identity-protective reasoning within local communities is the role of dominant political, intellectual, and media elites. According to this perspective, narrative pluralism beyond the courtroom is likely to be exacerbated where group cohesion and polarisation is maintained in the aftermath of a conflict, the elites of the groups in question are the same or substantially similar to those in power when the atrocities occurred, the post-conflict society is characterised by an authoritarian absence of pluralism, and the elites in question perceive the work of the international criminal court as a threat to their own power and authority.[188]

As this brief perusal of social psychological and practical factors reveals, judicially constructed narratives are neither self-validating nor static but subject to an ongoing process of interpretation and contestation within audiences beyond the courtroom. As a result, rather than a bulwark against denialism, it is more common for both the authority and interpretation of historical narratives within international criminal judgments to remain disputed long after their initial construction.[189]

III. Conclusion

International criminal courts author historical narratives about the culpability of particular individuals and the mass atrocity contexts within which they once operated. As Doris Buss explains, these courts are increasingly expected to provide 'a careful accounting of the patterns of the conflicts, the nature of the different harms suffered, the circumstances that lead to the violence and the roles of different individuals, armies and militias in creating the conditions in which crimes were committed'.[190] Yet, despite their aspirations towards establishing historical closure, this chapter has demonstrated how the narratives constructed within international criminal judgments have often been subject to a process of ongoing contestation both within and beyond the courtroom.

The narrative pluralism illuminated in this chapter demonstrates a need for humbling the expectations that are often placed on international criminal courts both with respect to the construction of narratives within the courtroom and their reception beyond it.[191]

[188] Milanović (2020) (n 155).

[189] D Luban, 'Demystifying Political Violence: Some Bequests of ICTY and ICTR' (2016) 110 *AJIL Unbound* 251, 254 (arguing that while international criminal courts may help fight denialism amongst global audiences, they are unlikely to succeed within the affected populations. As a result, we should 'think globally, hope locally—but don't be surprised if trying to establish the truth locally fails in the face of ongoing identity politics.')

[190] Buss (n 4) 23.

[191] On the importance of modesty within the field of international criminal justice, see generally, B Sander, 'International Criminal Justice as Progress: From Faith to Critique', in M Bergsmo et al (eds), *Historical Origins of International Criminal Law: Volume 4* (Torkel Opsahl Academic EPublisher 2015) 749; DS Koller, 'The Faith of the International Criminal Lawyer' (2008) 40 *New York University Journal of International Law and Politics* 1019; S Kendall and SMH Nouwen, 'Speaking of Legacy: Toward an Ethos of Modesty at the International Criminal Tribunal for Rwanda' (2016) 110 *American Journal of International*

Within the courtroom, while consistency in the interpretation of legal and evidentiary frameworks is important for ensuring fairness towards the accused,[192] a degree of narrative pluralism is likely to be unavoidable. In particular, narrative pluralism is likely to arise from even slight variations in the evidentiary, charging, and interpretative decisions of the different actors who interact in each new case. In addition, a unique historical perspective is almost inevitable when viewing similar mass atrocity incidents through the prism of determining the culpability of different accused individuals. Importantly, a degree of narrative pluralism need not necessarily be a cause for concern. In fact, narrative pluralism can even serve to enrich the historical record of an international criminal court. As Lawrence Douglas argues, '[p]articularly in the case of traumatic or sensational history, it seems the law often only reaches a satisfactory result and understanding through a process of revisiting and re-trying the contested events'.[193]

Beyond the courtroom, international criminal courts undoubtedly have the potential to ignite public discourse,[194] stimulate social awakening,[195] and initiate civilised debate on what has happened during a particular mass atrocity situation.[196] However, it is important to recognise that whether this potential is fulfilled in practice will almost entirely depend upon factors beyond the control of international criminal courts, including most prominently the reaction of local elites.[197]

Law 212; and L van den Herik, 'International Criminal Law as a Spotlight and Black Holes as Constituents of Legacy' (2016) 110 *AJIL Unbound* 209. See also, S Moyn, 'On a Self-Deconstructing Symposium' (2016) 110 *AJIL Unbound* 258, 262 (pointing to 'the intuition that what people need is not exactly a legacy monument for the ICTY or the ICTR so much as a reality check about what it might actually take to improve a recalcitrant and violent world').

192 See generally, M Cupido, 'Facing Facts in International Criminal Law: A Casuistic Model of Judicial Reasoning' (2016) 14 *Journal of International Criminal Justice* 1.

193 Douglas (n 8) 198–199.

194 See, for example, S Landsman, 'The *Eichmann* Case and the Invention of the Witness-Driven Atrocity Trial' (2012–2013) 51 *Columbia Journal of Transnational Law* 69, 111 (noting, with regard to the *Eichmann* trial, that '[w]hether it was the key to the ignition of public discourse is open to question, but that it significantly contributed to the movement in that direction seems beyond serious doubt').

195 See, for example, J O'Connell, 'Gambling with the Psyche: Does Prosecuting Human Rights Violators Console their Victims?' (2005) 46 *Harvard International Law Journal* 295, 232 (discussing trials as 'stimulants of social awakening').

196 See generally, M Osiel, *Mass Atrocity, Collective Memory, and the Law* (Transaction Publishers 1997), 36–55 and 283–301.

197 Milanović (2020) (n 155) 290 ('by themselves international criminal tribunals have little, if any, power to shape local public opinion. In other words, their relative success or failure in gaining acceptance for their findings among target audiences is not really *their* success or failure') (emphasis in original).

8
Conclusion

The field of international criminal justice is at a critical juncture. From an institutional perspective, the field has exceeded all expectations, achieving a degree of judicialisation that few thought imaginable. Yet, at the same time as the field has established itself as a dominant frame for responding to situations of mass atrocity, there has been a growing sense that the field's normative aspirations far exceed what can realistically be achieved in practice.[1] Amidst rising frustrations and disillusionment, the glow that once accompanied international criminal justice has faded, the unflinching enthusiasm has been tempered.[2]

Set in this critical climate, this book has sought to understand international criminal courts through the prism of their *historical function*—exploring, in particular, how such courts confront the past by constructing historical narratives concerning both the culpability of the accused and the broader mass atrocity contexts in which they are alleged to have participated. The book has argued that international criminal courts are host to *struggles for historical justice*, discursive contests between different actors vying for judicial acknowledgement of their preferred interpretations of the past. By examining these struggles within different institutional settings, the book has sought to surface the *legitimating qualities* of international criminal judgments—illuminating, in particular, what tends to be foregrounded and included within, as well as marginalised and excluded from, the historical narratives constructed by international criminal courts in practice.

Focusing on the relationship between legal categories and historical narration, the preceding chapters have revealed how history within international criminal courts has been constructed in a legal idiom and structured according to the adjudicative questions of whether particular categories of crimes have been committed (the *crime* question) and whether criminal responsibility for their commission may be attributed according to particular categories of culpability (the *culpability* question) to particular categories of persons (the *prosecutorial targets* question). By exploring how different actors interact over these questions, this study has revealed some of the dynamics of struggles for historical justice in different institutional contexts and the legal forms of legitimation that result.

In drawing the book to a close, this final chapter begins by exploring what this study has revealed about the legitimation function of international criminal courts (Section I), before offering some reflections on the implications of the study for the field of international criminal justice going forward (Section II).

[1] B Sander, 'International Criminal Justice as Progress: From Faith to Critique', in M Bergsmo et al (eds), *Historical Origins of International Criminal Law: Volume 4* (Torkel Opsahl Academic EPublisher 2015) 749.
[2] D Luban, 'After the Honeymoon: Reflections on the Current State of International Criminal Justice' (2013) 11 *Journal of International Criminal Justice* 505.

Doing Justice to History. Barrie Sander, Oxford University Press (2021). © Barrie Sander.
DOI: 10.1093/oso/9780198846871.003.0008

I. The Legitimation Function of International Criminal Courts

Through the practice of historical narration, international criminal courts reveal their productive power—their expressive capacity to construct and shape the identities of individuals, groups, and the relations between them, and to define and delineate boundaries between guilt and innocence, blamers and blamed, and victims and perpetrators.[3] To recognise the productive power of judicial narratives is to appreciate their particularity—their legitimation of particular perspectives and understandings of mass atrocity situations at the expense of others.

The legitimation function of law has been widely recognised in international legal scholarship.[4] Hilary Charlesworth, for example, has observed how a tendency on the part of international lawyers to focus on crises as the engine of progressive development can lead to international law serving merely as 'a source of justification for the status quo'.[5] In the human rights context, Wendy Brown has discussed how the ideology of human rights activism, by failing to address the structural constraints of individual agency, largely codifies those constraints.[6] Similarly, Susan Marks has critiqued the 'justificatory exceptionalism' of former US President George Bush and former US Secretary of Defence Donald Rumsfeld, which they exhibited in their apologies for acts of torture committed by US soldiers at Abu Ghraib.[7] By characterising the abuses at Abu Ghraib as exceptional departures from normal US military practices, their apologies served a number of legitimating functions—obscuring the fact that allegations of torture were far more widespread and systematic at Abu Ghraib, concealing the conditions that lay behind those acts of torture, and diverting attention from other forms of violence that are enabled and normalised within the international political order.[8]

Within the literature pertaining to mass atrocities, a significant body of scholarship has surfaced the legitimating qualities of *domestic* atrocity trials and judgments.[9] In particular, a number of studies have revealed how international criminal prosecutions before domestic criminal courts have been carefully orchestrated to legitimate

[3] See, in this regard, M Foucault, *Discipline and Punish: The Birth of a Prison* (Penguin 1991) 194 ('We must cease once and for all to describe the effects of power in negative terms: it "excludes", it "represses", it "censors", it "abstracts", it "masks", it "conceals". In fact, power produces: it produces reality; it produces domains of objects and rituals of truth. The individual and the knowledge that may be gained of him belong to this production.')

[4] See generally, S Veitch, *Law and Irresponsibility: On the Legitimation of Human Suffering* (Routledge-Cavendish 2007); and C af Jochnick and R Normand, 'The Legitimation of Violence: A Critical History of the Laws of War' (1994) 35 *Harvard International Law Journal* 49, 56–59.

[5] H Charlesworth, 'International Law: A Discipline of Crisis' (2002) 65 *Modern Law Review* 377, 391.

[6] W Brown, '"The Most We Can Hope For ...": Human Rights and the Politics of Fatalism' (2014) 103 *South Atlantic Quarterly* 451, 455. See also, S Marks, 'Four Human Rights Myths' (2012) *LSE Law, Society and Economy Working Papers: Working Paper No 10/2012*, 12–17; and B Rajagopal, *International Law from Below: Development, Social Movements, and Third World Resistance* (CUP 2003) 186.

[7] S Marks, 'Apologising for Torture' (2004) 73 *Nordic Journal of International Law* 365, 376*ff*.

[8] Ibid 378–383.

[9] See generally, B Sander, 'Justice as Identity: Unveiling the Mechanics of Legitimation in Domestic Atrocity Trials' (2018) 16 *Journal of International Criminal Justice* 203.

particular understandings of the past in line with the interests of the States in which and on whose behalf such prosecutions were conducted. A prominent theme in such cases has been the construction of narratives of the past that serve to strengthen and protect particular conceptions of the national identity of the States in which the trials were convened, reflecting a notion of 'justice as identity' whereby the criminal courtroom is transformed into a didactic mechanism of nation-building.[10]

The present study has sought to reveal some of the legitimating qualities of the judgments of *international* criminal courts. Reflecting on the different themes examined in the preceding chapters, three strands of legitimation stand out. In particular, the histories produced by international criminal courts have generally been *apologetic* to State interests, focused on *spectacular* forms of violence, and *narrowly contextualised* in ways that emphasise the individual agency of military and political actors operating at the local level of mass atrocity situations.

A. Apologetic Histories

First, the narratives constructed within the judgments of international criminal courts have tended to be *apologetic* historical accounts, shaped and restricted in significant respects in accordance with the established relations of domination that exist both between and within States in the international political order at particular moments of time.[11]

This strand of legitimation has been particularly apparent with respect to *prosecutorial targets*. In particular, *situational* selectivity within international criminal courts has rarely conflicted with the interests of powerful States. As Gerry Simpson explains, while millions have died as a consequence of Great Power intervention or an indirect consequence of coups and military action, 'not one single national of a permanent Security Council member has been tried before an international criminal court since 1945'.[12] At the same time, *case* selectivity has generally been oriented *factionally* in accordance with the interests of States on whose cooperation prosecutors have been reliant and/or those which are particularly powerful within the international community more generally. While accident has played a role in defining which individuals have been prosecuted before international criminal courts—for example where a suspect or defendant has passed away prior to prosecution or judgment—in general, moments of anti-impunity against individuals belonging to weaker factions within mass atrocity situations have been accompanied by moments of impunity for individuals belonging to factions aligned or protected by more powerful actors within the international community.[13] As Adam Branch argues with respect to the International

[10] Ibid.

[11] On the ways in which meaning can establish relations of domination within international law, see generally, S Marks, *The Riddle of all Constitutions: International Law, Democracy, and the Critique of Ideology* (OUP 2000).

[12] G Simpson, 'Linear Law: The History of International Criminal Law' in C Schwöbel (ed), *Critical Approaches to International Criminal Law: An Introduction* (Routledge 2014) 159, 173.

[13] See similarly, K Engle et al, 'Introduction', in K Engle et al (eds), *Anti-Impunity and the Human Rights Agenda* (CUP 2016) 1, 5 ('each historical moment of "anti-impunity" may be more accurately described as one gripped simultaneously by "impunity"'); and Z Miller, 'Anti-Impunity Politics in Post-Genocide

Criminal Court (ICC), 'in every case in which the ICC has become involved, the court has either aligned itself with the interests of the powerful or, when it has tried to prosecute those with power, faced disaster', a trend that has risked sending the message that 'the best way to avoid prosecution is not to abide by the law but to win on the battlefield, to sign up to the War on Terror or to offer up suspects to the ICC'.[14]

In practice, situational and case selectivity have profoundly shaped the scope and content of the historical narratives constructed within the international criminal judgments, ensuring that judges avoid scrutinising the behaviour of particular actors—whether Allied personnel at the Nuremberg International Military Tribunal (IMT) and Tokyo International Military Tribunal for the Far East (IMTFE), North Atlantic Treaty Organization (NATO) personnel at the International Criminal Tribunal for the former Yugoslavia (ICTY), members of the Rwandan Patriotic Front at the International Criminal Tribunal for Rwanda (ICTR), peacekeepers at the Special Court for Sierra Leone (SCSL), or factions aligned with referring entities at the ICC. Whether by means of formally restricting the jurisdictional requirements by which situations and cases have been defined and selected or by exerting informal pressure through the obstruction or selective provision of cooperation, the balance of power between and within States beyond the courtroom has profoundly influenced the individuals targeted for prosecution and the orientation of historical narratives within it.

Beyond prosecutorial targets, the *overarching thematic paradigms of criminality* examined within international criminal courts have also been shaped in accordance with the balance of power within the international political order.[15] To be sure, the precise genealogy of particular crimes is generally traceable to longer-term currents of thought and epistemic communities.[16] Yet, questions of inclusion and prioritisation of particular categories of crime within the jurisdictional frameworks of international criminal courts have ultimately been matters of political negotiation. At Nuremberg and Tokyo, for example, the aggressive war paradigm reflected in the primacy afforded to crimes against peace was driven by the political interests of the United States, which viewed the crime as a means of validating its foreign policy during the Second World War and punishing acts of Nazi and Japanese aggression. The subsequent shift to an atrocity paradigm focused on the prosecution of war crimes, crimes against humanity, and the crime of genocide at the ad hoc tribunals and the ICC may also be

Rwanda', in Engle et al (n 13) 149, 165 ('Anti-impunity all too often brings with it a high degree of impunity'); A Branch, 'The African Criminal Court: Towards an Emancipatory Politics', in CC Jalloh et al (eds), *The African Court of Justice and Human and Peoples' Rights in Context* (CUP 2019) 198, 205 ('the ICC's practice has conformed most closely not to the liberal rule of law but to international lines of force, ushering in not a post-Westphalian order but a new geography of de facto impunity').

[14] Branch (n 13) 204.

[15] See similarly, R Liss, 'Crimes Against the Sovereign Order: Rethinking International Criminal Justice' (2020) 113 *American Journal of International Law* 727 (arguing that international crimes are best understood as 'crimes against the sovereign order of their era').

[16] See, for example, K von Lingen, 'Legal Flows: Contributions of Exiled Lawyers to the Concept of "Crimes Against Humanity" During the Second World War' (2020) 17 *Modern Intellectual History* 507 (identifying exiled lawyers within the United Nations War Crimes Commission during the 1940s as decisive for the emergence of crimes against humanity as a legal category); and F Hirsch, *Soviet Judgment at Nuremberg: A New History of the International Military Tribunal after World War II* (OUP 2020) 8 and 35 (identifying the roots of the category of crimes against peace in work of Soviet lawyer, Aaron Trainin).

viewed through the prism of the interests of powerful States in the contemporary era, which have generally been more comfortable addressing atrocities committed during situations of mass violence rather than resolving questions of responsibility for their outbreak that are more likely to implicate areas of law that could interfere with their freedom of action on the international plane.

The *specific crimes* charged have also been influenced by the political environment in which international prosecutors operate. At Nuremberg and Tokyo, the Allied powers directly steered the scope and content of the indictments in accordance with their interests. As Francine Hirsch has observed, 'the four wartime Allies understood that in putting together the case against the Nazi elite and their organizations, the prosecutors were also setting out a version of events for prosperity'.[17] At the ad hoc tribunals and the ICC, the interests of powerful States in shaping indictments have also been reflected, albeit in somewhat subtler terms, within what Christiane Wilke refers to as the 'deep architecture of the rules of international law' that shapes the visibility of different types of violence.[18] For example, the dearth of war crimes charges concerning the conduct of hostilities adjudicated within international criminal courts may be rooted at least partially in the deliberately intricate judgments required by the relevant underlying international humanitarian law norms, which render their application in the criminal law context both uncertain and complex.[19] As a result, international criminal judgments have rarely delved into the intricacies of armed conflict decision-making concerning the propriety of particular objectives and means of warfare, except for the clearest cases of attacks directed against civilians or civilian objects.[20]

In light of the political constraints that have informed the overarching thematic paradigms of criminality adjudicated within international criminal courts, together with the orientation of some of the specific charges, contestation over the interpretation of crime categories within international criminal proceedings has generally avoided encroaching on the interests of the most powerful States in the international community. At the ad hoc tribunals, for example, judges relied on a flexible approach to custom, a diversity of interpretative techniques, and a relaxed conception of the principle of legality to progressively adapt the categories of war crimes and crimes against humanity to the privatisation of contemporary violence, expand the crime of genocide to encompass more localised contexts, and modernise the underlying prohibited acts of general crime categories to reflect more diverse forms of criminality. While these decisions were undoubtedly significant, it is nonetheless notable that many of the most innovative of these interpretative acts—such as the recognition of war crimes in non-international armed conflicts—were aligned with the interests of the States who established the tribunals to ensure that the atrocities committed in the situations in the former Yugoslavia, Rwanda, and Sierra Leone did not go

[17] Hirsch (n 16) 83.

[18] C Wilke, 'Asymmetric Legality: The Invisibility of High-Tech Violence in Afghanistan' *Public Seminar* (2 May 2019).

[19] P Akhavan, 'The Dilemmas of Jurisprudence' (1998) 13 *American University International Law Review* 1518, 1520.

[20] C Ponti, 'The Crime of Indiscriminate Attack and Unlawful Conventional Weapons: The Legacy of the ICTY Jurisprudence' (2015) 6 *Journal of International Humanitarian Legal Studies* 118, 145.

unpunished.[21] By contrast, little or no attention was devoted to areas of law in which powerful States arguably had more at stake, such as the crime of aggression and the law governing the conduct of hostilities.[22]

Taken together, these trends reveal how international criminal courts have generally produced apologetic or 'hegemonic' histories within their judgments,[23] privileging perspectives of the past that tend to be circumscribed in ways that accord with the contemporaneous balance of power between and within States in the international community.

B. Spectacular Histories

The narratives constructed within international criminal judgments have also focused primarily on *spectacular* harms—foregrounding a narrow set of egregious physical, direct, and immediate forms of violence.[24] Importantly, the particular types of spectacular violence foregrounded within international criminal judgments have not remained static but evolved over time. The marginalisation of sexual and gender-based crimes at Nuremberg and Tokyo, as well as the fluctuating records of the ad hoc tribunals and the ICC, for example, reveal the contingency of the precise thematic orientation of judicial narratives on a diversity of factors, ranging from the shifting investigative strategies and priorities of different international prosecutors to the variable impact of judicial oversight, pressure from victim legal representatives and civil society movements, and witness testimony. Yet, while the micro-politics of meaning production has proven important, fluctuations in the visibility of violence have generally occurred within what Christine Schwöbel-Patel refers to as a 'dominant aesthetic',[25] privileging spectacular physical violence to the marginalisation and neglect of other types of harm.

For instance, although economic, social, and cultural forms of violence have not been completely neglected within the judgments of international criminal courts, rarely have they formed the focus of international prosecutions—a trend illustrated in particularly clear terms by the scarcity of attention devoted to environmental harms. In part, the marginalisation of these forms of violence is an act of choice that flows from drafting and charging decisions. In terms of charging, it is clear that international prosecutors have had at their disposal the doctrinal tools to bring charges concerning a range of economic, social, and cultural harms that fall squarely within the ambit of existing international criminal law.[26] Their reticence to use these tools has

[21] AM Danner, 'When Courts Make Law: How the International Criminal Tribunals Recast the Laws of War' (2006) 59 *Vanderbilt Law Review* 1, 45.

[22] Ibid 44; S Darcy, *Judges, Law and War: The Judicial Development of International Humanitarian Law* (CUP 2014) 326.

[23] Simpson (n 12) 170.

[24] On 'spectacle' and 'spectacular crimes' in international criminal law, see generally, C Schwöbel-Patel, 'Spectacle in International Criminal Law: The Fundraising Image of Victimhood' (2016) 4 *London Review of International Law* 247; and C Schwöbel-Patel, 'The Core Crimes of International Criminal Law' in KJ Heller et al (eds), *The Oxford Handbook of International Criminal Law* (OUP 2020) 768.

[25] Schwöbel-Patel (2020) (n 24) 788.

[26] See generally, E Schmid, *Taking Economic, Social and Cultural Rights Seriously in International Criminal Law* (CUP 2015).

resulted from a range of factors, including the perceived lower gravity of economic, social, and cultural forms of violence, evidentiary and legal challenges, and resource limitations.[27]

At the same time, while a certain amount of space has existed for prosecutors to direct greater attention towards economic, social, and cultural forms of violence, it is also the case that the jurisdictional frameworks of international criminal courts have been circumscribed in ways that exclude particular types of harm. That drafting decisions are important may be illustrated by comparing the narrow jurisdictional boundaries of the international criminal courts examined in this study with the more expansive jurisdiction envisaged by the Malabo Protocol, which proposes to establish international criminal jurisdiction within the yet to be established African Court of Justice and Human and Peoples' Rights.[28] In particular, the proposed International Criminal Law Section will have jurisdiction over not only natural persons but also corporations,[29] not only Africans but also under certain circumstances individuals and corporations globally,[30] and not only war crimes, crimes against humanity, genocide, and the crime of aggression, but also a broader set of crimes including mercenarism, trafficking in hazardous wastes, and money laundering.[31] While the Malabo Protocol also includes more restrictive elements and could potentially be instrumentalised to serve the interests of African security States and Western security regimes, its expansive personal and subject-matter jurisdiction illustrates how drafting decisions may open up or restrict political and narrative possibilities in legal contexts.[32]

Ultimately, however, while the marginalisation of particular forms of violence has to a certain extent resulted from situated choices in the form of drafting and charging practices, it is also the case that certain types of harm have proven an awkward fit for the vocabulary of international criminal law. As Mark Drumbl explains, some of the most prominent collective challenges confronting societies around the world, ranging from climate change to global health pandemics, 'are not crimes of intent, or conduct, or full expression of free will', but rather result from 'small daily acts ... in which everyone is slightly complicit and slightly victimized, that then become aggregated into collective security threats that the criminal law generally cannot respond to'.[33] In other words, while space exists for greater attention to be directed towards direct and immediate forms of economic, social, and cultural violence within the bounds of existing international criminal law, it remains the case that the paradigm of criminal responsibility is generally ill-equipped to address violence that is structural and slower in nature.

As a result, absent other societal mechanisms for confronting and addressing structural and slow violence, the risk arises that international criminal judgments may serve

[27] Ibid 326–329.

[28] African Union, Protocol on Amendments to the Protocol on the Statute of the African Court of Justice and Human Rights (27 June 2014) ('Malabo Protocol'). See generally, CC Jalloh et al (eds), *The African Court of Justice and Human and Peoples' Rights in Context* (CUP 2019).

[29] Article 46C, Malabo Protocol (n 28).

[30] Article 46E*bis*, Malabo Protocol (n 28).

[31] Article 28A, Malabo Protocol (n 28).

[32] Branch (n 13) 208*ff*.

[33] T Cruvellier, 'Mark Drumbl: "Law Cannot Solve The Biggest Problems We Face"' *JusticeInfo.net* (16 July 2019).

to reassure, console, and soothe societal audiences by focusing on what they classify as the exceptional actions of a handful of individual perpetrators of spectacular physical, direct, and immediate forms of violence, whilst at the same time naturalising the chaotic social, economic, and political structures that create the conditions of possibility for atrocities to occur in different societal contexts around the world.[34]

C. Narrow Histories

Finally, the narratives constructed within the judgments of international criminal courts have also tended to be *narrowly contextualised* in ways that risk inflating the agency of the individuals on trial at the expense of the broader context in which mass atrocities occur. Importantly, the histories produced in international criminal judgments are not completely decontextualised. Rather, they are *selectively contextualised* in a number of respects.

For example, through the recognition and development of culpability categories—in particular, modes of participation doctrines and grounds for excluding responsibility and mitigating punishment—judges within international criminal courts have typically emphasised the ways in which the collective and systemic qualities of system crimes may *expand* individual agency, whilst attaching limited weight to the ways in which coercion-based and cognition-based situational pressures may *reduce* individual agency in particular mass atrocity settings. The implication of this perspective has been to convey the message that most situational pressures encountered in mass atrocity environments are reasonably resistible by the individuals on trial, the accused's social context deemed merely explanatory of their behaviour—and therefore legally irrelevant—rather than exculpatory or mitigating.

In addition, with the gaze of international criminal courts understandably fastened towards adjudicative questions of criminal responsibility, attention has rarely been directed towards the roles performed by *bystanders* and *resisters* in mass atrocity contexts. As a result, international criminal judgments have tended to offer limited space for critically reflecting on the widespread societal acquiescence that characterises many mass atrocity situations, the dilemmas and ambiguities of agency experienced within the spectrum of human relationships that exist in mass atrocity situations that is rarely reducible to a simple victim-perpetrator binary, or the possibilities that may exist to exercise agency and build solidarity to resist passivity, conformism, and authority structures in mass atrocity environments.[35]

[34] See similarly, I Tallgren, 'The Sensibility and Sense of International Criminal Law' (2002) 13 *European Journal of International Law* 561, 593–595; T Krever, 'International Criminal Law: An Ideology Critique' (2013) 26 *Leiden Journal of International Law* 701, 720 and 722; and G Baars, 'Making ICL History: On the Need to Move Beyond Pre-Fab Critiques of ICL', in Schwöbel (n 12) 196, 206.

[35] See generally, LE Fletcher, 'From Indifference to Engagement: Bystanders and International Criminal Justice' (2005) 26 *Michigan Journal of International Law* 1013; LE Fletcher, 'Facing Up to the Past: Bystanders and Transitional Justice' (2007) 20 *Harvard Human Rights Journal* 47; B Leebaw, 'Lost, Forgotten, or Buried? Transitional Justice, Agency, and the Memory of Resistance' (2013) 2 *Politica & Società* 237; B Leebaw, 'Justice and the Faithless: The Demand for Disobedience in International Criminal Law' (2018) 24 *European Journal of International Relations* 344; B Leebaw, 'If Only More Such Stories Could Have Been Told: Ways of Remembering Resistance' (2019) 15 *Law, Culture and the Humanities* 448.

The narratives constructed in international criminal judgments have also been narrow in terms of the *actors* and *geographical spaces* that have formed their focus—predominantly examining the behaviour of political and military figures at the expense of economic actors and directing their attention towards localised systems of criminality rather than broader international networks. For example, rarely have international prosecutors targeted private business actors, a trend rooted in a diversity of factors including the perceived lower gravity of their interventions, evidentiary and legal obstacles to their prosecution, and State preferences for nurturing relationships with business communities rather than holding them to account in the aftermath of episodes of mass violence.[36] Where economic actors have been the focus of attention, for example the prosecution of individuals associated with Rwandan media entities at the ICTR, the focus has been on local apparatuses of power to the neglect of broader international interventions—whether international financial institutions, private security firms, or illicit arms and diamonds trade networks. Indeed, even with respect to political and military interventions, the narrative frame of international criminal courts has remained firmly fastened on local power structures,[37] with only marginal attention devoted to international peacekeeping forces or colonial actors, for example.[38]

Taken together, the apologetic, spectacular, and narrow qualities of the histories constructed within international criminal judgments reveal a somewhat ironic picture: courts promoted as mechanisms to challenge denial have risked becoming forms of selective amnesia,[39] instruments of legitimation that reflect and potentially reinforce patterns of domination in the existing international political order, displace attention from structural and slow forms of violence, marginalise the ambiguities and possibilities of individual agency in mass atrocity contexts, and understate the contributions of economic and international actors towards episodes of mass violence.

[36] See generally, JG Stewart, 'Atrocity, Commerce and Accountability: The International Criminal Liability of Corporate Actors' (2010) 8 *Journal of International Criminal Justice* 313; W Kaleck and M Saage-Maaß, 'Corporate Accountability for Human Rights Violations Amounting to International Crimes: The Status Quo and its Challenges' (2010) 8 *Journal of International Criminal Justice* 699; C Burchard, 'Ancillary and Neutral Business Contributions to "Corporate-Political Core Crime": Initial Enquiries Concerning the Rome Statute' (2010) 8 *Journal of International Criminal Justice* 934; MB Taylor et al, *Overcoming Obstacles to Justice: Improving Access to Judicial Remedies for Business Involvement in Grave Human Rights Abuses* (FAFO 2010); G Baars, *Law(yers) Congealing Capitalism: On the (Im)possibility of Restraining Business in Conflict through International Criminal Law* (University College London Doctoral Thesis 2012); E Schmid, 'Distinguishing Types of 'Economic Abuses': A Three-Dimensional Model' (2015) 26 *Criminal Law Forum* 225; and LA Payne et al, *Transitional Justice and Corporate Accountability from Below: Deploying Archimedes' Lever* (CUP 2020) 32–38.

[37] See similarly, S Ming Yau, 'The Decentralisation of International Crimes: A Shift from the Central Criminal Apparatus at the ICC?' *EJIL:Talk!* (27 December 2018).

[38] See, in this regard, AG Kiyani, 'International Crime and the Politics of Criminal Theory: Voices and Conduct of Exclusion' (2015) 48 *NYU Journal of International Law & Politics* 129, 175 ('while the prosecutions at the Nuremberg and Tokyo Tribunals arguably constituted a legal response to colonial crimes, the judicial condemnation only occurred when imperial excess challenged Western interests').

[39] See similarly, B Leebaw, *Judging State-Sponsored Violence, Imagining Political Change* (CUP 2011) 175; M Drumbl, 'Collective Responsibility and Postconflict Justice', in T Isaacs and R Vernon (eds), *Accountability for Collective Wrongdoing* (CUP 2011) 23, 37; and F Mégret, 'International Criminal Justice: A Critical Research Agenda', in Schwöbel (n 12) 17, 30.

D. The Limits of the Legitimating Power of International Criminal Judgments

The legitimating qualities of international criminal judgments are defined as much by what they marginalise and exclude as by what they recognise and emphasise.[40] Critically reflecting on the legitimation function of international criminal courts, however, it is important to guard against overstating the power of international criminal judgments to divert attention from specific agendas and injustices. For example, while it is indisputable that structural forms of violence have consistently fallen beyond the purview of international criminal judgments, less clear is the extent to which this silence has itself been complicit in a more general neglect of structural violence during periods of transition.[41]

International criminal courts undoubtedly arrest attention through their seductive legalism,[42] as well as an aesthetic bias that privileges the spectacle of physical violence over the complexity of structural injustices.[43] International criminal courts also capture attention by offering a simple and highly communicable frame for understanding mass atrocities.[44] As Keck and Sikkink explain, 'problems whose causes can be assigned to the deliberate (intentional) actions of identifiable individuals are amenable to advocacy network strategies in ways that problems whose causes are irredeemably structural are not'.[45]

Nonetheless, to focus narrowly on the distracting qualities of international criminal judgments may be to neglect or at the very least understate other factors that have proven instrumental in marginalising issues of structural violence during periods of transition. Indeed, it is interesting to note that several of the legitimating characteristics of international criminal judgments are also identifiable within other justice modalities that have been established in the aftermath of episodes of mass violence. A recent volume edited by Engle, Miller, and Davis on anti-impunity and the human rights agenda, for example, illuminates a number of 'mechanisms for human rights adjudication or transitional justice that appear to operate outside the retributive criminal

[40] Simpson (n 12) 173 ('International criminal justice is probably best defined by what it cannot do, by what it is prevented from doing and by what it refuses to do.')

[41] See also, the parallel debate in the field of human rights concerning the relationship between human rights and neoliberalism. See, in particular, Marks (n 6) 9 (arguing that Naomi Klein's work identifies the emergence of the human rights movement to be 'part of the context for the consolidation of neo-liberalism itself'); S Moyn, 'A Powerless Companion: Human Rights in the Age of Neoliberalism' (2014) 77 *Law and Contemporary Problems* 147, 169 (arguing that human rights have been 'a powerless companion' to neoliberalism); and T Dickson, *On the Poverty, Rise, and Demise of International Criminal Law* (Portland State University: Dissertations and Thesis Paper 2016) 119 (arguing that the human rights movement 'was reckless, if not more, but it was also opportunistic in marginalizing socio-economic rights').

[42] On seductive legalism, see generally, K McEvoy, 'Beyond Legalism: Towards a Thicker Understanding of Transitional Justice' (2007) 34 *Journal of Law and Society* 411, 416–4417 (noting how the 'seductive qualities of legalistic analysis lend themselves particularly well to transitional contexts... [including] values and working practices such as justice, objectivity, certainty, uniformity, universality, rationality, and so on').

[43] Schwöbel-Patel (2020) (n 24) 788.

[44] See generally, AB Houge and K Lohne, 'End Impunity! Reducing Conflict-Related Sexual Violence to a Problem of Law' (2017) 51 *Law & Society Review* 755.

[45] ME Keck and K Sikkink, *Activism Beyond Borders: Advocacy Networks in International Politics* (Cornell University Press 1998) 27, cited in Houge and Lohne (n 44) 781.

framework, but nevertheless end up mimicking aspects of it'.[46] Mahmood Mamdani, in particular, reveals how South Africa's Truth and Reconciliation Commission 'understood violence as criminal, not political; as driven by individual perpetrators, and not groups of beneficiaries; as targeting identifiable, individual victims, and not entire groups . . . [and] focused on violence as excess, not as norm'.[47] In a similar vein, Marcos Zunino's recent genealogy of transitional justice identifies a number of 'constant features that constitute a gravitational centre' within the discourse of transitional justice that closely resemble the legitimating qualities of international criminal judgments, including the predominance of legalism, an emphasis on violations of civil and political rights involving instances of physical violence to the neglect of structural harms, and a tacit endorsement of prevailing economic structures.[48]

These trends point to the importance of identifying a broader set of variables to account for the general neglect of structural violence in transitional contexts. Pádraig McAuliffe, for example, identifies a range of international and domestic political and economic configurations that have undermined efforts to address structural violence during periods of transition.[49] Peace agreements, for instance, have typically been negotiated by 'military and political elites who benefit from the existing order and whose existing advantages are increased by the opportunities created by marketization and privatisation'.[50] The consequent marginalisation of structural violence in peace negotiations is reflected by the fact that only 25 per cent of peace agreements negotiated in the last forty years have expressly addressed economic issues.[51] Resistance to addressing structural violence has also arisen in the form of informal war economies. These economies encompass new structures of political power that emerge during conflicts, and may persist in the form of clandestine coercion, bribery, and nepotism in post-conflict societies in ways which circumvent and undermine structural reforms.[52] Finally, international financial institutions, such as the World Bank and International Monetary Fund, often wield significant influence over States emerging from mass violence, exerting considerable pressure on them to adopt neoliberal economic policies, notwithstanding the fact that 'in many cases the pathologies of liberalization may have caused or exacerbated the conflict or repression before transition'.[53]

Beyond taking into account these wider political and economic factors, it is also important to remember that the authority and influence of the narratives constructed within international criminal judgments are not given, but subject to contestation both within and beyond the courtroom.

[46] K Engle et al, 'Introduction', in Engle et al (n 13) 1, 4

[47] M Mamdani, 'Beyond Nuremberg: The Historical Significance of the Post-Apartheid Transition in South Africa', in Engle et al (n 13) 329, 348.

[48] M Zunino, *Justice Framed: A Genealogy of Transitional Justice* (CUP 2019) 42–43, 49–51, and 53–56.

[49] See generally, P McAuliffe, *Transformative Transitional Justice and the Malleability of Post-Conflict States* (Edward Elgar 2017).

[50] P McAuliffe, 'Weighing Domestic and International Impediments to Transformative Justice in Transition' (2015) 3 *London Review of International Law* 169, 184.

[51] Ibid.

[52] Ibid 189–192.

[53] Ibid 194.

Within the courtroom, international criminal proceedings create space for the expression of a plurality of narratives,[54] including those that oppose or resist the versions of history ultimately authorised in judgments. As Gerry Simpson argues, 'Trials retain at their core a symmetry that can never quite be dissolved by the political elites who convene the trial ... Law's adversarialism, its commitment to equality of participation, and its openness mean it creates the occasional space for hitherto obscured "dissenting judgments".'[55] Whether taking the form of rebuttal or a more radical rupture strategy, counter-narratives have the potential to live on in the public domain as 'counter-memories',[56] undermining or at the very least weakening the legitimating messages transmitted by international criminal judgments. In addition to contestation at trial, space for the construction of counter-narratives also resides in the ability of judges to deliver separate and dissenting opinions,[57] as well as the possibility that later judgments within the same or different judicial institutions may challenge narratives constructed in earlier cases.[58]

Beyond the courtroom, the narratives constructed within international criminal judgments are transmitted to a range of audiences, who will often continue to contest their meaning and relevance long after the original narratives have been rendered. In practice, the social reception and ongoing contestation of judicial narratives amongst different audiences tend to vary depending on a diversity of factors, including social-psychological biases and the interventions of local carrier groups such as media outlets and national politicians. Although the impact of these factors is typically beyond the control of international criminal courts, in some contexts it may be possible for international criminal judgments to act as a discursive beginning for broader critical conversations concerning not only structural violence, but also the involvement and responsibility of States, international organisations, corporations, and bystander communities within particular mass atrocity contexts. According to Robert Cryer, for example, the work of the ICTY and ICTR helped the conflicts in the former Yugoslavia and Rwanda remain in the public eye, triggering 'at times agonised reflection on what states, through the UN, ought to have done to prevent those offences'.[59] Indeed, there is little to suggest that the silences of international criminal judgments themselves

[54] See similarly, S Löytömäki, 'The Law and Collective Memory of Colonialism: France and the Case of "Belated" Transitional Justice' (2013) 7 *International Journal of Transitional Justice* 205, 209 ('trials convey a plurality of narratives and social meanings and should be understood as forums where a variety of social, political and other actors promote their particular narratives in order to advance different causes').

[55] G Simpson, *Law, War & Crime—War Crimes Trials and the Reinvention of International Law* (Polity Press 2007) 93. See also, M Koskenniemi, 'From Impunity to Show Trials' (2002) 6 *Max Planck Yearbook of United Nations Law* 1; J Cockayne, 'Hybrids or Mongrels? Internationalized War Crimes Trials as Unsuccessful Degradation Ceremonies' (2005) 4 *Journal of Human Rights* 455; and F Mégret, 'Practices of Stigmatization' (2013) 76 *Law and Contemporary Problems* 287.

[56] N Henry, *War and Rape: Law, Memory and Justice* (Routledge 2011) 63 (citing Michel Foucault's notion of 'counter-memory' to describe 'challenges to official history through subjugated or disqualified knowledge').

[57] See, in this regard, Simpson (n 55) 92–101; H Mistry, The Paradox of Dissent: Judicial Dissent and the Projects of International Criminal Justice' (2015) 13 *Journal of International Criminal Justice* 449; N Jain, 'Radical Dissents in International Criminal Trials' (2017) 28 *European Journal of International Law* 1163.

[58] L Douglas, 'Truth and Justice in Atrocity Trials', in WA Schabas (ed), *The Cambridge Companion to International Criminal Law* (CUP 2016) 34, 46.

[59] R Cryer, 'International Criminal Law vs. State Sovereignty: Another Round?' (2006) 16 *European Journal of International Law* 979, 997.

pose significant obstacles to reliance being placed on other emancipatory vocabularies and initiatives directed towards addressing structural injustices.[60] As James Stewart argues, not only does there seem to be 'no reason why accountability need *necessarily* crowd out distributive justice projects', but also 'with care, consciousness, and a modicum of coordination, it is at least conceivable that these things might peaceably coexist, or even operate synergistically'.[61]

To be clear, cautioning against overstating the displacing power of international criminal judgments is not to be equated with a call to neglect the legitimation function of international criminal courts. In a world of limited resources, reliance on international criminal courts and the production of narratives within international criminal judgments clearly arrests some attention away from other emancipatory vocabularies and institutions.[62] Moreover, surfacing the legitimating qualities of international criminal judgments serves a number of important functions. For one, it may trigger changes in the practices of international criminal courts—for example, the emergence of thematic prosecutions in response to under-prosecuted economic, social, and cultural forms of violence. Equally, revealing the marginalising tendencies of international criminal judgments and the limits of the vocabulary of international criminal law may inspire creative thinking *beyond* the confines of anti-impunity frameworks—for example, the establishment of people's tribunals that seek to address structural causes of violence, or the possibility of other justice modalities operating outside the retributive blueprint.[63] In addition, raising awareness of the legitimating qualities of international criminal judgments may prompt greater reflexivity amongst actors participating in the field—not only reducing the emancipatory expectations placed on international criminal courts, but also generating a growing sensibility for the potentially darker sides of their interventions in different societal contexts. The point I seek to emphasise in this section, however, is that it is also important to acknowledge the limits of the legitimating power of international criminal judgments so as not to occlude or understate broader political and economic configurations at play in transitional contexts, as well as to ensure that attention is directed towards spaces

[60] See similarly, N Sedacca, 'The "Turn" to Criminal Justice in Human Rights Law: An Analysis in the Context of the 2016 Colombian Peace Agreement' (2019) 19 *Human Rights Law Review* 315, 321 (noting how critiques relating to international criminal law's focus on particular atrocities rather than broader structural and redistributive issues 'militate against a focus *only* or even primarily on individual criminal law . . . [and] do not necessarily preclude the use of criminal law as part of a broader strategy aimed at more strategic and redistributive goals') (emphasis in original). See also, P O'Connell, 'Human Rights: Contesting the Displacement Thesis' (2018) 69 *Northern Ireland Legal Quarterly* 19, 27 (discussing 'emancipatory or critical multilingualism').

[61] Stewart (n 36) 139–140 (emphasis in original). See also, JG Stewart, 'Towards Synergies in Forms of Corporate Accountability for International Crimes' *Blog of James G Stewart* (23 February 2019) (discussing 'synergistic accountability').

[62] SMH Nouwen and WG Werner, 'Monopolizing Global Justice: International Criminal Law as Challenge to Human Diversity' (2015) 13 *Journal of International Criminal Justice* 157, 174 ('The real issue is not whether both restorative justice and distributive justice, as well as equality before the law and retributive justice can be pursued—which is obviously possible—but which conception of justice prevails in times of clashes or limited resources. In a world of horrific constraint, conceptions of justice compete for their realization.')

[63] See generally, D Otto, 'Impunity in a Different Register: People's Tribunals and Questions of Judgment, Law, and Responsibility', in Engle et al (n 13) 291.

within and beyond international criminal courts that offer opportunities for ongoing narrative contestation.

II. Ways of Seeing International Criminal Justice

Operating under the cover of an idealised global community, international criminal courts have been structurally unable to transcend the inequalities of the actually existing international political order. As a result, the narratives constructed in international criminal judgments have tended to be apologetic in nature—oriented and circumscribed in ways that reflect the patterns of domination within the political environments in which international criminal courts operate.

Responding to concerns about the emancipatory limits of international criminal justice, proponents of international criminal courts have tended to fall back on the evolutionary claim that such restrictions represent only a temporary state of affairs on the road to a system of truly global justice free from State interference.[64] Critically examining this argument in the context of the ICC, Adam Branch explains how '[t]he evolutionary claim translates the gap between the ICC's current—partial—practice and impartial justice into a temporal gap between the imperfect present and an inevitable future in which the ICC will overcome the political interests of weak and strong states alike'.[65] The difficulty with the evolutionary claim is that it is based on a faith in the potential of the field of international criminal justice that lacks any empirical grounding.[66] The findings of the present study suggest that the accommodation of international criminal courts to the balance of power between and within States is a constitutive condition for their existence and operation. According to this perspective, the ultimate constituents of international criminal courts are not victims or conflict-affected communities but States, which constitute the 'shareholders' of international criminal courts and limit their 'material conditions of possibility'.[67]

Reflecting on the subordination of international criminal courts to the balance of power that exists between and within States beyond the courtroom, this final section concludes the study by elaborating two perspectives that may open up avenues for orienting the practices of international criminal courts towards a more emancipatory politics: first, a strategic expressivist perspective of international criminal justice; and second, a critical perspective of the historical narratives constructed in the judgments of international criminal courts.

[64] See, for example, R Cryer, *Prosecuting International Crimes: Selectivity and the International Criminal Law Regime* (CUP 2005) 230–231. For a critique of this argument, see S Nouwen, 'Legal Equality on Trial: Sovereign and Individuals before the International Criminal Court' (2012) 43 *Netherlands Yearbook of International Law* 151, 179.

[65] A Branch, *Displacing Human Rights: War and Intervention in Northern Uganda* (OUP 2011) 206.

[66] Nouwen (n 64) 179.

[67] S Kendall, 'Commodifying Global Justice: Economies of Accountability at the International Criminal Court' (2015) 13 *Journal of International Criminal Justice* 113.

A. A Strategic Expressivist Perspective of International Criminal Justice

Although international criminal courts tend to be structurally constrained in their ability to address demands for historical justice that challenge the existing international political order within their judgments, the broader international criminal justice process may still provide opportunities for such demands to be articulated and granted a degree of legitimacy. In particular, actors may be able to harness the *expressive* power of international criminal justice processes as one component of a broader *strategic* agenda for sociopolitical change.[68]

Expressivism is rooted in a range of ideas from different disciplines.[69] However, the animating assumption shared by most strands of expressivist thought is simple: social practices carry meanings and transmit messages quite apart from their consequences.[70] Importantly, from an expressivist perspective, *all* social practices are signifying practices. As David Garland explains, 'even the most mundane form of conduct in the social world is also a possible source of expression, of symbolization, and of meaningful communication—every action is also a gesture'.[71] As such, rather than focusing narrowly on the narratives constructed in the judgments of international criminal courts, expressivism is concerned with the symbolic and aesthetic meanings generated by the broader range of social practices that comprise and surround international criminal proceedings.[72] Moreover, expressivism is interested not only in the *construction* of messages within international criminal courts, but also with their *reception* amongst different audiences beyond the courtroom.[73] As James Boyd White famously observed, 'the text does not conclude the difficulties of the real world, but begins a process, a process of its own interpretation'.[74]

While it is possible to examine the field of international criminal justice from a range of expressivist perspectives, a *strategic* expressivist perspective is concerned with whether and how different actors in the field may mobilise the expressive power

[68] This section is adapted from B Sander, 'The Expressive Turn of International Criminal Justice: A Field in Search of Meaning' (2019) 32 *Leiden Journal of International Law* 851. For a detailed study of the expressivist functions of international criminal justice, see generally, C Stahn, *Justice as Message: Expressivist Foundations of International Criminal Justice* (OUP 2020).

[69] On the disciplinary origins and influences of expressivist theories, see generally, DM Amann, 'Group Mentality, Expressivism, and Genocide' (2002) 2 *International Criminal Law Review* 93, 117–124.

[70] CR Sunstein, 'On the Expressive Function of Law' (1996) 5 *East European Constitutional Review* 66, 66; and DM Kahan, 'What Do Alternative Sanctions Mean?' (1996) 63 *University of Chicago Law Review* 591, 597.

[71] D Garland, *Punishment and Modern Society: A Study in Social Theory* (Clarendon Press 1990) 255.

[72] F Mégret, 'In Defense of Hybridity: Towards a Representational Theory of International Criminal Justice' (2005) 38 *Cornell International Law Journal* 725; and AB Houge, 'Narrative Expressivism: A Criminological Approach to the Expressive Function of International Criminal Justice' (2019) 19 *Criminology & Criminal Justice* 277.

[73] RD Sloane, 'The Expressive Capacity of International Punishment: The Limits of the National Law Analogy and the Potential of International Criminal Law' (2007) 43 *Stanford Journal of International Law* 39, 84; and Amann (n 69) 118.

[74] J Boyd White, *Heracles' Bow: Essays on Rhetoric and Poetics of the Law* (University of Wisconsin Press 1985) 185.

of the vocabulary and practices of international criminal justice processes to advance their strategic social and political agendas.

In this context, it is important to specify the meaning of 'strategic'. A useful point of departure is the use of the term 'strategic' in the field of international human rights where 'strategic human rights litigation' has generally been relied upon to refer to 'litigation that pursue goals—or which concerns interests—that are broader than ... the particular victims or applicants at the centre of the particular case'.[75] Importantly, strategic human rights litigation generally constitutes only one change agent deployed in concert with other processes and forms of advocacy.[76] The term 'strategic' has also been deployed in the field of international criminal justice. Megan Fairlie, in particular, has recently examined the emergence of so-called 'strategic communications' before the ICC, a term used to refer to 'highly publicized investigation requests aimed not at securing any ICC-related activity, but at obtaining some non-Court related advantage'.[77] Although not identical in meaning, these conceptions of 'strategic' are united by the idea of using litigation or particular aspects of legal processes to generate political and social change that extend beyond the immediate goals of an individual case or request.[78]

Further unravelling the meaning of 'strategic', recent Marxist international legal scholarship draws a distinction between 'strategy' and 'tactics'. As Robert Knox explains, in this context '*strategy* refers to the achievement of long term, structural (or organic) goals, whereas *tactics* refers to the achievement of short term, conjunctural ones'.[79] Relying on this distinction, John Reynolds emphasises the importance of strategy and tactics being considered in tandem so that tactics become 'pragmatic and opportunistic interventions aimed at more immediate results that can contribute towards attainment of the larger strategic outcome'.[80] According to this view, while litigation is often purely tactical in nature because it is concerned with achieving a more immediate short-term end, what matters is the extent to which a tactical legal intervention has been dictated by and contributes towards a broader strategic objective.[81]

[75] H Duffy, *Strategic Human Rights Litigation: Understanding and Maximising Impact* (Hart 2018) 3.

[76] Ibid 41 and 46. See also, W Kaleck, 'Seizing Opportunities and Broad Strategy Both Essential in Human Rights Litigation' *Open Global Rights* (26 February 2019).

[77] MA Fairlie, 'The Hidden Costs of Strategic Communications for the International Criminal Court' (2016) 51 *Texas International Law Journal* 281, 283. Fairlie's deployment of the term 'strategic' is, therefore, relatively narrow, excluding communications submitted to the ICC that are made with the genuine aim of securing action from the Court. See also, MA Fairlie, 'A Newly-Revealed Cost of Article 15 Communications' *IntLawGrrls* (29 June 2018).

[78] For an examination of the different levels of impact that strategic litigation may contribute towards, see generally Duffy (n 75) Chapter 4 (outlining eight levels of impact: on victims, law, policy and practice, institutions, information gathering and truth telling, social and cultural change, mobilisation and empowerment, and democracy and the rule of law).

[79] R Knox, 'Strategy and Tactics' (2010) 21 *Finnish Yearbook of International Law* 193, 227. For a recent example of reliance on the strategy-tactics distinction in the international law context, see C Schwöbel-Patel, 'Populism, International Law and the End of Keep Calm and Carry on Lawyering' (2018) 49 *Netherlands Yearbook of International Law* 97.

[80] J Reynolds, 'Anti-Colonial Legalities: Paradigms, Tactics & Strategy' (2015) 18 *Palestinian Yearbook of International Law* 8, 35.

[81] R Knox, 'What Is to Be Done (with Critical Legal Theory)?' (2011) 22 *Finnish Yearbook of International Law* 31, 44 (explaining how legal tactics may be '*dictated by* a broader political logic, which may at times be unconventional or even counterproductive in legal terms') (emphasis added); and Duffy (n 75) 41 ('What we explore then may be not so much whether litigation provided a *solution* (which will only rarely be the case, given the broad-reaching social or political problems that underpin many rights violations), nor

Drawing on these perspectives, 'strategic' in the present context may be understood to refer to the ways in which the expressive power of the language and institutions of international criminal justice may be invoked and mobilised by different actors in line with their longer-term political and social agendas.[82]

A clear illustration of a strategic expressivist intervention in the field of international criminal justice is provided by the communication to the ICC Prosecutor jointly submitted by the Global Legal Action Network (GLAN) and the Stanford International Human Rights Clinic (Stanford).[83] The communication called for the ICC Prosecutor to open an investigation into alleged crimes against humanity committed by Australian officials and private companies against refugees and asylum seekers held offshore in Nauru and Manus Island. One of the reasons motivating the communication was to expressively counter the potential of the Australian immigration system 'to set a precedent, and to normalise subjecting vulnerable refugee populations to inhumane detention practices in order to deter future refugee flows'.[84] By relying on the vocabulary of international criminal law, the communication sought to label the actions of Australia as 'crimes against humanity' in an effort to expressively counter the possibility of Australian policies 'being influential and being replicated elsewhere, specifically in other states that are receiving refugee flow'.[85] The communication also sought to recalibrate the prosecutorial policy of the ICC away from an exclusive expressive focus on 'spectacular violence, occurring in some of the poorer and less developed states in the world', towards a broader vision that includes the investigation and prosecution of 'banal' violence, encompassing acts that are 'potentially replicated, normalised and perceived as an acceptable, or at least inevitable, consequence of the current international system'.[86]

Importantly, the communication was submitted to the ICC Prosecutor as one limited tactical component of a broader strategic struggle for emancipatory change and with an awareness of the geopolitical constraints of the institution. At the launch event of the communication,[87] Kevin Jon Heller—one of the signatories to the

whether change is *caused* by or attributable to it; rather we should consider the *contribution*—perhaps indirect and gradual—that litigation may have made alongside and in relationship with other processes and factors') (emphasis in original). See also, Knox (n 79) 227–228 ('actualising strategic concerns does not necessarily mean jettisoning practical interventions in everyday legal struggles, but rather *framing* these struggles in terms of the overall strategic goal') (emphasis added).

[82] See also, S Vasiliev, 'The Crises and Critiques of International Criminal Justice', in KJ Heller et al (eds), *The Oxford Handbook of International Criminal Law* (OUP 2020) 626, 644 (noting how critical voices in the field rarely demand the dismantling of the system of international criminal justice and 'still deploy it to promote a specific agenda—for example, in strategic litigation—albeit without a true attachment to the discipline').

[83] GLAN and Stanford International Human Rights Clinic, 'The Situation in Nauru and Manus Island: Liability for Crimes Against Humanity in the Detention of Refugees and Asylum Seekers' *Communiqué to the Office of the Prosecutor of the International Criminal Court under Article 15 of the Rome Statute* (13 February 2017).

[84] Ibid 114.

[85] Ibid.

[86] Ibid 115.

[87] 'The Refugee Crisis and International Criminal Law' City University of London, 13 February 2017. A recording of the event is accessible online at the following link: https://echo360.org.uk/media/825021ac-6d90-4b4e-a9fa-a9b4a02ba001/public (last accessed 30 May 2020).

communication—acknowledged that his goals for the communication were self-consciously 'very modest'.[88] In particular, Heller accepted that there were obstacles to the ICC Prosecutor opening an investigation into the situation, not least the damage it might cause to the relationship between the ICC and Australia, which had traditionally been a strong supporter of the Court.[89] However, Heller added that the communication need not lead to a formal investigation to have an expressive impact: 'Just a statement from Fatou Bensouda taking it seriously and the media coverage ... , this has a real significant effect on the behaviour of the Australia government.'[90]

On 12 February 2020, the ICC Prosecutor formally responded to the communication, concluding that there was no basis to proceed with an investigation at that time. Nonetheless, in its letter setting out its conclusions, the ICC Prosecutor confirmed its view that the conditions of detention on Nauru and Manus Island were sufficiently terrible to qualify as the underlying act of the crime against humanity of imprisonment or other severe deprivations of physical liberty.[91] As such, although the GLAN-Stanford communication did not trigger the opening of an investigation, lead to any prosecutions, or result in any judgments, it was still able to generate headlines confirming the ICC Prosecutor's view that Australia's offshore detention regime is unlawful.[92] In this way, the communication achieved one of its aims: to expressively support other social movements in Australia that have been campaigning at the domestic level for changes in Australian immigration and asylum practices.[93]

The GLAN-Stanford communication offers a useful illustration of how the expressive power of an international criminal justice *process* may be harnessed in a modest way to further a strategic agenda that seeks to hold accountable and challenge the domestic policy of a powerful State within the international political order. While the likelihood of an investigation and prosecutions was always slim, the GLAN-Stanford intervention illustrates the possibilities of 'emancipatory multilingualism', namely the capacity of social movements to utilise a particular emancipatory vocabulary—in this case, international criminal law—as part of a broader mobilisation of multiple, complementary (and sometimes contradictory) discourses in their struggles for strategic change.[94]

[88] Ibid 1 hour 28 minutes.

[89] Ibid 57 minutes.

[90] Ibid 1 hour 28 minutes. For media coverage of the communication, see B Doherty, 'International Criminal Court Told Australia's Detention Regime Could Be a Crime Against Humanity' *The Guardian* (13 February 2017); and R Hamilton, 'Australia's Refugee Policy Is a Crime Against Humanity' *Foreign Policy* (23 February 2017).

[91] ICC Office of the Prosecutor, Ref. OTP-CR-65/17, 12 February 2020, accessible online at the following link: https://twitter.com/GLAN_LAW/status/1229454798895927299?s=20 (last accessed 30 May 2020).

[92] B Doherty, 'Australia's Offshore Detention Is Unlawful, Says International Criminal Court Prosecutor' *The Guardian* (15 February 2020).

[93] 'The Refugee Crisis and International Criminal Law' (n 87) 1 hour 23 minutes. See also, Duffy (n 75) 44 (observing how the failure of strategic litigation in the courtroom may still serve the function of 'exposing to public criticism and international scrutiny the extent of the denial of justice, or paving the way for ... other forms of pressure'); and A Deeks, 'The Observer Effect: National Security Litigation, Executive Policy Changes, and Judicial Deference' (2013) 82 *Fordham Law Review* 827, 830 (examining the application in the legal field of the 'observer effect', namely 'the changes that an act of observation makes on the phenomenon being observed').

[94] P O'Connell, 'Human Rights: Contesting the Displacement Thesis' *Critical Legal Thinking* (18 June 2015).

While the GLAN-Stanford communication to the ICC offers an example of a proactive intervention in the field of international criminal justice,[95] strategic expressivism also encompasses *defensive* interventions. Adam Branch, for example, argues that Dominic Ongwen—the former child soldier and adult commander of the Lord's Resistance Army, currently on trial at the ICC—could have utilised a 'trial of rupture' tactic whereby his defence would have been conducted in the form of an attack on the system represented by the prosecution's case.[96] The aim would have been to place Ongwen's alleged crimes 'in the context of the violence committed by those putting on and benefitting from the trial—the Ugandan government, its western supporters, even the ICC itself'.[97] In this context, rather than relying on the expressive power of legal *arguments*, the legal *situation* would have been instrumentalised to directly promote the defendant's political goals.[98]

In practice, whether a particular intervention in the field of international criminal justice is likely to support the broader strategic objectives of a particular actor will often depend on the context and may itself become a matter of contestation. Importantly, however, an intervention in the field of international criminal justice need not harbour overly ambitious objectives for this purpose. For example, a social movement might utilise the vocabulary and institutions of international criminal justice to garner media attention around a particular conflict or type of criminality as one limited tactical component of a broader strategic struggle for emancipatory change. At the same time, as Helen Duffy cautions, it is important to remember that a legal intervention 'is not a neutral enterprise that at worst does little good, while not doing any harm'.[99] Any legal intervention, even if intended to positively contribute towards a strategic objective, has the potential to be counter-productive and generate negative repercussions—whether by over-inflating victim and community expectations, establishing regressive jurisprudence, or providing a veneer of legal legitimacy around the practices under scrutiny.[100]

Ultimately, determining whether a particular intervention in the field of international criminal justice has a reasonable prospect of advancing an actor's broader strategic agenda will require assessing a range of factors, including weighing the potential positive and negative effects that different stages of international criminal processes may generate, as well as the extent to which a particular intervention is likely to facilitate or frustrate other forms of advocacy that are attempting to contribute towards the attainment of the same strategic objective.[101] Going forward, as actors become savvier to the limitations and legitimating qualities of international criminal courts, it is suggested that strategic expressivism offers a perspective that could enable actors to look

[95] For further examples of proactive strategic interventions in the field of international criminal justice, see M Kersten, 'Making a Distinction: The Rome Statute Is Not the ICC: It Is Much More Than That' *Justice in Conflict* (17 July 2018) (discussing the strategic deployment of the Rome Statute at the domestic level in India and the Democratic Republic of the Congo).

[96] A Branch, 'Dominic Ongwen on Trial: The ICC's African Dilemmas' (2017) 11 *International Journal of Transitional Justice* 30, 49.

[97] Ibid.

[98] Knox (n 79) 225.

[99] Duffy (n 75) 5.

[100] See generally, Duffy (n 75) 5 and 77–80; and Fairlie (n 77) 291–298.

[101] See generally, Duffy (n 75) 39–45 and Chapter 10.

beyond the narrow confines of securing favourable judgments within international criminal courts towards considering how the expressive power of broader dimensions of international criminal justice processes may be harnessed in support of their strategic agendas.

B. A Critical Perspective of International Criminal Justice

Beyond viewing international criminal justice institutions from a strategic expressivist perspective, this study also highlights the importance of continuing to develop a critical awareness of both the limits and legitimating qualities of the historical narratives constructed in the judgments of international criminal courts.

The scope and content of judicial narratives inevitably depend on the contexts and situated choices of the actors who interact in international criminal proceedings. Accordingly, the judgments of international criminal courts always construct particular readings of the past, foregrounding some voices, interpretations, and experiences, at the expense of others. Over time, historical narratives may shift and evolve—whether between different courts due to differences in their statutory and interpretative frameworks, or between different cases within the same court in response to changes in charging, interpretative, or evidentiary practices. Moreover, beyond the courtroom, judicial narratives often continue to be contested because they resonate differently depending on social psychological biases and local carrier groups through whom narratives tend to be filtered before reaching different audiences.

With these insights in mind, rather than expecting international criminal courts to deliver improbable moments of historical closure, this study suggests a need for greater critical contextualisation of the historical narratives constructed within international criminal decisions and judgments, whether by looking *backwards* to the process through which such narratives were constructed, *forwards* to their ongoing contestation both within and beyond the courtroom, or *sideways* to other societal mechanisms tasked with constructing atrocity narratives about particular episodes of mass violence. Rather than mechanisms of narrative closure, international criminal courts should be viewed in more modest terms as at best a *discursive beginning* for individuals and communities to engage with and debate the past. From this critical, but also humbler, perspective, international criminal justice processes may be likened to public monuments, which, once constructed, permit debates over memory and the past, and potentially conflicting and diverse meanings and understandings of the underlying events.[102]

Ultimately, international criminal courts represent just one of many societal platforms for confronting the past, none of which can produce a definitive version of 'what happened' because they are each subject to their own particular institutional constraints.[103] Looking ahead, therefore, the challenge is to become more conscious

[102] M Minow, *Between Vengeance and Forgiveness: Facing History after Genocide and Mass Violence* (Beacon Press 1998) 139.

[103] See similarly, M-B Dembour and E Haslam, 'Silencing Hearings? Victim-Witnesses at War Crimes Trials' (2014) 15 *European Journal of International Law* 151, 170.

of these constraints, to develop a critical capacity for unveiling and questioning the forms of legitimation embodied within the historical narratives constructed within different societal platforms relied upon to address past episodes of mass violence, whilst constantly striving to situate such platforms within wider horizons of possibility.[104]

[104] See similarly, C Turner, 'Deconstructing Transitional Justice' (2013) 24 *Law and Critique* 193, 208 ('The challenge to remain open to critical engagement is rooted in the idea of an infinite idea of justice that is irreducible to law. It is in this ongoing process of questioning that justice lies—in the openness to the other, the existence of whom is immanent to the idea of transition'); and Mégret (n 39) 46 (noting that the challenge for critique is 'to upset international criminal justice's balance, expose some of its contradictions, increase its anxiety, and situate it within a larger horizon of possibilities').

Select Bibliography

Acquaviva G, 'At the Origins of Crimes Against Humanity: Clues to a Proper Understanding of the *Nullum Crimen* Principle in the Nuremberg Judgment' (2011) 9 *Journal of International Criminal Justice* 881

Adams A, 'The Legacy of the International Criminals of the Former Yugoslavia and Rwanda and their Contribution to the Crime of Rape' (2018) 29 *European Journal of International Law* 749

af Jochnick C and Normand R, 'The Legitimation of Violence: A Critical History of the Laws of War' (1994) 35 *Harvard International Law Journal* 49

Ainley K, 'Individual Agency and Responsibility for Atrocity', in Jeffery R (ed), *Confronting Evil in International Relations: Ethical Responses to Problems of Moral Agency* (Palgrave Macmillan 2008) 37

Ainley K, 'Excesses of Responsibility: The Limits of Law and the Possibilities of Politics' (2011) 25 *Ethics & International Affairs* 407

Akande D, 'Sources of International Criminal Law', in A Cassese (ed), *The Oxford Companion to International Criminal Justice* (OUP 2009) 41

Akande D, 'The International Criminal Court Gets Jurisdiction Over the Crime of Aggression' *EJIL Talk!* (15 December 2017)

Akhavan P, 'The Dilemmas of Jurisprudence' (1998) 13 *American University International Law Review* 1518

Aksenova M, 'The Modes of Liability at the ICC: The Labels that Don't Always Stick' (2015) 15 *International Criminal Law Review* 629

Allott P, *The Health of Nations: Society and Law Beyond the State* (CUP 2002)

Alvaŗez JE, 'Rush to Closure: Lessons of the Tadić Judgment' (1997–1998) 96 *Michigan Law Review* 2031

Alvarez JE, 'Crimes of States/Crimes of Hate: Lessons from Rwanda' (1999) 24 *Yale Journal of International Law* 366

Amann DM, 'Group Mentality, Expressivism, and Genocide' (2002) 2 *International Criminal Law Review* 93

Ambos K, *Treatise on International Criminal Law: Volume I: Foundations and General Part* (OUP 2013)

Ambos K, *Treatise on International Criminal Law: Volume II: The Crimes and Sentencing* (OUP 2014)

Amenge Okoth JR, *The Crime of Conspiracy in International Criminal Law* (Springer 2014)

Amnesty International, 'Bemba Appeals Judgment Highlights the Challenges of Charging Sexual Violence Crimes' *Human Rights in International Justice* (3 October 2018)

Andersen R, 'How Multilateral Development Assistance Triggered the Conflict in Rwanda' (2000) 21 *Third World Quarterly* 441

Anghie A and Chimni B, 'Third World Approaches to International Law and Individual Responsibility in Internal Conflicts' (2003) 2 *Chinese Journal of International Law* 77

Arajärvi N, *The Changing Nature of Customary International Law: Methods of Interpreting the Concept of Custom in International Criminal Tribunals* (Routledge 2014)

Arbour L, 'Progress and Challenges in International Criminal Justice' (1997) 21 *Fordham International Law Journal* 531

Arbour L, *War Crimes and the Culture of Peace* (University of Toronto Press 2002)

Arendt H, *Eichmann in Jerusalem: A Report on the Banality of Evil* (revised and enlarged edition, Penguin Books 1994)

Arendt H, 'Personal Responsibility Under Dictatorship', in J Kohn (ed), *Hannah Arendt: Responsibility and Judgment* (Schocken Books 2003) 17

Arnold R, 'The Judicial Contribution of the Special Court for Sierra Leone to the Prosecution of Terrorism', in Jalloh CC (ed), *The Sierra Leone Special Court and its Legacy: The Impact for Africa and International Criminal Law* (CUP 2014) 260

Ashworth A and Horder J, *Principles of Criminal Law* (7th edn, OUP 2013)

Askin KD, *War Crimes Against Women: Prosecution in International War Crimes Tribunals* (Martinus Nijhoff Publishers 1997)

Askin KD, 'Prosecuting Wartime Rape and Other Gender-Related Crimes under International Law: Extraordinary Advances, Enduring Obstacles' (2003) 21 *Berkeley Journal of International Law* 288

Baars G, 'Capitalism's Victor's Justice? The Hidden Stories Behind the Prosecution of Industrialists Post-WWII', in Heller HJ and Simpson G (eds), *The Hidden Histories of War Crimes Trials* (OUP 2013) 163

Baars G, *The Corporation, Law and Capitalism: A Radical Perspective on the Role of Law in the Global Political Economy* (Brill 2019)

Bachmann K and Fatić A, *The UN International Criminal Tribunals: Transition without Justice?* (Routledge 2015)

Bachmann K et al, 'Like Dust before the Wind, or, the Winds of Change? The Influence of International Criminal Tribunals on Narratives and Media Frames' (2019) 13 *International Journal of Transitional Justice* 368

Backer LC, 'The Führer Principle of International Law: Individual Responsibility and Collective Punishment' (2003) 21 *Penn State International Law Review* 509

Badar ME, '"Just Convict Everyone!"—Joint Perpetration: From *Tadić* to *Stakić* and Back Again' (2006) 6 *International Criminal Law Review* 293

Baines E, 'Complex Political Perpetrators: Reflections on Dominic Ongwen' (2009) 47 *Journal of Modern African Studies* 169

Bantekas I, 'Defenses in International Criminal Law', in McGoldrick D et al (eds), *The Permanent International Criminal Court: Legal and Policy Issues* (Hart Publishing 2004) 263

Bantekas I, 'Reflections on Some Sources and Methods of International Criminal and Humanitarian Law' (2006) 6 *International Criminal Law Review* 121

Bass GJ, *Stay the Hand of Vengeance—The Politics of War Crimes Tribunals* (Princeton University Press 2000)

Bassiouni MC, 'Negotiating the Treaty of Rome on the Establishment of an International Criminal Court' (1999) 32 *Cornell International Law Journal* 443

Bassiouni MC, 'The Need for International Accountability', in Bassiouni MC (ed), *International Criminal Law: Volume III, International Enforcement* (Martinus Nijhoff Publishers 2008) 3

Bassiouni MC, *Introduction to International Criminal Law* (2nd edn, Martinus Nijhoff Publishers 2013)

Bensouda F, 'Gender Justice and the ICC' (2014) 16 *International Feminist Journal of Politics* 538

Berger J, *Ways of Seeing* (BBC and Penguin Books 1972)

Bianchi A, 'Textual Interpretation and (International) Law Reading: The Myth of (In) Determinacy and the Genealogy of Meaning', in Bekker PHF et al (eds), *Making Transnational Law Work in the Global Economy: Essays in Honour of Detlev Vagsts* (CUP 2010) 34

Bianchi A, 'Reflexive Butterfly Catching: Insights from a Situated Catcher', in Pauwelyn J et al (eds), *Informal International Lawmaking* (OUP 2012) 200
Bianchi L, 'Challenging Impunity for Crimes of Sexual Violence: The Efforts of Prosecutor Jallow to Set the Record Straight', in Jalloh CC and Marong ABM (eds), *Promoting Accountability under International Law for Gross Human Rights Violations in Africa* (Brill 2015) 355
Bieber F, 'Do Historians Need a Verdict?', in Waters T (ed), *The Milošević Trial: An Autopsy* (OUP 2014) 349
Bilsky LY, *Transformative Justice: Israeli Identity on Trial (Law, Meaning, and Violence)* (University of Michigan Press 2004)
Bloxham D, *Genocide on Trial: War Crimes Trials and the Formation of Holocaust History and Memory* (OUP 2001)
Boas G, *The Milošević Trial: Lessons for the Conduct of Complex International Criminal Proceedings* (CUP 2007)
Bohrer Z, 'Is the Prosecution of War Crimes Just and Effective? Rethinking the Lessons from Sociology and Psychology' (2012) 33 *Michigan Journal of International Law* 749
Boister N, 'The Application of Collective and Comprehensive Criminal Responsibility for Aggression at the Tokyo International Military Tribunal: The Measure of the Crime of Aggression?' (2010) 8 *Journal of International Criminal Justice* 425
Boister N, 'The Tokyo Trial', in Schabas WA and Bernaz N (eds), *Routledge Handbook of International Criminal Law* (Routledge 2011) 17
Boister N and Cryer R, *The Tokyo International Military Tribunal—A Reappraisal* (OUP 2008)
Bonafè BI, *The Relationship Between State and Individual Responsibility for International Crimes* (Brill 2009)
Borgwardt E, 'Re-examining Nuremberg as a New Deal Institution: Politics, Culture and the Limits of Law in Generating Human Rights Norms' (2005) 23 *Berkeley Journal of International Law* 401
Bosco D, *Rough Justice: The International Criminal Court in a World of Power Politics* (OUP 2014)
Bourdieu P, 'The Force of Law: Toward a Sociology of the Juridical Field' (1987) 38 *Hastings Law Journal* 805
Bourdieu P and Wacquant LJD, 'The Purpose of Reflexive Sociology', in Bourdieu P and Wacquant LJD, *An Invitation to Reflexive Sociology* (University of Chicago Press 1992) 60
Boyd White J, *Heracles' Bow: Essays on Rhetoric and Poetics of the Law* (1985)
Boyd White J, *Justice as Translation: An Essay in Cultural and Legal Criticism* (University of Chicago Press 1990)
Bradfield P, 'Alternative Charges and Modes of Liability in the Latest CAR Case at the ICC—Trouble Ahead?' *EJIL: Talk!* (21 January 2020)
Branch A, 'Against Humanitarian Impunity: Rethinking Responsibility for Displacement and Disaster in Northern Uganda' (2008) 2 *Journal of Intervention and Statebuilding* 151
Branch A, *Displacing Human Rights: War and Intervention in Northern Uganda* (OUP 2011)
Branch A, 'Dominic Ongwen on Trial: The ICC's African Dilemmas' (2017) 11 *International Journal of Transitional Justice* 30
Branch A, 'Truth Beyond the ICC' *Humanity* (10 July 2017)
Branch A, 'The African Criminal Court: Towards an Emancipatory Politics', in Jalloh CC et al (eds), *The African Court of Justice and Human and Peoples' Rights in Context* (CUP 2019) 198
Brooks P, 'The Law as Narrative and Rhetoric', in Brooks P and Gewirtz P (eds), *Law's Stories—Narrative and Rhetoric in the Law* (Yale University Press 1996) 14
Brooks RE, 'Law in the Heart of Darkness: Atrocity & Duress' (2003) 43 *Virginia Journal of International Law* 861
Brown W, '"The Most We Can Hope For ...": Human Rights and the Politics of Fatalism' (2014) 103 *South Atlantic Quarterly* 451

Browning CR, *Ordinary Men: Reserve Police Battalion 101 and the Final Solution in Poland* (Harper Perennial 1998)
Brownmiller S, *Against Our Will: Men, Women and Rape* (Penguin Books 1976)
Burchard C, 'Ancillary and Neutral Business Contributions to "Corporate-Political Core Crime": Initial Enquiries Concerning the Rome Statute' (2010) 8 *Journal of International Criminal Justice* 934
Burgis-Kasthala M, 'Scholarship as Dialogue? TWAIL and the Politics of Methodology' (2016) 14 *Journal of International Criminal Justice* 921
Buruma I, *The Wages of Guilt: Memories of War in Germany and Japan* (Atlantic Books 2009)
Bush JA, 'The Prehistory of Corporations and Conspiracy in International Criminal Law: What Nuremberg Really Said' (2009) 109 *Columbia Law Review* 1094
Buss D, 'Performing Legal Order: Some Feminist Thoughts on International Criminal Law' (2011) 11 *International Criminal Law Review* 409
Buss D, 'Expert Witnesses and International War Crimes Trial: Making Sense of Large-Scale Violence in Rwanda', in Zarkov D and Glasius M (eds), *Narrative of Justice In and Out of the Courtroom: Former Yugoslavia and Beyond* (Springer 2014) 23
Campbell K, 'Victims and Perpetrators of International Crimes: The Problem of the "Legal Person"' (2011) 2 *International Humanitarian Legal Studies* 325
Campbell K, 'Reassembling International Justice: The Making of "the Social" in International Criminal Law and Transitional Justice' (2014) 8 *International Journal of Transitional Justice* 53
Carr EH, *What Is History?* (2nd edn, Palgrave 1986)
Cassese A, 'The International Criminal Tribunal for the Former Yugoslavia and the Implementation of International Humanitarian Law', in Condorelli L et al (eds), *The United Nations and International Humanitarian Law* (Editions Pedone 1996) 230
Cassese A, 'On Current Trends Towards Criminal Procedure and Punishment of Breaches of International Humanitarian Law' (1998) 9 *European Journal of International Law* 2
Cassese A, 'The Statute of the International Criminal Court: Some Preliminary Reflections' (1999) 10 *European Journal of International Law* 144
Cassese A, 'The ICTY: A Living and Vital Reality' (2004) 2 *Journal of International Criminal Justice* 585
Cassese A, 'The Proper Limits of Individual Responsibility under the Doctrine of Joint Criminal Enterprise' (2007) 5 *Journal of International Criminal Justice* 109
Cassese A, *International Criminal Law* (2nd edn, OUP 2008)
Cassese A, 'The Nexus Requirement for War Crimes' (2012) 10 *Journal of International Criminal Justice* 1395
Cassese A et al, *Cassese's International Criminal Law* (3rd edn, OUP 2013)
Charlesworth H, 'International Law: A Discipline of Crisis' (2002) 65 *Modern Law Review* 377
Chlevickaitė G, Holá B, and Bijleveld C, 'Judicial Witness Assessments at the ICTY, ICTR and ICC' (2020) 18 *Journal of International Criminal Justice* 185
Chossudovsky M, 'Dismantling Former Yugoslavia: Recolonising Bosnia' (1996) 31 *Economic and Political Weekly* 521
Chossudovsky M, 'Economic Genocide in Rwanda' (1996) 31 *Economic and Political Weekly* 938
Clancy D, '"They Told Us We Would Be Part of History": Reflections on the Civil Society Intermediary Experience in the Great Lakes Region' in de Vos C et al (eds), *Contested Justice: The Politics and Practice of International Criminal Court Interventions* (CUP 2015) 219
Clapham A, 'Issues of Complexity, Complicity and Complementarity: From the Nuremberg Trials to the Dawn of the new International Criminal Court', in Sands P (ed), *From Nuremberg to The Hague: The Future of International Criminal Justice* (CUP 2003) 30
Clapham A, 'Concluding Remarks: Three Tribes Engage on the Future of International Criminal Law' (2011) 9 *Journal of International Criminal Justice* 689

Clark JN, 'From Negative to Positive Peace: The Case of Bosnia and Hercegovina' (2009) 8 *Journal of Human Rights* 360

Clark JN, 'Plea Bargaining at the ICTY: Guilty Pleas and Reconciliation' (2009) 20 *European Journal of International Law* 415

Clark JN, 'The Impact Question: The ICTY and the Restoration and Maintenance of Peace', in Swart B et al (eds), *The Legacy of the International Criminal Tribunal for the Former Yugoslavia* (OUP 2011) 55

Clark JN, 'The ICTY and Reconciliation in Croatia: A Case Study of Vukovar' (2012) 10 *Journal of International Criminal Justice* 397

Clark P, *Distant Justice: The Impact of the International Criminal Court on African Politics* (CUP 2018)

Clarke KM, *Fictions of Justice: The International Criminal Court and the Challenge of Legal Pluralism in Sub-Saharan Africa* (CUP 2009)

Clarke KM, '"We Ask For Justice, You Give Us Law": The Rule of Law, Economic Markets and the Reconfiguration of Victimhood', in de Vos C et al (eds), *Contested Justice: The Politics and Practice of the International Criminal Court* (CUP 2015) 272

Clarke KM, 'Power Politics and its Global Shadows: From Margins to Center' *Blog of James G Stewart* (20 February 2015)

Cockayne R, 'Hybrids or Mongrels? Internationalized War Crimes Trials as Unsuccessful Degradation Ceremonies' (2005) 4 *Journal of Human Rights* 455

Cohen S, *States of Denial: Knowing About Atrocities and Suffering* (Polity Press 2001)

Cohn I, 'The Protection of Children and the Quest for Truth and Justice in Sierra Leone' (2001) 55 *Journal of International Affairs* 1

Combs NA, *Fact-Finding Without Facts—The Uncertain Evidentiary Foundations of International Criminal Convictions* (CUP 2010)

Combs NA, 'Deconstructing the Epistemic Challenges to Mass Atrocity Prosecutions' *Humanity* (11 July 2017)

Combs NA, 'Grave Crimes and Weak Evidence: A Fact-Finding Evolution in International Criminal Law' (2017) 58 *Harvard International Law Journal* 47

Côté L, 'Reflections on the Exercise of Prosecutorial Discretion in International Criminal Law' (2005) 3 *Journal of International Criminal Justice* 162

Cover R, 'Nomos and Narrative', in Minow M et al (eds), *Narrative, Violence, and the Law: The Essays of Robert Cover* (University of Michigan Press 1993) 95

Cowell F, 'Inherent Imperialism: Understanding the Legal Roots of Anti-Imperialist Criticism of the International Criminal Court' (2017) 15 *Journal of International Criminal Justice* 667

Craven M et al (eds), *Time History and International Law* (Martinus Nijhoff Publishers 2007)

Cruvellier T, *From the Taylor Trial to a Lasting Legacy: Putting the Special Court Model to the Test* (ICTJ 2009)

Cruvellier T, 'Mark Drumbl: "Law Cannot Solve The Biggest Problems We Face"' *JusticeInfo.net* (16 July 2019)

Cryer R, *Prosecuting International Crimes: Selectivity and the International Criminal Law Regime* (CUP 2005)

Cryer R, 'International Criminal Law vs. State Sovereignty: Another Round?' (2006) 16 *European Journal of International Law* 979

Cryer R, 'Sudan, Resolution 1593, and International Criminal Justice' (2006) 19 *Leiden Journal of International Law* 195

Cryer R, 'The Philosophy of International Criminal Law', in Orakhelashvili A (ed), *Research Handbook on the Theory and History of International Law* (Edward Elgar 2011) 232

Cryer R, 'International Criminal Tribunals and the Sources of International Law: Antonio Cassese's Contribution to the Canon' (2012) 10 *Journal of International Criminal Justice* 1045

Cryer R et al, *An Introduction to International Criminal Law and Procedure* (3rd edn, CUP 2014)

Cupido M, 'Pluralism in Theories of Liability: Joint Criminal Enterprise versus Joint Perpetration', in Sliedregt E and Vasiliev S (eds), *Pluralism in International Criminal Law* (OUP 2014) 128

Cupido M, 'The Contextual Embedding of Genocide: A Casuistic Analysis of the Interplay between Law and Facts' (2014) 15 *Melbourne Journal of International Law* 1

Cupido M, 'Facing Facts in International Criminal Law: A Casuistic Model of Judicial Reasoning' (2016) 14 *Journal of International Criminal Justice* 1

Cusato ET, 'Beyond Symbolism: Problems and Prospects with Prosecuting Environmental Destruction before the ICC' (2017) 15 *Journal of International Criminal Justice* 491

d'Aspremont J, 'The Multidimensional Process of Interpretation: Content-Determination and Law-Ascertainment Distinguished', in Bianchi A et al (eds), *International in International Law* (CUP 2015) 111

Damaška M, 'What Is the Point of International Criminal Justice?' (2008) 83 *Chicago-Kent Law Review* 329

Damaška M, 'Unacknowledged Presences in International Criminal Justice' (2012) 10 *Journal of International Criminal Justice* 1239

Dannenbaum T, 'Against Modesty at the ICC' *Opinio Juris* (11 April 2020)

Danner AM, 'Beyond the Geneva Conventions: Lessons from the Tokyo Tribunal in Prosecuting War and Terrorism' (2005) 46 *Virginia Journal of International Law* 83

Danner AM, 'When Courts Make Law: How the International Criminal Tribunals Recast the Laws of War' (2006) 59 *Vanderbilt Law Review* 1

Danner AM and Martinez J, 'Guilty Associations: Joint Criminal Enterprise, Command Responsibility, and the Development of International Criminal Law' (2005) 93 *California Law Review* 75

Darcy S, *Collective Responsibility and Accountability under International Law* (Transnational Publishers 2007)

Darcy S, *Judges, Law and War: The Judicial Development of International Humanitarian Law* (CUP 2014)

Darrow M, *Between Light and Shadow: The World Bank, the International Monetary Fund, and International Human Rights Law* (Hart Publishing 2006)

Dauphinee E, 'War Crimes and the Ruin of Law' (2008) 37 *Millennium: Journal of International Studies* 49

de Brouwer A-M, *Supranational Criminal Prosecution of Sexual Violence: The ICC and the Practice of the ICTY and the ICTR* (Intersentia 2005)

De Smet S, 'The International Criminal Standard of Proof at the ICC—Beyond Reasonable Doubt or Beyond Reason', in Stahn C (ed), *The Law and Practice of the International Criminal Court* (OUP 2015) 861

de Vos C, 'Investigating from Afar: The ICC's Evidence Problem' (2013) 26 *Leiden Journal of International Law* 1009

de Waal A, 'Moreno-Ocampo's Coup de Theatre' *African Arguments* (29 July 2008)

Deeks A, 'The Observer Effect: National Security Litigation, Executive Policy Changes, and Judicial Deference' (2013) 82 *Fordham Law Review* 827

DeFalco R and Mégret F, 'The Invisibility of Race at the ICC: Lessons from the US Criminal Justice System' (2019) 7 *London Review of International Law* 55

deGuzman MM and Schabas WA, 'Initiation of Investigations and Selection of Cases', in Sluiter G et al (eds), *International Criminal Procedure: Principles and Rules* (OUP 2013) 131

Del Ponte C, 'Investigation and Prosecution of Large-scale Crimes at the International Level: The Experience of the ICTY' (2006) 4 *Journal of International Criminal Justice* 539

Del Ponte C, *Madame Prosecutor: Confrontations with Humanity's Worst Criminals and the Culture of Impunity* (Other Press 2009)

Dembour M-B and Haslam E, 'Silencing Hearings? Victim-Witnesses at War Crimes Trials' (2014) 15 *European Journal of International Law* 151

Des Forges AL, *"Leave None to Tell the Story": Genocide in Rwanda* (Human Rights Watch 1999)

Des Forges AL, 'Shame: Rationalizing Western Apathy on Rwanda' *Foreign Policy* (May/June 2001)

Dickson T, *On the Poverty, Rise, and Demise of International Criminal Law* (Portland State University: Dissertations and Thesis Paper 2016)

Dinstein Y, *The Defence of 'Obedience to Superior Orders' in International Law* (AW Sijthoff-Leyden 1965)

Dixon P and Tenove C, 'International Criminal Justice as a Transnational Field: Rules, Authority and Victims' (2013) 7 *International Journal of Transitional Justice* 393

Doak J, 'The Therapeutic Dimension of Transitional Justice: Emotional Repair and Victim Satisfaction in International Trials and Truth Commissions' (2011) 11 *International Criminal Law Review* 263

Douglas L, *The Memory of Judgment: Making Law and History in the Trials of the Holocaust* (Yale University Press 2001)

Douglas L, 'Perpetrator Proceedings and Didactic Trials', in Duff A et al (eds), *The Trial on Trial: Volume 2: Judgment and Calling to Account* (Hart Publishing 2006) 191

Douglas L, 'The Didactic Trial: Filtering History and Memory into the Courtroom' (2006) 14 *European Review* 513

Douglas L, 'From IMT to NMT: The Emergence of a Jurisprudence of Atrocity', in Priemel KC and Stiller A (eds), *Reassessing the Nuremberg Military Tribunals: Transitional Justice, Trial Narratives, and Historiography* (Berghahn Books 2012) 276

Douglas L, 'Truth and Justice in Atrocity Trials', in Schabas WA (ed), *The Cambridge Companion to International Criminal Law* (CUP 2016) 34

Drumbl MA, 'Waging War against the World: The Need to Move from War Crimes to Environmental Crimes' (1998) 22 *Fordham International Law Journal* 122

Drumbl MA, 'Pluralizing International Criminal Justice' (2005) 103 *Michigan Law Review* 1295

Drumbl MA, *Atrocity, Punishment, and International Law* (CUP 2007)

Drumbl M, 'Collective Responsibility and Postconflict Justice', in Isaacs T and Vernon R (eds), *Accountability for Collective Wrongdoing* (CUP 2011) 23

Drumbl MA, 'The Effects of the Lubanga Case on Understanding and Preventing Child Soldiering' (2012) 15 *Yearbook of International Humanitarian Law* 87

Drumbl MA, *Reimagining Child Soldiers in International Law and Policy* (OUP 2012)

Drumbl MA, 'The Curious Criminality of Mass Atrocity: Diverse Actors, Multiple Truths, and Plural Responses', in van Sliedregt E and Vasiliev S (eds), *Pluralism in International Criminal Law* (OUP 2014) 68

Drumbl MA, 'Victims who Victimise' (2016) 4 *London Review of International Law* 217

Dudai R, '"Rescues for Humanity": Rescuers, Mass Atrocities, and Transitional Justice' (2012) 34 *Human Rights Quarterly* 1

Duffy H, *Strategic Human Rights Litigation: Understanding and Maximising Impact* (Hart 2018)

Dworkin R, *Law's Empire* (Harvard University Press 1986)

Elberling B, *The Defendant in International Criminal Proceedings: Between Law and Historiography* (Hart Publishing 2012)

Eltringham N, *Accounting for Horror: Post-Genocide Debates in Rwanda* (Pluto Press 2004)

Eltringham N, '"We Are not a Truth Commission": Fragmented Narratives and the Historical Record at the International Criminal Tribunal for Rwanda' (2009) 11 *Journal of Genocide Research* 55

Engle K et al, 'Introduction', in Engle K et al (eds), *Anti-Impunity and the Human Rights Agenda* (CUP 2016) 1
Eser A, 'Individual Criminal Responsibility', in Cassese A et al (eds), *The Rome Statute of the International Criminal Court* (OUP 2002) 767
Eser A, 'Mental Elements—Mistake of Fact and Mistake of Law', in Cassese A et al, *The Rome Statute of the International Criminal Court* (OUP 2002) 889
Evans RJ, 'History, Memory, and the Law: The Historian as Expert Witness' (2002) 41 *History and Theory* 326
Fairlie MA, 'The Hidden Costs of Strategic Communications for the International Criminal Court' (2016) 51 *Texas International Law Journal* 281
Fairlie MA, 'A Newly-Revealed Cost of Article 15 Communications' *IntLawGrrls* (29 June 2018)
Farhang C, 'Point of No Return: Joint Criminal Enterprise in *Brđanin*' (2010) 23 *Leiden Journal of International Law* 137
Fehl C, 'Explaining the International Criminal Court: A Practice Test for Rationalist and Constructivist Approaches', in Roach SC (ed), *Governance, Order, and the International Criminal Court: Between Realpolitik and a Cosmopolitan Court* (OUP 2009) 75
Felman S, 'Theaters of Justice: Arendt in Jerusalem, the Eichmann Trial, and the Redefinition of Legal Meaning in the Wake of the Holocaust' (2000) 1 *Theoretical Inquiries in Law* 465
Felman S, *The Juridical Unconscious: Trials and Traumas in the Twentieth Century* (Harvard University Press 2002)
Fenrick WJ, 'The Crime against Humanity of Persecution in the Jurisprudence of the ICTY' (2001) 32 *Netherlands Yearbook of International Law* 81
Ferdinandusse WN, *Direct Application of International Criminal Law in National Courts* (TMC Asser Press 2006)
Festinger L, *A Theory of Cognitive Dissonance* (reprint edn [1957] Stanford University Press 1962)
Finley LM, 'Breaking Women's Silence in Law: The Dilemma of the Gendered Nature of Legal Reasoning' (1989) 64 *Notre Dame Law Review* 886
Finnin S, *Elements of Accessorial Modes of Liability: Articles 25(3)(b) and (c) of the Rome Statute of the International Criminal Court* (Martinus Nijhoff Publishers 2012)
Fish S, *Is there a Text in this Class? The Authority of Interpretive Communities* (Harvard University Press 1980)
Fish S, *Doing what Comes Naturally: Change, Rhetoric, and the Practice of Theory in Literary and Legal Studies* (OUP 1989)
Fisher KJ, *Moral Accountability and International Criminal Law: Holding Agents of Atrocity Accountable to the World* (Routledge 2012)
Fiss O, 'Objectivity and Interpretation' (1982) 34 *Stanford Law Review* 739
Fiss OM, 'Conventionalism' (1985) 58 *Southern California Law Review* 177
Fitzmaurice G, 'The Future of Public International Law and of the International Legal System in the Circumstances of Today', in Institut de Droit International, *Livre du Centenaire de l'Institut de Droit International 1873–1973* (1973) 197
Fletcher GP, 'The Right and the Reasonable' (1985) 98 *Harvard Law Review* 949
Fletcher GP, *Basic Concepts of Criminal Law* (OUP 1998)
Fletcher GP, 'The Storrs Lectures: Liberals and Romantics at War: The Problem of Collective Guilt' (2002) 111 *Yale Law Journal* 1499
Fletcher GP, *The Grammar of Criminal Law: American, Comparative, and International: Volume One: Foundations* (OUP 2007)
Fletcher LE, 'From Indifference to Engagement: Bystanders and International Criminal Justice' (2005) 26 *Michigan Journal of International Law* 1013

Fletcher LE, 'Facing up to the Past: Bystanders and Transitional Justice' (2007) 20 *Harvard Human Rights Journal* 47

Fletcher LE and Weinstein HM, 'Violence and Social Repair: Rethinking the Contribution of Justice to Reconciliation' (2002) 24 *Human Rights Quarterly* 573

Fletcher LE and Weinstein HM, 'A World unto Itself? The Application of International Justice in the Former Yugoslavia' in Stover E and Weinstein HM (eds), *My Neighbour, My Enemy: Justice and Community in the Aftermath of Mass Atrocity* (CUP 2004) 29

Ford S, 'A Social Psychology Model of the Perceived Legitimacy of International Criminal Courts: Implications for the Success of Transitional Justice Mechanisms' (2012) 45 *Vanderbilt Journal of Transnational Law* 405

Ford S, 'Fairness and Politics at the ICTY: Evidence from the Indictments' (2013) XXXIX *North Carolina Journal of International Law and Commercial Regulation* 45

Ford S, 'The Complexity of International Criminal Trials is Necessary' (2015) 48 *George Washington International Law Review* 151

Foster D, 'Rethinking the Subjectivity of Perpetrators of Political Violence', in Smeulers A (ed), *Collective Violence and International Criminal Justice: An Interdisciplinary Approach* (Intersentia 2010) 39

Foucault M, *Discipline and Punish: The Birth of a Prison* (Penguin 1991)

Fournet C, *The Crime of Destruction and the Law of Genocide: Their Impact on Collective Memory* (Ashgate 2007)

Fournet C, 'Mass Atrocity: Theories and Concepts of Accountability—On the Schizophrenia of Accountability', in Henham R and Findlay M (eds), *Exploring the Boundaries of International Criminal Justice* (Ashgate 2011) 27

Frankenberg G, 'Human Rights and the Belief in a Just World' 12 *I-CON* (2014) 35

Friedlander S, 'Introduction', in Friedlander S (ed), *Probing the Limits of Representation: Nazism and the 'Final Solution'* (Harvard University Press 1992) 1

Friman H et al, 'Charges', in Sluiter G et al (eds), *International Criminal Procedure: Principles and Rules* (OUP 2013) 381

Fry E, 'Legal Recharacterisation and the Materiality of Facts at the International Criminal Court: Which Charges Are Permissible?' (2016) 29 *Leiden Journal of International Law* 577

Funkenstein A, 'History, Counterhistory, and Narrative', in Friedlander S (ed), *Probing the Limits of Representation: Nazism and the "Final Solution"* (Harvard University Press 1992) 66

Gaeta P, 'Serious Violations of the Law on the Conduct of Hostilities: A Neglected Class of War Crimes?', in Pocar F et al (eds) *War Crimes and the Conduct of Hostilities: Challenges to Adjudication and Investigation* (Edward Elgar 2013) 20

Galbraith J, 'The Good Deeds of International Criminal Defendants' (2012) 25 *Leiden Journal of International Law* 799

Gallant KS, *The Principle of Legality in International and Comparative Criminal Law* (CUP 2009)

Gallmetzer R, 'Prosecuting Persons Doing Business with Armed Groups in Conflict Areas: The Strategy of the Office of the Prosecutor of the International Criminal Court' (2010) 8 *Journal of International Criminal Justice* 947

Galtung J, 'Violence, Peace, and Peace Research' (1969) 6 *Journal of Peace Research* 167

Garland D, *Punishment and Modern Society: A Study in Social Theory* (Clarendon Press 1990)

Gaynor F, 'Uneasy Partners—Evidence, Truth and History in International Trials' (2012) 10 *Journal of International Criminal Justice* 1257

Gevers C, 'International Criminal Law and Individualism: An African Perspective', in Schwöbel C (ed), *Critical Approaches to International Criminal Law: An Introduction* (Routledge 2014) 221

Gewirtz P, 'Narrative and Rhetoric in the Law', in Brooks P and Gewirtz P (eds), *Law's Stories—Narrative and Rhetoric in the Law* (Yale University Press 1996) 2

Gil A and Maculan E, 'Current Trends in the Definition of "Perpetrator" by the International Criminal Court: From the Decision on the Confirmation of Charges in the *Lubanga* case to the *Katanga* Judgment' (2015) 28 *Leiden Journal of International Law* 349

GLAN and Stanford International Human Rights Clinic, 'The Situation in Nauru and Manus Island: Liability for Crimes Against Humanity in the Detention of Refugees and Asylum Seekers' *Communiqué to the Office of the Prosecutor of the International Criminal Court under Article 15 of the Rome Statute* (13 February 2017)

Glasius M, *The International Criminal Court: A Global Civil Society Achievement* (Routledge 2006)

Glassborow K, 'ICC Investigative Strategy Under Fire' *Institute for War & Peace Reporting* (27 October 2008)

Golder B, 'Beyond Redemption? Problematising the Critique of Human Rights in Contemporary International Legal Thought' (2014) 2 *London Review of International Law* 77

Goldstone R, 'Acquittals by the International Criminal Court' *EJIL:Talk!* (18 January 2019)

Gourevitch P, *We Wish to Inform You that Tomorrow We Will Be Killed with Our Families* (Picador 1998)

Grabert A, *Dynamic Interpretation in International Criminal Law: Striking a Balance between Stability and Change* (Herbert Utz Verlag 2015)

Gready P and Robins S, 'From Transitional to Transformative Justice: A New Agenda for Practice' (2014) 8 *International Journal of Transitional Justice* 339

Greenawalt AKA, 'Justice Without Politics: Prosecutorial Discretion and the International Criminal Court' (2007) 39 *NYU Journal of International Law and Politics* 583

Grey R, *Prosecuting Sexual and Gender-Based Crimes at the International Criminal Court: Practice, Progress and Potential* (CUP 2019) 76

Grey R et al, 'Evidence of Sexual Violence against Men and Boys Rejected in the Ongwen Case' *Human Rights in International Justice* (10 April 2018)

Grover L, 'A Call to Arms: Fundamental Dilemmas Confronting the Interpretation of Crimes in the Rome Statute of the International Criminal Court' (2010) 21 *European Journal of International Criminal Law* 543

Grover L, *Interpreting Crimes in the Rome Statute of the International Criminal Court* (CUP 2014)

Guariglia F and Rogier E, 'The Selection of Situations and Cases by the OTP of the ICC', in Stahn C (ed), *The Law and Practice of the International Criminal Court* (OUP 2015) 350

Guilfoyle D, 'Responsibility for Collective Atrocities: Fair Labelling and Approaches to Commission in International Criminal Law' (2011) 64 *Current Legal Problems* 255

Guilfoyle D, 'Part II—This Is Not Fine: The International Criminal Court in Trouble' *EJIL:Talk!* (22 March 2019)

Haack S, 'Epistemology Legalized: Or, Truth, Justice, and the American Way' (2004) 49 *The American Journal of Jurisprudence* 43

Hagan J and Levi R, 'Crimes of War and the Force of Law' (2005) 83 *Social Forces* 1499

Hamilton R, 'Australia's Refugee Policy Is a Crime Against Humanity' *Foreign Policy* (23 February 2017)

Hart HLA, *Punishment and Responsibility: Essays in the Philosophy of Law* (2nd edn, OUP 2008)

Hartmann T, 'Abdicated Legacy: The Prosecution's Use of Evidence from Milošević', in Waters T (ed), *The Milošević Trial: An Autopsy* (OUP 2014) 465

Haslam E, 'Silences in International Criminal Legal Histories and the Construction of the Victim Subject of International Criminal Law: The Nineteenth-Century Slave Trading Trial of Joseph Peters', in Schwöbel C (ed), *Critical Approaches to International Criminal Law: An Introduction* (Routledge 2014) 180

Hausner G, *Justice in Jerusalem* (Harper & Row 1966)

Hayden P, 'Political Evil, Cosmopolitan Realism, and the Normative Ambivalence of the International Criminal Court', in Roach SC (ed), *Governance, Order, and the International Criminal Court: Between Realpolitik and a Cosmopolitan Court* (OUP 2009) 157

Hayes N, 'Creating a Definition of Rape in International Law: The Contribution of the International Criminal Tribunals', in Darcy S and Powderly J (eds), *Judicial Creativity at the International Criminal Tribunals* (OUP 2010) 129

Hayes N, '*La Lutte Continue*: Investigating and Prosecuting Sexual Violence at the ICC', in Stahn C (ed), *The Law and Practice of the International Criminal Court* (OUP 2015) 801

Heikkilä M, *Coping with International Atrocities through Criminal Law: A Study into the Typical Features of International Criminality and the Reflection of these Traits in International Criminal Law* (Åbo Akademi University Press 2013)

Heller KJ, 'Beyond the Reasonable Man? A Sympathetic but Critical Assessment of the Use of Subjective Standards of Reasonable in Self-Defense and Provocation Cases' (1998) 26 *American Journal of Criminal Law* 1

Heller KJ, '*Prosecutor v. Karemera, Ngirumpatse & Nzirorera*. Case No. ICTR-98-44-AR73(C). Decision on Prosecutor's Interlocutory Appeal of Decision on Judicial Notice' (2007) 101 *American Journal of International Law* 157

Heller KJ, 'Mistake of Legal Element, the Common Law, and Article 32 of the Rome Statute' (2008) 6 *Journal of International Criminal Justice* 419

Heller KJ, 'The Role of the International Prosecutor', in Romano CPR et al (eds), *The Oxford Handbook of International Adjudication* (OUP 2013) 669

Heller KJ, 'The ICC in Palestine: Be Careful What You Wish For' *Justice in Conflict* (2 April 2015)

Heller KJ, 'Russia's Short-Sighted Approach to the Georgia Investigation' *Opinio Juris* (13 February 2016)

Heller KJ, 'The Rome Statute's Flawed Amendment Regime—Starvation in NIAC Edition' *Opinio Juris* (7 December 2019)

Heller KJ, 'Who Is Afraid of the Crime of Aggression?' *Amsterdam Law School Research Paper No 2019-49* (2019)

Heller KJ, *The Nuremberg Military Tribunals and the Origins of International Criminal Law* (OUP 2011)

Heller KJ and Simpson G (eds), *The Hidden Histories of War Crimes Trials* (OUP 2013)

Henderson I, 'The Firebombing of Tokyo and Other Japanese Cities', in Tanaka Y et al (eds), *Beyond Victor's Justice: The Tokyo War Crimes Trial Revisited* (Martinus Nijhoff 2011) 311

Henry N, *War and Rape: Law, Memory and Justice* (Routledge 2011)

Higgins G, 'The Impact of the Size, Scope, and Scale of the *Milošević* Trial and the Development of Rule 73*bis* before the ICTY' (2009) 7 *Northwestern Journal of International Human Rights* 239

Higgins N, 'The Responsibility of the Netherlands for the Actions of Dutchbat: An Analysis of Nuhanović and Mustafić' (2014) 14 *International Criminal Law Review* 641

Hillebrecht C and Straus S, 'Who Pursues the Perpetrators? State Cooperation with the ICC' (2017) 39 *Human Rights Quarterly* 162

Hirsch F, *Soviet Judgment at Nuremberg: A New History of the International Military Tribunal after World War II* (OUP 2020)

Hisakazu F, 'The Tokyo Trial: Humanity's Justice v Victors' Justice', in Tanaka Y et al (eds), *Beyond Victor's Justice? The Tokyo War Crimes Trial Revisited* (Martinus Nijhoff Publishers 2011) 3

Hoare MA, 'Florence Hartmann's "Peace and Punishment"' *Greater Surbiton: The Perfect is the Enemy of the Good* (10 January 2008)

Hodžić R, 'A Long Road Yet to Reconciliation: The Impact of the ICTY on Reconciliation and Victims' Perceptions of Criminal Justice', in Steinberg RH (ed), *Assessing the Legacy of the ICTY* (Martinus Nijhoff Publishers 2011) 115

Hoffmann T, 'The Gentle Humanizer of Humanitarian Law—Antonio Cassese and the Creation of the Customary Law of Non-International Armed Conflict' *SSRN* (15 December 2009)

Hol A, 'The Theatre of Justice: On the Educational Meaning of Criminal Trials', in Brants C et al, *Transitional Justice: Images and Memories* (Ashgate 2013) 71

Hola B, 'Sentencing at the ICTY: Doing Justice to Complex Realities of International Crimes?' *Humanity* (4 July 2017)

Holá B et al, 'International Sentencing Facts and Figures: Sentencing Practice at the ICTY and ICTR' (2011) 9 *Journal of International Criminal Justice* 411

Hoover J, 'Reconstructing Responsibility and Moral Agency in World Politics' (2012) 4 *International Theory* 233

Hoover J, 'Moral Practices: Assigning Responsibility in the International Criminal Court' (2013) 76 *Law and Contemporary Problems* 263

Houge AB, 'Narrative Expressivism: A Criminological Approach to the Expressive Function of International Criminal Justice' (2019) 19 *Criminology & Criminal Justice* 277

Houge AB and Lohne K, 'End Impunity! Reducing Conflict-Related Sexual Violence to a Problem of Law' (2017) 51 *Law & Society Review* 755

Human Rights Watch, *Bringing Justice: The Special Court for Sierra Leone: Accomplishments, Shortcomings, and Needed Support* (September 2004)

Human Rights Watch, *Uprooted and Forgotten: Impunity and Human Rights Abuses in Northern Uganda* (September 2005)

Human Rights Watch, *Youth, Poverty and Blood: The Lethal Legacy of West Africa's Regional Warriors* (March 2005)

Human Rights Watch, *The Rwandan Genocide: How It Was Prepared* (April 2006)

Human Rights Watch, *Unfinished Business: Closing Gaps in the Selection of ICC Cases* (September 2011)

Human Rights Watch, *Justice After Genocide: 20 Years On* (28 March 2014)

Human Rights Watch, *Making Justice Count: Lessons from the ICC's Work in Côte d'Ivoire* (August 2015)

Hunt D, 'The International Criminal Court: High Hopes, "Creative Ambiguity" and an Unfortunate Mistrust in International Judges' (2004) 2 *Journal of International Criminal Justice* 56

Husak D, 'Partial Defenses', in Husak D, *The Philosophy of Criminal Law: Selected Essays* (OUP 2010) 311

Ignatieff M, 'Articles of Faith' (1996) 25 *Index on Censorship* 110

International Bar Association, *Fairness at the International Criminal Court* (August 2011)

International Commission of Jurists, *Report of the Expert Legal Panel on Corporate Complicity in International Crimes: Volume 2: Criminal Law and International Crimes* (International Commission of Jurists 2008)

International Crisis Group, 'The Special Court for Sierra Leone: Promises and Pitfalls of a "New Model"' *ICJ Africa Briefing* (4 August 2003)

Jackson M, *Complicity in International Law* (OUP 2015)

Jackson RH, *The Nürnberg Case* (Alfred A Knopf 1947)

Jain N, *Perpetrators and Accessories in International Criminal Law: Individual Modes of Responsibility for Collective Crimes* (Hart Publishing 2014)

Jain N, 'Radical Dissents in International Criminal Trials' (2017) 28 *European Journal of International Law* 1163

Jalloh CC, 'Special Court for Sierra Leone: Achieving Justice?' (2011) 32 *Michigan Journal of International Law* 395

Jalloh CC et al (eds), *The African Court of Justice and Human and Peoples' Rights in Context* (CUP 2019)

Jallow HB, 'Prosecutorial Discretion and International Criminal Justice' (2005) 3 *Journal of International Criminal Justice* 145

Jenkins K, *Refiguring History: New Thoughts on an Old Discipline* (Routledge 2003)

Jessberger F, 'On the Origins of Individual Criminal Responsibility under International Law for Business Activity' (2010) 8 *Journal of International Criminal Justice* 783

Jessberger F and Geneuss J, 'Introduction' (2010) 8 *Journal of International Criminal Justice* (2010) 695

Jochnick C and Normand R, 'The Legitimation of Violence: A Critical History of the Laws of War' (1994) 35 *Harvard International Law Journal* 49

Johns F et al, 'Introduction', in Johns F et al (eds), *Events: The Force of International Law* (Routledge 2011) 1

Johnson LD, 'Ten Years Later: Reflections on the Drafting' (2004) 2 *Journal of International Criminal Justice* 368, 378

Jordash W, 'Insiders: The Special Court for Sierra Leone's Dirty Laundry' *JusticeInfo.Net* (30 April 2020)

Jordash W and Martin S, 'How the Approach to JCE in *Taylor* and the RUF Case Undermined the Demands of Justice at the Special Court for Sierra Leone', in Jalloh CC (ed), *The Sierra Leone Special Court and its Legacy: The Impact for Africa and International Criminal Law* (CUP 2014) 96

Jørgensen NHB, 'Genocide as a Fact of Common Knowledge' (2007) 56 *International and Comparative Law Quarterly* 885

Kahan DM, 'What Do Alternative Sanctions Mean?' (1996) 63 *University of Chicago Law Review* 591

Kaleck W, 'Seizing Opportunities and Broad Strategy Both Essential in Human Rights Litigation' *Open Global Rights* (26 February 2019)

Kaleck W and Saage-Maaß M, 'Corporate Accountability for Human Rights Violations Amounting to International Crimes: The Status Quo and its Challenges' (2010) 8 *Journal of International Criminal Justice* 699

Kalpouzos I and Mann I, 'Banal Crimes against Humanity: The Case of Asylum Seekers in Greece' (2015) 16 *Melbourne Journal of International Law* 1

Kamola IA, 'Coffee and Genocide: A Political Economy of Violence in Rwanda' (2008) 99 *Transition* 54

Keck ME and Sikkink K, *Activism Beyond Borders: Advocacy Networks in International Politics* (Cornell University Press 1998) 27

Keen D, 'Greedy Elites, Dwindling Resources, Alienated Youths: The Anatomy of Protracted Violence in Sierra Leone' (2003) 6 *International Politics and Society* 67

Keen D, 'Liberalization and Conflict' (2005) 26 *International Political Science Review* 73

Kei-ichi T, 'Reasons for the Failure to Prosecute Unit 731 and its Significance', in Tanaka Y et al (eds), *Beyond Victor's Justice: The Tokyo War Crimes Trial Revisited* (Martinus Nijhoff 2011)

Kelman HC, 'The Policy Context of International Crimes', in Nollkaemper A and van der Wilt HG (eds), *System Criminality* (CUP 2009) 26

Kelsall T, *Culture under Cross-Examination: International Justice and the Special Court for Sierra Leone* (CUP 2009)

Kendall S, 'Critical Orientations: A Critique of International Criminal Court Practice', in Schwöbel C (ed), *Critical Approaches to International Criminal Law: An Introduction* (Routledge 2014) 54

Kendall S, 'Commodifying Global Justice: Economies of Accountability at the International Criminal Court' (2015) 13 *Journal of International Criminal Justice* 113

Kendall S and Nouwen S, 'Representational Practices at the International Criminal Court: The Gap between Juridified and Abstract Victimhood' (2013) 76 *Law and Contemporary Problems* 235

Kendall S and Nouwen SMH, 'Speaking of Legacy: Toward an Ethos of Modesty at the International Criminal Tribunal for Rwanda' (2016) 110 *American Journal of International Law* 212

Kennedy D, *The Dark Sides of Virtue: Reassessing International Humanitarianism* (Princeton University Press 2004)

Kersten M, 'In the ICC's Interest: Between "Pragmatism" and "Idealism"?' *Justice in Conflict* (16 July 2013)

Kersten M, 'Why Is the International Criminal Court Stepping out of Africa and into Georgia' *Justice in Conflict* (6 February 2016)

Kersten M, 'A Missed Trial or a Mistrial? The End of the ICC Cases against Ruto and Sang' *Justice in Conflict* (7 April 2016)

Kersten M, *Justice in Conflict: The Effects of the International Criminal Court's Interventions on Ending Wars and Building Peace* (OUP 2016)

Kersten M, 'Will the International Criminal Court's Latest Target in Libya Be Brought to Justice?' *The Washington Post: Monkey Cage* (31 August 2017)

Kersten M, 'Making a Distinction: The Rome Statute Is Not the ICC: It Is Much More than that' *Justice in Conflict* (17 July 2018)

Kirby P, 'Refusing to Be a Man?: Men's Responsibility for War Rape and the Problem of Social Structures in Feminist and Gender Theory' (2012) 16 *Men and Masculinities* 93

Kirchheimer O, *Political Justice: The Use of Legal Procedure for Political Ends* (Princeton University Press 1961)

Kirsch P and Oosterveld V, 'The Preparatory Commission for the International Criminal Court' (2002) 25 *Fordham International Law Journal* 563

Kiyani, AG 'International Crime and the Politics of Criminal Theory: Voices and Conduct of Exclusion' (2015) 48 *NYU Journal of International Law & Politics* 129

Kiyani A, Group-Based Differentiation and Local Repression: The Custom and Curse of Selectivity' (2016) 14 *Journal of International Criminal Justice* 939

Klabbers J, 'Book Review' (2004) 15 *European Journal of International Law* 1055

Klabbers J, 'The Meaning of Rules' (2006) 20 *International Relations* 295

Klamberg M, *Evidence in International Criminal Trials: Confronting Legal Gaps and the Reconstruction of Disputed Events* (Martinus Nijhoff Publishers 2013)

Klarin M, 'The Impact of the ICTY Trials on Public Opinion in the Former Yugoslavia' (2009) 7 *Journal of International Criminal Justice* 89

Knoops G-J, *Defenses in Contemporary International Criminal Law* (2nd edn, Martinus Nijhoff Publishers 2008)

Knox R, 'Marxism, International Law, and Political Strategy' (2009) 22 *Leiden Journal of International Law* 413

Knox R, 'Strategy and Tactics' (2010) 21 *Finnish Yearbook of International Law* 193

Knox R, 'What Is to Be Done (with Critical Legal Theory)?' (2011) 22 *Finnish Yearbook of International Law* 31

Koller D, '... and New York and The Hague and Tokyo and Geneva and Nuremberg and ...: The Geographies of International Law' (2012) 23 *European Journal of International Law* 97

Koller DS, 'The Faith of the International Criminal Lawyer' 40 *New York University Journal of International Law and Politics* (2008) 1019

Kopelman ES, 'Ideology and International Law: The Dissent of the Indian Justice at the Tokyo War Crimes Trial' (1991) 23 *NYU Journal of International Law and Politics* 373

Koskenniemi M, 'From Impunity to Show Trials' (2002) 6 *Max Planck Yearbook of United Nations Law* 1

Koskenniemi M, 'Hersch Lauterpacht and the Development of International Criminal Law' (2004) 2 *Journal of International Criminal Justice* 810

Kratochwil FV, *Rules Norms, and Decisions: On the Conditions of Practical and Legal Reasoning in International Relations and Domestic Affairs* (CUP 1989)

Kreß C, 'The Crime of Genocide under International Law' (2006) 6 *International Criminal Law Review* 461

Kreß C, 'On the Outer Limits of Crimes against Humanity: The Concept of Organization within the Policy Requirement: Some Reflections on the March 2010 ICC Kenya Decision' (2010) 23 *Leiden Journal of International Law* 855

Krever T, 'International Criminal Law: An Ideology Critique' (2013) 26 *Leiden Journal of International Law* 701

Krever T, 'Unveiling (and Veiling) Politics in International Criminal Trials', in Schwöbel C (ed), *Critical Approaches to International Criminal Law: An Introduction* (Routledge 2014) 117

Krever T, 'Africa in the Dock: On ICC Bias' *Critical Legal Thinking* (30 October 2016)

Kuhn T, *The Structure of Scientific Revolutions* (50th anniversary edition, University of Chicago Press 2012)

Kyriakakis J, 'Justice after War: Economic Actors, Economic Crimes, and the Moral Imperative for Accountability after War', in May L and Forcehimes A (eds), *Morality, Jus Post Bellum, and International Law* (CUP 2012) 113

Labuda P, 'The Flipside of Complementarity: Double Jeopardy at the International Criminal Court' (2019) 17 *Journal of International Criminal Justice* 369

Labuda P, 'The ICC's 'Evidence Problem': The Future of International Criminal Investigations after the Gbagbo Acquittal' *Völkerrechtsblog* (18 January 2019)

Lacey N, 'In Search of the Responsible Subject: History, Philosophy and Social Sciences in Criminal Law Theory' (2001) 64 *Modern Law Review* 350

Landsman S, 'The *Eichmann* Case and the Invention of the Witness-Driven Atrocity Trial' (2012–2013) 51 *Columbia Journal of Transnational Law* 69

Laverty C, 'What Lies Beneath? The Turn to Values in International Criminal Legal Discourse' *EJIL Talk!* (23 April 2018)

Lee RS, 'The Rwanda Tribunal' (1996) 9 *Leiden Journal of International Law* 37

Leebaw B, *Judging State-Sponsored Violence, Imagining Political Change* (CUP 2011)

Leebaw B, 'Lost, Forgotten, or Buried? Transitional Justice, Agency, and the Memory of Resistance' (2013) 2 *Politica & Società* 237

Leebaw B, 'Justice and the Faithless: The Demand for Disobedience in International Criminal Law' (2018) 24 *European Journal of International Relations* 344

Leebaw B, 'If Only More Such Stories Could Have Been Told: Ways of Remembering Resistance' (2019) 15 *Law, Culture and the Humanities* 448

Lehnhardt C, 'Individual Liability of Private Military Personnel under International Criminal Law' (2008) 19 *European Journal of International Law* 1015

Levi P, *The Drowned and The Saved* (Rosenthal R trans, Abacus 1988)

Levi R et al, 'International Courts in Atypical Political Environments: The Interplay of Prosecutorial Strategy, Evidence, and Court Authority in International Criminal Law' (2016) 79 *Law and Contemporary Problems* 289

Liss R, 'Crimes Against the Sovereign Order: Rethinking International Criminal Justice' (2020) 113 *American Journal of International Law* 727

Locke J, 'Indictments', in Reydams L et al (eds), *International Prosecutors* (OUP 2012) 604
Löytömäki S, 'Legalisation of the Memory of the Algerian War in France' (2005) 7 *Journal of the History of International Law* 157
Löytömäki S, 'Law and Memory: The Politics of Victimhood' (2012) 21 *Griffith Law Review* 1
Löytömäki S, 'The Law and Collective Memory of Colonialism: France and the Case of "Belated" Transitional Justice' (2013) 7 *International Journal of Transitional Justice* 205
Löytömäki S, *The Law and Politics of Memory: Confronting the Past* (Routledge 2014)
Luban D, 'The Legacies of Nuremberg' (1987) 54 *Social Research* 779
Luban D, *Legal Ethics and Human Dignity* (CUP 2007)
Luban D, 'State Criminality and the Ambition of International Criminal Law', in Isaacs T and Vernon R (eds), *Accountability for Collective Wrongdoing* (CUP 2011) 61
Luban D, 'After the Honeymoon: Reflections on the Current State of International Criminal Justice' (2013) 11 *Journal of International Criminal Justice* 505
Luban D, 'Demystifying Political Violence: Some Bequests of ICTY and ICTR' (2016) 110 *AJIL Unbound* 251
Luft A, 'Dehumanization and the Normalization of Violence: It's Not What You Think' *Items* (21 May 2019)
Lyons BS, 'Enough is Enough: The Illegitimacy of International Criminal Convictions: A Review Essay of *Fact-Finding without Facts, The Uncertain Evidentiary Foundations of International Criminal Convictions* by Nancy Amoury Combs' (2011) 13 *Journal of Genocide Research* 287
MacKinnon CA, 'Defining Rape Internationally: A Comment on *Akayesu*' (2006) 44 *Columbia Journal of Transnational Law* 940
Mahoney C, 'Sierra Leone: The Justice v. Reconciliation Archetype?' (2015) *TOAEP Policy Brief Series No 33*
Maier CS, 'Doing History, Doing Justice: The Narrative of the Historian and of the Truth Commission', in Rotberg RI and Thompson D, *Truth v. Justice: The Morality of Truth Commissions* (Princeton University Press 2000) 261
Mamdani M, *Saviours and Survivors: Darfur, Politics, and the War on Terror* (HSRC Press 2009)
Mamdani M, 'Beyond Nuremberg: The Historical Significance of the Post-Apartheid Transition in South Africa' (2015) 43 *Politics & Society* 61
Mani R, *Beyond Retribution: Seeking Justice in the Shadows of War* (Polity Press 2002)
Marks S, *The Riddle of all Constitutions: International Law, Democracy, and the Critique of Ideology* (OUP 2000)
Marks S, 'Apologising for Torture' (2004) 73 *Nordic Journal of International Law* 365
Marks S, 'Human Rights and Root Causes' (2011) 74 *Modern Law Review* 57
Marks S, 'Human Rights in Disastrous Times', in Crawford J and Koskenniemi M (eds), *The Cambridge Companion to International Law* (CUP 2012) 309
Marks S, 'Four Human Rights Myths' (2012) *LSE Law, Society and Economy Working Papers: Working Paper No 10/2012*
May L, *Crimes against Humanity: A Normative Account* (CUP 2005)
May L, *Genocide: A Normative Account* (CUP 2010)
May R and Wierda M, 'Evidence before the ICTY', in May R et al (ed), *Essays on the ICTY Procedure and Evidence: In Honour of Gabrielle Kirk McDonald* (Kluwer 2001) 249
McAuliffe P, 'From Watchdog to Workhorse: Explaining the Emergence of the ICC's Burden-Sharing Policy as an Example of Creeping Cosmopolitanism' (2014) 13 *Chinese Journal of International Law* 259
McAuliffe P, 'Weighing Domestic and International Impediments to Transformative Justice in Transition' (2015) 3 *London Review of International Law* 169
McAuliffe P, *Transformative Transitional Justice and the Malleability of Post-Conflict States* (Edward Elgar 2017)

McDermott Y, *Fairness in International Criminal Trials* (OUP 2016)
McDermott Y, 'The International Criminal Court's Chambers Practice Manual: Towards a Return to Judicial Law Making in International Criminal Procedure?' (2017) 15 *Journal of International Criminal Justice* 873
McDermott Y, 'Gbagbo's Acquittal Isn't Bad for the ICC. But Problems around Evidence Remain' *The Conversation* (24 January 2019)
McEvoy K, 'Beyond Legalism: Towards a Thicker Understanding of Transitional Justice' (2007) 34 *Journal of Law and Society* 411
Meernik J, 'What Kind of Bargain Is a Plea?' (2014) 14 *International Criminal Law Review* 200
Mégret F, 'Three Dangers for the International Criminal Court: A Critical Look at a Consensual Project' (2001) XII *Finnish Yearbook of International Law* 193
Mégret F, 'The Politics of International Criminal Justice' (2002) 13 *European Journal of International Law* 1261
Mégret F, 'In Defense of Hybridity: Towards a Representational Theory of International Criminal Justice' (2005) 38 *Cornell International Law Journal* 725
Mégret F, 'Beyond "Fairness": Understanding the Determinants of International Criminal Procedure' (2009) 14 *UCLA Journal of International Law and Foreign Affairs* 37
Mégret F, 'Practices of Stigmatization' (2013) 76 *Law and Contemporary Problems* 287
Mégret F, 'International Criminal Justice: A Critical Research Agenda', in Schwöbel C (ed), *Critical Approaches to International Criminal Law: An Introduction* (Routledge 2014) 17
Mégret F, 'What Sort of Global Justice is "International Criminal Justice"?' (2015) 13 *Journal of International Criminal Justice* 77
Mégret F, 'International Criminal Justice as a Juridical Field' (2016) XIII *Champ Pénal*
Mégret F, 'International Criminal Justice as a Peace Project' (2018) 29 *European Journal of International Law* 835
Mégret F, 'Is the ICC Focusing Too Much on Non-State Actors?', in deGuzman MM and Amann DM (eds), *Arcs of Global Justice* (OUP 2018) 173
Meijers T and Glasius M, 'Trials as Messages of Justice: What Should Be Expected of International Criminal Courts?' (2016) 30 *Ethics & International Affairs* 429
Meisenberg SM, 'Joint Criminal Enterprise at the Special Court for Sierra Leone', in Jalloh CC (ed), *The Sierra Leone Special Court and its Legacy: The Impact for Africa and International Criminal Law* (CUP 2014) 69
Meloni C, 'Fragmentation of the Notion of Co-Perpetration in International Criminal Law?', in van den Herik L and Stahn C (eds), *The Diversification and Fragmentation of International Criminal Law* (Martinus Nijhoff Publishers 2012) 481
Merkel R, 'The Law of the Nuremberg Trial: Valid, Dubious Outdated', in Mettraux G (ed), *Perspectives on the Nuremberg Trial* (OUP 2008) 555
Meron T, 'Answering for War Crimes: Lessons from the Balkans', in Meron T, *War Crimes Law Comes of Age: Essays* (OUP 1998) 278
Meron T, 'The Humanization of Humanitarian Law' (2000) 94 *American Journal of International Law* 239
Mettraux G, *International Crimes and the Ad Hoc Tribunals* (OUP 2006)
Mettraux G, 'Trial at Nuremberg', in Schabas WA and Bernaz N (eds), *Routledge Handbook of International Criminal Law* (Routledge 2011) 5
Milanović M, 'State Responsibility for Genocide' (2006) 17 *European Journal of International Law* 553
Milanović M, 'Establishing the Facts about Mass Atrocities: Accounting for the Failure of the ICTY to Persuade Target Audiences' (2016) 47 *Georgetown Journal of International Law* 1321
Milanović M, 'Courting Failure: When Are International Criminal Courts Likely to Be Believed by Local Audiences?', in Heller KJ et al (eds), *The Oxford Handbook of International Criminal Law* (OUP 2020) 261

Milgram S, *Obedience to Authority: An Experimental View* (Tavistock Publications 1974)
Miller Z, 'Effects of Invisibility: In Search of the "Economic"' in Transitional Justice' (2008) 2 *International Journal of Transitional Justice* 266
Miller Z, 'Anti-Impunity Politics in Post-Genocide Rwanda', in Engle K et al (eds), *Anti-Impunity and the Human Rights Agenda* (CUP 2016) 149
Ming Yau S, 'The Decentralisation of International Crimes: A Shift from the Central Criminal Apparatus at the ICC?' *EJIL:Talk!* (27 December 2018)
Minow M, *Between Vengeance and Forgiveness: Facing History after Genocide and Mass Violence* (Beacon Press 1998)
Minow M, 'The Work of Re-Membering: After Genocide and Mass Atrocity' (1999) 23 *Fordham International Law Journal* 429
Mistry H, The Paradox of Dissent: Judicial Dissent and the Projects of International Criminal Justice' (2015) 13 *Journal of International Criminal Justice* 449
Moffett L, 'The Role of Victims in the International Criminal Tribunals of the Second World War' (2012) 12 *International Criminal Law Review* 245
Mohamed S, 'A Neglected Option: The Contributions of State Responsibility for Genocide to Transitional Justice' (2009) 80 *University of Colorado Law Review* 327
Mohamed S, 'Deviance, Aspiration, and the Stories We Tell: Reconciling Mass Atrocity and the Criminal Law' (2015) 124 *Yale Law Journal* 1628
Moyn S, 'A Powerless Companion: Human Rights in the Age of Neoliberalism' (2014) 77 *Law and Contemporary Problems* 147
Moyn S, 'On a Self-Deconstructing Symposium' (2016) 110 *AJIL Unbound* 258
Moyn S, 'From Aggression to Atrocity: Rethinking the History of International Criminal Law', in KJ Heller et al (eds), *The Oxford Handbook of International Criminal Law* (OUP 2020) 341
Munslow A, *Deconstructing History* (2nd edn, Routledge 2006)
Musahara H and Huggins C, 'Land Reform, Land Scarcity and Post-Conflict Reconstruction: A Case Study of Rwanda', in Huggins C and Clover J (eds), *From the Ground Up: Land Rights, Conflict and Peace in Sub-Saharan Africa* (Institute for Security Studies 2005) 269
Mutua M, 'Never Again: Questioning the Yugoslav and Rwanda Tribunals' (1997) 11 *Temple International & Comparative Law Journal* 167
Nagy R, 'Transitional Justice as Global Project: Critical Reflections' (2008) 29 *Third World Quarterly* 275
Nesiah V, 'The Trials of History: Losing Justice in the Monstrous and the Banal', in Buchanan R and Zumbansen P (eds), *Law in Transition: Human Rights, Development and Transitional Justice* (Hart Publishing 2014) 289
Nesiah V, 'Doing History with Impunity', in K Engle et al (eds), *Anti-Impunity and the Human Rights Agenda* (CUP 2016) 95
Neumann K, 'Historians and the Yearning for Historical Justice' (2014) 18 *Rethinking History* 145
Nielsen CA, 'Can We Salvage a History of the Former Yugoslav Conflicts from the Milošević Trial?', in Waters T (ed), *The Milošević Trial: An Autopsy* (OUP 2014) 326
Nixon R, *Slow Violence and the Environmentalism of the Poor* (Harvard University Press 2011)
No Peace Without Justice, *Impact and Legacy Survey for the Special Court for Sierra Leone* (August 2012)
Nollkaemper A, 'Introduction', in Nollkaemper A and van der Wilt HG (eds), *System Criminality* (CUP 2009) 1
Noor M et al, 'When Suffering Begets Suffering: The Psychology of Competitive Victimhood between Adversarial Groups in Violent Conflicts' (2012) 16 *Personality & Social Psychology Review* 351

Norrie A, *Crime, Reason and History: A Critical Introduction to Criminal Law* (2nd edn, CUP 2001)

Nouwen S, 'Legal Equality on Trial: Sovereign and Individuals before the International Criminal Court' (2012) 43 *Netherlands Yearbook of International Law* 151

Nouwen S, *Complementarity in the Line of Fire: The Catalysing Effect of the International Criminal Court in Uganda and Sudan* (CUP 2014)

Nouwen SMH, '"As You Set Out for Ithaka": Practical, Epistemological, Ethical, and Existential Questions about Socio-Legal Empirical Research in Conflict' (2014) 27 *Leiden Journal of International Law* 227

Nouwen SMH and Werner WG, 'Doing Justice to the Political: The International Criminal Court in Uganda and Sudan' (2010) 21 *European Journal of International Law* 941

Nouwen SMH and Werner WG, 'Doing Justice to the Political: The International Criminal Court in Uganda and Sudan: A Rejoinder to Bas Schotel' (2011) 22 *European Journal of International Law* 1161

Nouwen SMH and Werner WG, 'Monopolizing Global Justice: International Criminal Law as Challenge to Human Diversity' (2015) 13 *Journal of International Criminal Justice* 157

Nowrojee B, '"Your Justice Is Too Slow" Will the ICTR Fail Rwanda's Rape Victims?' *United Nations Research Institute for Social Development Occasional Paper Series 10* (November 2005)

O'Brien M, 'Prosecutorial Discretion as an Obstacle to Prosecution of United Nations Peacekeepers by the International Criminal Court: The Big Fish/Small Fish Debate and the Gravity Threshold' (2012) 10 *Journal of International Criminal Justice* 525

O'Connell J, 'Gambling with the Psyche: Does Prosecuting Human Rights Violators Console their Victims?' (2005) 46 *Harvard International Law Journal* 295

O'Connell P, 'Human Rights: Contesting the Displacement Thesis' *Critical Legal Thinking* (18 June 2015)

O'Connell P, 'Human Rights: Contesting the Displacement Thesis' (2018) 69 *Northern Ireland Legal Quarterly* 19

O'Keefe R, *International Criminal Law* (OUP 2015)

Obote-Odora A, 'Case Selection and Prioritization Criteria at the International Criminal Tribunal for Rwanda', in Bergsmo M (ed), *Criteria for Prioritizing and Selecting Core International Crime Cases* (2nd edn, TOAEP 2010) 45

Ohlin JD, 'Three Conceptual Problems with the Doctrine of Joint Criminal Enterprise' (2007) 5 *Journal of International Criminal Justice* 69

Ohlin JD, 'Joint Intentions to Commit International Crimes' (2011) 11 *Chicago Journal of International Law* 693

Ohlin JD, 'Second-Order Linking Principles: Combining Vertical and Horizontal Modes of Liability' (2012) 25 *Leiden Journal of International Law* 771

Ohlin JD, 'LJIL Symposium: Where to Find the Liberal Principles of Criminal Law' *Opinio Juris* (10 April 2013)

Ohlin JD, 'Co-Perpetration: German *Dogmatik* or German Invasion?', in Stahn C (ed), *The Law and Practice of the International Criminal Court* (OUP 2015) 517

Ohlin JD et al, 'Assessing the Control Theory' (2013) 26 *Leiden Journal of International Law* 725

Olásolo H, *The Criminal Responsibility of Senior Political and Military Leaders as Principals to International Crimes* (Hart Publishing 2009)

Oosterveld V, 'Gender-Sensitive Justice and the International Criminal Tribunal for Rwanda: Lessons Learned for the International Criminal Court' (2005) 12 *New England Journal of International and Comparative Law* 119

Oosterveld V, 'The Gender Jurisprudence of the Special Court for Sierra Leone: Progress in the Revolutionary United Front Judgments' (2011) 44 *Cornell International Law Journal* 49

Oosterveld V, 'Evaluating the Special Court for Sierra Leone's Gender Jurisprudence', in Jalloh CC (ed), *The Sierra Leone Special Court and its Legacy: The Impact for Africa and International Criminal Law* (CUP 2014) 234

Oosterveld V, 'Sexual Violence Directed against Men and Boys in Armed Conflict or Mass Atrocity: Addressing a Gendered Harm in International Criminal Tribunals' (2014) 10 *Journal of International Law and International Relations* 107

Orentlicher DF, *Shrinking the Space for Denial: The Impact of the ICTY in Serbia* (Open Society Justice Initiative 2008)

Orford A, 'Locating the International: Military and Monetary Interventions after the Cold War' (1997) 38 *Harvard International Law Journal* 443

Osiel M, *Mass Atrocity, Collective Memory, and the Law* (Transaction Publishers 1997)

Osiel M, *Making Sense of Mass Atrocity* (CUP 2009)

Osiel M, 'Choosing among Alternative Responses to Mass Atrocity: Between the Individual and the Collectivity' *Ethics & International Affairs* (18 September 2015)

Osiel MJ, 'Obeying Orders: Atrocity, Military Discipline, and the Law of War' (1998) 86 *California Law Review* 939

Osiel MJ, *Mass Atrocity, Ordinary Evil, and Hannah Arendt: Criminal Consciousness in Argentina's Dirty War* (Yale University Press 2001)

Otomo Y, 'The Decision Not to Prosecute the Emperor', in Tanaka Y et al (eds), *Beyond Victor's Justice: The Tokyo War Crimes Trial Revisited* (Martinus Nijhoff 2011) 63

Otto D, 'Impunity in a Different Register: People's Tribunals and Questions of Judgment, Law, and Responsibility', in Engle K et al (eds), *Anti-Impunity and the Human Rights Agenda* (CUP 2016) 291

Overy R, 'The Nuremberg Trials: International Law in the Making', in Sands P (ed), *From Nuremberg to The Hague: The Future of International Criminal Justice* (CUP 2003) 1

Papa MI, 'The *Mothers of Srebrenica* Case before the European Court of Human Rights: United Nations Immunity versus Right of Access to a Court' (2016) 14 *Journal of International Criminal Justice* 893

Payne LA et al, *Transitional Justice and Corporate Accountability from below: Deploying Archimedes' Lever* (CUP 2020)

Pearson Z, 'Non-Governmental Organizations and the International Criminal Court: Changing Landscapes of International Law' (2006) 39 *Cornell International Law Journal* 243

Pendas DO, *The Frankfurt Auschwitz Trial, 1963–1965: Genocide, History, and the Limits of the Law* (CUP 2006)

Perriello T and Wierda M, *The Special Court for Sierra Leone Under Scrutiny* (ICTJ 2006)

Peskin V, 'An Ideal Becoming Real? The International Criminal Court and the Limits of the Cosmopolitan Vision of Justice', in Pierik R and Werner W (eds), *Cosmopolitanism in Context: Perspectives from International Law and Political Theory* (CUP 2010) 195

Pillay N, 'Equal Justice for Women: A Persona Journey' (2008) 50 *Arizona Law Review* 657

Pocar F, 'Completion or Continuation Strategy? Appraising Problems and Possible Developments in Building the Legacy of the ICTY' (2008) 6 *Journal of International Criminal Justice* 655

Ponti C, 'The Crime of Indiscriminate Attack and Unlawful Conventional Weapons: The Legacy of the ICTY Jurisprudence' (2015) 6 *Journal of International Humanitarian Legal Studies* 118

Powderly J, 'Judicial Interpretation at the Ad Hoc Tribunals: Method from Chaos?', in Darcy S and Powderly J (eds), *Judicial Creativity at the International Criminal Tribunals* (OUP 2010) 17

Powderly J, 'The Rome Statute and the Attempted Corseting of the Interpretative Judicial Function: Reflections on Sources of Law and Interpretative Technique', in Stahn C (ed), *The Law and Practice of the International Criminal Court* (OUP 2015)

Powderly J and Hayes N, 'The Bemba Appeal: A Fragmented Appeals Chamber Destabilises the Law and Practice of the ICC' *PhD Studies in Human Rights* (26 June 2018)

Power S, 'Accessory to Murder' *New York Times* (11 February 2001)

Power S, 'Bystanders to Genocide: Why the United States Let the Rwandan Tragedy Happen' *The Atlantic* (1 September 2001)

Priemel KC, *The Betrayal: The Nuremberg Trials and German Divergence* (OUP 2016)

Priemel KC and Stiller A, 'Introduction: Nuremberg's Narratives: Revising the Legacy of the "Subsequent Trials"', in Priemel KC and Stiller A (eds), *Reassessing the Nuremberg Military Tribunals: Transitional Justice, Trial Narratives, and Historiography* (Berghahn Books 2012) 1

Prosperi L and Terrosi J, 'Embracing the "Human Factor": Is there New Impetus at the ICC for Conceiving and Prioritizing International Environmental Harms as Crimes Against Humanity?' (2017) 15 *Journal of International Criminal Justice* 509

Rajagopal B, *International Law from Below: Development, Social Movements, and Third World Resistance* (CUP 2003)

Raman R, 'What Is Next for Félicien Kabuga? Socratic Connivance and Rupture in International Criminal Trials' *IntLawGrrls* (21 May 2020)

Ramulić E, 'Victims' Perspectives', in RH Steinberg (ed), *Assessing the Legacy of the ICTY* (Martinus Nijhoff Publishers 2011) 103

Rauschenbach M, 'Individuals Accused of International Crimes as Delegitimized Agents of Truth' (2018) 28 *International Criminal Justice Review* 291

Rauxloh RE, 'Negotiated History: The Historical Record in International Criminal Law and Plea Bargaining' (2010) 10 *International Criminal Law Review* 739

Reiter EH, 'Fact, Narrative, and the Judicial Uses of History: *Delgamuukw* and Beyond' (2010) 8 *Indigenous Law Journal* 55

Reydams L, 'The ICTR Ten Years On: Back to the Nuremberg Paradigm?' (2005) 3 *Journal of International Criminal Justice* 977

Reydams L, 'Politics or Pragmatism? The International Criminal Tribunal for Rwanda and the Burying of the Investigation into the Assassination of President Juvénal Habyarimana' (2018) 40 *Human Rights Quarterly* 989

Reynolds J, 'Anti-Colonial Legalities: Paradigms, Tactics & Strategy' (2015) 18 *Palestinian Yearbook of International Law* 8

Reynolds J and Xavier S, '"The Dark Corners of the World": TWAIL and International Criminal Justice' (2016) 14 *Journal of International Criminal Justice* 959

Richards P, 'To Fight or to Farm? Agrarian Dimensions of the Mano River Conflicts (Liberia and Sierra Leone)' (2005) 104 *African Affairs* 571

Robinson D, 'The Identity Crisis of International Criminal Law' (2008) 21 *Leiden Journal of International Law* 925

Robinson D, 'Legality and Other Contradictory Commitments: Some Thoughts about How We Think' (2009) *ASIL Proceedings* 104

Robinson D, 'Essence of Crimes against Humanity Raised by Challenges at ICC' *EJIL Talk!* (27 September 2011)

Robinson D, 'How Command Responsibility Got So Complicated: A Culpability Contradiction, Its Obfuscation, and a Simple Solution' (2012) 13 *Melbourne Journal of International Law* 1

Robinson D, 'A Cosmopolitan Liberal Account of International Criminal Law' (2013) 26 *Leiden Journal of International Law* 127

Robinson D, 'International Criminal Law as Justice' (2013) 11 *Journal of International Criminal Justice* 699

Robinson D, 'Crimes against Humanity: A Better Policy on "Policy"', in Stahn C (ed), *The Law and Practice of the International Criminal Court* (OUP 2015) 705

Robinson D, 'Inescapable Dyads: Why the International Criminal Court Cannot Win' (2015) 28 *Leiden Journal of International Law* 323

Robinson P and Ghahraman G, 'Can Rwandan President Kagame Be Held Responsible at the ICTR for the Killing of President Habyarimana?' (2008) 6 *Journal of International Criminal Justice* 981

Robinson PH, *Criminal Law Defences* (West Group 1984)

Rodenhäuser T, 'Beyond State Crimes: Non-State Entities and Crimes against Humanity' (2014) 27 *Leiden Journal of International Law* 913

Rodenhäuser T, 'Squaring the Circle? Prosecuting Sexual Violence against Child Soldiers by their "Own Forces"' (2016) 14 *Journal of International Criminal Justice* 171

Rodman KA, 'Justice as a Dialogue between Law and Politics: Embedding the International Criminal Court within Conflict Management and Peacebuilding' (2014) 12 *Journal of International Criminal Justice* 437

Röling BVA and Cassese A, *The Tokyo Trial and Beyond: Reflections of a Peacemonger* (Polity Press 1993)

Röling BVA, 'The Nuremberg and the Tokyo Trials in Retrospect', in Mettraux G (ed), *Perspectives on the Nuremberg Trial* (OUP 2008) 455

Rorty R, *Contingency, Irony, and Solidarity* (CUP 1989)

Rosenberg ST, 'The International Criminal Court in Côte d'Ivoire: Impartiality at Stake?' (2017) 15 *Journal of International Criminal Justice* 471

Rousso H, *The Haunting Past: History, Memory and Justice in Contemporary France* (Schoolcraft R trans, University of Pennsylvania Press 2002)

Ryngaert C and Spijkers O, 'The End of the Road: State Liability for Acts of UN Peacekeeping Contingents after the Dutch Supreme Court's Judgment in *Mothers of Srebrenica* (2019)' (2019) 66 *Netherlands International Law Review* 537

SáCouto S, 'The Impact of the Appeals Chamber Decision in Bemba: Impunity for Sexual and Gender-based Crimes?' *International Justice Monitor* (22 June 2018)

SaCouto S, Sadat LN, and Sellers PV, 'Collective Criminality and Sexual Violence: Fixing a Failed Approach' (2020) 33 *Leiden Journal of International Law* 207

Sadat LN, 'Crimes against Humanity in the Modern Age' (2013) 107 *American Journal of International Law* 334

Sadat LN and Jolly JM, 'Seven Canons of ICC Treaty Interpretation: Making Sense of Article 25's Rorschach Blot' (2014) 27 *Leiden Journal of International Law* 755

Sadat Wexler L, 'The Interpretation of the Nuremberg Principles by the French Court of Cassation: From Touvier to Barbie and Back Again' (1994) 32 *Columbia Journal of Transnational Law* 289

Saland P, 'International Criminal Law Principles' in Lee RS (ed), *The International Criminal Court: The Making of the Rome Statute: Issues, Negotiations, Results* (Kluwer 1999) 189

Sander B, 'International Criminal Justice as Progress: From Faith to Critique', in Bergsmo M et al (eds), *Historical Origins of International Criminal Law: Volume 4* (Torkel Opsahl Academic EPublisher 2015) 749

Sander B, 'The ICC's Crisis Mentality and the Limits of Global Justice' *Justice in Conflict* (9 March 2015)

Sander B, 'History on Trial: Historical Narrative Pluralism Within and Beyond International Criminal Courts' (2018) 67 *International and Comparative Law Quarterly* 547

Sander B, 'Justice as Identity: Unveiling the Mechanics of Legitimation in Domestic Atrocity Trials' (2018) 16 *Journal of International Criminal Justice* 203

Sander B, 'The Method Is the Message: Law, Narrative Authority and Historical Contestation in International Criminal Courts' (2018) 19 *Melbourne Journal of International Law* 299

Sander B, 'Unveiling the Historical Function of International Criminal Courts: Between Adjudicative and Sociopolitical Justice' (2018) 12 *International Journal of Transitional Justice* 334

Sander B, 'The Expressive Limits of International Criminal Justice: Victim Trauma and Local Culture in the Iron Cage of the Law' (2019) 19 *International Criminal Law Review* 1019

Sander B, 'The Expressive Turn of International Criminal Justice: A Field in Search of Meaning' (2019) 32 *Leiden Journal of International Law* 851

Sander B and Holtermann JvH, 'Symposium: Doing Justice to Truth in International Criminal Courts and Tribunals' *Humanity* (3 July 2017)

Savelsberg JJ and King RD, 'Law and Collective Memory' (2007) 3 *Annual Review of Law and Social Science* 189

Schabas W, 'Customary Law or "Judge-Made" Law: Judicial Creativity at the UN Criminal Tribunals', in Doria J et al (eds), *The Legal Regime of the ICC: Essays in Honour of Prof. I.P. Blishchenko* (Brill 2009) 77

Schabas W, *Unimaginable Atrocities: Justice, Politics, and Rights at the War Crimes Tribunals* (OUP 2012)

Schabas WA, 'Was Genocide Committed in Bosnian and Herzegovina? First Judgments of the International Criminal Tribunal for the Former Yugoslavia' (2001) 25 *Fordham International Law Journal* 23

Schabas WA, 'A Synergistic Relationship: The Sierra Leone Truth and Reconciliation Commission and the Special Court for Sierra Leone' (2004) 15 *Criminal Law Forum* 3

Schabas WA, *The UN International Criminal Tribunals: The Former Yugoslavia, Rwanda and Sierra Leone* (CUP 2006)

Schabas WA, 'Prosecutorial Discretion v. Judicial Activism at the International Criminal Court' (2008) 6 *Journal of International Criminal Justice* 731

Schabas WA, 'State Policy as an Element of International Crimes' (2008) 98 *Journal of Criminal Law & Criminology* 953

Schabas WA, 'Victor's Justice: Selecting "Situations" at the International Criminal Court' (2010) 43 *John Marshall Law Review* 535

Schabas WA, *An Introduction to the International Criminal Court* (4th edn, CUP 2011)

Schabas WA, 'Charles Taylor Judgment Suggests a more Modest Level of Participation in the Sierra Leone Conflict' *PhD Studies in Human Rights Blog* (28 April 2012)

Schabas WA, 'The Contribution of the Eichmann Trial to International Law' (2013) 26 *Leiden Journal of International Law* 667

Schabas WA, 'Selecting Situations and Cases', in Stahn C (ed), *The Law and Practice of the International Criminal Court* (OUP 2015) 365

Scharf MP, *Customary International Law in Times of Fundamental Change: Recognizing Grotian Moments* (CUP 2013)

Scharf MP, 'Forced Marriage as a Separate Crime against Humanity', in Jalloh CC (ed), *The Sierra Leone Special Court and its Legacy: The Impact for Africa and International Criminal Law* (CUP 2014) 193

Schmid E, 'Distinguishing Types of "Economic Abuses": A Three-Dimensional Model' (2015) 26 *Criminal Law Forum* 225

Schmid E, *Taking Economic, Social and Cultural Rights Seriously in International Criminal Law* (CUP 2015)

Schmid E and Nolan A, '"Do No Harm"? Exploring the Scope of Economic and Social Rights in Transitional Justice' (2014) 8 *International Journal of Transitional Justice* 362

Schomburg W and Peterson I, 'Genuine Consent to Sexual Violence under International Criminal Law' (2007) 101 *American Journal of International Law* 121

Schwöbel-Patel C, 'Spectacle in International Criminal Law: The Fundraising Image of Victimhood' (2016) 4 *London Review of International Law* 247
Schwöbel-Patel C, 'Populism, International Law and the End of Keep Calm and Carry on Lawyering' (2018) 49 *Netherlands Yearbook of International Law* 97
Schwöbel-Patel C, 'The Core Crimes of International Criminal Law', in Heller KJ et al (eds), *The Oxford Handbook of International Criminal Law* (OUP 2020) 768
Sedacca N, 'The "Turn" to Criminal Justice in Human Rights Law: An Analysis in the Context of the 2016 Colombian Peace Agreement' (2019) 19 *Human Rights Law Review* 315
Shklar JN, *Legalism—Law Morals, and Political Trials* (Harvard University Press 1964)
Shraga D and Zacklin R, 'The International Criminal Tribunal for the Former Yugoslavia' (1994) 5 *European Journal of International Law* 360
Shraga D and Zacklin R, 'The International Criminal Tribunal for Rwanda' (1996) 7 *European Journal of International Law* 501
Simpson G, 'War Crimes: A Critical Introduction', in McCormack TLH and Simpson GJ (eds.), *The Law of War Crimes: National and International Approaches* (Martinus Nijhoff 1997) 1
Simpson G, *Great Powers and Outlaw States: Unequal Sovereigns in the International Legal Order* (2nd edn, CUP 2006)
Simpson G, *Law, War & Crime—War Crimes Trials and the Reinvention of International Law* (Polity Press 2007)
Singer PW, *Corporate Warriors: The Rise of the Privatized Military Industry* (Cornell University Press 2008)
Simpson G, 'Men and Abstract Entities: Individual Responsibility and Collective Guilt in International Criminal Law', in Nollkaemper A and van der Wilt HG (eds), *System Criminality* (CUP 2009) 69
Simpson G, 'International Criminal Justice and the Past', in Boas G et al, *International Criminal Justice: Legitimacy and Coherence* (Edward Elgar 2012) 123
Simpson G, 'Linear Law: The History of International Criminal Law', in Schwöbel C (ed), *Critical Approaches to International Criminal Law: An Introduction* (Routledge 2014) 159
Sivakumaran S, 'Sexual Violence against Men in Armed Conflict' (2007) 18 *European Journal of International Law* 253
Sivakumaran S, *The Law of Non-International Armed Conflict* (OUP 2012)
Skouteris T, *The Notion of Progress in International Law Discourse* (TMC Asser Press 2010)
Skouteris T, 'Engaging History in International Law', in Beneyto JM and Kennedy D (eds), *New Approaches to International Law* (TMC Asser Press 2012) 99
Sloane RD, 'The Expressive Capacity of International Punishment: The Limits of the National Law Analogy and the Potential of International Criminal Law' (2007) 43 *Stanford Journal of International Law* 39
Smeulers A, 'Punishing the Enemies of All Mankind' (2008) 21 *Leiden Journal of International Law* 971
Smeulers A, 'Why Serious International Crimes Might Not Seem "Manifestly Unlawful" to Low-level Perpetrators: A Social-Psychological Approach to Superior Orders' (2019) 17 *Journal of International Criminal Justice* 105
Smeulers A et al, 'Sixty-Five Years of International Criminal Justice: The Facts and Figures' (2013) 13 *International Criminal Law Review* 7
Smeulers A et al, 'The Selection of Situations by the ICC: An Empirically Based Evaluation of the OTP's Performance' (2015) 15 *International Criminal Law Review* 1
Smeulers A and Holá B, 'ICTY and the Culpability of Different Types of Perpetrators of International Crimes', in Smeulers A (ed), *Collective Violence and International Criminal Justice: An Interdisciplinary Approach* (Intersentia 2010) 175

Smeulers A and Werner W, 'The Banality of Evil on Trial', in Stahn C and van den Herik L (eds), *Future Perspectives on International Criminal Justice* (TMC Asser Press 2010) 24

Smeulers A and Grünfeld F, *International Crimes and Other Gross Human Rights Violations: A Multi- and Interdisciplinary Textbook* (Martinus Nijhoff Publishers 2011)

Smith BF, *Reaching Judgment at Nuremberg: The Untold Story of How the Nazi War Criminals Were Judged* (Basic Book 1977)

Smith T, 'Why the International Criminal Court is Right to Focus on the Environment' *The Conversation* (23 September 2016)

Soares PP, 'Tangling Human Rights and International Criminal Law: The Practice of International Tribunals and the Call for Rationalized Legal Pluralism' (2012) 23 *Criminal Law Forum* 161

Southwick KG, 'Srebrenica as Genocide? The *Krstić* Decision and the Language of the Unspeakable' (2005) 8 *Yale Human Rights & Development Law Journal* 188

Stahn C, 'Between "Faith" and "Facts": By What Standards Should We Assess International Criminal Justice?' (2012) 25 *Leiden Journal of International Law* 251

Stahn C, 'Justice Delivered or Justice Denied? The Legacy of the *Katanga* Judgment' (2014) 12 *Journal of International Criminal Justice* 809

Stahn C, *A Critical Introduction to International Criminal Law* (CUP 2019)

Stahn C, *Justice as Message: Expressivist Foundations of International Criminal Justice* (OUP 2020)

Starr S, 'Extraordinary Crimes at Ordinary Times: International Justice Beyond Crisis Situations' (2007) 101 *Northwestern Law Review* 1257

Steinke R, *The Politics of International Criminal Justice: German Perspectives from Nuremberg to The Hague* (Hart Publishing 2012)

Stewart F, 'The Root Causes of Conflicts: Some Conclusions' *QEH Working Paper Series: Working Paper Number 16* (1998) 12

Stewart F, 'Root Causes of Violent Conflict in Developing Countries' (2002) 324 *British Medical Journal* 342

Stewart JG, 'Atrocity, Commerce and Accountability: The International Criminal Liability of Corporate Actors' (2010) 8 *Journal of International Criminal Justice* 313

Stewart JG, *Corporate War Crimes: Prosecuting the Pillage of Natural Resources* (Open Society Justice Initiative 2011)

Stewart JG, 'The End of "Modes of Liability" for International Crimes' (2012) 25 *Leiden Journal of International Law* 165

Stewart JG, 'A Pragmatic Critique of Corporate Criminal Theory: Lessons from the Extremity' (2013) 16 *New Criminal Law Review* 261

Stewart JG, 'Ten Reasons for Adopting a Universal Concept of Participation in Atrocity', in van Sliedregt E and Vasiliev S (eds), *Pluralism in International Criminal Law* (OUP 2014) 320

Stewart JG, 'Commerce and Atrocity: The Elephant in the Room' *Blog of James G Stewart* (5 March 2015)

Stewart JG, 'Towards Synergies in Forms of Corporate Accountability for International Crimes' *Blog of James G Stewart* (23 February 2019)

Stimson HL, 'The Nuremberg Trial: Landmark in Law', in Mettraux G (ed), *Perspectives on the Nuremberg Trial* (OUP 2008) 617

Stolk S, '"The Record on Which History Will Judges Us Tomorrow": Auto-History in the Opening Statements of International Criminal Trials' (2015) 28 *Leiden Journal of International Law* 993

Stolk S, 'The Victim, the International Criminal Court and the Search for Truth: On the Interdependence and Incompatibility of Truths about Mass Atrocity' (2016) 13 *Journal of International Criminal Justice* 973

Storey A, 'Economics and Ethnic Conflict: Structural Adjustment in Rwanda' (1999) 17 *Development Policy Review* 43
Stover E, *The Witnesses: War Crimes and the Promise of Justice in The Hague* (University of Pennsylvania Press 2005)
Stuart HV and Simons M, *The Prosecutor and the Judge: Benjamin Ferencz and Antonio Cassese, Interviews and Writings* (Pallas Publications 2009)
Stuckenberg C-F, 'Cumulative Charges and Cumulative Convictions', in Stahn C (ed), *The Law and Practice of the International Criminal Court* (OUP 2015) 840
Subotic J, 'Expanding the Scope of Post-Conflict Justice: Individual, State and Societal Responsibility for Mass Atrocity' (2001) 48 *Journal of Peace Research* 157
Sunstein CR, 'On the Expressive Function of Law' (1996) 5 *East European Constitutional Review* 66
Swart M, 'Is there a Text in this Court? The Purposive Method of Interpretation and the Ad Hoc Tribunals' (2010) 70 *Heidelberg Journal of International Law* 767
Tallgren I, 'The Sensibility and Sense of International Criminal Law' (2002) 13 *European Journal of International Law* 561
Tallgren I and Skouteris T (eds), *The New Histories of International Criminal Law: Retrials* (OUP 2019)
Tanaka Y, 'The Atomic Bombing, the Tokyo Tribunal and the *Shimoda* Case: Lessons for Anti-Nuclear Legal Movements', in Tanaka Y et al (eds), *Beyond Victor's Justice: The Tokyo War Crimes Trial Revisited* (Martinus Nijhoff 2011) 293
Taylor MB et al, *Overcoming Obstacles to Justice: Improving Access to Judicial Remedies for Business Involvement in Grave Human Rights Abuses* (FAFO 2010)
Taylor T, *The Anatomy of the Nuremberg Trials: A Personal Memoir* (Skyhorse Publishing 1993)
Teitel R, *Transitional Justice* (OUP 2000)
Thompson S, 'Forced Marriage at the Special Court for Sierra Leone: Questions of Jurisdiction, Legality, Specificity, and Consistency', in CC Jalloh (ed), *The Sierra Leone Special Court and its Legacy: The Impact for Africa and International Criminal Law* (CUP 2014) 215
Tiemessen A, 'The International Criminal Court and the Politics of Prosecutions' (2014) 18 *International Journal of Human Rights* 444
Totani Y, 'The Case against the Accused', in Tanaka Y et al (eds), *Beyond Victor's Justice? The Tokyo War Crimes Trial Revisited* (Martinus Nijhoff Publishers 2011) 147
Tournaye C, 'Genocidal Intent Before the ICTY' (2003) 52 *International and Comparative Law Quarterly* 447
Triffterer O, 'Prosecution of State for Crimes of State' (1996) 67 *Revue internationale de droit penal* 341
Tsereteli N, 'Pre-Trial Chamber of the International Criminal Court Authorizes Initiation of Investigation in Georgia' *EJIL Talk!* (1 February 2016)
Turner C, 'Deconstructing Transitional Justice' (2013) 24 *Law and Critique* 193
Turner JI, 'Defense Perspectives on Law and Politics in International Criminal Trials' (2008) 48 *Virginia Journal of International Law* 529
Turner JI and Weigend T, 'Negotiated Justice', in Sluiter G et al (eds), *International Criminal Procedure: Principles and Rules* (OUP 2013) 1375
Tyson L et al, 'Conditionality and Adjustment in Hungary and Yugoslavia', in Brada JC et al (eds), *Economic Adjustment and Reform in Eastern Europe and the Soviet Union: Essays in Honor of Franklyn D. Holzman* (Duke University Press 1988) 72
Uvin P, *Aiding Violence: The Development Enterprise in Rwanda* (Kumarian Press 1998)
Uvin P, 'Reading the Rwandan Genocide' (2001) 3 *International Studies Review* 75
van den Berg S, 'Netherlands Court Backs Decision Not to Prosecute Dutchbat Soldiers over Srebrenica Deaths' *International Justice Tribune* (4 May 2015)

van den Herik L, *The Contribution of the Rwandan Tribunal to the Development of International Law* (Martinus Nijhoff Publishers 2005)
van den Herik L, 'A Quest for Jurisdiction and an Appropriate Definition of Crime: Mpambara before the Dutch Courts' (2009) 7 *Journal of International Criminal Justice* 1117
van den Herik L, 'Economic, Social, and Cultural Rights: International Criminal Law's Blind Spot?', in Riedel E et al (eds), *Economic, Social and Cultural Rights in International Law: Contemporary Issues and Challenges* (OUP 2014) 343
van den Herik L, 'International Criminal Law as a Spotlight and Black Holes as Constituents of Legacy' (2016) 110 *AJIL Unbound* 209
van den Herik L and Dam de Jong D, 'Revitalizing the Antique War Crime of Pillage: The Potential and Pitfalls of Using International Criminal Law to Address Illegal Resource Exploitation During Armed Conflict' (2011) 15 *Criminal Law Forum* 237
van den Herik L and Stahn C, '"Fragmentation", Diversification and "3D" Legal Pluralism: International Law as the Jack-in-the-Box', in van den Herik L and Stahn C (eds), *The Diversification and Fragmentation of International Criminal Law* (Martinus Nijhoff 2012) 21
van der Wilt H, 'Joint Criminal Enterprise: Possibilities and Limitations' (2007) 5 *Journal of International Criminal Justice* 91
van der Wilt H, 'Joint Criminal Enterprise and Functional Perpetration', in Nollkaemper A and van der Wilt HG (eds), *System Criminality* (CUP 2009) 158
van der Wilt H, 'The Continuous Quest for Proper Modes of Criminal Responsibility' (2009) 7 *Journal of International Criminal Justice* 307
van der Wilt H, 'War Crimes and the Requirement of a Nexus with an Armed Conflict' (2012) 10 *Journal of International Criminal Justice* 1113
van der Wilt H, 'Corporate Criminal Responsibility for International Crimes: Exploring the Possibilities' (2013) 12 *Chinese Journal of International Law* 43
van der Wilt H, 'The Spider and the System', in Waters T (ed), *The Milošević Trial: An Autopsy* (OUP 2014) 484
van der Wilt H, 'Srebrenica: On Joint Criminal Enterprise, Aiding and Abetting and Command Responsibility' (2015) 62 *Netherlands International Law Review* 229
van Schaak B, '*Crimen Sine Lege*: Judicial Lawmaking at the Intersection of Law and Morals' (2008) 97 *Georgetown Law Journal* 119
van Schaak B, 'Engendering Genocide: The Akayesu Case before the International Criminal Tribunal for Rwanda' (2008) *Santa Clara University School of Law*
van Sliedregt E, 'The Curious Case of International Criminal Liability' (2012) 10 *Journal of International Criminal Justice* 1171
van Sliedregt E, 'Perpetration and Participation in Article 25(3)', in Stahn C (ed), *The Law and Practice of the International Criminal Court* (OUP 2015) 499
van Sliedregt E, *Individual Criminal Responsibility in International Law* (OUP 2012)
van Sliedregt E and Vasiliev S, 'Pluralism: A New Framework for International Criminal Justice', in van Sliedregt E and Vasiliev S (eds), *Pluralism in International Criminal Law* (OUP 2014) 3
van Tuyl P, *Effective, Efficient, and Fair? An Inquiry into the Investigative Practices of the Office of the Prosecutor at the Special Court for Sierra Leone* (War Crimes Studies Center 2008)
van Verseveld A, *Mistake of Law: Excusing Perpetrators of International Crimes* (TMC Asser Press 2012) 96
Vanacore G, 'Legality, Culpability and *Dogmatik*: A Dialogue between the ECtHR, Comparative and International Criminal Law' (2005) 15 *International Criminal Law Review* 823
Vasiliev S, 'Victim Participation Revisited—What the ICC Is Learning about Itself', in Stahn C (ed), *The Law and Practice of the International Criminal Court* (OUP 2015) 1133

Vasiliev S, 'The Making of International Criminal Law', in Brölmann C and Radi Y (eds), *Research Handbook on the Theory and Practice of International Law-Making* (Edward Elgar 2016) 354

Vasiliev S, 'The Crises and Critiques of International Criminal Justice', in KJ Heller et al (eds), *The Oxford Handbook of International Criminal Law* (OUP 2020) 626

Veitch S, 'Judgment and Calling to Account: Truths, Trials and Reconciliations', in Duff A et al (eds), *The Trial on Trial: Volume 2: Judgment and Calling to Account* (Hart Publishing 2006) 155

Veitch S, *Law and Irresponsibility: On the Legitimation of Human Suffering* (Routledge-Cavendish 2007)

Ventura MJ, 'Specific Direction à la Perišić, the Taylor Appeal Judgment and what it Could Mean for the ICTY Appeals Chamber in Šainović et al.—Part I' *Spreading the Jam* (8 January 2014)

Venzke I, *How Interpretation Makes International Law: On Semantic Change and Normative Twists* (OUP 2012)

Venzke I, 'Between Power and Persuasion: On International Institutions' Authority in Making Law' (2013) 4 *Transnational Legal Theory* 353

Verini J, 'The Prosecutor and the President' *The New York Times* (22 June 2016)

Vest H, 'Business Leaders and the Modes of Individual Criminal Responsibility under International Law' (2010) 8 *Journal of International Criminal Justice* 851

Vest H, 'Problems of Participation—Unitarian, Differentiated Approach, or Something Else?' (2014) 12 *Journal of International Criminal Justice* 295

Vinjamuri L, 'The International Criminal Court and the Paradox of Authority' (2016) 79 *Law and Contemporary Problems* 275

von Hebel H and Robinson D, 'Crimes within the Jurisdiction of the Court', in Lee RS (ed), *The International Criminal Court: The Making of the Rome Statute: Issues, Negotiations, and Results* (Kluwer Law International 1999) 79

von Lingen K, 'Legal Flows: Contributions of Exiled Lawyers to the Concept of "Crimes Against Humanity" during the Second World War' (2020) 17 *Modern Intellectual History* 507

Wald P, 'Note from the Bench', in Darcy S and Powderly J (eds), *Judicial Creativity at the International Criminal Tribunals* (OUP 2010) xxxv

Wald PM, 'International Criminal Courts: Some Kudos and Concerns' (2006) 150 *Proceedings of the American Philosophical Society* 241

Wald PM, 'Foreword: War Tales and War Trials' (2008) 106 *Michigan Law Review* 901

Waller J, *Becoming Evil: How Ordinary People Commit Genocide and Mass Killing* (OUP 2002)

Waller JE, 'The Ordinariness of Extraordinary Evil: The Making of Perpetrators of Collective Violence', in A Smeulers (ed), *Collective Violence and International Criminal Justice: An Interdisciplinary Approach* (Intersentia 2010) 19

War Crimes Studies Center, *Interim Report on the Special Court for Sierra Leone* (War Crimes Studies Center April 2005)

Waters T (ed), *The Milošević Trial: An Autopsy* (OUP 2014)

Waters TW, 'A Kind of Judgment: Searching for Judicial Narratives After Death' (2010) 42 *George Washington International Law Review* 279

Weigend T, 'Intent, Mistake of Law, and Co-Perpetration in the *Lubanga* Decision on Confirmation of Charges' (2008) 6 *Journal of International Criminal Justice* 471

Weigend T, 'Kill or Be Killed: Another Look at *Erdemović*' (2012) 10 *Journal of International Criminal Justice* 1219

Weigend T, 'Indirect Perpetration', in Stahn C (ed), *The Law and Practice of the International Criminal Court* (OUP 2015) 538

Weiner P, 'The Evolving Jurisprudence of the Crime of Rape in International Criminal Law' (2013) 54 *Boston College Law Review* 1207

Werle G and Burghardt B, 'Establishing Degrees of Responsibility: Modes of Participation in Article 25 of the ICC Statute', in van Sliedregt E and Vasiliev S (eds), *Pluralism in International Criminal Law* (OUP 2014) 301

Werle G and Jeßberger F, *Principles of International Criminal Law* (3rd edn, OUP 2014)

West R, *A Train of Powder* (Viking Press 1955)

Wharton S, 'The Evolution of International Criminal Law: Prosecuting "New" Crimes before the Special Court for Sierra Leone' (2011) 11 *International Criminal Law Review* 217

Wharton S and Grey R, 'The Full Picture: Preliminary Examinations at the International Criminal Court' (2019) 56 *Canadian Yearbook of International Law* 1

White H, 'The Fictions of Factual Representation', in White H, *Tropics of Discourse: Essays in Cultural Criticism* (John Hopkins University Press 1978) 121

White H, 'The Historical Text as Literary Artifact', in White H, *Tropics of Discourse: Essays in Cultural Criticism* (John Hopkins University Press 1978) 81

White H, 'Narrativity in the Representation of Reality', in White H, *The Content of the Form: Narrative Discourse and Historical Representation* (John Hopkins University Press 1990) 1

White H, *The Content of the Form: Narrative Discourse and Historical Representation* (John Hopkins University Press 1990)

White H, 'Historical Emplotment and the Problem of Truth', in Friedlander S (ed), *Probing the Limits of Representation: Nazism and the "Final Solution"* (Harvard University Press 1992) 37

White H, 'Response to Arthur Marwick' (1995) 30 *Journal of Contemporary History* 233

White H, 'Postmodernism and Textual Anxieties', in Strath B and Witoszek N (eds), *The Postmodern Challenge: Perspectives East and West* (Rodopi BV 1999) 27

Whiting A, 'Dynamic Investigative Practice at the International Criminal Court' (2013) 76 *Law and Contemporary Problems* 163

Whiting A, 'The ICC in Kenya: Institutional Promises and Limitations' *Just Security* (15 September 2015)

Whiting A, 'An ICC Investigation of the U.S. in Afghanistan: What does it Mean?' *Just Security* (3 November 2017)

Whiting A, 'Crime of Aggression Activated at the ICC: Does it Matter?' *Just Security* (19 December 2017)

Whiting A, 'Appeals Judges Turn the ICC on its Head with Bemba Decision' *Just Security* (14 June 2018)

Whiting AG, 'Finding Strength within Constraints' *International Criminal Justice Today* (23 November 2016)

Whitney CR, 'Panel Finds French Errors in Judgment on Rwanda' *New York Times* (20 December 1998)

Wilke C, 'Asymmetric Legality: The Invisibility of High-Tech Violence in Afghanistan' *Public Seminar* (2 May 2019)

Wilke C, 'High Altitude Legality: Visuality and Jurisdiction in the Adjudication of NATO Air Strikes' (2019) 34 *Canadian Journal of Law and Society* 261

Williams S and Woolaver H, 'The Role of the *Amicus Curiae* before International Criminal Tribunals' (2006) 6 *International Criminal Law Review* 151

Wilson RA, *Writing History in International Criminal Tribunals* (CUP 2011)

Women's Initiative for Gender Justice, 'A Review of the International Criminal Court's Current Jurisprudence and Practice: Modes of Liability' *Expert Paper* (November 2013)

Women's Initiative for Gender Justice, *Gender Report Card on the International Criminal Court 2014 Anniversary Edition* (December 2014)

Women's Initiatives for Gender Justice, 'Letter to ICC Prosecutor' (August 2006)

Woodward SL, *Balkan Tragedy: Chaos and Dissolution After the Cold War* (The Brookings Institution 1995)
Yanev L, 'A Janus-Faced Concept: Nuremberg's Law on Conspiracy *Vis-à-vis* the Notion of Joint Criminal Enterprise' (2015) 26 *Criminal Law Forum* 419
Yanev L and Kooijmans T, 'Divided Minds in the *Lubanga* Trial Judgment: A Case Against the Joint Control Theory' (2013) 13 *International Criminal Law Review* 789
Yee S, 'The *Tu Quoque* Argument as Defence to International Crimes, Prosecution or Punishment' (2004) 3 *Chinese Journal of International Law* 87
Young IM, *Responsibility for Justice* (OUP 2011)
Zacklin R, 'The Failings of Ad Hoc International Tribunals' (2004) 2 *Journal of International Criminal Justice* 541
Zahar A and Sluiter G, *International Criminal Law: A Critical Introduction* (OUP 2008)
Zarkov D and Glasius M (eds), *Narratives of Justice in and out of the Courtroom* (Springer 2014)
Zimbardo P, *The Lucifer Effect: Understanding How Good People Turn Evil* (Random House 2007)
Zolo D, *Victors' Justice: From Nuremberg to Baghdad* (MW Weir trans, Verso 2009)
Zunino M, *Justice Framed: A Genealogy of Transitional Justice* (CUP 2019)

Index

For the benefit of digital users, indexed terms that span two pages (e.g., 52–53) may, on occasion, appear on only one of those pages.